Encyclopedia
of PlayStation
cheats, tips & solutions

 second edition

FKB Publishing
F2 Wellpark, Willeys Avenue, Exeter EX2 8BE

Encycopedia of PlayStation Cheats, Tips & Solutions second edition
© **2000 FKB Publishing Ltd.**

Managing Editor: Johnny Morrisey
Deputy Editor: Ina Oltack
Solutions Editor: Andrew Dixon
Design: Mark James
Contributors: Brett Hardwell and Lawrence Brunt

ISBN 1 902160 28 2

Printed and bound in the UK by The Bath Press.

Encyclopedia
of PlayStation

cheats, tips & solutions

 second edition

CONTENTS

CONTENTS

3D LEMMINGS

Passwords for each level are as follows:
Fun
LEWISIAN; BLIMBING; FANAGALO; DRICKSIE; KURTOSIS; GREGATIM; WALLAROO; AVENTAIL; GAZOGENE; JINGBANG; DIALLAGE; BUNODONT; NAINSOOK; YAKIMONA; FUMITORY; CINGULUM; BESLAVER; ANABLEPS; QUINCUNX; TARLATAN.

Tricky
KAMACITE; GUMMOSIS; PRODNOSE; NGULTRUM; COTTABUS; BEDAGGLE; EPICALYX; HOMALOID; LALLYGAG; BILABIAL; CACAFOGO; METAVURT; SLOWBURN; PELLUCID; MAKIMONO; KHUSKUS; DISPLODE; RACAHOUT; ORGULOUS; DUNCEDOM.

Taxing
CABOCEER; GEROPIGA; BONTEBOK; EMPYREAL; LANGLAUF; NANNYGAI; SARATOGA; QUINTAIN; MUSQUASH; ZOMBORUK; SKILLING; WOBEGONE; BINDIEYE; FRAXINUS; LINDWORM; CURLICUE; HANEPOOR; IDEMQUOD; BLANDISH; MALAGASY.

Mayhem
CHORIAMB; GARGANEY; KAOLIANG; MAROCAIN; OBTEMPER; TASTEVIN; VELLOZIA; BORACHIO; JACKAROO; COOLAMON; BANAUSIC; FABURDEN; RECKLING; MIRLITON; OPAPANAX; BIMBASHI; CAATINGA; PENSTOCK; SPRINGAL; BABIRUSA.

Animations
For the Space, Egyption, Army and end-of-game animations, enter the codes SPACEAAA, EGYPTAAA, ARMYAAAA and MAZEAAAA respectively at the password screen.

Level Select Code
To choose which level to start on, enter LAMPWICK at the password screen.

A BUGS LIFE

Extra Lives
When you begin to run low on lives, replay the training level and collect the letters to spell out the name FLIK for an extra life. Repeat the process until you have enough lives.

ACE COMBAT 2

Free Mission
Find the secret ending by completing the Kingpin mission. A 'Free Mission' option will appear after you start the game allowing you to play any mission.

Track Sampler
Finish the game with a rank higher than First Lieutenant and a new feature will appear in the options menu called 'Music Player', where you can sample any of the tracks in the game.

Model Display
Completing the game on General will allow you to view and get information on every plane in the game.

Secret Missions
Complete all the missions in Free Mission mode on Easy, Medium and Hard. You will now receive two bonus missions.

Freeze Replay View
Hold down the map button during a replay to freeze the camera angle.

Alternate Map View
Press **Select** while highlighting the mission option on the Mission Select screen.

ACE COMBAT 3

Replay Controls
Press ■, ▲, ●, ✖, **L1** during a replay to change the camera angles. Pressing **L2** adds a filter and **R2** adds motion blurring.

Mission Simulator
Complete the game five times viewing each of the five different endings to unlock the mission simulator.

ACTUA GOLF 3

Unlock Canada and Colorado courses
Qualify as a professional by getting a handicap of 0.

Putt off the Green
If your ball falls just short of the green it is still possible to putt it. You cannot putt if you are in the rough however.

ACTUA ICE HOCKEY

Extra Teams
On the menu screen, hold ■ + ▲ + ●. After a few seconds you should hear a conformation sound.

ACTUA SOCCER

Dream Team
To gain access to the hidden Gremlin Star XI team, press **Select** and ↖ simultaneously on the title screen.

ACTUA SOCCER 2

All of the following Cheats must be entered from the Main Menu:

Beach Ball Mode
←, →, ←, ↑, ←, →, ■, ■.

Black and White/Colour T.V modes
↑, ↓, ↑, ■, ●, ↑, ↓, ↑.

Dwarfed Players
●, ↓, ↓, ■, ↑, ↑, ←, →.

Giant Players
↑, ↓, ↓, →, ■, ■, ●, ●.

Floodlight Failure
←, ←, ←, ●, →, →, →, ■.

Gremlin XI
←, →, ■, ●, ↑, ↓, ■, ●.

Invisible Players
■, ●, ↓, ●, ↑, →, ■, ←.

Super Furry Animals
←, ←, ■, →, →, ●, ↑, ↓.

Best Formation (Attack): 4-4-2
Best Formation (Defence): 5-4-1
Best Formation (Overall): 4-4-2

Easiest Goal: From the kick off move towards the goal then when you are on the edge of the penalty area shoot as hard and straight as you can. If the keeper is suspect the ball will fly in.

Crossing: Get to the edge of the penalty area and as close to the by-line as possible. When the cross is released repeatedly press shoot to enable a header or volley at goal.

Corners: Aim for a player between the 6-yard box and the penalty spot. Once the corner is taken repeatedly press the shoot button. If this is done correctly a diving header or volley should follow.

Free Kicks: There is no definitive way of scoring from free kicks so try to aim towards a player near the goal and start praying.

Route One: Very effective. A big hoof from your keeper will see your striker given a head start on the defenders.

Long Shots: When they are on target they can produce some goals of the season. However, due to the tricky shooting controls they are more likely to end up in row 12 of the stands or bouncing out for a throw-in.

Special Moves: Most of these come from high balls. Their activation depends on where the player is and when the button is pressed so a lot is left to fate. Only practice will help you master them.

ACTUA SOCCER 3

Enter these codes as a custom team name on the Team Creation screen to unlock the bonus teams.

Team	Code
Busby Babes	SIR MATT
Blackburn 94 95	SHEAR CLASS
Chelsea 44-99	FOREIGN LEGION
Liverpool 77-99	SCOUSE PERMS
Leeds 44-99	BREMNERS BOOT
Arsenal 70-90	TEA TOTAL
Derby 44-99	RAM RAIDERS
West Ham 44-99	WRIGHT BUY
Leicester 44-99	FRUIT N VEG
Villa 44-99	BIT OF CLARET
Newcastle 44-99	DOWN THE TOON
Dons 44-99	FASH THE CASH
Soton 44-99	DELL BOYS
Coventry 44-99	LADY GODIVA
Boro 44-99	EMMERSONS
Wednesday 44-99	BARMY ARMY
Forest 44-99	MEN IN TIGHTS
Everton 44-99	DUNCNDISORDER
Spurs 44-99	DIAMOND LIGHTS
Charlton 44-99	VALLEY BOYS
Ipswich 44-99	BALD FRITZ
Wigan 78-98	EGG CHASERS
5 Nations	RULE BRITTANIA
Shearer XXX	SEXY FOOTBALL
FC Gremlin	I MADE THIS
Cyborg Rovers	METAL HEADS
Skeletons	GRIM REAPER
Greenhouse Test	OZONE LAYER
Maddness Friday	IMPOSSIBLITY
Ledbury FC	SINK OR SWIM
Heavenley HTFC	LEE THE PIG
Fighting Forth	FLAGSTONING
Duds Spuds	SHUT IT
The Hardmen	SHADWELL TOWN
Dicks Pick N Mix	CANDY MAN
Gremlin Staff 1	WIDE BOYS
Gremlin Staff 2	DOUBLE TROUBLE
Pattis Shandi Men	CPU STUD
Virtual Blades	CHIP BUTTY
Actua Soccer Web	SPIT N SPIN
Top 50 Babes 1	PLEASE
Top 50 Babes 2	NO THANKS
Doncaster Rovers	SHAME

Arsenal Ladies	**LONDON GIRLS**
Food Group	**BINMAN**
Boat Racers	**TFF HOBBY**
Rushden	**NICE GEM**
Bore Crust	**LETS NOT PLAY**

ADIDAS POWER SOCCER

Dream Team

Press **L2**, **R2**, ■ and ✖ simultaneously at the Player Select screen. 'Dream Team' will become the name of your team if you do this several times.

Female Commentary

Press **Select** during an Arcade match to go to the in-game options. Go to Audio, highlight Commentary and then press ■ and ● together. You should now have the choice of French, German or British girls who will give their comments throughout the match.

ADIDAS POWER SOCCER '97

Hidden Shots

Use the following combinations to make special moves:
Juggling: Press ■ + ✖ on a low pass.
Backheel: Press ■ + ✖ when you are in possession of the ball.
Kick In The Head: Press ■ + ✖ when you are about to tackle.
Hand Of God: Press▲ + ● on a high kick.
Super Volley: Press ▲ + ● on a low kick.
Flick: Press ▲ + ● when in possession of the ball.
Pull Shirt: Press ▲ + ● when about to tackle.
Bicycle: Press ✖ + ▲ on a high kick.
Diving Head: Press ✖ + ▲ on a low kick.
Predator Kick: Press ✖ + ▲ when in possession of the ball.
Mega Run: Press ■ + ● when in possession of the ball.

AGILE WARRIOR

Passwords

Level 2: 5433
Level 3: 0007
Level 4: 1213
Level 5: 1224
Level 6: 7154

B1 Airstrike

To bring on the Stealth bomber for a devastating attack, pause the game and press ←, ■, ■, ■, ■, ↑, ▲, ▲, ▲, →, ●, ↓, ✖, ✖, ✖, ✖, ✖, ✖.

Hover Code

To reduce the minimum speed to zero, pause the game and press ←, ■, ■, ■, ■, ↑, ▲, ▲, ▲, →, ●, ↓, ✖, ▲, ▲, ▲, ✖. Press **L1** to hover.

Invincibility

Pause the game, then press ■, ■, ■, ■, ▲, ▲, ▲, ●, ↓, ✖, ▲, ▲, ▲, ■.

Maximum Fuel and Armour

Pause the game, then press ←, ■, ■, ■, ■, ↑, ▲, ▲, ▲, →, ●, ↓, ✖, ▲, ▲, ▲, ●.

Maximum Weapons (999)

Pause the game and press ←, ■, ■, ■, ■, ↑, ▲, ▲, ▲, →, ●, ↓, ✖, R1, R1, R1, R1, L1, L1, L1, L1, R2, R2, R2, R2, L2, L2, L2, L2, for an unlimited supply of all weapons.

Mesh Fog Editor

Pause the game and press ←, ■, ■, ■, ■, ↑, ▲, ▲, ▲, →, ●, ↓, ✖, ↓, ↓, ↓, ▲, ▲, ▲. Then to alter the graphical shading, use the buttons ■, ▲, ●, and ✖.

Mission Complete

To instantly complete all mission objectives pause the game and press ←, ■, ■, ■, ■, ↑, ▲, ▲, ▲, →, ●, ↓, ✖, ▲, ▲, ▲, ↓, ↓, ↓.

New Camera Angles

Pause the game and press the following sequence repeatedly for new camera angles. ←, ■, ■, ■, ■, ↑, ▲, ▲, ▲, →, ●, ↓, ✖, ↑, ↓, ←, →.

Overhead Map Translucency

To see through the overhead map when it is brought up, pause the game and press ←, ■, ■, ■, ■, ↑, ▲, ▲, ▲, →, ●, ↓, ✖ + ● five times.

Sexy Dancer

To see the FMV game ending, pause the game and press ←, ■, ■, ■, ■, ↑, ▲, ▲, ▲, →, ●, ↓, ✖, ↓, ✖, ↓, ✖, ↓, ✖, ↓, ✖, ↓, ✖. Enter the code and complete the current mission. On the next mission briefing you will see a sexy blonde girl dance for you.

AIR COMBAT

Change Two-Player Planes

After you select the two-player mode, hold **R1** and ●. You will see another loading screen with bouncing CD's. Now press ←, →, ←, →, ↓, ↑, ↓, ↑, ●, ●, ▲, ▲, ▲.

Change Wingman's Colour

Hold **R1** and ● while the game is loading to make the CD's bounce. Then press and hold → and press **Start** ten times. Now you can change the wingman's colour.

Different Coloured Planes

As before, hold **R1** and ● while you press ↑, ↓, ←, →, ↑, ↓, ←, →, then release **R1** and ● and press **R1**. In the lower

← corner a small jet icon should appear and will give you a differently coloured plane to fly with.

Extra Game
Hold **R1** and ● buttons when the game is loading. Press ↑, ←, ↓, and → when CD's start flying around the screen and you will have an extra game the next time the game loads. Use **L2** and **R2** to control the game icon. Your aim is to destroy as many bombers as possible.

Full Money
To have maximum money, press **R1** and ● when the game loads, to make the CD's bounce. Next enter ●, ▲, ▲, ▲, ●, ▲, ●, ▲, (● and ▲ together), and (● and ▲ together).

Play with all the Planes
Finish the game and sit through the credits. You will see 'EXTRA 010' in the top right corner of the title screen. To play with all the planes go back to the select screen and you should have ten extra to choose from.

AKUJI THE HEARTLESS

Debug Mode
Pause the game, hold **L2** and press ←, ↑, ↑, ▲, →, ■, ←, ▲, ↑, ↓, →, →.

Infinite Spirit Spells
Once you have the Spirit spell, pause the game holding **L2** press ←, ▲, ←, ←, ●, ←, ▲, →, ●, ↑, ↑, ↓.

Invincibility
Pause the game then while holding **L2** press →, →, ←, ▲, ✕, ↑, ●, ←.

ALIEN TRILOGY

The Ultimate Cheat
To have all the weapons, unlimited firepower, invincibility and complete access to every level enter the password 1GOTP1NK8C1DBOOTSON at the correct screen.

Jump Levels
To jump to the level number you entered, type GOLVL then a level number in the password section. However, your only weapon will be a pistol!

Xenomania Setting
Level 2: J3BBBBBBBDWP8903BBBBBBBBBMBBBXJBBB
Level 3: LZBBBBBKCPB9N3DBBBCGBBMBBCD1BBB
Level 4: FBBBBBBBBMCPB9XLDBBBFBBBMBBCX1BBB
Level 5: 7LBB7BBB84PB9K3GBBBDLBLMBBDB1BBB
Level 6: 1LBBBBBB6WPB7F3GBBBJ2BBBBBDX1BBB
Level 7: YGBJLBBB7OPB9R3CQVCBG9BBDBQFJ9CLB
Level 8: WGBBBBBBBOHPBJLBLL3BTGBLMBVFX9DVB

Level 9: XQBJLBBBMHPBJNVFQVBTGBLMCBGD9HBB
Level 10: 4BBBGBBBBFWPBQHLPN2BTLBLJCGG29FBB
Level 11: 3ZBJLBBB4HPBQQ3PQVBTLBLJCGHJ9FBB
Level 12: O3BJGBBBHWPB9BBOH3BTLBLDCBHZ9GVB

Section 2
Level 1: Z3BBSBBB74PB9GVTJVBBBBBBDB7JG9BVB
Level 2: 4BBLGBBBB8PB91B4PVBBBBBBMB3JZ9C3B
Level 3: 4GBKVBBBZRPB9BB5QVBBBBBKCGKG9GLB
Level 4: 2BBQGBBBSRPBBBBB5BBBBBBBBBBKZ9GVB
Level 5: OZBBBBBBD9V8PB9QWDHBBTLBLBCGLH9G36
Level 6: O3BQVBD9VHPB9QWJM7BTLBLGCGLO9HBD
Level 7: 1LBHXBD354PBJBCLPQBTBBLBB3MH9HBD
Level 8: RQBBBBD988PBJCCVDBBTBBLBBVMO9CBH
Level 9: 4BBQVBFGX4PBJJMVQGBTLBLBCGNH9FVK
Level 10: 77BQVBDMYMPBDJ24XPQBRLBLBBZNY9HBD

Section 3
Level 1: 8ZBCLBC8RMPBDKMPBD3BS1BLBB3PF9HBF
Level 2: H7BBBBCSFRPB9DWLP3BC7BBLBLPO9GVB
Level 3: NQBBBBCSLMPBQHCLP3BC7BBLBQQH9GVB
Level 4: OGBBBBFGK8PBLH4KK2BBBBBLB7QO9CBC
Level 5: KBBBBBFGCWPBLH4KJVBBBBBLB3RH9B3C
Level 6: KVBBBBBRLOPB9BBBCLBSQBBMB3RO9CLB
Level 7: O3BBBBBB8CPB9BBXDQBSQBBMCBSK9CLB
Level 8: WVBBBBBBY8PB9BBXL33BN3BLMB75O9CBB
Level 9: TQBBBBBB4MP9P3BDQBBBBBMCGTH9BBB
Level 10: 4VBJLBFGDMP89XVNQVBJLBBMCBT49F3J
Level 11: 4VBFNBCSZ4PB94BNF7BQVBBMB7VH9F3J
Level 12: S3BBBBFGSOPB94BNKZBQVBBMBZVO9HBL
Level 13: Q3BQVBDXRCPB94BNQVBTLBLMBGWH9GBL
End Sequence: QZBPSBBYRCPBZXBBBVBMNBBMBVW49DLK

ALONE IN THE DARK: JACK IS BACK

General tips
When fighting, get close to your enemy and punch as fast as you can. Always take whatever a dead person leaves behind. To get through certain doors and walls you must do a dive attack whilst holding the sword.

1) Kill the man with your bare hands.
2) Take his gun, the clip and the flask.
3) Run to the big statue of an anchor
4) Push it and enter the gardens. If you are quick enough, you can avoid the gunmen.
5) Kill the man behind the corner before he comes into view.
6) Take the picture.
7) Turn right.
8) Kill the gunman.
9) Take the clip and the flask.
10) Go towards where the gunman came from.
11) Take the rope. Don't forget the diamond card.
12) Go back to where you found the picture.
13) Walk to the crossroads and cross.

14) Shoot the man.

15) Go to the top of the screen.

16) Stay to the left wall and kill the next gunman. He is a real pain but if you don't kill him now he will get you later.

17) Go to the dead end and take the clip.

18) Go back to the crossroads and go to the bottom of the screen.

19) Kill the man in the trench.

20) Continue until you find the grapplin hook.

21) Another man will appear. Step on the diamond card if you don't want to shoot him.

22) Go directly forward and kill the green man.

23) Take the flask.

24) Go to the other part of the cave.

25) Make the altar raise by pushing the chest.

26) Shoot the ghost.

27) Take the pirate's saber.

28) If there are people at the entrance use the magnetic jack on the altar so you can escape via the other trap. If not, leave.

29) Make your way to a 3-way intersection.

30) Go in the L-path, be scared by the demonic face and turn left.

31) Shoot the fat gangster and move on.

32) Cut the branches with your saber.

33) SAVE!

34) Wooden Leg behind the trees is quite tough to kill. Hide behind the statue and use every weapon you've got, especially the revolver.

35) Take the flask and use the grapplin hook.

36) Use the grapplin hook again to make the statue's arm move.

37) Enter.

38) Take a nickel, a crank and a paper bag.

39) Take the notes and pipe cleaners from the corpse.

40) Use the paper under the door then use the pipe cleaners. You should get the key and get inside.

41) To get rid of the sitting man go behind the barrel, just beside the lever. Use the paper bag twice, wait until the man gets up then push the lever.

42) Take the shotgun, the book and the flask.

43) Go behind the grandfather clock.

44) Use the crank to open the secret passage.

45) Go there and take the shotgun shells.

46) Get rid of Musician by tearing the paper you used to get the key.

47) Take the hook.

48) Take the beater and go to the door.

49) Stay in the doorway, shoot the first man, then walk backwards and wait for the other man to show up.

50) Try to align 4 diamonds to open the door. Ninety degree rotations are possible with good positioning.

51) Kill the man and go into the cellar.

52) Get the flask.

53) Use the nickel in the slot machine to get two tokens.

54) Take the book located in the back of the room.

55) Go back to the shooting gallery.

56) Kill the man and get the bag.

57) Open the bag.

58) Put on the Father Christmas suit. This will prevent the chap upstairs from blowing the whistle on the blag.

59) Go right and head towards the kitchen. Dodge the statue by walking near the door

60) Once In the kitchen, take the frying pan and go close to the eggs.

61) Listen to what the guy tells you and prepare to fight him. (It is best to use the pan as it will block the darts.)

62) Take the wine from the stove and the poison from beside the dumbwaiter.

63) Use the poison with the wine.

64) Go to the door in front of the statue

65) Drop your special wine and wait for the outcome.

66) Dispose of the little pest walking down the hall and neutralise the statue. Do it by waiting until he walks past the statue, then start running to blast the trident. Dodge back into the kitchen and wait.

67) Go through the door you opened with the wine.

68) Use your two tokens in the jukebox in front of the statue. (The golden token will make a doubloon appear and the wooden token will open the door).

69) Get in the new room and take the bullet-proof vest, clip and gun.

70) Go next to the statue with the trident and take the crown.

71) Go upstairs

72) Kill the laughing zombie by repeatedly closing in on him and punching. It will take some time but you won't be harmed.

73) Open the door and go into the hall.

74) Open the door in the middle hall.

75) A man will throw a gun. Take it and use it quickly.

76) Take the sword.

77) Find the scroll and book on the bookshelf.

78) Go back to the hall and open the nearest door.

79) There are two ghost arms protecting the other half of the scroll. Use the sword to kill the arms. Stick close to the window, then keep slashing and retreating

80) Use the crown on the white statue. Go to the magic room and get the amulet.

81) Take the flask and the note.

82) Open the door, go directly to the left and take the gun with the clip.

83) Don't move and get ready to kill two baddies.

84) Take the grenade and the key.

85) Go into the open room and use the doubloon in the jack-in-the-box.

86) Take the pompom.

87) Open the door and go inside the room. The only way to get rid of the clown is to throw the pompom through the archway. Finding the right position is difficult. When the clown goes after the pompom, use the grenade in the chimney.

88) SAVE

89) Go down.

90) The best way to kill all of the baddies is to get out as fast as you can and wait in the kitchen or the lobby. When they

go through the door slash them. The beater is one of the best weapons because it's fast.

91) Take the red ball from the Christmas tree

92) Go upstairs into the poolroom.

93) Use the ball on the big box with holes.

94) Use the key on the door and go inside. Wait for result.

95) Listen to Jack and when he's finished, use the hook to get out.

96) You'll always get captured by Elizabeth. Your best plan of action is to go downstairs and walk toward the kitchen.

97) You are now Grace Saunders. Try out all your moves.

98) Push the plank so you can get out.

99) Go near to the parrot and take the seeds, sandwich and pepper.

100) Give the seeds to the parrot.

101) Leave the room and IMMEDIATELY and go to your left.

102) Hide in the small alcove until the pirate stops walking.

103) Return to the ladder at the end of the hall as fast as you can. The pirate will soon start chasing you again.

104) Don't tease the pirate

105) Climb the other ladder.

106) You must find a safe way to the open hatch without being noticed. Go behind the sitting man then go to the edge of the ship and hide behind the boxes.

107) Before going down, take the flint and steel on the deck.

108) Take the small cannon from the chest, the vase from the shelf and the stick next to the bed.

109) Position yourself in front of the door and put down the cannon.

110) Use the pepper on the cannon.

111) Throw the vase

112) When the pirate gets near use the flint and steel on the cannon.

113) Take the bell and leave of the room.

114) Enter the door in front of you.

115) Take the chicken's foot and get close to the blue plate.

116) Ring the bell and get inside the dumbwaiter.

117) Take the key.

118) Use the key on the locker in the kitchen.

119) Get the molasses and the freezer.

120) When you try to leave the kitchen, you'll be seen. Return to the kitchen and use the freezer in the doorway.

121) Go upstairs and do the same thing with the molasses.

122) Go to the poolroom.

123) Go into the room with the cell

124) Go to the corner of the room and use the stick behind the desk with the broken plate.

125) Find the key and another book.

126) The door to the chamber and magic room is now open.

127) Go into the magic room and use the stick on the plate.

128) Get back in the kitchen and hope you placed the ice at the right spot.

129) Go beside the dumbwaiter and ring the bell again.

130) Captured

131) Back as Carnby. Get the key and free yourself

132) Kill the pirate with your bare hands.

133) Take the sword.

134) Use the sword

135) Follow Grace outside. (Don't worry if you lose Grace.)

136) Kill everything that comes at you.

137) Get the fuse the man outside leaves behind.

138) Go through the door in front of you.

139) Kill both men

140) Get the fire-iron and the pliers

141) Get the key in the corner of the room then get out.

142) Go through the door next to the alcove where Grace hid.

143) Dispose of the man and take all of his possessions.

144) Push the barrel to the left

145) Get the chainmail.

146) Enter the door at the end of the hallway.

147) Kill the pistol-wielding pirate with your sword.

148) Take the ammo and the flask.

149) Go to the locked door on that deck. Use the key to get inside.

150) Don't use you're gun as you are in the gunpowder room.

151) Use the sword to kill the swordmaster.

152) Get the book and the gunpowder barrel.

153) Get onto the upper deck.

154) Open all the doors possible. There are two rooms you can enter.

155) Enter the room with a cannon.

156) Kill the man sleeping next to the cannon.

157) Use the pliers to free the cannon.

158) Push the cannon to the left (again, the right position is essential).

159) Drop the barrel anywhere in the sleeping room.

160) Use the fuse on the cannon and use the fire-iron.

161) Go into the remains of the sleeping room.

162) Take the flask and the gold pieces.

163) Use the gold pieces near the locked doors.

164) Kill the two dwarves.

165) Go to where they came from and take the flask.

166) Kill the cook behind the door

167) Take the metallic diamond card and use it on the last locked door.

168) Enter and fall under Elizabeth's spell.

169) As Grace again use the stick on the statue.

170) Enter the room and use the chicken's foot.

171) Run away from the ghost.

172) Climb the ladder to go to the main deck.

173) Kill everyone on the bridge.

174) Get the hook and climb up the mast.

175) Wait for the man, when he arrives hit him once with your sword to make him fall.

176) Use the hook on the rope.

177) Kill the next chap.

178) Jump down and take Nichol's sword.

179) Free Grace with the pliers.

180) Run to the cannons to stop the fuse.

181) Kill One-Eye Jack! Don't forget to use Nichol's sword and look out for pretend corpses.

182) Hurrah!

ANDRETTI RACING

Car Editor Menu

The car editor menu gives you control over settings such as downforce, tyre wear and fuel consumption. You can bring up the menu by pressing **Start** to pause the game while racing, and then moving the cursor to Race Statistics. Next press and hold the following: **L1 + L2 + R1 + R2 + ✖ + ← + Select**.

Different Coloured Cars

Start a new race and then select the Begin Career option. At the Register screen enter either **Go Bears!** (for stock cars), or **Go Bruins!** (for Formula One cars). There should now be cars with a variety of different logos and colours at the car selection screen.

ANNA KOURNIKOVA SMASH TENNIS

Safe Serving

Use ▲ for a second serve that is guaranteed to go in. This allows you to use a ● for a risky hard first serve.

Accurate Serves

Start a serve using ✖ to throw the ball into the air. As soon as you have done this, hold ← or → until you use ● or ✖ to serve. The ball will fly either down the inside or edge of the court. If you had pressed the ← or → at the same time as throwing the ball up, it would go out.

Extra Characters and Equipment

To unlock new characters, win any of the tournaments. The more wins you have, the more characters and equipment you will get. The characters are unlocked in this order:

Asaka Temple
1.Celeste 2.Robyn 3.Clara 4.Red Ace 5.Dragon 6.Heihachi
Times Square
1.Peach 2.Sasha 3.Acea 4.Eddy 5.Reikon 6.Pac-man
Osaka Bridge
1.Owen 2.Tara 3.Emilie 4.Sam 5.Troy 6.Richard
Theme Park
1.Xiomin 2.Tiffany 3.Coach 4.Lamar 5.Sherudo 6.Yoshimitsu

When you have won a character go to the character select screen and press **L2+R2** to view their locations.

APE ESCAPE

Cheeky Monkey!

When you fall off a cliff quickly press **Start** and choose EXIT. You will be able to restart at the time station without forfeiting a life.

Secret Tunnel

In Thick Jungles Level 2 push ↓ at the stop sign to find the tunnel.

Defeating the Machine

In Specter's First stage in the level MONKEY MADNESS charge at the Machine using your Super Hoop instead of using the Slingshot.

RC Car Bomb

When you are using the RC car you can move it near a monkey and then hit it with the stun club.

APOCALYPSE

Full Health

Pause the game, hold **L1** and press ✖, ▲, ●.

Infinite Lives

Pause the game, hold **L1** and press ▲, ●, ✖, ■

Restart Point

Continue to play the game after you lose a life, pause, hold **L1** and press ■, ●, ✖. You will be given the option to continue where you died.

Coordinates Display

Pause the game, hold **L1** and press ↓, ↓, ▲.

AREA 51

Secret Mode

In the first level shoot just the first three S.T.A.A.R. members, you will then enter a secret mode called Kronn Hunter.

Shotgun cheat

To get a shotgun puse the game and press ▲, ■, ▲, ←, R1.

ARMOURED CORE

First Person Perspective

Press ● + ▲ + **Start** then unpause. You should now have a pilots eye view.

Fixed Camera

Pressing ● + ✖ + **Start** will fix the camera position.

Design Your Own Background

Once you have designed an emblem in the Design Emblem press **L1 + R1 + Select** your emblem will now appear as the background.

Sad Bonus
Losing the game with debts of more than 50,000 choam will set off a short FMV sequence. When the game restarts you will have bonus items to compensate for your lack of ability.

Big Head Mode Aliens	■, ●, ●, ■, ↑, ■, ●, ●, ■, ✕.
Flat Characters	↑, ↑, ↓, ↓, ←, →, ←, →, ✕, ●.
Greyscale Graphics	✕, ✕, ▲, ▲, ■, ■, ●, ●, ↑, ↓.
Faster Run	✕, ■, ▲, ●, ✕, ■, ▲, ●, L2, R2

(press ● to run faster).

ARMY MEN 3D

Cheats
Pause the game before entering any of the following cheats:

Level Select	■, ●, R1, L1, then hold R1 and press R2
Total Invincibility	■, ●, L1, then hold L1 + L2
All Weapons	■, ●, R1, R2, then hold R1and press R2
Unlock All War Zones	Hold ▲ + ■ + ● and press L1 + L2 when you get to the difficulty screen.

First person View
Hold Start + ● + ■, the game will pause. Unpause and the game will switch to first person perspective.

ARMY MEN: AIR ATTACK

Passwords

All Co Pilots	↑, ↓, ↑, ↓, ↑, ↓, ↑, ↓
All Helicopters (2 player mode)	↓, ↓, ↓, ↓, ✕, ✕, ●, ●
All Missions and Helicopters	▲, ↓, ▲, ↓, ■, ↑, ■, ↑
Secret Ending	■, ↓, ✕, ↓, →, →, ↑, ↑

ARMY MEN: SARGE'S HEROES

All Weapons
Pause the game and press ■, ●, R1, L1 to get all the weapons with infinite ammunition.

Debug Menu
Pause the game and press L1, L2, R1, R2 or on the title screen hold ▲ + L1 + L2 + R1 + R2. You'll here Sarge shout "Retreat".

ASSAULT

Cheat Mode
Enter these codes quickly on the 'Press Start' screen.

Retro Mode	← x 10
Big Head Mode Players	■, ●, ●, ■, ↑, ■, ●, ●, ■, ▲.

ASSAULT RIGS

All Weapons
To gain access to all weapons press the following sequence: ←, →, ←, ←, →, ←, →, →, ↑, ↓, ↑, ↑, ↓, ↑, ↓, ↓.

Invincibility
To be invincible, pause the game and then press ←, ✕, ←, ✕, ←, ←, ✕, →, ✕, →, ✕, ✕. You will know that it has worked if you see a message on the screen.

Level Codes

Welcome	●, ●, ●, ●, ●, ●
Park A Lot	■, ■, ▲, ●, ■, ▲
Nextgen	■, ✕, ■, ✕, ▲, ■
Zamcam	●, ✕, ✕, ✕, ✕, ▲
This Way	▲, ■, ■, ●, ●, ▲
Shoot Me	▲, ■, ■, ▲, ▲, ▲
Joy Joy	▲, ■, ▲, ▲, ●, ▲
Wild	▲, ●, ▲, ▲, ●, ■
Noddy	■, ▲, ▲, ▲, ✕, ▲
Oil Rig	■, ●, ●, ✕, ●, ✕
Wastelands	▲, ■, ●, ●, ✕, ■
Right Way	✕, ●, ■, ▲, ▲, ■
Vertigo	✕, ■, ■, ▲, ●, ▲
Waste Two	■, ●, ■, ▲, ▲, ▲
Gem Tower	▲, ■, ✕, ■, ▲, ▲
Dodge	▲, ■, ●, ✕, ●, ●
Bridge	■, ▲, ■, ✕, ▲, ✕
Air	■, ●, ✕, ●, ✕, ▲
Obliterate	▲, ▲, ●, ■, ✕, ■
Jump	●, ■, ✕, ▲, ▲, ▲
Arena	▲, ▲, ✕, ▲, ●, ■
Room 101	▲, ■, ✕, ●, ■, ▲
PBM	●, ■, ▲, ▲, ▲, ●
Firepower	✕, ✕, ▲, ✕, ✕, ■
Ramps	▲, ■, ●, ✕, ▲, ■
Wave	✕, ●, ■, ●, ●, ■
Oasis	▲, ▲, ✕, ■, ■, ✕
Push Off	●, ▲, ✕, ▲, ✕, ▲
Halls	●, ✕, ▲, ▲, ▲, ▲
Perimeter	✕, ▲, ▲, ✕, ✕, ■
Coaster	●, ■, ●, ●, ●, ■
Spiral	✕, ▲, ▲, ✕, ▲, ■
Mine	▲, ▲, ▲, ●, ▲, ▲
The Castle	■, ▲, ■, ▲, ■, ✕
Look Up	■, ●, ■, ✕, ■, ▲
Fortress	■, ✕, ▲, ✕, ✕, ▲

Deadline	✖, ✖, ■, ✖, ▲, ●
Lifts Ahoy	▲, ✖, ▲, ●, ■, ✖
Fort	✖, ■, ✖, ▲, ▲, ■
Push Me	●, ✖, ▲, ●, ▲, ■
Stairway	▲, ■, ▲, ■, ▲, ▲

ASTERIX

Level Select Cheat
Go to the Language Select screen., Now while holding ▲ press ↑, ➡, ↓, ⬅, ⬅, ↓, ➡, ↑. If it has worked you will see the message Cheat Mode Active. You will now have access to all the levels.

ASTEROIDS

Excalibur Ship
On the title screen, hold **Select** and press ▲, ●, ●, ▲, ■, ●, ■

Level Select
On the title screen, hold **Select** and press ■, ▲, ●, ▲, ▲, ■, ●. During the game, hold **Select** and press **Start** to access the level select menu.

Classic Asteroids
On the title screen, hold **Select** and press ●, ●, ●, ▲, ■, ■, ●.

Classic Asteroids Cheats
Pause the game then enter:

Extra Life - ↑, ↓, ⬅, ➡, ●, ■, ✖, ▲.

99 Lives - ↑, ✖, ↓, ▲, ⬅, ■, ➡, ●.

Invincibility - ↓, ↓, ↑, ↑, ●, ■, ▲, ▲.

AUTO DESTRUCT

To access all of the cheats, firstly pause the game and enter ↑, ↓, ⬅, ➡, ↓, ➡, L1, R1, R1. The cheat menu will now be activated, and the following cheats can be entered by pausing the game:

Blood Mode
  L1, ↓, R1, ⬅, L1, ➡, R1.
Immortal
  ➡, R1, ↑, L1, ↑, ➡, R1, ↓, L1.
Angels
  ↑, R1, ↓, L1, ↑, ⬅, R1, ➡, L1.
Swarmers x5
  ↑, ↓, ↑, ⬅, ➡, R1, L1, R1, L1.
Double Lasers
  R1, L1, R1, L1, ↑, ↓, ↑, ⬅, ➡.

Car Select
  ⬅, R1, ➡, R1, ⬅, R1, ➡, R1.
New York Time Trial
  L1, ➡, ↓, ⬅, ↑, R1.
Tokyo Time Trial
  L1, ⬅, ➡, R1, ⬅, ➡, L1.
Subway Time Trial
  L1, ⬅, L1, R1, ➡, R1.
Debug Menu
  ↑, ➡, ⬅, ↓, ●, L1, R1, R1, L1, ●, ↓, ⬅, ➡, ↑.
Choose Mission
  ↑, ↓, ●, L1, R1, L1, ●, ↓, ↑.
Next Mission
  ■, ●, R1, L1, ●, ↓, L1, ↑.
Extra Nitros
  L1, ●, ↓, L1, ↑, ■, ●, R1.
All Money
  L1, R1, ↑, ●, ↓, ■, ➡, R1, L1.
Extra Time
  ↓, L1, L1, ●, ●, R1, ↑, ■, L1.
Invincibility
  L1, L1, L1, L1, ⬅, ●, ●, ■, L1.
Infinite Fuel
  L1, ●, ⬅, L1, ●, R1, L1, ↑, R1, ↓.
All Time Trials
  R1, L1, ●, ⬅, ●, ●, ⬅, L1, ●.
Tune Up Menu
  L1, R1, L1, ↑, ↓, ●, ↓, ➡, ⬅, ■, R1.

Passwords

Level	Code
2	sXFVgffPh
3	sXFVffhPt
4	sXBKgfhPh
5	gSKKJffsp
6	rmFJkHCrP
7	rmFJhHCrb
8	sXBVgrfPk
9	kRfXrWYPs
10	gFFVkrFVY
11	sSSPhtZNb
12	gSTBXrfmq
13	gXTCTTZmY
14	gXWBXWfrz
15	sSSFJWLLNZ
16	gSTRghCfm
17	gSFXTMBKH
18	sVHtsMMKC]
19	gSFXTMBKH
20	gSBMVMFKS
21	sPCgfghggr
22	gSFMgkHZP
23	sPHgfgfgS
24	gXBTgshCM
25	gSJVfVYZN

B MOVIE

Level Select
On the GT/King of the Jungle screen, press **L1, R1, L2,R2, ▲, ✖, ●, ■, ■, ●, ✖, ▲, Start.**

All Ships And Weapons
On the GT/King of the Jungle screen, press **L1, R1, L2, R2, ⬆, ⬇, ➡, ⬅, ➡, ⬇, ⬆.**

BALLBLAZER CHAMPIONS

Master Dome
To enable this cheat, enter the following code on the Password screen:
**●, L1, L1, R1, R2, L2,
✖, ■, ■, R1, R2, R1,
R2, ▲, L2, R1, L2, ●,
L2, R2, R1, ✖, L1, R2,
■, L2, R1, ✖, R1, R1.**

Shrinking Rotofoil
Again, this cheat must be entered on the Password screen:

**✖, ●, ✖, ✖, ●, ✖,
✖, ✖, ✖, ✖, ✖, ✖,
✖, ✖, ▲, ▲, ✖, ✖,
■, ✖, ✖, ✖, ✖, ■,
✖, ■, ■, ■, ■, ✖.**

BASES LOADED `96

Cheat Mode
To access the cheat mode, play a normal game then enter this code on controller two: **▲, ■, ✖, ●, ●, ●.** A piano tone will sound, indicating that the cheat mode is active.

BATMAN AND ROBIN

Invincibility
On the title screen press **L1, R2, R1, L2, Select, ✖, ●.**

BATTLE ARENA TOSHINDEN

Play as Gaia
To play as Gaia, the following code must be entered very quickly at the Title screen, as the text to highlight the options comes in from either side of the screen: **⬇, ⬉, ⬅, ■.** (**■** Being the default setting for weak slash). If entered correctly, a voice should say "fight!" Now enter the character select screen, highlight Eiji, then select him whilst pressing **⬆.** His picture should go blank, with the name Gaia appearing underneath.

Play as Sho
To play as Sho, enter the same code for Gaia (above), then allow the game to run the demo mode. Whilst the demo is running, press **Start** on controller 2 to re-enter the Title screen. Now Quickly enter the following code as the text to highlight the options comes in from either side of the screen: **⬅, ➡, ⬅, ➡, ⬅, ■.** (Again, With **■** Being the default for weak slash). A voice should say "fight" if the code is entered correctly. Now go to the Character Select screen, highlight Kayin, and select him whilst pressing **⬇.** Kayin`s picture should go blank, with the name Sho appearing underneath.

BATTLE ARENA TOSHINDEN 2

Access the last Boss
At the title screen, press **⬆, ⬇, ⬆, ⬇, ⬆+▲.**

Select the Bosses
To do this you must first complete battle mode on skill level 4. Then, at the character select screen, the random select will show the two bosses Uranus and Master, which are now selectable. Complete battle mode on skill level 6 (using no continues!), and two more bosses will be selectable: Vermillion and Sho. Next, to access the last secret character, Grim, Battle Mode must be completed on level 8, using Vermillion. After completion, go to the title screen and press **⬅, ⬅, ➡, R1, ▲, L2, ■.** You should then hear a bell sound, indicating that you have done everything correctly. Now, to select a boss, highlight the **?** on the Character Selection screen and hold down **Select** in order to slow down the scrolling. Finally, press **■, ▲, ●,** or **✖,** when the desired boss appears.

Quick selection of Uranus and Master
At the Title screen, as the menu items fly in from the left, quickly press **R1, L2, ✖, L1, R2, ●.** A jingle will play if it has worked. Next, go to the Character Select screen and highlight the random box. By correctly timing your button press, you should be able to select Uranus or Master.

Quick selection of Sho and Vermillion
Once the above code for Uranus and Master has been entered, wait until the menu items run in from the left again, and quickly enter this code on controller 2: **●, R2, L1, ✖, L2, R1.** Again, a jingle will sound if it has worked. Now go to the Character Select screen and highlight the random box. By correctly timing your button press, you should be able to select Sho or Vermillion.

BATTLE ARENA TOSHINDEN 3

Random Select
Hold down **L1+ L2+R1+R2** at the Character Select screen, then

press ■, ▲, ✖, or ● while the selection box is moving.

Play as the sub-bosses
Complete the game with each basic character at level 3 to use that character's sub-boss.

Play as Shou
After unlocking all of the sub-bosses, complete the game as Vermillion at level 3.

Play as Abel
Complete the game as Shou at level 7.

Play as Veil
Complete the game as Abel at level 7.

Play as Naru
Complete the game as Veil at level 7.

BATTLE TANX GLOBAL ASSAULT

Cheat Passwords
Level Select	BCKDR
Unlimited Ammo	BLTFD
All Tanks	THRTN
Access Brandon's Team	SMSLGNG
All Weapons	SRTHMB
Loads of Tank Books	DPPCKTS
Access Cassandra's Team	NSTYGRL

BEAT MANIA

Double Play Mode
On the 'Press Start' screen, hold down ← + ■ + ✖, release then press ← + →.

Hidden Mode
On the 'Press Start' screen, hold ← + → + Start, release and then press ← + ✖.

BIO FREAKS

Alternative View
Hold L2 + R2 + ← during a bout. Hold L2 + R2 + ↓ to return to normal view.

Fight Clonus
Hold Select while selecting your opponent to battle their clonus version.

BLACK DAWN

All Weapons
To gain access to all weapons press the following sequence:
←, →, ←, ←, →, ←, →, →, ↑, ↓, ↑, ↑, ↓, ↑, ↓, ↓.

Cycle Gun Modes
To cycle gun modes, pause and press Select, L2, Select, R2, Select, Select, Select.

Maximum Fuel and Ammo
For maximum fuel and ammo, pause the game and press Select, L2, Select, R2, then ▲, ▲, ▲, ●.

Maximum Weapons
For maximum weapons, pause and press Select, L2, Select, R2, L1, L2, R1, R2.

Mission Complete
To complete the mission, pause and press Select, L2, Select, R2, ▲, ▲, ▲, ↓, ↓, ↓.

Screen Mode Toggle
Pause and press Select, L2, Select, R2, ↓, R1, R2 to toggle the screen mode.

Summon Wingman
To summon the wingman, pause the game and press Select, L2, Select, R2, ■, ■, ■, and ●.

Upgrade Current Weapon
To upgrade, pause the game and press Select, L2, Select, R2, L1, L1, R1, R1.

Passwords
To get to any listed level enter the following passwords:
Urban Shield:	1018
Black Out:	1006
Ice Storm:	1213
Desert Fury:	0203
Tiger Trap:	0917
Crack Down:	0254

BLAM! MACHINEHEAD

Passwords
To get to the location in the game that you want, enter the following codes at the password screen:

Level 2 (1.2)	SQDZFO5TJJ
Level 3 (1.3)	HYM7GODECM
Level 4 (1.4)	WFHIHOPOJC
Level 5 (2.1)	I54FHOD5BF
Level 6 (2.2)	E94FHOLLKJ
Level 7 (2.3)	MHLFHODTCM

Level 8 (2.4)	ALLFHOXGPU
Level 9 (2.5)	BDNJHOLLPU
Level 10 (3.1)	8JGIHO9B4V
Level 11 (3.2)	E9GGHOJIQH
Level 12 (3.3)	9FOJGOLZJD
Level 13 (3.4)	SKAGHO9P4O
Level 14 (4.1)	JJOBNN9FCM
Level 15 (4.2)	EYWJHOP7BF
Level 16 (4.3)	JQNFHOT7BF
Level 17 (4.4)	7G9DAOMOCE
Game Over	6H9DAOQJ2F

BLAST CHAMBER

Infinite Lives
Use controller one to go to the main menu and enter the following code: ■, ←, ■, →, ●, ↓, ●, ↑. Now go to the game options and select solo survivor. You should now have infinite lives.

BLAST RADIUS

Access All Upgraded Ships
On the title screen press →, L1, ↑, ↑, ↓, →, R2, L2, R2, ↓, ↑, ↓. Start the game with any ship and then quit the game. Begin again and you should have all four upgraded ships and start on Sector 5.

Wraith Ship
Enter the Upgraded Ships code and then on the title screen enter ←, →, L1, ←, →, L1, R2, R2, L2, ←, →, ↑. Start the game and then quit the game. When you start again you'll be able to select the wraith ship and begin on Sector 8.

Programmer Planets
On the title screen enter ↓, ↑, L1, →, L1, ↑, →, Select, →, R2, L1, L2. All the planets will be replaced with the heads of the programmers. This cheat will not work if either the Upgraded Ships cheat or the Wraith cheat has been entered.

Additional Missions
On the title screen enter L1, ←, L2, ↓, Select, ←, ↓, R2, R2, R2, Select, ↑. This gives you four extra missions. This cheat will not work if either the Upgraded Ships cheat or the Wraith cheat has been entered.

BLAZING DRAGONS

End of Tournament
To get straight to the end of the tournament, enter the following password: V?U5MK 4N6LUL OHW5CB.

BLOODY ROAR

Big Head Mode
Go to the Character Selection screen and hold down L2 and press ● to select your fighter.

Kids Mode
Go to the Character Selection screen and hold down R2 and press ● to select your fighter.

Big Ring
Defeat ten or more characters in Survival Mode to get a larger ring.

Small Ring
Finish the game with Greg at skill level 4+ to get the small ring option.

Open Ring
Finish the game as Mitsuko at skill level 4+ to get a ring without walls.

Invisible Walls
Complete the game with Fox at skill level 4+ to get an arena with invisible walls.

Healing Mode
Complete the game with Bakuryu at skill level 4+ to fight with slowly increasing energy.

No Health
Complete the game with Yugo at skill level 4+ to fight without energy bars.

Camera Control
Complete the game with Alice at skill level 4+ to be able to position the camera.

Lightning Control
Finish the game with Long at skill level 4+ to turn off the lightning.

No Blocking
Complete the game with Gado at skill level 4+ to prevent blocking.

Mad Mode
Complete the game with all of the fighters at skill level 4+ to get strange backgrounds.

Long Arm of the Law
Complete the game at a skill level of 4+ with no continues used to get long arms.

Sakura Mode
Finish the Time Attack mode in less than ten minutes to get Alice in her school uniform.

Moves
All moves are based on your character facing to the right, reverse all direction controls when facing left.

Basic Moves
Forward Dash = →, →
Run = →, Hold →
Retreat = ←, ←
Low Crouch = ↓, Hold ↓
Standard Throw = ■ + ✖
Throw Crouching Opponent = ↓ + ■ + ✖

Landing From Air Juggle = ■ + ✖ **(In Air)**
Jumping Attack On Prone Opponent (Beast Mode) = ↑ + ■ /
✖ / ●
Low Attack On Prone Opponent = ↓ + ■ / ✖ / ●

Air Attacks
Overhead Attack (In Air) = ➡ + ■ / ⬅ + ■
Kick And Reverse Roll (In Air) = ➡ + ✖
Reverse Kick And Forward Roll (In Air) = ⬅ + ✖
Low Punch (Just Before Landing) = ↓ + ■
Foot Sweep (Just Before Landing) = ↓ + ✖

Character Moves
Fox
Basic Attacks
High Jab = ■
Mid Stomach Slash = ➡ + ■
Upwards Mid Chest Slash = ↘ + ■
Low Punch = ↓ + ■
Two Strike Low Slash = ↙ + ■
Turning Upward Slash = ⬅ + ■
Head Kick = ✖
Power High Kick = ➡ + ✖
Stomach Kick = ↘ + ✖
Low Kick = ↓ + ✖
Low Sweep = ↙ + ✖
Spinning Round House Kick = ⬅ + ✖
Flip Kick = ↑ + ✖
Forward Cart Wheel Kick = ↗ + ✖

Beast Mode
Waist Kick = ●
Lunging Attack = ➡ + ●
Low Swipe = ↘ + ●
Low Backhand Attack = ↓ + ●
Sacrifice Kick = ↙ + ●
Spinning Backhand Swipe = ⬅ + ●

When Facing Away From Your Opponent
Turning Punch = ■
Turning Low Punch = ↓ + ■
Super Smash Kick = ✖
Low Spinning Reverse Take ↓ = ↓ + ✖
Turning Overhead Attack = ●
Leg Removal Sweep = ↓ + ●

Special Moves
Triple Strike = ↓, ↘, ➡ + ■
Power Attack = ↓, ↙, ⬅ + ■
High Rising Kick = ↓, ↘, ➡ + ✖
Reverse Spin Kick = ↓, ↙, ⬅ + ✖
Forward Charging Slash = ↓, ↘, ➡ + ●
Reverse Roll = ↓, ↙, ⬅ + ●
Pounce (After Rolling) = ●

Rushing Attacks
Rushing Backhand Attack = **Running** + ■
Running Flip Kick = **Running** + ✖
Jumping Head Butt = **Running** + ●
Forward Dash Lunging Punch = ➡, ➡ + ■
Rising Knee = ➡, ➡ + ✖
Forward Rolling Foot Slam = ➡, ➡ + ●
Reverse Handspring Kick = ⬅, ⬅ + ●

Long
Basic Attacks
High Punch = ■
Reverse High Punch = ➡ + ■
Spinning Ground Punch = ↘ + ■
Low Punch = ↓ + ■
Ground Uppercut = ↙ + ■
Super Double Palm Power Thrust Punch = ⬅ + ■
Floating Head Jab Punch = ↑ + ■
Back Leg Tiger Kick = ✖
Spinning Cart Wheel Kick = ➡ + ✖
Mid Kick = ↘ + ✖
Low Ankle Kick = ↓ + ✖
Foot Sweep = ↙ + ✖
Spinning High Crescent Tiger Kick = ⬅ + ✖
Leaping Reverse Tiger Bite Kick = ↑ + ✖

Beast Mode
High Cat Slash = ●
Reverse Leg Slash = ➡ + ●
Twin Jaws Attack = ↘ + ●
Low Slash = ↓ + ●
Reverse Leg Sweep = ↙ + ●
Reverse Upward Orbit Kick = ⬅ + ●
Tiger Flip Kick = ↑ + ●

When Facing Away From Opponent
Turning Elbow = ■
Spin, Spin Punch = ↓ + ■
Spinning Roundhouse Kick = ✖
Leg takedown = ↓ + ✖
Power Tiger Shoulder = ●
Low Slash = ↓ + ●

Special Moves
Leaping Forward Punch = ↓, ↘, ➡ + ■
Super Power Elbow = ↓, ↙, ⬅ + ■
Leaping Double Kick = ↓, ↘, ➡ + ✖
Head Stomp = ↓, ↙, ⬅ + ✖
Pouncing Throw = ↓, ↘, ➡ + ●
Jungle Earthquake Stomp = ↓, ↙, ⬅ + ●

Rushing Attacks
Charging Punch = **Running** + ■
Leaping Kick = **Running** + ✖
Forward Somersault Roll = **Running** + ●
Elbow Dash = ➡, ➡ + ■

Step Into Sweep = →, → + ✖
Forward Lunging Uppercut Slash = →, → + ●
Backwards Flip Shoulder Charge = ←, ← + ●

Bakuryu
Basic Attacks
Head Punch = ■
Spinning Backhand Slap = → + ■
Spin Punch = ↘ + ■
Low Punch = ↓ + ■
Low Slash = ↙ + ■
Backhand Claw = ← + ■
Forward Character Flip = ↑ + ■
High Heaven Kick = ✖
Forward Flip Kick = → + ✖
Shin Kick = ↘ + ✖
Low ↓ Kick = ↓ + ✖
Take ↓ Sweep = ↙ + ✖
Side Rib Thrust Kick = ← + ✖
Mystic Flip Kick = ↑ + ✖

Beast Mode
Head Swipe = ●
Forward Lunging Mole Punch = → + ●
Foot Slide = ↘ + ●
Low Swipe = ↓ + ●
High Rising ↑percut = ↙ + ●
Counter Lower Block Over Head Attack = ← + ●
Leaping Slash = ↑ + ●

When Facing Away From Opponent
High Punch = ■
Lunging Punch = ↓ + ■
Reverse Spinning Roundhouse = ✖
Foot Sweep = ↓ + ✖
Turning Attack = ●
Crawl Away = ↓ + ●

Special Moves
Air Throw = ↓, ↘, → + ■
Powered Palm Punch = ↓, ↙, ← + ■
Forward Teleport = ↓, ↘, → + ✖
Teleport Kick = ↓, ↙, ← + ✖
Impaler Throw = ↓, ↘, → + ●
Clawing ↑percut = ↓, ↙, ← + ●

Rushing Attacks
Charging Leg Sweep = **Running** + ■
Running And Leaping Kick = **Running** + ✖
Forward Dive Kick With Spring Back = **Running** + ●
Twin Palm = →, → + ■
Dark Rising Kick = →, → + ✖
Double Clawed Ken = →, → + ●
Leaping Claws = ←, ← + ●

Yugo
Basic Attacks
Head Jab = ■
Strong Mid Punch = → + ■
Weak Mid Punch = ↘ + ■
Low Punch = ↓ + ■
Spinning Low Punch = ↙ + ■
Spinning Backhand = ← + ■
Flying Elbow = ↑ + ■
Sky Kick = ✖
Axe Kick = → + ✖
Mid Stomach Kick = ↘ + ✖
Low "Towards The Floor" Kick = ↓ + ✖
Feet Take ↓ = ↙ + ✖
Roundhouse Kick = ← + ✖
Leaping Spin Kick = ↑ + ✖

Beast Mode
Chest Slash = ●
Jumping Double Claw = → + ●
Low Groin Slash = ↘ + ●
Lifting Claw = ↓ + ●
Kick Out = ↙ + ●
Backhand Slash = ← + ●
Flipping Wolf Kick = ↑ + ●

When Facing Away From Opponent
Reverse Spinning High Punch = ■
Reverse Spinning Low Punch = ↓ + ■
Spinning Turn Kick = ✖
Foot Sweep = ↓ + ✖
Turning Face Claw = ●
Rising Wolf Handspring Kick = ↓ + ●

Special Moves
Charging Elbow = ↓, ↘, → + ■
Power Wolf ↑percut = ↓, ↙, ← + ■
Jumping Knee = ↓, ↘, → + ✖
Reverse Flip Kick = ↓, ↙, ← + ✖
Wolf Teeth Face Mutilation = ↓, ↘, → + ●
Leaping Defence = ↓, ↙, ← + ●

Rushing Attacks
Rushing Shoulder = **Running** + ■
Running Slide = **Running** + ✖
Somersault Kick = **Running** + ●
Wolf Punch = →, → + ■
Knee Attack = →, → + ✖
Claw Smash = →, → + ●
Reverse Low Slash = ←, ← + ●

Gado
Basic Attacks
High Punch = ■
Elbow = → + ■
Mid Stomach Punch = ↘ + ■

Low Punch = ↓ + ■
Backhand Punch = ↙ + ■
Slow Spinning Elbow = ← + ■
Leaping Hand Slice = ↑ + ■
High Lion Kick = ✖
Forward Knee = → + ✖
Body Blow Roundhouse Kick = ↘ + ✖
Low Kick = ↓ + ✖
Foot Sweep = ↙ + ✖
Reverse Roundhouse Kick = ← + ✖
Drop Kick = ↑ + ✖

Beast Mode
Slash = ●
Claw Stab = → + ●
Double Claw Slash And Claw = ↘ + ●
Low Slash = ↓ + ●
Leg Sweep = ↙ + ●
Reverse Backwards Roundhouse = ← + ●
Flip Kick = ↑ + ●

When Facing Away From Opponent
Spinning Backhand = ■
Low Punish = ↓ + ■
Reverse Strike Kick = ✖
Opponent Take ↓ = ↓ + ✖
Reverse Drop Kick = ●
Low Slash = ↓ + ●

Special Moves
Double Strike and Throw = ↓, ↘, → + ■
Super Lion Punch = ↓, ↙, ← + ■
Double Axe Kick = ↓, ↘, → + ✖
Lion Triple Kick = ↓, ↙, ← + ✖
Neck Rip = ↓, ↘, → + ●
↑percut Slash = ↓, ↙, ← + ●

Rushing Attacks
Diving Tackle = **Running** + ■
Ground Slide = **Running** + ✖
Leaping Dive = **Running** + ●
Shoulder Charge = →, → + ■
Rising Knee = →, → + ✖
Head Butt = →, → + ●
Double Slash = ←, ← + ●

Greg
Basic Attacks
Head Punch = ■
Heavy Punch = → + ■
Mid Punch = ↘ + ■
Low Punch = ↓ + ■
Mid Backhand = ↙ + ■
Double Fist Pound = ← + ■
Leaping Strike = ↑ + ■
High Kick = ✖

Skip Jump = → + ✖
Low Kick = ↘ + ✖
Shin Kick = ↓ + ✖
Low Kick = ↙ + ✖
Gorilla Kick = ← + ✖
Leaping Skyward Kick = ↑ + ✖

Beast Mode
Face Swipe = ●
Reverse Fist = → + ●
Two Clawed Hammer Horror Smash = ↘ + ●
Low Swipe = ↓ + ●
Twin Fist = ↙ + ●
Face Slap = ← + ●
Twin Loader = ↑ + ●

When Facing Away From Opponent
Forward Face Strike = ■
Low Twisting Punch = ↓ + ■
Twisting Crescent Kick = ✖
Foot Sweep = ↓ + ✖
Spinning Backhand = ●
Low Ground Power Punch = ↓ + ●

Special Moves
Spinning Throw = ↓, ↘, → + ■
Wind ↑ Monkey Punch = ↓, ↙, ← + ■
Gorilla Hug = ↓, ↘, → + ✖
Power Kick = ↓, ↙, ← + ✖
Triple Ground Slam = ↓, ↘, → + ●
Hair Throw = ↓, ↙, ← + ●

Rushing Attacks
Floor Dive = **Running** + ■
Leaping Drop Kick = **Running** + ✖
Stomach Slam = **Running** + ●
↓ Town Punch = →, → + ■
Jump Kick = →, → + ✖
Gut Punch = →, → + ●
Retreating Back Flop = ←, ← + ●

Mitsuko
Basic Attacks
High Punch = ■
Uppercut = → + ■
Juggling Starter Punch = ↘ + ■
Low Punch = ↓ + ■
Over Head Smash = ↙ + ■
Double Ken Slam = ← + ■
Leaping Double Ken = ↑ + ■
High Boar Kick = ✖
Mid Knee = → + ✖
Shin Kick = ↘ + ✖
Low Kick = ↓ + ✖
Double Crouching Kick = ↙ + ✖

Reverse Kick = ← + ✖
Drop Kick = ↑ + ✖

Beast Mode
Head To Head = ●
Forward Stepping Head Butt = → + ●
Boar Horn Lift = ↘ + ●
Shoulder Lift = ↓ + ●
Low Forward Charge = ↙ + ●
Forward Mounting Charge = ← + ●
Lift = ↑ + ●

When Facing Away From Opponent
Backhand Lift = ■
Lower Body Punch = ↓ + ■
Retreating Attack = ✖
Foot Sweep = ↓ + ✖
Stomping Kick = ●
Low Swipe = ↓ + ●

Special Moves
Choking Slam = ↓, ↘, → + ■
Power Grand Slam = ↓, ↙, ← + ■
Frankenstiener = ↓, ↘, → + ✖
Boar Quake Stomp = ↓, ↙, ← + ✖
Horn Carry = ↓, ↘, → + ●
Head Butt = ↓, ↙, ← + ●

Rushing Attacks
Shoulder Charge = **Running** + ■
Drop Kick = **Running** + ✖
Diving Head Butt = **Running** + ●
Spinning Punch = →, → + ■
Forward Kick = →, → + ✖
Dashing Headbutt = →, → + ●
Retreating Headbutt = ←, ← + ●

Alice
Basic Attacks
High Punch = ■
Strong Mid Strike = → + ■
Mid Strike = ↘ + ■
Low Punch = ↓ + ■
Spinning Leg Punch = ↙ + ■
Stomach Strike = ← + ■
Leaping Head Attack = ↑ + ■
High Bunny Kick = ✖
Forward Flip Kick = → + ✖
Shin Kick = ↘ + ✖
Low Kick = ↓ + ✖
Spinning Leg Kick = ↙ + ✖
Backwards Retreating Roundhouse Kick = ← + ✖
Bunny Kick = ↑ + ✖

Beast Mode
Forward Face Punch = ●

Leaping Elbow = → + ●
Low Fur Kick = ↘ + ●
Low Ground Punch = ↓ + ●
Twisting Low Kick = ↙ + ●
Face Stomp = ← + ●
Forward Rabbit Hop = ↑ + ●

When Facing Away From Opponent
Face Punch = ■
Low Punch = ↓ + ■
Rabbit Kick = ✖
Foot Sweep = ↓ + ✖
Stomp Kick = ●
Low Slash = ↓ + ●

Special Moves
Rising Spin Attack = ↓, ↘, → + ■
Mid Power Shoulder Attack = ↓, ↙, ← + ■
Flip Kick From Handstand Position = ↓, ↘, → + ✖
Rabbit Flip Kick = ↓, ↙, ← + ✖
Reverse Somersault From Chest Bounce = ↓, ↘, → + ●
Super Bunny Flip Kicks = ↓, ↙, ← + ●

Rushing Attacks
Shoulder Slam = **Running** + ■
Side Attack = **Running** + ✖
Dashing Flip Kicks = **Running** + ●
Dashing Low Punches = →, → + ■
Dashing Knee = →, → + ✖
Rising Bunny Kick = →, → + ●
Retreating Uppercut = ←, ← + ●

The Beast Rave
When you're in beast mode hit ✖ to enter your characters rave mode. This makes yours character even faster and with a reduced recovery time on your moves. Your beast meter will deplete quicker when hit by your opponent.

Reversal
When your opponent attacks hit → immediately. Your character will side step the oncoming attack with your opponent open to a counter attack.

BOMBERMAN RACE FANTASY
Double Your Money
Save the game twice onto two separate memory blocks. Go to the bank and select Money Transfer. The money from one memory block will be transferred to the other, doubling your money.

Unlock Black Kangaroos and the White Dinosaur
Buy all five kangaroos and all five dinosaurs to unlock the two hidden variations.

BOMBERMAN WORLD

Passwords

Bonus Versus Level: **5656**
Bonus Battle Level: **4989**
Battle Royal Mode: **1616**
Maniac Mode: **4622**

Planet Forest
1 - 1 = **8010**
1 - 2 = **1180**
1 - 3 = **8086**
1 - 4 = **2919**
1 - 5 = **1021**

Planet Wind
2 - 1 = **0127**
2 - 2 = **1220**
2 - 3 = **1018**
2 - 4 = **0804**
2 - 5 = **0714**

Planet Fire
3 - 1 = **1027**
3 - 2 = **2413**
3 - 3 = **3009**
3 - 4 = **6502**
3 - 5 = **6809**

Planet Ocean
4 - 1 = **0627**
4 - 2 = **8808**
4 - 3 = **3674**
4 - 4 = **4891**
4 - 5 = **0605**

Planet Black
5 - 1 = **0730**
5 - 2 = **2151**
5 - 3 = **3562**
5 - 4 = **3812**
5 - 5 = **2203**

BRAHMA FORCE

Easy mode
To reduce the skill of enemy drones, press ↗ + ✖ + ■ then press **Start** on the "Press Start" screen.

Hard Mode
Why? Press **L1**, **R1**, **L2**, **R2**, ■, ✖, ▲, ● on the Title screen.

Hover Mode
If you finish the game in under an hour and a half, hold **L1**+**R2** and press ✖ on pad 2. Then, when you start a game you can use

R2 and **L1** to raise and lower your mech. Also, pressing **Start** on the title screen will access an FMV, play all level and sound options menu. All secret areas will also be visible on the map.

Level Skip
To skip to the next level, select the memory card options from the select screen and load up the level you are currently on from your saved games. Whilst the card is loading, keep pressing **Start** until the "Save game" message appears. Select yes or no and exit. You will be whisked away to begin the next level.

BREATH OF FIRE 3

Dauna Mines
After being released from the crystal, attack the two miners. Search the right corpse for a **Melted Blade**. Head right and out of the mines. Defend against Bull and you'll be knocked out by the crane operator. You'll find yourself caged and on a small train, rock the d-pad left and right to knock the cage off the train and into the woods.

Woods
You'll be rescued by Rei from a pack of wolves and he'll take you home. At this point you change from a dragon into a small boy.

Rei's House
When you wake, search the desk in the bottom right for the diary and save. Leave through the door at the top of the room and travel down the bottom path and travel to on Mcneil Town.

Mcneil Town Area
Here you'll meet up with Rei and Teepo. Rei will rob the town merchant for some equipment. Head east to the Yraall Road. Hide behind the trees and talk to Rei. After talking to Bunyan return through Mcneil Town and up to Cedar Woods. Head east and have Rei pick the front door. Once inside climb down the ladder in the top right. Search the shelves for a **Beef Jerky** and talk to Rei and Teepo. After Rei and Teepo leave, climb up the ladder and exit the house. Talk to Bunyan. Rei will be sent to Glaus Mountain while you and Teepo will chop logs. Wait until the log begins to tip before you strike with your sword. Chop enough logs and Bunyan will allow you to leave. Head north onto the world map and enter the path marked ?. Select Teepo and cross the small bridge. Strike the small rock under the boulder and then walk down the stream bed. Climb out of the river bed and follow the path until you reach a chest. Open the chest and collect the **Weather Vane**. Return back along the river bed and search the area for stones. Kick these to discover items hidden in holes. Head to the top left to return to the world map. Head towards Glaus Mountain.

Glaus Mountain

Cross over the bridge and search the area for **Antidotes**, these will increase your characters skill levels. Head to the northern cliff, cross the rope bridge and enter the house. Talk to Rei and rest for the night. As morning breaks the house will be attacked by the Nue. Have Rei attack using his basic attack whilst using Teepo's flare attack. Use Ryu's basic attack until one of your characters sustains major damage, then use his healing spell. After the Nue has lost around 150 hit points it will retreat. Save using the statue at the rear of the house. Follow the Nue up the mountain till you reach a cave. Enter the cave and follow the trail of blood. Take the first left and search the pile of bones to discover a **Bent Sword** and a **Molotov**. Return back to the main cavern and continue to follow the blood stains. Search the skeleton and collect **200 Zenny**. Return to the main cavern. Walk right and then up the left path. Leap into the water and enter the cave at the bottom of the waterfall. Use the same tactics as before. If you are low on AP points for Ryu and can't perform his healing spell, get him to use Healing Herbs instead. After defeating the Nue enter the cave at the top of the screen. Return back to the water and swim downstream. Talk to Bunyan.

Spring Time

Go upstairs and save. Leave the house and head towards McNeil. On the way, talk to both the Goblin and the Blob in the woods for useful information. Enter the McNeil and talk to the town folk. Visit the various houses and purchase items from the shops. Talk to Loki and accept his offer. Leave the town and head just left of McNeil to the '?'. Talk to the old man. He is one of the worlds seventeen masters who can teach your character special power in return for all your money. Return to McNeil, head south and enter the shed near the crop fields. Talk to Loki about stealing the tax money from the manor.

Outside The Mansion

Search the wall till you find the newly repaired wall. Talk to Rei and Teepo, Rei will fall through the wall as he lays on it. Enter the manor grounds. Bribe the first guard, talk to the second and he'll turn his back. Climb the stairs and head left, search the corner for a **Wallet**. Walk right and give the wallet to the guard, he'll allow you to pass. Past the stairs and approach the guard holding the lantern. Wait until he faces away from you. With his back turned, run past him. If you are seen you will be thrown out of the manor grounds and have to start again, which includes bribing the guard again. Go down the stairs and continue downwards, avoid the guards as you go. Climb the ladder and strike the bell. One of the guards will leave. Walk through the gap and talk to the smoking guard. Walk towards the gate and fight the dog using basic attacks. Return and talk to the smoking guard. Head to the top right corner and talk to the guard in front of the chicken house. Then walk to the two people near the maze. Talk to both of them and then return to the guard at the chicken house. Once he leaves enter the chicken house. Inside you'll be attacked by a giant chicken. Use Rei's basic attack and Teepo's Simoon spell. If you're turned into an egg use either antidote or croc tears

to restore your character. Once the giant chicken has been killed, the small chickens will escape and distract the guards. Head up the stairs and to the right, open the chest and collect the **Firecracker**. Return past the smoking guard and up the stairs. Rei will distract the guards near the entrance while Ryu and Teepo sneak in.

Inside The Mansion

After entering the house, go through the door on the right. Go right and up the small hallway to the bed. Rest and save. Enter into the room at the top left and search the drawer for **120 Zenny**. Return down the small hallway and climb the two sets of stairs into a storeroom. Search the crates for **Eye Drops** and a **Taser**. Return down the stairs to the main hallway near the mansion's entrance. Climb the stairs and you'll be attacked by a ghost. Use Teepo's Simoon spell while Ryu uses his basic attack and Healing spells. Once defeated climb the stairs and up the left staircase. Continue left then through the second left doorway. Walk to the end of the room and you'll face McNeil. McNeil will transform into a ghost. Use the same tactics as you did with the ghost in the main hallway. Continue forward and into the room at the end. As you try and climb down the stairs, you'll be attacked by another ghost. Unlike the other ghosts you've encountered this one is resistant to magic attacks. Use both your characters basic attacks and when low on health have Ryu use his Healing spell or healing herbs. When you have defeated the ghost head down the stairs. Walk down the corridor, as you pass search the cupboard for a **MultiVitamin**. Exit through the door and then through the one to the left. Once in the kitchen, talk to the chef then go through the doorway. You'll be attacked by another ghost, just use the same tactics as before. Follow the ghost flame to a lift and ride it to the top. Climb the stairs to a storeroom and save/rest. Climb the ladder to the roof. Walk to the top of the roof and head to the far right. Go next to the end window and pick up the **Grappling Hook**. Rei will appear and help you across to the opposite roof. In the lower left corner is a **Swallow Eye**, collect this and then head to the top of the roof and descend the stairs. Walk into the main room and talk to McNeil. You'll be attacked by a super ghost. Have Rei and Ryu use their basic attack, when you lose health have Ryu cast his Healing spell or use healing herbs. Use Teepo's Simoon spell until he runs out of AP, then have him use his basic attack. Once you've destroyed it, talk to McNeil and collect the stolen money.

Go upstairs and save. Leave the house and head to McNeil Town. Talk to all the villagers, then go to the farm and speak with Loki. Enter the hut and Bunyan will warn the characters. Return home to find your house on fire. You'll be confronted by Sunder and Balio and be beaten in battle. Ryu will awaken in Bunyan house. Go outside and talk to Bunyan. Then head to the Yraall road past the farm. Head right to Mount Myrneg. Once there head right and speak to the monster next to the chest. Open the chest to collect an **Icicle**. Climb the mountain till you reach Sunder. Speak to Sunder and he'll knock you out, you'll turn into a dragon and be taken to the castle.

Castle Wyndia

When you wake you find yourself in Castle Wyndia and back as a boy. You'll be sent to the dungeons. Nina will come and attempt to release you. She'll be kidnapped by Sunder and Balio. Charge the door twice to open the cell door. When you're free, enter the top cell and collect the **Skill Ink** and save. Head down the right passage and down the stairs. Here you'll confront Sunder and Balio. Attack them and Nina will hide, when you are killed Nina will restore your health. Together you escape the castle.

Graveyard

Examine the grave stones and answer using the green words. After you have examined seven grave stones return to the first grave and select the green answer. You'll then be dropped to a new section of the graveyard. Open the chest and collect the **Light Bangle**, then continue to the right. Climb the ladder and open the chest to receive a **Glass Domino**. Climb up to the mound with two grave stones and push the words: Red, Climbing, I, Is, Look, Beneath, This. You should then fall to a new area. Walk to the lower left and fall through the hole. Talk to Nina then follow the path out of the crypt.

Wyndia

Enter the inn and rest/save. Visit the shops and buy items. Talk to the group of children and join their game of hide and seek. One is hidden at the right of the three shops near the beggar and one at the opposite side. Another is near the cafe in the right corner behind a tree. The final child is in the top right next to the line of trees. Leave the city and walk between the wall at the edge of the city to the ? Enter the hut where you will meet another one of the masters. Leave the hut and return to the main road. Enter Eygnock Road. Enter the house then leave after hearing the scream. Outside you'll will be confronted by Sunder and Balio. Again you're be beaten till unconsciousness and then taken to Genmel.

Genmel

Once you escape from the pub, visit the inn, weapon shops and learn more about 'The Contest'. Leave Genmel through the bottom right gates and head towards Mount Boumore. Climb to the top of the mountain till you reach a hut. Speak to the two men and you'll be allowed to spend the night in their hut. In the morning, try to open the door and you'll discover that Mason has locked you in and fetched Sunder. Go through the open door at the rear of the room and up to the cable car control panel. Nina will use her magic on the control panel and you'll escape to the opposite mountain. Climb to the top of this mountain and you'll be cornered by Sunder. Both Ryu and Nina will escape by jumping down the mountain. When you recover, leave the mountain and head left till you reach a clearing with two trees and a '?'. Enter and follow the trail and you will arrive at a crystal. Examine the crystal and Ryu will learn a new Gene. Return to the world map, head right and enter the tower.

Tower

You can buy items from the fish creature at the base of the steps. Climb the steps, walk right and enter the door near the pond. Walk to the crystal, select Nina and strike the crystal with her magic. Once lit, walk left to the staircase and exit the tower by the bottom door. Run to the pond and strike the four crystals with Nina's wand. If you do this fast enough, the pond water will drain, revealing a chest. Head left towards the main tower entrance and speak to the robot who will reveal enemy weaknesses. When you have finished, enter the tower and climb the stairs. Here you'll reach a save point, search the bookshelves for info on machines and magic. Continue up the stairs until you reach a door, a robot should exit then return through the door. Enter the room and speak to Momo. Momo will join your party. Return to the corridor and enter the room next along. Read the sign then turn all the tiles in the mosaic grey. Once you've solved the puzzle correctly, enter through the door which opens at the top. Search the three chests then return to the corridor. Walk to the end of the corridor and up the stairs. Walk up to the orb and activate the second from the left switch. Then the switch on the far right. Walk across the hallway, up the stairs and into the next room. Hit the two switches and enter the corridor in the top wall. Once in the corridor, enter the first door. Search the bookcase for more info on chrysm energy. Return to the corridor and enter the next door. Inside the chest are some Zenny. Return to the switch room and climb the stairs. Keep walking till you reach a room with moving platforms. Step onto the grey platform to reach the opposite side. Continue up the stairs till you reach a yellow crystal. Examine the sign next to it, then strike the crystal eight times with Nina's wand to reach the staircase on the opposite side of the room. If you strike the crystal only twice you can collect the **Breastplate** from the chest or strike the crystal six times to collect the **Dice**. Once up the stairs collect the **Rod** from the room above then continue up until you reach the room with the energy beams. If you touch the beams you'll be poisoned. Use Nina's wand to activate and deactivate the beams until you reach the opposite side. Go through the door and enter the library. To escape the tower, examine behind the desk and push the switch.

Once your characters have recovered, walk up and collect the Gene from the crystal. Return to the world map and move up till you reach a hut near the mountains. Enter this area. Enter the coffee shop and take a seat. A scientist friend of Momo will appear and will tell you about the trouble at the plant. Speak to the women upstairs. She is one of the masters and will train you if you have more than fifteen weapons in your inventory. Leave the coffee shop and return to the world map.

The Plant

Head down and go into the plant. To reach the scientist friend of Momo, use the conveyer belts and switches. Select Momo and talk to the scientist. He'll tell you to visit the dump. Leave the plant and go down to the dump. Once at the dump head right down the corridor. Walk down and at the first junction walk up. When you reach the switch, press it twice. Go through the gap and search the chest to receive **1,200 Zenny**. Return to the cave entrance and walk around the top of the cave. Use the crates to cross to the chest, inside are **High Boots**. Return to the switch area and enter through the gap to the left, continue left until you leave the cave. Head down towards the magma pit and enter the root cave on the right. Once inside, you'll be attacked by a mutant onion. Use fire and earth attacks to cause the most damage. When you run out of AP, use edged weapon attacks. When the mutant onion has been defeated, he begs you to kill him. Place the mutant onion in the lava. At this point a smaller onion will jump out of the lava, Peco will join your party. Leave the cave and go onto the world map. Walk towards the large tree near the plant and enter the '?'. Select Peco and speak to the giant redwood at the end of the trail. The giant redwood is another master and he will train anyone in return for a Wisdom Fruit. Return to the plant and talk to the scientist. He will offer you safe passage back to Wyndia. In the morning you hide in an old wagon but are attacked by Sunder and Balio and taken to Genmel.

The Contest

The Unicorn brothers will agree to let you participate in the 'contest'. Once in the town visit the stores and stock up on weapons, health and armour. When finished go to the contest area. Walk into the dressing room near the four body builders and talk to the show girl. She will explain the rules and the lead character will be sent to the fire pit to do battle. The first fighter is Claw, beware of her double strike. The second fighter is a fat wizard, attack the body builder beneath him and he will attack the body builder which will consume all his AP. Once this is done attack him using your basic attack. The last fighter is extremely strong, if playing Ryu turn into a dragon and throw everything at him. After the firepit has been completed, walk back to the main hallway to the rest of your party and save the game. When you have finished walk to the null magic hall. Enter the dressing room and speak to the showgirl. She'll explain the rules to you. When the game begins, turn into a dragon and cast the counter attack move. Concentrate on attacking the wizard until he's defeated. When he's gone, his two golems will attack each other. Heal your injured party members and then finish them off. Heal your characters and save. Proceed to the final dressing room and speak to the show girl. She'll tell you about your opponent Garr. The final battle has been rigged so you cannot win. Once you've been defeated, Garr will take your party as prizes. After you've been released, follow Garr to the Unicorn brothers office to be reunited with your kidnapped party members. Leave Genmel.

Head down from Genmel and left towards the bridge. Cross the bridge and enter Maekyss Gorge. Here you'll be attacked again from Sunder and Balio. Defeat the first wave of their troops and Garr will appear and defeat the rest of the Unicorn brothers army. Garr will then join your party. Sunder and Bailo will merge into Stallion. Change Ryu in to his dragon form and go all out offensively. Use Garr's blades attack but keep his health at max.

After Stallion has been defeated, walk down the side of the bridge and towards the house on the right. Search the bush outside the house for a **Frost Gene**, enter the house and talk to the couple inside. Remember the wife's name is Kimiko. Search the cabinet for **800 Zenny** and head outside. Return across Maekyss Gorge and towards the top of the mountain. Enter the '?' area next to the tree. Select Peco and head butt the tree near the tent to reveal a **Flower Gem**. Go into the tent and collect the Wisdom Fruit from the cabinet. Return back across Maekyss Gorge to Wyndia.

Wyndia

Once you've reached Wyndia, pay a visit to Durandol if any of your characters is his pupil. Select Nina and enter the castle. Talk to the guard at the castle entrance and your characters will be treated to a feast. After the feast, Nina will retire to her royal chambers. You'll hear a crash, walk downstairs and go right into the blue carpeted dining room. Speak to the maid by the broken plate and Honey will appear. Head right up the staircase and talk to the women in the bed. Collect the items from the cabinets before leaving. Return to the dining room and go down the stairs at the bottom of the screen. Search the barrels opposite the drunk, then talk to the mouse and collect the **Cheese**. Return back to Nina's chambers and go through the left door. Walk along the ramparts and talk to Honey. Nina will join the party after Honey falls from the battlements.

Visit Mygas, if one of your characters is his pupil. Go to Bunyan house and speak to Bunyan, he will offer to be one of your characters master. When you are finished head to Wyndia. When you reach the checkpoint Garr will bluff his way past the guards. When you reach the bridge he will reveal more about himself and his people. Cross the bridge and enter the small hut on the hill. Enter the '?' area and head towards the fishing hut. Walk behind the hut and down the stairs where you'll find the **Thunder Gene**. Return to the world map and head down to the fishing area. Enter the '?' area and talk to the fish creature. Say yes when he asks you a question and he'll offer to train your characters, but only if they have reached the rank of master fisherman. Return to the world map and walk to the top right and enter the port of Rhapala.

Rhapala

Walk through the port and head to the inn. Walk downstairs and speak to the sailor in the red lifejacket. Leave the inn and walk left across the stone bridge. Enter the shipyard and walk to the top of the docks, talk to the women stood behind the body builder. You'll then be introduced to Beyd the book keeper. Ask him about the guild and then return to the town. Speak to Shadis and then enter the inn. Talk to Sinkar then leave the town. Return to the world map, the characters will discuss what to do and return to Rhapala in the morning. Head towards the wharf, speak to Beyd and agree to help him train to get into the lighthouse. Beyd will meet you in the town square at night once you've brought weapons for him. Training Beyd consists of twenty rounds of combat. Use light attacks to lower his HP, then use a rejuvenation spell to raise his health. When you are finished, return to camp and rest. Return to the wharf and speak to Beyd. At this point you can train again or head to the lighthouse. Beyd should be trained three or four times before going to the lighthouse. When you're ready to leave, Zig will try to stop you and challenge Beyd to a duel. Your party can help Beyd by attacking Zig. Once Zig has been defeated head to the wharf and talk to Beyd to receive a pass to get to the lighthouse. Search the chest for some extra weapons.

The Lighthouse
Walk to the left from the wharf to get to the lighthouse. Show the guild badge to the guard and continue to the left. Go to the tower, enter through the door and read the sign inside. Descend the stairs and head south west through the complex. Open the chests to reveal a **Fire Chrysm**, head back inside the complex and walk to the top left. Enter the door on the right and climb the ladder to reach the boiler. Read the sign then return to the hatch with a downward arrow on it. Examine the hatch then place the chrysm inside. Walk over to the switch and watch the blimp. Every fourth time the blip reaches the centre of the screen, the edges will flash. Press the switch when the dot is at the highest point in the centre of the screen. When done correctly the power will be restored to the first part of the circuit. Climb down the ladder and follow the glowing circuit till you reach another switch. Press this switch and follow the circuit to the next one. Press the switch and then climb the stairs into the lighthouse. As you approach the lighthouse you'll be attacked by the Glazer. Use blind and jolt attacks to weaken it. Once you've defeated the Glazer, walk up the stairs, walk to the left of the tower and collect the **Eldritch Gene**. Press the switch and a small fairy will appear and drop a **Tiara**. Return to the world map.

Go to the flower circle and use the tiara to enter it. You will be transported to the world of the fairies. Enter the small shack on the hill. Talk to the fairy and agree to slay the sea beast. Head down until you reach the beach and wait for the sea beast to arrive. Talk to the sea beast and wait until Momo and Nina leave. Speak to the sea beast again in English and it will threaten the fairies. Use fire and electric magic whenever it rises from the sea. When the beast is dead , return to the fairy hut and talk to the fairies inside. Return to the world map.

Return to the coffee shop and enter the '?' area just left of the shop. Hack away the bushes and follow the path to the river. Select Peco and head butt the rock into the river. A fairy will rise from the water and ask you for a flower gem, give it to her and she offers to train your characters.

Return to Rhapala and talk to Beyd. Speak to Sinkar at the inn about the volcano and he'll eventually give you a letter. Leave Rhapala and head to Mount Zublo in the top right. Climb the temple steps and head right. Reach the mountain entrance by following the path to the right and up the steps. Walk forward

and then right. Follow the magma. Enter the cave and head to the right, avoid the yellow gas from the pipes and continue down the ledge. Search the chest for a **Fire Ring**. Climb the ladders and head left into the next cave. Walk around the fire pit and collect the **Miracle gene**. Equip the Fire ring and open the chest across the fire pit for the **Fire Talons**. Continue to walk round the fire pits and head up. You'll be confronted by an old man. He'll unleash two fire creatures, use ice magic on them and attack the old man using wind magic. Walk through the cave and leave the mountain.

Enter the city in the top left. Walk to the right and enter the temple. At the top of the stairs is a master who will train you if one of your characters has the backhand skill. Select Garr and climb the ladder behind the master. Use Garr to move the rock and enter the meditation chamber. Speak to Sudama then leave the town. Camp for the night and Garr will explain more about his past and Ryu's destiny.

Walk to the top right and enter the Angel Towers. Talk to the guards next to the staircase then climb the stairs. Go through the gap in the banister and talk to the guard. If you drop down to the left you can collect a **Dice**, the right holds a **Wisdom Seed**. Drop off the ledge near the second staircase, walk in line with the stairs and go down the hole near the bottom of the cliff. Examine the pyramid and then go up the stairs at the top of the room. Follow the corridor and go down the first set of stairs, walk left and then select Momo. Shoot through the crumbling wall and collect the **Diamond Ring** and the **Moon Tears** from the chests. Return to the main staircase. Continue through the temple until you reach a hole in the ground surrounded by pillars. Climb down and walk up. Select Garr and push the grey block to the left. Push the next block forward until it's just below the two walkways. Walk to the highest block and push it down. Use these two blocks to create a bridge, Return to the first block and push it in place. Head left and climb the steps to reach the staircase. Walk down the stairs and leave Momo behind. Examine the tablets and Garr will reveal the history of the dragons. When Garr attacks you, transform into a dragon and use the Miracle Gene to counter Garr's attacks. When Garr has been defeated Ryu will enter into the realm of dreams.

Garr will ask for your forgiveness once you wake. Collect the items he leaves and then follow him. Continue right until you reach the crane which knocked you out at the beginning of the game and head down to the elevator. Ride the elevator to basement 1, follow the railway tracks until you reach the miner's camp. Enter the hut and search the cupboard for **200 Zenny**. You can buy items from the fish creature. Return to the elevator and ride down to basement 2. Enter the door at the top, rest and save. Leave and walk right to the main cavern. Continue right until you reach the rock with the chest on it. Line up the rails by pressing the nearest leaver, walk over to the mine cart and get Garr to push it. Cross the ledge and search the chest for a **Feather Sword**. Return the mine cart to it's original position and reposition the levers so the mine cart has a clear path to the top left corner. Push the mine cart and pull the lever when it stops, push the cart again and it will open the cave entrance. You'll be attacked by a dragon spirit, Use ice magic to defeat it. Once it is dead collect the **Shadow Gene** it leaves behind. Speak to the women and she'll give you the **Fusion Gene**.

Exit through the hole in the wall and head right. Enter through the first door and search until you find the **Lion Belt** and some **Protein**. Walk down and then head right. Enter the next room and use the lever three times to raise the platform outside, cross the platform and leave the mine. Talk to the foreman and head to the office, speak to the mine manager and collect the reward. Leave the office and enter the hut next door. Rest and save.

Head right and enter '?' area, enter the hut. Inside is Emitai the wizard who agrees to train you if you give him 10,000 Zenny. Leave the hut and return to the world map. Head to Syn city. Enter the city and speak to the beggar in the centre of the market. For every 20 Zenny you give him he will give you more information on the beast on Ogre Road. Visit the shops. Leave the city and head up to the bridge, walk right from the bridge and enter Ogre Road. Use Ryu's sword to cut down the three bushes on the darken patch of ground and collect the **Horseradish**. Follow the path to the edge of Ogre Road and you'll be attacked by the beast. When it takes too much damage it will retreat, continue down the road and enter the world map.

Go to Mount Levett, walk up to the top of the mountain and go right. Follow the path down to reach the exit. Enter Yraall road and talk to the guard, you'll be told the road to Wyndia is blocked, head to McNeil village and head to the inn. Speak with the landlady outside and she'll tell you about the weretiger. Enter the inn, talk to her again then rest and save. Leave the inn and enter Cedar woods. Walk towards Rei's tree house, leave Garr on the path and enter the tree house. Speak to Rei and ask about Syn city. After Rei leaves, go back to Garr and walk to the farm. Talk to the villagers in the field and walk to McNeil's mansion. Talk to Nina and she'll tell you that McNeil was arrested. When you wake, leave the mansion and return to Syn city.

Syn City
When you reach Syn city you discover the city has been attacked by the weretiger. Walk around the town and talk to the survivors. Enter the building with the panther mouth and talk to the man inside who will tell you his boss has left for the checkpoint. Search the chest then leave the city. Head to and enter the check point area. Rei will attack the gang leader, Mikbah. He'll be stunned and you'll be attacked. Use earth and wind magic and then your basic attacks once you've run out of AP. Once defeated, Rei will join your party. Select Rei and pick the lock on the checkpoint hut and search the hut. Leave

and walk to Eygnock road.

Talk to Nina then head towards the plant. Walk round the conveyer belts and speak to Momo and Honey. After Momo joins the party, go to the world map and enter the tree master's area. Speak to Peco, then select Peco and Momo to be in the main party. Return to the plant. Speak to the scientists who will tell you about the chrysm gas leak in the green houses. Use the conveyer belts to reach the green houses. When you reach the green houses get Peco to push a rock onto the cross written on the ground. Then head butt the rock into the green house. Once the gas has been released, head down to the next green house. Repeat as before to release the gas. When both green houses have been cleared enter the boiler room. Search the cupboards, then use Momo's cannon on the fireplace. Once the smoke has cleared, climb through the gap.

Climb down the ladder and head right. Follow the corridor until you reach the computer room. Select Momo and examine the switched on computer. Once Mom has entered the password return back to the beginning of the complex and head left. Walk down the corridor and down the stairs. You have only fifteen seconds to search the room before you're affected from the released chrysm energy. Examine the plant trays and examine the onion for the second password. Return to the computer room and enter the password. Enter the door to the right of the second door with the number one. Enter the number two door and press the switch. Return to the previous room and go down the staircase. When you reach a group of grey beams, cross the top beam and examine the maintenance document. Enter through the door at the side of the room and walk over to the document. Collect the document for the third password and go to the conveyer belt. Across the girder is a **Force Gene**. Walk back to the computer room, enter the password and go through the door marked three. Examine the three energy banks then head towards the door at the top end of the room. A deadly gas will fill the room and you'll be attacked by a massive slug. Use ice magic and electricity against him. Once dead, return to the previous room and go up the stairs in the bottom left corner. Collect a **Wisdom Ring** from the chest at the top of the stairs. Return to the computer room and have Momo enter 1-3-2-5-4. Door four will open. Enter through the door behind the computers and save. Climb the ladder and head towards door four. Enter the control room and battle against Palet. Use fire and earth magic to weaken his roots. Once Palet has been destroyed, press the switch to kill his mother and leave the plant.

Head for Wyndia and visit Durandol. Nina and Rei will enter the castle together. Talk to the children. If you agree to play their game, four of them will hide on the world map. Once found they'll return to the fountain and offer to train your characters. One is hiding in the grave yard underneath castle Wyndia. The second is in the third basement of the Duana mine. The third hidden near the bridge which connects Wyndia to Rhapala. The last one is hidden in Junk town. Select Nina and go to the castle entrance, talk to the guard and enter the castle. Speak to the King. After Nina offers Rei a guided tour, head to the kitchen and meet Honey. Nina will pick up Honey. Search the cells and if you want enter the graveyard and find the hiding child. Select Nina and head to Sheila's bedroom. Talk to Sheila, then return downstairs and speak to the King. When Honey appears head to the cellar. Go through to the basement and let Honey into the locked room. Enter the teleporter and you'll be transported to the basement underneath Durandol's house. Leave the house and head down to join up with the rest of your characters.

Camp for the night, then in the morning enter the checkpoint area. Talk to the guards and you'll be allowed through the checkpoint. Head towards Urkan Tapa. Select Garr and talk to Sudama. Leave Urkan Tapa and head for Angel Tower. With Garr, talk to the guards at the top of the stairs and you'll be allowed through. Garr will prey when he reaches the top. Return to Urkan Tapa and have Garr talk to Sudama. He will give you a clue to where the first guardian is located. Return to the world map and walk right to the east coastline. Walk down along the coastline till you reach the tidal caves.

Enter the caves and talk to the fish creature. He'll tell you about the tides. Wait until the tide is at it's lowest level before looking around. Head up into the cave and follow the passage to the far side of the cave. Wait until the tide drops then climb down the ladder. Walk up to the raft and use Ryu's sword to sever the guide rope. Ride the raft to the ledge on the left. Enter through the door on the left and up the ladder. Collect the **Gross Gene** from the corridors and follow the path to the world map. Walk to the cliff area just below the tidal cave. Select Garr and enter the cave at the far end of the village. Talk to Gaist. He'll then talk to Ryu. Return outside and speak to Garr. After talking to Garr then return to the cave and talk to Gaist. He will then turn into a demon and attack you. Use ice and wind magic to put out the torches. This will stop Gaist from regenerating. Attack Gaist using Ice Gene, Lightning Gene and Thorn. Once destroyed Garr will suggest they return to Angel tower. Examine Gaist remains before you leave to receive the **Beast Spear.**

Return to Angel tower. Enter the tower and go to the room with the naked woman. Approach the pyramid to release the woman. She'll tell you to meet her at Mount Zublo. Walk to Mount Zublo and enter the temple at it's peak. Read the inscription and Ryu will enter Deis's chamber who will bestow him the power of Prana. Leave Mount Zublo and head to Urkan and enter Junk town. Visit the shops once you've reached Junk town. Walk down until you meet Beyd, talk to the merchant and then follow them to the docks. Select Momo and enter the docks. Talk to Beyd and he will ask Momo to look at the engine. Momo will then give Ryu a list of parts needed to fix the engine. Leave the docks and speak to the watchman. He'll tell you to return to Junk town and talk to the Guildmaster. The Guildmaster is in a hut in the lower left corner of Junk town. He will give you

permission to search Steel Beach. Leave Junk town via the lower exit and walk to the left. When you reach the rock face head down and enter the hut. Behind the sheet is another Dragon Gene. Return to the rock face and enter Steel Beach.

Steel Beach

Ensure Garr is in your party before you enter. Head into the cave and talk to the guard, when he lets you through head up the beach and collect the Dragon Gene. When you reach the crane talk to the Minotaur wearing the cap. He'll ask Garr to help him pull something out of the water, wait until the red flag is raised before pulling. Defeat the sea creature you pull from the sea, then talk to the Minotaur. He will allow you to enter the freighter. Part A is just left of the Minotaur on the beach. Part B is in the pile in front of the old man with the stick. Part F is next to the wielder. Left of the wielder in the cliff is Part C. Just above here is Part H. Enter the freighter and near the entrance is Part D. Head up and collect Part B from the dead end corridor. Walk down and go down the ladder. Collect Part D from the left side of the central lever. Then search behind the central lever for Part F. Head down right and collect Part H below the second lever. Pull the two lower levers and cross over to the top lever, behind this is Part G. Search the chest behind the crates for a **Wind Robe**. Near the chest are two parts, Part C and Part E. Pull the lever and travel across the gap and climb the ladder. At the top crate is Part A. Part C is hidden near the next set of crates. Return to the top lever and lower the girder. Climb back up the ladder and cross the crates and collect Part F. Return to Momo at the docks and give her the parts.

Once the engine has been repaired, Beyd will take the boat back to Rhapala to re-crew. During the voyager talk to Nina. When Beyd has re-crewed, board the boat and speak to Zig and he'll start the engines. Zig asks you to talk to all the other characters, do this then talk to Zig again. When you gain control of the boat, steer the boat up towards rough sea. Zig will suggest getting a navigator, head across from Rhapala and dock at Parch. Walk to the top of the town and enter the mayor's house. Talk to the mayor's aide who will inform you he won't talk to anyone until he's eaten. Talk to the mayor. You need to find out what the mayor eats. Head back to Rhapala via the boat, Walk to central Wyndia and go to Maekyss gorge. Above the river is a small house, go under the bridge and enter the house. Talk to the woman inside and she'll explain where to collect the ingredients. You should have collected the Horseradish from Ogre Road. The Shaldy seeds are hidden behind the woman's house. Use Peco to head butt the seeds from the tree. Leave the gorge and enter the fishing area across the bridge, Use the rod and line to collect the Mackerel. Travel to the coffee house and walk to the well on the hill below, Select Garr and speak to the women. Draw some water from the well and she'll give you the Vinegar. Return to the woman's house and she'll tell you the correct ratio of ingredients needed. Walk to Durandol's house and use the teleporter to reach the palace. Enter the kitchen and talk to the chef who will agree to train you if you collect some ingredients for him. The Beef Jerky was taken from Bunyan's house at the beginning of the game. The Swallow Eye can be brought from a shop if you don't possess one. The Martian Squid can be caught by fishing just outside the castle. The Angler can be caught by fishing near Angel tower. Once this is done return to Rhapala and take the boat to Parch.

Return to the Mayor's house and talk to the aide. He'll tell you how to mix the ingredients. Present the Shisu to the Mayor and in return he'll give you a set of charts. Take the boat through the rough sea and sail between the two rocks and enter the '?' area. You have thirty seconds to reach your destination before the tide turns. The mariner's cabin is hidden in the top left waterway. There are other items hidden throughout the waterways which can be collected. When you reach the mariner's cabin, speak with him and he'll tell you that you need the black ship to cross the channel. You'll come face to face with the black ship. Ram the ship from behind using the turbo boost, once it's wrecked go to the engine room and help Momo. Return to the deck and choose Momo and another character and board the black ship.

The Black Ship
Once on board go through the door at the top left. Walk down the staircase and enter the room at the bottom. Select Momo and examine the computer, select the second program and then step onto the grey platform to reach the other side of the room. Enter into the next room, walk to the slot machine and collect the ID Card. Return to the computer and select the fourth program. Ride the platform and open the chest to collect a **Skill Ink**. Return to the computer and select program three, Ride the platform to the power room and activate the crane. Go back to the platform and walk back to the stairs. Return to the top deck, go through the door and activate the crane. Move the crane and pick up the four boxes from the centre of the room. The fourth one will smash and reveal an item. Walk across the bridge of crates and enter the door at the top. Head left and collect the **Star Shells** from the chest. Return to the crane room and exit via the right corridor. Climb the stairs and enter the first room on the left, search the shelves and collect the **Ammonia**. Leave and enter the next door along and examine the machine. Return to the corridor and climb the stairs. Use the ID Card on the machine, enter the elevator and select Momo. Use Momo to examine the elevator, then return down the elevator and enter the room with the counting device. Make a note of the number showing and return to the elevator. When the blimps reach 99 walk up the stairs and talk to Momo. The engines should start and your party will board the ship.

While on your journey an alarm will sound, Speak to Momo and you'll be told that the ship has hit something. Enter the crew quarters and save. Enter through the door Momo opened. Walk to the top left of the ship and go on deck, head to the bow of the ship and look in the water. You'll be attacked by two squid creatures. Move away slowly until you reach the other end of the ship. Attack the two creatures and you'll have back up from the two deck guns. Once destroyed, the ship will reach shore.

Walk up from the docks and enter the town. Continue up to the top right and enter the alley way between the two houses. Talk to the robot and then select the second response. The robot will give you **Homing Missiles**. Visit the shops and speak to the town folk, then leave. Camp for the night and rest. Head up and enter the '?' area. Walk to the tree in the clearing and collect the **Trance Gene**. Select Momo and enter the steel grave area. Take the left path and enter the building at the top. Climb up the ladder and collect the **UV Glasses**. Head right and climb the ladder, go down the hole and have Momo shoot the panel in the left wall. Search the chest for a **Spanner,** then head back up the ladder and up to leave the grave. Go to Colony. Select Momo, climb the steps and examine the radar dish. Return down the steps and enter the door beneath the radar. Collect the key then leave. Walk left then down the ledge, continue left and collect the **Failure Gene**. Follow the ledge round and enter through the first door. Exit through the door opposite the passage. Walk left, across the ledge and search the chest. Return to the gap in the ledge and jump down. Have Momo examine the lever you land next to. Use the key on the lever and align the rotating blades, A beam should hit a fuse and the teleporter above will be activated. Head upstairs and enter the teleporter.

Select Momo and examine the control panel, Leave through the door in the bottom right. Follow Honey down the hallway, climb the ladder and enter the door at the end. Talk to Momo then return to the hallway. Head away from the teleporter chamber and follow the corridor round. Climb the left staircase and enter the control room. Pull the blue lever, then the light blue lever and then the dark red lever to raise the girders. Go up the stairs to the left of the girders, continue up the stairs and then take the left corridor. Move the platforms and ride the one directly adjacent to the central platform, standing on the central platform will open the door. Go through the door. Continue round and up the stairs till you reach the top of the building. Move the radar dish so it faces the top left and begins to transmit. Return to the teleporter chamber and have Momo examine the control panel again. Set the destination co-ordinates to the container yard and enter the teleporter.

Head to the lower left of the teleporter and collect the **Radiance Gene**. Return to the teleporter and go to Dragnier. Once you've left the teleporter, talk to the old man. He'll invite you to eat with him, during the meal he will reveal that the villagers are members of the brood. In the morning, search the shelves for a **Skill Ink.**. Leave the tent, then talk to Rei. Head up, climb the stairs and talk to Garr. You'll be told to go to the village well in the centre of the village. Leave the village and save. Select Nina and Garr and enter the village and go down the well. Climb down the ladders, then move up the corridor and through the doorway. Enter the room to the left, select Ryu and talk to Jono. Select Garr, talk to Jono then finally have Nina talk to him. Jono will transform into a dragon and attack you. During this battle Ryu will be unable to change into dragon form. Once the dragon has been slain, it will turn to chrysm, collect this and receive **Infinity Gene**. Leave the well.

Speak to the elder once you reach the top of the well then go to the teleport chamber. Enter the door at the top. If you've collect all the genes, Ladon will offer to train your characters. Walk over to Horis and ask him to lead you to the desert. Once on the world map, enter the factory. Take Momo and Peco with you. Take the lower path, enter the factory, climb the stairs to the room and collect some **Ammonia**. Return to the lower floor and go down the corridor. Enter the door near the stairs, continue down and search the chest for the **Rockbreaker**. Return upstairs, take the main corridor and go through the door near the lever. Follow the passage and enter the cave with the central staircase. Go up the stairs and enter the room with three switches. Quickly pull the first two switches. Exit through the door at the bottom and head right. Take the lower corridor and through the door. Pass the electrified room and climb the ladder. Walk to the top left, pull the lever and return to the electrified room. Climb to the high platform and examine the control panel. These control the robot outside. Move the robot and pull the three switches to turn off the power. Go up the ladder, then through the top right door. Climb the stairs, select Momo, use her cannon to shoot the emergency switch and open the door.

While you are camped talk to Horis then examine the jug near his tent to collect some water. When you reach the desert you'll need to use the stars to navigate. You need the north star and false north star at the same height with the three stars between them. At this point you'll be attacked by the desert boss. After the boss has been defeated, Nina will fall ill. Have Ryu talk to Momo then head outside and speak to Rei. Walk behind the camel and use Ryu's sword to collect the meat. Take this to Nina to revive her. Make your way to the Oasis. Once you've reached the oasis rest and save. Nina will recover from her illness and rejoin the party. Select your party which includes Garr then follow the path up the mound. Head up right and enter the '?' surrounded by buildings. Go into the house and with Garr, destroy the crate next to the teleporter. If you have met all sixteen masters, return through the teleporter to Wyndia and speak to the remaining master standing in the courtyard. Return through the teleporter and climb the ladder.

Enter Caer Xhan and visit the two robot shops. Head right and enter the building at the top of the map. Examine the robot which resembles Honey, then walk to the left and enter the room with the square floor. Climb down the stairs and enter the next room. Press the switch and the lights will go out. Return upstairs and you should be able to see the infra red beam. Move around the beams and up the stairs on the right. Head up and enter the building. Walk to the console and turn

the power back on. Use the controls to open the gates to the city. Exit and drop off the ledge to the left. Walk up, enter the control centre, use the console to unlock the gate then enter through the open gate. Go into the elevator.

Station Myria

Once in the station, climb the stairs and pull the lever at the top. Return downstairs and examine the hole in the floor. The elevator will move. Select the arrival desk and enter the elevator. From the chest collect the **Wisdom Fruit**. Return to the control panel and select the maintenance deck. Enter the elevator. Walk up and enter the second elevator. Follow the corridor through the door at the top then up the stairs past the two locked doors. Look at the two consoles and deactivate the lasers. Return to the main entrance where you entered. At the two locked doors head down the left corridor and enter the door on the right. Rest and save. Continue down the corridor, up the stairs and enter through the door. Follow the yellow path up the stairs and ride the conveyer belt to the next yellow path. Enter the door at the end of the yellow path. Search the cage for an **ID Card**. Turn off the gas in the cage and exit the room. Enter the next door along and look at the console. Match the diagram using the console in both rooms. Pass through the electronic walkway in the cage and ride the elevator down. Head down the lower corridor and enter the left area. In the corner is a **Skill Ink**. Return to the middle corridor and head up through the next room. Ride the elevator up, kill the creature at the top and collect it's **ID Card**. Return to the elevator and go down, enter the storage area and collect the **HE Rounds**. Go through the bottom door. Use Rei to unlock the cage and collect the items inside. Return to the save point at the bottom of the stairs. Select Momo and Rei, head to the two locked doors and use the ID Card to open the door. Speak to the robot and you'll be given a robot guide. Search the chest for a **Demon Bane**. Leave the room and climb the stairs. Follow the green path and ride the escalator up. Equip Momo with the HE Shells and use her cannon to clear away the plants blocking your path. Head through the door, take the top passage and have Rei open the door in the corner. Search the shelves for a **Wisdom Fruit** and **Ginseng Root**. Exit through the far door. Travel left across the garden From the hill head up and enter through the door. Search the chest for a **Dragon Spear**. Return to the garden and climb the hill. Head right, up the staircase and exit through the door at the end. Ride the elevator up. In the top right is a **Soul Gem** and in the bottom left is **Force Armour**. Collect both then cross the bridge at the top left. Speak to Teepo and you'll be transported to another realm.

Teepo Returns

Head left and talk to Nina. Examine the dragon statue to the left, then continue left. When you return to the statue, examine it again. Walk right. Speak with Rei then use the dragon statue to save. Walk left and examine the two stone tablets. Head left and fall down the hole. Examine the dragon and answer yes to his question. Search the chest then enter the glowing pillar. Go up, walk left and examine the dragon statue. Stand in front of it for 20 seconds then enter the area which appears behind it. Search the chests and walk left to the glowing pillar. Walk on the yellow teleporter and talk to Garr. Step on the teleporters in this order: purple, green, blue. Enter through the glowing pillar at the end. You'll meet Teepo and he'll summon a skeleton rider to attack you. Once the skeleton rider is destroyed you'll be transported back to the garden. Teepo will appear, transform into a dragon and attack your party. Once he's dead, collect his armour, weapons and the key card from his remains. Return through the second locked door.

Open door A and collect the **Light Bangle** from the chest. Return to the corridor and climb the stairs near the save point. Head down right near where the green and yellow paths start. Use the second ID Card to open the locked door. Take the top left path then the bottom left. Enter the door at the end. Continue forward through three doors until you reach a room with a ladder. Climb the ladder and enter the room to the left. Collect the **Moon Tears** from the chest, then leave through the other door. Climb down the ladder and save. Climb down the second ladder and enter the underground tunnels.

Final Battle

Follow Honey to the lift and ride down the lift. Talk to the hologram, follow the passage round and speak to the second hologram. Continue to follow the passage round and follow the right hand path when you reach the split. Here you'll learn more about chrysm. Continue right and ride the elevator to Myria. After speaking to Myria, talk to all the characters in turn. Myria will talk to you again and will give Ryu a choice. If you choose to give up your power, the game will end. If you choose to keep it you'll fight Myria.

If you defeat Myria, she'll be banished back to her own realm. Your characters find themselves in the desert. As they walk into the sunset a small seed sprouts in the desert sand.

BRIAN LARA'S CRICKET

Cheat codes

Uncatchable Slippery Ball	**DROPBALL**
World X1 Team	**PENSIONS**
Unbreakable Stumps	**SOILDOAK**
Beach Pitch	**SUNSHINE**
Big Ball	**BIGBALLS**
Super Batsman	**SUPERMAN**
Helmet Camera View	**CHRISREA**
Unlock All The Classic Matches	**NOWAYEAS**

BROKEN SWORD

Advice: Exploration and conversation are the key to advancing. Vital information can lie anywhere!. Examine everything and talk to everyone about everything!

Act 1: Paris

First collect the newspaper by the lamppost. Talk to the detective in the cafe, then talk to the photographer (Nicole) about the clown and it's assistant until you get her phone number. Give the newspaper to the man at the roadworks, and take his tool from the tent. Use the tool to uncover the manhole in the alley by the cafe. Collect the following things:

Sewer Area 1 - clown's nose
Sewer Area 2 - tissue and material

Give Rosso's card to the concierge in the courtyard, and also show him the material. Go to the roadworks once you have asked him about the jacket, and get Nico's address by phoning her from the workman's phone.

Go to Rue Jarry. Get into Nico's apartment by asking the flower seller about Nico.

Show Nico the material, and take the photograph. Show her the nose, then go to Risee du Monde. Ask the costumier about the clown and show him the photograph. Take the buzzer and go to Nico's.

Phone the tailor and ask him about Khan.

Go to Ubu Hotel. Show Piermount the key and talk to her about the key and the assassin. When the receptionist leaves, use the key to open the door up the stairs.

Climb out of the window and enter the window just to the right. Upon leaving this room an assassin will appear. Once he leaves, get the ID and matchbook from his trousers. Ask the receptionist about the ID and the safe, and show the ID to Piermount. This should help to get the manuscript from the safe. Drop the manuscript from the window ledge in Ubu Hotel. After being searched, get the manuscript from the alleyway. Show Nico the manuscript.

Look at the tripod in the museum by going to the map. Go to Ireland via the airport; tell Nico you are going.

Act 2: Ireland

Talk to Maguire, MacDevitts and Ron the poacher. If you continuously wait, Ron will leave a snare on the table, which you can take when he sneezes. Talk to Sean and Pat, and offer Pat a beer. Take the towel from under Pat's elbow. Ask Sean about the dig, then talk to Maguire. Talk to Sean about the gem and the package. Once Maguire comes in, go outside and hit the switch next to the pub door.

Go back in and get a drink off Mick. After showing him the ID you should be able to use the snare on the washer's plug.

Unlock the trapdoor in the cellar, then open it from the outside. Collect the gem from the cellar, then get the towel wet using the tap.

Make your way to the castle gate. Talk to the farmer, climb the haystack and jump over the wall by inserting the tool into the wall. Approach the hatch, and as the goat knocks you over quickly click on the far-left machinery to trap it so that you can enter the excavation via the ladder.

Push the statue onto the sand to make some imprints. Put the plaster into the imprints and put the wet towel on the plaster. Use the plastercast on the holes in the wall to find the hidden room.

Act 3: Paris

After showing Nico the gem, go to Moue at the police station and talk to him. Now ask the hospital receptionist about Marquet. Use your ID if necessary, and get some directions from her.

Talk to Sam the cleaner, turn off his cleaning machine and when he leaves, get a doctor's uniform from the cupboard. Talk to the man in the reception doorway. Now try to walk through the ward. Talk to Benoir. Talk to the big-guy at the reception, then give the cuff to Benoir; tell him to use it on Eric. Now you can go to Marquet's room and talk to him.

Talk to Lobineau at the museum, then open the window and hide in the sarcophagus.

During the raid, push the totem pole.

Talk to Nico again and go to Montfaucon.

Act 4: Montfaucon

Go to the juggler and try a bit of juggling. Show the gendarme the red nose. Try juggling again. When they leave, use the sewer key to get underground and examine the right hand arch. You should be able to break a hole in the plaster and pull the lever. Get onto the boat and attach the chain to the cog. Turn the winch and enter the next room.

Spy on the meeting through the hole in the wall. When they leave, go down the steps, put the tripod on the stand, and the gem on the tripod.

Talk to Andre until he talks about Spain.

Act 5: Spain

Use the cuff on the hosepipe and go down the passage at the back of the house.

Some dogs will scare George into the hallway.

Click on the armour. Talk to the Countess upstairs.

Pick up the bible and examine the lectern.

Talk to the Countess while Lopez gets something.

To solve the chess puzzle, white can only go on the centre column. Knight goes in the middle, King below, and bishop above.

Go to Marib in Syria.

Act 6: Syria

Go up the stairs and let the carpet-seller see the matchbook.

Try to go to the toilets at Club Alamut. Ask Ultar about the sign and return to the street.

Talk to Arto, the kebab man.

Mention Arto to Nejo. Offer Nejo the red-ball. After using the phrase on Arto, talk to Nejo and then give the club's toilet brush to the club manager.

Take the towel from the toilet and go back to Nejo. Stroke the cat, ring the bell, and use the tissue on the statuette. Sell the statuette to Duane for $50.

Show Ultar the photograph, get him to take George to Bull's Head Hill and give him the $50. When you meet up with Ultar again give him the towel. Use the stick or towel on the crack so that you can climb down.

Pull the ring in the crack in the rock. Next you should search Klausner's body. Read the inscription.

Whatever you do don't lie to Khan.

Agree to shake the man's hand, and during the pause get the buzzer and then jump off the cliff.

Act 7: Montfaucon Church

Let the priest see the chalice and clean it.

Look at the rear tomb and look at the scroll in the statue's hand. Use the scroll with the lens. Get the chalice back and examine the tomb again.

Find Lobineau in the museum and talk to him about Baphomet. Go to the Baphomet site.

Act 8: Excavation

Walk to the lobby and click on the toilet door.

Use the guard's keys to get in the toilet.

Use the excavation room key with the soap and plaster to get a copy of the key.

Give the keys back to the guard. Try to use the copied key on the painter's pot.

Phone Nico from the lobby, then dip the key in the paint to make it look more realistic.

Look at the thermostat in the lobby and ask the guard about it. Turn it to cold. Get the keys, go to the toilet and swap the plaster key for the real excavation key. Give the guard back the keys.

Phone Nico again. Now you'll have to hang around for a while. Use the real key on the Left lobby door and go in. Put the new clean chalice on the patch on the floor so that you can see the projection. This should send you back to Nico's. Go to Spain again.

Act 9: Spain

Get the mirror from the utility room. After chatting to the countess go to the Mausoleum.

Close the window with the hook. Put the tissue on the hook and set it alight with the candle by the lectern. Using the flaming hook, light the big candle to receive the stone key. Give the bible to the Countess and let her look up the references. Chat to Lopez about wells. Get a twig from the hazel tree and show it to Lopez.

Pull the tooth in the lion's head and move away quickly.

There is a shaft of light coming down from the well. Use the mirror to show up the keyhole in the wall. Touch the secret door and use the stone key to get in. Return to Nico's. Now you can go to Bannockburn via the airport.

Act 10: Train

Leave the compartment and go left down the walkway. You should meet a guard and Guido on your way.

Once you know Ekland is aboard go back to your compartment. Talk to Geordie in the 2nd compartment, then climb out of the window. Go right along the roof. Re-enter into the baggage car. Guido will be thrown off, pull the brake cord.

Try to leave the carriage, talk to Nico, and then leave.

Act 11: Scotland

Go to the church tower and break the wheel mechanism by turning it. Take the first cog and spindle and get the second cog from the rubble. Use both cogs and the handle on the demon statue. Now you should go to the crypt and to the exit.

The Final Task

When you see Guido again, get the torch and throw it on the gunpowder and get out.

BROKEN SWORD 2

Fire! Fire!

Kick the wooden block away from under the cupboard. It will fall over and kill the poisonous spider. Free yourself by using the sharp wall-bracket. Go to the writing desk. Drink the tequila and pick up the worm. In the drawer is a decorated pot. Examine it and get the key. Pick up the dart from the corner of the rug. Examine the handbag near the curtain and take the lipstick, note, and knickers. Open the cupboard near the fire with the dart. Pick up the green cylinder by using the knickers. Combine the cylinder with the siphon and extinguish the flames. Kick the door down. Pick up the eclipse-article and phone Lobineau. Use the key to open the front door.

Garcon!

Talk to the old guy about everything. Talk to the waiter a couple of times and he will serve you a coffee. Once he leaves, Lobineau will arrive. Show him the pot and try to leave. Use the Gendarme icon and take the flask from his table. Talk to him again and go to the Glease Gallery.

The Gallery

Find the fat bloke in the gallery. Use your flask on his drink a couple of times and he will fall over and smash the case. Now talk to Monsieur Glease. In the storeroom area there is a clue in the form of a label in a case.

Marseilles

You can't climb the fence as the guard-dog is suffering from a headache and doesn't want to be disturbed. Look into the hut and talk to the night watchman. You can get the bottle by using the hook, which is in the water down the stairs. Use the bottle with the chimney in order to get the Cone. Leave the bottle in the chimney pot. The hut now fills with smoke. You can enter the hut through the trapdoor once the man leaves.

Get the dog biscuits and feed the dog from under the hut. You can get rid of the dog by using the hook on the platform under the dog. Climb over the fence and go up the ladder. Use the hook on the fan by looking through the window. Go back and knock on the door. Go back up and grab the pulley. Knock the boy into the water and enter the warehouse.

The Warehouse

Find the key from the drawer and use it to free Titipoco. Jam the lift door with a crate. Put the light on. Examine the map on the wooden wall area. Go through the secret door. Talk to Nico and untie her. Grab the flint. Tie the rope to the statue. Put the tape on the electric detector at the base of the lift to stop it being called away. Get the crate from the lift and use it with the other crate. Move the last crate out of the way. Hit the lever under the statue and tie the statue to the pulley. Get Nico to help you push the statue. Using the manacles, slide down into the water.

Quaramonte

Go over to the band and ask them about their jailed pipe player and the mine accident. Talk to Mrs. Henderson about Duane. Duane is in the truck. Ask him about the truck, music and Miguel. Go to the Tourist Information building and ask about Oubier. Talk to the bloke on the right hand side about pyramids and try to look at the chart on the wall. Talk to Duane about the General, to Nico about the chart, and to the woman in the mine office about professor Oubier. Ask Duane about detonators, then the woman in the mine office about detonators and the chart. Talk to the General and get Nico to leave with him. Talk to Renaldo and Pearl about pyramids. When Pearl goes off with Renaldo, look at the chart. Talk to Concha in the mine office about the chart. Take the detonator and give it to Duane.

Go to the Police Station and down the passageway. Talk to Miguel and get captured.

Character Setup

Talk to the General about the items in the room until his mum arrives. As George, talk to Miguel. Get the noose and tie it to the bars on the window. Switch control to Nico by putting the speech icon over the window. Watch the sequence.

Root of the Problem

Get the rope from the wheel and use it with the stones to make a drive belt. Put the statement on the damp leaves. Use the fetish from the water wheel to light a fire. Talk to Hubert about Nico. You need to find a root to help Nico. Press the collar between the stones using the cross and give it to the Priest. Get him to take you to the village.

Shaman Bob

Talk to the native about Nico. Try to see the Shaman and give the biscuits to the native. Put the Mayan Stone in the empty packet and use it on the native. Talk to the Shaman and find out about the Legend of Tezcatlipoca and his kids. Ask about the Jaguar Stone, the Eagle Stone and the root. Go back to the treehouse and put the cone under the stones. Press the root and take the cone. Give it to Nico.

Ketch's Place

Look into the Theodolite. Examine the plans and talk to Bronson about the Theodolite. Go up the steps. You can socialise with the cat, well.....not literally but anyway, try to open the door and talk to the old biddies. Go down the steps to the jetty. Ask the boy about everything in this order:

1. Treasure
2. Ketch
3. Sisters
4. Plans
5. Bronson

Talk to Bronson about the sisters and the plans. Go up the steps and tell the old biddy that you like cats. Talk about Rio, Emily and the cat. Talk to Rio at the jetty about fish, Emily and lipstick. If you go away and then come back and talk about the fish, you can the innertube from the wheel. Get the fish from Rio and ask him about the innertube. Go back up the ladder and use the innertube with the flagpole. Put the fish on the innertube. Get the cat's ball. Get the innertube back and use it with the tree to make a catapult. Use the cat's ball to knock the Theodlite target. While Bronson is busy, remove the ladder. Get the marker and the Theodolite. Talk to Bronson, then get the plans. Give the plans to the old biddies.

British Museum

As Nico, examine the cabinet on the right hand side. Talk to the attendant and choose the stone icon. Talk to professor Oubier. Ask the attendant about the stone again. Get the cabinet key and get the Obsidian Dagger from near the phone. Get the key and talk to the attendant to trigger the phone. Use the dagger with the hidden doors.

Ketch Museum

Get the Quill from the table. Find Emily in the chest and talk to her. Look at the portrait of the Captain. Go out and break the quill by tickling the cat with it. Find Rio and give him the bits of quill. Get the conch and find Emily. Talk to her. Put the map on the table. Put the lantern in the ink well and the cross in the penholder. Talk to Rio.

A Quick Glance

Get Rio's net and use it to climb over the obstruction.

The Underground

As Nico, use your hairclip on the slot machine. Get the penny and use it on the weighing scales. Use the dagger and the card to unlock the cupboard. Press the button and get the train.

Zombie Island Close Up

As George, go to the forest. Get the reed, then go right. Put the reed in the hole under the tree. Go back to the clifftop, then go south-east. Use the reed with the dart on the boar. Grab the branch above you. Go right, then up to find the stone

needle. Try grabbing the vine. Combine the net with the marker and put it on the vines. Throw one end over the stone needle. Go back through the exit that the boar created. Put the Theodolite on the top of the hill and use it to look at the stone needle. Click on the marker. Take the right-hand exit.

Docks By Night

Wait for the night watchman to go past, then get behind the crate and open the cupboard near the ladder. Go up onto the roof. Shut the guard in the cupboard with the mop. Looking in through the porthole lets you see the professor being killed. Go into the cabin area. Examine him and get the stone. Stab Karzac with the stone.

Lights, Camera, Action!!

As George, talk to Hakes and Haiku. When you're told to get out of the way, examine everything. Get the bun, pancake and syrup from the table. Put the syrup on the pancake and give it to Bert. Talk to Hawkes. Disturb the hornets by throwing buns in the bush. When you're on the beach ask Bert about the stone pillar. Talk to Hawkes and then Bert and then Hawkes again. Even more talking follows: talk to the cameraman about the pillar, the portable camera and Hakes. Talk to Hawkes about everything. Talking about the right things will get you hired!

Village Ruins

Get the pants. Get Titipoco to help you tip the barrel. Pick up the once-hot stone and then go to where Titipoco is pointing.

Base of the Pyramid

Remove the cylinder from the generator. Get some fuel into the cylinder by taping the fuel pipe with your dagger. Use the fuel with the lift-engine and press the button. Hit the lever and then switch it off again. Give Titipoco the rope so that he can climb up using the scaffolding. Tie the rope to the wheel. Talk to Titopoco and get on the lift.

Top of the Pyramid

Grab the ammo from the crate and get in the lift. Once the guards see you, pick up the torch. Titipoco will light it. Once the fire is lit, use the ammo to make some fireworks. Talk to the General and use the dagger to free George.

The End is Nigh!

Get George to help you pull the levers on the wall to open the secret door. To solve this tedious puzzle, you must hit the four tiles on the far right. Clicking on the wheels will turn them left or right. Pressing a letter tile requires you to identify and press the two appropriate number tiles. Pressing a number tile requires you to move the wheels so that the corresponding symbols meet at the centre-line.

To create fewer problems, here are the codes:

A	2+5
B	3+10

C	1+8
D	6+9

Solving the puzzle opens a secret door. Upon picking up the torch, get Titipoco to light it and hit the lever on the wall. Using your torch, light the one on the wall. At the centre of the back wall is a lever. Hit it and go through the left-hand door. Pull the right, then left lever, and go through the door. Pull the next lever, go through, and then down the right-hand stairs. Hit the lever and go down the steps to the centre of the pyramid. Tada! The End!

BUBBLE BOBBLE

Cheat Mode
Firstly, press ↓, ↑, ↓, ↑, ➡, ↓, ⬅, ↓, ↑, ↓ a message will tell you if you have been successful. Next, start a game and during play press the following buttons; **R1** to skip level, **L1** to return to the previous level, **R2** to bring up an options menu and **L2** to confirm selections on the options menu.

BUBSY 3D

Secret Passwords
Choose Load Game from the main menu and enter the following passwords:

Password	Action
XXMUCHOLIFE	Gives you 99 lives
XXTOOROCKER	Gives you all the rocket parts
XXBNSCHTMMM	Go bonus rounds
XXLVLCHTMSB	Level select
XXZOOMMERKB	Level warp (press ⬅ and **Start** during the game to warp to differenet parts of that level)

BUGS BUNNY: LOST IN TIME

Maximum carrots
Go to the Level Selection Screen. Hold **L2 + R1** and press ✖, ■, R2, L1, ●, ✖, ■, ■, ●

Level select
Hold **L2 + R1** and press X, ■, R2, L1, ●, ✖, ■, ■, ■

All abilities
Go to the Level Selection Screen. Hold **L2 + R1** and press ✖, ■, R2, L1, ●, ✖, ■, ●, ■

Full energy
Go to the Level Selection Screen. Hold **L2 + R1** and press ✖, ■, R2, L1, ●, ✖, ■, ●, ●

Extra key
Go to the Level Selection Screen. Hold **L2 + R1** and press ✖, ■, R2, L1, ●, ✖, ●, ■, ■

BURNING ROAD

Mirror Mode
Select Practice Mode, and choose your track, car and transmission. As soon as the race itself starts, turn your car around and drive the wrong way round the track. As soon as you pass through a checkpoint you will be placed in first, and the other racers will turn and follow you. Now, race as normal and you will have three more tracks to race on.

BUSHIDO BLADE

Play a link-up game using only one CD.
Load the game on the first machine and select Link-Up mode. Remove the disk and load it on the other machine. Select Link-Up mode. After selecting weapons and characters the game should freeze. Put the disk back in the first PlayStation and the game should load.

BUST A MOVE 2

Character Select
To choose a character, start a Puzzle game and when the stage map appears press ⬅, ⬅, ↑, ↓. Next press **L1**, **L2**, **R1** and **R2** together and a Character Select screen should appear. To choose your character use the ⬅ and ➡ buttons, and press ✖ to continue. When you play the game the new character will appear.

Extra Credits
To gain up to twenty nine credits, highlight Credit in the Option mode, and press ⬅, ➡, R1, R2, L2, L1, ↑, ↓. Next press ✖ repeatedly as quickly as you can until the timer runs out.

Modified Levels
Press **R1**, ↑, **L2**, ↓, on the selection screen where you see Game Start, Time Attack etc. The words 'Another World' should now be below the single-player 'story mode' which contains modified versions of the levels.

BUST A MOVE 4

Bonus world
On the title screen, press ▲, ⬅, ➡, ⬅, ▲. If you entered the code correctly, you will hear a sound and a small face will appear at the bottom right corner of the screen.

Bonus characters

On the title screen, press ➡, ➡, ➡, ▲, ⬅, ⬅, ⬅.

Character select

On the title screen, press ➡, ➡, ▲, ⬅, ⬅.

BUST A MOVE: DANCE AND RHYTHM ACTION

Dance Preview

Complete the game on easy difficulty setting.

Play as Capoeira

Complete the game on normal difficulty setting.

Play as Robo-Z

Complete the game on hard difficulty setting.

Play as Burger Dog

First complete the game on both the normal and hard difficulty settings. Then select Hamm and complete the game again on the normal difficulty setting.

Play as Columbo

First complete the game on both the normal and hard difficulty settings. Then select Shorty and complete the game again on the normal difficulty setting.

Alternative Costume

Highlight a character, then hold **Select** and press ●.

Level Skip

In a one player game, hold **L2 + R2 + Select** during a dance to skip to the next level.

Winning Pose Close Up

Hold ● after winning a dance.

CARDINAL SYN

Select Sub-Bosses

Input these codes on the 'Press Start' screen.

Kahn:	⬆, ⬆, ⬇, ⬇, ▲
Stygian:	⬅, ➡, ⬅, ➡, ▲
Redemptor:	⬆, ⬇, ⬅, ➡, ●
Juni:	⬆, ⬅, ⬅, ⬆, ■
Mongwan:	⬇, ⬇, ⬇, ⬆, ▲
Vodu:	⬅, ⬅, ⬅, ⬆, ●
Bimorphia:	➡, ➡, ➡, ⬇, ■
Moloch:	⬆, ➡, ⬇, ⬅, ■

CASTLEVANIA

Play as Richter Belmont

Save any game with 190% or more completion. Next, start a new game and enter your name as Richter, and he can be controlled when the new game commences.

Passwords

After completing the game, these passwords can be entered:

New Armour	AXEARMOR
Hard Game	X-X!V'
Extra Luck	X-X!V"

CASTROL HONDA SUPERBIKE RACING

Wheelies

On a straight section of road going 100mph let go of the throttle for a couple of seconds then hit the gas again.

CHAMPIONSHIP BASS

Challenge Level Codes:

Level 2 – **WK7GuHcbZo7a**

Level 3 – **JZsVh*romb82**

Level 4 – **cMB4UBWVTuB** ▲

CHAMPIONSHIP MOTORCROSS FEATURING RICKY CARMICHEAL

Enter your name as one of these codes in championship mode.

Big Head Mode	**GROSSE TETE**
Extra FMV	**LIVE ACTION**
All Classes	**ALL EVENTS**
Mirror Tracks	**OPPOSITE LOCK**
Open All Tracks	**DIRT TRACKS**

CHEESY

Level Codes

Level 1	WESTONMARE
Level 2	FOUNDATION
Level 3	PANTALOONS
Level 4	POLYNESIA7
Level 5	LANDSCAPES

CIRCUIT BREAKERS

Activate All Tracks

On a one player game, pause the game and go to options.

Select 'Sound' and highlight 'FX Volume', then press **L1 + L2**. The game will be 400% complete and all the tracks will be activated.

Night Racing
On the circuit selection screen, hold **L1 + L2 + R1 + R2** until a headlight appears in front of the car, now when you play all the races will take place at night.

COLIN MCRAE RALLY

Hidden Cars
Win the Super Special Stages with a fast time to reveal the following cars:

Greece	Ford Escort MkII
Australia	Ford RS2000
Corsica	LanciaDelta Integrale
UK	Audi Quatro

Passwords
Enter your name as any one of these passwords to activate some strange cheats:
BACKSEAT = Nicky Grist driving the car.
PEASOUPER = All the tracks in fog.
BUTTONBASH = Tap ✖ and ● alternately to accelerate.
DIRECTORCUT = You can edit the replay.
KITCAR = Special full customised Rally Edition car.
TROLLEY = Four wheel steering.
FORKLIFT = Rear wheel steering.
HELIUMNICK = Co driver Nicky Grist has a high pitched voice.
MOREOOMPH=Turbomode.
BLANCMANGE = Green jelly car.

Super Jumps
Enter your name as **KITCAR**. During a race press **Select** to perform a Knight Rider super jump.

Unlock All The Tracks
Enter your name as **OPENROADS**. All the tracks will now be unlocked.

Unlock Bonus Cars
Enter your name as **SHOEBOXES**. Enter time trial and you will be able to drive the four bonus cars.

Low Gravity
Enter your name as **MOONWALK**.

Increased Frame Rate
Enter your name as **SILKYSMOOTH**.

Mirror Tracks
Enter your name as **WHITEBUNNY**.

Reverse Tracks
Enter your name as **SKCART**.

All Tracks Set At Night
Enter your name as **NIGHTRIDER**.

Tinfoil Car
Enter your name as **TINFOILED**.

Micro Machine Style Cars
Enter your name as **DIDDYCARS**.

Hovercraft Mode
(mmm.. easy to remember..)
Enter your name as **HOVERCRAFT**.

COLIN MCRAE RALLY 2.0

Extra Cars
Enter these codes at the Create New Driver Profile screen.

All Tracks Unlocked	**HELLOCLEVELAND**
All Cars Unlocked	**ONECAREFULOWNER**
Mirror Tracks	**RORRIMSKCART**
Cat Silhouette	**HELLO_RAZU_AND_FLEA**
Lancer Road Car	**OFFROAD**
Sierra Cosworth	**JIMMYSCAR**
Ford Puma	**COOLESTCAR**
Mini Cooper	**JOBINITALY**

Cheats
Enter these on the Cheat Options screen.

Shoot Fireballs	**GREATBALLSOF**
Bouncing Collisions	**RUBBERTREES**
Monster Truck Wheels	**EASYROLLER**
Low Gravity	**MOONLANDER**
Aggressive Computer Controlled Cars	**NEURALNIGHTMARE**
Turbo Mode	**ROCKETFUEL**
Faster Game	**PRUNEJUICE**

Shadow Mode
When racing, switch to an external view and then press **R2 + ▲**. The car will disappear. To return to normal keep pressing **▲**.

COLONY WARS

Cheat Codes

Commander*Jeffer	Level Select.
Hestas*Retort	Invincibility.
Memo*X33RTY	Infinite Missiles.
Tranquillex	Infinite Laser.

COLONY WARS: RED SUN

On the main menu press **R2, R2, L2, L2, R1, R1, Select, Select**. A cheat option will appear, select this and enter one of these cheats.

All Ships	**Greyam_Beard**
All Weapons Loaded on Ship	**Big_Daddy**
Infinite Afterburners	**Jalferezi**
Infinite Hull and Shields	**Awra**
No weapons overheat	**ROCKWROK**
Upgrade Ship	**Break_and_Enter**
Infinite Secondary Weapons	**Sly_n_Devious**
End Current Mission	**Quickie**
Hub Select	**Move_House**
Disable All Cheats	**All_Cheat_Off**

COLONY WARS: VENGEANCE

Enter these on the password screen:

All Weapons	**Tornado**
Infinite Afterburners	**Avalanche**
Infinite Secondary Weaponry	**Chimera**
Infinite Shield Energy	**Vampire**
No Gun Overheat	**Dark*Angel**
Activate All Cheats	**Blizzard**
Deactivate All Cheats	**Stormlord**
Activate All Ships	**Thunderchild**
Maximum Tech Specs	**Hydra**
Select Any Level	**Demon**
One Hit Destroyed Ships	**Tsunami**

COMMAND AND CONQUER

GDI Passwords

Level 2 - Estonia	X2CJOKTLU
Level 3 - Latvia	A8RPQIPCT
Level 4A - Poland	FBPC8RSK8
Level 5A - Germany	8PHJDBOHU
Level 6 - Czech Rep	87Q7T7TED
Level 7 - Czech Rep	OX3CS3D4G
Level 8A - Austria	GTJ2NBE51
Level 8B - Slovakia	8PZA9MQY7
Level 9 - Hungary	WJ6Q1M17L
Level 10A - Slovenia	UKKRMGUZK
Level 10B - Romania	LW32DZZSX
Level11 - Greece	SH4AD9KVC
Level 12A - Albania	MWRUN47H6
Level 12B - Bulgaria	C9NPZHVN9
Level 13 - Yugoslavia	OMB4I1IMS
Level 14 - Yugoslavia	SH4K6CSUZ
Level 15B - Bosnia	W1N4QEMR3
Level 15C - Bosnia	OX3CCPYK9

NOD Passwords

Level 3- Sudan	GB4V1S7TT
Level 4- Chad	YK4BRTQCT
Level 5- Mauritania	W15DASRS8
Level 6C- Nigeria	AQINN7NKU
Level 7A- Gabon	GTJKWOJDK
Level 7B- Cameroon	OX3UJOV6Q
Level 8A- Zaire	GTK1EGBQN
Level 8B- Zaire	C982ETIMY
Level 9- Egypt	OFDWQOJNK
Level 10B- Tanzania	QG9KTOPTY
Level 11A- Namibia	OX3UKOP94
Level 12- Botswana	MEY28UCVF
Level 13A- S. Africa	45P58LIUG

Covert Operations
To access extra Covert Operations missions in GDI or NOD mode, enter the password **COVERTOPS**.

Guerilla Missions
In the missions where there is no option to build your army, place your army so that they fight and hunt together. When you have tanks, protect them by putting infantry in front or around them. This helps in close range attacks.

The following codes can be used for both GDI and NOD sides. To use them, pause the game and then enter the desired code:

Extra $5000
➡, ⬇, ⬇, ⬅, L1, ⬅, ➡, ⬇, ⬅
Instant Air Strike
➡, ⬇, ⬅, ⬅, ⬇, ➡, ➡, ⬇, ⬅, ✖, ■, ●
Instant Ion Cannon
➡, ⬇, ⬅, ⬅ ⬇, ➡, ➡, ⬇, ⬅, ✖, ■, ▲
Reveal All Of the Map
●, ●, ●, ⬆, ●, ■, R1, ●, ●, ●

Hidden Mission
When you have completed the final GDI mission enter **PATSUX** on the password screen.

All FMV
Enter **CINEMA** on the password screen. Then enter either **WHOAMI**, **JC** or **SG**.

Map Code
On the title screen hold **L1 + L2 + R1 + R2 + ■ + ●**, then press **Start**. Select either 'Password' or 'New Game'. Continue to hold all six buttons until the level begins.

Instant Nuclear Strike
Enter during play ➡, ⬇, ⬅, ⬅, ⬇, ➡, ➡, ⬇, ⬅, ✖, ⬆, ✖

Japanese Troops

Enter the password **GODZILLA** and all your troops will speak in Japanese.

Kane Intro

When the game is loading hold **Select** on pad 1 until Kane appears.

COMMAND AND CONQUER: RED ALERT

Soviet Passwords

Level 2:	17DUXFJ6C
Level 3:	VMBWOQ284
Level 4:	XN37MCCS0
Level 5:	LH06FZZQL
Level 6:	BUVV20LFF
Level 7:	AVYQ10YA8
Level 8:	LZRJTMQAN
Level 9:	YQX4C9GFH
Level 10:	1QES08LE0
Level 11:	RKPOUOXJA
Level 12:	CDLKYL7Q4
Level 13:	8T5GGDK25
Level 14:	X5CDEOKN8

Allies Passwords

Level 2:	LZ9SWDNVK
Level 3:	3AH5VCCYG
Level 4:	X63VC9XJI
Level 5:	DV795V0EE
Level 6:	17DCPX2Z8
Level 7:	90BAZDHP3
Level 8:	9000DSR5H
Level 9:	SRS80SSQT
Level 10:	5SOSL9GZ8
Level 11:	HFZNFE4HS
Level 12:	5RNZ2K1A4
Level 13:	3AS0QJC80
Level 14:	59EW5K6G1
Level 15:	M3102QMBV

Cheats

A-Bomb launch	●, ✖, ●, ▲, ■, ▲.
Win the Battle	✖, ■, ■, ●, ▲, ●.
Cash	■, ■, ●, ✖, ▲, ●.
Time Warp	▲, ●, ●, ■, ■, ✖.
Remove Shroud	■, ▲, ●, ✖, ▲, ■.
Parabomb	■, ✖, ●, ●, ✖, ▲
Turn Ore Into Beer	■, ●, ■, ✖, ●, ●
Ore into Men (Link-up only)	✖, ●, ▲, ▲, ●, ✖

COMMAND AND CONQUER: RETALIATION

Power Stations

A Power Station is a key target for the enemy. By building more than you actually need you will be able to suffer losing some while still keeping Power.

Spies

By sending in a spy to your enemy's base you can learn where the main structures and power supplies are. Crippling these first is almost always the best route to victory.

Destroy Enemy Natural Resources

You can blow up enemy mineral fields by sending in two of your tanks, having one drive around, while the other fires on it. As you cannot fire directly at minerals this way missed shots will blow the minerals up.

Field Mechanics

Take plenty of field mechanics with you when you attack with a group of tanks. They will be able to constantly repair them during the battle.

CONTRA 3D

Cheat Codes

Enter these codes at the Title Screen:

Weapon Select	L2, R2, L1, L2, ⬆, ⬇, ⬇, ⬆
Infinite Continues	L2, R2, L1, R1, ⬅, ➡, ➡, ⬅
Movie Player	L2, L1, R1, R2, ⬆, ⬅, ⬇, ➡
Bamboo Arcade	R2, R1, ➡, ⬅, L1, L2
Bamboo Gyruss	L2, L1, ⬅, ➡, R1, R2

COOL BOARDERS

Change Announcer's Voice

Go to the options menu and press **Select** approximately forty times until you hear a noise.

COOL BOARDERS 2

Hidden Characters-Alien and Snowman

To play as an alien or snowman, complete all 100 moves in Master Mode and set all of the records in Freestyle mode. Alternatively, get a score of 40.0 or more on the half-pipe.

Mirror Mode

Simply complete the Competition Mode in first place. Also, complete mirror mode in first place to make the game harder.

Bossman
To play as the boss character, complete Mirror Mode in first place. Now select him in Freestyle Mode.

Extra Track
To get course ten dive into the cave. You must complete all 100 tricks in Big Air or Master Mode.

Extra Boards
Complete Freestyle mode in first place for the Trick, Total and Time categories for three new boards. They are not available for use in Competition mode though.

COOL BOARDERS 3

All Courses
Select the Tournament Mode and enter your name as **WONITALL**. If you enter the code correctly you will hear "Cheater".

All Boards and Boarders
Select the Tournament Mode and enter your name as **OPEN_EM**. If you enter the code correctly you will hear "Cheater".

Big Head Mode
Select the Tournament Mode and enter your name as **BIGHEADS**. If you enter the code correctly you will hear "Big Head Mode".

Control The Replay
Hold ← during a replay to go to slow motion or ↓ to pause.

COOL BOARDERS 4

Cheat codes:
ICHEAT   Enter as your name to unlock all the mountains, boards and riders.
IMSPECIAL   Enter as your name to unlock all the special events.

COURIER CRISIS

No Timer
Press **L1 + R2** at the neighbourhood selection screen.

Taunt
Press and hold **L1 + L2** or **R1 + R2** during the game to taunt at the traffic.

CRASH BANDICOOT

Super Password
To gain access to any level, 100% complete score, both keys and all gems, go from the main menu to the Password screen. Enter the following:
▲, ▲, ▲, ▲, ✕, ■, ▲, ▲.
▲, ▲, ■, ✕, ▲, ●, ▲, ▲.
▲, ●, ■, ▲, ✕, ✕, ✕, ✕.

CRASH BANDICOOT 2

Extra Lives
To gain ten extra lives, simply jump on the baby polar bear's head in the second warp room (levels 6-10).

Extra Shield
To get a little extra help, press ↑+● when you die. You will reappear sporting a mask.

Self Inflicted Torture
If you wish to fight the bosses again, stand on the appropriate pad and press **L1+R1+L2+R2+▲** and tap ↑.

CRASH BANDICOOT 3: WARPED

Hot Cold bonus level
On Level 14 ride half way through the level to an alien crossing sign on the left. Run into the sign to be transported to level 31.

Eggipus Rex bonus level
On Level 11 take the yellow gem ride. Continue until reaching the area where the huge dinosaur chases Crash. Allow the second pterodactyl to capture Crash and get to level 32.

105% completion:
Collect all relics and gems including those from the Hot Cold and Eggipus Rex bonus levels. The relics that are collected must be at least gold or platinum. Now approach Crash's sister next to the save spot for another clear gem. Collect the gem with 105% completion status and a great ending.

CRASH TEAM RACING

Secret Characters
On the main menu hold **L1 + R1** and enter one of the following codes to unlock the corresponding hidden character.
Penta Penguin – ↓, →, ▲, ↓, ←, ▲, ↑
Ripper Roo – →, ●, ●, ↓, ↑, ↓, →
N Tropy – ↓, ←, →, ↑, ↓, →, →
Papu Papu – ←, ▲, →, ↓, →, ●, ←, ←, ↓
Komodo Joe – ↓, ●, ←, ←, ▲, →, ↓
Pinstripe – ←, →, ▲, ↓, →, ↓

Gameplay Cheats

Scrapbook – ↑, ↑, ↓, ➡, ➡, ⬅, ➡, ▲, ➡

Bonus Tracks – ➡, ➡, ⬅, ▲, ➡, ↓, ↓

Invisibility – ↑, ↑, ↓, ➡, ➡, ↑

Always Get Invisible Power Ups – ↓, ⬅, ➡, ↑, ↓, ➡

Infinite Masks – ⬅, ▲, ➡, ⬅, ●, ➡, ↓, ↓

Infinite Bombs – ▲, ➡, ↓, ➡, ↑, ▲, ⬅

Infinite Wumpa Fruits – ↓, ➡, ➡, ↓, ↓

Super Turbo Pads – ▲, ➡, ➡, ●, ⬅

Display Turbo Counter – ▲, ↓, ↓, ●, ↑

Spyro 2 Demo – ↓, ●, ▲, ➡

Extra Battle Arenas

Complete Arcade mode on all three difficulty settings, and get all four cups. You will now be able to select four new battle arenas.

CRIME KILLERS

Passwords

Level 2 = ●, ■, ✕, ▲, ✕, ▲, ■, ▲, ■.
Level 3 = ●, ●, ■, ✕, ▲, ●, ●, ●, ●, ●
Level 4 = ●, ●, ■, ▲, ●, ●, ■, ▲, ■, ✕.
Level 5 = ▲, ●, ●, ●, ●, ●, ●, ●, ■, ▲.
Level 6 = ■, ▲, ■, ▲, ●, ■, ✕, ✕, ✕, ▲.
Level 7 = ●, ●, ●, ●, ■, ✕, ▲, ●, ●, ●.
Level 8 = ■, ▲, ■, ✕, ▲, ■, ✕, ▲, ■, ✕.
Level 9 = ✕, ✕, ▲, ●, ■, ✕, ▲, ■, ▲, ●.
Level 10 = ●, ▲, ●, ●, ■, ✕, ▲, ●, ●, ●.
Level 11 = ■, ▲, ■, ▲, ●, ●, ■, ▲, ■, ▲.
Level 12 = ■, ▲, ■, ▲, ■, ▲, ●, ■, ▲, ■.
Level 13 = ✕, ✕, ✕, ▲, ●, ●, ●, ■, ✕, ✕.
Level 14 = ✕, ✕, ✕, ✕, ▲, ●, ■, ✕, ✕, ✕.
Level 15 = ✕, ▲, ■, ✕, ✕, ▲, ●, ■, ✕, ✕.
The End = ✕, ▲, ●, ■, ▲, ■, ✕, ▲, ■, ▲.

CRITICAL DEPTH

Cheats

Enter these cheats during play:

Enemies Drop Pods	L1, R1, L1, R1, ↑, ↓, ⬅, ↑.
More Firepower	R1, R2, R1, R2, ↑, ↓, ↑, ↓.
Invincibility	L1, R1, L1, R1, ↑, ↓, ⬅, ➡.
Infinite Weapons	L1, R1, L1, R1, ↑, ↓, ⬅, ↓.

CROC

Level Passwords

World One

1-2	ULLLLDDULURDRRU
1-3	RULULUURLRURLUD
1-b1	DLURLDRLRLRRDLL
1-s1	LURURUDRLDULULD
1-4	ULDLLDDRLLRDRRU
1-5	RUDULUUULDURLUD
1-6	DLRRLDRDRURRDLL
1-b2	LDUURRDRLLURULD
1-s2	URLRULDRLDRDRRU

World Two

2-1	RDLDURUULLURLUD
2-2	DRULULRDRRRRRDLL
2-3	LURDDRDRLDULULD
2-b1	ULDRULDRLLRDRRU
2-s1	RDDDURUULDUUDUD
2-4	DRRLULRDRURULLL
2-5	LDUDDUDRDLUDRLD
2-6	ULLRDUDRDDRLURU
2-b2	RULDDDUUDLUUDUD
2-s2	DRULDULDURRURLL

World Three

3-1	LURDUDURDDUDLLD
3-2	ULDRDUURDLRLDRU
3-3	RUDDDDDUDDUUUUD
3-b1	DLRLDULDUURURLL
3-s1	LUDDULURDLUULDD
3-4	URRRURURDDRLDUU
3-5	RDRDULDUDLUUURD
3-6	DRDLURLDURRURDL
3-b2	LULDDLURDDUDLDD
3-s2	URURURULDLRLDDU

World Four

4-1	RDUDULDDDDUUULD
4-2	DRLLURLUUURURUL
4-3	LDDDDDULLLRULUD
4-b1	UURRDDULLDULDDU
4-s1	RRRDDULDLLRUULL
4-4	DDDLDDDURRUURUD
4-5	LLLDUURLLDRDLUL
4-6	UUURDDRLLLULDDR
4-b2	RLUDDULDLDRUULL
4-s2	DDLDDDDURUUURUU

World Five

5-1	LLDLURRLLLRULUR
5-2	UDRUULRLLDULDDL
5-3	RRRLURLDLLRUULR
5-4	DDDDULDURRUURUU
5-b1	LLLLDRRLLDRDLUR

CROC 2

Cheat mode:

On the Title Screen hold **L1** and press ▲, ⬅, ⬅, ➡, ■, ↑,

⬆, ⬅, ●. Then, hold **L2** and press **R2** during the game to access a cheat menu.

Unlimited crystals:
On the Title Screen hold **L1** and press ■, ■, ●, ⬇, ⬅, ➡, ⬅. Then hold **R2** and press ■ during the game play to get an extra hundred crystals.

Unlimited lives:
On the Title Screen hold **L1** and press ●, ⬇, ⬅, ⬆, ➡, ▲, ⬇

Croc vs. Dantini boat race:
In the waterfall in Sailor Village find the last coloured crystal.

CROW: CITY OF ANGELS

Level Codes
When at the Main Menu screen, highlight the continue option in order to enter a password.

Pier	▲, ✖, ▲, ▲, ●, ■, ✖, ●
Boat	✖, ✖, ✖, ✖, ▲, ■, ✖, ●
Tomb	▲, ●, ▲, ●, ■, ▲, ▲, ●, ✖, ●
Grave	✖, ▲, ✖, ▲, ■, ✖, ✖, ▲, ■, ●
Church	▲, ▲, ▲, ▲, ●, ■, ▲, ■, ●, ●
Day o` Dead	✖, ▲, ✖, ▲, ■, ●, ●, ✖, ■, ●
Club	▲, ●, ▲, ●, ●, ▲, ✖, ●, ■, ●
Tower	✖, ✖, ●, ✖, ■, ■, ✖, ▲, ●
Borderland	▲, ✖, ✖, ✖, ●, ■, ▲, ■
Finale	✖, ✖, ✖, ●, ■, ■, ✖, ✖, ▲, ●

CRUSADER: NO REMORSE

Mission Passwords
Select 'Load Game', and then 'Teleport To Mission' before entering these level passwords:

LEVEL	PASSWORD	LEVEL	PASSWORD
2	FWQP	3	PLRQ
4	SZNF	5	TD5S
6	J1BT	7	K2CV
8	N3DW	9	M4FX
10	X5GZ	11	C6HQ
12	D7J1	13	F8K2
14	FGL3	15	JFM4

CYBERSLED

Extra Sleds
Wait for the game to load, and when you see the screen with the 'Press **Start** Button' message, press the following for five new sleds to choose from:

⬆, ⬅, ⬇, ➡, ⬆, ▲, ⬆, ➡, ⬇, ⬅, ⬆, ●.

CYBERSPEED

Compilation Date
To show the compilation time and date on any menu screen, press ⬆, ⬅, ➡, ▲, ●, ■, ⬅, ➡, ■, ●.

Fly As A Cow
On the ship select screen, press ⬆, ⬅, ⬇, ⬆, ⬅, ⬇, ➡, ⬅, ⬇, ➡, ■, ✖, ● to fly as the cow.

Play Movies
To play all the intermission movies, press ●, ■, ▲, ⬅, ➡, ⬆, ■, ➡ on the language select screen.

DARK FORCES

Cheat Menu
A cheat menu can be accessed by pressing ⬅, ●, ✖, ➡, ●,.✖, ⬇, ●, ✖ during play. The options will be:
Invincible- can not be killed (deflects weapon attacks)
Coords- provides position coordinates
Supermap- fills in HUD map completely
Pogo- propels you to normally inaccessible heights
Pal Mode- changes video mode (not recommended)
Max Out- gives you maximum weapons and equipment
Game Won- see Level Skip cheat below
Ponder- think about it!
Return to Game- resume gameplay

Level Select
To have the choice of all fourteen levels, select Restore Game and enter P3NDLDQNY2.

Level Skip
In the cheat menu, toggle the Game Won option to green. Then exit the menu and pause the game and another menu will provide you with options:
Game Paused
Return to Game
Next Mission
Abort Mission

Passwords

Talay: Tak Base	Y7B5T7S183
Nar Shaddaa	W9F635SZB5
Anoat City	!VHDBMBMXZ
Jabba's Ship	V!Q534TOF6
Research Facility	9WJHBLCNO0
Imperial City	NVHL4LFQ1R
Gromas Mines	8XKGBKDPZ1
Fuel Station	MYGM!KBR2S
Detention Centre	7YBKBJFL22

The Executor	LXFN4JCSZT
Ramsees Hed	Y7C4L7Q193
The Arc Hammer	205F6HJTOV
Robotics Facility	X8D3L6R2C4

DARKLIGHT CONFLICT

To see a secret menu full of cheats, go to the options menu and press ↓, ↑, ↓, ■, Left, ←, L1, R1, ●. Now exit to the previous menu.

DARKSTALKERS 3

Unlock Shadow
On the character selection screen, highlight the random character space and press **Select** five times, then press any button.

Unlock Marionette
On the character selection screen, highlight the random character space and press **Select** seven times, then press any button.

Vampire Hunter Style Characters
There are Vampire Hunter variations for Lillith, Victor, Talbain, Rikuo, Bishamon, Huitzil and Donovan. To access simply hold **Select** when choosing your character.

EX Options, Collection 2, 3, 4 And DX Options
Enter Original Character mode and select a character. After customising your character you can fight against the computer and gain experience points. The more experience points you gain the more powerful your custom character becomes. Earning experience points also unlocks the EX Options, DX Options and the Collections.

DAVE MIRRA FREESTYLE BMX

Extra bike and Slim Jim
Beat the game with any character to get Slim Jim and a bonus bike.

Extra points
When the time is just about to run out press ✖ to bunny-hop and hold ↓ + ✖ or ↑ + ✖ and you will now continue to get points even after the time has expired.

DEAD BALL ZONE

All Teams and Stadiums
Highlight Italian on the language select screen and press and hold **R1 + L2 + ■** for eight seconds to unlock all the teams and the stadiums.

DEAD OR ALIVE

Extra Costumes
Complete the game on the default settings to gain a new costume for that character.

Raidou
Gain all the costumes for every character to unlock Raidou.

Ayane
Gain all the costumes for Raidou to unlock Ayane.

Extra Config Options:
Fighting Order = Default/Random/Manual
Complete the game once with any character. When the game has been played for over three hours.
Safety Zone Size = Normal/Nothing/All
Complete the Time Attack on the normal difficulty setting in under five minutes. When the game has been played for over six hours.
Danger Damage = No Damage/Small/Normal/Large/Critical
Complete the game with all ten basic characters on default settings. Complete Survival mode with all basic characters. This only works when the game has been played for over nine hours.
Danger Zone Bounce = No Bounce/Normal/High
Complete Kumite mode with an 80% win rating. This only works when the game has been played for over twelve hours.
System Voice = Normal/Wakana/Sakura
Wakana/Kasumi: Complete the game once with any character. Sakura/Ayama: Play Kasumi 100 times or when the game has been played for over fifteen hours.
Extra Voices
Perform all the moves for a chosen character in the 'Command Mode' of the Training mode to unlock their extra voice option.
CG Gallery
Gain all the costumes for Ayane.

Wallpaper
Insert your Dead or Alive CD into a PC or Mac and you can use artwork from the game as your on screen wallpaper.

DEATHTRAP DUNGEON

Level Select
On the main menu screen press **L1, R1, ▲, ▲, ■, ●, R1, L1.** When you go to the Load Game option all the levels will be available.

Spire 1
Run past the fireballs and past the crumbling floor.

Spire 2

Jump from the stone pillars to platforms in the cage room to collect goodies. Go down the ramp through the left gate and flick the lever at far end. Flick the switch at opposite recess. Take the lift up and go left to the grey lever. Back at the cage room go up in the brickwork lift. Go left to SAVE, then go up again in the brickwork lift. Jump across the platform to the lever. Climb the rocks by the arrow and hit the switch opposite the pit. Go down in the lift into the passage then back to the entrance. Go past the right-hand sliding wall and go left to flick the switch. Follow the arrow to open the wall. Go back up in the lift. Drop down the rocks. Flick the lever in the middle of the main room and go through the gate. Open the wall and hit lever. Go through the portcullis for treasure. Climb up the stairs from the main room and open the gate. Go up in the lift and ride the moving platforms until you reach the top. Open the gate and Teleport.

Spire 3

Avoid the knackerers and open the portcullis past the central pillar. Stand at the side of the lift. Jump to the ledge. Move the platform over to the portcullis using ■. SAVE game at the skull up the ramp. Go right to the lift and drop down. Flick the two switches behind the moss coloured buildings. Go up the new stairs and up the lift then pull the lever. Go down stairs, then up the ramp and SAVE. Go to the top of the next ramp and then up on the lift. Pull the two-floor lever to burn the imps.

Spire 4

Save at the skull. Dodge the swinging axes and avoid the light spots in the crusher room. The easiest way to kill the snake women is to lure them into the crushers. The teleports in the alcoves will help you out of any tight spots. Go left past the gate and up in the lift. Flick the switch round the outside. Go back down the lift and into the room with the pillars opposite you. Get the silver sword in the furthest chest. Go to the torchlit passage by opening the blue panel next to the exit and hit the switch. Go along the passage to the third gate in the main room. Flick the yellow switch to exit.

Labyrinth 1

Save at skull. Minotaurs are released when the clock strikes six. Go down the right ramp, avoiding the flames to open the door. Once in the passage get the warding spell in the first door on the left. Turn the wheel in the right portcullis. There is a treasure chest in the gate at the end of the passage. Go back to the opposite ramp in the main room. Flick the first switch and kill the escaping minotaur. Flick the switch in his cell. Flick the other switch and defeat the other escaping minotaur. Drop into the cave through the arch and flick the switch on the middle pillar. Flick the switch where you dropped down to Teleport. Climb onto the raised floor in the main room and go through the right hand window. Jump over the weak floor just past the arch. Hit the switch up and to the left. Get the blunderbuss bullets to the left of the weak floor. Stick close

to the right wall to dodge the flames. Open the door, kill the imps and go through. Go up both lifts to get health potions. Go right to find the wooden bridge.

Jump onto the stone lift to your right. Go up to the ledge and flick the yellow switch further along. Go up the stone lift at the other side of the wooden bridge. The secret warhammer is on a weak floor behind the bright wall on the right. Jump to the alcove at the other end of the ledge and push the switch. Get the blunderbuss. Go to the wooden lift and go down. Don't touch the switch past the wooden bridge or the floor will collapse. Go into the passage. Activate the dark wall in the left-hand door. Climb up the wall and flick the yellow switch. Drop down and flick the switch through the grey door. Do a running jump to the left of the wooden bridge. Get the golden key in the alcove. Open the golden lock at the end of the passage. Exit the level via lift.

Labyrinth 2

Save at the skull. Try to open the left door and the imps will attack you from the right door. Kill the imps and go through to flick the switch. Hit the gold switch through the left door. Go through the centre door and get the golden key. Get the goodies through the gold door. Watch out for the weak floor after the minotaur. Go to the right passage and get the health potion. Climb up and flick the switch. Flick the switch beyond the weak floor. Turn around and jump left to collect the coin and hit the switch. In the large room don't go along the centre bridge. Use the sliding platforms instead. Go right through the entrance and flick the switch by climbing up at the end. Go to the left passage and turn the wheel. Go left and climb up to push the switch. Run over the weak floor and land on the platform with health and charm of icy cool. Jump to the lower platform, turn and jump to get the red key. Drop down and flick switch through the right door.

Go through the portcullis into the Teleport room and Teleport up to the entrance next to the bridge room. SAVE at the skull after jumping over the pit. Flick the switch on the far ledge in the bridge room along the platforms on the left. Go through the exit to a new passage. Use the Teleport at the top of the wooden lift. Open the sliding wall then go back to dodge the spikes. Open the sliding wall on the left to get treasure. Defeat the zombie with your warding spell. Go back down the passage and left to the bridge. When you are in the centre of the bridge kill to the two droid's which appear in the corners behind you. Go to those corners and flick the switches. Kill the droid on the left platform. Open the red key door through the portcullis and collect. Go to the crate room along the passage. Flick switch through the right hand wall. Shoot the Droid on the opposite platform at the high bridge and go through the portcullis. Go left and through the right door to hit the switch. Go through this door and flick the switch. Open the door previously protected by flames at the bridge. Attempt to open the portcullis. Kill the zombie to open portcullis and exit level via lift.

Circus 1

Flick the right hand switch. Go through the left gate and SAVE. Kill the snake women with the venom sword. When you are in the centre of the main room the left door will open. Go through and collect. SAVE at the skull. Enter the door ahead and drop down to the left avoiding the spikes. Flick the yellow switch. Use the Teleport. Open the portcullis back at the skull. Go through the next one and drop onto the treasures. Back at the path follow the passage through the unlocked door. Kill the snake women behind the next door and get the sword. Kill the snake women behind the fire door. Go back, go right then left into a passage. Go left and run across the weak floor to open door, run back then quickly jump across. Open the next door and run right. Keep going until you find locked doors. Go back through and open the jack-in the box. Head right back to the skull and SAVE. Open the far door at the paths over the circus. There is a bomb in the box so leave it. Use the firefly through the next door. Follow the passage, collect the health at the right fork, and take the left fork. Kill the snake woman and exit the level.

Circus 2

Go down and SAVE at the skull. Turn right at the end of the corridor and flick the switch. Avoid the knackerer and pull the lever. Follow another knackerer along the passage and go right opposite the portcullis. Flick the switch but don't open the box. When the knackerer has passed run right and open the right-hand box. Go back to switch. When the knackerer passes flick the switch and make it to the portcullis before it shuts. Go back to the passage through the first knackerer room. SAVE back at the skull. Enter the door down the clown corridor and open the wall on the right. Stand to one side to dodge the knackerer. Trap it in the left passage by hitting the switch. Go right and turn the wheel. Head right through the passage to the portcullis. Open the sliding wall, go right past the portcullis, then right again. Open the sliding wall. Open the door at end of passage. Go through gate and through door. Go through the right door and step to one side to dodge the lightning bolt. Use the warding spell or fireballs to defeat the priestess. Collect. Defeat the next priestess. Hit switches to raise the curtains. Flick again to open more curtains outside. Go back to the left door and open. Go to the exit.

Circus 3

SAVE at skull. Go around the sword building anti-clockwise and open the grey gate to the far right. Open the brown wall in the corridor to get the red key. Drop off the ledge onto the venom sword and use it to kill the snake women. Flick the switch and go through portcullis. The doors opposite this lead to a trap. Open the opposite grey gate to the left of the original entrance. Ignore the other gates. SAVE at the skull. Go up the the lift then up the next lift. Drop down the hole and collect. SAVE at the skull. Head left and go down in the lift. Open the red key door. Open the side gates. Go through the arenas slaying and killing. In the fourth arena kill the reptile with war pigs, spells and bombs.

Pit 1

Go through door, open the wall in the alcove opposite the gate for goodies. Go through gate and down either passage. Kill the priestesses by luring them into the corridor then kill the high priestess. Activate the altar front for a lift to a secret area. Go out of the room via the gate then turn left and open the left wall. Find a switch by shooting the barrels and flick it. SAVE at the skull. Head left, go through the door, and collect the coin by the altar. Enter the gate and kill the princesses. Collect in the alcove. Go back through the gate then through right gate. Go through the chapel to the stone lift collecting the coin and warhammer from behind pillar on the right. Grab the flamelance when you flick the far yellow switch. Go up the stonelift then climb up to wooden exit lift.

Pit 2

Go down in the lift that will appear when you go forward. Head down the passage and through room full of priestesses to arch alcove in the corner. Go through the now open wall to turn the wheel. Flick the switch around from the stone lift. Go back to the wooden lift and open the left and right walls. Climb onto the ledge, ring the bell, and flick the switch. Go back to the level start and through opposite gate. Follow the passage right, open the corner wall and flick the switch. Get the coins on the left ledge at the bottom of the ramp. Open the gate, then open the near-right wall and tug the lever. Open the wall in the far-right corner. Exit the room, turn left, open the right door, then climb onto the ledge for a secret SAVE. Open the door opposite the silver portcullis. Open the far gate and get health from the recess on left. Open the wall to the left of the right doorway entrance. Pull the grey lever around to the right. Go through the silver portcullis and use the silver sword to kill the skeletons. SAVE at the skull.

Head along the passage ringing the bell on the way. Drop down by the first bell. Find and defeat the high priestess. Use the anti-magic charm on her if you have it. Use the red key she leaves to open the red portcullis. Go up the ramp, over to the platform then over to the new white platform. Flick the switch then jump back across to the platform then onto moving platform. Ride to the right and open the wall for goodies. Ride back to other side, flick the switch, then leap across to the ledge opposite. Leap back to the red save point, open both right walls, and flick the switch. Go back to other side and turn the wheel. Hit the yellow switch and get the golden key. Open the gold portcullis near the start.

Pit 3

Kill the demon to open the alcove and SAVE at the skull. Stand on the block in corner of the large chamber and press ■ to raise. Jump to the block for goodies. Exit room and go down the left passage. Open the wall opposite and flick the switch. Climb on the red square and hit the switch. Open the right hand door back up the passage and kill all the skeletons and axe chuckers to bring down the lift. Go up and the flick switch. Go right at the end of the passage and flick the switch. Return and go down the left passage to kill the high priestess. Go down passage, kill the high priestess and open the wall to SAVE. Mind the trap when getting the silver sword. Head down and attempt to open the left wall. Kill, then open the left wall to flick the switch. Go up the lift at the start of the passage. Leap to the left alcove and open the left wall to SAVE. Collect the key from up the back of the alcove and open the wall behind. Jump across and collect the silver sword by the red key gate. Walk down the right corridor through the red gate, avoid the skeletons, and climb up to the left of the room. Leap over the gap then jump across the next gap to the alcove and flick the switch. Press ■ to lower lift. Exit the level via the new lift.

Pit 4

Go through the gate and grab the silver sword. Hug the left wall at end of corridor and drop down. Mind the trap by the chest. Flick the switch and also flick the switch in left passage. Defeat the skeletons and ghost to obtain the silver sword and the red key. Pull the lever through the portcullis. Go back to the switch and use the Teleport. Use the red key outside the doorway, then head down the steps. Go around to the left of the passage and flick the switch by the mural. Kill the spiders and go around the wooden door for goodies. Collect the golden key from far the alcove. Go down and up in the lift, then go to golden arch to Teleport. Drop down to the lower floor and SAVE at the skull. Drop onto the ledge via the new step then open the wall in the step. Jump to the left ledge by the pit and flick the switch. Follow the corridor to the portcullis, open, then go right. Flick ONLY the yellow switch then ride the platform outside to the other side. SAVE at the skull and open the wall. Drop to the left step from the ledge and open the door in corridor. Beware of the edge when grabbing health. Go through the doorway and head left to open the portcullis with the silver sword inside. Flick the switch to the left of the portcullis. Get the silver key and go through the silver portcullis. Go back through the left door and open the silver lock doors. Get the red sword and use on the ghosts. Pull the lever by the door round to the left. Head back and SAVE at the red skull. Drop down the left step onto the stone lift and go down.

Pit 5

Drop down the ledge. Carry on past the hidden door on the left then open it after dodging the bolts. Jump away to avoid more bolts then enter the door and flick the switch. Hug the wall through the gate and flick the switch opposite the treasure chest. Go back down the passage and enter the newly opened gate. At the end of the passage quickly open and pull the switch. Open the wall opposite and flick the switch. Go through the last gate and open the end wall to flick a switch. SAVE at the skull and leave.

Drop off the ledge to the right, go through the back arches and open the left wall to reveal the rocket launcher. Go through

the right doorway and open the wall in the left of the centre alcove. Flick the switch then go up the ramp and jump onto the platform with the skeleton after killing it. Get the silver key and use it. Return to the ledge and drop down right to another ledge. Flick the far switch then the near one. Step on the lift. Follow the steps down to the passage and SAVE at the red skull. Flick switch. Open the right chest then hit the left switch. Exit to the ledge and enter the portcullis. Go through the last arch and run past the flames. Drop right and open the end gully. Teleport then go past the flame traps and jump over to the sandy block. Open the wall to collect secrets. Return to the ledge and onto the lift.

Pit 6

Stay on top of the pit and head through the different passages collecting the treasures. Be extra careful of the sliding walls. When you get to the area that has the chest with the Greater Razorspell and Warding, open the wall. Dodge the fireballs and collect the rockets. Once you have collected everything ride the lift down to the SAVE skull. To kill the first pit monster run forward and through the arch furthest to the right. Flick the switch at the end of the passage to lower it into the flames. Go through the passage, SAVE, then go to the main area and kill the second monster in the same way. Get the red key when the lift comes up. Get the goodies in the passages then SAVE. Go through the red portcullis and up the ramps to flick the switch. Go through the portcullis and up in the lift. When battling Agrash get the warding and ankh of vitality by opening the walls on the ledges.

Belfry 1

Pull the lever by the blank wall and avoid the lever marked by skulls. Be quick when you go up the lift and across the drawbridge. Kill the knights across the bridge through the portcullis. Collect the goodies including the golden key in the room beyond the next portcullis. Go across the bridge beyond the left portcullis and kill the knight to enter the room. Go through the far right gate and push the block into the corner to Teleport to a secret area. SAVE at the skull down the lift. Go through the gate and flick the switch. Go outside and right to enter the gold portcullis and get the silver key. Ride up the lift in the previous room and get the red key. Open the portcullis to the right of the chest across bridge. Fight the Knight, open the red portcullis, then Teleport.

Belfry 2

Save at the skull and go right to the pit. Press the golden switch and ride the lift to a secret. Run past the pit and around the path, then jump across the weak path where the monster will meet his maker. SAVE then open the doors. Flick the switch, go out into the courtyard, and head left. Collect warpigs from behind the walls. Go around to the right and open a wall to reveal a red portcullis. Get the red key and goodies from the chest. Avoid the pit after the red portcullis. Go up in the chequered lift and collect the goodies from the chests. Go through the gate, kill, then go through two more gates. Go through the opposite gate and SAVE at the red skull. Go through the portcullis. Carefully jump via the revolving platform to the left ledge to flick a switch, being aware of the weak floor. Go to the opposite ledge then to the last ledge. Go right into the open passage and through the portcullis to the lift.

Belfry 3

SAVE at the skull. Leap across the rafters into the passage. Find the silver sword and use it to kill the red knight. Go back to the rafters and across the weak platform. Go right, left, right, then round the passage to the coffins. Go down the lift and defeat the green hands by luring them onto the weak platforms. Open the gate and SAVE at the red skull. Go up the red lift and flick the switch to the back of the arches. Flick the switch past the portcullis, climb up the step, and turn the wheel. Jump to the sandstone path and go up to press the gold button. Go back and drop to the first lift. Open the gate opposite the red lift and open the right wall. Flick the switch. Go towards the demon picture to open the passage. Go through and press the gold button. Open the first left gate in the courtyard and go up the lift. Open the next gate in the courtyard then open the left end wall. Go along the corridor and climb the right wall. Press the button at end of the room, then take the lift down and jump over the weak floor. Head right then take the lift to exit.

Sewer 1

SAVE at the skull. Go right and climb to the passage. Throw bombshots into the lower room. Go through the portcullis and into the passage. Hug the right wall through the maze. Go through the banner room and go up in the lift. Get the red key. Hug the left wall back through maze. Go back to the start and SAVE at the skull. Go through the red door room and drop off the bridge. Go through the door and up in the lift into a passage. Jump to the bridge and go up in the lift. Collect the golden key and go through the golden key gate at the start.

Sewer 2

Go down the lift and climb up. SAVE at the skull. Climb up the opposite side of the lift. Climb up the stone ledge at the end of the passage. Collect the silver sword and hit both switches. Climb through the arch and go through the right hand doors. Open the middle left coffin. Use the silver sword on the ghosts. Go right at the bottom of the slopes. Hit the switch through the portcullis. Go left at the junction and hit both switches in the large room. Go through the gates and fall through the weak floor.

Sewer 3

Kill the insects and get the flame thrower from the opposite force field. Head through the passage, down the slope through the passage and SAVE at the skull. Kill all ants in the purple cavern then fall through the weak floor. Push the left wall past the giant spiders. Go back to left fork and climb up the block. Shoot the stalactites to drop on the insect queen.

Sewer 4

The glare from the green haired Medusa will turn you to stone so avoid it. Collect treasure though the red portcullis, after killing all the Medusas. Follow the left wall from the entrance and go up the steps. Follow the left wall past the double doors for treasure. Go up the lift through the double doors. Drop off to the right in the pillar room and hit the switch. Kill the archers and warrior though the portcullis. Use anti-magic charm on Shaman and kill him with your sword. Hit the gold button.

Trench 1

Kill ratmen that attack you in the trench. Climb out and go up to the next level. Go down in the lift and get the red key in the room with the giant rat. Follow the right passage and go through the left portcullis. Jump out of the lift before you are spiked. Go up to the ledge via the next lift and drop onto the silver key. Collect the golden key from beneath the bridge and cross to the ledge with the graves. Open the gate and go up in the lift.

Trench 2

SAVE at the skull. The lift is a Teleport. Press ■ to be Teleported to the ledge. Then go up the lift. Go left and down the ramps. Kill the rat ogre and carry on through to the crossroads. SAVE at the skull. Go down the opposite corridor and up in the lift to press the gold switch. SAVE at the skull. Go left avoiding the mine pit and go down in the lift. Drop down the hole behind the control room. Take the lift down.

Trench 3

SAVE at the skull. Pull all four levers. Climb to the exit. Step on to the wall through the large room. Kill the rats to open the red portcullis by enticing them into crumbling traps. SAVE at the skull. Get the red key in the room past the grey gate. Go through the red portcullis. Open the gate to the rat kings chamber. Kill the Rat King. Hit the gold switch through the gate.

Inversion 1

Go down in the central lift and SAVE at the skull. Go through the portcullis and shoot the barrels to reveal the chest. Go through the wooden doors and get the red key. Go through the red portcullis, across the bridge, and through next portcullis. Pull the right lever to open the wall. Pull the right lever at the junction and go through the portcullis to collect shot. Go to the portcullis opposite and exit.

Inversion 2

To set off flame traps, approach then wait. Go through the doors and kill the army of ratmen by running down the corridor and releasing bombs. Find the silver key in the wall. Take the chequered lift through the grey gate. Go through the passage and around to the right to the coffin room. Open the coffin to the right of the wall with eyes, then open the wall and edge towards the silver sword. Kill the ghosts in the coffin room with the silver sword. Open the gate over the bridge and go down on the chequered lift. Beware of the weak floor and go through the left silver portcullis. Kill the rat ogres through the middle door and exit.

Inversion 3

Shoot the rat musketeers across the bridge. Shoot the musketeers in the far right wall and flick the switch. Go up in the lift and SAVE at the skull. Go through the portcullis and go left to get the golden key. When the imp kicks you open the wall on the left and head back to the skull. Head right over a weak floor, then up in the lift. Go through the gold portcullis, avoiding the middle coffin. Go through the doors, through the gate, and on through the gate on the other side of the bridge.

Inversion 4

Hit the switch and go down on the lift. Go through the gate on the bridge. Drop left off the bridge to collect rockets on the bridge below, then Teleport. Don't enter the Teleport through the door at end of the bridge. Open the wall between the locked portcullis and take the lift up. Pull the right lever through the portcullis. Hit the switches through the doors with one torch above them. Hit the switches through doors with two torches above them. Quickly run through the doors with three torches above them and avoid the weak floor. Step onto the Teleport and collect the golden key. Open the opposite portcullis then go around to the lift and go down. Go through the left gold portcullis to treasure. Return to the lift and go through the right gold portcullis. Run left past the monsters and through the wooden door.

Inversion 5

Drop off at the white arrow for treasure. Use invisibility to kill the rat ogres then hit the switch in the right pillar. Go through the portcullis and get the golden key. Open the wall to the right of the entrance. Open the right gold portcullis. Go through the next portcullis and kill the ratmen behind you. Go through the portcullis. Hit the golden switch and go back to the bridge. SAVE at the skull through the gold portcullis. Go up in the lift. Jump over the alcove with two torches and hit the switch. Jump back to the lift quickly, then go left to hit the switch. Jump back to the lift. Go though the portcullis to get the red key. Pull the lever and Teleport to the lift. Go down, SAVE, then go through the red portcullis.

Inversion 6

Ride the turtle. Open the left gate being aware of the ratmen, and collect the fireflies. Follow the passage and SAVE at the skull. Activate the banners for secrets. Head on through the passage and open the left wall at end to return to the start. RESAVE at the skull then activate the banner to open the doors.

Inversion 7

Collect warding off the lower bridge then Teleport. Go through the gate at end of bridge and SAVE at the skull. Hit the two switches, run quickly to the left and Teleport. Retreat from the

window, open the gate and ride the turtle to the ledge with the opening gate. Open the right wall through the gate. Collect the bomb through the portcullis. Open the wall and flick the switch in the passage near the grenade launcher. Go through the doors and Teleport. Launch grenades into the open doorways to kill the robots. Drop down and go through the gate. Open the right coffin then go into the Teleport. Go through the gate, and head around the passage through the wooden door.

Inversion 8

Drop off the middle bridge and SAVE at the skull. Teleport then go through the gate. Go down on the lift and collect the goodies. When the central right lift begins to lower go back on the lift then lower it without you on it. Destroy the giant robot by the arsenal. As soon as the robot is destroyed get on the lift as fast as possible. Do a standing jump to the turtle and ride him out of the level.

Inversion 9

SAVE at the skull and ride the turtle while shooting and collecting as you go. When the words WATCH OUT appear on the screen jump to another turtle. When the turtle reaches the edge jump off and SAVE. Retreat from the flaming robots and destroy them. Destroy all the large robots from the safety of the corridor. Exit on the far right corner lift.

Dragon 1

Kill all the knights then open the hidden door to the right of the hidden passage. Open the wall while avoiding the flame trap, then hit the switch and SAVE at the skull. Take the central lift down in the main room. Run through the flames without using the lever. Collect all the treasure. Go back up the lift by pressing the right hand switch. Open wall to the left of the portcullis and flick the golden switch. Grab the golden key through the portcullis then open the golden portcullis. Hack the blood beast's forehead using the venom sword avoiding the bolts from its tail. Enter the portcullises to collect treasure. Head towards the steps on the far side of the cave taking care not to drop into the pit. Take the lift down to finish the level.

Dragon 2

Go down lift and pull the lever by the far pillar. Flick the golden switch on right side of the room near the rockets. Pull the lever at top of the lift then go down into the passage behind the portcullis before the door closes. Flick the levers in the corners of the dragons arena then hit the central lever to open the door at the end of the arena. Hit six golden switches and go through the portcullis to collect the red sword. Slay the hydra dragon in the arena avoiding the flames from its nostrils. Go back through the doors to Teleport, then through the doors to the lift.

Dragon 3

SAVE at the skull. Head left in the arena then go up twice on the lift. Flick the switch to the right, then go through the door at the back of the lift shaft. Flick the switch and dodge the bolt trap. Switch the gold switch behind you. Turn right on the walkway and open the gate. Flick the switch then go to the top level via the lift. Flick the gold switch at the back of the lift shaft. Go to the corner furthest right from where you entered the arena and flick the switch. Take the red lift to the ledge and flick the switch to reveal a gold switch. Go back to the arena and follow the left wall to the gate. Take the lift to the middle level and hit the switch at the back of the lift shaft. Go to the top and take the black sword. Use cannons, warding and above all the black sword to kill the dragon. Exit via the far portcullis.

Dragon 4

Keep moving and SAVE at the skull. Flick the switch on the left. Avoid the stone blocks on the walkway and pull the lower lever. Run back past the lift to find the silver key. Go back and pull the upper lever, then go through the wall and through the portcullis. Go down in the lift. Run and jump over the light coloured slab. Pull the lever under the block and remain stationary. Climb onto the block and pull the lever. Enter the portcullis and pull the lever on the right. Flick the other switch and go through the open wall. Pull the lever. Climb up the right end of the new block and immediately jump back. When the second block slides across, jump to the high block and pull the lever. Go through the door in the red room and collect the golden key and the charm of icy cool. Open the golden key wall and edge to the magic charm. Jump over the pits and return to the arena. Use the Teleporters to move between the walkways and the platform. Collect the red key on the lower walkway and go through the door. Climb up to the left side then open the hidden door dodging the fire trap. Flick the switch and run to the other hidden door on the other side of the ledge. Flick the switch then go to the hidden door on the other ledge. Use the charm of icy cool on the flame traps. When the floor lowers quickly pull the switch. Run to the last door before your time expires and pull the final lever. Collect the goodies and the red sword. To kill the dragon fire flamelance from the middle walkway until it lands on the central platform. Jump to the central platform and use strength, warding, charm of icy cool and anti magic charm. Hack with the red sword. Repeat as necessary.

DEMOLITION RACER

Unlock Everything

On the main menu, press ✖, ✖, ■, ■, ▲, ▲, ●, ●

DESTREGA

Random Level Select

Press Start on the level select screen to randomly select a battleground.

Secret Characters

Complete the one player game with any character. Play again and highlight the character you used to complete the game with. Pressing **Start** will enable you to play with an alternative version of that character.

DESTRUCTION DERBY

Extra Points
To gain four points, hold Accelerate and ➡ for 3 seconds at the beginning of each race.

Passwords

For some useful cheats, enter any of the following words as your name at the password screen:

!DAMAGE!	stops your car from being damaged
NPLAYERS	you can choose up to twenty opponents (only Practice Mode)
REFLECT!	access the Ruined Monastery track (only Practice Mode)

Record Cheat

To put an impressive 599.99 seconds on the lap record table, select Total Destruction and quit out of it immediately by repeatedly pressing **Start** as 'GO' scrolls.

DESTRUCTION DERBY 2

Passwords

Enter Race Type and select Championship mode. Enter one of the following passwords as your name:

MACSrPOO	to access all tracks

You must go back and start a new Practice race for the tracks.

CREDITZ!	animated credits
ToNyPaRk	to view FMV movies

DIABLO

Infinite Gold

Begin a new two player game and load up a previous saved character with gold in their inventory. Drop the gold and get the second player character to pick up the gold, save and then quit the game without saving player one's character. Repeat until you have enough gold.

DIE HARD TRILOGY

Die Hard Level Codes

At the password screen enter the following codes. (The symbol _ denotes a space).

Level 2-Reception
ZN1!6HTWZJ!HF
GK5N5W7CX7JZR
V!CYHPZRV!CXH
KZRV!CYHPZRVJ

Level 3-Const.
T41X_3_4TD1DP
5B9W974MM6DT7
4XMLG9T74XMMG
FT74XMLG9T74J

Level 4- Office
Q_1WSX3WQK!CD
!6FSS!M1FFPQ2
SC1D5JQ2SC1F5
NQ2SC1D5JQ2S_

Level 5-Maint. 1
Y41!ZDT3YJMZZ
Y!BPYY6MW7DY7
NZMVH9Y7NZMWH
FY7NZMVH9Y7NJ

Level 6-Comp. 1
F8279HY3FLM6X
15K1!TGNWWHF9
P6NVMBF9P6NWM
GF9P6NVMBF9P_

Level 7-Exec. 1
74225VHK7WVMW
H7GRVLCLH1X74
XMLG9T74XMLH9
Y74XMLG9T74XJ

Level 8-Const. 2
TN1ZN9JCSJ_XL
7X5R9N4WL68TR
6XWMGFTR6XWLG
9TR6XWMGFTR6J

Level 9-Office 2
H425H75XGGVRV
BXK479!L!3XH5
XRLZCTH5XRL!C
YH5XRLZCTH5XJ

Level10-Ballroom
3D231ZZ!23CK!
8BS_QV9Q7JZ3D
FKQ6SW3DFKQ7S
!3DFKQ6SW3DFJ

Level 11-Maint. 2
W82GN88TVSCFX
WCM79Q5PRZ!WC
FFPQQVWCFFPRQ
ZWCFFPQQVWCF

Level 12-Office 3
942RCHX88Z14N
RL3WL4XLM2D95
4NLLB9954NLMB
F954NLLB9954J

Level13-Const.3
TJ2HGH_DSD1DP
Z_VN45NTLG9TM
6DTM6DTM6DTL6
8TM6DTM6DTM6_

Level 14-Vault
DX22HW5SGZPQ7
Z5NGQZGSM2DY
MQGTW7DYMQGSW
3DYMQGTW7DYMJ

Level 15-Comp.2
BX21PND98VGP_
4ZB1QDYGNLLBY
CPGPVRBYCPGNV
MBYCPGPVRBYCJ

Level 16-Exec.2
XJ2BXT9SZXPG5
DJ6S_Z69SH1XM
LG9T74XMLG9S7
XMLG9T74XML_

Level 17-Office 4
RS2GX9C5P9SCJ
S3X65LMYGYWRV
!CYHPZRV!CYGP
VRV!CYHPZRV!_

Level 18-Maint.3
FS237Z5NHGKQR
871JV7ZXVWCFT
R6XWMGFTR6XVM
BFS6XWMGFS_

Level 19-Comp.3
B42_RJ498VGPC
7S8DVXY2P2NB5
8P2NBKB58P2PB
PB58P2NBKB58J

Die Harder Level Codes

Level 2-New Wing
14_JJ2JB144JL
289144JB_F1_
4JLKT3GS9_L38
F144JL289144J

Level 3-Tunnel
SS_XHKG5SW3DF
KQ6SW3F!QQ1SM
3DDQRNCCVDFJQ
2SW3DFKQ6SW3

Level 4-Runway
F416QVMBF5NQL
VC9F5NNSLCHF9
NQM1W6TDP6LWC
F5NQLVC9F5NJ

Level 5-Plane
N_V38Y3N2JB1
85_N2J955Y1NL
JB_1L4Q7TV195
4N2JB185_N2J_

Level 6-Church
8N_N8KL68P2NB
KB58P2RQ!L581
2NB698681NBJB
18P2NBKB58P2J

Level 7-Snow
8D142J2_8F1N6
JV38F1JJ3B_8P
1N7BGCBSV46KV
78F1N6JV38F1J

Level 8-Intercept
N_1B58Y3N2JB1
85_N2JHHXP2NZ
JB_76LXXNV195
4N2JB185_N2J_

Die Hard With A Vengeance Level Codes

Level 2-Central Park 1
XJ1GFT!7XMLG9
T74XMLD3K72X!
LG82RC8VMZKSH
HXWQZWM7GVHSJ

Level 3-Chinatown 1
T81XMLG9TC5DP
LQBTC5G!VQDT7
5DN965F24Y7QQ
7TW1X6CK5JV6J

Level 4-Uptown 1
ZS1!CYHPZWWHF
YRQZWWF7PRJZR
WHD67TBLVY7QR
TZ3!!!BK!_2BJ

Level 5-Central Park2
KS28P3DFKV78Y
3NGKV7BRCN8KQ
78XS415M6VCC4
YHN57PC2XX9MH
_K63SGSJDFD2J

Level 6-Chinatown 2
Z41!5XRLZ7S!3
XHKZ7SY9NHRZC
S!27!ZBGTD7LR

J!7XHK!CVWFG_

Level 7-Urban 2
!81!MZHT!CYHP
ZRV!CYF!QRX!7

TZ3T!7VPFC4H_

Level 8-Uptown 2
5422VBKB54NLL
B9954NJS29H58
NLMKT6KFP6VT1
C48J2198NRN6J

Level 11-Aqueduct 2
8J24_KV78K248
K248K262T228Y
249BLCXS3K66L
3996NV535LHKJ

Level 9-Aqueduct 1
S82DFJG1SC1D5
JQ2SC1GHSQ4S7
1D4C6FD2_SM_6
7TW5XQ4QGC62_

Level 12-Gruber
9N24LMLG9P6NV
MBF9P6QJWBC9T
6NW8V2YX72L82
C89248C9MQZN_

Level 10-Wharf
7N23LHKZ7NZMV
H9Y7NZKJ79W7S
ZMWNTLMY!6ST9
T6_V38MH9T9RJ

Die Hard Cheats

Coordinates:

To put coordinates and strange wire objects on the screen, pause and hold the **R2** button. Next press ←, ●, ↓, ■

Fifty Grenades:

For fifty standard grenades, pause and hold the **R2** button. Next press →, ■, ↓, ●.

Floating Dead:

To make the baddies float when killed, pause the game and hold the **R2** button, then press ↓, ■, ▲, ↓.

Invincible Mode:

To be invincible, pause and hold the **R2** button before pressing →, ↑, ↓, ■.

Lardy Mode:

To make Bruce and the hostages fat, pause the game and hold the **R2** button, then press →, ■, ■, ↓.

Level Skip:

To access a level skip option, pause the game and hold **R2**, then press ↓, ●, ←, ■, ↑, ■, ←. When you press **Start** the option appears. Use → to move through the levels.

Skeleton Mode:

To turn the baddies into red skeletons and the hostages blue, pause the game and hold the **R2** button. Press ▲ ten times and ➡ four times.

Speech Speed:
Pause the game and hold the **R2** button. By repeatedly pressing the sequence ⬇, ■, ■, ➡, you alter the speed of speech from very slow to very fast.

Stupid Mode:
To make the bad guys fire between their legs, pause and hold the **R2** button, then press ⬇, ●, ●, ⬇, ▲, ⬇.

Unlimited Weapons:
To have a shotgun and unlimited shells, pause the game and hold the **R2** button. Press ➡, ⬆, ⬇, ⬇, ■, ➡. To change to different weapons re-enter the same sequence. Each weapon has unlimited ammunition.

Wailing Plants:
Pause the game and hold the **R2** button. If you press ●, ●, ■, ■, ➡, the plants will now scream when shot.

Die Harder Cheats
Fergus Mode:
To make everyone look like Fergus McGovern (the Probe Entertainment boss), pause and hold the **R2** button. Then press ●, ⬇, ⬇, ■, ✖, ■.

Invincible Mode:
To guard against dying when you lose all of you lives, pause the game and hold the **R2** button, Then press ⬇, ▲, ➡, ■. Re-enter the sequence to return to normal.

Map Editor:
For access to the Map Editor, pause and hold the **R2** button. Next press ➡, ⬆, ⬇, ■ and **Start**. Coloured lines show the movements of the baddies on the current level. You can scroll around and move objects. To move freely in 3D press **Select** and use ⬆ and ⬇ to zoom in and out. Use **L1** and **R2** to enable you to look up and down.

Maximum Specials:
To gain ninety nine grenades and ninety nine rockets, pause and hold the **R2** button before pressing ➡, ■, ⬅, ●, ▲, ⬇.

Reverse Controls:
If you would like to reverse your controls, pause and hold the **R2** button, then press ➡, ■, ▲, ➡. To return them back to normal repeat the sequence.

Skeleton Mode:
To turn everyone into skeletons pause and hold the **R2** button, then press ▲, ⬅, ⬅, ⬇, ■, ▲, ⬇. To put them back to normal enter the same sequence.

Weird Shaped People:
To make everyone either very tall, short or fat, pause and hold the **R2** button, then press ⬅, ▲, ➡, ⬇.

X-Files Mode:
Use the Level Skip to get to the Central Park 1 level, where you can use this cheat. Next, pause the game and highlight 'Quit'. Press and hold **R2** on controller 1, then press the following: ➡, ■, ▲, ⬇, ✖, ✖, ✖. This should bring up a 'Roswell' screen with aliens being blown up.

Die Hard With A Vengeance Cheats
Extra View:
To choose a new Chase Car view, pause the game and hold the **R2** button. Next press ⬇, ●, ⬇, ●.

Fergus Mode:
To make everyone look like Fergus McGovern (the Probe Entertainment boss) and also have hundreds of Fergus faces floating around the screen, pause the game and hold the **R2** button. Then press ●, ⬇, ⬇, ▲, ✖, ■.

Flat Shade Mode:
To turn off the texture-mapping graphics, pause and hold the **R2** button, then press ⬇, ⬆, ⬅, ⬅, ⬇, ⬆, ⬅, ⬅, ⬇, ⬆, ⬅, ⬅.

Hello Mode:
To have a 'hello' message on the compass and various numbers on the screen (the bottom pair are your coordinates), pause the game and hold the **R2** button, then press ➡, ⬆, ⬇, ■.

Infinite Lives:
To have infinite lives, pause the game and hold the **R2** button. Then press ⬅, ●, ⬆, ⬇, ■, ➡.

Infinite Super-Turbos:
To jump over traffic at a high speed, pause the game and hold the **R2** button, then press ●, ⬅, ⬇, ■, ▲, ⬅.

Infinite Turbos:
To gain some extra speed to reach the bombs, pause and hold the **R2** button. Then press ●, ●, ■, ■, ⬇, ⬇, ✖, ✖.

Jumbo Cars:
To make all the cars massive, pause and hold the **R2** button, then press ⬅, ▲, ➡, ⬇.

No Clock and Level Skip:
Pause the game and hold the **R2** button. When you press ➡, ⬆, ⬇, ■, some numbers and letters will appear on the screen. Now press **Start** on the second controller. When the cheat options appear, press ▲ to toggle the clock on or off. To advance through the different levels use ➡, and to advance to the next bomb press ● on the second controller.

Odd Mode:
To try some strange views pause the game and hold the **R2** button, then press ●, ↓, ↓, ■, ➡. To switch between flattened, stretched, and close-up, repeat the sequence.

Slow Motion:
To play in slow motion, pause the game and hold the **R2** button. Then press ⬅, ↑, ⬅, ⬅, ■, ↓.

Toy Car Hanger:
To have a toy car hanging inside the windscreen (on the inside view), pause and hold the **R2** button. Then press ➡, ●, ⬅, ⬅, ■, ↓.

Weird Buildings:
To give some of the buildings a strange appearance, pause the game and hold the **R2** button, then press ➡, ■, ⬅, ▲, ✖, ■, ↓.

DIE HARD TRILOGY 2

Level Select and Movie Player
On the main menu press **L1, L1,** ●, ●, ■, ■. Select movie player to view all the games cut scenes or direct level access to skip to a later level.

Action Mode Cheats
Pause the game and enter one of the following codes:
All Guns – ■, ■, ●, ●, **L1, L1**
Unlimited Energy – ▲, ▲, ●, ●, **L1, L2**
Unlimited Ammo – **L1, L1, R1, R1,** ●, ●
Deactivate Laser Sight – **L1, L1,** ▲, ▲, **L1, L1, L1**
First Person View – ●, ▲, ▲, ■
Big Head Enemies – **R1, R1, L1, L1,** ▲, ▲
Blow Enemies Heads Off – ■, ■, ●, ●, **R1, R1**
Electric McClane – ■, ■, **L1, L1, R1, R1**
Skeleton McClane – ●, ■, ▲, ▲, ■, ●

Gun Mode Cheats
Unlimited Energy – ▲, ▲, ●, ●, **L1, L2**
All Weapons – ■, ■, ●, ●, **L1, L1**
Infinite Ammo – **L1, L1, R1, R1,** ●, ●
Auto Reload – ■, ■, ▲, ▲, ●, ●
Slow Motion – ▲, **L1,** ▲, **L1,** ▲, **L1**

Driving Mode Cheats
Indestructible Car – ▲, ▲, ●, ●, **L1, L2**
Disable Clock – **L1, R1,** ■, ■, **R1, L1**
Full Nitro Tank – **L1, L1, R1, R1,** ●, ●
Rainy Weather – ■, ■, **L1, L1,** ▲, ●
Wheels Only – **L1, R1, R1, L1, L1, R1**

DIGIMON WORLD

Learn by raising Digimon rookies a couple of stats at a time. Always raise your Digimon in HP and MP, then choose a stat to work with. If you train an Agumon in defence, you will get a completely different Digimon than if trained in brains. By experimenting you will both expand your knowledge of the game and raise your tamer rank.

Expand your technique list as quickly as possible. More techniques make it easier to digivolve later in the game. Techniques also give you a greater choice of attacks for your Digimon.

Battle as well as train. Train often at the training sites, but do not underestimate the importance of battles for your Digimon. Through battles you can win bits, items, and occasionally new techniques.

Keep an eye on the weight of your Digimon. Your Digimon may well fade away without asking for food, so it is up to you to look after this. Healthy weights are in the region of 30 for rookies and 60 for champions. Some Ultimate Digimon will need lighter weights however.

Pay close attention to Digimon care. Work out where the closest toilet is and keep food and recovery items handy. Consider carrying portable potties with you for safety.

Talk to Yuramon, Tsunomon, Angemon, and read Shellmon's bulletin board often. These Digimon are there to help you out.

Caring for your Digimon costs money. To accumulate a lot fairly quickly you can collect DigiMushrooms, and then take them to the south-eastern Mojyamon. He will trade you a Medium Recovery for each mushroom you bring to him. Take the Medium Recoveries to the south-western Mojyamon. Trade him the medium recoveries for Super Defence Disks. Return to File City and sell them at the Item Shop. Each disk can be sold for 2,000 bits.

To see your opponents HP rating press **SELECT** during battle.

Be patient when trying to make ultimate Digimon. You will have to have amazing stats for your Digimon to digivolve to ultimate. Be patient, learn techniques, and save stat chips. Using stat chips can be helpful as your Digimon can digivolve to ultimate when it is just 11 or 12 days old. This allows you to fight tougher opponents for longer.

DINO CRISIS

Infiltration

When you finally reach the fence surrounding the complex, your team finds the area deserted. Gail scouts ahead. With the area clear for now of any hostile forces, Rick enters the main complex and tries to find the control room. Head to the left and talk to Gail. Gail is examining a clean tear in the fence. After a brief conversation, head through the green double doors to the right. You will find yourself in a storeroom. Push the shelf to reveal a medic pack and collect the key found on a shelf in the corner of the room. Exit the storeroom and head towards the gate to the left. Rick will tell you via his radio that the complex is deserted. Gail appears and will take the key you found in the storeroom from you. Follow Gail through the gate. Head through the gate to the right. Follow the path around and you will find a disembodied corpse. Speak to Gail. He will tell you to enter the generator room and get the power on while he will stay outside and cover you. Head through the door straight in front of you.

Generator Room

Make your way to the opposite side of the room. Examine the glass panel. You will need to move the four coloured plugs into the correct order (left to right) Red – Blue – Green – White. Then pull the four levers to the right of the glass panel. The generator will now be activated. Make your way outside. As you near the door you will hear a gun shots.

First Encounter

When you get outside you will discover Gail and the corpse missing. Before you have time to react a Raptor will pounce from above. You have a choice of either standing your ground and killing the Raptor, or running past the beast and towards the gate at the end of the path. If you decide on the latter, once you are through the gate, the Raptor will jump over the fence after you. Quickly turn around and dive through the gate on the right. For a moment the Raptor will consider chasing you further but will decide not to and stalk away. Rick will contact you and tell you he has gained access to the control room but is not inclined to believe your story about giant lizards. Head forward and enter the complex.

The Main Complex

Follow the corridor to the right and you will come across a laser fence. Stand on the air vent cover and climb up into the airshaft. Follow the shaft around and drop down through the first hole. Ignore the door behind you and head forward. Collect the 9mm shells and enter the door on the right. You are now in the control room.

Control Room

Inside you will find Rick. You will agree to search the area. Exit the control room and head back towards the airshaft but enter the double doors. You will find yourself in the first save room. Collect the DDK-H disk from the desk then press the switch to

the right of the door. Power will be restored to the room and you can access the computer. Enter the second part of the room and pick up the 'LEO' key next to the corpse. Leave via the opposite door that you entered through. Rick will then unlock the laser fence next to you. Kill the Raptor stalking the corridor and then enter the room to the right. This room is filled with lockers. Collect the DDK-H from above one of the lockers and collect the darts found in the corner of the room. Read the file on the table, inside you will find the code to unlock the safe in the save room.

Exit the room and enter the save room. Unlock the safe using the combination '0375'. Inside you will find the lobby key. Exit via the door you came through and deactivate the laser fence. Head through the double doors. You will find yourself in the lobby. Unlock the main doors and head outside. Make your way around to the left. Collect the DDK-N disk near the corpse and read the pad. The pad will reveal another code – '47812'. Return back inside. Go up the stairs.

Top Floor

Make your way through the door to the right. Inside you will encounter a Raptor. Kill the Raptor then head into the room on the left. Inside you will find a second Raptor. Once it is dead, walk up to the bar and read the yellow pad. Open the safe on the back of the wall using the code '7687'. Inside you will find a weapon modifier. Return to the corridor and head out the door at the end of the passage. Enter the room on the left. Read the yellow folder, it will explain the code system. Exit and head back into the corridor. Examine the blue panel to the left of the door. Enter the password 'HEAD'.

Top Floor Office

Inside you will find a mortally wounded scientist. He will give you a 'SOL' key. Collect the DDK-N disk, and then examine the medals in the corner of the room. Insert the 'SOL' key into the left slot and the 'LEO' key into the right slot. Then enter the code '705037'. Inside you will find a key labelled 'L'. As you leave the T-Rex will come crashing through the large glass window. There are two ways to escape from the jaws of the T-Rex. Wait until the T-Rex is about to strike then fire a round into its jaws. When it reels back dash for the door. You will have to be quick or you will become the T-Rex's next meal. Alternately wait until the T-Rex is about to strike and fire a round into its jaws. Continue to fire into its mouth and eventually the T-Rex will retreat. Exit the room and head into the lobby. Descend the stairs. Head towards the double doors under the stairs and examine the panel to the right. Enter the password 'NEWCOMER' to unlock the door.

Training Area

Inside you will find another corpse and two elevators. Take the map from the centre of the room, then head out the single door. Turn off the laser fence and head through the door on the left. Kill the Raptor you find inside. Read the file on the table and the writing on the white board. This will reveal another code

– 1123. Exit via the door you entered through and head down the corridor. Kill the Raptor, which inhabits the corridor. Enter the room on the left. Go to the front of the room and take the key near the white board. Suddenly a Raptor will attack from above. Struggle out of its grasp and Gail will appear and kill the beast. Gail will tell you to return to the control room. Exit the room.

Take the key from the corpse. Enter the airshaft further down the corridor. Follow the shaft and drop through the vent. You will find yourself in the toilets. Exit through the door. Deactivate the laser fence. Enter the save room and exit via the door opposite. Make your way down the corridor and enter the control room. Inside you will find Rick and Gail. You will now need to restore power to the lower level.

Restoring Power to the Lower Level

Leave the control room and climb up into the airshaft near the door leading to the save room. Drop down the vent at the far end. Head outside. Go up at the intersection and go through the gate. Climb down the ladder. Take the plug from the lone panel with the flashing light. Insert the plug into the panel at the far end. Then move the plugs into the correct order (left to right) Red – Blue – Green – White. The generator will now be activated. Rick will contact you and ask you to return to the control room. Retrace your steps back to the control room. When you enter the complex, a Raptor will smash through the glass window. Struggle from its grip and kill it. When you reach the control room you will be presented with two choices, either follow Gail down into the basement after Doctor Kirk or go with Rick and answer the distress call.

Follow Gail

Exit the control room and head to the right. Go down the stairs. When you turn the corner you will spy a pack of small dinosaurs called compys, dining on a fallen Raptor. Shoot them all using your pistol then enter the room on the right. Collect the ID card from the desk then read the yellow folder. Exit the room and head through the door at the end of the passage. You will be reunited with Gail but before you can act, Doctor Kirk drops a grill separating you from Gail. Enter through the door to the right. As you walk down the passage, a Raptor will leap out from behind an abandoned elevator. Struggle from its grasp and it will be electrocuted as you push it away. Deactivate the laser fence, then head through the double doors. You will find yourself in a room filling with large storage containers. Examine the corpse to the left then exit via the single door to the left. Now head through the single door opposite and you will find yourself in the 2nd generator room.

Climb the ladder up and head through the gate. Return inside the building. Enter the airshaft at the end of the corridor. Ignore the first vent and drop through the 2nd vent. Head to the end of the corridor and enter the door next to the door, which leads to the toilets. Inside, collect the DDK-E disk and the finger print machine. Read the yellow file and use the

emergency box if you need too. Exit and head back down the corridor. Go through the double doors. Head through the double doors opposite, then down the corridor and outside. Head through the gate to the left. Rick will contact you and explain that he found Tom but was too late to save him. Make your way out through the gate to the right. You will face two Raptors along this path. Collect both cases of shotgun shells. Make your way through the double doors at the end. As soon as you enter you will be taken unaware by a Pterodactyl. Struggle from its grip before you are thrown towards the wall. When you are free, retrieve your gun and dive through the door in the right corner.

Examine the corpse and you will find a DDK-L disk. The body is that of the under cover agent Tom. Take the second DDK-L disk from the counter and head through the next door. Collect the map and head through the door at the end of the room. Avoid the Pterodactyl and enter the room on the far left. Descend the ladder. When you reach the bottom, collect the control card to your right. You will be faced by six consoles, each console has three different coloured buttons. When you press one of the buttons, a pipe will descend from above. Your aim is to lower all six pipes. Stand in the centre of the room so you have three consoles to your left and three to your right. On each side there is a top console (at the top of the screen), a middle console and a bottom console (at the bottom of the screen).

First: Go to the bottom left console and activate the red button.
Second: Go to the top right console and activate the red button.
Third: Go to the centre left console and activate the green button.
Fourth: Go to the centre right console and activate the green button.
Fifth: Go to the top left console and activate the blue button.
Finally: Go to the bottom right console and activate the blue button.

With all the pipes in position the power will be restored. Return back up the ladder and exit the room. Outside, you will be grabbed by a Pterodactyl that plans to grind you in the giant fan. Struggle free in time and the Pterodactyl will nose dive to a gory death. Make your way through the door to the far right. Make your way through the computer room and outside. If you try to leave via the path you came by, the ground beneath you will crumble away and you will have to fight to prevent yourself falling. Go to the console and activate the elevator. You will find yourself in the room filled with large storage containers you were in earlier. Climb the ladder to the left. Run to the left and use the control card on the console. You will now be in control of the crane. You need to use the crane to move the containers and clear a path to the doors on the right.

First: Choose Up, Down, Left, Hook.
Second: Choose Left, Release.
Third: Choose Up, Hook.
Finally: Choose Exit.

Return back to the ladder and climb down. Make your way past the crates and through either of the doors at the end. Head down the passage past where you electrocuted the Raptor and through the door at the end. Run to the end of the passage and go up the stairs. Enter the save room at the end of the corridor. Exit via the door opposite. Enter the lobby through the double doors. Go through the double doors under the stairs. . Head through the single door. Enter through the door on the left. To gain access to the elevators you will need to update your ID card. To update your ID card, go to the computer on the opposite side of the room and insert your ID card. You will first need to input one of these pass codes. '47812' or '46907'. You will also need to use the finger machine on either of these corpses. Tom found in the computer room near where you first encounter the Pterodactyls. The corpse found opposite the elevators and the body outside near the main lobby. You will need to use a combination of a pass code and a fingerprint to update the ID card in your possession. With your updated ID card exit via the door you entered through. Go through the door on the right. Enter the left elevator and ride down to the floor below.

Follow Rick

Exit the control room. Go left up the corridor and enter airshaft. Follow the shaft to the vent above the corridor that leads outside. Drop through the vent and out the door to the left. Head through the gate to the left. You will notice Rick walking off to the right. Follow him through the gate on the right. Along this path you will face two Raptors and find two boxes of shotgun shells. Enter through the double doors at the end of the path. Before you have time to react you will be knocked to the ground. A Pterodactyl will drop from above and grab you. During the attack you will drop your gun. Struggle free before the winged beast throws you against the wall. Once you are free, reclaim your gun and dive through the door in the top right corner.

Inside you will find Rick and a badly wounded but still alive Tom. Tom will give you a DDK-L disk. You will find another DDK-L disk on the console. Enter the second part of the room and take the map from the wall. Go through the door opposite. Avoid the Pterodactyl and go through the door on the far left. Descend the ladder. Collect the control card to your right. You will be faced by six consoles, each console has three different coloured buttons. When you press one of the buttons, a pipe will descend from above. Your aim is to lower all six pipes. Stand in the centre of the room so you have three consoles to your left and three to your right. On each side there is a top console (at the top of the screen), a middle console and a bottom console (at the bottom of the screen).

First: Go to the bottom left console and activate the red button.
Second: Go to the top right console and activate the red button.
Third: Go to the centre left console and activate the green button.
Fourth: Go to the centre right console and activate the green button.
Fifth: Go to the top left console and activate the blue button.
Finally: Go to the bottom right console and activate the blue button.

With all the pipes in position the power will be restored. Return back up the ladder and exit the room. Outside, you will be grabbed by a Pterodactyl that plans to grind you in the giant fan. Struggle free in time and the Pterodactyl will nose dive to a gory death. Make your way through the door to the far right. Make your way through the computer room and outside. If you try to leave via the path you came by, the ground beneath you will crumble away and you will have to fight to prevent yourself falling. Return through the door. Activate the console then return into the computer room. Regina and Rick will help Tom out onto the elevator. You will find yourself in the room filled with large storage containers. Climb the ladder to the left. Run to the left and use the control card on the console. You will now be in control of the crane. You need to use the crane to move the containers and clear a path to the doors on the right.

First: Choose Up, Down, Left, Hook.
Second: Choose Left, Release.
Third: Choose Up, Hook.
Finally: Choose Exit.

Return back to the ladder and climb down. Make your way past the crates and through either of the doors at the end. The game will switch to Rick and Tom. As they enter the save room on this level they inadvertently wake a sleeping Raptor. The game will switch back to Regina. Head up the passage and through the door at the end. Head past the large grill and through the door. Before you there will be a dead Raptor being eaten by a pack of compys. Shoot the compys with your pistol and enter the save room on the right. Inside you will find Rick standing over the body of Tom who died fighting the Raptor they woke. Rick will return to the control room. Take the ID card and read the yellow folder. Exit the room and head back through the door you entered through. Walk up to the large grill. Gail will contact you. You will make the decision to use the elevator rather than try and move the grill.

Return back through the door and up the stairs at the end of the corridor. Run past the control room and into the save room found at the end of the corridor. Go through the door opposite. Head to the right and through the left door at the end. Collect the DDK-E disk and the finger print machine. Exit the room and go through the double doors at the end of the corridor. You will now be in the lobby. Go through the double doors underneath the stairs. Head through the single door. Enter through the door on the left. To gain access the elevators you will need to update your ID card. To update your ID card, go to the computer on the opposite side of the room and insert your ID card. You will first need to input one of these pass codes. '47812' or '46907'. You will also need to use the finger machine on either of these corpses. Tom found in the save room on the level below. The corpse found opposite the elevators and the body outside near the main lobby. You will need to use a combination of a pass code and a fingerprint to update the ID card in your possession. With your updated ID card exit via the door you entered through. Go through the door on the right. Enter the left elevator and ride down to the floor below.

Basement Level 1

Before you get a chance to exit the elevator, a Raptor will tear through the roof of the elevator. Struggle free from its grasp and then kill the beast. Read the yellow folder. Go up to the double doors and examine the panel. Enter the password 'LABORATORY'. In the next corridor you will be faced with two Raptors separated by laser fences. Wait until the Raptors collide with the laser fences, then while they are stunned deactivate the laser fence and attack. Enter the first door you run into. You will find yourself in an electronic locker room. Slip around to the top and you will be positioned behind the lone Raptor stalking this room. Once it is dead, search the room for a pistol upgrade. Exit via the single door. You will face two more Raptors in the follow corridor. Deactivate the laser fences and enter the first door you encounter. Inside, collect the DDK-E disk, the emergency box key from the shelf and read the yellow file. Before you leave examine the console and you will discover another pass code '5037'. Return to the corridor and enter the room at the end. Collect the emergency box key and the screwdriver from the red toolbox. Activate the lit console next to yellow folder. Enter the code '5037'. Exit via the door you entered and return to the room down the corridor. You can now enter the door on the other side of the room.

Containment Chamber

You will find yourself in a containment/gas chamber. Inside the chamber is a scientist, but before you can enter you will need to decontaminate the chamber. Examine the console. Push the middle button, then the left button and finally the right button. Once the chamber is decontaminated, enter inside. The scientist inside will give you a key with '3695' inscribed on it. The scientist will unfortunately die. Search his body for a key. This key will open one of the small wooden boxes in the save room near where you found the compys dining on a dead Raptor. As you try to leave, you will be faced by a Raptor, which has followed you into the room. Escape its grip then run to the containment room controls. You will find the Raptor is locked in the chamber. You have a choice to leave the Raptor where it is or gas it to death; the latter is far more fulfilling. Press the right button to gas the Raptor quickly or play with the controls for a far slower death. Once you have finished with

your torturous exploits, exit the room. Return to the corridor. Head up the corridor and enter the electronic locker room.

Electronic Locker Room

Examine the computer on the left of the room. Insert the key with '3695' inscribed on it and then enter '3695'. You are faced with a puzzle in which you need to match the two images.
First: Press the 2nd from bottom twice.
Second: Press the 3rd from bottom once.
Finally: Press the 5th from bottom once.
One of the lockers will light green. Use the '3695' key on the lit locker to open it. Inside you will find a key labelled 'R'. Exit through the single door and head to the room at the end of the corridor. Go up to the big screen. Use the 'L' labelled key in the left panel. To gain access to Doctor Kirk's laboratory both the 'L' and 'R' keys need to inserted simultaneously. To do this, Regina contacts Gail and asks him to help. Once both keys are inserted you will be faced by another panel requiring a password. Enter 'ENERGY'. Enter Doctor Kirk's laboratory.

Doctor Kirk's Laboratory

Read the brown folder and then examine the console. Enter 'Gamma', 'Beta', then finally 'Alpha'. Exit the laboratory. Once outside the laboratory, all the doors will shut tight. Use the screwdriver on the panel just left of the door. The next puzzle requires you to over lay three panels that will match the one shown. Do not touch the left panel, turn the middle panel to the right once and the right panel to the right once. Then place down the right panel, then the left panel. Finally lay down the middle panel. The doors will now be released. You will then have two choices placed before you.

Agreed With Gail

Exit via the door on the left. The whole area is now overrun with Raptors and are usually found in pairs. The best strategy is to avoid their attacks and run, very, very fast. Run down the corridor avoiding the Raptors. Head through the door into the locker room. Avoid two more Raptors and head out the double door to the left. Avoid the Raptors and head through the door at the end. You will now be opposite the elevators. Head through the open grill and through the single door. Head down the passage and through the double doors at the end. You will be reunited with Gail who has found your quarry, Doctor Kirk. You will receive an ID card from Doctor Kirk which will give you access to the elevator in the control room. You will now need to return to the control room. Head through the single door on the left. Then go into the generator room via the next single door. Climb the ladder and then through the gate. Head into the complex. Climb up into the airshaft. Drop through the first hole. Enter the control room.

Agreed With Rick

Return into Doctor Kirk's laboratory and go to the computer in the left corner of the room. To unlock the emergency exit you will need to remember the letter combinations that flash on screen (it is advisable to write down each letter when they flash on screen). There are three different sections and you only get two chances. Once you have unlocked the emergency exit, climb down the ladder. You will find yourself in the room filled with the large containers. Before you get a chance to catch your breath you will run into Doctor Kirk. Before he gets a chance to escape, Gail appears and takes him into custody. Gail will ask you to signal the extraction team. You will receive an ID card from Doctor Kirk. You will now need to return to the control room. Head through the single door on the left. Then go into the generator room via the next single door. Climb the ladder and then through the gate. Head into the complex. Climb up into the airshaft. Drop through the first hole. Enter the control room.

Signalling the Extraction Team

Once in the control room, enter the elevator opposite the door. You will find yourself in another computer filled room. Open the box on the wall near the door and take the 'Drive' key. Exit the room. You will find yourself on the top of the complex. Run to the far left and enter the left door. Insert the 'Drive' key into emergency panel. This will activate the emergency satellite dish. Exit the room. For no apparent reason all the doors on the top level will automatically lock.

The T-Rex Strikes Back

This would not be so much of a problem except for the fact that the T-Rex has decided to make an untimely appearance. After diving aside from its first attack, run to the far right. When you reach the door you will find it locked, but Rick is working on it, you just need to buy some time. With your back to the wall, wait until the T-Rex strikes and fire a round into its jaws. After several assaults, Rick will eventually unlock the door and you can dive to relative safety. Its time to try and escape. Rick will tell you to use the gate outside the main entrance to reach the helicopter pad. Ride the elevator down to the control room. Exit the room and go down the passage and enter the save room. Exit via the door opposite.

Go out the double doors into the lobby. Go out the main entrance. Avoid the Pterodactyls and make your way around to the left. Enter through the large gate. Follow the path to the end. When you turn the first corner, a Raptor will leap over the wall. Avoid its attacks and continue forward. As you go onward another Raptor will pounce at you; just keep running until you reach the doors at the end. Dive through the door on the right. You will find yourself in a warehouse with your route to the helicopter pad barred by a number of movable wooden crates. First you have two wooden crates, a higher and a lower crate. Push the higher crate forward, then the lower crate down. Then you will have two more crates in front of you. Push the 2nd lower crate forward, and then push the 2nd higher crate up. Make your way through the door in the right corner.

Helicopter Pad

You will now be on the helicopter pad and you will be reunited with Rick and Doctor Kirk. The helicopter will appear. You escape? Game over? No! Before the helicopter gets a chance to land, the T-Rex appears and chomps on it. Leaving you without an escape route and out in the open before a hungry T-Rex. Startled by the appearance of the T-Rex, Doctor Kirk slips away unnoticed. Run around the helicopter wreckage avoiding the T-Rex. You will need to occupy the T-Rex until Rick can repair the elevator. When he signals to you, run to the elevator. Walk forward. When you turn the corner you will be overrun by a group of compys. Shoot them all, then continue forward. Enter the door on the right. Inside you will find more compys. Deal with the compys first then collect the 'EV' card and read the notes on the floor. Return to the passage and enter the door at the end. You will find Rick working on another elevator. As you ride the elevator down a fuse blows. You will find yourself in a large hangar. Rick will try to restore power but needs a plug. Go through the door in the corner of the hangar, right of where you entered. Take the plug you find inside and return to Rick. With power restored you can go through the door in the top right corner of your present position.

The New Strain Raptors

Collect the two sets of control cards then talk to Rick. Exit via the door on the left. Here will be your first encounter with a stronger, more dangerous type of Raptor. First though you will need to dive out from under a falling storage container. Then you will have to fight two of the horned Raptors. Kill both beasts then head through the large door at the end. You will face another horned Raptor. If you have plenty of ammunition kill the creature, if not, grab the control cards and the key then dive back out of the door. Climb the ladder and head left. Climb the second ladder up into the control room. Insert control card 1 into the console. To reach the corpse on the floor below you will need to move some of the containers surrounding him.

First: Choose Right, Hook.
Second: Choose Left, Release.
Third: Choose Up, Hook.
Fourth: Choose Release.
Fifth: Choose Right, Up, Hook.
Sixth: Choose Up, Down, Release.
Seventh: Choose Right, Up, Down, Hook.
Finally: Choose Exit.

Climb down both ladders. Follow path around the containers to reach the corpse. Collect DDK-W disk. Return to the save room and exit via the door on the right. Make your way around the room and through the door in the opposite corner of the room. Run down the passage avoiding the purple Raptors, and through the door at the end. Collect the emergency box key from the corpse and the level map. Go through the only other unlocked door. Head down the passage and turn right. You will find a set of stairs in front of you. Climb the stairs. Kill the lone Raptor lumbering along the corridor and through the door at the end. You will find yourself in another save room. Go through the door into the second part of this room. Collect the DDK-S disk, the 'B2-1' key near the corpse. Go around the console and deactivate the alarm. Leave the room via the door you entered through. Enter the airshaft.

Follow the shaft to the end and drop through the vent at the end. When you try to take the level 'C' card a Raptor will spring out from beneath the grating on the right. Kill the giant lizard then collect the level 'C' card. Go through the door opposite. Collect DDK-W disk, then exit. Head down the passage and enter the room at the end. You will be reunited with Gail. After he has left, exit and return up the airshaft. Drop down the vent at the end. Return down the stairs and go through the door at the top, while avoiding the two purple Raptors. Once through the door you will face a lone purple Raptor. Kill it then examine the panel next to the door opposite. The password is 'WATERWAY'. Collect the emergency box key from the corpse. Rick will enter. Collect the 'B2-11' key and exit. Go through the door on the right. Follow the passage and head out the door at the end. The large shutter will rise to reveal the T-Rex. After striking a power coupling, the T-Rex will be left stunned and for the moment unconscious. Walk up to the glass panel and take the plug from inside. Go through the single door in the corner. Insert the plug into the glass panel. The combination is A-C-D. Turn to your right and activate the power button. Exit the room.

Go through the large shutter. Collect the 'Port' card and the DDK-S disk from the corpses you find. The third corpse holds a security key. Exit through the shutter. You will now need to head back to Rick in the save room. Go through the door in the top left corner. Enter the door at the end of the passage. Enter the save room. With the 'Dock' key in hand, Rick will open the door leading to the docks, but your route will be blocked by an energy field. Take the DDK-S disk next to you and return to the save room. Exit through the door to the right. A purple Raptor will enter the room. Exit through the door opposite. Head down the passage and up the stairs. Go through the door at the end of the passage. You will now be in this level's save room. Examine the panel next to the door opposite you. The password is 'STABILIZER'. Before leaving, enter the second part of this room. You will see a large computer screen on the left wall. Insert the 'B2-1' card into the left panel and the 'B2-11' key into the right panel. Activate the computer and key in '0392'. You will face another puzzle like the one you encountered in the electronic locker room.

Left Column
First: Press the 2nd from bottom twice.
Second: Press the 3rd from bottom once.
Third: Press the 4th from bottom once.
Fourth: Press the 3rd from bottom twice.
Fifth: Press the 4th from bottom twice.

Right Column
First: Press the bottom twice.
Second: Press the 2nd from bottom twice.

Third: Press the 5th from bottom once.
Fourth: Press the 4th from bottom once.
Fifth: Press the 3rd from bottom twice.
Finally: Press the 4th from bottom twice.

At this point all the white sections will be at the bottom of the left column and all the red sections will be at the bottom of the right column. Now, trade the white sections from the left column with the clear sections from the right column. With the puzzle completed, exit via the door on the left. Continue through the next room and into the corridor beyond. Go up the corridor and deactivate the laser fence at the end. Enter the room at the end. Kill the purple Raptor then collect the DDK-D disk. Search the room for the safe and open it with the code '1281'. Inside you will find a gun modifier. Attach the modifier to your shotgun. Return to the corridor and back through the door you entered by. Go left and examine the panel by the door. Enter the password 'DOCTORKIRK'. Once inside, insert the 'B2' key into the green panel and the 'B1' key into the next. Make your way through the room. Press the switch to extend the bridge. Continue forward and through the lone door in the corner. Descend the stairs.

Take the 'level B' card from the computer. Return back up the stairs. Collect the emergency box key, then head through the door near the elevator. Reading the yellow folder reveals another code '78814'. Examine the board. You will be faced by another puzzle like the one you encounter when you left Doctor Kirk's laboratory. You are faced with three overlaying panels. Turn the left panel to the left once. Turn the middle panel once to the left. Do not touch the right panel. Then place down the middle panel and then the right panel. Finally place down the left panel. Take the map then leave. Examine the computer opposite. Return to the room you just left and you will find the wounded person has been shot dead. Suicide or murder? Examine the corpse and you will find a bloody note with '1281' written on it. Use the fingerprint machine on the circuit board near the corpse. Walk towards the far right door. Go through the door and head to the end of the corridor. Doctor Kirk will surprise you and put a gun to your head. Gail will fortunately appear and disarm the Doctor. You will receive a 'level A' card. You will be presented with two choices.

Agreed With Gail
Go through the door on the right. Enter through the door on the opposite side of the room. Enter the elevator found in the opposite corner of the room. Ride the elevator down to basement 3. You will now be located outside the save room. Go out through the door on the right. Follow the passage to the end and out of the door. Run past the comatose T-Rex and into the other save room. Go out the left door. Kill or avoid the two purple Raptors and dive through the door to the right of the ladder. Enter the small security 'A' door. Go into the second part of this room and ride the small elevator up. Take the Stabilizer and the Initializer. Return down the small elevator. Go out the door and then through the door at the end

of the passage. Head through the next room back into the save room. Go out the right door. Race past the still dormant T-Rex and out the door in the opposite corner of the room. Run down the passage and through the door at the end. Enter the elevator and ride back up. Head out the door opposite the stairs. Run to the opposite side of the room and go through the left door. Enter the door found at the end of the passage. Go down and through the right door. Continue forward until you reach the save room.

Agreed With Rick

Head out through the door on the right. Enter the door on the left. Head down passage and through the door at the end. Enter the level A room on the left. Enter the disk into the computer. The pass code is '367204'. Take the two component parts. Return into the corridor. Go left and out via the door at the end of the corridor. Head up and then right. Enter the room. Insert the disk into the computer in the corner of the room. Input the code '0204'. Take the two component parts. Insert the disk into the computer opposite the entrance. Input the code '0367'. Take the component from the console. Leave the room and enter the room at the top of the corridor. Enter the second part of the room. Insert the disk into the green lit disk drive. Take the final component needed to construct the Stabilizer and Initializer. Insert the first component into the computer around to the right. You will finally need to construct the Stabilizer and Initializer. Simply rotate the main component around so that the additional parts slide into place. Once you have both the Stabilizer and Initializer in your possession return back into the corridor. Run down the corridor and enter the door on the left. Go through the door at the end of the passage leading back to the save room.

Activating the Third Energy

Enter the second part of the room and insert the ID card into the computer next to the corpse. Enter the code '78814'. Exit via the door on the left. Run down the corridor and through the door at the end. Go through the door at the end of the passage. Dash along the gantry and through the single door at the end. Activate the computer panel next to the yellow folder. Exit via the door you entered through. Run across the bridge and press the green switch. Insert the white Stabilizer. Return back across the bridge. Make you way past the two doors and you will find an elevator. Ride the elevator down. Follow the path around and you will find another green switch. Press the green switch and insert the blue Initializer. Activate the computer to the right. Collect the emergency box key and ride the elevator back up. Head across the bridge and activate the computer. Head towards the two doors and enter the right door. Go through into the next room. You will find Gail badly injured and Doctor Kirk missing. Gail will give you a tracker which to locate the Doctor. Regina will help Gail to the save room where Rick is working on removing the energy field blocking the passage that leads to the docks. Gail argues to recapture the Doctor while Rick disagrees and proposes to leave him behind and just try to escape. You have two choices presented before you. Your choice will decide on which ending you will receive.

Agreeing With Gail (First Ending)

If you agree with Gail's decision to recapture Doctor Kirk, Regina will allow Gail to leave. Use the tracker to discover where Doctor Kirk is located. Make your way to his location and you will find Gail holding Doctor Kirk at gunpoint. During the ensuing conversation, Regina discovers the real reason of their mission. Gail will give you a disk containing all the information regarding the third energy project. Gail will unfortunately die shortly after. You will return to the save room with Rick. Rick will escort the Doctor to the boat. Head through door on the left. Follow the passage to the end and go through the door. You will find yourself in the loading bay of the docks. To the left, you will notice a presumed dead T-Rex. Make your way around to the opposite side of the loading bay and through the single door. When you leave the T-Rex stirs into consciousness. Descend the stairs and climb on board the boat. As you speed away from the island you will come under attack from the submerged T-Rex. Collect the grenades for your grenade launcher and head out onto the side of the boat. The T-Rex will rise out of the water and chase behind the boat. Using the grenade launcher, fire continuously until the T-Rex falls. The T-Rex provides a final challenge but Regina finally causes its extinction with the help of some plastic explosives.

Final Mission Status

Doctor Kirk: Captured
Gail: Deceased
Rick: Alive
Tom: Deceased
Cooper: Condition Unknown

Agreeing With Rick (Second Ending)

If you agree with Rick, Regina knocks out Gail. Preventing him from chasing after Doctor Kirk. Follow Rick through the door to the left. Follow the passage and through the door. Head through the door at the end. You will find yourself in the loading bay of the docks. Run to the opposite side of the docks and through the single door. Once inside, descend the stairs and walk towards the boat. Rick will throw you a canister. You will need to fill the canister with fuel for the boat. Return up the stairs and through the single door. Littered around the loading bay are grey and red canisters. Use the canister on one of these to fill it with fuel. Return back through the single door and give the canister to Rick. The room will then start to shake signalling the return of the T-Rex. Rick will throw you a metal case. Inside you will find grenades for your grenade launcher. Return up the stairs and out through the door. Outside, you will come face to face with the final confrontation with the T-Rex. Armed with the grenade launcher continually fire at the T-Rex as it stomps towards you. When the T-Rex gets close, retreat around the centre crates and continue to fire at the gigantic beast. Once you have caused enough damage, Rick will appear and provide much needed additional missile support.

Final Mission Status

Doctor Kirk: Condition Unknown.
Gail: Alive.
Rick: Alive
Tom: Deceased
Cooper: Condition Unknown

Third Ending (Best Ending)

Agree with Rick, but instead of heading towards docks use the tracer to locate Doctor Kirk. You will have to use the tracer several times to discover Doctor Kirk's final destination. When you reach Doctor Kirk, you will find him trying to escape by helicopter. Regina tries to sneak up on him but her position is blown by an untimely radio message from Rick. Dinosaurs may take serious firepower to bring down but scientists only need a good spin kick to the face and the fight is over. Take the grenades from the metal case and exit through the door. Rick and Gail will appear closely followed by an old friend, the T-Rex. Armed with your grenade launcher open fire at the T-Rex as it chases you. Once you have caused enough damage you and your team will escape via the helicopter but it takes a bomb dropped from the helicopter to finally make the T-Rex extinct.

Final Mission Status

Doctor Kirk: Captured
Gail: Alive
Rick: Alive
Tom: Deceased
Cooper: Condition Unknown

Secrets

Army and Battle Costumes
Complete the game once with any ending and you will receive two different costumes.

Ancient Costume
Complete the game a second time with a different ending and you will receive another costume.

Super Weapon
Complete the game a third time with the final ending and you will receive the super weapon.

Operation 'Wipeout'
Complete the game with the third and best ending in under three hours, with less than three saves and three continues and you will be assigned a new mission. Operation 'Wipeout' is a battle mode in which you need to hunt down a target number of dinosaurs with a limited amount of ammunition.

DINO CRISIS 2

Access the Dino Coliseum
Beat the game once to unlock the Dino Coliseum.

Access Dino Duel Mode
Buy Rick, Gail and the Tank for the extra Crisis games at the Player Entry screen. You will now get a new row of dinosaurs to select from. Use your Extinct points to buy dinosaurs then fight them in Dino Duel.

Unlimited ammo
Complete the game and collect all 11 Dino files. You now have unlimited ammo. The EPS Platinum Card is now available on the Save Screen, giving you unlimited ammo

Unlock Triceratops and Compsagnathus
In Hard Mode buy all the other dinosaurs for Dino Duel and Dino Coliseum to access Triceratops and Compsagnathus.

DISCWORLD

Act 1
1) Take the pouch from the cupboard.
2) Talk to the Arch Chancellor.
3) Get your luggage from your room and give the banana to the librarian. Show the book to the Arch Chancellor.
4) Staff: Exchange the broom with the Windle Poon's magic staff.
5) Imp: Talk to the apprentice in the garden. Take the frog. Go to the livery stable (outside the castle walls) and collect some corn. Talk to the alchemist in the alley. Avoid the jumping plate. (If you don't you can get down by entering one of the windows.) Use the corn with the flask to wake the imp. If you go to the market you can throw a tomato at the tax collector. Take the worm from under the second tomato, then get some string from the toy shop. Use the worm and string to lure the imp out of the mouse hole.
6) Dragon Breath: Go to the palace and get the mirror. Get to the flagpole on the tower via the jumping plate. Annoy the dragon by putting the mirror on the end of the flagpole. Knock down the ladder on your way down.
7) Magic Coil: The street urchin can teach you how to pickpocket. Get the barber talking about his milkmaid then pick his pockets.
8) Metal Container: Talk to the psychiatrickerist twice to get the net. Use your ladder on the university rear window to get the pancake. Go to the kitchen to get the frying pan. Upon receiving the items, the Arch Chancellor will give you a dragon detector. Its lair is at the bottom left corner of the map.

Act 2: Golden Items
1) Talk to the guy in the library about his golden banana. Exchange your gold for the banana, and use the banana to allow you to enter L-space. A thief will steal the book, but don't

take it back! Push the book - this will open the staircase. Find the thief's hideout.

2) Put the frog in the drunkard's mouth. Use the butterfly on the street corner lamp, then take the pot from the window ledge.

3) Go back to 'Present' and get the black robe from the clothesline. Get a drink from the Broken Drum and take the tankard. Talk to the barman about the Counterwise wine and take the glass.

4) Go back to the hideout in the past. Use the pipe on the right drainpipe, and turn the left drainpipe so that you can hear the secret password. Put the robe on and join the ceremony to find the identity of the brotherhood.

5) Mason: Present time, talk to the scared guy in the pub. Take a bed sheet from the inn, and go into the past. Use the sheet, go to the inn and do what the scared guy said. Go back to the present, talk to him again, now go to the past and try again.

6) Use the pass to get past the present gate guards. Shake the coconut tree, get a coconut with the net. Go to the mountain pass, collect an egg and a feather. Use the screwdriver from the barn to put a hole in the coconut.

7) Talk to street-starfish in the market, and try to learn the secret handshake. Go upstairs in the psychiatrickerist's and get the inkblots. These will help you get into the palace. Talk to the peasant inside.

8) Get some cornflower from the kitchen. Read the graffiti on the past toilet door. Go to the House of Negotiable Affection in 'Shades'. Give Big Sally the coconut, cornflower and the egg.

9) The bloomers will allow you to learn the secret handshake. Visit the mason in Shades, use the handshake and take the golden trowel.

10) Thief: Found in the hovel. Use the ladder to drop the bra in the hovel. Use the feather to turn the thief around, get the golden key. Collect the ladder.

11) Dunnyman: Get a doughnut from the Dibbler. Give it to the dunnyman. Get a note from the milkmaid and give it to the barber, now get the golden tooth.

12) Fishmonger: Start a fight in the past Broken Drum by turning the little guy's glass. When the troll joins in, use the ladder to get the drumstick. Use the stick to ring the gong in present university. Now you can get the prunes. Go to Nanny Ogg's (Dark Woods). Fill your pot with custard, put this in the fishmonger's toilet. Tie the octopus up and put it in the toilet. Put prunes in his caviar and get the golden belt.

13) Fool: Get bubble bath from the inn. Get a bin from the back of the university. Show the second inkblot to the other guard. Put the bin on the fool, use the bubbles in his bath and get the golden bell.

14) Chimney Sweep: Get the following things: doll from the toy maker, fireworks and gunpowder keg from city gate, matches from Broken Drum
Get onto the roof of the alley and put the doll in the alchemist's chimney. Put the keg in the alchemist's fireplace and light the fuse. The golden brush is yours.

15) Give the golden items to the dragon. Buy the carpet from Nanny in the market and steal her custard book. Time-travel to get the Dragon-Summoning book. Exchange the covers of the two books, and the thief will take the custard book.

Act 3: Hero Items
1) Go to Nobby and solve his riddle.
2) Magic Talisman: Get a custard tart from the hideout. Tell the alchemist where there is more corn and nick his camera. Read the bumper of the donkey cart at the stables. Talk to Lady Rankin at the Dragon Sanctuary. Go to the back, and talk to her again. Knock on the door to distract her, then steal the rosette, leash and nail.
Buy some cactus juice from the bar to get the worm. Buy the bag of leaches from the Dibbler. Use them to knock out the palace guards. Go to the dungeons and use the worm to catch the new imp. Put the imp in the camera. Get the octopus picture from the fishmonger's.
Talk to Nanny Ogg about the Truth Potion. Get it. Put the rosette on the sheep and take a photo. Take the mallet.
Hang the framed picture in the pub using the nail. Frame it using the octopus picture.
Mix Braggart's beer with Truth Potion. Talk to him then go to the temple. Use the carpet on the bridge to get rid of the monk. Tie the leash on the luggage and put the blind fold on. Fill your pouch with sand and replace it with the eye.
3) Moustache: Go to the woods and fill the pot with wishing-well water. Use the pot with the soap at the inn. Get the bath-brush from the palace, and use it on the soapy water. Use the brush on the livery stables donkey cart and read the sticker. Go to the hovel in Shades. Take the knife. Use the knife on the rooftops to cut the ladder. Give the assassin the information. Get the scissors from the barber's shop and cut the donkey's tail in the market to get a moustache.
4) Birthmark: Get a bone from the dungeons. Use the bone with glue from the toy-maker. Give it to the dog from the inn. Talk to the sailor to get a parrot whistle.
Get a snake from the market by trying to get an egg. Get the fertilizer from the back of the university. Light the lamp in the closet and get the starch. Use the fertilizer and starch on the snake, exchange it for the Windle Poon's staff. The broom handle can be used to elongate the butterfly net.
Get the hat from the Arch Chancellor's room, then go to the edge of the world. Attract the parrot by using the whistle, and throw a firework at it. Catch the parrot and go to the sailor. Go back to the edge of the world, and put the magic-hat on the lamp. Climb down to get the whistle and give it to the sailor.
Show the milkmaid the barber's appointment book. Show the barber the signed book. Now go to the barber's shop and talk to him. Talk to the street starfish. Cut the rubber band on the Custard-King machine. Climb up the tower and bungee-jump off the top to get the birthmark.
5) Magic Spell: In the library, hidden where the sleazy guy was.
6) Camel-Flage: Collect the spatula in the kitchen. Use it on the mural in Shades. Take the soot.
7) Magic Sword: Use the screwdriver on the well in the woods. A sword can be found if you use the crank from the well on the

dungeon racks. Get to the Dwarves by talking to the city guard's carrot.

8) Elderberry Wine: Tell the barman that the cellar is full of foxes. Talk to the person in the inn, use the screwdriver on the door. Tell the bogeyman to scare the foxes away. Fill your tankard with elderberry wine. Give it to the dwarf Smith who will enhance your sword.

Act 4

1) Go to the square and take left. Take the key off Lady Ramkin. Open the dragon's door, and get past the pile by using the magic carpet. Use the little mambo on the dragon in the square. Give mambo a firework, and use both on the dragon. Then use the love custard tart on the dragon.

DISCWORLD 2

Act 1

1) Go to the High Energy Facility. Take the test-tube, magnet, and bellows.
2) Use the magnetic-force on the imp in the garden.
3) Get the flamingo, fish and incense from the travel shop outside. Try to get the candles off the old biddy.
4) Find Dibbles in the Plaza and talk about everything.
5) Get the saw then the clay pot from the beggar area in Shades.
6) Get the knife from the mortuary.
7) Get some scissors from Mrs. Cakes. Get the ironing board and the petticoat. Observe the genie bottle and use the saw with the mannequin. Talk to Mrs. Cake.
8) Steal the hooter from the Fools Guild. Get the brick and use it on the fool. Go down the hole and use the bellows on the grate. Get out.
9) Use the brick on the accelerator back at the High Energy Facility.
10) Give the ectoplasm to Mrs. Cakes.
11) Near the beggars, use the imp boots on the bottle in Shades. Take this bottle and try it out with Foul Ole Ron. Get the chilli powder off Gimlet and talk to Gimlet.
12) Go to Shades and talk to Casanunda in the pub. Get the matches and talk to the troll.
13) Make your way to the docks. Use the knife to get the net. Use the net to get the shark and use the stuffed fish to get the bird.
14) Get out your beer and use it on the corn in the University gardens. Use this corn to feed the rooster. Use the shark on the Bursar. Then use the flamingo on the Dean and the Bird on the Librarian.
15) Travel to the beehives and use the booklet with the beekeeper. The flowers might need a bit of chilli powder.
16) Find Rincewind and give him the petticoat. Light the incense and use it on the bees. Use the clay pot on the hive and get some wax.
17) Give the wax to the women in the travel shop.
18) Find the beggars and use the coffee tin with the rooster. Use the rooster with the vampirical block in the pub.

19) Get the pick from the cemetery. Go to the crypt and climb the ladder up the coffin to get the false teeth. Get some mouse blood using the teeth and the test tube.
20) Give the mouse blood, mallet, and smell glitter to the Arch Chancellor.

Act 2

1) Go to the warehouse via the hole in Fools Guild. Use the pick on the ice.
2) Talk to the dead collector in Shades. Talk to the mortician about death certificates. Use the mirror on the bunsen and put in down again. Now use the slab.
3) Use the dummy-part and the ice on Rincewind.
4) Give the dead collector the death certificate.
5) Go to the Camel Park at Djelibeybi and talk to the salesman.
6) Go to the hill. Use the knife on Bone Idle once you've talked to him.
7) Get the glue from the pyramid and use the bandage with the scissors. Bandage the wooden arm and use it on the rotten arm at the oasis.
8) Look at the horse in the costume room at Holywood. Ask the dwarf about it. Use the rotten arm. Use the 10 from the post box on the weight. Give the dwarf the ring.
9) Get the camera from the imp trainer in the make-up room. Talk to him about catching imps.
10) Examine the sticks in XXXX. Look at the baskets and ask Point about them.
11) Go to the University gardens via Ankh-Morpork. Grab the hoops. Talk to the librarian about the horse. Get the food using the basket.
12) Go to the shop at Djelibeybi. Steal the poster. Find Uri and give him the hoops. Talk about music. Look at the candy. Talk to the rock-seller and get the stake from the stoning place. Go to the wheel in the desert.
13) Travel back to the Unseen University Gardens in A. Morpork. Put the stake in the compost.
14) Talk to the Casanunda in the mortuary. Talk to the witch about elves.
15) Use the weight on the hook at the docks and get the novelty item.
16) Put the Suffrajester in the stake's place at the stoning area. Grab the rope.
17) Go to the imp place at Holywood. Use the boomerang on the paint and then on the imp. Give the troll the candy. The trailer door is locked so get the key off the troll. Use the rope on the troll and go into the trailer. Give the girl the troll's tooth.
18) Use the food basket on the anthill in XXXX. Use the saw on the ironing board. Use the board as a surfboard at the beach. Take a picture of the cave paintings and store the camera in your inventory. Make your way to the elven-circle and use the glue on the hooter. Now use the hooter with the horse costume. Use the costume with the librarian and put it in your inventory. Use the costume with Rincewind and the camera on the Elf Queen.

19) Go to the Unseen University and to the High Energy Facility. Use the ant basket on Hex as well as the honey and the pyramid. Use the wire on the pyramid: plan to do this. Talk to Skagg and answer the Hermit's question.

20) Give Dibbler the novelty item, the band, jingle and the babe. Give the girl in the make-up room the pictures of the Elf Queen. Talk to Dibbler.

21) Go to Shades. Use the certificate on the door at the top of the steps. Talk about stunts to the sheep and give it the cave photos. Use the reel on the device and then use the Elf Queen film on the device.

Act 3

1) Get the key from the mat outside the house. Get the ink from the hourglass room and ring the bell.

2) Get the sugar and the oily rag from the kitchen. Look in the oven.

3) Get the scythe and the curtains.

4) Go up to Susan's room, get the rabbit, and get the pyjamas off it. Grab the string.

5) Get Rincewind's book from the book-room (it's the middle one).

6) Talk to Albert.

7) Go to the stables and give the sugar to Binky. Grab the rope and put the glue on the saddle. Use the saddle with Binky.

8) Go into the garden and set fire to the rag. Put the pyjamas on and use the rag with the hive. Get the wax and the honey and put the wax on the string.

9) Get the gnome's rod from the pond. Use the rod and honey on the soul-pool.

10) Look at the cart and talk to the girl about it. Show her the book.

11) Put the ink in the pond as well as the curtains.

12) Light the candle in the book-room and put it in the inventory. Open the door with the key. Get Rincewind to use the lit candle and get the tablet. Give it to Susan in the garden.

13) Use the boomerang with the rope, then use this on the chimney. Click on the chimney.

14) Show Albert the scythe and the robe. Use them. Use the cart and scythe combination with the corn. Give Albert the ant souls.

Act 4

1) Get the cork from Bonestock.

2) Get the canteen from the prospector in Djelibeybi. Use the arm on his saddlebag.

3) Use the cork on the fountain of youth.

4) Use the hourglass with the sand.

Epilogue

1) Look at the raven and talk to the witch about it. Steal the broomstick.

2) Talk to Dibbler and use the canteen with the bladders. Put them in Rincewind's pocket. Use the broomstick with the tower.

DISRUPTOR

Float Around
To float around, during the game press **Select** and go to Map Mode. When you press **L1** and ▲ you return to the game with floating ability. Use **L1** and **R1** to move up and down.

Passwords
Level 1- ■ ■ ▲ ✘ ● ● ▲ ✘ ✘ ● ✘ ✘
Level 2- ✘ ▲ ● ▲ ✘ ✘ ▲ ● ● ■ ● ●
Level 3- ▲ ✘ ● ✘ ▲ ■ ● ● ✘ ▲ ▲ ■
Level 4- ● ✘ ● ▲ ● ✘ ✘ ✘ ■ ▲ ■ ●
Level 5- ✘ ■ ● ● ✘ ▲ ▲ ■ ● ✘ ● ■
Level 6- ✘ ■ ● ● ✘ ▲ ✘ ● ● ✘ ● ■
Level 7- ✘ ✘ ▲ ● ● ✘ ▲ ▲ ● ■ ✘ ●
Level 8- ▲ ● ✘ ● ✘ ▲ ● ■ ▲ ✘ ■ ✘
Level 9- ● ✘ ✘ ✘ ● ● ▲ ■ ✘ ● ✘ ▲
Level 10- ✘ ■ ✘ ▲ ● ■ ▲ ✘ ● ● ● ✘
Level 11- ▲ ● ● ▲ ✘ ✘ ● ● ✘ ✘ ▲ ●
Level 12- ● ▲ ● ▲ ✘ ● ✘ ■ ▲ ● ✘ ■

DOOM

Level Map
For a level map, pause and press ▲, ▲, L2, R2, L2, R2, R1, ■.

Map Plus Objects
To display a level map with objects included on it, pause and press ▲, ▲, L2, R2, L2, R2, R1, ●.

All the Weapons and Ammo
To have all weapons and ammunition, pause the game and press ✘, ▲, L1, ↑, ↓, R2, ←, ←.

Invincibility
To be invincible Pause the game and press ↓, L2, ■, R1, →, L1, ←, ●.

Level Warp
To select the start level, pause and press →, ←, R2, R1, ▲, L1, ●, ✘.

X-Ray Vision
To have x-ray vision, pause the game and press L1, R2, L2, R1, →, ▲, ✘, →.

DRIVER

Cheats
On the Main Menu enter one of the following cheats. The cheat will then become available on the cheats screen.

Invincible
L2, L2, R2, R2, L2, R2, L2, L1, R2, R1, L2, L1, L1.

No police
L1, L2, R1, R1, R1, R1, L2, L2, R1, R1, L1, L1, R2.

Rear wheel steering
R1, R1, R1, R2, L2, R1, R2, L2, L1, R2, R1, L2, L1.

Mini cars
R1, R2, R1, R2, L1, L2, R1, R2, L1, R1, L2, L2.

High suspension
R2, L2, R1, R2, L2, L1, R2, R2, L2, L2, L1, R2, R1.

Upside-down screen
R2, R2, R1, L2, L1, R2, L2, L1, R2, R2, L2, R2, L1.

View credits
L1, L2, R1, R2, L1, R1, R2, L2, R1, R2, L1, L2, R1.

Getaway Techniques:
1. If the Police are chasing your car from behind, slam the brakes, wait for him to run into the back of your car, then slam into reverse. If all goes well the policeman will say that he lost you. Accelerate away free.

2. You can brush up against the cars coming towards you. The cops will follow, usually ramming the opposite traffic.

3. Move your car behind a lamppost and watch the cops crash into it. You can then drive away.

4. Taking your car up onto a footpath and keeping it there for ten seconds or so will make the police turn around to go in another direction saying that they have lost you.

DUKE NUKEM: TIME TO KILL

Level Select
Pause the game and press **↑ x9, ↓**, then exit the game. Select the 'Time To Kill' option.

Invulnerability
Pause the game and press **L2, R1, L1, R2, ↑, ↓, ↑, ↓, Select x2.**

Temporary Invulnerability
Pause the game and press **R1, L2, L1, L2, R1. L1, R1, L2, L1, L2.**

Invisibility
Pause the game and press **L1, R1, L1, R1, L1, R1, L1, R1, L1, R1.**

Unlimited Ammunition
Pause the game and press **←, →, ←, →, Select, ←, →, ←,**

→, Select.

All Weapons
Pause the game and press **L1, L2, ↑, L1, L2, ↓, R1, →, R2, ←.**

Super Weapons
Pause the game and press **R1, R2, L2, L1, R1, R2, L2, L1, Select x2.**

All Items
Pause the game and press **R1 x5, L2 x5.**

All Keys
Pause the game and press **↑, →, ↑, ←, ↓, ↑, →, ←, →, ↓.**

Holo Duke
Pause the game and press **L2, R2, L2, R2, L2, R2, L2, R2, L2, R2.**

Big Head Mode
Pause the game and press **R1 x9, ↑.**

Small Head Mode
Pause the game and press **R1 x9, ↓.**

Big Head Enemies
Pause the game and press **R1 x9, ←.**

Small Head Enemies
Pause the game and press **R1 x9, →.**

Rogue Trip Trailer
Press **L1 + L2 + R1 + R2** at the GT Interactive logo.

DUKE NUKEM: TOTAL MELTDOWN

Super Kick
During the game, hold **L1 + L2 + R1 + R2** and press ■

EHRGEIZ

Alternative Costumes
Hold **↑** while selecting a character on the character selection screen.

Hidden Characters
Kouji Masuda
Complete the game with any male character
Clair Andrews
Complete the game with any female character

Yuffie Kisaragi
Complete the game with Cloud Strife
Vincent Valentine
Complete the game with Tifa Lockheart
Django
Complete the game using all eight non Final Fantasy characters
Zack
Complete the game using all the Final Fantasy characters

ESPN EXTREME GAMES

All Vehicles
To have all vehicles, a super athlete, $5030, and wins in the first and second races, enter the password 237 190 190 080 000 000 176 113 219.

Extra Money
To get £1,110, complete the first race after entering the password 229 013 066 016 000 000 000 000 031.

Final Race
To enter only the final race of the season which is in San Francisco, use the following password: 254 071 216 094 085 177 113 104.

Money Round
When you have passed through all the gates on a course, enter the bonus Cash Course. This consists of $5 and $10 gates.

Race Alone
Would you like to be the only one in the race, and always finish first? If so, go to the TV-1 in the equipment room and press ✖ Next go to the equipment selections and press ✖ to deactivate each CPU player. Choose a course to start racing.

ESPN X GAMES PRO BOARDER

Unlock circuit
Enter ✖, ●, ✖, ▲, ▲, ■ as a password.

All tracks and circuits
Enter ■, ▲, ✖, ■, ●, ● as a password.

Super Circuit and bonus boarders
Enter ▲, ✖, ■, ✖, ▲, ● as a password for the Super Circuit and Ollie B.

EURO 2000

Euro Classics Mode
Win the Euro 2000 mode on any skill level to unlock the classic mode. Winning the classic 1960 match will unlock the following European match and so on up to 1996.

EVERYBODYS GOLF

Mirror Courses
On the Course Select screen when you select the course hold: **L1 + L2** then press ✖. You will now get a mirrored version of the selected course.

Variable Handed Golfers
When selecting a character hold **L1** and press ✖. This switches between left and right handed golfers.

EVIL ZONE

Extra Costumes
Complete the game with any character to unlock their hidden costume.

Play as the Boss and Unlock the Hidden Stage
Complete the game three times using three different characters.

Play as Ihadurca
Complete the game using Setsuna.

EXCALIBUR 2555 AD

Level Codes
Use the following codes to access the levels:

Level	Code
Level 1 – Ort Underworld	✖ ✖ ✖ ✖ ✖
Level 2 – Death Crypt	▲ ■ ✖ ● ● ▲
Level 3 – The Trappings	● ■ ✖ ● ● ▲
Level 4 – The Sewer	■ ✖ ▲ ▲ ✖ ●
Level 5 - Eco Sector	● ✖ ● ▲ ■ ✖
Level 6 - Fabian Water Hold	✖ ● ▲ ■ ● ●
Level 7 - Fabian Central	■ ■ ● ● ✖ ▲
Level 8 - The Prison	● ✖ ■ ▲ ▲ ■
Level 9 - Elysian Labyrinth	▲ ✖ ▲ ● ■ ▲
Level 10 - Subterrania	▲ ● ● ■ ▲ ✖
Level 11 - The Vault	✖ ■ ■ ✖ ▲ ■
Level 12 - Delavars' Lair	● ▲ ✖ ● ■ ●
Level 13 - Project Eden	■ ▲ ● ✖ ✖ ✖

Press **Start** to pause the game before entering one of the following codes. Then select 'Continue' and press ✖ to activate the cheat, or press **Start**. Rember you can only enter one cheat at a time, so pause, enter the first cheat, and unpause. Repeat this method to enter further cheats :

Full Health:	▲,▲,▲,■,■,■,■,■
Full Sword Power:	▲, ▲, ■, ■, ←, ←, ■, ■
Show Collision Boxes:	←, ←, ←, ←, ■, ←, ←, ■
Skip Level:	■, ←, ■, ▲, ←, ▲, ▲, ▲

F1 RACING CHAMPIONSHIP

All Arcade Tracks
Select Arcade Mode and on the track select screen, press ↑, ↑, ↓, ↓, **L1, R2, L2, R1.** Now all the tracks and all difficulty levels will be selectable.

FADE TO BLACK

The following passwords will give you access to the levels:

Level 1- ■ ● ▲ ✖ ● ■   Level 8- ■ ■ ✖ ▲ ■ ■
Level 2- ▲ ● ✖ ● ■ ✖   Level 9- ▲ ✖ ✖ ▲ ● ▲
Level 3- ✖ ● ✖ ● ▲ ✖   Level 10- ✖ ▲ ■ ● ▲ ✖
Level 4- ✖ ■ ▲ ● ● ▲   Level 11- ● ■ ✖ ✖ ■ ✖
Level 5- ■ ■ ▲ ✖ ✖ ●   Level 12- ✖ ▲ ✖ ■ ● ✖
Level 6- ▲ ✖ ✖ ✖ ✖ ●   Level 13- ✖ ✖ ● ▲ ● ▲

Infinite Shield
For infinite shields, enter the cheat activation code ■, ▲, ●, ✖, ●, ▲ at the password screen. As before, leave this screen and re-enter it immediately, then enter ■, ●, ●, ■, ▲, ✖. Again, you can ignore all 'Invalid Code' messages.

Invincibility
To be invincible, enter the cheat activation code ■, ▲, ●, ✖, ●, ▲ at the password screen. Leave and enter the password screen, and then enter ▲, ✖, ▲, ▲, ■, ●, ignoring the 'Invalid Code' messages.

Level Select
To select the start level, enter the cheat activation code ■, ▲, ●, ✖, ●, ▲ at the password screen. Leave and re-enter the screen as before, and enter the code ●, ●, ▲, ✖, ■, ■. Ignore the 'Invalid Code' messages.

Play All Movies
To play all movies, enter the cheat activation code as follows at the password screen: ■, ▲, ●, ✖, ●, ▲. Next you must leave the password screen, but immediately re-enter it. Then enter ■, ✖, ●, ▲, ●, ✖. After entering the codes you may see 'Invalid Code' messages, which can be ignored.

FEAR EFFECT

Cheats
Go to the option screen and select credits. As the credits roll enter one of the following cheats:

Infinite Ammo – **L1**, ▲, ↑, ↓, ●, ●, ▲, ■, ←, ▲
No Fear – **L1**, ▲, ↑, ↓, ●, ●, ▲, ■, →, ■
One Shot Kills – **L1**, ▲, ↑, ↓, ▲, ■, ↓, **R1**
Super Ammo – **L1**, ▲, ↑, ↓, ●, ●, →, **R1, R2**
Harder Enemies – ↓, ↓, ↓, ▲, ↓, ↓, ↓, ■, ←, →

Instant Puzzle Solution – **L1**, ▲, ↑, ↓, ●, ●, ↓, ↓, ↓, ↑

FELONY 11~79

Long Distance Camera View
Hold **Select** and press ▲ while playing.

Select All Vehicles
Plug in two control pads and delete any Felony save files from your memory card. On the title screen, with control pad two, hold ▲ and then quickly press **R1 + R2 + L2** together and then release but continue to hold ▲. Then press **R2, L2, R1.** If done correctly you should hear a rumbling sound.

FIFA '97

Adjust Shadows
To alter the length of your players' shadows, start a match and go to Instant Replay mode. Next hold **R1** and move ↑ and ↓ to alter shadow lengths. To continue, exit Instant Replay.

John Motson Crooning
Hear Motty singing by putting the CD in a player and selecting track 6.

John Motson Playing
To see John Motson playing select a friendly match and choose either Dallas or New York from the USA league.

FIFA '98

Unlimited Player Attributes
To get infinite points to allocate to your players, got to the Player Edit screen and press **L1, L2,**✖, ■ and ✖.

Alter Floodlights
At the In-Game Options screen enter the code ■, ▲, ✖, ■, ▲, ▲, ✖, ✖, ■, ■, ■, ■, ■, ▲, ▲, ▲, ▲, ▲.

Loads'a Money!
To get rich quick, go to the Customise Squad option from the Main Menu, then Team Edit. Pick the club team of your choice and press ■, ✖, ■, **L2, L1.** Beware however, as if you toggle the shirt/shorts/socks option you'll return to your original bank balance.
Best Formation (Attack): 4-3-3
Best Formation (Defence): 5-4-1
Best Formation (Overall): 4-4-2

Easiest Goal: A through-ball from your midfield man will usually result in your striker running onto the end of it from the edge of the penalty area. If he's got the legs to stay in front of the defenders a speed burst followed by a quick tap on the shot button, with a bit of aftertouch, should suffice. It is advisable to keep your strikers fresh by substituting them during the game. Beware in world class mode as the defenders are more adept at cutting this out.

Crossing: When running down the flank press the chip button. This will generally give you a perfectly weighted cross towards the back post. With the right timing your striker will rise above the defenders and score a goal that the great John Wark would've been proud of.

Corners: Although not easy to head goals directly from the corner, a nicely flighted inswinger towards the penalty spot will usually result in a goalmouth scramble where anything could happen.

Free Kicks: If you want to try and curl one keep it low and don't use too much power.

Route One: A big hoist from the keeper or shot from the edge of your own penalty area will quite often send your striker on his way goalwards.

Long Shots: A shot from the corners of the penalty areas will sometimes find the back of the net. It is only worth trying a shot from anywhere around the edge of the box but as a last resort as the keeper will probably deal with it easily.

Special Moves:
Double Tap
●: Lob.
R1: Flick.
R2 or **L2**: Shimmy to left or right.
L2+▲: 360 spin.
L2+■: Flick up for overhead kick.
L2+●: Jink.

FIFA '99

Atlanta Attack Team
Win the Champions Cup as Brazil on the Professional difficulty setting. Then select the Custom Cup and choose International Team.

Formation
The best attacking formation is 4-3-3. Push both wings out, and have the centre forward further up than your other two strikers.
The best midfield formation is 4-4-2. Push both attackers forward and keep your midfield as a flat wall. Send your defence back and keep them tight.
The best defence formation is 5-3-2. Push your defence back and keep your left and right backs close to the rest of your defence. In the midfield send your wingers out wide and have

a fast centre. Leave your attackers as they are.

Defending
1. When defending a corner select a player in the centre of the box and use either short pass or long pass to clear the ball.
2. If defending a free kick select a man in the centre of the wall, and use the shoot button to clear the ball.
3. If the opposition has the ball using the shoot button will result in you winning ball with a clean tackle.
4. When your opposition get past all of your defenders press and hold R1 to make your keeper run out and close the angle of the shot.
5. Set your strategy on offside trap, and try to catch the opposition offside.
6. When the opposition break your defence and there is no way you can reqain possession use L1 to perform and illegal foul. This usually results in a red card.

Midfield
1. When taking a free kick close to the opponents goal hold down shoot until the arrow is fully stretched. You can now angle the perfect shot. Aim for the bottom corner that is unmarked.
2. The best way to get the ball to your forwards is to pass up and down the field until a forward is in position then use a through ball.
3. Use a long ball to switch the ball to either wing enabling you to get in a good position for a cross.
4. If you haven't quite mastered controlling the ball in the air use ground passes.
5. Press L1 when in possesion to make your player jump in the air to avoid tackles. Be careful because when you perform this move you will lose control for a moment.

Attacking
1. When taking a corner, if you are on the right side of the goal use the ground pass and put a little curl on the ball to the right. Place the ball to the right of the two defenders through to your player. When it touches his feet tap shoot and it should go in back of the net.
2. Use your midfield to pass the ball around until one of your forwards are in position. Pass it through and tap shoot to drill it into the bottom corner.
3. Take a winger down the line and put a ground pass into the box. When it approaches one of your players hit shoot to play a first time shot.
4. An alternative strategy when taking a corner is to send in a high ball to the centre of the box. This should result in a scramble. Keep tapping the shoot button and, if one of your players is quick enough, he should get a shot in.
5. If your attacker is your only player in the box tap long pass to attempt to lob the keeper. If you succeed it should go in the top corner.

THE FIFTH ELEMENT

Cheat Menu
Press **L1, L2, R2, R1, Select** at the main menu. Select New Game and a cheat menu will appear.

FIGHTERS IMPACT

Alternative Costumes
To change fighters' clothes, highlight a character then hold down ● + ■ and press **Start**.

Cardboard Cut-out style Characters
For wafer-thin action, press ➡ ten times at the Title screen. A chime will confirm that the cheat is active.

Deformed Characters
For strangely shaped characters, press **Select** ten times at the Title screen. A chime will confirm that the cheat is active.

Hidden Characters
To access four new characters, simply complete the game four times.

Stickman Characters
For that Lowry effect, push ⬅ ten times at the Title screen. A chime will confirm that the cheat is active.

Tiny Characters
For small fighters, highlight a character then hold ⬇ + ✖ + ● and press **Start**.

FIGHTING FORCE

Cheat Menu
To access the cheat menu hold down ⬅ + ■ + L1 + R2 at the Main Menu screen. The words "cheat mode" should then appear at the bottom of the screen. Next, go to the Options screen and you should be able to select invincibility, and go to the stage you wish to play.

FINAL DOOM

All the Map
To see a map level, pause the game and press ▲, ▲, L2, R2, L2, R2, R1, ■.

All Map Plus Objects
Foe a level map with objects included, pause the game and then press ▲, ▲, L2, R2, L2, R2, R1, ●.

All Weapons and Ammo
For all weapons and ammunition, pause the game and press ✖, ▲, L1, ⬆, ⬇, R2, ⬅, ⬅

Invincibility
To be invincible, pause the game and press ⬇, L2, ■, R1, ➡, L1, ⬅, ●.

Level Warp
To select the start level, pause the game and press ➡, ⬅, R2, R1, ▲, L1, ●, ✖.

X-Ray Vision
For x-ray vision, pause the game and press L1, R2, L2, R1, ➡, ▲, ✖, ➡.

Master Level Codes

LEVEL	HEALTH	PASSWORD	TITLE
2	125%	LB173PPWPM	Virgil
3	200%	ZSNDHQW820	Canyon
4	200%	KS5WZH4RRKH	Combine
5	150%	J!670JKQJG	Catwalk
6	200%	5VJTMOOW64	Fistula
7	200%	4FHDW39X35	Geryon
8	200%	W9NRG2W820	Minos
9	200%	C958ZKCRKH	Nessus
10	200%	W!PQH1V71Z	Paradox
11	200%	C!670JBQJG	Subspace
12	200%	W7LTJOY!02	Subterra
13	200%	K394TB8MFC	Vesperas

TNT Level Codes

LEVEL	HEALTH	PASSWORD	TITLE
14	200%	Y8PQH1V71Z	System Control
15	200%	F8670JBQJG	Human Barbeque
16	200%	WXJCL68W64	Wormhole
17	200%	CX1W3PRCPM	Crater
18	200%	WYKBM57V53	Nukage Processing
19	200%	Y2V4NQBNL	Deepest Reaches
20	200%	WVGFN4!Y46	Processing Area
21	200%	CVZY5MTFMP	Lunar Mining
22	200%	WWHDP39X35	Quarry
23	200%	CWOX6LSDLN	Ballistyx
24	200%	W1DHQ!40!8	Heck

Plutonia Level Codes

LEVEL	HEALTH	PASSWORD	TITLE
25	200%	!LQP7W26WY	Congo
26	200%	W2FGR93Z97	Aztec
27	200%	C2YZ8SLGSQ	Ghost Town
28	200%	WZBKS8628!	Baron's Lair
29	100%	HXZY5MMFMP	The Death Domain
30	100%	OYHDP33X35	Onslaught

FINAL FANTASY VII

Essential Tips:
1) Experience Points: These are only obtained through battle. Acquiring a certain number of experience points will put your

level up, resulting in a higher HP max capacity and MP max capacity.

2) Battles: In Final Fantasy VII as in all Final Fantasy games battles are random and cannot be avoided. They can be minimised by running. Once in battle it is possible to run away by holding L1 and R1. However, avoiding battles means fewer experience points and a lower HP max. So only run away if you are low on time or energy.

3) Healing: Along your way you will pick up potions, ethers, curative materia, etc. Use them when you are low on energy. As enemies get harder, this boundary line will get higher, but it is generally about a quarter of your energy.

4) Materia: Materia are ancient gems which slot into your weapons and armour and allow you special abilities such as magic, stealing, analysing etc. Find them or buy them at immense costs. Equip them as you see fit. When a character leaves the party, they will be automatically unequipped.

5) Armour/Weaponry: These can be bought and found and as long as they are more powerful, should be equipped immediately. Sell the old armour and weaponry, as you will not need it.

6) Saving: Save points are represented by a spinning question mark. Save whenever you can, as you never know what is around the corner.

7) Always have "Hypers" on your party. This gives your party "Fury" and helps gain Limit-Breaks.

Section One

Reactor No. 1

You start the game as Cloud, a former member of Soldier now seemingly turned Avalanche. To start with you know little about yourself, but all will be revealed as the game progresses. Follow the others off the train and on to your first battle. Only attack, save your magic for later on. Follow Biggs, Jessie and Barret into the reactor. Talk to Biggs and Jessie to get through any locked gates. After the second gate and just before the elevator, there is an area to your right where a Phoenix Down can be found. Get in the elevator. Follow Jessie down the stairs and into the reactor. Jump across the gaps and follow the path. Save at the save point and continue along the pipe. Collect the materia, which unfortunately cannot be used at the moment. Setting the bomb triggers an alarm, alerting the boss.

Boss 1: Guard Scorpion

Now it's time to use your magic! Use Cloud's Bolt magic and Barret's normal attack. If the boss raises it's tail don't attack, as it will counter with a powerful laser for massive damage. Wait until it drops it's tail. If your HP goes below 100, heal yourself with potions.

After destroying the boss, equip Barret with the new Assault Gun. You now have ten minutes to get out. Go the same way as you came in, remembering to get Jessie on the way.

Getting To Sector 7

Once the rest have left, go up the steps. Buy a flower from the girl. In the next area collect the potion. Go south and fight all of the guards. Now jump on the train and get out of there. You should have plenty of potions by now, so you should have no problems with health. Once you are on the train talk to everyone a couple of times.

Sector 7 Slums

Get off the train and follow the rest to the village. Buy three iron bangles from the weapon shop and equip Cloud with one. Go to the hideout. Give Marlene the flower that you bought. Now try to leave. Have a drink with Tifa, then go down the secret chute. Once you've talked to Tifa, go back up, talk to her again and get your pay off Barret. Now go to the second floor of the weapon shop to find out anything that you need to know. Make sure that you get the materia and ether. Go to the first floor and sell all three of your bronze bangles. You will need to have equipped Tifa and Barret with iron bangles in order to sell these. Buy a Fire and Ice materia from the Materia Shop, and equip them as you see fit. If you have more money, buy more. On your way back to the train, head north and save. To the train!

Reactor 5

Move up the train within the time limits and then jump out of the door. Make sure that you run down the track, then left down the chute. Follow the path, talk to Wedge, and go up the ladder. The enemies in this sector don't do much damage. Magic attacks are much more effective than standard attacks. Talk to Jessie and climb down the lower left ladder. Talk to Biggs and get the tent. Go up the small ladder and slide down the chute. From now on, the layout is much the same as reactor 1. The enemies here require the standard attack, not magic. Make your way to the reactor, saving on the way. The flashback explains some of Tifa's history, and her feelings toward the mysterious Sephiroth. Set the bomb for detonation. Now get out of the way as you did for reactor 1 (up the stairs). The next part is different. Go into the left area and hit the buttons simultaneously to open the gate. Go through the gate, save and heal. Follow the path, go to the second boss.

Boss 2 - Air Buster

If you've got Limit Breaks, this boss is very easy. Otherwise, just use Bolt magic and standard attacks. It will be over all too soon. However, what lies ahead isn't so good!

Sector 5 Slums

When you wake up, talk to Aeris until Reno and his merry band turn up. Talk to Reno, then leave by the back exit. Go up the stairs. When Aeris falls, tell her to fight them. As Cloud, go to the top. The second time, tell her to fight, the third tell her to run. When she joins you on the beams, get out by the hole in the roof. Run along the ruins. Go west and save. In the small town, buy some materia and Titan Bangles. Equip and sell everything you don't need. Aeris's house is by the north east exit. Get the materia from the garden and equip it. Talk to Aeris's mum and stay the night. You must do as Aeris's mum says and try to leave. Learn where the loose floorboards are and go downstairs.

Go through the town to the south, then head west. Aeris just happens to be waiting for you.

Sector 6 Slums

The enemies in sector 6 can cause a lot of damage, so get rid of them as quickly as possible with magic. Go to the town and talk to everyone. Buy some new weapons if you have the money. At Don's mansion you find that only girls can enter. Take a trip to the clothes shop and talk to the girl about her dad. Now go to the bar and persuade the shop owner to make you a dress. Go back to the clothes shop to collect it. To get a wig, go to the gym and challenge the black guy to a squatting contest. Win or lose, you'll get the wig. Go to the clothes shop and put the outfit on. Now go to Don's mansion.

Don Corneo's Mansion

Go in and find Tifa. Collect the ether and go to Don's room. You get taken to the employee's room. Throw off your disguise and fight them all. Collect the Phoenix Down and go to the cellar to get Aeris. Now go to Don Corneo's room and get the information you need. Unfortunately the old 'trap door where you are standing' has been installed, and you fall into the sewers.

Sewers
Boss 3 - Mutant

As soon as you get up, the boss will attack. It is vulnerable to fire magic and Limit Breaks, especially Cloud's Cross Slash. If you have learnt it Aeris's Healing Limit Break will also come in handy.

Make your way through the sewage system, collecting the Steal materia on the way. Climb up the ladder to the Train Graveyard.

Train Graveyard

There's no simple route through this, it's just a matter of trial and error. Save and be on your way. Try to collect all the items. On the second part you should try to jump into the engine train to push the carriage out of the way. Go to the next engine train and move it backwards. Jump onto it from the adjacent carriage and then onto the station at sector 7.

Save Sector 7

As you would have found out earlier, Shinra are trying to crush sector 7 to wipe out Avalanche by destroying the pillar that holds up the plate. Save, and get to the top as quickly as possible. Be sure to give Tifa any of Aeris's materia as she won't need them.

Beat the guards on the way up by using magic to destroy their rotors and then attacking normally.

Boss 4 - Reno

Reno is vulnerable to fire magic. If he casts Pyramid on someone, you can break it by attacking the inflicted person. Reno will run off. Grab the wire and swing to safety.

Pick up the Sense materia from the playground. Now make your

way through sector 6 to Aeris's house and talk to her mum. The story that follows should fill you in on the ancients and Aeris's potential powers.

Go upstairs, talk to Barret and Marlene, and get some rest in the spare room.

Straight to the Top!

Now you must get to Shinra Headquarters. Head to Wall Market via sector 6. Stock up on new weapons, armour, materia and items. Save. Now go to the exit to the right of the entrance to Don's Mansion. Some kids will show you the way. Climb up the wire. You'll find that you need a battery, so go to the weapon shop and the bald bloke will sell you some. Now it's back up the wire. Place the batteries in the right place, then get to the top.

Shinra Headquarters

Enter by the side entrance, and go up the seemingly endless staircase. Pick up a welcome elixir on the way up. Make your way to floor 60 in the lift. Go into the room on the left and do as Barret says. After removing all the guards, go up the stairs to 61. Talk to everyone and get the Keycard 62. Talk to the Mayor of Midgar on floor 62. Don't give his assistant any money! The password is BEST. On floor 63 you can get items by opening a maximum of three doors. By using the air-ducts you can get all three items. Remember to exchange the coupons. Save on floor 64. Check the lockers for items and go to floor 65. This floor houses enemies, so beware!

In the centre is a model of Midgar. In one chest on this floor is one of the missing pieces. Slot this piece in and another chest will open. Repeat this process until you have Keycard 66. Go to the toilet cubicle on floor 66 and listen in on the executive meeting. Go to floor 67 and follow Hojo. Get the materia, save and go up the lift.

Boss 5 - Jenova Specimen

Vulnerable to fire, about ten attacks should take it out.

Equip Red XIII and get Keycard 68 from the assistant. The enemies on this floor all fear fire, so use Red's Fire All magic. Go to the 66th floor elevator to meet the rest. Unfortunately Tseng and Rude intercept you. It's off to the president we go! You will be slammed in the brigg. Sleep off your anger. You'll awaken to find the scene set for an episode of the X-Files! Free the others and investigate. Go to the specimen tank, then save. Go up the lift and follow the trail of blood to the president... the ex-president, that is. It seems that the order of hierarchy has shifted slightly! The mysterious Sephiroth has returned. Go out to the helicopter and have the pleasure of meeting Rufus. You'll be seeing a lot of him in the future. You are now missing Cloud for the first time in the game. Leave Cloud's materia as it is. Equip your team with Bolt, and if you have it, Restore and Sense. The first maintenance robot is vulnerable to lightening. Try to cure yourself with potions until you can use Aeris's Healing Wind Limit Break.

The second robot is also weak against Lightening. If it sends you to sleep, hit that person to wake them. As Cloud, make sure you have Bolt and Cure. Use Bolt on Rufus as well as Cross-Slash Limit Break. Once he has gone, meet up with Tifa. This is where the game gets really good!

Rebel Riders
This is really easy. Left and right and slash left and slash right. Don't let the enemy get to your party.

Boss 6 - Armoured Tank
Weak against lightening and Limit Breaks. Well that's it. The first small section of the game is complete. You can now leave Midgar. Choose your team and equip. Make sure that you swap team members occasionally so as to familiarise yourself with their new abilities.
Note: On the world map you can save at any time so get into the habit of saving regularly.

Section 2 - The Search for Sephiroth
Who Is Sephiroth?
Get onto the world map by leaving Midgar, and save. Head northeast towards a town called Kalm. Go to the inn and meet up with the gang. What follows is a lengthy story about Cloud's involvement with Tifa, Soldier, and Sephiroth. Remember that it's a story, but you do take control in parts of it. These flashbacks take a good half an hour to get through.

To Catch A Chocobo!
If you have any money, buy new materia such as Earth, and weapons. Talk to everyone. It seems that Sephiroth has been here and went east. Travel east through the valley to Chocobo Farm. Say 'wark' to the Chocobi and receive a Summon materia. You can now summon a giant Chocobo or Mog once a battle. Talk to Chocobo Bill, then go to see his stables. Ask about how to use Chocobo's. He'll sell you the Chocobo Lure for 2000 Gil, which you probably won't have. Get the money by fighting on the Chocobo tracks. Use the Summon materia to quickly end the battle. A couple of battles should do it. Buy the materia and some greens. Now get into a battle over the Chocobo tracks. Immediately give the Chocobo some greens. To catch it you must fight off some other enemies. Use standard attacks only, otherwise you'll scare it off.
Once you have caught a Chocobo, go southwest to the marshes and leg it to the other side before the serpent can get to you. Save, and go into the cavern.

The Caverns
Find your way through the caverns. Explore to find all the items and materia. Leave by the way Rude shows you. Elena says something about Sephiroth going to the harbour, so that is your destination.

Save the Condors!
Go south to Fort Condor. Agree to help them fight Shinra. Rest and save. Go to the top of the mountain. You probably won't have enough money at the moment, but find out all you can and leave. Come back later in the game.

Junon Harbour
Make you're way northwest to the harbour. Talk to the girl down by the seashore.

Boss 7 - Bottomswell
A massive sea serpent that is only vulnerable to the elements and Limit Breaks. If it casts a white sphere around you, you're in trouble. All you can do is wait for that person to slowly die, and then bring them back to life. Your HP should be above 500 by now so the other attacks shouldn't be a problem.
Bring Priscilla back to life and go to see her dad. Stay the night, then go outside and find Priscilla. Equip the Shiva materia and get on the tower using the dolphin. Use the shadows of the beams to help you.

Infiltrating the Base
Get into the base by climbing up the tower. Put on a uniform and follow the guards.
Once you're back in the locker room, learn the new moves and then make your way to the dock. On your way, visit all the shops and save. It is vital that you go to the basement of one of the soldiers quarters and learn about advanced fighting techniques.
At the dock do the performance well, and you'll get a HP Plus materia. Get onto the cargo ship.

Crossing the Ocean
Collect the materia and find your friends. Go upstairs, then back down to talk to Aeris. Go back up, and the guard who was in the way will have gone. Talk to Barret until the alarm sounds. Choose your party and go downstairs to the door that was previously guarded.

Boss 8 - Jenova: Birth
Being a Cetra, Jenova fears nothing. Standard attacks will do the same damage as magic attacks. You should have three Summon materia by now. Use those and Limit breaks. Having 4000 HP, the battle could last a while.

A New Continent
At the resort, get some Carbon bangles from the guy in the bar, and talk to Hojo on the beach. He'll tell you to go west. Find your way onto the mountain track and to the reactor. You can't get in here yet, so carry on over the train rack until you get to the rest of your party. On the way you can pick up some cool stuff. The chest at the top holds a gun-arm for Barret. The other side holds a turbo-ether and a Transform materia. If you fall through the track, push and hold left/right and tap the ● button repeatedly to get a Wizard Staff for Aeris, and a Star Pendant. You will have to close the bridge to cross the water by hitting the switch in the small hut. When you've done that, climb the wall to the bird's nest and take the treasure. Go back across the bridge, and cross the other, now closed, bridge. Take the track that goes down to the water and into the cave. Get the items, then go back up and follow the track to the suspension bridge. Don't fight the fireballs on this bridge. Run away as they

do massive damage when they die.

Carry on to North Corel. Here, Cloud can get a new sword. On to the Gold Saucer!

Section 3 - The Gold Saucer And Beyond

Is Barret Guilty?

You will need 3000 Gil to get into the Gold Saucer. If you don't have enough get into a couple of fights first. Once you are in, go to the Wonder Square and play in the arcade to get some GP's. You need GP's to go on the rides. Now go to the Battle area. Here you discover that a man with a gun-arm has killed everyone. Could it be Barret? Dio, the owner of the Saucer throws you out to the desert below. Find Barret and get him to explain what is going on. Form a party, and go back the way you came to where the guarded gate was. Go through this and on to confront Dyne.

Boss 9 - Dyne

Because he is constantly attacking you, you should get Limit Breaks quite often. Use these along with any magic you have got.

Cloud, Chocobo Racer

Sort out Mr. Coates and go up the escalator with Ester. The best way to win is to use sort bursts of turbo and then hold down turbo as you come to the last corner. Alternatively just put it on Auto. When you win Dio will give you a buggy and tell you where Sephiroth is.

Gongaga

Head south across the river in the buggy. Go south a little further and there is a settlement encircled by a forest. This is Gongaga. You will bump into Reno and Rude. They will take a lot of damage before they retreat so use Summons and Limit Breaks. Go left and follow Rude and Reno. Get the materia and buy anything you need from the village. Now take the other road to the reactor. After Scarlet has left get the Titan materia and leave.

Cosmo Canyon

Carry on in the buggy, cross another river, and on the top of the hill is Cosmo Canyon, Red X111's hometown. There are some really good weapons and materia here. Go to see Bugenhagen and he will show you his observatory. When you have finished go to the Cosmo Candle. Bugenhagen will take you underground. Fight every battle you get into. You can get lots of money and learn loads of spells by doing this properly. Explore everywhere and get all the items.

Boss 10 – Gi Nattack

Vulnerable to Limit Breaks, Summons, and most magic. However, it loves fire, so whatever you do don't cast fire. Ignore the two Flames and just go for the main boss. You should have loads of money now so buy any equipment you need.

Home, Sweet Home

Carryon in the buggy and cross another river towards the

Nibelheim Mountain range. Nibelheim will seem familiar to you, as it is the town in Cloud's stories. It is Cloud's home, which had supposedly burnt to the ground. Talk to everyone and get all the items. Go to the mansion. The first thing to do is to get all the treasures and go to the basement to see Sephiroth. He will give you a Destruct materia. Now go to the area near the front door where there is a note from Sephiroth. The solutions to the clues are as follows:

1) "On the lid of the box with the most oxygen."
   On the lid of the chest in the plant room
2) "Behind the ivory's short of tea and ray."
   Behind the piano in the tea room with the rays of sunshine
3) "Near the creaky floorboard on the second floor"
   Go to the room with the stone door leading to the basement. The chair in this room has a loose floorboard next to it. You'll have to press the Confirm button to find it. Just above the room to the left of here are some more loose floorboards. The number lies here.
4) No clue given
   The clue is written in invisible ink. Just put the cursor down to where clue 4 should be and it will appear.

The combination is therefore:
1) R36 – Turn right to 36
2) L10 – Turn left to 10
3) R59 – Turn right to 59
4) R97 – Turn right to 97

Before you open the safe, check your materia. If you have not done it already make sure someone has Restore combined with All so you can use this person as a healer.

Boss 11 – Lost Number

Open the safe and come face to face with this freak of nature. It fears nothing and only Summons and Limit Breaks will do any sort of damage. This battle will take a while, and you'll have to be healing constantly.

Get Vincent

Collect the key and the materia. Odin is tremendously powerful so equip it straight away. Go to the basement and talk to Vincent in the previously locked room. When he says, "leave me to sleep" leave the basement. He will follow you.

Mount Nibel

Explore every pathway. Some frustratingly lead to dead ends, but others will lead to cool treasure e.g. a new sword for Cloud. Eventually you will come to a room with ladders and pipes with a giant insect in the corner. Don't go anywhere near the insect at the moment. Go to the top and go down the first pipe so that you can save. Use a tent here also. Now go to the insect.

Boss 12 – Materia Keeper

This is by far the hardest boss so far. It is not only the fact that it has a HP of nearly 8000, but it has got some really powerful attacks, taking up to 800 HP. It heals itself with Cure-2 every couple of rounds and it fears nothing.

However, keep your head and it can be done. Firstly make sure someone has the Enemy Skill materia. They should learn Trine quite quickly. This does about 500 HP damage, so use it all the time. Magic doesn't really do much even on level 2, but it all counts. Limit Breaks will pop up often and Cloud should have learnt level 2 Limit Breaks by now. These take off anything up to 900 HP. Summons magic is useful, especially Odin which takes off over 1000 HP. This will take a long time and you will use a lot of Phoenix Down, Ethers, Turbo Ethers, and Restore Magic.

The Mako Fountain

Save!! Instead of taking the exit you have just cleared take the one next to it and follow the path. You will come to the fountain that was in Cloud's story. Take the Elemental materia and go back to the boss room. Take the other exit and travel to the Rocket Launch site just around the corner.

The Tiny Bronco

Talk to all the people and buy some armour. Go to see the plane in one of the back gardens. Talk to Cid in the rocket and ask to borrow the Tiny Bronco. Go back to the plane and Cid will follow you. Go out to see Rufus and you will then have to go up against Palmer.

Boss 20 – Palmer

For a small fat bloke he is dead hard! He fears nothing, but Summons and Limit Breaks will sort him out.

Get the Keystone

Follow the shoreline and find the small house. The bloke will tell you that Dio, the owner of the Gold Saucer has taken the Keystone, which is the key to the Temple of the Ancients. Your buggy should be parked outside Nibelheim, so head back there, park on the shore and drive the buggy back to North Coral. Go up to the Gold Saucer and visit Dio's museum in the Battle Area. The owner will give you the keystone once you have fought in the Battle Arena. Now go outside and save. You may need to get some GP's first.

Upon trying to leave you will find that the tram is broken, so you'll have to stay in the hotel for a while. During the night Tifa's emotions get the better of her and she drags Cloud out to take part in a play and to go for the free rides. When you get back to the station Cait Sith is acting strangely. Follow it and you'll find it to be a robotic spy for Shinra. You've now lost the Keystone.

The Sleeping Forest

Travel in the buggy back to the plane. Use the plane to get to the far northern continent. There is a settlement in the middle of the forest called Bone Village. Here you can buy some Diamond Bangles and find out about the location of the Temple of the Ancients and the Sleeping Forest. Go into the Sleeping Forest via the village and run into the screen a couple of times. Occasionally you will see a red dot crossing the screen. Grab it and you will receive an immensely powerful new Summon materia. However, you can't get through this forest, as you don't possess the Lunar Harp yet.

Find Yuffie

Drive the plane south, back to Nibelheim where you should have left your buggy. The plane can be driven up the river where the buggy is and through the continent to the eastern side. Once you're on the other side travel southeast to a large island with a forest and a pyramid in the middle. If you get into a fight in this forest you should go up against a ninja girl by the name of Yuffie. Once you have beaten her tell her the following things:

1) You are not interested in fighting again
2) She petrifies you
3) Wait a second
4) You have to hurry on

Yuffie will join your party

Temple of the Ancients

Go into the pyramid in the centre of the forest. Put the keystone at the altar. Follow the wizard guys. When you catch them rest and save. When you get to the time guardian use the ▲ button to select a time period. Visit them all. Most are treasure rooms. One room contains a series of caves and a wizard. Catch the wizard by figuring out his pattern. Once caught you can rest and save. Now go through the large doors and face Sephiroth.

Boss 21 – Red Dragon

If you have learnt Trine on your enemy-skill materia then use that. Otherwise, only physical attacks, Summons and Limit Breaks will hurt it. Try and equip two people with Restore All magic. Just keep attacking and healing, even if you are not low on energy.

Equip the Bahamut materia and make sure that someone has Death Blow materia. Go back to the wizard, rest and save. If your HP max isn't up to at least 1400 by now spend some time in the Red Dragon Boss corridor and get into fights until you've gained a couple of levels. Ideally you should build up your limit gauges until they are full, but don't use them. Use magic instead. Now go to the time-guardian. The clock will be set and you will have to go straight ahead.

Boss 22 – Demon Gate

This boss is seemingly impossible to start with. His Demon Rush almost kills you outright! Sometimes this boss is really hard and attacks relentlessly. Other times it will be kinder to you, but it is still very hard. If Tifa's in your team her water kick should remove 1200 of the 10,000. Clouds level 2 Limit should take off about 1400. Bahamut should remove 2500. That is half of its HP in three attacks. Death Blow should take about 600 every time. Getting energy off the boss isn't hard. It is just staying alive long enough to do it. Cure everyone all the time and only attack when your HP is full. This may take some time.

Black Materia
Once Cait Sith has done his bit you can get the black materia. However, Sephiroth intervenes.

Lunar Harp
You will wake up in Gongaga village. Get the Tiny Bronco and go back up to Bone village. You can get the harp by hiring some men to dig for it. Place your men in the upper part of the village and dig in the area that the smoke floats in front of. Once you have got the harp you can pass through the Sleeping Forest

Forgotten Capital
Explore every pathway, rest and save at the save point, and get all the treasures. Equip Cloud with Comet materia and the Water Ring. Now go to the main building and walk down the transparent blue stairway to get to Aeris. Once again Sephiroth intervenes.

Boss 23 – Jenova
The only person who will survive Jenova's water attacks will be Cloud, who has the Water Ring. In fact Jenova's attacks give Cloud energy! Use Bahamut and Comet to kill Jenova.

The North Limit
Follow the path that Sephiroth took. Climb up the spinney-shell and into the cave. Negotiate the cracks in the walls and get all the treasures. At the bottom of the ladder is a Magic Plus materia. On the world-map travel west to the small village. Buy some equipment. Get the map and the snowboard and then go snowboarding. Using the map to identify the landmarks and get to the area with a red tick on it. Going the long way round lets you find more items. Once you get to the red-tick talk to the mountain-climber in the hut.

Gaea's Cliff
Nothing much to say about this. Explore, equip new treasures, explore, fight, save. By the time you get to the top you should have 2000 HP max.

Boss 24 – Schizo Twins
Similar to recent bosses. Equip Cloud with an Aurora Armlet and the Water Ring and use Comet, Bahamut and Odin as well as Limit Breaks. The other two members of the party will die, but cloud will gain energy. Schizo's dying spell takes off 1200 HP, so use Sense and cure accordingly before finishing them off. On completion go back to the area near the save point to restore your health. Then save and continue on.

Whirlwind Maze
Get the Neo-Bahamut materia and equip it. Save. Cross the chasms by watching the wall of wind. As soon as it starts to slow down, run for it.

Boss 25 – Jenova: death
Use the same tactics as previous bosses. This time however use Cure All as your whole team can survive this. Neo-Bahamut, Bahamut, Odin, any enemy-skills and Limit Breaks will finish it off quite quickly. Get the reflect-ring, equip it and save. Move on to Sephiroth.

Weapon Awakens
What follows is a very lengthy flashback section and some amazing FMV footage. It does answer some of the questions, but completely re-writes what you may have been thinking before, and poses yet more questions.

Section 4 – Meteor's Approach
On Death Row
Make your way to the main hall. When Cait Sith appears equip it. Then make your way to the airport, finding and equipping Yuffie on the way. As Tifa, use the appropriate buttons to grab the key and get out of the chair. Run all the way down to the edge of the gun.

On the Highwind
Once you have talked to everyone on the bridge, go to operations and sort out your team and save. Your first port of call should be Chocobo Ranch. Hire some stables, catch some Chocobo and breed them. This will take a while and will use up a lot of money, but you should be rich by now anyway. Make sure you talk to the young boy in the stables as he has some vital information.

Mideel
Travel to the far south to a continent you couldn't get to before. It is a village in the middle of a forest. Scratch the white Chocobo behind the ears to get a Contain materia. Buy any equipment you need and go to the clinic.

The Huge Materia
Get a team ready and go to the Coral Reactor. Defeat the enemies within the time limit and stop the train. The young boy will give you an Ultima materia, which you should equip. Now go to Fort Condor. Defeat the troops and collect the Phoenix materia. The old man will give you the huge materia. Go to see Tifa and Cloud.

Earth to Cloud
Weapon will attack Mideel. Use your most powerful Summons to scare it off. Unfortunately Weapon has made the lifestream unstable and Tifa and Cloud fall into it during a massive earthquake. After Cloud has found himself you will understand a lot more about what is and has gone on.

Stop, Thief!
Travel to Wutai, which is a resort in the far northwest. Yuffie will steal all your materia. Go into town and look everywhere for her. When you eventually corner her she will trick you and run away again. Go towards the large tower. On the left is a

structure with a gong. Hit the gong, and a secret door will appear. Corneo is in here. Chase him to the mountain.

Boss 26 – Corneo's Pet
You have no materia, so just attack and use your items to heal yourself. A Limit Break or two should do it.

Underwater Reactor
Re-equip your materia and go to Junon. Go down the runway, past the shops, towards the cargo ship. Then go left and you'll come to some guards practicing a drill. Go through the door and onto the lift and the underwater tunnel. When you get to the underwater glass-pipe keep getting into fights until you go against rowing-skeleton. Analyze him to get his HP-max. Attack him as normal, but finish him off with the Morph command. This will turn him into a GuideBook that you will need later in the game. Further exploration will lead you to lots of treasure and eventually, Reno.

Boss27 – Dock Loader
This boss has got one powerful attack, which is his laser. Cure often to survive. Ignore the arms. Go straight for the body with Limit Breaks Summons and Comet and Comet 2. Make sure you get the items from chests outside the sub. Destroy the enemy submarines and go to the area where the Highwind was once kept, in Junon. You will arrive in time to see the cargo plane depart. Get in the submarine and locate the red-leader submarine. Get the Huge materia and go to the rocket launch-pad area.

The Last, Best Hope
Go to the rocket. Defeat Rude by using Summons and Limit Breaks. Once the rocket is in space make your way to the huge materia. The combination for the security system can be learnt from Cid if you pay attention.

You should now have all three huge materia. Now go to the escape-pod. Fly to Cosmo Canyon and give the huge materia to Bugenhagen to put in his observatory. Look at all the materia. You will receive Bahamut Zero from the blue materia. Return to Junon and the guard will tell you that the canon is aimed at the Northern Limit and that Shinra is getting an army together at Midgar. To get into Midgar you will need a key. This key can be found in the same place as the Lunar Harp, (Excavation Camp, path of the smoke). Use the key to get in to Midgar. You will be able to buy a Sneak Glove from the weapon store in Wall Market for 129,000 Gil. This is an accessory that increases your ability to steal.
Now go to Junon and get into the submarine. Avoid Weapon and travel to where Bone Village and the Forgotten City would be. Around here is a small gap, which leads to a seemingly dead end. Adjusting the camera allows you to see a cave. Inside this cave is the Key to the Ancients. Take it, go back to the Highwind and visit the large crystal in the Forgotten City. Here you will find out about Holy magic and

how to use it.
However, Sephiroth is blocking the course of nature, so he must be removed first. Thankfully President Rufus intends to do something about the barrier protecting Sephiroth. When you try to leave Bone Village Weapon will surface and charge towards Midgar. Fly to Midgar and save. When Weapons comes ashore fight it.

Boss 28 – Weapon
Weapon has about 25,000 HP max. Always keep your HP above 1800 as it has some very powerful attacks. Limit Breaks, Kjuta, Bahamut, Neo Bahamut, Bahamut Zero, Odin, Comet, Comet 2 and Ultima should do the job nicely. You may have to fight Weapon three or four times. When you fight it above Cosmo Canyon you will know that it's the last time. On defeating Weapon you will get loads of money and masses of experience points. You should gain about two experience levels. The explosion leaves a crater in the ground which allows you to get up the hill in the forest.

The Secret Forest
Pick up the frogs and put them in the picture-plants in order to get across the gaps. Another way to cross the large gaps is to wait for the frogs to get restless so that they jump up, catapulting you in the process. Blocks can be thrown into the Venus Fly-Traps to close them. Use the select button to help you find the exits. From this forest you can get Slash All materia and Typhoon Summon.

Shut Up Midgar
Go to the Northern Limit. Watch the enemy's plans, then go back to Midgar.

Sector 8
Explore and battle. Make sure you get all of the treasures as a good gun for Barret is amongst them. The difficulty is in proportion to the first reactor battles. They are just difficult enough to warrant curing after each battle. When you meet up with the Turks avoid a battle. When you get to Yuffie take the left path and go up the ladder.

Boss 29 – Proud Clod
Heineggar's Weapon Beater is just as big as Weapon, and even stronger. There are two parts to this boss, both having about 40,000 HP max. The same technique as Weapon should be used.

Stop Hojo!
Get all the treasures; there is a new gun for Barret and a new sword for Cloud. Go to Hojo via the stairway.

Boss 30 – Hojo
Only 13,000 HP max, so nothing to worry about.

Boss 31 – Helletic Hojo
Relatively easy. Use the same tactics as for Proud Clod.

Boss 32 – Whipping Boy
30,000 HP max You will need to use anti-poison magic as you will be poisoned a lot. Cure all the time and remember that if you are put to sleep the only cure is to hit that person.

Anywhere you haven't been yet?
Near the Northern Limit lives the Chocobo Sage. His Chocobo will give you an Enemy Skill materia. There is a cave on a barren plain and a small hill on a plateau near Cosmo-Canyon, but the Highwind cannot land on these. They are also not accessible by foot or buggy. Make sure you get loads of Hi-potions, Tents, and Phoenix Downs before you go to the Northern cave.

Final Fantasy Secrets
1. Near the Northern Limit lives the Chocobo Sage. You can get an Enemy Skill materia off his Chocobo. He also gives you tips on breeding special Chocobo's.
2. If you have not already done it, find the Sunken Shinra cargo plane (Gelnika) using the submarine. You can get loads of experience and Hades Summon, as well as Yuffie's Ultimate Weapon.
3. Have you solved the Pagoda problem yet? PutYuffie in your party and go to the Pagoda in Wutai. Make your way to the top and get Yuffie's Level 4 Limit Break and Leviathan Summon.
4. Now that you have defeated Weapon you can take part in the Special Battle at the Battle Arena (Gold Saucer). As long as you are powered up enough this shouldn't be a problem. Special Battle puts you up against some tough enemies, ending with Proud Clod. It may be better to do this after you have solved the Gold Chocobo problem. Defeating Special Battle will earn you Final Attack materia. This is vital for defeating the other Weapons. As well as this, get 32,000 or 64,000 battle points on the normal battle to earn Cloud's Level 4 Limit Break (Omnislash) and W-Summon materia respectively. The best way to get points is to get the worst handicaps. Eg. All materia Break or No MP. Equip yourself with Ribbon and Haste, Curse 3 and a couple of each type of materia.

5. **Breeding Gold Chocobo's**
   First make sure you have about 200,000 Gill. Go to the Chocobo Stables and hire six stables. Now equip yourself with Chocobo Lure materia. Preferably it should be mastered. Below is where to find the appropriate Chocobo:
   Good Chocobo: Gold Saucer Area – Capture Rate _
   Great Chocobo: Mideal Island – Capture Rate 1/4
   Wonderful Chocobo: Northern Limit – Capture Rate 1/12
   The Capture-Rate is the chance you have of getting the applicable Chocobo as opposed to getting a bad chocobo.
   Shown Below is an exact guide of how to get a Gold Chocobo. It will cost a lot of money, but you will be

unable to defeat Emerald and Ruby Weapon without it.

Key: (Z) - Letters in brackets stand for the Class Rating of the Chocobo. Raise your rating by racing at the Gold Saucer.
Carob/Zeio – These are the nuts that you have to feed Chocobo's in order to breed them.

Carob nuts can be found in the grass area around Bone Village. Get into a fight with the Red Dragons, then either defeat them or steal from them to get the nut. Unfortunately you won't always fight the Red Dragons as squirrels turn up quite a lot. Zeio nuts are found on an island in the northeast corner of the map. You have to fight the goblins to get them. In order to raise the Class-Rating of your Chocobo go to see Esther at the Chocobo Races and register your Chocobo. Ideally you should feed your Chocobo with 15 Sylkis greens to get their stats up. Get these greens from the Chocobo Sage.

In the races you can get infinite stamina by holding **R1** and **R2** while racing. When you race select "short race" and press **Select** to go to "manual mode". Then press and hold **R1** and **R2** and the speed-up button. Do not sprint, as you will lose stamina. As long as you have fed your Chocobo enough greens you will have no problems. Winning three races moves you up a class. There are four ranks, C, B, A, and S. Whenever you win take the GP and not the items.

Once you have bred a pair of Chocobo's you can't breed them again for a while. While you are waiting for them to rest go to Mideel and Power-up your materia by getting into loads of fights.
1. Good (C) x Great (C) - Carob – Good/Great (C)
2. Good/Great (C) x Great (C) - Carob – River (C)
3. Good/Great (A) x Great (A) - Carob – Mountain (C)
4. River (S) x Mountain (S) - Carob – Black (C)
5. Black (S) x Wonderful (S) - Zeio – Gold (C)
NB: You will not always be successful on your first attempt. You may have to do it 2 or 3 times.

6. Once you have the Gold Chocobo go and get the special materia from the materia caves.
   Knights of the Round (Summon) – This is not on the map. Go to the top right of the map. There is a crater with a cave.
   Mime (Command) – Just south of Wutai is a cave that's out on a peninsular.
   HP-MP (Purple) – A cave on the desert area that you could never get to. The last special materia can be found in a cave near Mideel. Just follow the land east from Mideel.
7. Using your Gold Chocobo race up to S-Class. You will now be able to win vital items such as elixirs,

megalixirs, counter/magic counter materia. If you already have these take your GP for items in the Wonder Square. These include Carob nuts, Gill Plus materia and EXP Plus materia.

8. Go to Kalm and find the old man. He is upstairs in one of the houses. Give him the Guide Book to get the Underwater materia.

9. Go to the Northern Limit and make your way dow use the Save Crystal. Avoid the Stone Demons as they will use Level 4 Death on you. When you split up take your team left and then up. This is the safest way. The route holds Magic Pots that will attack you. Give them elixir then kill them. This will give you loads of AP. Eventually you will come to an open area with a bright light in the centre. You can get two materia here: W-Magic and Mega-All. Don't go any further as you won't be able to get out. Explore the two other routes by going back up to the Highwind and then going down again. There is a lot of treasure to get.

Boss 33 – Emerald Weapon

Before you even attempt this make sure you have the following:
1. All characters with maximum HP and MP
2. All characters with Cure 3/Regen All
3. At least two characters with Ribbon
4. All characters with Ultimate Weapons
5. All characters with decent chain-combos e.g. counter+deathbow, counter+slash all, magic counter+cure, magic counter+ultima
6. W-Summon, Knights of the Round, Final Attack and Pheonix really need to be powered up to at least Level 3, preferably higher.

An example of a good set up is as follow:
Cloud: Level 99/ Level 4 Limit
Ultimate Weapon + Mystile + Ribbon
Counter+Deathblow/ Knights of the Round+MP Turbo/ W-Summon+HP Plus/ Final Attack+Pheonix/ Cure+All

Yuffie: Level 99/ Level 3 Limit
Conformer + Wizard Bracelet + Tetra-Elemental
Counter+2-Cut/ HP Plus+Mime/ Cure+All/ Haste+All/ Bahamut Zero+Quandra/ Underwater

Red X111: Level 99/ Level 3 Limit
Limit Moon + Fourth Bracelet + Ribbon
Magic Counter+Ultima/ W-Magic+Mime/ Mega-All+Cure/ W-Item+HP Plus/ MP Turbo+Barrier

Fill up the other slots with commands or supports. The above are the essentials. Note that some multi-hit Level 3 Limit Breaks take off more than the one hit Level 4 Limit Breaks. Equipping the Underwater materia removes the time limit so you are able to take your time. Using the submarine, drive into Emerald Weapon. Immediately cast W-Summon with Knights of the Round and Mime it. This will remove one half of its energy. Then cast Regen and Wall using W-Magic. Your healer's job is

to cast Wall and Regen every round and to use W-item and cast Megalixir and elixir when needed. Your primary-attack character should cast W-Summon with Knights of the Round and should keep the party alive by casting Pheonix and Final Attack.

Your secondary-attack character should mime the primary attacker and cast four Bahamut Zeros. If at all possible the healer should mime this for an amazing eight Bahamut Zero's. This boss is relatively easy if you follow these guidelines. Using W-Summons + Knights of the Round + Mime twice will finish it off. Emeralds Weapon's eyes will die after removing 9999 from each. The only problems they prove to have is that they drain loads of MP. The main body has some awesome attacks that it uses sparingly. These can only be countered by using Final Attack and Pheonix.

Emerald Weapon has 1,000,000 HP max. On defeating it you will get the Earth Harp. Take it to the old man in Kalm to get a set of Master materia.

Boss 34 – Ruby Weapon

Get your most powerful character and set them up based on the following example:

> Cloud: Level 99 Level 4 Limit
> Ultimate Weapon + Mystile + Ribbon
> Master Summon+MP Turbo/ Master Magic+MP Turbo/ Mega-All+HP Plus/ Final Attack+Pheonix/W-Magic/W-Summon/W-Item/Counter+4-Cut

This boss is surprisingly easy. You just need to cast W-Summon + Knights of the Round four times. Attack the main body. It is only vulnerable to attacks when it's hands are in the ground. Get it's hands in the ground by attacking. One problem you will encounter is that Ruby Weapon uses Whirlsand to remove two of your characters at the start. The selection is random so you will have to keep trying it until you are left with the character that you need. The way to finish it off is to cast Wall and Regen and use a Megalixir with Haste when needed. When you get a chance, cast W-Summon + Knights of the Round. Defeating this boss is easier than defeating Emerald Weapon and thus the reward is pretty lame. You will get the Desert Rose. Exchange this with the man in Kalm for a Gold Chocobo (?!?)

And thus Final Fantasy V11 is well and truly sussed! All that remains is to kick Sephiroth's butt. After Weapon, Sephiroth's 60,000 HP max is not a great problem. Make your way down the crater.

Boss 35 – Jenova

Has a 40,000 HP max. Use 4-Cut and Mime it.

Boss 36 – Sephiroth Combo

Another 40,000 HP max. Use Knights of the Round.

Boss 37 – Ultimate Sephiroth

Has a HP max of 60,000. Use Knights of the Round.

If you want a Job Done

Even after that Sephiroth still remains to prevent Holy doing its work. Cloud is summoned for a one-on-one battle with True Sephiroth. Hammer the buttons to build your limit up and then let rip with the mighty Omnislash. You can now sit back and enjoy the excellent twenty-minute end sequence.

FINAL FANTASY VIII

Characters

Name: Squall Leonhart
Age: 17
Sex: Male
Height: 5'10" (177cm)
Birth Date: August 23rd
Blood Type: AB
Weapon: Gunblade

Squall is a hero who wants no part of heroism. Deeply introverted, Squall is emotionless not allowing anyone see his true feelings. Squall's name means 'passing shower'. Squall bears a facial scar inflicted by Seifer Almasy during a heated training session.

Name: Rinoa Heartilly
Age: 17
Sex: Female
Height: 5'4" (163 cm)
Birth Date: Unknown
Blood Type: Unknown
Weapon: Blaster Edge

Rinoa is the leader and Princess of a resistance group in the Galbadian controlled town of Timber known as the Forest Owls. She is also the daughter of General Caraway a commander of the Galbadian army based in Deling City. Before Rinoa met Squall she had a close relationship with his rival, Seifer Almasy.

Name: Zell Dincht
Age: 17
Sex: Male
Height: 5'6" (167cm)
Birth Date: March 17th
Blood Type: B
Weapon: Gloves

Zell entered the Garden military academy at the age of 13. An impressive martial artist Zell is constantly practising his moves. He hates Seifer who calls him a 'chicken punk' because of his hair style.

Name: Seifer Almasy
Age: 18
Sex: Male
Height: 6'1" (188cm)
Birth Date: December 22nd
Blood Type: A
Weapon: Gunblade

Seifer is obsessed with becoming the greatest soldier ever and has started an unhealthy rivalry with Squall Leonhart. He received a gunblade scar between his eyes from Squall during a deadly training session. Seifer has a hatred for authority, which brings him into conflict with the teachers at Garden.

Name: Laguna Loire
Age: 18
Sex: Male
Height: 5'11" (181cm)
Birth Date: January 3rd
Blood Type: B
Weapon: Machine Gun

A former Galbadian soldier, Laguna traded his gun for a pen and became a journalist. His best friends are two of his former army comrades Ward Zaback and Kiros Seagul. Laguna was deeply in love with a musician named Julia. On several occasions when they were stationed nearby, Laguna would drag his two friends with him all the way to Deling City to hear her play.

Name: Selphie Tilmett
Age: 17
Sex: Female
Height: 5'1" (157cm)
Birth Date: July 16
Blood Type: B
Weapon: Nunchaku

Despite her natural clumsiness and carefree outlook on life, Selphie remains a dedicated student. Selphie started her studies at Travia Garden and transferred to Balamb to sit the SeeD entrance exam. She loves trains.

Name: Irvine Kinneas
Age: 18
Sex: Male
Height: 6'0" (185cm)
Birth Date: November 24th
Blood Type: O
Weapon: Shotgun

An expert marksman, Irvine studied to become a member of Seed at the Galbadian Garden. On the surface full of confidence and a resounding hit with the women, Irvine hides a sensitive and low esteem personality behind that cowboy hat.

Name: Quistis Trepe
Age: 18
Sex: Female
Height: 5'6" (172cm)
Birth Date: October 4th
Blood Type: A
Weapon: Chain Whip

Incredible ambitious, Quistis enrolled in Garden at the age of ten. At fifteen she graduated as a member of SeeD. Later, Quistis became a teacher blossoming into a skilled instructor. She has been warned many times for not being strict enough with her students. Well respected by her students, they have formed a 'Quistis Trepe' fan club. Quistis has strong feelings for her student, Squall Leonhart.

Walkthrough

Infirmary: The game begins with Squall recovering in the infirmary after being wounded during training with his rival Seifer. Doctor Kadowaki will enter and ask Squall if he is feeling okay. Answer with 'Yeah'. After Doctor Kadowaki leaves, a girl will peep into Squall's room. Quistis, one of Squall's teachers will enter. She will instruct Squall to follow her.

Classroom: Squall will eventually find himself in a classroom. Quistis will tell the class that the SeeD entrance examination will start in the evening. All the students will stand up and leave. Walk up to Quistis and she will explain that you will have to visit the 'Cave of Fire' or you will not be able to sit the SeeD entrance examination. Go back to your desk. From here you can view the various tutorials and collect your first two Guardian Forces, Shiva and Quetzalcoat. When you have finished leave the classroom via the door to the far right. As you head towards the elevator you will literally run into a girl. Ask her if she is okay then agree to show her around the campus. Talk to the student near the elevator and he will give you a pack of cards. You can now play the card battle game. When you want to challenge someone to a game, walk up to them and press square button. Enter the elevator. When you reach the first floor, walk up to the lobby directory. Squall will explain the different locations and their purpose.

Dormitory: This is where you will find Squall's room. You can return here and rest restoring Squall's and party member's health points (HP).

Parking Lot: This is where the SeeD vehicles are stored. Occasionally you will need to come here to be transported to your next mission.

Training Centre: You can visit here to increase your fighting experience. Be warned the creatures here are real and you can die while fighting them. Lurking in the training centre is a huge T-Rex known as T-Rexaur. If you encounter this beast early on in the game it is best to run, but it is possible to defeat. The T-Rexaur has between 10,000 and 17,000 HP when you first encounter it.

Library: Come here to find useful information and magazines. Search the second bookcase for a copy of Occult Fan 1. You might find it an interesting read.

Infirmary: You will find the campus physician here.

Quistis's Classroom: Located on the second floor. Before you leave the campus be sure to collect Squall's first two guardian forces from his desk.

Head Master Cid's Office: Located on the third floor, you will only visit here when you are sent for.
Cafeteria: You will usually find Zell here trying to get his favourite food, Hot Dogs here.

Quad: This is the location of the 'Garden Festival'.

When you have finished, the girl will thank you and leave. If you want to you can explore the area. When you are done head

down towards the main gate. You will find Quistis waiting for you. Quistis will tell you that the 'Cave of Fire' can be found east of Garden. Before you leave Garden, Quistis will give you a brief tutorial. Once on the world map be sure you have equipped your guardian forces. Give one to Squall and the other to Quistis for the moment. By junctioning a guardian force you are then given the option to draw magic, cast magic, summon guardian forces and use items from you inventory during battles. On your way to the 'Cave of Fire', participate in some random battles until you are comfortable with drawing magic, junctioning magic to your attributes and summoning your guardian forces. If you encounter any Fastitocalon-F's or Glacial Eyes be sure to draw Blizzard from them, it will make the upcoming battle with the guardian force Ifrit a lot easier.

The Cave of Fire
When you reach the cave entrance, the guard will ask you to choose a time limit between 10 and 40 minutes in which to complete the cave (the time you select will effect your SeeD ranking). The timer will continue to go down during battles and will only stop once you leave the cave. Once in the cave just follow the path to its end. Here you will face the games first boss, Ifrit.

Ifrit
HP: 1,068
Attacks: Fire
Weakness: Ice
Draw: Fire, Heal, Sense.
AP Gain: 20
Strategy: Make full use of the guardian force Shiva and any drawn ice magic such as Blizzard and you should find Ifrit easy.

Once you have defeated Ifrit, he will join your party as a Guardian Force. Follow the path back out of the cave. Return back to Garden. When you reach Garden, Quistis will ask you to change into your uniform and meet her in the first floor lobby. Head to your dormitory. Use the lobby directory if you do not know where to go. Once you reach your dormitory you can rest and restore your HP. Change into your uniform and then head back to the first floor lobby.

The SeeD Entrance Examination
When you reach the first floor lobby you will be introduced to a new team member, Zell Dincht. Seifer, the man responsible for your facial scar will enter with his two friends, Fuujin and Raijin. Before Seifer and Zell get into a fight, the school Headmaster appears. Headmaster Cid will briefly explain your mission. Squall will follow the group to the parking lot where they will board a vehicle. Drive the vehicle to the Balamb town/port, just follow the path leading from the school.

When you reach the port you will board a heavy built boat. Inside, you will be briefed on the situation before you by a lady named Xu.

'For the past 72 hours, Dollet has been under attack by the Galbadian army. 49 hours after the outbreak of war, the city of Dollet was evacuated. At the present time, they are hurrying to take refuge in the outlying mountain area'.

Liberation of Dollet

When Xu has left talk to Zell. Seifer will begin taunting Zell. Quistis will ask you to go on deck. Answer with 'Sure' and head out onto the deck. The fleet of boats will land on the shore of Dollet town.

Your performance at Dollet is closely being watched by your SeeD instructors. Your grade is determined on how well you follow orders, number of battles, outwitting your opponents, if you talk to anyone during the examination, and your route to your objective.

Follow Seifer, the mission leader through the city streets. You will face Galvadian soldiers as you go. You should have no trouble dispatching them. Once you have reached the town square you will need to take out the guard found to the right. Talk to Seifer. He will admit to finding the mission boring. Talk to Zell. The dog will bark and howl as Galbadian soldiers move through the square towards a facility located on the mountaintop. Seifer will decide to ignore his orders and find out why the enemy is so interested in the facility. Follow Seifer up towards the Communication Tower. You will need to fight through several random battles until you finally catch up with Seifer. Talk to the wounded soldier and then to the soldier at the top of the stairs. Before you can continue you have to fight a huge snake creature called an Anacondaur.

Anacondaur
HP: 1,000+
Attacks: Bite, Grab and Twist. Poison Breath
Weakness: Ice Attacks
Draw: Fire, Heal
AP Gain: 4
Strategy: Just summon your guardian forces and draw Heal from the Hedgeviper.

Enter Selphie

Continue up the path until you reach the cliff opposite the Communication Tower. Seifer will run off. A girl will appear behind you and fall down from the steep slope. She will give a 'kawaii' smile. She will introduce herself as Selphie, a messenger from Squad A (she is also the girl you showed around the campus). Just as she asks about your squad captain, you will see Seifer enter the Communication Tower. Selphie will jump off the cliff after him. You will be given the choice of jumping over the cliff after Selphie or following the path down to the Communication Tower. You will be deducted points for jumping off the cliff after Selphie. Either way, once you reach the Communication Tower, Selphie will join your party, replacing the hot-headed Seifer.

Communication Tower

When you enter the tower the scene will switch to two Galbadian soldiers, Biggs and Wedge high up on the Communication Tower. Wedge will report that a monster of some type has been spotted on the Communication Tower. Once inside the tower you will find a magic stone on the left and a save point on the right. Before riding the elevator up, distribute your guardian forces between your party. When you reach the top of the Communication Tower, Major Biggs will activate the satellite dish. First, you will face Biggs.

Biggs
HP: 450 – 700+
Attacks: Machine Gun, Charge
AP Gain: 4
Strategy: His most damaging attack is a running charge. Attack with your basic attacks and magic. Once you have caused enough damage he will call for his colleague, Wedge.

Wedge
HP: 400 – 600+
Attacks: Flame, Sword Swipe.
AP Gain: 4
Strategy: You need only to defeat either Biggs or Wedge. Once one of them fall they will be dragged away by a small whirlwind and you will face the monster Wedge reported. The Elvoret is the first creature you may find challenging.

Elvoret
HP: 1,500 – 3,500
Attacks: Bolt, Claw Swipe, Storm Breath (attacks all), Fire.
Weakness: Wind Attacks. Invulnerable to Poison.
Draw: Bolt, Heal, Double, Siren.
Strategy: Use your Guardian Forces and magic. Keep restoring your health as Elvoret's Storm Breath can cause 200+ damage to all party members. If you draw from the Elvoret you can get a guardian force, Siren.

Evacuation

Once the battle is over, Selphie will relay her message to Seifer that all the SeeD troops and SeeD candidates must withdraw and assemble at the beach. Seifer will give you 30 minutes for you to reach the beach. During your ride down to the ground floor, Biggs will activate a giant mecha crab to go after you. Before exiting the radio tower, save and restore your health using HP potions. Once outside the giant mecha crab Biggs activated will drop from above.

X-ATM092
HP: 5,492
Attacks: Desperate Charge, Claw Attack, Leg Swipe.
Weakness: Lightning.
Strategy: The X-ATM092 is susceptible to lighting. Use both Quetzalcoat and bolt magic to cause the mecha crab to its knees. Once it is down you will need to flee by pressing **L2** and **R2**. Run down the path towards the beach. If you are quick enough, you can reach the beach in around five minutes and facing X-ATM092 only once. You are more likely to face X-ATM092 three or four times, just use the same tactic as before, causing the mecha crab to its knees and then flee. It is possible though to only face the mecha crab once. You cannot avoid fighting X-ATM092 when it first appears. You can though avoid any other encounter.

1. After fleeing once, run around the path until you reach the cliff Selphie jumped off. The X-ATM092 will leap at you here. If you continue to run to the left you will exit the screen just before it has a chance to catch you.
2. As you make your way down the leftmost path walk and do not run. The mecha crab's heavy steps will cause your party to lose their balance if they are running.
3. Finally as you run across the bridge, the X-ATM092 will leap over you blocking your way. Turn around and run back across the bridge. The X-ATM092 will leap back over you. At this point

turn and run across the bridge towards the town. Run through the town and towards the beach.

Once you reach the beach, Squall will board the evacuation boat just in time for Quistis to blow the X-ATM092 away.

Balamb

Harbour: You will be returned to the harbour of Balamb. Seifer will be met by his two friends, Raijin and Fujin. Then Seifer heads back to Garden. Follow the path up into the town.

Talk to the man sitting on the bench and draw from the magic stone.

Zell's House: Enter the house on the right. Inside you will meet Zell's mother. Zell will not let you upstairs to his room. It is far too sacred. You can play Zell's mother at a game of cards and win Zell's card. While in Zell's home, search for the old copy of 'Timber Maniacs'.

Train Station: The train station is found to the far left. Here you can catch a train for towns such as Timber and Deling. At this point there are no trains to catch, but you can find the very first issue of 'Timber Maniacs' next to the signpost.

Item Store: Visit and buy some items such as Potions and Phoenix Downs.

Queen of Cards: Standing between the item store and train station is the mysterious 'Queen of Cards'. She monitors and enforces the various rules throughout the world. You can pay her and she will introduce a new rule to the land. You can even challenge her to a game of cards if you think you are good enough.

When you have finished in Balamb, head back to Garden. Once you reach Garden, Zell and Selphie will say their farewells. Head to the lobby. When you reach the lobby you will be met by Quistis, Cid and Xu. Once you have finished talking with Cid and Quistis head towards the library where you will find Seifer. Cid, Quistis and Xu will enter and lecture Seifer about his behaviour at Dollet. An announcement will signal all students to assemble in the second floor hall. Head to the elevator and ride up to the second floor.

Examination Results

The test results will be read out and Squall, Zell, Selphie and a fourth student who have passed will attend the award ceremony with Cid. You will be given a SeeD ranking. Your test result depends solely on your performance at Dollet..

There are five categories
1. Conduct – You need to reach the beach from the Communication Tower in less than 5 minutes and only encounter X-ATM092 once.
2. Judgement – Complete the 'Cave of Fire' in under 30 minutes with an experience level of 8 or 9.
3. Attack – Defeat 60 enemies in Dollet.
4. Spirit – Never flee during a battle (the battle against X-ATM092 is the only exception).
5. Attitude – Do not talk to any members of team A or C (Selphie is the exception) and do not jump off the cliff opposite the Communication Tower. Instead, take the path around.

If you get a low SeeD ranking you can take a written test. Available later in the game, the written test involves you answering ten questions. If you get them all right your SeeD ranking will increase one level.

Your SeeD ranking will determine how much Squall will be paid. Return downstairs to be congratulated by Seifer's friends Fujin and Raijin. Head back to your dormitory. Go into your room and change into your graduation uniform. Talk to Selphie who will compliment you on your appearance.

The Inauguration Ball

You will find Squall standing alone in the corner of the hall. Zell will approach Squall and offer him his hand in friendship now they are in SeeD. Squall, cold as ever refuses. Zell will leave and Selphie will appear and try to get Squall to participate in the festival committee. Agree and she will leave. A beautiful girl (Rinoa Heartilly) will approach Squall and ask him to dance.Not taking no for an answer she drags Squall onto the dance floor, but when the dance slows Rinoa suddenly departs leaving Squall alone. While Squall stands alone on the balcony, Quistis appears and ask Squall to go to her 'secret place'. Head back to your room and change into your casual clothes. Quistis asked you to meet her in the corridor leading to the training centre.

The Training Centre

The 'secret place' is on the other side of the training centre. Once inside head left. Most of the time you will face plant creatures throughout the training centre but occasionally you will stumble across a T-Rex creature known as T-Rexuar. The T-Rexuar has between 10,000 to 17,000 HP so it is best to flee rather then fight. If you decide to fight it use a combination of guardian forces and drawn magic to defeat this prehistoric creature. When you reach the save point you will see a path that leads up. The path leads to the 'secret place'. Quistis reveals she has been dismissed as a teacher because she was not strict enough with her students. Squall, cold as ever offers no shoulder to cry on. When you return to the training centre, head right. When you near the exit (the training centre is circular) you will find a girl cornered by a huge dragonfly. You might recognise the girl, she peeped into the infirmary at the beginning of the game.

Granaldo
HP: 1,500 – 10,000
Attacks: Kick the Raid, Fire Throw, Fire
Weakness: Wind Attacks
Draw: Sleep, Darkness, Shield.

Raldo
HP: 100 – 6,500
Attacks: Swipe
Draw: Fire, Bolt, Barrier
Strategy: The Granaldo is accompanied by three armadillo creatures called Raldos, which it can throw at you. Concentrate on Granaldo using drawn magic and guardian forces. The battle ends when all of them are killed.

Once the battle is over, the girl will be escorted out by two guards dressed in white. Who is the mysterious girl? and what connection does she have to Squall's past? Once you leave, Zell will tell you that since you are now a member of SeeD you have been moved to a private room. Squall's private room is still located at the dormitory.

The Trepies, Selphie's Diary and Beating Head Master Cid
Once awake, you need to head to the main gate for his first official job. Before you leave collect a copy of 'Weapons Monthly' from the table. Before you rush off on your first assignment you might want to try a few of these.

1. If you want to increase your SeeD ranking you can take the written test. You can access the test either via Squall's desk in Quistis classroom or from the tutorial section from the main menu.
2. If you agreed to help Selphie with the Garden Festival you can check out Selphie's online diary from Squall's desk.
3. You can win Quistis card from one of her fan club members. They are known as the Trepies and are the two girls found in Quistis's classroom and the day dreaming boy in the cafeteria.
4. Head Master Cid holds Seifer's card but is quite a good player. If you do not challenge him now you will not get the chance to again until much further in the game. By then, the dreaded 'Random' rule may be inforced.

Train to Timber
At the main gate you will be met by Head Master Cid. Cid will brief you on your upcoming mission. Your mission is to travel to the town of Timber and rendezvous with the local resistance movement there. Before you leave Cid will give you a Magic Lantern which contains a new guardian force, Diablo. You will need to defeat Diablo before you can summon it. Diablo is quite powerful so you might want to postpone fighting it until you are more experienced.

An important thing to remember is that as your characters become more experienced so do the creatures of the Final Fantasy 8 world. If you challenge Diablo now his HP will be low but your characters are still quite weak. If you wait until your characters are more powerful until you challenge Diablo, then you will find Diablo has become more powerful.

Diablo
HP: 1,600 – 80,000+
Strategy: First, draw Demi magic and cast it back against Diablo. Summon your guardian forces and cast any wind magic you might possess. When your health is low you can unleash your limit breaks. Have Selphie cast Full Cure (You will need to use the Do Over option until you find a Full Cure spell). Once you have defeated Diablo you will be able to summon it and you will receive the Diablo card.

Once on the world map, head to Balamb. Once there, continue left past the man on the bench towards the train station. Buy any items you might need from the shop. You will need to pay the conductor 3,000 gil before you can board the train to Timber. Once on the train head to SeeD's personal cabin. You will find Selphie loves trains so much that she sings for most of the journey about trains. Once in the cabin, talk to Zell. You will find him making himself comfortable on the couch. Zell will ask you if you know anything about the town of Timber. All he knows is that there are a lot of resistance movements

in Timber. Once Selphie enters, the group collapses into unconsciousness.

Enter Laguna
You find yourself in control of a totally new character, Laguna Loire. Laguna has two colleagues, the giant Ward Zaback and Kiros Seagul. You will find Laguna has the same attacks, spells and guardian forces as Squall commanded. Ward will command Zell's attacks and Kiros will command Selphie's. Laguna and co will find themselves alone in a forest. Follow the path drawing from any magic stones you find. As you go you will encounter numerous random battles. Eventually you will find a truck. Once in the truck you will be transported to Deling City.

Deling City
Once in Deling, you will need to find a hotel called 'The Galbadia Hotel'. In the main lobby of the hotel you will find a save point. Once you have saved your position, descend the stairs to the right. Talk to the waitress and she will take you to a table, thank her. A lady dressed in red will appear and begin to play the piano. Her name is Julia and Laguna is deeply in love with her but is too shy to talk to her. Kiros and Ward try to pressure him into speaking with her. Laguna will approach the stage but gets a cramp in his leg (he always gets a cramp when he is nervous). Once Laguna has shuffled back to his friends, Julia will approach him and invite him to her room. Once Julia has left, head up the stairs and go up to the main desk. Answer the clerk with 'I'm looking for Julia's room'. The clerk will tell you to go ahead. Once there, Julia will reveal that she always noticed Laguna looking at her and Laguna will tell her that he wants to be a journalist. Julia will ask Laguna if he will write lyrics to her music. The dream sequence ends when Kiros knocks on the door and tells Laguna that they have new mission orders.

The Forest Owls
Squall, Zell and Selphie awaken back in the train cabin. Before the train arrives in Timber, the group discovers that they all had the same sort of dream. Once at Timber Station you will be met by a member of one of Timber's many resistance groups. He is a member of the Forest Owls and requires a password. Answer with 'But the Owls are still around'. You will be taken to the Forest Owls headquarters, a train. Once on the train you will have a brief conversation with two of the resistance members. Zone is the man dressed in blue, he seems to always have a stomach ache and pukes in the corner of the room. The other man, wearing the yellow cap is Watts, he is the groups intelligence agent. Zone will ask you to wake the Princess who is in her cabin, much to Squall's annoyance. Head up the stairs and through the door. The room to your left contains a save point and the other members of the Forest Owls. Continue through the door at the end and you will find yourself in the Princess cabin.

The Princess
The Princess is Rinoa, the girl who danced with Squall at the inauguration ball. When she awakens and notices Squall, she runs up to him and flings her arms around him. The ensuing conversation reveals that Rinoa was at the ball to see Head Master Cid and that she is an acquaintance of Seifer (boo). Rinoa seems sad that he has not come with you. Before you leave, Rinoa introduces you to her partner, her dog named

Angelo. Rinoa's limit breaks involves her pet dog. You can teach Angelo new attacks by collecting Pet Pals magazines. Back at the entrance Squall will introduce Zell and Selphie to Rinoa. In the briefing room Zone will explain their plan to kidnap the President of Deling. The plan involves switching the President's carriage with a replica while it is on route to Timber. Once the briefing is over save your position and prepare your team. Back at the entrance, talk to Watts.

Kidnapping the President of Deling
You will find yourself on the top of the train. Once you have jumped onto the Galbadian train you will need to disconnect the President's carriage. This is done by lowering yourself down the side of the train and inputting the code shouted to you by Rinoa.

Keys

▲ - enters 4
● - enter 1
■ - enters 3
✖ - enters 2
L1 - looks left
R1 - looks right
↑ – moves Squall up the train
↓ - lowers Squall down the train

You have to do this whilst avoiding being seen by the two Galbadian soldiers patrolling the corridor. Once you have begun inputting a code you cannot pull yourself up. Use the shoulder buttons to look left and right and always pull yourself up to the top of the train if you see either of the guards walking towards you. You will have to disconnect both ends of the President's carriage before you can switch it with the decoy carriage. For the first carriage you will need to input three codes and then five codes on the second carriage. Once the trains have been switched you will be returned to the entrance of the Forest Owls train. Head to the save point and save your position. Return to the entrance and talk to Watts. Rinao will enter and ask you if you are ready. Answer with 'Okay'. Once in the President carriage you will discover it is not in fact the President but a fake.

Fake President Deling
HP: 458
Attacks: Charge, Life Drain
Draw: Heal
Strategy: The fake President only has several hundred HP but once you have depleted this, the fake President transforms into a zombie called Gerogero.

Gerogero
HP: 2,450
Attacks: Claw Swipe, fire, Bolt, Flood Breath, Blind, Beserk.
Weakness: Fire, Earth, Holy.
Draw: Cure, Double, Berserk, Drain.
AP Gain: 20
Strategy: Use a barrage of fire-based attacks and guardian forces. Use Cure if any of your party becomes inflicted with Sadness, Silence or Blinded. It is possible to instantly kill Gerogero by throwing a Phoenix Down at it.

Back in the briefing room the Forest Owls are stunned at being tricked. Watts discovers the President's destination, the broadcasting office in Timber. Squall will ask Rinoa to show him her contact with Garden. A letter from Head Master Cid reveals that the team dispatched to her from Garden (Squall and co.) are permanently there until Timber wins its independence. Choose your party members then save. Watts will tell you that you can reach the broadcast station via a local train but at the moment neither the local or transcontinental trains are running. When you are ready tell Watts. You will be returned to the Timber station.

Timber and the Broadcast Station
Once you have reached the Timber station, the scene will switch to a group of Galbadian soldiers and reveals that they are aware of your presence in the city. This means you are likely to be involved in several random battles. First, head to the Pet Shop and buy some items. In the Pet Shop you can buy items for your guardian forces such as GF Potions and GF Phoenix Down. Once done, head right across the bridge towards Timber hotel. You will find a weapon shop nearby and a card player near the signboard. At the moment you cannot stay at the Timber Hotel because it is full of men from Galbaidia. Outside, make your way to the right, you will find a group of Galbadian soldiers harassing some Timber guards. When you draw closer you will be brought into combat. After the battle, the Timber guards will explain that they cannot allow you through. Head back to the train station and take the path in between the tracks. You will find yourself in front of a building that says 'Timber Maniacs'. Enter the building to the right. The women inside will ask you if you are going to the TV station. Go upstairs and look out the window. You will see an alley leading from the bar towards the TV station. Once outside, head right. Descend the stairs and head into the bar. Inside you will find a drunk blocking the way to the alley. Approach the drunk and start a conversation. Tell him about the card. The drunk will move aside allowing you to pass. Once in the alley you can save your position. You will find another card player sitting in the alley.

Want to get lots of cards without any risk? The drunk in the alley holds a lot of good cards and there is a save point directly opposite him. Save your game then challenge him. If you win, pick a card then save your game. If you lose load up your last save game and continue. Once you have all his good cards you can go and challenge some of the better players. You can use this strategy against most players but you might need to trek further to and from a save point. The majority of people in Timber are card players. The best players in Timber are the girl in the Timber Hotel looking at the model train set, and the teenager on the screen where you find the Timber Owls train. If you have lost any good cards while in Timber win them back before heading to the Broadcast Station because you will not return until much later in the game.

Go through the gate at the end of the alley, then make your way up the winding stairs. As you run up the stairs, a large TV screen comes to life with a strange written message. Rinoa decides to change her plan much to the dismay of Squall. Upset, Rinoa runs off, just as Zell/Selphie arrives. The President's broadcast will start. As the President begins, Seifer appears takes out the guards and restrains the President. Quistis will appear and try to prevent Seifer from killing the President. Once in the TV studio Quistis will tell you how Seifer escaped a discipline chamber, injuring some people in the process and she has followed him in the attempt to take him back to Balamb garden. Suddenly a mysterious women appears and casts a spell on Seifer. With Seifer in a trance like state he waves goodbye to Squall and then disappears through a magic portal along with the mysterious women. The President is left unharmed.

Escaping Timber
Outside the TV station, Squall and co will discover the Forest Owls hideout has been discovered and ransacked. Head back through the alley into the bar. Leave the bar and go into the building next to the 'Timber Maniacs' building. Inside, the owner will offer you sanctuary from the Galbadian forces (she is a member of one of Timber's many resistance movements, called the Forest Fox). A conversation will ensue regarding Seifer and the Sorceress. Talk to Quistis then try to leave. Squall and Quistis decide to head for Galbadian Garden. Reorganise your party then as you leave the owner will give you a Phoenix Down, a Potion, a Soft, an Antidote and a Remedy. Outside you notice a Galbadian soldier who turns out to be Watts. He will inform you that all the trains are about to be shut down except for the 'Campus East' train which leaves shortly. Head right and you will discover Zone disguised as an old man. He will provide everyone with passes. Head right, then up and around the bridge to reach the train platform. Once on the train speak to everyone leaving Zell until last. Select 'Wait for a while'. The train will stop at the Campus Station East. You will find yourself standing at a station on the world map. You will need to head to the mountains, Galbadian Garden is on the other side. The only way to reach Galbadian Garden is via a small forest leading through the mountains. Once in the forest Squall and co will collapse. The scene will fade.

Laguna's Fate
You will find yourself back in control of Laguna. Follow the path down into the industrial structure. In this area you will encounter Esther soldiers which mine this area. You should have no trouble defeating them. At the fork in the road head right and descend the ladder. Laguna will hurt his foot. When you reach the bottom, follow the path and then go up. From here head right until you reach a save point. Once you have saved take the next passage. Laguna and co will find themselves at the edge of a cliff looking out over the ocean. Miners will pile in behind you. You will have to fight them in a series of battles. First one miner, then two miners, one miner, two miners again then finally another two miners. When you defeat the last miner, it will perform a desperation attack called a Soul Crush against Kiros and Ward reducing their health to 1HP (unless their health is already dangerously low). Cornered and badly wounded, Laguna throws his friends over the cliff. Before Laguna can pluck up the courage to jump he slips and falls to his fate.

Far East Academy (Galbadian Garden)
Squall and co awaken from their slumber. You will need to restore your party's health because their health has been reduced to 1HP. Follow the path through the forest and you will find yourself on the other side of the mountains. Travel west and you will find a building similar to Balamb Garden. This is Galbadian Garden known as the Far East Academy. Once

you reach Galbadian Garden you will be greeted by a number of flying mecha. You will discover via a conversation between a couple of students that the President has formed an allegiance with the Sorceress. Organise your party then enter. An announcement will inform Squall and co to wait in the second floor reception. Ignore this if you want to play cards with several of the students.

Head down the right corridor. A male student will explain about 'character' cards and another about 'monster' cards. Ignore the two male students as they hold average cards but play the female student. The female student will claim she has no good cards. This is not true. Play her to win cards such as the Fujin/Raijin card and many of the boss cards. You can find a save point in the main hall.

From the main hall head up to find a set of stairs. Once upstairs enter the room opposite. You will find yourself in the reception area. Once there, Quistis will reveal that the Galbadian government has charged Seifer with the attack on the President and that he has been executed. At this point everyone except Squall says how much they liked Seifer even Zell admits to not entirely hating Seifer. The worst blow comes from Rinoa who admits she may have been in love with him. Squall storms out into the corridor. When you return into the reception area, only Quistis is left and she tells you to assemble at the main gate when you hear the announcement. There is another student who holds the rest of the boss cards. Make your way down the stairs and you will find Zell and a group of students performing press ups. A small boy will appear from the stairs. Challenge this demure card player and once you have all his good cards you should be in possession of all the level 1,2,3 and 4 monster cards, all the boss cards, and a few guardian force and character cards.

Enter Irvine Kinneas
Head towards the main hall and you will meet Raijin and Fujin. They have new orders for you from Headmaster Cid. They of course do not believe Seifer is dead and tell Squall they are off to Galbadia to find him. Head for the main gate. Follow Quistis to the others. Talk to Rinoa and a car will approach. The Headmaster of Galbadian Garden steps out. Headmaster Martine explains your new orders which involves the assassination of the Sorceress when she is in Deling City. Martine offers you the services of Galbadian Garden's best sniper, Irvine Kinneas. Irvine will introduce himself and causes the female characters hearts to race. After debriefing your party organise them (Squall does not quite appreciate Irvine's own party set up). Leave Galbadian Garden and head for the Far East Academy station. Head towards the train. You will have to pay 3,000 gil to buy a ticket to Deling from the train conductor. Once on the train follow Selphie and Irvine towards the cabin. Talk to Selphie then return to the rest of the group. Once there, Irvine will explain how lonely his life is and Zell in frustration nearly damages the train with one of his punches. The train will finally reach the Galbadian capital, Deling City.

Deling City
Once on the platform, the station attendant will inform you that both trains are at present undergoing maintenance. Leave the station via the escalator to arrive in the city centre of

Deling (You will find yourself in the same city where Laguna and co visited to hear Julia play). From here you will need to proceed to General Caraway's mansion located in the official district. Head to the bus stop. Wait until a bus pulls up, then speak to the bus stop attendant. He will ask you if you want a ride, answer with yes. The General's mansion is located on the first screen after the bus departs. Once you are off the bus head right towards the path. The General will not see you until you have proved your merit. The guard requires you to obtain a password. The guard tells you to travel to the 'Tomb of the Nameless King' and search for what is left of a Galbadian Garden student who has not returned from his test at the tomb. The password can be found on an item left near the tomb's entrance. The guard will give you a map of the tomb. The guard will give you the option to buy a hint or purchase a 'present location display device'. It is advisable to purchase a present location display device but if you are well prepared you will find negotiating the tomb quite easy. Once you are ready ask the guard to lead you to the city limits. The guard will suggest you hire a car as the wilderness is filled with monsters. You can hire a car for 3,500 gil. You can travel quickly and safely in a car but if you fight your way there you can gain experience and drawing opportunity. Exit Deling City to the left.

The Tomb of the Nameless King
When you reach the tomb, you will see two Garden students fleeing from the tomb. The monsters in the tomb are quite tough so rely on your guardian forces and drawn magic. Head inside the tomb. You should find yourself on a straight path into the tomb. When you reach the junction you should stumble across a gunblade. The gunblade should have a three-figure number inscribed on it, this is the password you are searching for. The password is randomly generated every time you play (so write it down). You can decide to head straight back to Deling City but the tomb holds another guardian force if you wish to search for it. You can exit the tomb quickly by pressing **Select** and then press ✖, but this will effect your SeeD ranking.

The Minotaur Brothers
This part of the game is optional, and is for those who want to collect the Minotaur Brothers guardian force. If you to skip this optional quest, go to 'The Assassination Plan'. Take a look at the map of the tomb given to you by the General's guard (press Select to view the map). At the bottom is the tomb's entrance. There are four areas you need to take note of: An area to the far right of the tomb, an area to the far left, an area at the very top, and finally an area in the centre of the tomb. You first need to head towards the far right of the tomb. At the first junction head right, follow the passage until you reach the next junction. Head right again. Once you reach the area on the far right of the tomb you will find a small room with a statue. Talk to the statue and it will move. This is where you fight the first boss of the tomb. This creature is called Sacred and is a minotaur.

Sacred
HP: 800 – 37,000
Attacks: Regeneration, Basic Attack
Weakness: Poison and Wind attacks. Absorbs Earth based attacks.
Draw: Shield, Barrier, Berserk, Life
AP Gain: 20

Strategy: Sacred will cast regeneration on itself so to prevent this cast Silence/Dispel. Thrash the beast using your guardian forces and drawn magic.

Once defeated, Scared will flee swearing he will remember you. Restore your characters health and then head towards the north section of the tomb (at the very top of your map). Once there you will find a small room containing a chain locking a barrier. The barrier is holding back a wall of water. Unlock the chain (using ✖) to free the water. You will now need to negotiate to the far left of the tomb. Here you will find a set of gears and a lever. Activate the gears (using ✖) The released water will flow in, lowering the drawbridge to the brothers hideout. The drawbridge is located opposite the entrance in the centre of the tomb. Once there, you will encounter Sacred again, but this time he calls for his big brother, Minotaur for help.

Sacred
HP: 800 – 37,000
Attacks: Regeneration, Basic Attack
Weakness: Poison and Wind attacks. Absorbs Earth based attacks.
Draw: Shield, Barrier, Berserk, Life

Minotaur
HP: 500 – 28,000
Attacks: Basic Attack
Weakness: Poison and Wind attacks. Absorbs Earth based attacks.
Draw: Shield, Barrier, Berserk, Life
Combined Attack: Earthquake
AP Gain: 40
Strategy: Concentrate your attacks against Minotaur, he is the most dangerous. Cast Silence on them to prevent them regenerating their health. Summon your guardian forces as much as possible because they will cause damage to both minotaurs.

Once you have defeated both brothers, you will have released the spirit of the nameless King. As a reward, the King gives you the brothers as guardian forces and their playing card. Now make your way out of the tomb.

The Assassination Plan
Once outside the tomb, save your position and restore your party's health. Trek back to Deling City. Make your way back to the General's mansion. Walk up to the General's guard and tell him the password (the three-figure code found on the gunblade in the tomb). You will need to tell him the password in reverse for example, if the password is 123 you need to tell the guard '3', '2', '1'. If you tell him correctly, the guard will allow you to continue to the mansion. Once in the mansion, Rinoa will leave and 'complain' about being made to wait. General Caraway will then enter. Squall and co will discover General Caraway is Rinoa's father and he does not want her participating in the mission.

General Caraway will explain the specifications of the assassination mission. You also will discover the Sorceress is called Edea. General Caraway will take you on a guided tour of Deling City and explain the mission further. With the briefing over, you are free to explore the city, buy supplies, play cards etc. When you are done head back to the General's mansion. Once back at the mansion, General Caraway will split your party into two groups consisting of Squall and Irvine as the sniper team and then Zell, Quitis and Selphie as the arch team.

Squall will leave and you will take control of Quistis. As you leave, Rinoa will come running in. Quistis calls Rinoa a rebellious daughter then leaves, leaving Rinoa alone, unwanted and feeling useless. The scene will switch to Squall, who believes there is no good or evil, just personal viewpoint. General Caraway will continue to brief Squall and co about the mission ahead. Control will switch to Quistis. Head back to the General's mansion. Once there, Quistis, Zell and Selphie, become trapped in the mansion by the automatic lock intended for Rinoa, who leaves just before Quistis and co arrive.

Rinoa Confronts Edea
You will now be in control of Rinoa. Rinoa decides to prove herself by presenting Edea with the Odyne Amulet. Rinoa believes the amulet will restrict Edea's magic powers. You can save your position using the save point to the left. To reach Edea's apartment you will need to climb up the crates and then jump to the ledge. From the ledge head left, then climb the ladder. Climb up to the roof. Rinoa will find herself in a large room, in front of her is a throne where Edea is sitting. Rinoa approaches Edea, amulet in hand but before she can place it around Edea she is thrown across the room. Edea's beak like mask slides back revealing the face of a beautiful young women. She rises from her throne and steps out of the room. Rinoa, deep within Edea's powers follows trance like. Hidden deep within the crowd, Squall and Irvine get their first glance of their target, the Sorceress Edea. Before the crowd, Edea begins to ridicule them calling them 'Shameless, filthy wretches', much to the dismay of President Deling. When President Deling tries to interrupt her, Edea summons a ball of energy and electrifies him. Leaving President Deling a smouldering corpse and the crowd cheering louder than before, Edea returns to her chamber. Edea animates two stone gargoyles, which bound over the crowd and take up position around her chamber.

The scene will switch back to Quistis and co locked in the General's mansion. Look at the painting on the right. The painting is of a statue in the image of a girl holding a glass. There is a similar statue in the corner of the room. Take a glass from the cabinet and place it on the statue. This will reveal a secret passage behind the statue. Enter the passage. In the passage you will find a save point. Once you have saved your position, head down the ladder. The passage leads into the sewers. Climb over the gear to reach the other side of the tunnel.

Saving Rinoa
Back in the control of Squall, follow Irvine through the crowd and through the main gate. Save your game and equip Irvine's guardian forces (everything will be reset). Follow Rinoa's route up the crates and up onto roof. Once on the roof Squall and Irvine will find President Deling lying dead on the floor. Head towards the door. Once at the door follow the red carpet into Edea's chamber (note there is a hatch to the right). In the chamber you will find Rinoa being attacked by the two animated gargoyles.

Iguions
HP: 1,000+
Attacks: Bite, Whip, Acid Breath
Draw: Heal, Cure, Petrify, Carbunkle

AP Gain: 20 (10 AP each)
Strategy: Attack with guardian forces and when you are low on HP, draw Heal spells. If either of your characters are turned in to stone from the Iguions's acid breath use Cure, which you can also draw. Remember to draw the guardian force Carbunkle.

With both creatures defeated the heroes will run to Rinoa's side. Rinoa is overcome with fear. She desperately pleads with you not to leave her. Head towards the entrance and use the hatch to the right. This is a secret passage to the clock room. In the clock room you will find the rifle for Irvine.

Lost in the Sewers
Back to Quistis and co lost in the sewers. The ladder leading up is found to the right of the first junction. Head left. When you have passed the ladder it will fall across the sewage. Cross the ladder and head left to find a magic stone. The head left then up. From here continue up. Head right and continue right again. Ride the left cog up then ride the right cog down. Head right. Ride the cog up. Continue up until you reach the ladder. Remember you can climb across some of the gears as long as they turn in the same direction as you want to go. Many of the doors can be opened and if you find yourself at a dead end then you have gone the wrong way. If you encounter a huge spider while trekking through the sewers, it is advisable to flee rather than fight, you will find it will take ages to defeat it. Once you have reached the ladder, save your game and climb up. You will find yourself in the arch. Climb up to the next floor. Look through the window. The time will hit 20.00.00. As Edea's float passing under the arch. Press the switch in the room to drop the gate and trap the Sorceress.

The Trapped Sorceress
The time has come, the clock room rises giving Irvine a clear shot at the Sorceress. Fear overcomes Irvine who admits to not having the confidence to fire the killing shot. Calmly, Squall convinces him to fire. The shot is deflected by Edea. Before continuing organise your party. Squall will fight Seifer alone but the battle against Edea is a team effort with Irvine and Rinoa. Squall is forced to fight the Sorceress hand to hand. Leaping from the clock room, Squall jumps into a nearby car and drives towards the arch and the Sorceress. Before facing Edea you will face her knight and Squall's rival Seifer.

Seifer
HP: 200 – 1,200
Strategy: Squall faces Seifer alone. Seifer's physical attacks are pretty weak and his HP quite low. Simply summon your most powerful guardian force and Seifer should quickly bow out.

Edea
HP: 1,500 – 7,000
Attacks:
Draw: Cura, Dispel, Double, Life.
AP Gain: 20
Strategy: During this battle Squall will be joined by Rinoa and Irvine. Cast Carbunkle (if you drew it from the Iguions), this will create a barrier that will deflect magic attacks back at its caster. This prevents you from casting healing magic on your characters as it will be deflected at Edea. If you need to

restore a characters HP use a potion. Edea may cast Dispel but can only cast it against a single character. Edea will spend three turns removing your barrier. While she is occupied doing this, summon your guardian forces and draw magic from her. Edea possess some good magic so take time to draw from her. If you lose the battle it is not game over but you will miss out on 20 AP.

As the battle ensures, Edea summons large shards of ice and projects them at Squall and Rinoa. Rinoa narrowly misses being hit, but Squall is impaled and falls to the ground below.

The Monster Rancher of Winhill

The scene returns to Laguna. A small girl Ellone will enter and tell 'Uncle' Laguna that she is going to the pub to see Raine. Follow the girl downstairs. You will find a magic stone in the cupboard. Talk to Ellone then go outside. Follow Ellone into the pub next door. Here you meet Raine, the women responsible for looking after Laguna after the incident in Esther. Kiros will enter. During the ensuing conversation you will get the chance to ask him about Ward and Julia. Ward is well and working in a Galbadian Prison. He can no longer talk. Julia, believing her love died in the Timber war married General Caraway after his comforting her. Without the men to defend the town monsters have invaded and Laguna has become the resident monster hunter. Kiros will join Laguna with his monster hunting. Leave the pub and head towards the bridge. Laguna's route takes him towards the flower shop and down to the item shop at the end of the village then back to the pub. Laguna must defeat any monsters he encounters on his patrol. The majority of monsters you will encounter are Caterchipillars and Bite Bugs. During their patrol, Kiros will converse with Laguna about his future. Head upstairs and talk to Raine. Talk to Ellone then return downstairs. Exit the pub and return to Laguna's room in the house next door. Save then rest.

Prisoners of Edea

The scene returns to Zell, Selphie, Quistis and Rinoa imprisoned by the Galbadian army. You will find yourself in control of Zell. Talk to everyone then talk to Rinoa again. The scene will switch to Squall who is being held in a portable cell. Back to Zell and co. Three Galbadian guards enter and try to take Rinoa. Due to Zell's resistance against them taking Rinoa they start to beat him. Seifer enters Squall's cell and throws him against the cell wall. Unconscious, Squall is dragged from his cell by two orange creatures known as Moombas. Squall awakens hung up on a torture wall. Seifer begins torturing Squall demanding the meaning of SeeD. Back with Zell and co. Selphie tries to heal Zell using her magic but is getting limited success due to the magic barrier around the cells. A Moomba enters their cell carring a tray. When the Moomba trips and drops the tray a guard will enter and try to punish the Moomba. Decide to help the Moomba. Seifer will continue to torture Squall. As Zell talks to Quistis then talk to the Moomba. The group will decide to try and retrieve their weapons held on the eighth floor. Once Zell escapes his cell make sure you junction a guardian force and some magic. Head up the stairs to the eigth floor. You will find your weapons being guarded by two Galbadian soldiers. You should have no trouble defeating the two soldiers (Just summon a GF like Shiva or Ifrit). Squall will escape his torture with the help of three Moombas who continue to call him Laguna? Back in the cell, Zell will return

Quistis and Selphie's weapons. Before you can go in search of Squall, Biggs and Wedge enter the cell.

Biggs
HP: 1,400 – 2,300
Attacks: Machine Gun, Charge
AP Gain: 5

Wedge
HP:1,400 – 2,200
Attacks: Flame, Sword Swipe.
AP Gain: 5
Strategy: Biggs and Wedge are tougher than they were at the Communication Tower in Dollet but you should still have no trouble defeating them, Either cast a couple of guardian forces or try this. Wedge feels Biggs bullies him so cast Confuse on either of them and when one attacks the other, the other will counter attack. If Biggs strikes Wedge, Wedge will yell at Biggs to stop picking on him.

When defeated, Biggs will sound the alarm. Now is your chance to find Squall who is being held captive on the thirteenth floor. Follow the Moombas up the stairs to the thirteenth floor. Higher up, you will find a wall stopping you from heading straight up the stairs and forcing you around the ledge. Here you are likely to be involved in more random battles. Once on the thirteenth floor head to the right and enter the door surrounded by Moombas (still chanting Laguna, is he here or do the Moombas mistake someone else for him?) Inside you will find Squall. Zell will throw Squall his gunblade. Outside Squall's cell the group will decide to try to escape using the portable cell Squall was transported in. Zell heads to the control room where he can operate the portable cell. Once in the control room press the red button on the control panel. Once you are on the ground floor open the gate. Coal will pile out revealing the prison is built into the ground. You will find yourself back in control of Zell. Run around the ledge to the left. You will notice Zell is being chased by Galbadian guards. Near the stairs Zell will be knocked out by a warden, suddenly Squall will appear and save Zell. Just as Selphie and Quistis appear everyone will be pinned down by gunfire until Irvine appears and opens fire. Rinoa appears behind Irvine and then promptly kicks him down the stairs. The group will split into two teams. Squall, Rinoa and one other member will head up to the fourteenth while Irvine and two other members will head down towards the third floor. Have Squall's party fight their way up the prison. When you reach the thirteen floor the scene will switch to Irvine and his party. As you go check the other cells. There are a couple of card players who will charge you to play them, a Combat King 001 and magic stones. Once Irvine's team reaches the third floor the scene will switch back to Squall's team. On the fourteenth floor, talk to the Moombas to receive a guardian force rename card and a tent. Head up the stairs situated at the bottom of the screen. Continue up until you find yourself outside. Here you will face a Galbadian Commander and two GIM52A.

Galbadian Commander
HP: 250 – 5,000
Attacks: Machinegun Fire, Charge, Fire Blast, Heal, Aura, Shield
Draw: Fire, Bolt, Ice
AP Gain: 2

GIM52A x2
HP: 1,500 – 20,000
Attacks: Charge, Rocket Missiles
Draw: Haste, Sense
AP Gain: 2
Strategy: Concentrate your attacks on the Commander. He has a tendency of casting invincibility on the two GIM52A and their dead seeker missile can cause 300+ damage. Just summon a couple of powerful guardian forces such as Quezacotl and lightning magic against the GIM52A's.

After the battle, head back down to the control room. Head back outside and make your way across the bridge. As you cross, the prison will start to submerge. The bridge will collapse leaving Squall hanging. Quickly shimmy to the right, towards the flashing green light. If you are not quick enough the prison will submerge into the ground and it will be game over. Your party will appear from a garage. Your party will split up and take the two vehicles inside. Your party will end up at a deserted road. Once in control of Squall, draw from the magic stone and then speak to Selphie. You will see a volley of missiles launched from the Galbadian Missile Base. Selphie becomes desperately worried about Trabia Garden. Selphie will suggest that the party splits into two groups. One will head to Balamb Garden and warn them of the missiles while a second group will head to the Galbadian Missile Base and try to destroy it to prevent the Galbadians from firing any more missiles. You will need to organise your party into two groups. Squall will go to Balamb and Selphie to the missile base. I would suggest you send your strongest characters with Squall. Squall's mission is tougher compared with Selphie's.

The Great Train Robbery
Squall's team will find themselves at a deserted train station. Make your way around the fence. Run left until you reach the engine. Once inside the train will begin to move. Irvine will taunt the chasing Galbadian soldier until he is forced to give up the chase.

The Galbadian Missile Base
With Squall and co on their way to Balamb the scene switches back to Selphie and her team. You will find yourself on the world map. The Galbadian Missile Base is located south of Deling City. Enter the missile base in the vehicle and Selphie's team will disguise themselves as Galbadian soldiers. Enter the building near where you stop. Inside, examine the door. One of your party members will reveal an ID Card. Use the ID Card and head inside. You will notice a Galbadian soldier guarding a door. Your objective is to sneak into the base and sabotage the missile launch. To do this you must follow any orders you are given and act inconspicuous. Throughout the base you will be given several options on how to act when you are prompted. It is always best to act cool as you will encounter random battles if you are revealed. You will need to decide on how to act as you passed the first guard. Once past the first guard head right. Continue right on the next screen. Opposite the stairs is a door which leads to a hangar containing missile warheads. The console to the right of the door is where you reprogram the missiles. The room to the right is where you activate the bases self-destruct. The passage to the left leads to the observation deck. Head down the stairs and go left towards the observation deck. Talk to the maintenance team there. Head back towards the stairs and enter the maintenance soldiers in the hangar. Return to the maintenance soldiers on the observation deck. Head back up the stairs and back towards the first Galbadian soldier. Talk to him and he will leave. You can now enter the control room. Inside approach the control panel. Smash the control panel. Eventually Selphie will cause a blackout. Outside the room you will be confronted by two Galbadian soldiers. When they enter the control room, follow them in and bundle them. Return towards the hangar. A Galbadian maintenance soldier will ask you to help with moving a dislodged missile. Agree and help push the missile back into place. Return outside and access the computer to the right of the door. First select 'Target'. Then select 'Set Error Ratio' and hold right to set the error ratio to maximum. Select 'Data Upload'. Then select 'Yes' to upload the data. Head upstairs and enter the room on the right. Here you will encounter two Galbadian soldiers and a commander. Remember when fighting any Galbadian soldiers to draw from them. Examine the control panel and enter the next room. Selphie will activate the base self-destruct. You can set the self-destruct between 10 to 40 minutes. You now need to exit the base. If you selected a time less than 20 minutes you can use the door in the self-destruct room. If you selected a higher time limit than 20 minutes you will need to backtrack through the base.

Selphie Exposed
If your disguise is revealed you will be unable to change the missile error ratio at first. Instead you will have to go directly to the self-destruct room and set a time limit. Then you will have to work your way back to the entrance of the base. During this time you will be involved in random battles with Galbadian soldiers while the self-destruct countdown continues. A good tactic is to flee rather than fight to save time. There, Selphie will remember that she needs to set the missile error ratio and you will have to work your way back through the base. To access the computer you will need an ID Card and a password. Outside the self-destruct room you will find a wounded guard. He will give you his ID card and the computer password 'EDEA'. Access the computer. First select 'Target'. Then select 'Set Error Ratio' and hold right to set the error ratio to maximum. Select 'Data Upload'. Then select 'Yes' to upload the data. When you are finished you will need to evacuate the base.

Outside the base, Selphie's team will be met by the disgruntled missile base commander and his new toy.

BGH251F2
HP: 4,000 – 8,500
Attacks: Machinegun Attack, Laser Beam
Draw: Protect, Barrier, Stop
AP Gain: 4
Strategy: Unleash guardian forces such as Shiva, Quezacotl and the Brothers. The BGH251F2's Laser Beam that can do up to 900+ damage. Have at least one character with the 'Item' ability so you can use a Phoenix Down on any fallen characters. Once you have destroyed the BGH251F2 you will face its crew, a Galbadian commander and two soldiers. If you defeated the BGH251F2 you should find defeating the three Galbadian soldiers 'a piece of Galbadian cake'.

You have two opportunities to increase your SeeD ranking while at the missile base. First, do not reveal your true identities while in the missile base, this requires you to follow any orders you are given. Second, you need to exit the base and defeat the boss in under ten minutes, no easy feat if you are relying on your guardian forces who can have some long attack animation.

Balamb - Garden versus SeeD

Squall's team arrives back at Balamb Garden to discover it is in total chaos, with Garden candidates hunting down SeeD candidates. Once inside, the Garden faculty will demand to know your allegiance, to Headmaster Cid or to Lord Norg. If you say your allegiance is with Cid you will encounter random battles in the campus, if you say it is with Norg you can freely move about. Your aim is to find Headmaster Cid and Xu. SeeD students are being attacked by Garden candidates all over the campus. You will need to visit each area and protect any SeeD candidates. In each area you will encounter a Garden Faculty Member who will summon a monster to fight you.

The Library: Here you will face a Grat. Talk to the SeeD candidates inside and you will receive a Remedy.

Training Centre: Inside you will find two Garden candidates and a Faculty Member. Follow them and you will find them attacking a SeeD candidate and two children. The Faculty Member will summon a T-Rexuar. Before you leave talk to the female cadet and she will give you a Remedy.

Parking Lot: You will face an Iguion here. You will find several students have a hologram of Headmaster Cid. Talk to the cadet and you will receive a Tent.

Dormitory: Here the Faculty Member will summon a Caterchipiller.

Cafeteria: The Faculty Member will summon a Bomb

Quad: You will not face a battle here. Head to the stage and three SeeD candidates will jump down. The middle cadet will give you a Hi-Potion.

Infirmary: Here you will face a Granaldo. Talk to Dr Kadowaki. And she will give you an Elixir.

Once you have settled all the fights, head to the elevator. You will get a glimpse of Xu entering the elevator. Follow her up. Head past Quistis's classroom and you will find Xu. Xu will take you to Cid who is hiding up on the third floor. Squall will tell Cid about the barrage of missiles heading towards Balamb Garden. Headmaster Cid will give Squall a key to unlock Balamb's defensive system situated deep below the campus. Save your game by talking to Cid then enter the elevator.

Balamb's Defensive System

While riding the down the elevator shuts out. Examine the hatch to reveal an escape route. Climb down the ladder, but be quick as the elevator will regain power and start to descend. Head down the passage and down through the hatch. In the room with the valve wheel, you will need to tap the ■ button quickly to open the hatch. If you fail, do not worry as one of your party members will join in and help. Once you have

succeeded climb down the ladder. Walk down the stairs, you will find a magic stone near the pillar. With Squall, climb the ladder. It will break and he will be thrown into a control room. Activate the console to the right then return down the ladder. Once down on the ground, look for a flashing green light. Examine the green light and you will find a ladder. Climb down. Push the lever to open the bay doors. Save your game then head across the bridge. On the bridge you will face two Oilboyles.

Oilboyles x2
HP: 1,000 – 5,000
Attacks: Grab and Bite
Draw: Esuna, Blind, Confuse
Weakness: Fire
AP Gain: 20
Strategy: Oilboyles weakness is fire. Summon Ifrit and cast fire magic such as Fire, Fira and Firaga. If any of your characters gets an abnormal status, simple draw the esuna spell form the Oilboyles and cast it on the affected member.

With the Oilboyles vanquished head across the bridge and down the ladder. Examine the console to start the gears into motion. Squall and co will be transported to the third floor. Suddenly, just as the Galbadian missiles hit their target, Balamb Garden takes off and begins to fly. Talk to Cid then exit. Take the elevator down to the second floor and head past Quistis's classroom. Head through the door at the end of the corridor. On the second floor deck, Squall and co will admire the Balamb scenery. If Rinoa is in your party you will get an extra scene with her admiring the beautiful scenery. Head back towards the elevator. You will be returned to Headmaster Cid's office, he will pass the controls of Balamb Garden to Squall. Balamb Garden will come to a halt, floating above the sea. Squall awakes back in his quarters. If Rinoa is in your party she will enter and drag Squall to the campus cafeteria. If Zell is in your party you will find him in line waiting for his favourite meal, Hot Dogs. Head to the lobby. There a Garden Faculty Member will tell you to go to the basement. Head towards the elevator. You will be rejoined by the rest of your party there. Use the elevator to reach the basement. Here you will face Master Norg.

Norg
HP: 4,000 – 13,000
Draw: Protect, Shell, Heal, Leviathan
AP Gain: 20
Strategy: Norg is the hardest boss you will have faced so far and requires strategic fighting rather than pure strength. Norg sits on an egg like throne. On either side of the throne are two Orbs. They change colour from blue to yellow to red. Once they turn red they unleash powerful magic spells against you. You can turn the orbs back to blue by using a strong attack. Summoning guardian forces will hurt Norg but not the two magic orbs. Before you can face Norg you must destroy the middle section protecting him. Have one character unleash powerful magic and summon guardian forces while the two other characters attack the magic orbs using psychical attacks. Using this strategy the orbs should be unable to cast any spells against you. Once you have destroyed the middle section of Norg's throne you will be able to attack him directly. You can cast Carbunkle on your party, this will reflect most of Norg's

and the left orbs magic back at Norg. You will still need to attack the right orb as this casts dispel, removing your reflect spell. The downside is that you will be unable to use healing spells, if you do so they will be reflected at Norg restoring his health. You can use potions though so at least one of your characters must be able to use items from your inventory. Remember to draw from Norg as you can get a new guardian force, Leviathan.

Edea's White SeeDs
Confused as ever, Squall decides to try and get some answer from Cid. Head to the elevator and ride up to the lobby. Head to Squall's room to rest and restore lost HP. Head to the Infirmary and talk to Doctor Kadowaki. Talk to Cid. Headmaster Cid will reveal that the sorceress Edea is his wife and that Norg was financially responsible for Garden. Cid also reveals that it was Edea's idea behind the creation of SeeD and ideologically more than simple mercenaries for hire. If you want to buy some items you will now find a item seller in the training centre by the wooden planks. Head towards the lobby and you will meet Xu. She will tell you to head to the second floor deck where a boat has requested to dock. Once there you will meet white SeeD's here to protect Ellone. Cid will enter and ask you to find Ellone. Ellone can be found in the Library. Once you have found her, squall will eventually leave with the white SeeDs (Ellone is the girl who peeped into the infirmary at the beginning of the game and the girl you saved in the training centre. Is she any relation to the Ellone in Laguna's time?). Once Ellone sails off into the sunset, Squall will return to his quarters. There he will dream of a small boy standing outside a house in the rain. Squall will be awoken by Rinoa (or Zell depending on who is in your party) and will drag Squall out for a walk. Their walk will be interrupted by an announcement from Headmaster Cid who has lost control of Balamb Garden and steered into Fisherman's Horizon (narrowly missing the town's fisherman master).

Fisherman's Horizon
Balamb Garden will dock at Fisherman's Horizon, a town situated in the centre of the ocean. Cid will ask Squall to enter the town and ask the Mayor for assistance with repairs to Balamb Garden. The Mayor's house can be found in the centre of Fisherman's Horizon. From the control room head down to the second floor and make your way past Quistis's classroom. Enter the door with the flashing light. Outside, head to the far right and ride the elevator down into the town. Cross the train tracks and head down the slope to the Mayor's house. Once inside, head up to the second floor. Here you will meet the Mayor who appears to be an ageing surf dude. He will offer assistance to the repairs on Balamb Garden, but demands you leave as quickly as possible. The Mayor feels that conflict can be resolved without violence and this is a contradiction to what SeeD and Garden stands for. Challenge the Mayor to a game of cards and you might be able to win the Quezacotl card from him. Leave the Mayor's house. Outside head to the right and you will find Martine, the Headmaster of Galbadian Garden. He holds all the level 7 cards but beware he is an excellent card player, (I hope the dreaded 'Random' rule has not spread this far yet).

Galbadian Army versus Ageing Surf Dude
At the peak of the slope, the Mayor and his wife will appear, the Galbadian army has arrived in Fisherman's Horizon. The Mayor will run off to talk things over (I do not think that will work). Follow him right, just follow the train tracks. At the end of the train track you will find the Mayor being threatened by a Galbadian Commander. Choose to intervene and the Galbadian Commander will call in the BGH251F2, well actually it's the same one that Selphie's team confronted at the missile base, looking not very hot. Just use the same tactics you used the first time you met this thing. It has between 5000 – 8000 HP and if you have the 'Mug' ability you can steal some Adamantine which you will need to remodel some of your weapons. Vanquished, the BGH251F2 submerges into the sea. Suddenly Selphie and her team (rather wet for wear) appear. Selphie and co are alive and somehow survived the missile attack on the missile base (probably by hiding in the BGH251F2). After the reunion everyone will leave except Squall and Rinoa. Talk to Rinoa then you can explore the town further.

You will find an issue of Timber Maniacs in the house at the end of the train tracks.
You will find a weapon smith at the end of the pier opposite the inn. Talk to the boy trying to fish.
When you have finished in the town head back to Garden. Along the way back, you will be met by Irvine. Once in Garden, head to the Quad. There you will find Selphie and the stage in ruins. Try to cheer Selphie up then head to the control room. Once there, Cid will promote Squall, putting him in charge of defeating Edea. Squall will return to his quarters.

Concert for Squall
Back in Fisherman's Horizon, Selphie and the rest of the group decide to cheer up Squall and congratulate him on his promotion by staging a concert. You must choose four instruments, one each for Selphie, Irvine, Zell and Quistis. There are eight instruments to choose from. For best results pick these instruments (any character can play any instrument).

Ballet – Sax, Electric Guitar, Piano and Bass Guitar.
Irish Folk – Guitar, Violin, Flute and Tap.

Rinoa will lure Squall to the concert. There they will talk and look at Irvine's dirty magazine.The evening ends with Squall quarrelling with Rinoa. Back in his bed, Squall will again dream of a boy standing in the rain. Once Squall is awake head to the control room. There, Xu will suggest Garden return back to Balamb. Selphie will go on vacation so you will be unable to use her in your party.

Zell's Troubled Home
Head back to Balamb town/port. Docked in the port you will find Galbadian Garden which has the ability to levitate. You will need to land just outside the town and enter on foot. Once in the town you will discover that the Galbadian army has taken control of the town and is preventing anyone from entering or leaving. Talk to the man and lady then talk to the Galbadian guard. Repeat and the guard will allow you to enter believing you have information on Ellone. Before you enter, Zell will appear and ask to be in your party (it is his home after all). Reorganise your party then continue. Enter Zell's house. The Galbadian army is using the hotel as a head quarters so you will be unable to stay there. Instead, Zell allows the party to

stay in his room. There you can save and rest. Before you leave you can punch his punching bag.

Leaving Balamb

If you need to leave Balamb for any reason you will first need to do this sequence. Head into the dining room of Zell's house. There his nephew will run out of the house. Head outside and enter the house next door. Inside you will find the daughter of the two people outside the Galbadian barricade. Zell's nephew will leave and head to the barricade. He will signal you to talk to the guard allowing him to give a message to the man and women outside. From then on just talk to Zell's nephew and he will distract the guard allowing you to leave.

Head to the hotel and try to find the Commander. The Commander is on his patrol. Head to the dock and talk to the soldier with the dog. Head back to Zell's house and talk to Zell's Ma. Head to the train station. From here go back to the dock. There the dog, catching a scent will run off. Follow the dog back to the train station. The dog will chase the Commander from his slumber in one of the train carriages. The Commander is non other than Seifer's buddy Raijin. Chase Raijin to the hotel. At the hotel you will face Raijin and two Galbadian soldiers.

Raijin
HP: 8,000 – 12,000
Attacks:
AP Gain: 12
Strategy: Summon all your guardian forces except Quezacotl as Raijin can absorb thunder attacks. Raijin relies on strong psychical attacks so draw Protect from him and cast it on your party. Raijin's spinning pole attack does 400+ damage.

Raijin will eventually retreat into the hotel, Squall and co will follow. Inside Raijin will be joined by Fujin.

Raijin
HP: 5,000 – 23,000 +
AP Gain: 12
Fujin
HP: 8,000
AP Gain: 10
Strategy: Concentrate your attacks against Raijin who's HP and high damaging attacks. Draw Pandemona from Fujin and Protect from Raijin. Cast Protect on all your party members. Fujin and Raijin each hold magic that can be drawn from one and cast against the other.

When both have been defeated the Galbadian forces will leave Balamb. Selphie will return from her vacation. Selphie will ask to visit her home, Trabia Garden.

Trabia Garden

Trabia garden is located on the large continent to the north of Balamb. Once there, Selphie will rush inside. Follow her over the wall. If Selphie was in your party, she will leave temporarily, do not worry about reorganising your party, you will not face any battle while in Trabia. Inside you will find Selphie talking with one of her friends. Talk to Selphie, she will ask you to wait for her at the basketball court. The basketball court is located on the left side of Trabia Garden. Before rushing to the basketball court take your time to explore Trabia Garden, draw

from magic stones and play cards against some of the students. Once there, Selphie will enter and Irvine will tell the group about his childhood growing up in an orphanage. Leave the house and walk down to the beach. Suddenly everything is revealed, the whole group including Seifer (except Rinoa) all grew up in the same orphanage before enrolling in Garden and by junctioning guardian forces blocks early memories. Even worse, the Matron of the orphanage is non-other than the sorceress Edea. Back in the present everyone will leave except Rinoa. Talk to Rinoa and the screen will fade.

Edea's Orphanage and Galbadian Garden

The orphanage is located to the west of the large southern continent. Here you will face the Galbadian Garden. From the control room ride the elevator down. Reform your party, then talk to Quistis. Now head down to the first floor and go to the Quad. There you will find Zell giving orders to Garden and SeeD cadets. Talk to Zell and then to Rinoa when she appears. A scene will take place where Zell gives Rinoa Squall's ring. Return to the control room. As Galbadian Garden nears Balamb, Galbadian soldiers riding motorcycles are jettisoned towards Balamb. You will be put in control of Zell, head left. Galbadian Garden will ram Balamb causing a potion of the Quad to be ripped apart. Rinoa falls and is left hanging for her life. Head right towards the lobby, here you will face random battles with Galbadian forces. There you will find Squall's party. Squall's party will need to head to the front gate. Reform your party and return to the lobby. Ride the elevator up and head to Quistis's classroom. Green rocket-pack clad Galbadian soldiers attack Balamb. You will face four of these green Galbadian soldiers in the classroom. After the battle talk to the lady and she will escort the children to safety. Return back to the control room and talk to Dr Kadowaki. She will have Squall motivate everyone. Squall rallies the cadets to take the battle from Balamb Garden to Galbadian Garden. Ride the elevator down to the second floor. Talk to the female student near the elevator then head past Quistis's classroom. Here you will find the missing boy. Suddenly, Squall will be ambushed by a Galbadian Paratrooper.

The Galbadian Paratrooper Minigame

After Squall has been hit, you will be given a choice of what to do next. First select ' Look around for another option', and then examine the emergency exit and select 'Press the button for the emergency exit'. Squall and the Paratrooper will tumble out of the exit and find themselves hanging from the Paratrooper's rocket-pack. During this mini game you will have three buttons at you disposal.
Punch - ✖
Block - ■
Kick - ▲
Punching is slow to perform but packs quite a punch. Kicking is faster but not as strong as a punch. There is a third attack at your disposal. After blocking several enemy attacks you will be able to unleash a Deathblow using ●. If you fail to beat the Paratrooper when the time runs out, who ever has the most health will be decided the winner. If you lose, you will get the chance to try again but with more health.
Squall will use the Paratroopers rocket-pack to fly to Rinoa's rescue. Squall and Rinoa glide over a huge battle pitched against SeeD and Garden cadets against Galbadian soldiers. Landing safely outside Galbadian Garden, Squall and Rinoa prepare to enter inside. Rinoa will try and return Squall's ring

who lets her keep it. You will get the chance to rename the lion that embellishes Squall's ring. It is originally a guardian force called Griever and is possessed by the games end boss. When you are ready enter Galbadian Garden.

Infiltrating Galbadian Garden

Once inside Galbadian Garden you will be rejoined by the rest of your friends and be asked to reorganised your party. Save your game before continuing.

Card Key 1

Head right. In the passage with three doors go right up the stairs. On the floor above you will find Fujin and Raijin. Talk to them, then go left down the passage. Enter the room on the right. Inside you will find a Garden cadet. Talk to him and he will give you the Card Key 1. Return to the save point.

Card Key 2

From the save point, head left. Enter the door on the left and you will find yourself in an ice ring. Cross the ice ring and go through the door on the right. Head right. The cadet in here will give you the second card key. Return back to the save point.

Card Key 3 and Cerberus

Head right and up the stairs. Continue up to the next floor. Go through the door and into the stadium. Jump down onto the field and head left into the building. Make your way down ignoring the stairs and continue until you reach the main hall. You will find Cerberus in the centre of the main hall. Before fighting him, circle around the hall to the save point behind Cerberus.

Cerberus

HP: 7,000 – 10,000
AP Gain: 30
Strategy: Battling Cerberus is optional but when summoned gives all your party members the ability to cast double and triple magic. Cerberus has some damaging attacks including Quake which causes 600+ damage to all party members, it can cast three times in a row if you allow it to cast triple on itself. When it does so counter with Dispel. Summon your guardian forces such as Ifrit but refrain from using Quezacotl and Pandemona.

Save your game and then head left. Enter the door on the left and the cadet inside will give you the third and final card key. With the third card key in hand return to the main hall and head up to the stairs. Head up to the next floor. Go left and ride the elevator up. You will find yourself in a chamber with Edea and Seifer at the other end. Save your game and then approach Seifer.

Seifer

HP: 1,500 – 10,500
AP Gain: 20
Strategy: Seifer has greatly improved since your encounter in Deling. Draw Haste from Seifer and cast it on all your party members so that you can summon your guardian forces quicker. Seifer concentrates his attacks against Squall including a special move that can cause 1,500+ damage. Cast Aura on Squall and unleash his limit break on Seifer.

With Seifer defeated, Edea will make good her escape. Save your game then ride the elevator down to the floor below. Head right and you will be on the balcony in the main hall. Make your way around the balcony to the auditorium at the other end. In the auditorium, approach the balcony, Edea will appear.

Seifer

HP: 1,200 – 7,500
Edea
HP: 500 – 16,000
AP Gain: 50
Strategy: Edea will be joined by Seifer, you must defeat him before you can face the sorceress. Seifer's HP is much lower than before. Use the same strategy as before. Once Seifer has been defeated, Edea will enter the fray. Edea's magic cannot be reflected so there is no point in casting Carbunkle. Use Dispel if Edea casts Reflect on herself. Draw Demi from Edea and cast it against her to reduce her health by a quarter. Summon Cerberus and then cast Aura on all your party, then unleash your limit breaks. Before the battle ends, draw the guardian force Alexander from her.

With Edea defeated, Rinoa runs to Seifer's side. Suddenly she collapses. Edea returns to the caring Matron who ran an orphanage and is no longer possessed by Ultimecia.

The Future

Back in Balamb Garden, Squall will go to Rinoa's bedside. Quistis will tell Squall to go to Edea's house. Form your party and head to Edea's house, you will be unable to select Rinoa for your party. Enter the derelict house. Head right and speak with Cid. You will then be able to talk to Edea. Edea will explain that a sorceress in the future known as Ultimecia is trying to compress time allowing people from the past, present and future to live in the same time. Ultimecia needs Ellone and her special powers. Ellone can send people back in time and view the lives of people she knows. It was Ellone who sent Squall back in time to view parts of Laguna's life. Once you have finished talking with Edea you can challenge her and Cid to a game of cards. Edea holds the Edea card and Cid holds Seifer's card. When you are done try to leave. Back in Balamb Garden, visit Rinoa in the infirmary. Squall will be transported back to Laguna's time.

Laguna the Movie Star

You will find Laguna preparing to star in a movie. Kiros leaves to get into a dragon costume. Laguna dressed as a knight in shining armour runs to the side of the damsel. Suddenly a huge Ruby Dragon thunders down the mountain. You will fight the Ruby Dragon in a mini game.
Attack – ▲
Defend – ■
Simply defend against the Dragon's attack and then counter attack. After the battle, Laguna will flee down the mountain. At the bottom you will face the Ruby Dragon again so you will need to junction your guardian forces, magic and ability for both Laguna and Kiros. The Ruby Dragon is a fire elemental, so cast ice magic and summon Shiva. Do not cast wind or fire magic or you will cure the Ruby Dragon.

The White SeeD Ship

Back as Squall, heal your party before returning to Edea's

house. Edea will tell you the location of the White SeeD ship and a letter. The White SeeD ship is located in a cove north of Edea's house. When you find the ship make contact and board. Once on board head to the rear of the ship and enter the cabin. Inside the White SeeD Leader will explain Ellone boarded a Esther Ship. Back in Balamb Garden head to the dormitory and save your game. Go to the infirmary and visit Rinoa. This is where the game gets a bit weird. Squall picks up Rinoa and goes in search for Ellone who might be in the mysterious city of Esther. Travelling through Fisherman's Horizon and desolate streets, Squall stops at a deserted train station. There, everyone including Edea catch up with Squall. Reform your party (which can include Edea if you wish). You will find yourself on the world map. Save your game before continuing.

Head towards the snowfield to the right. Head through the snowfield eventually stopping at a huge skeleton. Climb up the skeleton on the right and continue forward. Cross the bone bridge then drop off the cliff edge. Continue forward into the next screen. Go right to find a save point, then continue left until you are ambushed by an Abadon.

Abadon
HP: 15,000+
Strategy: The Abadon is an undead creature like the Gerogero and so can be heavily damage by health potions and spells. If you posses Leviathan's Recovery command you can defeat the Abadon with two attacks. Each Recovery command will cause 9999 HP damage. Use holy and fire magic and summon guardian forces such as Ifrit.

After the boss fight, go right and you will find a shape outlined in the background. Examine it and you will discover a ladder. Climb up and enter the air vent.

Esther
Follow the path forward until you reach an elevator. Ride the elevator into Esther. Squall and co will collapse signalling the return to Laguna's time. Laguna and co are being forced to work deep below Esther. Kiros and Ward will be moved to a different part of the complex. Talk to the guard in the right hand corner and then to the guard near the door on the left. Then talk to the Moomba and the prisoner. Talk to the Moomba again and eventually Laguna will fight one of the guards. Laguna will help the Moomba and the prisoner escape in the elevator. Kiros and Ward will enter triggering another battle with the guards. Junction your equipment before fighting. Ride the elevator up. Quietly creep out of the complex. Outside you will meet the Moomba and prisoner you help escape. One of Dr Odine's assistants will approach you. Draw from the magic stone and save before returning inside the complex. Ride the elevator down. Approach Dr Odine and you will encounter another battle. After the battle Dr Odine will escape in the elevator. Follow him out of the building. Laguna and co will jump in a car and race to Dr Odine's laboratory. Fight your way into the building. Sit on the portable elevator (it looks like a large teacup) and you will be transported to the floor above. Fight your way into the room and examine the blue screen. Ellone is being held inside. Examine the console to the right until you find how to unlock the chamber door. Return via the elevator to the first floor and head into the room in front. Inside Laguna will be reunited with Ellone.

Squall and co will regain conciseness. Dr Odine will appear and offer them a ride in his car. Talk to everyone and then head down. You will be told to visit Lunar Gate. Exit the building. Before rushing off to Lunar Gate take your time to explore the city. The quickest way around this huge city is using the teacup elevators. Visit the shopping mall and stock up on Hi-Potions and X-Potions. Before leaving the city rent a car (buy some fuel from the shopping mall). You have a long distance to cover and you will encounter some nasty monsters on route.

Lunar Gate
Lunar gate is situated south of Esther and has a ramp shooting off into the air. Enter the building and inside you will be met by an assistant. She will take you to a capsule room. You must select a third party member to join Squall and Rinoa up to the space station. Zell stays behind to watch Edea. Squall, Rinoa and co will be jettisoned up into space.

Lunatic Pandora
You will now be in control of Zell. Leave the building and make your way back to Esther. Head to Dr Odine's laboratory. Talk to the assistant and enter inside. Ride the teacup elevator up and enter the control room (this is the same place where Laguna found Ellone). Inside you will find Dr Odine. He will explain all you need to know about the Lunatic Pandora. The Lunatic Pandora has to pass through the city to reach Tears' Point. You can intercept the Lunatic Pandora at three points. You will encounter random battles as you run through Esther.

Intercept Point #1 15:00 – 12:00 From Dr Odine's laboratory head right. Take the path at the top of the screen. Go up the stairs and off to the left.

Intercept Point #2 10:00 – 5:00 From the first intercept point head right and back down the stairs. Take the path at the bottom and head right through the shopping mall to the intersection. Go left from the intersection.

Inception point #3 3:00 – 0:00 From the second intercept point head right and go right at the intersection.

Once you have reached the Lunatic Pandora you will have to fight some Galbadian soldiers before you can head inside. If you do not board the Lunatic Pandora do not worry, even if you do get inside, you will be jettisoned off.

Esther Space Station
Left floating in space, Squall and co are brought on board the Esther space station. Once on board talk to the station crew and then pick up Rinoa. Follow the crew to the med lab. Exit the room and follow the man dressed in white, Piet to the control room. Examine the console and then talk to Piet. Exit the control room and head up the stairs. Enter the room at the end. Inside you will find Ellone. Talk to Ellone then return to the med lab. You can win Laguna's card by playing Ellone. Rinoa will begin to move and make her way to the control room. If you try to stop her you will be thrown to the floor. In the control room Rinoa lowers the barrier surrounding the imprisoned sorceress Adel. On the red planet below millions of monsters begin to form. Leave the control room and head to the locker room on the right outside Ellone's room. Inside you will find Rinoa dressed in an anti gravity suit. Examine the

locker and Squall will change into an anti gravity suit. Follow her but you will be unable to stop her. Return back to the control room. Rinoa will release Adel. Everyone will evacuate the station. Talk to everyone and they will run to the escape pods. Talk to Ellone and then evacuate. Squall will plead Ellone to send him back to Rinoa's time to try and prevent Ultimecia from possessing her. Squall will see a scene where Rinoa persuades Irvine to return to the Galbadian desert prison. The scene will then switch to Rinoa floating out in space. Squall will exit the escape pod in an attempt to rescue Rinoa. You will rescue Rinoa in a very simple sub game. Line up Squall with the tumbling Rinoa. Reunited with Rinoa, the lovers drift in space until they find a derelict space craft, the Ragnarok.

The Ragnarok

Once on board Ragnarok save your game. The Ragnarok is home to eight nasty monsters known as Propagators. There is a special way of killing these creatures. Propagators come in pairs signified by their colour. You must kill one Propagator and then kill the other Propagator with the same colour. If you do not, the dead Propagator will be reanimated by its partner. When fighting the Propagators, unleash your guardian forces and strong magic. Try to keep all your characters at peak health, the Propagators attacks can do 1000+ damage and cause abnormal status. Head forward and down the stairs at the end. In the hangar bay you will face a Purple Propagator. After eliminating it head through the large door and quickly through the door on the left, avoiding the Red Propagator. In this room you will face the second Purple Propagator. Return to the previous room and fight the first Red Propagator. Head back up the stairs near the entrance and you will face the second Red Propagator. Head to the entrance and you will find the first Yellow Propagator. Return down stairs and past the room where you eliminated the second Purple Propagator. In the centre of the room is the elevator to the bridge. It is guarded by a Green Propagator. Creep past the Green Propagator and head through the left doorway. Inside you will face the second Yellow Propagator. With the Purple, Red and Yellow Propagators destroyed it is time to eliminate the Green Propagators. The first one is found guarding the elevator. The second Green Propagator is found through the small door under the stairs in the hangar bay. With the ship clear of monsters ride the elevator up to the bridge. On the bridge Squall will take control of Ragnarok. Squall and Rinoa will get very close!!!!

Squall will pilot the Ragnarok down to the planet surface. There, Rinoa will be taken into custody . Return inside the Ragnarok and head to the room to the left of the elevator. There the group will convince Squall to rescue Rinoa. Selphie will take control of the Raganarok. Before rescuing Rinoa from the Memorial you can take your last opportunity to complete some of the games optional side quests.

Sorceress Memorial

Once at the memorial, head inside and confront the scientists. Head left and free Rinoa. Leave the Memorial (hmm the large man seems familiar) and board the Ragnarok. Fly to Edea's house. Once there follow Angelo to the flower field. Once you are ready to leave return to the Raganrok and fly to the Esther. You can land at the Esther Air Station, it is a large building with a circular landing pad on top. Head for the

Presidential Palace. Once inside head left to the President's chamber. The President of Esther in non other than Laguna Loire. Laguna will brief you on the plan to stop Ultimecia.

Ragnarok versus Lunatic Pandora

Back in control of Ragnarok, fly to Tears' Point and Lunatic Pandora. The Ragnarok will unleash a volley of missiles and claws it way through Pandora's force field. As soon as you board the Lunatic Pandora, you will be confronted by Raijin and Fujin.

Fujin
HP: 18,000+
AP Gain: 8
Raijin
HP: 22,000+
AP Gain: 12
Strategy: Fujin and Raijin are slightly tougher than when you encounter them in Balamb and have a few new moves. Fujin possess a sai attack which reduces a characters health to 1 so be ready to restore their health. Fujin spends most of the round supporting Raijin with magic. Cast reflect on Raijin and Fujin to limit their spells effectiveness. Summon Cerberus and then cast Shell and Project on all characters. Summon your guardian forces such as Diablo, Cactus and Doomtrain (if you posses them). Cast Aura and unleash your special moves.

After the battle continue forward and then go left. Here you will find Biggs and Wedge but they are sick of being beaten by you. Save then head inside. Run to the second elevator and ride it up. Here you will encounter random battles against some of the toughest monsters in the game. If you possess the 'discover hidden points ability' you will find a save point here. Head up and you will find Fujin and Raijin. Instead of fighting you personally they summon an incredible tough robot to fight you.

Mobile Type 8
HP: 10,000 – 50,000+
AP Gain: -
Strategy: This boss is tough. Before it releases it probes, the Type 8 will counter any attacks to the main body. When the probes are released, the Type 8 can unleash the Corona. The Corona reduces all three party members to 1 HP. Summon Cerberus at the beginning of the round or cast Triple so that a single party member can cast Curage and restore all your characters health. Being a machine, the Type 8 is susceptible to Quezacolt and lightning.

Enter the chamber at the end of the passage. Inside you will find Seifer. Before facing Seifer make sure all your character's health is fully restored.

Seifer
HP:35,000+
AP Gain: 40
Strategy: If you took the time to acquire Odin, he will appear at the beginning of the fight only to be sliced in half by Seifer. Seifer is not that tough compared to Type 8. Draw Aura from him and cast it on your party. Then unleash a volley of special moves. If you possessed Odin a new being will take his place, Gilgamesh.

Believing Seifer has fallen, he surprises Squall and kidnaps Rinoa. Form a new party then exit the chamber. To the right of where you fought Type 8 will be a ladder leading up. Head up and continue forward to Adel's chamber. Inside, Seifer throws Rinoa before Adel who begins to junction with her.

Adel
HP: ??????
Strategy: Your characters basic attacks must be powerful inflicting 1000+ a hit if possible. Adel will drain 600+ health from Rinoa so you will find her health will dwindle. If you heal her with potions and spells you will heal Adel but you will not see any +HP appear on her. Concentrate on attacking her with your basic attacks, healing your party when attacked (Adel will unleash Meteor and Ultima magic). You will need to defeat Adel before Rinoa runs out of health. If Rinoa dies it is game over. The battle against Adel is incredible tough.

After the battle against Adel, time will begin to compress sending Squall and co back in time. You will eventually find yourself in a room filled with false save points. Run through the room and you will encounter Edea. You will then face various sorceresses across several areas. The sorceress are quite easy so just use basic attacks or a guardian force. The final sorceress's counterattack will cause 1000+ damage. When the final sorceress starts to count down she is preparing to unleash Ultima magic. When she is counting down she will not counter-attack. Once the final sorceress has been defeated you will be returned to Edea's house. Enter Edea's house and head to the right.

Ultimecia's Realm (ooooooh scary)
From Edea's house you will see the Castle of Eight Powers, Ultimecia's castle (again ooooooh scary). Scattered across the ground are the bodies of the White SeeD (in the future the White SeeD's must be defeated by Utimecia). There are huge chains leading from Edea's house to Ultimecia's castle. You can explore the world by stepping through one of the portals along the chain.
1st Portal – Leads to the north of Esther.
2nd Portal – Leads to the Sentora Continent.
3rd Portal – Leads to Galbadia.
4th Portal – This hidden portal found to the right of the chain leads to the Ragnarok.
Head up the chain and enter Ultimecia's Castle. Once in the castle you will find that all your abilities except the basic attack have been sealed. To unlock your abilities you will need to defeat each of the eight bosses that lurk the castle. Inside you will organise two separate parties. The green circles enable you to switch between parties or reorganise your groups. Place all your strong characters into your main party. With your main party head up the stairs and battle the first boss, Sphinxaur.

Sphinxaur
HP: 10,000
AP Gain: 30
Strategy: At this point you only have the basic attack command so just continue to attack until Sphinxaur falls.

Continue up the stairs through the door at the top. Stand on the huge chandelier and you will plummet to the floor below. Open the trap door and head down.

Tri-Point
HP: 2,000 – 23,000
AP Gain: 30
Strategy: Before fighting you should junction Thunder magic to your characters. When Tri-Point counterattacks, you will be healed. If you unlocked your guardian forces unleash Ifrit or Shiva.

Head back up stairs and go through the door to the left. Follow the passage around until you are returned to the main lobby. Switch to your second party and head up to the large chandelier. After falling to the floor below, go to the green circle and hold the lever down. Switch back to your main party and run up and across the large chandelier. Head through the door to the balcony. Here you will face Krysta.

Krysta
HP: 5,000 – 16,000+
AP Gain: 30
Strategy: Krysta will counter-attack any magic or physical attack causing 3,000+ damage. Summon your guardian forces to do your bidden or cast Tornado, Metoer or Ultima magic. Krysta's will cast Ultima magic as a final attempt to take you to the grave with him.

Head back across the chandelier and return to the lobby. Head through the door on the right. Head down the stairs and through the door in the middle of the room. You will find yourself in an art gallery. Examine every picture then examine the main, nameless picture. Select Vividarium, then Intervigilium and then finally Viator. The fourth boss, Trauma will appear behind you.

Trauma
HP: 5000 – 35,000
AP Gain: 30
Strategy: Summon your guardian forces but keep one of your characters as a medic healing themselves and the other two characters when Trauma unleashes its mega pulse cannon.

Go through the door in the centre of the room and head down the stairs in the centre of the room. In the dungeon, enter the left cell. Take the prison key from the corpse. Suddenly the Red Giant will appear.

Red Giant
HP: 30,000
AP Gain: 30
Strategy: Physical attacks against this beast are useless. Cast Silence and blind to try and stun the Red Giant then summon your guardian forces such as Quezacolt and Thunder magic. Return to the main lobby and head through the door in the centre of the room. Run past the fountain and into the abbey. Head up the stairs. The key to the armoury is on the edge of the shaky bridge. Walk slowly up to the key. Return to the dungeon where you fought Red Giant and unlock the right cell. Inside you will encounter a Vysage.

Gargantua
HP: 10,000 – 15,000+
AP Gain: 30

Strategy: Once you have destroyed all three parts to the Vysage, Gargantua will appear from the ground. This mummified creature will cast Berserk on your characters so be ready to cure your characters.

From the prison, head to the fountain outside the abbey. Search the fountain for a key. Head back to the main lobby and go through the lower door on the left. The treasure vault door is on the left of the tilted corridor. Inside you will find four boxes. First close box 1, then shut box 4, then shut box 2 and then finally open box 3. When all four boxes are open you will face Catoblepas.

Catoblepas
HP: 10,000 – 60,000
AP Gain: 30
Strategy: Summon Leviathan and the Brothers but avoid using Quezacolt and Thunder magic. Draw Meteor from Catoblepas and cast it back against it. Catoblepas will strike back with a final Meteor attack before it dies.

Head to the abbey and head up the stairs until you reach the bell. Jump from the ledge onto the bell. From the bell jump onto the small ledge. Head through the hole in the wall. Outside you will face the final boss, Tiamat.

Tiamat
HP: 20,000 – 90,000
AP Gain: 30
Strategy: Tiamat is Bahamut turned to the darkside by Ultimecia. Tiamat only has one attack, the Dark Flare. It takes time to charge the Dark Flare so unleash everything you have got. Just make sure your health is at its peak before Tiamat performs its Dark Flare.

With all eight bosses defeated you should now have unlocked all your abilities. Before you face Ultimecia you can try and defeat the Omega Weapon (this battle is optional). To face the Omega Weapon, firstly switch your main party at the fountain outside the abbey to your second party. Then take your second party to the room on the left of the castle with the two green circles. Pull the rope at the base of the stairs to ring the bell. Quickly switch to your main group. With your main group head into the abbey, inside you will face Omega Weapon who has over 1 million HP.

When you are ready to face Ultimecia, head up to the very top of the abbey. Save before entering Ultimecia's lair. Ultimecia is the toughest monster you will ever face in Final Fantasy.

Ultimecia and Griever
HP: 1,000,000- 2,000,000 + (and properly a bit more)
Strategy: In this battle you will use all six of your characters. Ultimecia will randomly challenge three of your characters. During the ensuing battle once one of your characters falls, you will get three or four turns to resurrect that character before they are replaced by a healthy character. Every battle previously should have prepared you for this fight. Protect your characters physically and magically, summon your guardian forces, cast level 3 magic and cast Aura to unleash your limit breaks. Once you have caused between 50,000 – 100,000 damage, Ultimecia summons her own guardian force, Griever (non other

than the creature engraved in Squall's ring), a gigantic sky blue lion with wings. The Griever casts powerful magic as Pain and Doom. Eventually Griever will junction itself with Ultimecia. The junctioned Ultimecia will cast Great Attraction, a planet splitting spell which causes 1,500 damage to all party members. Once near death the screen will begin to spin and the junctioned Ultimecia will explode. Spinning through space and time you will face Ultimecia's final form. In her final form Ultimecia will cast Hells Judgement which reduces all your characters to 1HP. You should then unleash your limit breaks. Squall should cause over 100,000 points of damage alone. Strangely Final Ultimecia seems content with continuing to cast Hells Judgement which is useless once your characters health is 1. Continue to unleash your limit breaks until Ultimecia is finally laid to rest.

Now sit back and watch the ending which will confuse you more than ever.

The Story Line?
So you have completed the game but still cannot grasp the story line. Here is a quick run down. 17 or 18 years before Squall graduates as a SeeD, Laguna Loire is in the service of the Galbadian army. While the Galbadian army fights for control of the town of Timber, Laguna falls in love with a pianist named Julia. Soon after Laguna and his friends stumble across the mysterious Esther forces raising up a strange craft (the Lunatic Pandora). During the ensuing battle, Laguna and his two friends Kiros and Ward are seriously wounded. Laguna finds himself in the village of Winhill where he is cared for by a girl named Raine. Laguna discovers that his love, Julia, believing he was dead, got married to General Caraway. Laguna becomes the villages monster hunter and quickly becomes close to Raine and her daughter, Ellone. Laguna and Raine eventually marry. During this time, the advanced city of Esther is controlled by an evil sorceress named Adel. Ellone is kidnapped by Esther forces. Ellone possess the power to transport a person back in time and experience the lives of the people she knows. Laguna, Kiros and Ward travel to Esther to rescue Ellone. Laguna leaves without knowing Raine is pregnant with their child. They are captured and force to work deep underneath the city. Laguna and co escape and rescue Ellone. Laguna joins the resistance movement building against Adel. Ellone is sent back to Raine in Winhill. The revolution succeeds and Adel is imprisoned in space. Laguna is elected president of Esther. Raine dies during childbirth and her new born child and Ellone are put in an orphanage. When Raine dies, Laguna decides to stay in Esther oblivious to the existence of his child. Years later, Ellone leaves the orphanage in search of Laguna. She leaves her younger brother Squall behind. Years later Squall enters Balamb Garden and trains to become a member of SeeD. He is reunited with the other children from the orphanage but their childhood memories are repressed when they begin junctioning guardian forces. Ellone uses her powers to send Squall back in time and experience important events in Laguna's life in the hope he can change those events. After defeating Ultimecia the sorceress from the future, Squall is sent back in time and meets Edea. Squall tells her about the future threat, Garden and SeeD. It is Edea who creates Garden and SeeD with financial help from Norg. Edea inherits her powers from Ultimecia and it is Ultimecia's soul who takes control of Edea and tries to use her to compress time. Squall

is Laguna's son, this is why the Moombas call him Laguna. Squall falls in love with Rinoa, Juila's daughter. So if Squall did not defeat Ultimecia she would not possess Edea who would then not pass on her powers to Rinoa. This would mean Squall would not be forced to defeat Ultimecia. If Squall does not defeat Ultimecia he would not go back in time and tell Edea about SeeD which he would join in the present.

FIRESTORM: THUNDERHAWK 2

Final Password
Input this code to view the end-game sequence:
1NOK20T5326M4MA.

FIRO AND KLAWD

Passwords

AREA	PASSWORD
Back alley	MOOMIN
Back street	MOONPIG
Back street B	MOONPINGEON
Back roof	SNUFFKIN
Main street	LITTLE-MI
Main street B	LITTLE-MO
Vinnie's scrapyard	SOUP-DRAGON
Vinnie's scrapyard B	SUPER-DRAGON

FORMULA ONE

Bike Mode
To race bikes that have two car wheels, choose a Single Race and on the Race Qualify screen hold **Select** and press ↓, ↑, ●, ▲, ➡, ↑, ■, ▲. An activation message should appear. To go back to using cars, go to the Race Qualify screen and re-enter the same code.

Bonus Track
To race on the Grand Champion Bonus Track, choose a Single Race in either Arcade or Grand Prix Mix, then choose any team, plus a driver and track. At the Race Qualify screen (Practice/Qualify/Race), hold down **Select** and press ◀, ●, ●, ▲, ▲, ●, ↑, ➡, to show a message that indicates that the cheat has worked. Next you must start the current race and then abandon it. Choose a Single Race in Arcade Mode and at the Circuit Select screen look through the tracks to find the Grand Champion Bonus Track, which will be in the shape of an F1 car.

Buggy Mode
To make overtaking easier by using slimmer buggies, go to the Race Qualify screen in a Single Race, and hold down **Select**. Then press ➡, ↑, ▲, ◀, ↑, ■, ▲, to show a message indicating that the mode has been activated. To return to the original cars, re-enter the same code sequence on the Race Qualify screen.

German Mode
If you would like a German commentator, go to the Race Qualify screen in a Single Race, hold down **Select**, and press ↓, ↑, ◀, ◀, ■, ●, ✖.

Gibberish Mode
To make Murray Walker talk a load of gibberish in his commentary, go to the Race Qualify screen, hold down **Select** and press ◀, ●, ↑, ↓, ↓, ➡, ●, ■, ■.

Lava Mode
To race on a track that is made of red hot lava and have flames jetting from your rear tyres, go to the Race Qualify screen in a Single Race, hold down **Select** and then press ■, ●, ↑, ➡, ➡, ●, ✖ to show a message indicating activation of the cheat. When you wish to quit lava mode go to the Race Qualify screen and enter the same code.

FORMULA ONE '97

Hidden Arcade Tracks and 60's Mode
To access the hidden track for each Arcade difficulty setting, you must come first in every race.

Cheat Options
To enter the following cheat codes, select "Grand Prix" mode from the Main menu, then choose "Select Driver". Edit the drivers' name and replace it with the cheat code.

Helicopter View:	ZOOM LENSE
Virtual Reality Graphics:	VIRTUALLY VIRTUAL
Wipeout 2097 Mode:	PI MAN
Background Music:	SWAP SHOP
Fat Tyres:	LITTLE WEELZ

FORMULA ONE '98

Secret Tracks
Enter the Driver/Team Select option and select Options, then Edit Driver Name. Change the name to enter one of these secret tracks.

Cheesy Poofs	Stunt Course
Go Cows	Roman Forum

FRENZY

Level Select
On the password screen enter **PICKLE**, you should be told that it is an incorrect password. Press ▲ to return to the main menu. Select cheat menu and choose level select.

FROGGER

Infinite Lives

To gain infinite lives in this classic game, press Pause then enter the following code: ➡, ■, ▲, ■, ▲, ✖.

Access all Levels

To play any level, Pause the game and enter the following code:
➡, ■, ▲, ■, ▲, R1, L1, R1, L1, ●.

GEX

Level Passwords

The following passwords will allow you to get to various stages in the game. The Rez code lets you into Rez's lair with the other levels complete.

SVZFKHGP -	Cemetery
BXRFYHGP	
ZVTCYHGP	
KXVKRHKP -	Jungle
CVHCSHKP	
SVKLPHKP	
CVBLPHKP	
RVTCSHGP -	Toonville
XVVBRHKP	
YTCHPHKP -	Kung Fu Land
ZTDHPHKP	
DXVGRHKP	
GYVYRHKP -	Rezopolis
PZYPRXYL -	Rez

99 lives

You can get ninety-nine lives by going to the two secret areas in the first stage several times. First run through, getting the collectables and free men, then get the bonus area by going to the area that is above the camera. Run through again and get everything you can, next go to the area that you crawl through, get the collectables and then the free man by running and jumping where the portal shows up. Next run and jump above the moon where you will see another portal. Do not go to this portal until you have gone through the level at least once, and then everything will be replaced.

More Infinite Lives

For infinite lives, jump into the rocket right after the third camera in the stage Rock It In New Toonland. You will see an arrow made of flies that points downward. Jump down to find a hole. When you are in the hole you will see a yellow thing that you must hit with your tail making it purple. Now you will see an opening on the right, inside of which are four extra lives with a remote control. Take these and jump into the spikes to die. You will now start back at the camera again. If you jump back into the hole, repeating the whole process, the lives reappear each time you die, so you can get as many as you like.

Various Pause Cheats

Press pause and hold the **R2** button before using the following sequences:

Electricity:	➡, ⬅, ➡, ●, ▲, ➡, ●, ⬇, ➡
Fire balls:	✖, ⬆, ➡, ⬆, ➡, ➡
Ice balls:	●, ●, ⬅, ⬇, ●, ⬆, ➡
Infinite lives:	⬆, ●, ▲, ⬇, ➡, ■, ⬇
Invincibility:	✖, ■, ⬇, ⬇, ⬆, ⬇, ➡
Super jump:	✖, ●, ⬆, ⬆, ⬇, ➡, ➡

GEX 3: DEEP COVER GECKO

To enable cheat modes, pause the game, hold the L2 button and press the following:

Debug mode

⬆, ●, ➡, ⬆, ⬅, ➡, ⬇. (Press **Select** for Debug menu)

Invulnerability

⬇, ⬆, ⬅, ⬅, ▲, ➡, ⬇

Select one-liners

⬇, ➡, ⬅, ●, ⬆, ➡ (Press **Select** for one-liners)

Vault Codes

When you have access to the vault, use the following codes:

10 Lives	■, ✖, ●, ●, ▲, ■
1 Life	▲, ●, STAR, ■, ■, ✖
Invincibility	■, STAR, ▲, ■, ▲, DIAMOND
Play as Alfred	■, ✖, ▲, ■, STAR, STAR
Play as Cuz	■, DIAMOND, ■, ■, ▲, DIAMOND
Play as Rex	■, STAR, STAR, ■, ▲, ▲
GEX Video 1	●, ▲, ■, STAR, DIAMOND, STAR
GEX Video 2	DIAMOND, STAR, ■, ✖, ▲, ●
GEX Video 3	✖, DIAMOND, STAR, ▲, ▲, ●
All GEX Videos	STAR, ✖, ✖, ●, ■, ▲
Eight Hit Paws	■, DIAMOND, ▲, ▲, STAR, DIAMOND

GEX 3D: ENTER THE GECKO

Invincibility

Pause the game, highlight quit then hold **L2** and enter the code
⬅, ➡, ▲, ⬇, ➡, ⬅.

Infinite Lives

Pause the game, highlight quit then hold **L2** and enter the code
⬆, ⬆, ⬇, ➡, ▲, ⬇

Level Select

Pause the game, highlight quit then hold **L2** and enter the code
➡, ➡, ⬅, ➡, ▲, ⬇, ➡.

Chatty Gex
Pause the game, highlight quit then hold **L2** and enter the code ▲, ←, ●, ↑, ↓. Press **Select** during the game For some words of Gecko wisdom

Babbling Gex
Pause the game, highlight quit then hold **L2** and enter the code ↓, →, ↑, ↓, →, ←, →, ↓, ↓.

GHOST IN THE SHELL

Mission Select and All FMV
On the main menu, press **R2, R1, ■, ■, ↑, ↓, ■, ■, R2, R2.** Every level can be accessed and you can watch all the movies from the Movie Replay sub menu.

Hidden Kusanagi Screen Shot
Complete the game from beginning to end without continuing to view an extra manga picture after the end credits.

GOALSTORM

Special Konami Team
On the 'Press Start' screen, enter the following sequence if you would like to play with a Konami team: ↑, ↑, ↓, ↓, ←, →, ←, →, ✕, ●. You can enter the sequence on controller 1 to have the home strip, and on controller 2 for the away strip.

G~POLICE

All Weapons and Ammo
To enable this cheat, go to the Weapons Loadout screen and hold down **L1, L2, R1, R2, ●, ▲, ■** and press ←.

Invincibility
To enable this cheat, go to the Mission Briefing screen and hold down **L1, L2, R1, R2, ●, ▲, ■** and press ←.

Secret Mission
Enter PANTALON on the Password Screen.

Passwords

Level	Password
1	MADGAV
2	DOLMAN
3	SONAGAV
4	ACEDUF
5	JOJOGUN
6	WENSKI
7	SAEGGY
8	MAZMAN
9	DAZMAN
10	DELUCS
11	ANDOOOO
12	KIMBCHS
13	ANDYMAC
14	YERMAN
15	OLLIEB
16	THEYOLK
17	TONYMASH
18	ANDYCROW
19	BIONIC
20	TSLATER
21	IAINTHOD
22	JONRITZ
23	CLAIREC
24	STEVEBOT
25	ANGUSF
26	EUANLEC
27	EDFIRE
28	STUBOMB
29	THONBOY
30	JIMMAC
31	PUGGER
32	ROSSCO
33	CAKEBOY
34	NIKNAK
35	SAGLORD

GRAND THEFT AUTO

Cheat M
Enter c   names.

M

GROOV

EATTHIS
BLOWME
CHUFF
TURF
CAPRICE
WEYHEY
FECK
TVTON

GRAN

Cheat C
Enter th

RAZZLE	All of the levels.
MAYFAIR	London levels 1-2.
PENTHOUSE	London levels 1-3.
MCVICAR	99 Lives.
BIGBEN	9,999,990 points.
SIDEBURN	Multiplier x5.
GRASS	No cops.
SWEENEY	Display the co-ordinates.
HAROLDHAND	All levels, all weapons, infinite ammunition, Get Out Of Jail Free card, armour x3, parrot image, 9,999,990 points, 99 lives, multiplier x5, no cops, display co-ordinates.
GETCARTER	All levels, all weapons, infinite ammunition, Get Out Of Jail Free card, armour x3, 99 lives, multiplier x5, maximum wanted level, display co-ordinates.
FREEMANS	All levels, all weapons, infinite ammunition, Get Out Of Jail Free card, armour x3, multiplier x5.
TOOLEDUP	All weapons, infinite ammunition, Get Out Of Jail Free card, armour x3.
SORTED	All levels, all weapons, infinite ammunition, Get Out Of Jail Free card, armour x3.

GRAN TURISMO

Tracks (Arcade Mode)
the four tracks grades

grades of

erent grades of

ption.

g on all

Spoon Honda S2000
To unlock the Spoon Honda S2000 get the gold rating on all B-Class license tests

Mitsubishi FTO LM Edition
to unlock the Mitsubishi FTO LM Edition get the gold rating on all International-A license tests.

Honda Del Sol LM
to unlock the Honda Del Sol LM Edition get the gold rating on all International-B license tests

Mitsubishi 3000 GT LM
to unlock the Mitsubishi 3000 GT LM Edition get the gold rating on all International-C license tests

Super License
Earn all licenses (A, B, International-C, International-B, International-A) to unlock the Super License.

Toyota GT-ONE
to unlock the Toyota GT-ONE get the gold rating on all Super License tests

GRIND SESSION

All Tricks
During Tournament mode, pause the game and then press
↓, ←, ↑, →, ↓, ←, ↑, →.

Master AO
To unlock this master skater you need to collect all the keys, photos and coins in the dreamhouse.

GUNSHIP

Invulnerability
To be invulnerable, press and hold the following sequence after you have recieved your mission orders at the loading screen: **L1, L2, R1, R2**. Keep the buttons depressed until the mission begins, then you will see 'CHEAT' in the top Left of the screen. This means the cheat has worked.

HARDCORE 4X4

Cheat Codewords
To activate each separate cheat, first select "Time Trial" from the Race Types on the Menu. Start the Time Trial, select "Edit Details", then "Edit Name", and then enter the desired code:

Mother Truck + Select Race Class
To race in the Pro and Extreme classes and gain the Mother Truck, enter "MAINLINE".

Raining Frogs
For some Biblical fun, enter the code "RAINFROG".

Secret Asteroids Game
Get back to the Old Skool! Enter the code "DUTCHMAN". Next, press ▲ until you come back to the first Menu. Select "Options" then "Credits" to play Asteroids. ✖ is Fire, and ● is boost.

HEART OF DARKNESS

Level And Screen Select
Hold **L1 + L2 + R1 + R2** on controller 2 and turn the Playstation on. Continue to hold all four buttons, enter the option screen and select 'Load Game'. Here you can select any level and then a starting point.

HERCULES

Passwords
Level 2 The Hero's Gauntlet:
  Serpent, Medusa, Coin, Medusa.
Level 3 Centaurs` Forest:
  Centaur, Hercules Silhouette, Minotaur, Archer.
Level 4 The Big Olive:
  Centaur, Coin, Serpent, Hercules Silhouette.
Level 5 Hydra Canyon:
  Coin, Gladiator Helmet, Coin, Soldier.
Level 7 Cyclops Attack:
  Gladiator Helmet, Pegasus, Hercules Silhouette, Archer.
Level 8 Titan Flight:
  Soldier, Coin, Coin, Lightning Bolt.
Level 9 Passageway Of Eternal Torment:
  Medusa, Soldier, Centaur, Pegasus.
Level 10 The Vortex Of Souls:
  Soldier, Lightning Bolt, Soldier, Centaur.

View All the Movie Clips
To view all of the in game cut scenes, enter the following password: **Pegasus, Soldier, Centaur, Soldier.**

HEXEN

Cheat Mode
To enable the cheat mode, firstly enter the Options screen from the Main Menu and select "Pad Config.". Hold **R2**, and press ➡, ⬇, ➡, ▲, ✖ whilst on the Pad Config. screen, and a sound will confirm correct entry of the code. Next, start the game and press Pause to access the cheat menu.

HOGS OF WAR

Early in the game water is harmful as the pigs can't swim. Use TNT or mines to send pigs into the water so that they drown or lose HP whilst swimming to safety.

If possible shoot or knife pigs next to minefields so that they are pushed into the mines.

Cluster grenades can be deadly on a group of pigs. Press ✖ to detonate the grenade and ✖ again to explode the cluster.

Make sure you have a plan before you start each pig off on their turn, Time is limited and gets shorter in later missions.

Enter the Following Team Names for Extras:
PRYING PIGS   See all the FMV scenes on the game use the team name.
WATTA PORK   View an extra scene.
MARDY PIGS   Unlock the secret Team Lard.

HOT WHEELS: TURBO RACING

Enter these cheats on the main menu:

Large Tyres	■, ▲, ■, ▲, R1, R1, L2, L2
Small Cars	■, R2, L2, ▲, ▲, L2, R2, ■
Unlimited Turbos	R2, L1, ■, ▲, R1, L2, L1, R2
Bonus 'Tow Jam' Car	■, ▲, L1, R1, L2, R2, ■, ▲
Gourad Shaded Style Cars	L1, R1, L2, R2, L1, R1, L2, R2

IMPACT RACING

Bonus Levels
To play each bonus level in turn instead of playing the main tracks, go to the password screen and enter BONUS.LEVELS.

Debug Mode
To alter the time limits, number of power-ups, enemy intelligence, or to switch the track type for each level, go to the password screen and enter RABBITBADGER. 'Debug Mode' will appear at the bottom of the main menu, and this enables you to make your changes.

Final Stage
To play the last stage of the game go to the password screen and enter ENDGAMELEVEL

Full Weapons
For a full supply of all the special weapons, go to the password screen, enter ALL.TOOLEDUP, and start the game.

Infinite Ammunition
For unlimited ammunition for a selected weapon, go to the password screen and enter LOADSOFSTUFF.

Invincibility

To be invincible, go to the password screen and enter I.AM.IMORTAL

Play your own CDs

When you complete the game you are rewarded with a Virtual Jukebox. At this point you can take out the game disc and replace it with any music CD. Watch the screen to see patterns reacting to the music. You can press **Select** to see the music track information, and use ← and → to choose the track that you want.

You can go directly to the Virtual Jukebox from the start, by entering JOURNEYS.END on the password screen.

Level Passwords

The codes are only given when you complete bonus levels. At the password screen, enter the following codes:

LEVEL	CAR	WEAPON	PASSWORD
2	AR12	Double Laser	000G4KB0M04Q
2	Destroyer	Double Laser	000G73BK26XK
3	Destroyer	Missiles	01F96MBWA79K
4	AR12	Missiles	1MAT6XCE3OIL
5	Destroyer	QuadLaser	02MO4CCLQ84A
7	Destroyer	Firewall	03HAV2DCMDU2
8	AR12	Quad Laser	OZMAQKDS00HG

INCREDIBLE HULK

Level Passwords

World	Easy	Medium	Hard
Castle:	70000F630A	60080FFB85	80100F8401
Ice:	A0000A352F	90080ACDAA	B0100A5626
UFOs:	C000010759	B008019FD4	D010012850
Maestro:	300006D8BD	F01005616D	101005F9E8

IN THE HUNT

Alter Speed

To speed up the game, pause and then return to the game while holding ▲ and **R2**. To slow down the game, pause and return to the game while holding ▲ and **L2**.

Extra Lives

If when using the above cheat you are still unable to finish the game in one-player mode, before you die press **Start** on controller 2. This gives you player 2's lives.

Stage Select

To have a stage select option, highlight the Start option and press ↖, ● and **Select** simultaneously.

Unlimited Continues

For extra continues, after you have died and you are at the countdown screen, hold ▲ and **Select** while pressing **Start**.

INDEPENDENCE DAY

After entering one of the following passwords, go to the game selection screen and quickly press ←, →, ■, ●, ▲, ▲, ↓.

City Select

Enter the password FOX_ROX as a player name.

Fast Reload, Damage Bonus, and Weapons

Enter the password GO_POSTAL as a player name.

Invincibility

Enter the password LIVE_FREE as a player name.

Plane Select

Enter the password MR_HAPPY as a player name.

INDY 500

Drag Race

This cheat has two separate codes, for a one or two player drag race. For a one player race, go to the Indy 500 Mode screen, highlight the Qualify option and hold **L1+L2+R1+R2** and press **Start**. For a two-player race, go to the Handicap screen, hold **L1+L2+R1+R2** then press **Start**.

Alternative Replay Angles

During the Replay hold **Select** and use **L1, L2, R1, R2, ▲, ■, ✖**.

Extra Menu Option

For an extra item at the menu, go to the title screen and press ●, ✖, ▲, ■ three times.

INTERNATIONAL SUPERSTAR SOCCER DELUXE

Dogs In Black

To transform the linesmen and referee into whimpering dogs, press the following at the title screen: ↑, ↑, ↓

INTERNATIONAL TRACK AND FIELD

Change Swimsuits

To give the swimmers bikinis, go to the Game Select screen and highlight 100m Freestyle. Then press the following: ↑, ↑, ↓, ↓, ←, →, ←, →, ✖, ●.

Hide Gauges

To remove the gauges from the screen, go to the title screen and select Start. Enter an event and pause the game, then press and hold **L1, L2, R1, R2, ■, ✖, ▲, ●**. While you are still holding the buttons press either ↑ or ↓ repeatedly.

See Birds
To see a flock of birds you must get a distance in the discuss event whereby the metres and centimetres have the same number e.g. 26.26.

See Gopher
To see a gopher, you must match the last three numbers of your distance in the triple jump.

See Space Shuttle
To see a space shuttle fly by, when you are pole vaulting clear the qualifying height of 4.5 metres, and on the second attempt set the pole to 5 metres and clear the jump again. The shuttle will fly by on the next pole setting.

See T-Rex
To make a huge T-Rex come into the stadium, you must get a distance in the shot put event that is composed of all the same numbers e.g. 44.44.

See UFO
Have a UFO crash land while you are in the javelin event, press a run button once to jog towards the foul line. As soon as the angle metre appears press and hold the Angle button so that it is above 73 degrees. As soon as the meter rises, press the Run button very quickly. When you are running at a fast speed let go the javelin before you reach the foul line. If you don't get it exactly right, try again.

INTERNATIONAL TRACK AND FIELD 2

Alternative Costumes
On the event select screen, highlight any event and press ↑, ↑, ↓, ↓, ←, →, ←, →, ●, ✖.

Hidden Mole
When participating in the long jump get a distance with identical digits and a mole will pop its head out.

IRON AND BLOOD

Play as Avatar
To play as the baldy-man, first go to the Character Selection screen. Next, hold ← and press ■. Release the buttons then press → + ●. The cursor should end up in the bottom left-hand corner of the screen to indicate success.

IRON MAN XO

Mega Passwords
These passwords give you full Armour, Boost, Weapons and 99

Lives. Simply enter a code on the Password screen:
One Player End Level
C04A7707777777777777777777
Two Player End Level
C02A77X777777777777777777

JACKIE CHAN'S STUNT MASTER

Build Up Your Lives
On any level where you find an extra life, collect the extra life, exit the level, re-enter the level. The extra life will have reappeared.

Unlock All Levels
On the title screen, press L2, ■, ▲, ●, ✖, R2, R2. You will be now able to instantly jump to any level.

Bonus Movie
On the title screen, press ←, →, R1, ●, ■, ▲, ▲. You will now be able to view a behind the scenes movie of Jackie Chan making the game.

JEREMY MCGRATH SUPERCROSS '98

Reversed Tracks
To be able to race backwards around the tracks complete the season in first place

Mirrored Tracks
Mirrored tracks are obtained by completing the season in first place using the reversed tracks.

Yamaha Z80 Bike and Race Against Jeremy Mcgrath.
Win the first race of advanced mode.

JET RIDER

Access all tracks
Go to the Options screen and set the difficulty to amateur. Now set the Trophy Presenter to be male and press **Start** to return to the main screen. Next press the following on the player one pad: ↑, →, ↓, ←, ↑, →, ↓, ←. Now go ← once and press ✖ to return to the Options screen. Set the difficulty to Professional, and the Trophy Presenter to Rider's Choice. Now press **Start** to go to the main screen, and enter the following on the player one pad: ↑, ←, ↓, →, ↑, ←, ↓, →. If you hear the 'ka-ching' sound, you know that the cheat has worked and you can race on all of the tracks.

Special Codes
To use the following codes, you need to win a Full Season at Professional Level on all of the ten tracks. Once you have achieved this you can enter any or all of the codes:

Air Brakes	R1, R2, ➡, L2, ⬆, ⬤, ⬆, ⬤.
Double Stunts Points	➡, ⬆, ⬤, L2, ▲, ⬤, R2, R2.
Ice Racing	⬆, R2, R1, ➡, L1, ■, ➡, ➡.
Rocket Racer	▲, ⬆, ⬆, L2, L2, ⬆, ⬆, ⬆.
Show-Off Camera Enabled	▲, ⬇, ■, ▲, L1, L1, R1, R1.
Super Agility	⬇, ⬤, ⬅, L1, ⬅, ➡, ⬅, ➡.
2 Player Computer Al Code	⬤, ■, R2, ⬤, ▲, L2, ➡, ⬆.
Unlimited Turbos	▲, ⬤, ➡, R2, ⬆, ■, ⬆, ▲.
Zero Resistance	■, L1, ▲, ➡, L1, ⬇, R2, ▲.

JOHNNY BAZOOKATONE

Bonus Level
To enter the bonus level, go to the right side of the wall at the beginning of level 1. Where the wall stops, jump up while holding ⬅ to jump onto a secret walkway. Next walk to the Left and jump up to enter the bonus level. If you lose a life in the bonus level it will not affecct the amount of lives you have in the rest of the game, so you can collect as much as possible. Collect 1000 music notes to get an extra life.

Invincibility
To be invincible, go to the password screen and enter PILCHARD

Level Select
For a level select option, go to the password screen and enter KRISTIAN.

Passwords
At the password screen enter the following codes to get to the desired level:

Hotel:	AFLEAPIT
Restaurant:	TEASPOON
Hospital:	SEDATION
Penthouse:	VERYNICE

JO JO'S BIZARRE ADVENTURE

Hidden Characters
To unlock these hidden characters you must acquire a certain amount of ability points in story mode:

Robber Soul – 350
Khan – 1,000
Hol Horse and Boingo – 1, 300
New Kakayoin – 1, 450

JUMPING FLASH

Begin On Any World
To enter any world or stage, go to the title screen and press the following: ⬆, ⬆, ⬇, ⬇, ✖, ✖, ⬅, ➡, ⬅, ➡, ✖, ▲, ✖,

▲. The screen should turn red, now press the **Start** button. Use ⬅ and ➡ to **Select** a level to start on.

Cloud Speeds
To change the speed of clouds on the title screen, hold **L1**, **L2**, **R1**, **R2**, and then press ⬆ and ⬇ to alter the speed.

Extra Stages
You can play extra stages if you kill the Baron in World 6 Stage 3. In these stages, some items are in different places eg. jetpods, exits, bonus levels. Some items will be new and others removed. You have five minutes to complete these extra stages.

Super Mode
To play in super mode where you have added abilities you must complete the game without using continue. Once in the super mode you will be able to jump six times in succession instead of the normal three. You can increase your speed of falling and therefore the impact upon creatures by pressing ▲ when falling. To run faster press **L1** or **L2** during play, and this also allows you to jump further and higher.

JUPITER STRIKE

Side View
To view the action from the side, press **Start** to pause, press **Start** again and hold for 10 seconds. Then press **L2** and **Start** together.

Top View
For a birds' eye view, press Start to pause the game, then press the **Start** button again and hold it for 10 seconds. Next press **L1** and **Start** at the same time.

JURASSIC PARK: THE LOST WORLD

Play as Human
Enter the password ⬤, ⬤, ✖, ✖, ▲, ■, ■, ■, ⬤, ⬤, ■, ▲,

Play as Raptor
Enter the password ■, ✖, ⬤, ▲, ✖, ⬤, ■, ▲, ✖, ■, ⬤, ✖.

Play as Male Human
Enter the password ⬤, ⬤, ✖, ✖, ▲, ■, ■, ■, ⬤, ⬤, ■, ▲.

View T-Rex Gallery
Enter the password ▲, ▲, ⬤, ■, ▲, ✖, ▲, ■, ■, ✖, ▲, ⬤.

View Prey Gallery
Enter the password ▲, ■, ⬤, ■, ✖, ▲, ▲, ⬤, ✖, ■, ▲, ▲.

View Raptor Gallery
Enter the password ⬤, ■, ▲, ✖, ⬤, ▲, ■, ✖, ⬤, ■, ✖, ▲.

View Hunter Gallery
Enter the Password ▲, ✖, ■, ▲, ●, ✖, ■, ●, ▲, ■, ✖, ●.

When entering the following codes the game will start with no sound effects. Exit the game and turn on the sound in the options menu. Re-enter the code to activate.

Play as Hunter
Enter the code ■, ✖, ●, ▲, ✖, ●, ■, ▲, ■, ✖, ●, ✖.

Play as T-Rex
Enter the code ▲, ■, ●, ■, ✖, ▲, ▲, ●, ■, ▲, ▲, ✖.

59 Lives
Enter the code ▲, ✖, ■, ▲, ●, ✖, ■, ●, ■, ▲, ✖, ●.

KENSEI: SACRED FIST

Hidden Characters

Akira	Complete the game with Yugo.
Quigtao	Complete the game with Yuli.
Cindy	Complete the game with Douglas.
Steve	Complete the game with Allen.
Arther	Complete the game with Ann.
Kornelia	Complete the game with Heniz.
Sessue	Complete the game with Hyoma.
Mark	Complete the game with David.
Genya	Complete the game with Saya.
Zhou	Complete the game with all nine standard characters then play with a standard character.
Kaiya	Complete the game with all nine standard characters then play with any hidden characters.
Kazane	Complete the game with Zhou.
Jelly/Billy	Complete the game with Kaiya.

Extra Mode
Unlock all 22 characters.

KILEAK THE BLOOD

All Items
To have all items right from the start, go to the title screen and where the little objects congregate, press ● 6 times. Rotate the controller 3 times clockwise from ➡, then press ▲, ■, ■, ▲, ✖, Start.

Invincibility
To make yourself invincible, when the intro screen appears press the following 3 times in under 5 seconds: ▲, ▲, ⬅, ➡, ■, ■, Select, L1, L2, R1, R2.

KING OF FIGHTERS '95

Boss Code
To play as the Boss, firstly go to the Character Selection screen. Next, choose "yes" to Team Edit, and hold Start whilst pressing ⬆ + ●, then ➡ + ■, then ⬅ + ✖, then ⬇ + ▲. There is no way of confirming this cheat on this screen, so if it doesn't work try again.

Extra Characters
To gain the extra characters Omega Rugal and Saisyu Kusanagi, firstly enter the Character Selection screen. Next, select Team Edit and enter the following code: ⬆, ■, ➡, ●, ⬅, ▲, ⬇, ✖.

Victory Clip Code
To disable the end of battle victory picture, go to the Options, then to the Configuration screen, and press L1+L2+R1+R2 simultaneously. A beep should sound, and the "Win Demo" menu will pop up.

Quit code
To exit the game to the Main Menu at any time, except during loading, hold ▲ + ● + ✖ + ■.

KING OF FIGHTERS '96

Play as the Bosses
To play as the Bosses, enter the Character Selection screen (in any mode) and press ⬆ + ●, then ➡ + ■, then ⬅ + ✖, then ⬇ + ▲. Goenitz will be selectable to the left of Athena, and Chizuru Kagura will be to the right of Clark. Happy hunting!

KLONOA

Bonus Game:
If you release all 72 Phantomilians then you will be able to play the level 'Extra Vision: Balue's Tower'

Music Player:
Get the Music Player by completing the 'Extra Vision: Balue's Tower' bonus game.

KNOCKOUT KINGS '99

Fight As A Bear
On the main menu, press ➡ + ■, ➡ + ●, ➡ + ✖.

Big Head Mode
On the main menu, press ⬅ + ●, ⬅ + ▲, ⬅ + ✖.

Taunt
During a bout press **R1** + **R2** + **✖**.

KNOCKOUT KINGS 2000

Extra Fighters
Enter these as your name at the creation screen in exhibition mode:

Clown	**SHMACKO**
Alien	**ROSWELL**
Throbbing Head	**THROB**
Gargoyle	**GARGOYLE**
Basketball Player	**TIM DUNCAN**
Comedian	**MARLON WAYANS**
Hip Hop Musician	**JERMAINE DUPRI**
Trible Quest Member	**Q TIP**
Music Composer	**O**
Founder of Ecko Clothes	**MARC ECKO**
Undefeated Boxer	**ED MAHONE**

KRAZY IVAN

Level Select
To enter your chosen level, start a game and chooe Russia at the mission choice screen. Next press ➡, ⬅, ⬇, ✖.

LEGACY OF KAIN

99 Items
To get 99 items from a spirit forge take over an enemy with the mind control or spirit rack spells and send them into the forge instead of yourself. You will lose their life but gain the items.

Access All Movies
To access all the video sequences in the Dark Diary, press ⬅, ➡, ■, ●, ⬆, ⬇, ➡, ⬅ at any point in the game.

Blood Refill
To refill Kain's blood during the game press ⬆, ➡, ■, ●, ⬆, ⬇, ➡, ⬅.

Extra Magic Energy
For Kain to have extra magic energy, press ➡, ➡, ■, ●, ⬆, ⬇, ➡, ⬅.

LEGEND OF KARTIA

Secret Spells
Create the following spells with these combinations:

Big Disaster   Quake + Big + Disaster

Big Quake	Quake + Mold + Big
Core Quake	Quake + End + World + Star + Law
Hell Quake	Quake + Intense + Violent
Ogre Cap	Hat + Skin + Goblin
Ogre Jacket	Jacket + Skin + Goblin
Ogre Shoes	Shoes + Skin + Goblin
Power Quake	Quake + Strong + Intense
Quick Quake	Quake + Goblin + Fast

LEGO RACER

Enter the following cheats on the 'Make License' screen.

Turbo Mode	**FSTFRWRD**
No Bricks, No Chassis	**NCHSSS**

LIBERO GRANDE

Play As Gregorio Zonaras
Complete Arcade mode on the normal difficulty setting.

Play As Arnold Lang
Score over 8,000 total points on the Player Challenge mode.

Play As Ruprecht Goes
Complete all nine events in the Player Challenge mode.

Play As David Magellan
Score over 1,150 points on every event in the Player Challenge mode.

Play As Roland, Edgard Cailaux, Powel Gardner and Gerald Wells
Win the International Cup with all countries on the normal difficulty setting.

LIFEFORCE TENKA

All Weapons
To gain the full arsenal, Pause the game and hold L1. Then press ▲, R1, ▲, ■, R1, ●, ■, ■, and release L1.

Level Warp
To skip levels, Pause the game and hold L2. Then press ●, ●, ■, ▲, R1, ■, ▲, ●, and release L2.

LOMAX

Helicopter Mode
You can only do this when you have activated the Level Skip cheat. Select the chopper, then press **L1** and ■ to enable you to fly around the levels.

Level Skip

During the game press ↓, **Start**, ↑, (hold), **L1** (hold), ▲, ●, ✖, ■. To the Left of Lomax a number will appear. Press and hold ↑, **L1**, **Select** and **Start**, to skip a level.

LONE SOLDIER

All Weapons

To have all weapons with maximum ammunition, pause the game and press ➡, ↓, ●, ▲, ↑, ➡.

Invincibility

To be invincible, pause the game and press ↑, ⬅, ●, ▲, ↑, ⬅.

Skip Level

To skip a level, pause the game and press ↓, ➡, ●, ▲, ↓, ➡.

LOST VIKINGS 2

Infinite Energy

Go to the password screen (select 'Load Game') and enter the code CH3T. Now enter one of the following level codes and you will have infinite energy:

LEVEL	CODE	LEVEL	CODE
1	NTRO	2	1STS
3	2NDS	4	TRSH
5	SW1M	6	WOLF
7	BR4T	8	K4RN
9	BOMB	10	WXRD
11	BLKS	12	TLPT
13	GYSR	14	B3SV
15	R3TO	16	DRNK
17	YOVR	18	OV4L
19	T1N3	20	D4RK
21	H4RD	22	HRDR
23	LOST	24	OBOY
25	HOM3	26	SHCK
27	TNNL	28	H3LL
29	4RGH	30	B4DD
31	D4DY		

MACHINE HUNTER

Infinite Continues

For unlimited Continues, enter this code on the Password screen: ****URANUS****

MADDEN '97

Block Every Field Goal

When in 3-4 formation, select 54 Angle Man (on the top row, using ✖), and choose to be the nose tackle (in the middle of the defensive line). When the computer snaps the ball, run down towards the kicker to block the kick.

Secret Teams

To choose from some secret teams, go to User Records and enter the code TIBURON in place of your name. When you go to the team selection screen there will be a list of teams.

Special Teams

To have one of the special teams, hold **L2** and **R2** when in Exhibition mode to make a random selection of teams. By repeating this several times you will eventually land on one of the special teams, which include Tibourn, EA Sports, All Pro, All 80's, All 50's, and All 60,s. You will find that you will be more likely to land on a special team if you choose and old team such as the 69 Chiefs, or the 68 Colts.

View Movies

For a choice of movies to watch, while the game is loading, and the Sony Playstation symbol appears, you need to hold down **R1** and **L1** for aproximately 1 minute. Next a screen should appear which shows you a choice of movies.

MADDEN '98

Hidden Teams

Go to the Create Player screen and enter the following names to access the following teams:

AFC Pro Bowl	LUAU
All Time Leaders	LEADERS
All Time All Madden	COACH
All 60's Team	PAC ATTACK
All 70's Team	STEELCURTAIN
All 80's Team	GOLD RUSH
EA Sports Team	ORRS HEROES
NFC Pro Bowl	ALOHA
Tiburon Team	LOIN CLOTH

MADDEN '99

Bonus Teams

Enter one of the following passwords.

Team	Code
NFC Pro Bowl	BESTNFC
AFC Pro Bowl	AFCBEST
All-Madden	BOOM
All-Time Stat Leaders	IMTHEMAN
60s Greats	PEACELOVE
70s Greats	BELLBOTTOMS
80s Greats	SPRBWLSHUFL
90s Greats	HEREANDNOW
All-Time Greats	TURKEYLEG

75th Anniversary Team	**THROWBACK**
NFL Equipment Team	**GEARGUYS**
1999 Cleveland Browns	**WELCOMEBACK**
EA Sports	**INTHEGAME**
Tiburon	**HAMMERHEAD**

Bonus Stadiums

Enter one of the following entries at the code screen.

Stadium	Code
EA Sports	**EA_STADIUM**
Tiburon	**OURHOUSE**
Cleveland	**DOGPOUND99**
RFK	**THEHOGS**
Original Miami	**NOTAFISH**
Original Tampa	**SOMBRERO**
Original Oakland	**STICKEM**
Astrodome	**FOR_RENT**

MADDEN 2000

Cheat Codes

Enter any one of these at the code entry screen:

Increased injuries	PAINFUL
Large vs. small team	MINIME
Bonus stadiums	MULENIUM
Dodge City stadium	WILDWEST
EA Sports stadium	ITSINTHEGAME
Marshalls fantasy team	COWBOYS
No interceptions	EXPRESSBALL
Less penalties	REFISBLIND
All '70s team	LOVEBEADS
All '60s team	MOJOBABY
100 yard field goals	BIGFOOT
100 yard passes	PIGSKINSFLY
5 yard first downs	POPWARNER
All '80s team	BIGHAIR
All '90s team	INTERNS
All-Madden team	TEAMMADDEN
Ball chase view	VERTIGO
EA Sports team	WEARETHEGAME
Easy to intercept	PICKEDOFF
Electric sidelines	STATICCLING
Fast passes	FASTFORWARD
Faster fatigue	FINALTIME
Floating heads	TALKINGWHAT
Frequent fumbles	ROLLERGIRL
Gridiron stadium	KLAATU
Harder to tackle players	TEFLON
Longer jumps	SPRONG
Madden Millennium team	TIMELESS
Maddenstein stadium	COUNTMADDEN
Monsters team	KTHULU
More defensive scoring	FRAPLPRO

Mummies team	WRAPPEDUP
NFL Millennium team	ALLTIMEBEST
Perfect passes	QBINTHECLUB
Praetorians team	DOASWEDO
Receivers catch better	MAGNASAVE
Salvagefield stadium	TETANUSHOT
Stiffer arm	SMACKDOWN
Sugarbuzz team	TREMENDOUS1_2
Super speed burst	NO2
Tiberium stadium	FEEDTHELIONS
Tiburon Bros. Stadium	COTTONCANDY
Tiburon stadium	WEPUTITTHERE
Tiburon team	SHARKATTACK
Toymakers team	XMASFILES

MADDEN NFL 2001

Enter one of the following codes at the code entry screen.

1957 49ers team	Goldrush
1957 Lions team	Lionpower
1958 Colts team	Stables
1958 Giants team	Jollygreen
1962 Oilers team	Therewasaman
1962 Texans team	Getem
1966 Chiefs team	Megiveyou
1966 Cowboys team	Whoshotjr
1966 Packers team	Champs
1967 Cowboys team	Tundra
1967 Packers team	Snowplow
1967 Rams team	Blitzer
1968 Colts team	Shocker
1968 Raiders team	Heidi
1968 Jets team	Tvtimeout
1969 Chiefs team	Nofluke
1970 Browns team	Mnf
1971 Chiefs team	Overtime
1972 Colts team	Airshow
1972 Dolphins team	Perfect
1972 Steelers team	Lucky
1974 Steelers team	Steelcurtain
1975 Cowboys team	Hailmary
1975 Vikings team	Purple
1978 Chargers team	Roller
1978 Oilers team	Earl
1978 Raiders team	Holy
1978 Steelers team	Dynasty
1979 Cowboys team	Comeback
1981 49ers team	Thecatch
1981 Bengals team	Tigers
1981 Chargers team	Ironman
1984 All-Madden team	Madden84
1984 Dolphins team	Dantheman
1985 Bears team	Upset
1985 Falcons team	Flyaway

1985 Patriots team	Blowout
1986 All-Madden team	86madden
1986 Broncos team	Thedrive
1988 All-Madden team	Madden88
1989 Broncos team	Crushed
1990 All-Madden team	90madden
1990 Bills team	Wideright
1991 Falcons team	Neonlights
1992 All-Madden team	Madden92
1992 Bills team	Comebackkid
1993 Bills team	Notagain
1994 All-Madden team	94madden
1994 Chargers team	Charge
1996 All-Madden team	Madden96
1996 Packers team	Almost
1996 Panthers team	Defense
1998 49ers team	Thecatchtwo
1998 All-Madden team	98madden
1998 Packers team	Noluck
1998 Vikings team	Missedchance
EA Sports team	Inthegame

MAGIC CARPET

Go to the options screen and enter the following code: ▲, ▲, ●, ■, ▲, ●, ▲, ■. You should now be able to select any level.

Use the level select code and then pause the game before entering the following codes:

■	for more mana
▲	for all spells
●	restores world

MAGIC THE GATHERING: BATTLE MAGE

Win All Duels
1. Save a tome to a memory card.
2. Start a new campaign or load one up.
3. Play until you are confronted by another wizard and begin a duel.
4. Once the duel has loaded, press both **Start** and **Select** to bring up the quit menu.
5. Press ▲ to reset the game.
6. Select 'Duel' from the main menu.
7. Load up your tome or for the computer wizard select all lands from the CD ROM.
8. Select the duel symbol.
9. Fight the duel, when you win you will be returned to the campaign.
10. Save the game and repeat to win all the duels you fight.

MARVEL SUPER HEROES

Hidden Characters
To gain three new characters follow the instructions below:

Doctor Doom
To play as Dr.Doom you will firstly have to complete the Arcade game at the Default settings. Next, save the game to your memory card and input the following code on the Character Selection screen: Tap ⬇ then press and hold ⬇ + Fierce Kick + Medium Kick + Light Kick. When all of the buttons are held, you will hear "Captain America!"

Thanos
To play as Thanos, (after having enabled Dr.Doom) go to the Character Selection screen and enter the following code: tap ⬆ then press and hold ⬆ + Fierce Punch + Medium Punch + Light Punch. With all buttons held, you will hear "Spider Man!"

Anita
To play as Anita, both Dr.Doom and Thanos must already have been enabled. Go to the Character Selection screen and input this code: Press ⬆, ➡, ⬇, ⬅, ⬆, ➡, ⬇, ⬅. Next, press and hold ⬆ + Light Punch + Medium Punch + Fierce Punch.

MARVEL SUPER HEROES VS STREET FIGHTER

Hidden Characters:
Armoured Spiderman
On the character select screen, highlight Spiderman, hold **Select** and press either punch or kick.

Mephisto
On the character select screen, highlight Omega Red, hold **Select** and press either punch or kick.

US Agent
On the character select screen, highlight Vega/M.Bison, hold **Select** and press either punch or kick.

Shadow
On the character select screen, highlight Dhalsim, hold **Select** and press either punch or kick.

Dark Sakura
On the character select screen, highlight Hulk, hold **Select** and press either punch or kick.

Mech-Zangief
On the character select screen, highlight Blackheart, hold **Select** and press either punch or kick.

Same Character Team Ups
Complete the game once and you will be able to select a

team consisting of two of the same characters.

Extra Options

Complete the game without losing a round and an extra option screen will appear on the option menu.

MASS DESTRUCTION

Level Select

To gain access to all the levels enter TTTTTTTTTTTTGP on the password screen.

MAX POWER RACING

Unlock All The Tracks

In Arcade mode, highlight Africa and press R1, R2, R1, L1, ■, L1.

Unlock All GTI Cars

In Arcade mode, highlight Rome and press L1, ●, R1, ■, L2, ■.

Unlock All Sports Cars

In Arcade mode, highlight the UK and press R1, ■, L1, ●, R2, ●.

Radio Controlled Cars

In Arcade mode, highlight the USA and press ■, L1, R2, L2, ●, R1.

Max Power Race

In Arcade mode, highlight Peru and press ●, ■, R2, R2, R1, R1.

MDK

Level Select

Obtain a level select option on the Main Menu by holding down L1, L2, R1, R2 and pressing ↑, ➡, ▲, ●, ➡. Then quickly release the buttons so that the Stage Select text remains. Now press ■ to change level and ● to change arena.

Full Cheat Codes

Pause the game at any time and enter ↓, L1, ↑, ■. Unpause then Pause again immediately. Now enter any of the following codes:

Full Energy
➡, L1, ■, ▲, L1, ↓.
Super Fast
➡, ●, ▲, ●, ✖.
Mega Gun
➡, ↑, ↓, L1, ↓, ●, ⬅, ⬅.

Nodie
●, ▲, ▲, ●, ➡, ↑, ⬅, L1, ■.
Smallest Nuke
↓, ↑, ■, ▲, ↓, ●, ●, ➡.
Interesting Bomb
↓, ➡, ●, ●, ⬅, ⬅, ↑, ■, ▲.
Hand Grenade
▲, ●, ■, L1, ➡.
Extra Airstrike
↓, ↑, ●, ↓, ↑, ↓, L1.
Chain Gun
⬅, L1, ↓, ■, ▲, ↑, ↓.
Homing Bullets
■, L1, L1, ➡.
Sniper Grenade
↑, ■, L1, ⬅, ●, ▲.
Mortar
⬅, L1, ▲, ■, ➡, ●, ⬅, ⬅.
Seal
●, ▲, ▲, L1, ➡.
Bones Seal
▲, ➡, ●, ⬅, ⬅.
EWJ Power Increase
↑, ↓, ↓, L1, ➡.

MECH WARRIOR 2

Enter the following codes at the password screen:

Cruise Control Throttle

Enter the following code and you will no longer need to hold the throttle button down: #AX0/A4YYA

Extra Chassis Variants

Enter this code and the next time you go to the Change Mech screen you will have a choice of extra chassis variants. Each has different weapons: T#X0/AX<<<

Extra Mech: Elemental

This is a small mech which is like a suit of armour: T/X0/AZ<#*

Extra Mech: Tarantula

For a spider mech: #/X0/A4<LY

Heavy Load Carrying Mechs

You can carry any amount with this code: #0X0/AX>TU

Invincibility

##X0/AXUZ

Jumpjets On All Mechs

#YX0/A>Y0L

Slower Overheating

This code slows down the heat production rate of your

weapons, thereby allowing you to fire more quickly without overheating: #XX0/A4>Y+ =EXTRA HEAT SINK

Unlimited Ammo
T0X0/AX>TU

Unlimited Fuel
TXX0/AZ>=X

Unlock All Missions
T<X0/AXA<=

MEDAL OF HONOR

Enter these codes at the password screen:

CAPTAINDYE	Same Health From The Previous Mission.
MOSTMEDALS	Invincibility
BADCOPSHOW	Infinite Ammunition
SPRECHEN	English Dialogue
TRACERON	Wire Frame Mode
ICOSIDODEC	Raid Fire
GOBLUE	Reflecting Shots
SPYSCHOOL	Theatre Arena in Multiplayer Mode

Multiplayer Codes – Hidden Characters

BEACHBALL	Noah
WOOFWOOF	Dog
BIGFATMAN	Colonel Muller
GUNTHER	Gunther
HERRZOMBIE	Otto
SSPIELBERG	Dinosaur
ROCKETMAN	Werner Von Braun
PAYBACK	Shakespeare
FINESTHOUR	Churchill
HOODUP	Wolfgang

Level Passwords

Level 2	**RETTUNG**
Level 3	**ZERSIOREN**
Level 4	**BOOTSINKT**
Level 5	**SENTGAS**
Level 6	**SCHWERES**
Level 7	**SICHERUNG**
Level 8	**EINSICKERN**
Level 9	**GESAMTHEIT**

DWIGALLERY	Staff Photos
CWIMOHTEAM	Team Photo
AJRULES	Adrian Jones
COOLCHICK	Lynn Henson

MEDIEVIL

Cheat Menu
Pause the game, hold **L2** and press ▲, ●, ▲, ●, ●, ▲, ←, ●, ↑, ↓, →, ●, ←, ←, ▲, →, ●, ←, ←, ▲, ●, ●, ↓, ●, ●, →. An extra option menu will appear.

MEDIEVIL 2

Cheat Menu
During the game, pause, hold **L2** and press ▲, ●, ▲, ●, ●, ▲, ←, ●, ↑, ↓, →, ●, ←, ←, ▲, →, ●, ←, ←, ▲, ●, ↓, ●, ●, →. A cheat option will appear at the bottom of the pause menu.

MEGAMAN X3

End Stage
To access the final stage of the game, enter the Stage Select screen and highlight the "X" logo. Next, quickly press ↓ + ■ + ✖. The cursor will move to the bottom of the screen if successful.

METAL GEAR SOLID

Entrance
Return into the water and collect the **Ration** from behind the steel drum. Crawl under the water tank, wait until the guard turns his back, grab him, then break his neck. Take out the second guard then wait until the elevator arrives. Wait until the guard moves away from the elevator and enter the elevator.

Heli-pad
Collect the **Chaff Grenades** from the heli-pad, then head up and enter the rear of the truck. Collect the **Socom Gun**. Head up to the top right and climb the stairs. Kill the guard or wait until he moves to the far left of the walkway. Crawl through the air vent and into the complex.

Complex
Crawl through the air vent and listen to the guards conversation. Collect the **Ration** and climb down the open vent. Collect the **Thermal Goggles** from the second room on the upper right. Make your way down the stairs, head to the elevator and select B1. Follow the corridor and climb the ladder in the bottom right corner. Crawl through the air vent and take the first left. Watch the guard on the toilet then continue forward and collect the **Socom Bullets**. Return back to the intersection and continue forward. Watch the girl, then continue forward and drop into Donald Anderson's cell. Anderson will give you a **Level 1 Keycard**. After Anderson dies, the girl in the next cell escapes and opens your cell. Collect the **Ration** from under the bed then exit the cell. You will be confronted by the girl from the adjacent cell who will introduce

herself as Meryl. Guards will then storm the cells in groups of three. After each group, collect the ammo and rations they drop before the next wave. Once Meryl has left, return using keycard 1 and enter the cells. Collect the ammo from the toilet and from near the computer. Return to the elevator and select floor 1. Enter the room in the lower right and collect the **Supressor**. If you have not alerted any guards the guard inside will be asleep and you will be able to crawl past him and collect the Supressor without waking him. Return to the elevator and select B2. There are three rooms you can enter using the level 1 keycard. Avoid the trap doors by running across them. Use the **C4** on the discoloured walls to gain access to hidden rooms. These lie in the top left and top right walls near the elevator and one in the bottom left. In the bottom left room use C4 on the discoloured wall halfway down the right wall. There are two walls at the end of the corridor which can be destroyed. The room above leads to the first boss character, the room to the right contains **C4** and a **Ration** guarded by two drone guns. Enter the boss room and prepare to face Revolver Ocelot.

Revolver Ocelot

Only move around the outside of the room. If you touch the trip-wires you will trigger the C4. As soon as you begin run left around the room and follow Ocelot around the room. Wait until he stops and turns to fire at you before firing. Continue to follow him and when he stops flashing fire another shot while running. Once Ocelot has lost his energy, Ninja will appear and release Kenneth Baker. Baker will give you a **Level 2 Keycard** before he dies. Talk to Natasha on radio frequency 141.52.

Return to the large storage room and enter the bottom right room. Equip the thermal goggles, crawl under the infra-red lasers and collect the **FA-MAS** rifle. Return to the elevator and ride up to floor 1. Head up the stairs and collect the **Cardboard Box** from the upper left room. Continue round the top of the room, enter the level 2 door in the upper top right and collect the **Mine Detector** and the **Ration**. Use your radio and contact Meryl on frequency 140.15, eventually she will open the large level 5 door. Head inside and use your thermal goggles to see the infra-red lasers. Once across the room use the level 2 keycard to leave the complex. Use the mine detector to avoid the mines. By crawling over the mines you can pick them up and add them to your inventory.

Vulcan Raven

Before facing Vulcan Raven make sure you have got two spare rations placed on stand by, full health and as many grenades you can carry. Head right and wait near the cliff safe from the shell blasts. Wait until the tank fires a shell before running forward and at the tank. Once you are up close the tank will open fire using its machine guns. Your target is the gunners who both can be killed with two grenades. The best strategy is to circle around the tank, avoiding it and the machine guns. When you are close to the turret throw a grenade at the gunner. It takes two grenades to kill the gunner and there are

two gunners. A direct hit with a grenade will kill the gunner instantly. If you become low on health or ammo, you can collect rations and grenades from the top area. Once you have killed the two gunners, collect any needed items and use the keycard Snake collects from the dead gunner to enter the second complex.

Second Complex

Head left up the walkway and collect the **Ration**. Head down and crawl under the partially open gate. You cannot use any weapons except chaff grenades in this area. If you alert any of the guards the room will fill with gas, so it is best to avoid any confrontations and rely on stealth. Head left and hide behind the crate until the guard walks past. Continue left and up the stairs, wait until the guard walks to the far right of the walkway, then run to the elevator. Once in the elevator select B1. Leave the elevator and enter the double doors. Enter all the rooms you can and collect all the items you find. In one room should be the **Nikita Launcher** and **Nikita Missiles**. Return to the elevator and ride it down to B2. To cross the electrified floor you will need to guide a Nikita missile around the room and destroy the power generator. Guide the missile down the corridor and then left. Destroy the three drone guns on the right then go for the power generator. The room is also filled with gas so after firing a missile you will need to leave the room and recover before returning and firing again. Once destroyed use the keycard to enter the room on the right and collect the **Gas Mask**. Alternate between the gas mask and keycard and explore the rooms on the left of this floor. When finished enter the door in the bottom right. Continue right then enter the top corridor. The room will be filled with dead guards, follow the corridor and enter the door at the end.

Ninja

Your guns will not work against Ninja, so you will need to get up close and use your punch, punch, kick combo (PPK combo). When he has lost 50% of his energy he will cloak himself, use the thermal goggles to find him and attack. Once he has lost another 30% energy, he will de-cloak and fight you hand to hand. When you try to attack him, he will dart behind you and attack you from behind. Throw a single punch then turn around as he darts around you and attack. When he is down to around 5% energy he will start to short circuit. Do not stand to close or you will be hit by his energy field, wait until it dies down, then either use grenades or run up and attack with a combo to finish him off.

Talk to the scientist Hal and he will give you a **Level 4 Keycard**. Collect the items from the room then collect the grenades from the level 4 room in the gas filled corridor. Return to the elevator and go up to floor B1. Be careful as Meryl is disguised as one of the guards on this floor. She should be on the left side of the lower computer room. When you find her, follow her to the ladies rest room. She will give you a **Level 5 Keycard** and the **Pal Key**. Return to the lower computer room and collect the **Diazepam** and the **Night Vision Goggles** from the side rooms. Return to the corridor and enter the level 5 room at the end of the corridor.

Psycho Mantis

Here you will be confronted by Psycho Mantis. As you enter he will possess Meryl and try to shoot you. Knock her out by using a stun grenade. Psycho Mantis will then attack you himself. You can avoid all his flying projectile attacks by laying on the floor, the only attack you need to worry about is the energy balls he fires at you. Learn his pattern and when there is an opening attack him with a PPK combo. This will take ages, so you will need to be patient. When he has lost half of his energy he will revive Meryl. Knock her out using a throw or a stun grenade before she shoots herself. He will then cloak himself and levitate around the room. Use the thermal goggles and attack him before he fires his energy ball. When he has only 10% energy left he will throw all his projectiles at you at once. Lay on the floor and when you see an opening, attack with a PPK combo.

Before Psycho Mantis dies he will open a secret door behind one of the bookshelves. Go through the secret door, collect the **Ration**, **Socom** and **FA-Mas Ammunition**, then use the level 5 keycard to open the door at the end. Use the equip and the night vision goggles and crawl under the rock wall. Use a stun grenade to knock out the wolves and head right. Crawl through the left gap and collect the **PSG1 Ammunition**. Return under the gap and crawl through the right gap and follow the wolf cub to find Meryl. Collect the **Ration** and enter through the level 5 door. Equip the thermal goggles, then crawl on the ground and collect the **Claymore Mines**. Meryl will be shot down, if you move near her you will be shot. Quickly leave back through the door and make your way back through the second complex to the first complex. Ride the elevator down to B2 and enter the top left room. The storage room is now guarded by heavily armoured troops. Once inside, equip the thermal goggles and crawl past the infra red laser. Collect the **PSG1 Sniper Rifle**, then leave. Head down through the bottom level 4 door into the room where you fought Ocelot. Head down and right into the small corridor with the two drone guns. Enter the level 4 room and collect the **Camera**. Head back to where you left Meryl, on the way collect any items you need.

Sniper Wolf

When you reach the area you discover Meryl has gone. Sniper Wolf is at the end of the stone passageway. Face forward then select the PSG1 to get into sniper mode. It takes six direct shots to defeat her. If she hits you, get up and reposition yourself. Do not try to re-aim in sniper mode once you get hit as it will take too long and you will be hit again. Once Sniper Wolf has fallen, run forward and collect any items you find. Try to enter the level 6 door and you will be captured.

Torture Room

Snake will be taken to the torture room in the first complex. Ocelot will torture Snake by electrocuting him. Tap ● as fast

as you can to keep Snake alive. You will have to do this three times, each time for a longer amount of time. If you survive you will be locked in a cell with the body of Anderson. After a few minutes you will be taken back to the torture room. Do the same as before and you will eventually be returned to your cell. The guard will run off to the toilet and while he is gone Hal will appear. Hal will give you a **Level 6 Keycard**, a **Cloth** and a bottle of **Ketchup**. There are three ways to escape. Hide under the bed and when the guard returns he will unlock your cell. Lay on the floor and use the ketchup, the guard will return, believe you are dead and open your cell. If you fail to escape you will be tortured again. When you return Ninja will appear and set you free. When you escape kill the guard and enter the torture room. Collect your belongings from the red box and dispose of the timed bomb in your inventory. Head back to the second complex and ride the elevator to floor B2. Collect the **Body Armour** from the level 6 room. Then return to the level 6 door where you fought Sniper Wolf.

As soon as you enter the building, the alarm will sound. Run down the corridor and collect the **Rope** as you go. Equip the body armour and run up the stairs. Ignore the first door and continue up the stairs. When you get guards in front of you, grab them and throw them down the stairs. This will usually knock down the guards behind you. When you reach the top use the FA-MAS to kill any guards behind you. Climb the ladder and head out onto the roof. Walk towards the Satellite dish and it will be destroyed. Use the rope to absail down the side of the tower. Use ✖ to kick your way down to the walkway below. Use the PSG1 to shoot at the guards at the end of the walkway. When they run off, move to the left and wait. When they return wait until they stop firing, then use the PSG1 to kill them in safety. When they are dead, follow the walkway up and left. Collect the **Stinger** and **Stinger Missiles** and enter through the bottom door. The elevator is inactive and the stairs up are blocked. Descend the stairs and you will discover the lower staircase has been destroyed. Return up to the lift and Hal will appear. He will move the blocked stairs for you. Use chaff grenades to disable the four sets of drone guns. Collect the ammunition and climb the ladder to the roof.

Gunship

Once on the roof you will be attacked by a gunship piloted by Liquid Snake. Stay in between the two buildings and use the stinger to lock onto the gunship. Keep out of the gunship's line of fire when it fires its minigun. If you run low on stinger missiles there are extra ones in the bottom right corner. Once you have destroyed the gunship, Liquid Snake will take unleash a bombardment of missiles at the roof. Take cover in the bottom left corner of the roof.

Return down the stairs to the elevator. Ride the elevator down and you will be attacked by four experimental cloaked shock troops. Throw the guards at each other, then you can grab them and break their necks. Collect the ration and ammunition and exit through the level 6 door. Disable the drone gun and continue through the corridor. Disable the three drone guns in the next corridor and exit through the door at the end.

Sniper Wolf

Use the same tactic as before. Watch for her laser trail to find where she is hiding. There are PSG1 ammunition and rations to the far left and right of the compound entrance.

Search the compound rooms and collect the items inside. Most of the rooms either have drone guns or claymores inside. Once you have collected everything head into the top left room. Disable the two drone guns and descend the stairs in the top right corner of the room. Head left and shimmy along the ledge. Duck under the counter weight as it passes you. If you choose you can use a stinger missile to destroy the counter weight but this will alert the guards. Walk down the stairs and kill the guard. If you are low on ammunition enter the door opposite the large double doors. Avoid the steam and crawl under the pipes on the left. Collect the ammunition and return to the double doors. Ride the platform lift down. As you descend you will be attacked by three guards. Grab them one by one and break their necks. When you reach the bottom, disable the drone gun then use the thermal goggles to avoid the claymore mines. Activate the second platform lift. Collect the items hidden around the crates and enter the double doors.

Vulcan Raven

The easiest way to beat Raven is to use stinger missiles. Wait until he appears around the corner and fire a stinger missile just as he turns to face you. Move around one of the crates and wait until he follows you around. Again as he turns to face you fire another stinger missile. Continue this method until he is dead. If you have run out of stinger missiles you can lay claymore mines around him. Another way is to guide nikita missiles around him and blow him up as he turns a corner. Before Raven dies he will give you the **Level 7 Keycard**.

Metal Gear Hanger

If you are low on ammunition you can return to the outside compound and open the level 7 room. Enter the door at the end of the Raven room. Disable the drone guns and watch out for the trap doors. Collect the stinger missiles and enter the level 7 door. Climb the ladders on the right side of the metal gear. Climb over the metal gear and kill the guard. Listen to the conversation between Liquid Snake and Ocelot. Ocelot will shoot the Pal Key from your grasp. Climb back down the ladders and search for the Pal Key in the water. Once you have found it, return to the control room. Disable the three drone guns and insert the Yellow Pal Key in the left lap top. The Blue and Red Pal Keys represents the appropriate temperatures needed for that key. Return to the Raven room and after a few minutes the Yellow Pal Key will turn blue. Return to the control room and insert the Blue Key Card in the central lap top. Head to the furnace room and the Blue Key Card will turn red. Return to the control room and insert the Red Pal Key into

the right lap top. Master Miller will reveal himself as a disguised Liquid Snake and the room will fill with gas. Contact Hal and he will open the doors. Follow Liquid Snake.

Metal Gear Rex

Use chaff grenades to disable the metal gear's missiles. Target the right dish and open fire with your stinger missiles. Ninja will then appear and attack the metal gear. After Ninja's/Fox's death use the same tactics as before. This time target Liquid Snake in the centre of the metal gear with your stinger missiles.

Liquid Snake

When you awake, you will find yourself on the top of the destroyed metal gear. You have to fight a one on one fight with Liquid Snake. Run up close and use a PPK combo. Throws are useless and Snake will escape if you try to grab him. When he is low on energy he will charge at you. Simple side step his attack and use a PPK combo.

The Escape

If Meryl is alive after you defeat Liquid Snake she will drive the jeep. If she is dead, Hal will appear and drive instead. Collect the **Ration** from the bottom of the stairs then enter the jeep compound. Throw the guards until Meryl/Hal starts the jeep. Jump on the back and shoot the barrels to blow up the gate. Use the first person view and kill the guards at the checkpoints. When Liquid Snake returns, continue to fire at him until you reach the tunnel entrance.

Bonus Item

If you rescue Meryl you will be given a **Bandanna** to use during your next game. If you escape with Hal you will obtain **Stealth**.

METAL GEAR SOLID VR MISSIONS

Frequencies
Campbell/Naomi 140.85
Mel Ling 140.96
Master 141.80
Otacon 141.12
Meryl 140.15
Nastasha 141.52
Deepthroat 140.48

MICRO MACHINES

The following codes can be entered at any time during a game, and can be cancelled by re-entering the same code.

Big Bounce: ■, ➡, ➡, ⬇, ⬆, ⬇, ⬅, ⬇, ⬇.
Change car into an object: ⬇, ⬇, ⬆, ⬆, ➡, ➡, ⬅, ⬅.
Double Speed: ■, ✖, ●, ■, ▲, ✖, ✖, ✖, ✖.

Lower camera: ←, →, ■, ●, ←, →, ■, ●.
Slow down CPU cars: ●, ▲, ■, ✖, ●, ▲, ■, ✖.

Debug Mode
To enter Debug mode enter the following code at any time: ■, ↑, ↓, ↓, ■, ●, ●, ▲, ✖. The following options are now available:
To blow up all the cars: ✖, ▲, ●, and ■
To look at a different car: **Select** and **L1/R1**
To move the camera: **Select** and **D-Pad**
To move the cameras in and out: **L2/R2**
To quit the race and still win: **Select** and ✖
To turn player's car into drone: **Select** and ■

Tanks On All Tracks
To have tanks on all of the tracks, enter **TANKS4ME** as a character name.

MICRO MANIACS

Infinite Power Ups
Go to the secret option screen, then hold **Select** and enter
●, ✖, ▲, ■, ✖, ←, ✖, ■, ■, ●, ←, ●, ↑, ▲.

MISSION IMPOSSIBLE

Cheat Codes
Select Load Game and enter these as a special password. Ignore the bad password response.

Super Jumps	**BIONICJUMPER**
Disable AL	**SCAREDSTIFF**
Turbo Mode	**GOOUTTAMYWAY**
Slow Motion Mode	**IMTIREDTODAY**
View In Game Movies	**SEECOOLMOVIE**
A Message from the Writer	**TTOPFSECRETT**

Level Codes

Subpen Area	**ABEMJQLNVTPG**
Russian Embassy	**OGLIESHVIRLL**
KGB Warehouse	**OQRFFSITJMNI**
KGB Headquarters	**EHNJHSURWJMP**
Security Hallway	**GDPSISJOWUAN**
Underground Sewage Plant	**GGHIHSJVWRML**
Security Hallway 2	**GQOFISKTLMAI**
KGB Headquarters	**IGCJMJMVMRBL**
Russian Embassy	**IQDSNJNTOMCI**
IMF Headquarters	**IJENMUNHONCJ**
IMF Headquarters 2	**IMQPNHNKOSCM**
Infirmary	**PBFROUOPPWDB**
CIA Rooftops	**PMGKPUPKQSDM**
CIA Mainframe Computer	**PJGNOUPHQNDJ**
CIA Rooftops	**KEJPPUPSRKEE**
Waterloo Station	**HDGGFPKQMOBC**

Train	**IGILGPMLMYBO**
Train 2	**HDGOFTKQMOBC**
Train Roof	**IGJDGTMLMYBO**
Lundkvist Base	**NGHSMGQTXMGI**
Tunnel	**MOEEOJGHVXJH**
Mainland	**MKEHTJSSVVJD**
Gunboat	**AFQMOJGPVTPG**

MONSTER TRUCKS

Go to the main menu to enter the following codes. You will need to do this each time you race.

CODE	ACTION
L1, R2, L2, R1, ↑	Extra tall trucks
L2, ←, →, ↑, ↓, R2	Greater durability of trucks
←, ←, ←, ↑, ↓, L1, R2	No damage
←, L1, R2, R1, ←, R2, R2, R2	Super-grip tyres
L1, L1, R1, R1, L2, L2, R2, R2	When you press ▲ you will be winched to the nearest checkpoint (Endurance races)

MORTAL KOMBAT MYTHOLOGIES
Passwords

Wind Level	THWMSB
Earth Level	CNSZDG
Water Level	ZVRKDM
Fire Level	JYPPHD
Prison level	RGTKCS
Fortress Level	XJKNZT
Fortress Stage	ZCHRRY
Lives	GTTBHR
Urns of Vitality	NXCVSZ
View Credits	CRVDTS

MORTAL KOMBAT TRILOGY

Access ? Screen
To access the '?' in the options screen, go to the options screen and highlight any box. Hold **L1, L2, R1,** and **R2** all at the same time, then press ↑. You should hear a boom and now you can access the '?'. The selections are:

One Button Fatalities ON/OFF
Instant Aggressor ON/OFF
Normal Boss Damage ON/OFF
Health Recovery ON/OFF
Low Damage

One Button Fatalities
Stand next to your opponent and press the relevant button:

HP - brutality
HK - fatality 1
LK - fatality 2
LP - stage fatality
R1 - friendship
R2 - animality
L2 - babality

Crispy

To hear Shao Kahn say 'Crispy', hold both the Run buttons after you do the stage fatality on Scorpion's Lair.
To make Dan Forden pop out and say 'Crispy', hold both of the punch buttons.
To hear Shao Kahn and Dan Forden say 'Crispy' together, hold both run buttons and both punch buttons.

Frosty

To make Dan Forden say 'Frosty' instead of 'Toasty', you must freeze your opponent when he or she is in danger.

Pit Fatalities

Perform the following for some spectacular fatalities:
Pit 1 - uppercut
Pit 2 - perform the stage fatality
Pit 3 - perform the stage fatality
Dead Pool - hold **LK**, **LP** and ⬇ then press **HP**
Kombat Tomb - perform the stage fatality
Shao Kahn Tower - perform the stage fatality
Subway - perform the stage fatality

Play As Chameleon

Choose either Human Smoke, Ermac, Classic Sub-Zero, Scorpion, Noob Saibot, Rain, or Reptile, and before the round starts, hold ⬅, **R1**, **R2**, ▲, and ■. You will find that Chameleon now has the abilities of the same colour Ninja that he morphs into.

Quick Exit

If you wish to exit a game during a match, press **Start** and then **Select** to be given an exit option.

Random Select

While the default players are highlighted, press ⬆ and **Start** at the select screen.

Shao Kahn's Treasure Chest

Once you have beaten Shao Kahn you can select a symbol:
Box 1 - character endings
Box 2 - fight Chameleon
Box 3 - MK1 classic endurance kombat
Box 4 - MK2 classic endurance kombat
Box 5 - random prize
Box 6 - fatality demo 1
Box 7 - fatality demo 2
Box 8 - fatality demo 3
Box 9 - super endurance kombat (all females and Robot Ninjas)
Box 10 - battle with Shokan champions (bosses)

Box 11 - mega endurance kombat (all Ninjas and Chameleon)
Box 12 - supreme fatality

Stage Select

To play in your own choice of background, highlight Sonya in the character select screen and hold the **Start** button, then press ⬆ on the control pad. You should hear an exploding sound. Once you have chosen your character you can choose a background. If there are 2 players, the person who enters the code will be the one to choose the background.

Ye Olde Characters

To reveal the 2 MK and 2 MK2 characters, press **Select** on the relevant character and you will find out their previous incarnation. The characters are Kano, Rayden, Kung Lao, and Jax.

MOTO RACER

All of the following cheats should be entered on the Start/Options screen using control pad one:
All Ten Tracks
   To race on all of the tracks press ⬆, ⬆, ⬅, ➡, ⬇, ⬇, ●, R2, ▲, ✖.
All Ten Tracks-Reversed
   For some backwards fun enter ⬇, ⬇, ➡, ⬅, ⬆, ⬆, ●, L2, ▲, ✖.
Night-time Racing
   For a shot in the dark, enter ⬆, ●, L1, ⬇, ▲, L2, ●, ⬅, R1, ✖.
Pocket Bike
   For tiny racing, enter the code ⬆, ⬇, R2, L2, ⬇, ⬆, L1, ✖.
Reverse Mode
   Use this code to drive backwards without gaining extra tracks: ⬅, ➡, ⬅, ➡, ■, ●, R1, L1, ▲, ✖.
Slow Opponents
   To make your opponents race at 50 km/h, enter ⬇, ⬇, ⬇, ●, L1, ●, L2, ⬇, ⬇, ✖.
Ultra-fast Bike
   For mega-speed, press ⬆, ⬆, ⬆, ▲, R1, ▲, R2, ⬆, ⬆, ✖.
View Credits Movie
   To view the game credits, enter ●, ▲, ●, ●, ▲, ●, ⬆, ➡, ⬅, ✖.
View Victory Movie
   To revel in glory, press ●, ▲, ●, ▲, ●, ▲, L1, ⬆, R2, ✖.

MOTO RACER 2

Passwords
Open all the tracks   **cdnalsi**
Mini Bikes   **ctekcop**

MOTORHEAD

Secret Codes And Passwords
Enter these on the password screen.
COWRULES to unlock division 2 cars and tracks.
FRAGTIME to unlock division 1 and 2 cars and tracks.
INSANITY to change the demo mode.
LASTCODE to unlock all cars and tracks.
SOFTHEAD to activate in game motion blur.
SUPERCAR to activate above the car camera view.
TURBOMOS to unlock Nolby Hills

Alternative Credits
On the credits screen, hold **L1 + L2 + R1 + R2 + ● + ■.**

Secret Message
Enter your name as **SH4** to replace the credits screen with a secret message.

MOTORTOON GRAND PRIX 2

Advanced Options
For an advanced options menu, hold **L1**, **L2**, **R1**, **R2** while choosing Options.

Expanded Options
For an expanded options menu, hold **L1**, **L2**, **R1**, **R2** and ✖ while choosing Options.

Extra Characters
To get the extra characters Vanity (motorbike), Billy the Tough (train), and Ching Tong Shang (F1 car), complete the game in Easy mode.

Extra Tracks
To use the first 5 tracks in reverse order and with different scenery and colours, you must complete the game in Normal mode.

MotorTooner
To race on a different version of Toon Island II in either an F1 or a stock car, complete the game in Export mode.

Submarine X
To play a linkable 3D version of the Battleships boardgame, complete the game in Professional mode.

Tank Combat
To play a linkable first-person perspective tank combat game, complete the game in Hard mode.

Sony Replays and Ghosts
To watch or race against ghosts of the Sony teams' best times, hold **R1** when you select any memory card accessing option. This lets you access the replays on the game CD.

MR DRILLER

If you time it right it is possible to drill a cube that's about to fall on your head. This can be very useful in tight situations. As timing is hard to judge you should only use it rarely though!

To open up new challenges you need to clear each stage in the Time Trial mode. You should make sure that you then save your progress.

MUPPET RACE MANIA

Cheat Codes
These must be entered on the main title screen before pressing **Start** to bring up the menu screen.

Unlock the Main 24 Courses.
●, ▲, ✖, ●, ▲, ✖, ●, ▲, ■, ✖

Unlock all the Muppets and Vehicles.
▲, ●, ▲, ■, ▲, ✖, ▲, ▲, ✖, ●

Unlock the Studio Course
■, ■, ●, ●, ✖, ●, ▲, ●, ▲, ■

Unlock the Arches Course.
■, ●, ✖, ●, ■, ▲, ●, ✖, ●, ▲

Unlock the Fraggle Rock Course.
✖, ■, ✖, ■, ✖, ■, ▲, ●, ✖, ■

End Credits and Overhead Tracks.
●, ▲, ■, ▲, ✖, ▲, ■, ●, ▲, ✖

On the main menu screen, select Options, then The End. During the credits, press Start and the view will switch to an overhead view.

N20

Level Passwords

Level 3	●, ✖, ●, ●, ■, ▲, ✖, ▲
Level 4	●, ●, ▲, ●, ▲, ●, ■, ■
Level 5	■, ▲, ■, ▲, ■, ▲, ▲, ●
Level 6	■, ■, ●, ■, ▲, ✖, ▲, ✖
Level 7	✖, ▲, ●, ■, ✖, ▲, ●, ▲
Level 8	■, ●, ●, ▲, ▲, ■, ▲, ■
Level 9	■, ●, ✖, ▲, ■, ■, ✖, ●
Level 10	✖, ▲, ■, ●, ▲, ✖, ✖, ✖
Level 11	●, ■, ▲, ■, ●, ▲, ■, ▲
Level 12	●, ✖, ✖, ✖, ▲, ✖, ✖, ■
Level 13	■, ▲, ▲, ●, ●, ✖, ●, ●
Level 14	■, ■, ▲, ●, ●, ▲, ●, ✖
Level 15	●, ▲, ✖, ■, ●, ▲, ▲, ▲

Level 16	●, ■, ▲, ✖, ●, ●, ●, ■
Level 17	✖, ●, ▲, ✖, ■, ■, ■, ●
Level 18	●, ▲, ●, ●, ▲, ■, ■, ✖

Cheats

Level Select	■, ●, ✖, ▲, ▲, ✖, ●, ✖
Extra Lives	●, ✖, ✖, ▲, ■, ▲, ■, ●
Water Mode	●, ✖, ■, ▲, ▲, ●, ▲, ●
Extra Weapons	■, ✖, ●, ■, ✖, ■, ●, ■
Firewalls	✖, ✖, ■, ✖, ✖, ✖, ▲, ▲

NAGANO WINTER OLYMPICS '98

Gold Menu
On the title screen, press ↑, ↓, ←, →, ▲, ●, ■, ←, ←, →, ✖, ↓, ↓, ↑, ▲, ✖.

Watch The Ending
At the options, press L1, R2, ●, ■, ▲, go to Event Select, choose Olympics. Enter your name as **TWY** from Russia. Go to the select screen to access the ending.

NAMCO MUSEUM VOLUME 4

Extra Continues
To earn extra Credits in any of the games, as often as desired, simply press select.

NASCAR RACING

Hidden Game
To bring up a Tron clone directly from the eighties, press ✖ on controller two during the start of the Title sequence, and race that Light Cycle.

NASCAR RACING '99

Extra Drivers
Select Single Race and choose the track relevant to the driver. Highlight 'Select Car' and enter the code below:

Bobby Allison, Charlotte
←, ↑, →, ■, ✖, ●, L1, L2, R2, R1.

Davey Allison, Talladega
↑, ✖, ↓, R1, ←, ●, →, ■, L2, R2.

Alan Kulwicki, Bristol (Day)
R1, R1, R2, R2, ■, ■, ●, ●, ✖, ✖.

Cale Yarborough, Darlington
↑, ↑, ↑, ■, ■, ■, ←, ●, ●, ←.

Richard Petty, Martinsville
↑, R1, →, ●, ↓, ✖, ←, ■, L1, R1.

Benny Parsons, Richmond
R2, R2, L1, L1, L2, L2, R1, R1, R2, L1.

Paintball Mode
Pause the game during a race and go to the Race Statistics screen. Press **L1 + L2 + R1 + R2**. Return to the race and by pressing ▲ you can fire paintballs.

NBA HANGTIME

Extra Players
To gain extra players, input the name of the desired player at the Enter Name screen, and PIN to gain access to him.

Name	PIN	Player
MRICH	2020	Dan AmricH
BARDO	6000	BardoCA
PESINA	1010	Carlos Pesina
DANR	0000	Dan Roan
DANIEL	0604	Daniel
ThompsonDIVITA	0201	Sal Divita
EDDIE	6213	Eddie Ferrier
EUGENE	6767	Geer
JAMIE	1000	Jamie Rivett
JAPPLE	6660	Japple
JC	0000	John Carlton
JFER	0503	Jennifer Hedrick
JONHEY	6000	Jon Hey
KOMBAT	0004	Ed Boon
MARTY	1010	Martinez
MEDNIK	6000	Mednik
MINIFE	6000	Minife
MORRIS	6000	Air Morris
MORTAL	0004	John Tobias
MUNDAY	5432	Larry Munday
MXV	1014	Vinikour
NICK	7000	Nick Ehrlich
NFUNK	0101	Neil Funk
PERRY	3500	Matthew Perry
PIPPEN	0000	Scottie Pippen
QUIN	0330	Kevin Quinn
ROOT	6000	John Root
SHAWN	0123	Shawn Liptak
SNO	0103	S. Oursler
TURMEL	0322	Mark Turmell

NBA JAM EXTREME

Extra Players
To gain a plethora of new characters, firstly start the game, then answer Yes to Keep Records? Next enter one of the

following records:

Character	Record
George Cervin	ICE Apr 7
XX Stinger	MSS Oct 26
Mr. Unhappy	GEM Nov 3
Dufus the Clown	GRR Jun 19
Three Feet Under	TOD Apr 17
Ooooh	jLH Jan 26
Who	WHO Jan1
Mark Canus	MMG Sep 16
Brained	BCS Jan 7
Monkey Boy	PJP Nov 2
Dwain Skinner	DAS Feb 21
John Elway	WAY Sep 30
Marv Albert	MRV Dec 31
Frank Thomas	BIG Dec 6
Newt Gingrich	NEW Aug 12
Pirate Bill	SAL Feb 2
Mr. Happy	MJT Mar 22
Rebecca Lobo	LOB Jul 4
Carol Blazejowski	BLzMar 1
Bob Lanier	LAN Sep 10
Air Nick	ARN May 18
Dave Ross	DJR Jun 8
Jeff Peters	JBP May 17
Daren Smith	DRS Apr 10
Mike Callahan	MWC May 1
The Tinman	TIM Jan 24
Roy Wilkins	RNW Sep 15
Rob Daurel	RAD Mar 19
Howie	BCE Jul 10
Jim Jung	JKJ Dec 13
Huh	CBR Jun 25
Cheryl Swoopes	SWO Jan 1
Junior Seau	JR Jun 1
XX Shamrock	JHG Aug 26
Diamond Dave	DJP Jun 29
Chris Slate	JCS Dec 8
Sausage Boy	TVC Oct 3
Richard Szeto	RTS Feb 25

NBA LIVE '98

Secrets

To access the secrets mode, firstly start a new game and select any teams. When you get to the User Setup screen, press ⬆ to change "Player 1" to "Start New", then press ✖ to enter your name as "Secrets" and **Start** to accept it. Next, press ● to open the new Secrets option at the bottom of the screen, highlight the "Enter Secret Code" option, and press ✖. Finally, enter any of the following codes and press **Start** to make the option appear on the Secrets menu. You can toggle its setting by highlighting it and pressing ⬅ or ➡:

Chameleon Mode

Enter "Lizard" and toggle the "Chameleon Home" option to make any or all of your players blend in with the court. Also, enter "Reptile" to enable the same options for the away team.

Change Costumes

Enter "Scary", and toggle the "Halloween Home" option to Clown, Alien or Mummy. Also, enter "Freaky" for the Halloween Away option for the visiting team.

Teddy Bear Players

Enter "Pin rocks" and choose the "He's both" answer. Toggle the "Loveable Pin" option to play as teddies. You must first have obtained the Halloween costumes option.

Wet Court

Enter "Seaweed" and toggle the Aqua Court to play underwater.

Hidden Teams

To gain access to the secret teams, firstly press ● on the Main Menu and choose Rosters, then Custom Teams. Next, enter the desired code:

City	Team
EA	Europals
Hitmen	Coders
Hitmen	Earplugs
Hitmen	Idlers
Hitmen	Pixels
QA	Campers
QA	DBuggers
QA	Testtubes
TNT	Blasters

Free Throw Tricks

Granny Throw

Hold **R1** during a free throw and you will throw the ball underarm.

Spinning Ball

Hold down **R1+L1** and press ✖ when the ball is moving on the aiming crosshair and you will spin the ball in your hands.

Warm-up Shot

Hold **L1** during a free throw and your player will bounce and play with the ball before making the shot.

NBA LIVE '99

Fake Out Defense

When you have got the ball, wait for a defender to come up to you, hold down **R2** and press the direction pad as if you were dribbling up court. Let go of **R2**, quickly press ■, then dribble up court the opposite way. The defender will be faked out, and you will have an open path to the hoop.

Fake Pass
During gameplay press **L2 + ✖** for a fake pass.

Sun's Gorilla
Go to the **Create a Player** screen and enter the name **BIG BOY**. Now enter Charles Barkley's attributes. You should have Phoenix's Gorilla mascot as a free agent.

NBA SHOOTOUT '97

All-Star Difficulty
To make the game insanely hard, firstly go to the Game Options screen. Highlight "Difficulty", and press **L1**, **R1**, **L2**, **R2**. The new skill level of "Super All-Star" should now be selectable.

NEED FOR SPEED

Extra Weight
Help your car to turn more sharply by adding weight to the front or rear. Go to Tournament mode and enter the code TSYBNS, then you may either continue in this mode or quit it. From the car selection screen, choose Car Showcase, and then Mechanical. Select Next Slide. You will see that you may now add the extra weight by pressing **L1** if you wish to add to the front of the car, or by pressing **R1** for the rear. The amount of weight is indicated by red triangles at either end of the car.

Lost Vegas Track
To select Lost Vegas, enter the password TSYBNS at the Tournament password screen, then go back to the Head-to-Head game. Lost Vegas will now be selectable as you cycle through the tracks.

Lunar Springs Track
To race on a track set in a lunar landscape, access the Tournament mode and enter the password SPKSHC. Next choose another mode, and on the track select screen highlight Rusty Springs. Press and hold **▲**, press **L1** and **R1**. Use **✖** to select Rusty Springs.

Machine Gun Code
Fire an invisible machine gun that removes cars and police vehicles from your pathway by choosing the Head-to-Head mode, and pressing and holding the following sequence immediately after selecting your opponents' car: **L1**, **●**, **■**, **↖**. Hold the buttons until loading is complete. Now you can fire the machine gun by using the horn button.

No Mercy Mode
To turn off the slower car catch-up, again enter the code TSYBNS, go to the Head-to-Head screen and hold down **L1** and **R1** to change the option to NO MERCY.

Oasis Springs Track
Enter the password TSYBNS at the Tournament password screen as before, then go to the Rusty Springs track while in Head-to-Head mode. To turn the track into Oasis Springs, hold down **L1** and **R2** together, and while holding them, press **Start**.

Rally Mode
To race on a muddy rally track, enter the password TSYBNS as before and enter the Head-to-Head mode. Choose a track and then hold down **L1** and **R1** to see RALLY MODE on the screen. Press **Start**.

Warrior Car
Enter TSYBNS as before, and go from Head-to-Head mode to the car selection screen. Hold down **L1** and **R1** to select the Warrior car.

Passwords

Track 1	WRDRTY
Track 8	KJPQND
Track 2	ZDPBWN
Track 9	SDQWCG
Track 3	MTQRZP
Track 19	SLZXDH
Track 4	JVPZLL
Track 11	SPZDFX
Track 5	ZYMNLH
Track 12	ZVGRGX
Track 6	WMRPGZ
Track 13	XJHVCK
Lost Vegas	YXGSJJ

NEED FOR SPEED 2

Extra Car
To win the tournament and have the Ford indigo, enter the password LILZIP.

Extra Track
To race on the Monolithic Stidios track, enter the password SHOTME.

Extra Vehicles
To drive one of the following vehicles, enter the corresponding password and start the race. For player two to drive one of these vehicles, replace the 'ME' part of each code with 'U', eg ARMYME becomes ARMYU.

VEHICLE	PASSWORD
Army truck	ARMYME
Audi Quattro	QUATME
BMW	BMRME
Bus	BUSME
Camper Van	VANME
Citroen 2CV	CITME
Comanche pick-up truck	JEPME
Crate	CRATME

Jeep	YJME
Limo	LIMOME
Log	LOGME
Mazda Miata	MAZME
Mercedes Benz	BNZME
Outhouse	OUTHME
Snow Truck	SNOWME
Stand A	STDAME
Stand B	STDBME
Stand C	STDCME
T Rex	TREXME
Toyota LandCruiser	LCME
Trabant	BEETME
Tram	TRAMME
Truck Cab	SEMIME
Volvo Estate	VOVME
VW Beetle	BUGME
Wagon	WAGOME

Faster Car

For a Pioneer engine that gives better acceleration in Arcade mode, and acceleration and top speed in Simulation, enter the password POWRUP.

More Camera Views

For an extra five camera angles, go to the main menu, start the race and then hold the following: **L1 + L2 + R1 + R2 + ✖ + ▲ + ■ + ●**. When the race starts, release the buttons. (These extra views will disappear if you restart the race.)

NEED FOR SPEED 3

Extra Cars

Jaguar XJR 15
   Win a tournament in Beginner Mode
Mercedes CLK-GTR
   Win a tournament in Expert Mode
Bonus Car
   Win a knockout contest in Expert Mode

Change Land Rovers

Select Hot Pursuit Mode then select Redrock Ridge. Press **Start** then instantly hold down the **↓ + R1 + L2** buttons until the loading screen appears. The Land Rovers should now be beige cop cars.

Germanic Police

Select Hot Pursuit Mode press **Start** to load the race then instantly hold down the, **↑ + R1 + L2** buttons until the loading screen appears. The Police should now speak with German accents.

Play The Game With The Replay Camera

Enter **SEEALL** as your name.

All Basic Cars and Tracks
Enter **SPOILT** as your name.

The Room Track
Enter **PLAYTM** as your name.

The Caverns Track
Enter **XCAV8** as your name.

The Scorpio-7 Track
Enter **GLDFSH** as your name.

The Space Race Track
Enter **MNBEAM** as your name.

The Autocross Track
Enter **XCNTRY** as your name.

The Empire City Track
Enter **MCITYZ** as your name.

Unlock The Mercedes Benz
Enter **AMGMRC** as your name.

Unlock The Jaguar
Enter **1JAGX** as your name.

NEED FOR SPEED: ROAD CHALLENGE

Enter these codes as a player name in the "User name" option. When the codes are entered you will not be able to save.

Police Helicopter
Whirly (only available in Test Drive mode)
Super Car
Hotrod
Titan Car
Flash
Dashboard view
At the Loading screen, press and hold **↑ + ▲ + ✖**.
Drunk mode
At the Loading screen, press and hold **↑ + L2 + R1**.
Turbo
Enable the Dashboard view then while driving press **↑**.
Slow CPU cars
At the Loading screen, press and hold **← + ■ + ●**.
Heavy car
At the Loading screen, press and hold **← + ■ + ●**.

Money Trick

Buy the best car you can and save it to a memory card. Copy the memory card data to a second memory card creating a clone of your original car. Enter High Stakes and race both your original car against the clone car. Come first with the original car and you will win the clone car. Sell the clone car and upgrade the original car with the extra money. Repeat again to gain more money.

NFL GAME DAY

Secret Options Menu

To enable several new options, including the ability to play against ickle rabbits, enter the following code as soon as the NFL Game Day logo appears on the screen: **R1**, **R1**, **L2**, **L1**, ▲, ●, ■, **L1**, **L1**, **L2**, **R1**, **R2**, **L1**, ▲, ▲.

NFL GAME DAY '97

Secret Passwords

To use the passwords, look out for a graphic at the top of the screen that tells you it is either Season or Preseason, and also look for the NFL logo spinning in the top left of the screen. Press **L1**, **R1**, **L2**, **R2**, then press ✖ to enter or remove the passwords shown below. Use ● when a letter or number is highlighted to select it.

BAZOOKA	strong passing arm
BIG GIRLS	extra big cheerleaders
BIG STARS	star players are large
BLIND REF	less penalties
BLIZZARD	very strong wind in the snow
BRITTLE	more injuries
BROADWAY JOE	increases quarterback accuracy
BUSY REF	more penalties
CREDITS	displays credits
CRUNCHY	hits are louder
DARK NIGHT	play in the dark
DEFENSE	better defense
ELECTRIC FB	players twitch
FLEA CIRCUS	tiny players
FRIDGE	extra big players
FROG	high long dives and hurdles
GB SPEED	speeds up the game
GD CHALLENGE	computer is hard to beat
GOLIATH	extra large players
HANGTIME	kicks go very high
HATCHET	players jump very high
HOGS	offensive line blocks are better
HOME COOKING	players are fatter
ICE SKATES	loose physics
INFAMOUS POP UPS	adds pop-ups from first game
JUICE	super fast speed bursts
KARATE	turns forearm shiver into a karate chop
MANDARICH	defensive lineman faster and stronger
NO TIME	game clock doesn't move
OFFENSE	better offense
PINBALL	forearm shiver is stronger on defense
REJECTION	jump higher
SAYERS	running back is faster and stronger
SHOUT	extra loud crowd
SLOMO	slow-moving players
STEROIDS	strong stiff arm

SQUALL	very strong winds in the rain
TIGHT COVER	players are closely covered
TORRETA	quarterback lobs passes
TWISTER	very strong winds

NFL GAME DAY '98

Cheat Codes

Firstly, you must activate the password screen by pressing **L1+L2+R1+R2** on the Main Menu. Next, enter the codes:

Code	Effect
HATCHET	Harder to tackle runners
LOUD MOUTH	Loud announcer
PSYCHIC	CPU cheats when calling plays
SHOW OFF	Dive, press jump in the air then keep running!
AIR ATTACK	CPU always passes
BETTIS	CPU runs stronger
BIG FOOT	Stronger Kicker
CPU OFFENCE	Better computer offence
QUIET CROWD	Shhhh!
BLIND REF	Get away with more
BUSY REF	Get away with less
CRUNCH TIME	Extra loud hits
COOKIE CUTTER	Players are 2-D
AHAB	Legless players
FLAT LAND	Players are flat
CPU DEFENCE	Better computer defence
DEEP GRAY	Computer remembers more plays
CLOUD OF DUST	CPU always runs
INVISIBLE	Shadows only!

N~GEN RACING

Cheat Codes

These need to be entered very quickly on the main menu:

All Championships and Permits
R1, L1, R1, R2, L2, R2, L2, L1

400 Million Credits
R2, L2, R2, L1, R2, R1, R2, L1

Bonus Jets
R1, R2, L1, L2, L2, L1, R2, R1

NHL '98

Cheat	Code
Big Heads	BRAINY
Big Players	BIGBIG
Change Tops	3RDEA
Blades Team	EAEAO

Kid Players	NHLKIDS
Mutant Players	PLAYTIME
Play Against England	GIPTEA
Programmers as Free Agents	FREEEA
View the Stanley Cup Video	STANLEY

NHL '99

Change Crowd Sounds

After scoring a goal press and hold the ▲.

Cheat Codes

Enter these codes on the password screen.

Code	Effect
STANLEY	View winning movie
GIPTEA	Easy win vs. team England
NHLKIDS	Players and goalies are tiny
PLAYTIME	Tiny players and large goalies
BIGBIG	Big players
BRAINY	Players have big heads
EAEAO	Activates the EA Blades team

NHL 2000

Taunt the opposition

Press ▲ after scoring a goal to laugh at the other team.

NHL FACE-OFF

Seven-Game Series

To obtain a seven game series start a seven game playoff before the end of the season. The option to "Continue Playoff" will appear. When the season ends the old playoff will be overwritten, but retain the seven game format.

NHL FACE OFF '98

Super Player Cheat

To create a plethora of super players, firstly choose Roster, then Create Player. Next, input any name from the list below:
RAJA ALTENHOFF
TOM BRASKI
STEVE BRASKI
DAVE BRICKHILL
CRAIG BROADBOOKS
PETER DILLE
JOSH HASSIN
JODY KELSEY
TAWN KRAMER
CRAIG OSTRANDER
JOHN REHLING
KELLY RYAN

ALAN SCALES
CHRIS WHALEY

Next press ▲ to exit and select Create Player again. Press **L1** to see the new players with a rating of 99 for their entire attributes. Don't change him to a goalie, or his stats will be wiped. To add the created players to your team, select Sign Free Agent from the Roster menu, releasing players if you have too many.

NHL OPEN ICE CHALLENGE

Super Speed

To speed across the ice, hold down ▲ + ■ + **Start** + **Select** when the game is loading.

Titchy Heads

On the "Tonight's Game" screen, and press **Turbo, Turbo,** ▲, **Shoot, Shoot,** ▲.

Big Heads

Go to the "Tonight's Game" screen, and press ▲ + **Pass** + **Turbo.**

Big Headed Goalies

To block up the goals with your keepers heads, go to the "Tonight's Game" screen and press **Pass, Pass, Pass, Turbo, Shoot, Pass.**

Extra-large Puck

On the "Tonight's Game" screen, and press ▲, ▲, ▼, ▼, **Turbo.**

Extra Players

To gain two extra players, Go to the "User Records" screen and enter the desired code:

Initials	MonthDay	Player
GH	Mar31	Gordie Howe
MJ	Jan21	Michael Jordan

NIGHTMARE CREATURES

Super Cheat

To get Infinite lives, Weapons and a level select enter ◀, ▲, ▲, ▼, ●, ▲, ■, ▼.

The Blur Mode

Input the 'Super Cheat Mode', then press **L1, L2, L2, L1, L2, L2, L1, Select.** Then select the 'Play j Blur' option.

Miniature Creatures

Input the 'Super Cheat Mode', then press **L2, L2, R1, R1, L1, R2, Select.** Then select the 'Reduce' option.

Music Select

Input the 'Super Cheat Mode' then press **L1, L1, L1, L1, R1, R1, R1, Select.** Then select the 'Play Track Option'. Start a new game and then pause. Select the 'Current Track' option and use left or right to select a different song.

Passwords
Ignatius

Level 2:	▲, ●, ▲, ←, ▲, ■, ✕, ■.
Level 3:	▲, ✕, ●, ▲, ▲, ↓, ■, ↑.
Level 4:	▲, ■, ▲, ←, ▲, ↓, ↑, ■.
Level 5:	▲, ↑, ▲, ↑, ▲, ↓, ↓, ✕.
Level 6:	▲, ↓, ▲, ✕, ▲, ↓, ←, ●.
Level 7:	▲, ←, ▲, ✕, ▲, ←, ▲, ●.
Level 8:	▲, →, ▲, ✕, ▲, ▲, ●, ●.
Level 9:	●, ▲, ▲, ✕, ●, ●, ■, ✕.
Level 10:	●, ●, ▲, →, ▲, ↑, ↓, ↓.
Level 11:	●, ✕, ▲, →, ▲, ↓, ←, ↓.
Level 12:	●, ■, ▲, ■, ▲, ↑, ▲, ■.
Level 13:	●, ↑, ▲, ■, ▲, ↓, ●, ■.
Level 14:	●, ↓, ▲, →, ▲, ●, ✕, ↓.
Level 15:	●, ←, ▲, ■, ▲, ▲, ■, ■.
Level 16:	●, →, ▲, ■, ▲, ●, ↑, ■.
Level 17:	✕, ▲, ✕, ■, ▲, ■, ↓, ↑.
Level 18:	✕, ●, ✕, ■, ▲, ↑, ←, ↑.
Level 19:	✕, ✕, ✕, ■, ●, ↓, ●, ↓.
Level 20:	✕, ■, ✕, ■, ●, ←, ✕, ↓.

Nadia

Level 2:	↑, ●, ▲, ←, ▲, ■, ✕, ■.
Level 3:	↑, ✕, ▲, ↑, ▲, ■, ■, ✕.
Level 4:	↑, ■, ▲, ↑, ▲, ↑, ↑.
Level 5:	↑, ↑, ▲, ↑, ▲, ↓, ↓, ✕.
Level 6:	↑, ↓, ▲, ↑, ▲, ←, ←, ✕.
Level 7:	↑, ←, ▲, ↑, ▲, ▲, ▲, ✕.
Level 8:	↑, →, ▲, ✕, ▲, ▲, ●, ●.
Level 9:	↓, ▲, ✕, ✕, ●, ✕, ■, ■.
Level 10:	↓, ●, ✕, ■, ▲, ■, ↓, ↑.
Level 11:	↓, ✕, ✕, ■, ▲, ↑, ←, ↑.
Level 12:	↓, ■, ✕, ■, ▲, ←, ●, ↑.
Level 13:	↓, ↑, ✕, ■, ▲, ←, ●, ↑.
Level 14:	↓, ↓, ✕, ■, ▲, ▲, ✕, ↑.
Level 15:	↓, ←, ✕, ■, ▲, ●, ■, ↑.
Level 16:	↓, →, ✕, ■, ▲, ✕, ↑, ↑.
Level 17:	←, ▲, ✕, ■, ▲, ■, ↓, ↑.
Level 18:	←, ●, ✕, ■, ▲, ↑, ←, ↑.
Level 19:	←, ✕, ✕, ■, ●, ↓, ●, ↓.
Level 20:	←, ■, ✕, ■, ●, ←, ✕, ↓.

NIGHTMARE CREATURES 2

Cheats Menu
Pause the game, then hold **L1 + R2 + ● + ■** and press **Select**. From the cheats menu you can select Hero Unlimited Life. From here enter the following cheats:

Enemy Unlimited Life	■ + ● + Select
Unlimited Power Ups	L1 + R1 + Select
Display Hero Life	L2 + R2 + ■ + Select

Unlimited Continues	L1 + R1 + R2 + Select
Kill Enemy	L1 + L2 + R1 + ■ + Select

NINJA

Level Select
On the 'Checking Memory Card' screen, press **L2, L2, L2, R2, R2, R2.**

All Weapons
Pause the game and press **R2, R2, R2, L2, L2, L2, R2, R2, R2, L2, L2, L2, L2, L2, L2.** Repeat the code to select the next available weapon.

Deformed Ninja
On the 'Press Start' screen, press **Select, Select, Select, L2, L2, L2, Select, Select, Select.**

Invincibility, Items And Skeleton Ninja
Pause the game and press **L2, R2, L2, L2, L2, R2, R2, R2, ●, ▲, ■, ●, ▲, ■.** If done correctly you will transform into a skeleton. To change back into a ninja repeat the code.

NOVASTORM

Level Select
To have a Level Select option go to the high score list and enter **TWIRLY** plus a space.

NUCLEAR STRIKE

Passwords

Level 2	CUTTHROATS
Level 3	COUNTDOWN
Level 3b	PLUTONIUM
Level 4	PUSAN
Level 5	ARMAGEDDON
Level 6	RMAGEDDON
Bonus Level	LIGHTNING

Unlimited Lives
Enter LAZARUS as a password.
Move Faster
Enter WARPDRIVE as a password.
Unlimited Ammo
Enter GOPOSTAL as a password.
Start with Five Credits
Enter the password WARRIOR.
No Enemy Fire
Enter the password PHOENIX.
Easy First Mission
Enter the password EAGLEEYE, or AVENGER to meet no enemy resistance.

Fly Further
Enter the password MPG.
Return to Previous Mission
Enter the password ANDREAS
Infinite Ammo, Fuel and Armour
Enter the password PACKISBACK

Cheat Passwords
BUCCANEER
HAMMERHEAD
CHEESYPOOF
OLDSCHOOL
BASTILLE
AFTERSHOCK
DIGIT
SHARKBAIT
CROSSEYED
NOMANSLAND
DETONATE
GUNSRUS
CHAINMAIL
MADBOMBER
CHESSPIECE
UNLEADED
APACHELITE
SURFIN
BLITZKRIEG

ODDWORLD: ABE'S EXODUS

Level Select
On the main menu, hold **R1** and press ↓, ↑, ←, →, ▲, ■, ●, ▲, ■, ●, ↓, ↑, ←, →.

View The Movies
On the main menu, hold **R1** and press ↑, ↓, ←, →, ■, ●, ▲, ●, ■, ●, ↑, ↓, ←, →.

Invulnerability
During the game, hold **R1** and press ●, ▲, ■, ✖, ↓, ↓, ↓, ●, ▲, ■, ✖.

Advance To The Next Section Of The Level.
During the game, hold **R1** and press ●, ●, ✖, ✖, ■, ■ to jump to the next section of the Level. Be warned, Mudokons will die and you will be unable to complete the game properly using this cheat.

ODDWORLD: ABE'S ODDYSEE

Level Select
At the Main Menu hold **R1** then press: ↓, →, ←, →, ■, ●, ■, ▲, ●, ■, →, ←. A menu will then appear, enabling levels to be chosen.

View all FMV
At the Main Menu hold **R1** then press: ↑, ←, →, ■, ●, ▲, ■, →, ←, ↑, →.

Voice Cheat
To get Abe to mime passwords, simply hold down **R1** and press ▲, ↑, ●, ←, ✖, ↓, ■, → during play.

ODT

Play Sophia Hawkins
On the main menu quickly press **L1, L2, R2, R1**. Then go to the character selection screen.

Play Karma The Ex-Deviant
On the main menu quickly press **R1, R2, L2, L1**. Then go to the character selection screen.

Upgrade Current Weapons
Pause the game, then press **R1, L1, R2, L2**, ←, →, ↑, ↓.

Upgrade Current Spells
Pause the game, then press ↓, ▲, **Select, L1, R1, Select.**

Full Energy
Pause the game, then press ←, →, ←, →, ■.

Full Ammunition
Pause the game, then press ←, →, ↑, ↓, ●, ■.

Full Experience
Pause the game, then press ●, ▲, **L1, L2, R1.**

Full Mana
Pause the game, then press ←, →, ←, →, ●.

OFF WORLD INTERCEPTOR

Level Passwords
1p5vk?pzqg41417p
nrqv!tb9mbjgkb8!
cqd?dc5kpl5kw741

Loads of Money
For loads of money, go to the option screen and press ■, ✖, ● six times and then press **L1**. This cheat also activates automatically if you beat the game.

OMEGA BOOST

U1 Zone
Finish the game on the hard difficulty level with 90 AP and without using any continues.

U2 Zone
Finish the game on the hard difficulty level with 60 AP.
U3 Zone
Finish the game on the hard difficulty level with 50 AP.
U4 Zone
Finish the game on the hard difficulty level with 90 AP and without using any continues.
U5 Zone
Finish the game on the hard difficulty level with 60 AP.
U7 Zone
Finish the game on the hard difficulty level without using any continues.
U8 Zone
Finish the game on the normal difficulty level.
U9 Zone
Finish the game on the normal difficulty level without using any continues.
V5 Zone
Finish the game with 60 AP
Inner Level A
Finish the game with 60 AP (with invincibility, all weapons at level 9)
Inner Level B
Finish the game on the hard difficulty level with 90 AP (with unlimited special attacks, all weapons at level 3)
Inner Level C
Finish the game on the normal difficulty level (with highest speed, all weapons at level 9)
Inner Level D
Finish the game on the normal difficulty level with 90 AP (with five-way attack, all weapons at level 9)
Inner Level E
Finish the game on the hard difficulty level (with improved speed when moving up, down, left, right, all weapons at level 9)

ONE

Cheat Passwords

All Weapons:	**Maxpower**
Level Select:	**Hevyfeet**
Extra 31 Lives:	**IMMORTAL**
Invincibility:	**NEVERDIE**

OVERBLOOD

You have woken from a cryogenic sleep in a scientific research facility. The blue bar at the top right corner of the screen must be turned red otherwise you will freeze to death. Kneel in front of the auxiliary power generator in the centre of the room (between cryo-pods 3 and 4) and inspect it. The generator will turn on, and the heat will rise to 0 degrees. Inspect the door with the round object attached to it. Your character will push it forward. Go through.

Kneel beside the case on the floor in the back right corner of the room. Take the recording chip to enable you to save the game. Open the case on the floor in the back left corner of the room. Take the vest to prevent you from freezing to death. Get the computer chip. Go to the robot body in the front corner and use the computer chip. This activates the robot. Go back to the first room. Change characters to the robot. Interface with the computer between cryo-pod 1 and 2. This unlocks one of the two main doors.

The door in front of Cryo-pod 2 is now open. Enter the hallway and go to the damaged section. Inspect the wreckage to find a security card. Now inspect the wreckage with the male character. You should now crawl over it and onto the raised section of the hall above. The robot will follows. Go through the door at the end of the hall, proceed to the door at the other end of the bridge and enter it. From the "T" shaped hallway go through the centre door that is straight up the hall. Go through the door at the end of the small hallway you just entered.

You are now in the elevator room of level B-04. Use the terminal between the two round doors. The door to the right will open and a dead mutated man tumbles out. Kneel down and inspect him. Here you will find a piece of paper with some numbers on it. Go back to the small hallway and then through to the "T" shaped hall. Turn left and go through the door at the end. Continue to the end of this short curved hallway and inspect the door. Enter the bottom number on the piece of paper from the dead mutant – 61891. Now press the large orange button on the keypad. Enter now unlocked door into the main hall.

Enter the door next to the door you just came in. Push the boxes to reach the back left corner of the storage lab. Change characters to the robot. Use the robot to inspect the wires showing through the broken glass of the power box. This reconnects the power. Change characters again. Go to the green cabinet on the right of the power. Use your security card in the card slot on the left side of it. The front of the cabinet opens. Inspect it to get the laser knife. Go back into the main hallway.

Go away from the storage laboratory through the door at the far end, right of the large hole. Stand in front of the floating statue just inside the door and push the statue over. Kneel in front of the stand it was on and inspect to find a green chip, (an anti-gravity device). Go back into the hallway. Stand on the edge of the hole in the floor and use the anti-gravity device to jump over the hole to the other side. The robot can not follow. Enter the door on the other side of the hole.

You are in the computer control centre. Inspect the terminals on the right of the door. Watch a cinematic sequence giving you the positions of switches to activate a door. At the terminals on the other side of the door inspect them until you find the switches to activate the lighting, doors and air conditioning. Push the switches until you align them as lighting-off, doors-on, and air conditioning-off. If you enter a wrong choice you must start again. Done correctly it unlocks two doors, one across from the keypad lock door and one in the stairway. At the back of the control centre inspect the computer bank to be given information about a malfunction in the main generator. Leave the control centre.

Use the anti-gravity device to jump back over the hole in the floor back to the robot. Go in the now unlocked door across from the keypad lock door. You are in a long hallway. Kneel and use the laser knife on the grate where the buzzing sound is coming from. Change characters to the robot and enter the open grate. Interface with the generator at the back of the shaft. Leave the shaft and switch back to the male character. Exit the hall the way you came in, going back through the keypad lock door.

Go back through the curved hall and into the "T" shaped hallway then through the door straight ahead of you. The hall will have a red emergency light flashing. Go down the hall, turn the corner and exit through the door at the other end, where you will find yourself on the stairway. Go to the edge of the ledge to your left and come to a broken section of railing. At the edge of this section use the anti-gravity device to jump to the girder and to the ledge opposite. Enter the door in front of you, which you unlocked by the switches in the computer control centre. Proceed until you come to a heavy rising door. Inspect the door to make it rise a little and fall back down. Use the anti-gravity device in front of the door so once the door has risen halfway you can kneel and crawl under it.

The door will fall down and trap you. The blue health bar returns and you are controlling the robot. You have to raise the door before the man is crushed. Inspect the 3 levers on the wall to the left of the door. Pull levers 1 and 3, so that they are in the sequence: 1: ↓ 2: ↑ 3: ↓ . The man can now escape.

You are now back in control of the man above a large drop. An open section of railing leads to a wide girder. Walk onto the girder and head across it. Halfway across the girder the robot becomes frightened and runs to the end of it. The whole complex begins to shake and the girder will start to break off. The blue health bar returns. You need to run to the end of the girder before it breaks under your feet. From the platform at the end of the girder look behind and right. See a large white pipe. Walk off the platform above it and you should drop down onto it. Go into the dark opening at the end of the pipe.

On the pipe you are heading towards the main generator. As you exit the tunnel into the generator room you will notice the generator controls. Jump down onto the generator to your right, then jump across the gaps until you are underneath the controls. Walk to the back edge of this section and jump to pull yourself up onto the small catwalk that houses the controls. Inspect the controls to turn the generator on. The sections of the generator now turn. Jump back down and go right. Jump across the sections until you see the robot on a catwalk above you. Jump up to the robot and go through the door at the back of the catwalk. Go through a dark carpeted hallway and to the door at the other end. This takes you back in the hall where you cut the grate open. Follow the halls back to the elevator room.

Back in the elevator room you are treated to a cinematic sequence. You then enter the elevator going to level B-3F. Go through the door in front of you into a long hallway. Change characters to the robot and interface with the control box on the wall to your right. This opens the door at the end of the hall. Control switches back to the man. Go through the door and control goes back to the robot. Press the control box to raise the door again. Control then switches again to the man. Switch quickly back to the robot and run through the closing door into another "T" shaped hallway.

Enter the door on the right into a hall with dead bodies on the floor. A cinematic sequence follows of you finding the bodies. Head towards the other end of the hall. A mutated creature will jump down from the ceiling and attack you. Another cinematic sequence follows showing the battle between your characters and the mutant. This ends in the death of your robot. Inspect the door at the end of the hallway to find it is locked. Exit the hall by the door you came in and then the door down the "T" shaped hall in front of you.

You are in the chemical storage area. Stand under the open air vent on the wall to your right and jump to climb into the air vent. Go towards the other end. Along the way you have to jump down a hole into a lower section of the vent. Crouch again after doing this to be able to fit into the shaft. Proceed to the light at the end of the shaft and jump into the room below.

There is a woman being attacked by a mutant. Fight hand to hand with the creature. When the mutant is dead kneel and inspect the woman until she regains consciousness. A sample tube will be added to your inventory. Get the key off the shelf near the fire extinguisher. On the desk at the back of the room you will get a detonator device. Inspect the door to get out. Go back through the "S" and "T" shaped halls, re-enter the chemical storage area, and have both characters stand on the lift. You will be lowered to the bottom section of this room. On the left side of this section use the silver key with the top grey box. Take the red tube of chemical explosives that are inside. Kneel and inspect the brown covered crate to the left of the boxes to find a can of oil. Kneeling and inspecting the white covered crate gives you first aid spray. Inspecting the device to the right of the lift causes the lift to rise. Use the oil on the hydraulics that are now visible under the lift. The lift ride is now smoother so that the chemical explosives will not be shaken. Back to the lift control device to lower the lift. Move both characters to the lift, go back to the upper section of the room, and go through the door on the air vent wall into the underground subway.

Jump onto the empty tracks and go towards the crashed subway car. Place the detonator device under the hole in the wall situated above the ledge to your right. Put the chemical explosives into the detonator. You need to get back up on the platform at the beginning of the tracks within nine seconds. To jump onto the platform press Inspect it. After the explosion, go back down to the scene of the blast and inspect the hole you created. Jump up onto the divider between the two sections of track. Jump down onto the tracks on the other side, in front of the parked subway car. Go down the tracks away from the car. The car's brakes will fail and it comes rushing towards you. Inspect to make your characters dive onto the tracks to avoid the car, which crashes into the wall. Enter the car by the back door. Inspect the box on the right hand wall of the car to find a gun and a red security card. Exit the front of the car, climb onto the platform, and go through the door into the computer room for air vents.

Get the man to use the computer to see a map of the central ventilation, freight transportation, and chemical storage area. Unlock and go through the door opposite the one you entered by using the red security card. You are now in a "Y" shaped hallway. The door to the left is unlocked. Go in and try to open the door at the back of the room. A cinematic sequence shows your characters deciding to split up. Once you regain control of the characters the woman no longer automatically follows the man.

Using just the man, leave this room and go back to the air vent in the computer room. Stand under it and jump, he will crawl into the vent. Crawl to the blocked passage to the left and inspect the door blocking your way. The door will close trapping you in the air vent. Switch control to the woman and go to the computer room. Use the computer to bring up the maps of the vents. You can now open the closed doors inside the air vents. Choose a door to try to press ● to open. You will randomly open one or more doors. Try until the 3 lowest doors on the ventilation map are opened. Press ✖ to exit the computer and switch back to the man.

Head down the now open shaft until you come to a bright light and jump into the fan room below. Two huge fans are here, one blowing you and the other sucking you. Kneel below the airflow. Crawl forward to the front of the room. Inspect the control panel in front of the blowing fan. This turns off both fans. Inspect the ladder you climbed down to climb back up into the air vents. Go back through the air vents until you reach the other exit. Here you will find the giant

fan in the floor, which was shut-off when you shut down the other two. Inspect the vent on the other side of it to continue down the shaft. Jump down out of the vent and into the research lab below. You will find a first aid spray if you kneel in front of the red tank. Go to the sample device on the end of the desk in front of the large window and use the DNA sample from your inventory. You get an interesting cinematic sequence.

You are in an atrium full of trees. Push the red button on the steel panel to drain the small pool of water in the centre of the atrium. Face the doorway and inspect the machinery on the wall to the left to find a clip of bullets. Go to the hole in the empty pool and climb down the ladder into a hallway. You are up to your knees in water. Kneel and inspect the broken grate at the opposite end of the hall to crawl under it into a room with a broken water pipe. Attempt to turn the valve behind the flow of water. It will be stuck so use your oil can on it. Turn the valve to raise the door in the rear of the room and go through it into a hallway. Halfway down the hall a giant object will rush towards you. As soon as you regain control of your characters jump to save your characters.

You find yourself in a small hallway. As you approach the door a mutant jumps from the ceiling. Use the man to fight the creature then exit the hall into the elevator room. Use the elevator controls to start another cinematic sequences. You are now on level B-2F. Exit the elevator room. You will now be in a hallway with lasers crossing the hallway blocking your way. Shut the lasers off by going to the control box next to them and entering the number from the top of the piece of paper from the dead mutant - 91861. Turn around and go to the hall to the right of the elevator room and through the door to the lounge. Look out of the window in this room to see an underground cave. Kneel in front of one of the coffee tables to find a clip of bullets. Exit this room through the door you came in.

Go through the door on the other side of the now defunct lasers onto a short bridge that has been destroyed. Run and jump over the broken section in the middle of it .You will start to fall but will grab the other edge and pull yourself up. Leaving the woman on the other side, go through the door on your side of the bridge into the hallways of the personnel quarters. You will be attacked by a mutant, kill it. Go down the right hand hall and go in the first door. Get the laptop computer and view the report on it. After the report kneel and grab the metal rods in the middle of the floor. Then kneel and inspect the grey dresser to find the stun gun. Exit and go to the room across the hallway. Kneel by the bed to find more bullets. Go down the hall a bit further to the next room. Pick up the metal grating on the floor in the room. Return to the broken bridge, lay the metal rods across the gap, and then the grating on top of the metal rods. This makes a bridge for the woman to cross. A cinematic sequence follows.

Go to the kitchen at the end of the hall, opposite the door to the broken bridge. Check the strawberry a few times. This eventually gives you a first aid spray. Go back to the room where you found the metal grating. Jump down the hole in the back of the room to a dark set of tunnels. Explore these tunnels to find two more open grates in the ceilings, a broken section of floor with a large pipe sticking out of it, and a sealed vent on a wall. Stand directly underneath the open grate in the ceiling and jump, then pull yourself up into the room above. Use the stun gun to open a steel box on a wooden shelf and get the lasercutter from the box. The door to this room can be opened from the inside. Return to the tunnels.

Pull yourself up into the open grate in the tunnels that you have not used. From this room go through the door into the smaller room connected to it. Inspect the laptop computer a few times and get the computer CD-ROM. Exit these two connecting rooms from the front door into the hallway. Return to the hallway with the elevator room door and enter the hall to the right. You will hear rushing water from this hall. Kneel and inspect the grated floor to see a card underneath it. Still kneeling use the lasercutter on the grated floor. Jump down the hole you have just made, kneel and pick up the yellow key card. Kneel and inspect the rock to the right of the water to find the clip. Jump back up the hole out of the cavern. Head towards the hallway across from where you just cut the grating. A cinematic sequence follows and you end up in the medilab.

Leave the medilab and enter the operating room through the automatic sliding door. Find the crowbar on the basin. Leave the operating room into the hallway near the elevator and go back to the tunnels under the private quarters. Use the crowbar to remove the vent on the wall in the tunnels. This allows you to enter the hole.

You are now on the girders below the broken bridge. Go forward, take your first right, continue down that girder, take your next right and carry on to the end of the girder. Enter the hole in the wall at the end of it. Once in the room go through the door at the side. Push the cabinet to the left of this room so it falls into the hole in the other doorway. Walk across the top of the cabinet and enter the door you were previously unable to reach. This will take you into the control room. Kneel in front of the machine to the right of the door to find a clip of bullets. Also kneel in front of the panel at the back right corner of the room to find a first aid spray. Use the CD-ROM at the centre of the main computer, which is up the steps. A cinematic sequence will follow. Leave the control room and go back to the now unlocked door at the end of the hallway. Go to the room where you found the metal grating.

Inspect the door and go through it into the suit hanger. Check the suits. There is a clip of bullets in the suit near the box on the wall. Go through the door with the round windows at the back of the room. You are now in a tunnel. You will find

a clip of bullets if you inspect the machine in this tunnel. Step into the darkness at the end of the tunnel. Walk onto the platform near where you entered and inspect the water skimmer number 3. This will enable you to find and remove the dead battery. Go back across to the tunnel. Exit by the door to the rear. You will be attacked by another mutant. Dust it up then kneel and inspect behind water skimmer number 1. You will find the live battery here. Leave by the door you came in and go back onto the platform where skimmer 3 is. Use the live battery on it. The battery will now be in the skimmer. You will now see a cinematic sequence of your characters escaping into the water on the skimmer.

Controlling the skimmer you are now on involves moving left and right, pushing up to go forward, and pressing down to slow. Steer the skimmer through the rocky water. Your blue health bar appears and for every rock you hit it decreases. After you have navigated the rocks, you will get a cinema sequence. At the skimmer landing pad go through the door to the next room.

You will enter a walkway above some giant cables. As soon as you enter you will be attacked by another creature. Kill him and go down the walkway and round the corner. Inspect the elevator door. This will trigger a cinematic sequence that will see your female friend captured by a mutant. When you regain consciousness enter the elevator and go to level B-1F. You will see another cinematic sequence at this point.

On arrival at level B-1F, go down to the door in the dome shaped section. You may have to kneel to enter the door area. Go through the door into a large cryogenic chamber. Go to the exit at the other side of this room. Enter the door to the left side of the hallway. You are now in the briefing room. If you inspect the man hunched over on the left twice you will find a clip of bullets. You will also find a first aid spray under the table. Inspect the man lying dead on the floor to get the ID passcard then return to the hallway. Go to the door at the end. Show the ID passcard to red robots guarding the door so they will move and let you pass

You will see the woman being held. You confront the man responsible, and in a cinematic sequence you learn an interesting fact. The scientist then mutates. Take control of your male character, equip the gun and fight him. After the scientist is defeated go to the back of the room and inspect the computer. Then use the robot's memory chip from your inventory on it. The robot will now infiltrate the system and destroy the facility. He will also unlock the door to the right so you can exit. A timer will begin to count down. This is how long you have until the facility is blown up. Go through the door that the robot unlocked.

You have now entered a rising freight elevator. It is not an easy ride! At the top you enter the hanger bay. Inspect the left side of the aircraft's cockpit. Fight the mutated scientist as soon as it appears. Once it is defeated it will come back at you again. You must lure him to the rear of the aircraft where the woman has got into the cockpit. When it is behind the aircraft, the woman will turn on the engine and fry the mutant. Escape and watch the facility explode.

PACMAN WORLD

99 Credits
Press **Select** before starting a game to increase your credits up to 99.

PANDEMONIUM

Level Passwords

Level 1	ADEAMIIE	Level 10	AIICBAJI
Level 2	EPIJAKCA	Level 11	FBIIAKCK
Level 3	FBIJAKCI	Level 12	FDIIAKDC
Level 4	KOCCCIEE	Level 13	FFIIAKDK
Level 5	NGIAIBJJ	Level 14	KACACIBA
Level 6	NIIAJBCB	Level 15	ADMCFAID
Level 7	KGCACICI	Level 16	EMIIEKBE
Level 8	AHICBAJE	Level 17	OEIBIBMJ
Level 9	AIICFAJG	Level 18	FAAIAKCE

Cheat Passwords

ALMABHOL	Access all levels
BODYSWAP	Press ▲ to swap characters during play
BORNFREE	You can select any world
CASHDASH	Jump to a bonus screen when you complete a level
CORONARY	Gives you extra hearts
EVILDEAD	Makes enemies invincible
HARDBODY	Makes you invincible
INANDOUT	Returns you to the map screen when you quit a game
OTTOFIRE	Automatic autofire
THE THING	To cycle through parts of the body hold **L2**, and press ●. To return to normal, hold **L2** and press ✖.
TOMMYBO	Finish a level and play pinball
TWISTEYE	To rotate the screen hold **L1** and **L2** and press ← or →. (↓ centres)
VITAMIN S	Gives you 31 lives

PANDEMONIUM 2

Invincibility
To live forever enter the password **NEVERDIE**, an offering of M.C Hammer's "You can't touch this" confirms your success.

Level Selection
To play any level you choose, enter the password **OCMCKKEJ**.

Passwords
Level 2 = **AJMABLOC**
Level 3 = **FAAAGCNA**
Level 4 = **LJABIDOA**
Level 5 = **LDBBJLAE**
Level 6 = **KLBFCCE**
Level 7 = **IEBBJLMF**
Level 8 = **POECHEJJ**
Level 9 = **FHCAODAC**
Level 10 = **AKAJDIJC**
Level 11 = **NIECGPCJ**
Level 12 = **FKDAGMNK**
Level 13 = **LKFBKLAM**
Level 14 = **BBAMFKDK**
Level 15 = **FPDAGMHC**
Level 16 = **APEMFINO**
Level 17 = **POGCLMEB**
Level 18 = **FMDAGPIM**
Level 19 = **FCLAGJNE**

PARAPPA THE RAPPER

Extra Special Bonus
To gain the bonus, you must first complete all six stages with a Cool rating. This gets a bonus stage where Sunny Funny and Katy are dancing. Finish each stage normally, then replay it to achieve a Cool rating. To do this you have to embellish the second line of each rap and keep rapping freestyle well enough until the end. The special embellishments are:

Level 1:	---/●-● ●/-●-●
Level 2:	---/▲-▲-/■-■ ■/-■-/■----
Level 3:	---/● ● ● ●/-● ●-
Level 4:	---/✖-✖ ✖/-■ ■-/-R R-/-L L-
Level 5:	---/-L L L/-L L-/-L-L L/-L L-
Level 6:	---/●---●/●---●/●---●/●----

Voice Change
Complete the first two levels with a cool rating. Press ✖, ✖, ✖, ▲, ●, ■, ■, R1, L1, ■ ✖ and finish the next level. On level four press ✖, ■, ▲, ●, ✖, Hold R1 and press ● or ▲ to cycle through the voices of the other characters in the game.

Play As Sunny Or The Ninja
1. Complete level 1 with over 3,000 points and a cool rating.
2. Complete level 2 on good with cool flashing.
3. Complete level 3 and 4 with over 2,000 points and a good rating.
4. Complete level 5 with over 4,000 points and a cool rating.
5. Complete level 6 with over 2,000 points and a cool rating.
6. Start a new game and both Ninja and Sunny will be selectable.

PARASITE EVE 2

You begin the game in the shooting gallery.

You can choose to continue with your training. There are five levels of training that you can participate in. Each level will train you in shooting multiple targets and getting you accustomed to the controls.

When you are finished with your training, exit via the door to the far right of the room. Head left and through the door at the end. Inside you will find Pierce. He will tell you your next assignment. Head out through the door in the top left of the room. Go through the door on the left marked 'Firearms Control'. In here a women named Jodie will explain BP (Bounty Points) to you. This is where you can spend any bounty points you earn and buy weapons, ammunition and equipment.

When you are finished, leave the room and head down the corridor. Here you will find the garage. Speak to Pierce. Tell him you are ready. Aya will drive her car to the crime scene.

From your car walk down the path and speak to the Police Sgt. He will allow you to enter the building. Walk up to the front entrance and talk to the Police Officer. He will tell you that SWAT entered the building moments before you arrived. He will step aside allowing you to enter the elevator. Once you have left the elevator head through the double doors. Inside you will find that the SWAT team has been massacred. Descend the stairs to the left. Head right and collect the unlimited box of ammunition. Head up the stairs on the right and examine the phone in the corner. Use the phone and talk to Baldwin, you will also be able to save your game. Head through the double doors. As you walk down the hall you will meet a surviving SWAT member, he will give you the Cafeteria Key. Return back through the double doors. Head down the stairs on the far left. Down here you will find a SWAT team member being attacked by a mutant creature. Kill the creature and then talk to the ravaged SWAT member. Unlock the door using the Cafeteria Key you collected earlier. Inside you will find a women sitting at a table. On closer examination, she falls to the floor and mutates. Use the tables to keep the creature from attacking you and unload all your ammunition into it until it falls. Collect the scientific journal from the table. Examine the fallen creature and you will find a Metallic Implant. Just as you leave, the creature stirs. Before it can attack, another hunter appears and kills it for good.

As you leave the Cafeteria, Aya will be attacked by two smaller creatures lurking on the roof. Once they are dead, head up the stairs at the end of the path and use the phone in the right corner. After saving your game head down the stairs on the right and head along the path. Kill the creature you find and head through the door opposite the stairs. Head around the fountain and through the door on the left. Kill the rats, then open the yellow box hanging on the wall and take the Blue Key

found inside. Head through the door on the left next to the water cooler. Inside examine the yellow flashing light and insert the Blue Key in the A slot. This will unlock the door to the escalator. Head back outside. The door at the end leads back into the Cafeteria. The door to the right of the Cafeteria door leads to a room with a creature and a dead body. The fridge contains a Stim. Head out the door to the right of the water cooler. Go right around the fountain and through the door. Go right and through the glass door and up the escalator. At the top of the escalator you will meet another creature. When the area is clear, search the dead body by the Coke machine for a tactical vest. Head down the escalator on the other side. Move in close before attacking the fat creatures. Once they are dead you will hear a gunshot from behind the wooden doors. Check the body in the corner and collect the Submachine Gun.

Inside you will find Rupert being attacked by a strange armoured assailant. Near Rupert you will find a Red Key. Return outside, up the path and back up the escalator. Make your way down the escalator on the opposite side. Head up the stairs and save at the phone. Return down the stairs and through the door opposite. Head around the fountain and through the door on the left. Go through the door on the right. Insert the Red Key to turn off the fountain. Head to the fountain and search by the blood stain to find the body of yet another SWAT member and a Grenade Launcher. Head through the door on the right. Head up the stairs and replenish your ammunition. Return down the stairs and head right up the escalator. Head down the opposite escalator and down the path. Go through the door on the left. Input the code 561 in the console to the right. The bridge will rise. Head across the bridge to the door opposite. Something will be thrown against the door. Go through the door. Kill the wounded creature and head up the stairs. Save at the phone. Continue up the stairs until you reach the roof.

Follow the gantry round to the elevator. You find the elevator is stuck on the level above. Head back to the stairs. Before you can reach the stairs you will be confronted by the mysterious armoured assailant which attacked Rupert. To defeat this green clad nemesis, keep your distance and fire from afar. When he moves past the power conducts, fire at the conduct to release a power cable that will swing into his path and electrocute him. Continue this pattern until you reach the elevator. Continually shooting the final conduct will spray water at the hanging power cable inflicting more damage. Once you cause enough damage, he will retreat to the helipad. The elevator will lower. Ride the elevator up to the helipad. The armoured assailant will escape by jumping over to the next building, leaving you seconds to escape by helicopter before the building explodes.

Back at headquarters you will have a meeting with Rupert and Baldwin who will assign you to Dryfield.

You will find yourself in the garage. Pierce will inform you all the SWAT weapons have been returned so sadly no Grenade Launcher and Machine Gun. Examine the boot of Aya's car, this is where you can store items. Go to the 'Firearms' room and talk to Jodie. Buy the Assault Rifle, ammunition and any other equipment you might need.

Head back to the garage and talk to Pierce. Tell him you are ready.

Dryfield

The box at your feet is your unlimited supply of ammunition. You can store items in the boot of the car. Head down the dusty street. There is a pay phone you can use to save your position. Head through the gate at the end of the street. A strange mutant dog will leap over the wall and attack you.

Head through the gate in the top right corner. Follow the alley until you reach a door and a well. If you examine the well a flood of bats will attacks you. Head through the door. You will find yourself in a garage. Go through the door in the fence and past the car. In the corner you will find the garage circuit breakers. Push these up. Go back towards the door you came in and examine the yellow light. Press the up button to raise the car, then the turn button. You should now be able to press the button next to the shutter. Open the door in the fence to your right. Return to the yellow light and press the turn button. By going through the door in the fence you should be able to enter the garage office via the shutter. Inside you will meet Douglas. He will give you the Motel Key 6. Head back out via the shutter and back out the door leading to the alley. Go left down the alley to the motel.

Fight your way through the giant scorpions and through the gate on the left. Go up the fire escape and open room 6 with the motel key. Inside, there is a phone next to the bed where you can save. Head out onto the balcony, you will see a water tower. Climb down the ladder. Head around the fence. You will find two dog creatures digging a hole under the fence. Kill these two then head through the gap at the end. Examine the control box and flip the switch. The fence on the opposite side of the courtyard will open. Run over to the opposite side of the courtyard avoiding the dog creatures as you go. You will more than likely be knocked off your feet as the dog creatures pass, so just get to your feet and run through the open gate before it closes. Inside the compound, the dog creatures will slip under the hole in the fence and attack you. Stand just below the hole and shoot the dog creatures as they enter. Either dodge their charges or replenish your health until the dog creatures stop their attack. Once the compound is clear, a ladder will lower. Climb the ladder. Once you reach the top of the water tower, walk around and talk to Kyle. Kyle will tell you that he is a P.I out of L.A and is in search of some kind of shelter. Climb the ladder to the top of the water tower. Search the corpse for a Key. Climb back down the ladder and activate the gate lever before climbing down from the water tower. At the base of the tower you will be attacked by a pack

of scorpions, use the fence to protect you from their attacks. Head around to the door near the hole under the fence and unlock it.

Inside you will encounter giant moths, kill these from the safety of the doorway. Search the locker for a recovery potion. Examine the fridge at the end of the room for a Coke Cola fridge magnet. Now go through the door to the left of the entrance. You will find yourself in the Saloon. Enter the toilet and examine the map on the wall. Head towards the Saloon entrance. You will disturb a group of moths as you pass the pool table. Kill these before unlocking the Saloon entrance. Now return through the stockroom to the water tower. Go through the gate to the left of the ladder that leads to the motel room. Just as you reach the door, a dog creature will attack. After disposing of it, use the intercom and speak to Mr Douglas. He will tell you to unlock the door using the key found to the left. To reach the Key you will need to use the Coke Cola fridge magnet. Guide the Factory Key to the right corner of the fence. Unlock the door. Head through the shutter behind the car. Kill the moths lurking in this room, then head out through the door at the top. You will find yourself outside where you will meet a dog. Follow the dog to Mr Douglas's trailer. Head inside. From Mr Douglas you can exchange your Bounty Points for guns, ammunition and equipment.

After hearing a scream from the nearby General Store, you will need to head off to the well, found behind the factory/garage. Head outside once you are finished. Flint, Mr Douglas's dog will show you the way. Flint will lead you to a Coil of Rope, but before you can collect it you must fight a pack of scorpions first. Head through the door on the right. Fight your way through the giant moths. Head through the shutter and out the door to the top left. You will find yourself in the alley by the well. If you want you can head down the alley, past the Motel and back to the main street. Save your game, collect more ammunition and then return back to the well. If you do not want to fight the two dog creatures sleeping in the Motel courtyard, you can carefully creep past them by keeping close to the wall.

Back at the well, use the rope and then descend into the darkness. Equip the M4A1 Rifle. The gate to the right is locked so head left down the dark tunnel. On the first turn you will be attacked by a group of bats. Take these down and continue forward. Climb the steps and through the gate at the end. You will find yourself in a stone tunnel. Something invisible will pass by you, a new type of ceiling walking creature which can turn invisible. Run down the tunnel, turn and try to aim, if you lock on, fire until it either gets close to you or you lose your lock. Run further away and try again. Continue this until it dies, then climb up the ladder into the Grocery Store.

Walk down the hall. At the end you will encounter a new type of parasite, one which explodes when it dies. Shoot them from a distance. Unlock the main door and head outside. Save your game and get any items you may need from the truck of your car. Back in the Grocery Store search the drinks cabinets for a Recovery 3 and Cola. Head out of the door in the corner. Outside, kill the two dog creatures. You will hear a scream from the end house but the door is locked. Go in the middle house and examine the closet in the corner of the room, you need to actually see the hinges keeping the closet pinned to the wall. Head back through the Grocery Store and go to Mr Douglas's trailer via the factory. Talk to Mr Douglas and ask for his permission to use his tools. Go back outside and into the factory. In the corner you will find his tools. Take the Monkey Wrench. Now go back through the Grocery Store to the house with the bolted closet. Use the Monkey Wrench to remove the bolts. Aya will move the closet revealing a hole in the wall. Head inside.

In the next room a women will stumble towards you before falling to her knees. From out of the shadow comes the mysterious assailant you fought in the city. He will reveal himself as No 9. Now this match is easy, simple stand in the corner of the room and continuously fire at No 9. His sword strikes should miss. When he gets close simple run around him into the opposite corner and start firing again. Eventually No 9 will refer to Eve. Aya will have a flashback and No 9 will burst into fire in the same way Eve could alight people in the first game. Aya will be awoken by Kyle who luckily survives from being set alight himself from Aya's power. Aya and Kyle decide to use her car to find the parasite nest. Leave by the door.

Outside you will encounter a group of scorpions, Kyle will help you fight them. Head into the Grocery Store. Fight your way outside where you will find your car trashed by a group of strange goblin parasites. You and Kyle must defeat around ten of these creatures before you can examine the car. The car is completely trashed. You need to head off to Mr Douglas's trailer. The phone has been cut off and you will not be able to save, so be careful as you fight your way through the town. Outside his trailer you will face two invisible creatures, simply target one and fire until it turns invisible whilst avoiding the other. As soon as the one you have targeting reappears start firing. Inside ask Mr Douglas for a car. He will tell you to check out the Motel Lobby. Buy any equipment you may need and save your game using the radio near the door. Now head to the Motel.

In the Motel courtyard, kill the moths firsts, avoiding the dog type creature and then when they are gone, concentrate on the dog, use the pillars to avoid his ramming attacks. Go through the gate. Run down the path and enter the Motel Lobby on the left. Go around the counter and examine the cash register. Input #3033 Total. Inside you will find a Key. Head outside and up the stairs. Go around the roof and through the double doors in the top right corner. Inside, pick up the Jerry Can found near the shelf. Suddenly three invisible creatures will drop in through the skylight. Once the area is clear, go to the safe near where you collected the Jerry Can. Use the

combination 4487. Inside you will find a bottle. Head back outside and down into the lobby. Save your game. Head back to your car and use the Jerry Can with the Petrol Pump next to your car. No go to Mr Douglas's red truck and give him the Jerry Can. You will find him around the other side, under the truck. Mr Douglas will tell you to get some rest so head back to the Motel, go up the stairs at the back and go into room no 6. Inside, save your game at the telephone and then examine the bed and select go to sleep.

While you sleep a huge, flame throwing behemoth will attack the town. You will battle this giant on the top floor of the Motel. This monster has two main attacks. He breaths fire, watch for a small spark from the nozzle in his mouth then run to either side as he breaths a wall of flames. His second attack is when he smashes down his fist. When he prepares to slam down his fist run in either direction. While avoiding his attack just let rip with your machine gun, grenades etc. His attacks don't do major amounts of damage. If you are hit simply heal yourself using your parasite energy. You should have enough magic points to last against this boss. Once vanquished, go back into your room and save. Climb down the ladder. Kill the three invisible parasites and go through the door which leads to the Saloon. Fight your way past the moths and rats in the stock room. Go through the door on the left and creep past the goblins. Go outside, fight the dog creature and the four scorpions. Go through the gate at the end. In the Motel courtyard you will find Mr Douglas who is mourning over the death of his dog, Flint. He will give you the Truck Key. Head back to the water tower the same way you came and go through the gate in the corner. Fight your way past the dog creatures and the moths and go through the door at the end. Go through the shutter to meet Kyle at the truck. If you want to buy any more equipment head through the door on the right and head to Mr Douglas's trailer. On the way examine the green car on the left by the trailer, you will find a Chicken Armour. When you are ready to leave go back and talk to Kyle.

Mesa – On the outskirts of Dryfield
You and Kyle will be pinned down by dog parasites next to a mine. Kyle will head into the bar while you are left to fight around twelve dog parasites in packs of two. Stay close to the fences and the truck so when they charge they knock themselves out. When you have killed them all enter the mine. Fight another two dog parasites and some moths. Head down the tunnel and through the gate straight in front. Run past the mine carts fighting the goblins. In the following room you will reach a broken bridge. Head back to the first tunnel and go left into the next room. Push the mine cart. At the end of this small tunnel you will find an oak board. Take this and head back to the broken bridge. Use the Oak Board to bridge the gap. As you cross the bridge you will be attacked by a flock of bats. Once across the bridge enter the door on the right. Once inside, save your game at the telephone and examine the terminal in the corner of the room. Take the plug from the top left corner and place it in the second from top socket. Head back outside and

through the main gate. Here you will face a boss in the form of a giant dog/horse parasite. This fight is quite easy. First run around the room and shoot all four of the barrels to light the room. The boss has three attacks, a charge, a pounce (where it grabs you and swing you around) and a stomp attack. Simply follow the boss as it moves around the room. When it stops, attack. When it moves in for an attack move in closer so its attack overlaps you and simply let rip with your weapon. When it falls, Aya will search the creature's body and discover Kyle's gun and another plug. But the creature is not dead and rises again. This time the creature runs around the screen. Just stay in one place, when the creatures moves towards you move close so it misses its attacks and when you lose sight of it prepare for it to jump down on you so keep moving. Continue to fire after it misses its attack and as it runs away. Was that thing Kyle??

Examine the motorcycle in the corner then leave the room. Head into the room on the right. Save your game then go to the terminal. Take the plug and slot it into the top socket. Place the other plug into the bottom socket. Now return back to the bike and press the switch. The door is hidden behind the wall. Before going any further make sure you have the grenade launcher because it will make the next fight easier. Go through the hidden door. As you turn the corner you will be attacked by an invisible parasite. This one can be tough because it does large amounts of damage and causes you to be poisoned when it hits you. Equip the grenade launcher and quickly fire, reload and fire again. Its not worth running because its so fast. So stand your ground and just heal yourself when your health gets low. At the end of the corridor is an elevator.

Head down the corridor and through the door on the left. Head down the corridor and through the door leading into the storeroom. Head through the door opposite. Fight your way down the hall and into the sleeping quarters. Make your way through the sleeping quarters and into the main hall. Go through the centre door. Go through the left door and go through the next. Save your game if you want and place any items in the strong box. Go through the door on the right. Go round the corner and use the elevator.

From the elevator, shoot the sentry guns and head right and through the door. In this room you will face a new enemy, a sea serpent style of creature which fires an electric bolt from its mouth. These are best avoided so run across the bridge into the next room. You only lose 10 BP's which you can make up for later. Head right and into the breeding room. Examine the desk and read the journal. Kill the worms that are hiding in the two holding cells and go through the door on the opposite side of the room. Run down the corridor. Suddenly you will be attacked by a strange creature from above. The creature will tell you in a hiss that you will soon die. Backtrack to the elevator and go up. Go through the door at the bottom of the screen. The room will fill with gas, so climb into the dust chute.

After you dust yourself off, start walking to the right. Suddenly a huge creature will appear from beneath the rubbish heap. Its attacks consist of sucking you towards it mouth. When it does this, target its mouth and open fire, just be ready to turn and run so it doesn't swallow you. After this attack, the camera view will switch to an above view as electric bolts fall from the sky. You will see the bolts shadow before they hit so move out of the way. Occasionally, two smaller creatures will jump out from the sides. Concentrate on these two, they are very easy but if the larger creature swallows them, his health will raise by 100 HP. When it starts to move towards you, just back off, turn and fire. Only attack when its mouth is open or you will cause no damage. Eventually it will collapse. Continue right and through the door. Continue right, as you do the large blast door behind you will open and the creature will start to give chase. Run to the right. The creature has a new attack, where it blows a green gas, which will poison you if you touch it. Continue to run down the corridor. Eventually you will come to a drop, to the right is a floor panel, stand on this and a platform will slowly rise. Avoid the creature's attack until the platform appears. Run across the platform and towards the door at the end. The creature will follow you, but the platform will lower trapping it. Stand on the second floor panel while avoiding the green gas and the creature will be crushed. Run to the door and shout for help until you are saved.

You will reunited with Kyle. Save you game at the telephone. Go left at the top of the screen and down the flight of stairs. Head through the door at the end. Head around and up the ladder. Go to the console and enter 18. The water level will lower, go down the stairs and through the gate. Go down once you reach the junction. Climb down the ladder. Head left through the door. Follow the path until you reach a locked door. Use the elevator to the right of the door. From here you split up from Kyle.

The first thing you need to do is go up to basement level 1 and search for the creature that told you that you were going to die, it's lurking in one of the corridors. Be careful because it has the ability to throw fireballs. Once it is dead you will find Bowman's card. Make your way down to basement 2 elevator hall and use Bowman's card to unlock the left door. Head down the corridor and through the door at the end. Fight your way through the operating room and go through the door into the Laboratory. Examine the white board, the computer system has a worm bug, but the magazine with the information has been borrowed by a employee. Head for the sleeping quarters and search the beds for the missing computer magazine. Go back to the Laboratory and examine the computer. The code is A3EILM2S2Y. Go to visitor section and answer the three questions. Kyle will contact you and ask you to meet him at the pod service gantry. Race there and meet Kyle. After talking to him you both go in search of the pilot. Head right into the control room and examine the camera screen in the right corner. Switch through the cameras, opening the doors and operating the lift. Leave the room and use the elevator. Run down the corridor and through the door at the end. Run along the gantry and through the door. Go left and use the elevator.

Neo Ark

Kyle stays behind. Head left, go through the arch and down the stairs. Follow the path and go through the door. Fight your way past the creatures and head inside the shrine. Go up and then left at the junction. Examine the stone opposite the locked door. Head back into the shrine but go down at the junction. Examine the puzzle on the wall. You need to move the red blocks into a diagonal pattern from the top right down to the bottom left. The creature sitting must be in the top right, the legs next, then the slim oval and finally the open rectangle in the bottom left. The empty space should be in the bottom right. You will hear a metallic sound. The locked door will now be open. Inside you will find a living generator. First destroy all the wall mounted devices then the machine to the creatures left. Then with everything destroyed, kill the creature. Head back through the shrine and return to the observation platform. Then go through the right arch and follow the path. In the jungle, kill the strange new creature you encounter then go through the gate to the right. Run down the path and follow until you reach a steel gate. Once on the other side, examine the disc to the left and spin it until the pattern matches. Go up onto the pyramid and step on the floor panels in this pattern.

Red, Yellow, Blue, White, Blue, White, Red, Yellow, White, Blue, Yellow, Red.

Head back down from the pyramid and through the steel gate. Follow the path and through the gate at the end. Head right and go down through the under water observation tunnel and up the stairs at the end. Go through the gate. Run down the gantry and through the gate at the end. Go through the door on the left. Head up the steps. You will find another generator. Destroy the wall devices then the machine. Then concentrate on the generator itself. Head back outside and backtrack your way to where you left Kyle and head up the elevator.

Your next step is to go down the elevator as indicated on your map (press **Select** to bring up your map), but take this chance to save your game and head up to the armoury and stock up on ammunition. You want a grenade pistol and at least 40+ grenades. Beware though as there are a lot of Dr Bowman style creatures lurking about.

Once at the bottom, you will be bombarded by waves that reduce your MP, if you haven't already you will have to destroy the sentry guns guarding the elevator. Ride down the elevator. Fight the two fat parasites then head into the next room. Here you will face what seems to be a huge Dr Bowman type creature defending or being powered by a small girl. Simply stand to the rear left of the giant creature and continuously fire grenades up at the creature. Eventually the creature will die and you

should lose the minimum of health, if any.

Aya discovers that the pilot is in fact Eve a clone of her DNA. Talk to Kyle, then the lights will flicker out. The room will fill with gas and No 9 style troops will storm the room. Keep talking to Eve until she follows you to the elevator. Once she is on board activate the elevator. Stay too long and Eve will die. You will appear from the elevator near the building that held the generators. Eve will run off. Run after her. In the underwater observation tunnel Eve will be kidnapped by No 9 (yes he's still alive). From here you must fight your way to the parking lot on basement level 1. The whole complex is filled with No 9 style troops, heavy armoured versions and even cloaked version which attack from behind. All the sentry guns have been reactivated also. To reach the parking lot you will have to make your way through the sleeping quarters via the storeroom. Once you reach the parking lot, you will have to examine the control panel to the right of the garage. You will need to select car no 3. Move the car onto the turntable then examine the panel to the right of the main parking lot door. Use Yoshida's card. Then use the car. From the car, run forward and use the emergency exit. Fight your way through the corridor and out the door at the end. Head down the screen and enter the door on the left. Head down and unlock the main door. Return outside and go through the large door. Run to the top left hand corner and open the gate onto the heliport.

After the cool cut scene you will find yourself in a military tent. Save your game and then examine the boxes in the corner for some grenade rounds. Leave the tent. Outside you will meet Rupert. He will give you a magnum and some ammunition. When you are ready to leave, activate the panel to the right of the main gate. Make your way back into the complex the same way you escaped. Back in the complex, fight your way to the Pod Service Gantry in basement 1. Save your game in the sterilisation room before continuing. Once you have reached the Pod Service Gantry you will be reunited with Eve, Kyle and the evil No 9. Once the sequence has finished you will find yourself back in the corridor. Heal yourself, then ride down the elevator to the left. Head through the door in front.

Here you will face the first of two the end of game bosses. Save the magnum for the very last boss. The boss has four attacks. The first is a purple beam fired from its head. As it powers up to attack, run to either side to avoid being hit. From its shoulders it releases a green gas which will choke you if you are hit by it. From its stomach it will spit a white liquid which will poison you and cause you to pause. Its other attack involves it swiping at you with its hands. First concentrate on its head. Avoid the beam and when it releases it gas, shoot the creature's head. It will only fire the white liquid if you are standing on the lower gantry. To avoid its hands, simply stand in the corner with your back to the wall. When you have removed the head, it will fire a bright yellow beam, simple run in either direction and continue to shoot at its neck. Eventually it will open its stomach. You will instantly die if you are hit from the beam it emits from its stomach. Stand at the top of the gantry and when it powers up, run to the lower gantry. The creature will slowly turn to face you and by the time it does the beam will have stopped so use this moment of safety to open fire at its vulnerable stomach. If you manage to destroy all the creature's body parts before you finally kill it you will be rewarded with loads of EXP and BP.

Once victorious, equip the magnum, shotgun, rifle and loads of ammunition. Walk along the gantry and press the button to open the bridge. Eve will be snatched and will become the last boss you will face. Immediately cast antibody and energy shot onto yourself. Equip the magnum and shoot her while avoiding her wing swipe attack. When she vanishes, stand still for a few seconds and then quickly move. She will appear in the same place you stopped in. Continue to avoid her moves and attack when you can. You will know she is close to dying when she creates a shadow version of herself. Kill the shadow and concentrate on Eve until she dies.

With the game completed you will unlock two extra game modes. These are:

Replay Mode – Start the game again but with bonus EXP, MP, BP and items.

Bounty Mode – Start the game with bonus BP as you hunt down the rogue armoured assailants.

PARODIUS DELUXE PACK

Hidden Stage
To have a go at a hidden section, shoot the ships in the first wave of stage 2, then shoot the first ship of the second wave while avoiding all the other ships. The enemies will explode and you will arrive in the hidden section.

Invincibility
To be invincible, pause the game and press the following sequence: ▲, ▲, ✖, ✖, ●, ■, ●, ■, ↓, ←. To return to normal just repeat the same code.

Maximum Power-Ups
To have the maximum power-ups, pause the game and press ↑, ↑, ↓, ↓, ←, →, ←, →, ✖, ●. You can repeat the sequence at any time.

Level Select
For a level select option, go to the title screen and press ■, ■, ■, ■, ■, ▲, ▲, ▲, ▲, ▲, ▲, ▲, ●, ●, ●.

PEAK PERFORMANCE

Special Class
To gain access to the special class, go to the Car Selection Screen, (Under class A, B or C) and simply press **L1** + ●.

Extra Cars
To gain extra cars, simply follow the instructions below. It is possible to tune up the extra vehicles, and also save them for easy access.

Nissan 240 ZX and Bus
Complete the Bay Area track in under 3 minutes

Lamborghini Diablo
Hold on to your potatoes! Firstly select a car and finish the uptown Driveway circuit in first place in all three difficulty settings, in one-player mode. Next, finish in first place in the next level. Finally, race the uptown Driveway track in Time Trial mode and find the parked Diablo.

Porsche
Finish the Seven Tight Corners track in first place in all three difficulty settings, in one-player mode. Next, race the same track in Time Trial mode, and find the Porsche at the Hotel.

McLaren and Truck
Finish the Pikes Hill Climb circuit in under 2 minutes 30. These vehicles will now be available for use in the Time Trial mode only.

Scooter
Race the Northern Country track in Time Trial mode in an Anticlockwise direction. Next, go through the gate near the river on the second lap to find the scooter.

PERFECT WEAPON

Level Codes

Level	Code
Ice Moon	✖, ■, ✖, ■, ■, ●, ■, ●.
Garden Mn.	●, ✖, ✖, ▲, ●, ●, ✖, ▲.
Forrest Mn.	●, ▲, ■, ●, ■, ■, ▲, ▲.
Desert Mn.	●, ✖, ✖, ✖, ▲, ●, ▲, ▲.
Morgone	✖, ✖, ■, ✖, ■, ■, ▲, ●.
Toran	▲, ▲, ✖, ■, ▲, ▲, ✖, ●.
Shiro	●, ●, ✖, ■, ✖, ✖, ●, ▲.
Renza-Fi	▲, ●, ✖, ✖, ▲, ■, ▲, ▲.
Sacra-Ja	●, ✖, ●, ●, ■, ●, ✖, ■.
Morgone O.	✖, ▲, ●, ✖, ▲, ●, ●, ▲.
Lizard Guard	●, ■, ■, ✖, ●, ✖, ✖, ●.
Final Level	■, ▲, ●, ✖, ■, ▲, ●, ✖.

PITBALL

View all FMV Sequences
To see all of the in-game movies, highlight any ending on the "FMV Test" screen, and press ←, →, ▓, ●.

Mini-Game
To gain access to an extra mini-game, firstly highlight any ending on the "FMV Test" screen and press ▓ + ●. The team ending highlighted determines the type of ship that will appear. Also, pressing ▓ + ● without a highlighted ending results in a first-person view.

PITFALL 3D

Enter the following Passwords on the Password Screen:

More Lives:	GIVEMELIFE
Big Heads:	BIGHEADHARY
Demo Mode:	VIGILANTE
Pitfall Original:	CRANESBABY
Disappear:	2DHARRY

PO'ED

Ammo Refill
Go to Foot Mode and perform a backflip using ▓ and **L2**, and press →, ✖, ● while your flip is in motion.

Farting Arses
To hear the walking arses make farting sounds when firing, go to the main menu and select Load Game. Press **L1**, **L2**, **R1**, and **R2** together.

Full Inventory
To have all the weapons to use, go to the map screen by pressing ▓ and **Select**, then press ← to make the arrow point at you. Next press **Start** and you will return to standard view. Press **L1**, ▓, ✖, ● while the camera is still rotating, then when you press ▲ you will have the weapons.

Health Refill
In Foot Mode do a backflip, and press ↓, ✖, **R2** while flipping.

Invincibility
If you want to be invincible you must have the drill. If you do not you can use the Full Inventory cheat to get it. Next you need to go somewhere safe and bring up the Weapon Select menu so that you can select Frying Pan with **L1** or **R1**. Return to the game and go to Weapon Select again. Cycle through the weapons by pressing ● and **R1** and you will see 999 flashing on your health counter. To return to normal again press ● and **R1**.

See the Final Sequence
Go to the main menu and select Load Game, then press → and hold while you press ●. Press ▲ to cancel. Then press ▓ and ← and release. When you press ▲ the final scene will appear.

Stage Select
To access the stage select, go to the main menu screen, simultaneously press **L1**, **L2**, **R1**, **R2**, and ↑, then release them. Press ● to start a game. When you see the difficulty screen, press **L1**, **L2**, **R1**, and **R2**, at the same time as you are pressing ↓. Select a difficulty, then you will be able to choose a level.

Turn Off Collision Detection
In jetpack mode, find a body and stand on it, then bring up the weapons selection by pressing ▲. Next press **L1**, → and ↓ and you will fall through the floor. You need to use the jetpack to move around. Bring up the weapons selection again with ▲, press **L1**, → and ↓ if you wish to turn the collision detection back on.

PONG

Pause the game at the zone selection screen before entering one of the following cheats:

Fill 1 bar of the Atari logo	**R1**, **L1**, **R1** (open level 1)
Fill 2 bars of the Atari logo	**L2**, **R2**, **L2**, **R2** (open level 2)
Fill 3 bars of the Atari Logo	**L1** + **R1** + **L2** + **R2** (open level 3)

Press **Start** and return to the zone selection.

POOL HUSTLER

Bowlliards Mode
On the title screen press ↑, ↑, ↓, ↓, ▲, ▲, ✖, ✖, ←, →, ▓, ●.

POOL SHARK

Unlock All The Locations And Tables
Rename your player as **CW12 4AP** including the space. When you return to the game you will have all the locations and all the tables.

POPULOUS 3D

Strategies
1. Always save your game before going into battle. If you get decimated you can reload your position and try a different approach

2. Increase the range of spells by casting from high ground
3. Place guard towers at all sides of the village to prevent any nasty surprises.
4. Place a preacher in the guard towers to convert any waifs and strays that come into the vicinity.
5. Keep all of your followers busy.
6. When Braves are in resting in huts or building they produce four times more mana.
7. Enemy spies take the form of suspicious looking braves. Unmask them using ✖
8. Use swamp spells to ward off any unwanted attacks, then use swarms to chase enemies into them.

A guide to magic

Angel of Death	Flies around picking off enemy followers one by one. Attack itwith firewarriors or your own angel of death.
Blast	Simple and powerful, kills most enemies with one hit.
Earthquake	Causes huge damage to anything in its wake.
Convert	Converts wildmen to your tribe.
Erode	Causes land to erode quickly, useful for attacking enemies on coastal or high ground.
Hypnotism	Enables you to get enemies into your control. Use preachers on hypnotised enemy to permanently convert them.
Invisibility	Makes followers invisible, very good when combined with Shield.
Landbridge	Gives access across water and levels the land between the Shaman and the place where the spell is cast.
Lightning and	Extremely powerful, sets fire to buildings trees.
Swamp	Places an uncrossable swamp in the path of your enemies to halt them in their tracks. Use the swarm to trick them into it.
Swarm	Scatters armies and evacuates buildings.
Sheild	Gives followers short-term invincibility. Spells cast at shielded followers will bounce back at the attacker
Tornado	Destroys buildings.
Volcano	Causes massive devastation to anything caught in its lava trail. Cast in the middle of a populated area.

PORSCHE CHALLENGE

Short Cuts
USA- Drain
Go past the first left corner and you will see a car park on your right. If there is a white truck in it you know that the Drain short cut is open. Take a sharp left through a gate in the wire fence when you are about level with the truck. Avoid the water, as this will slow your speed. The exit is by the railway station.

Japan- Temple
You can open the Temple Gate short cut by hitting the first basket on the left of the course. The basket will have an IO logo on it. The short cut begins just past the starting grid.

Alpine- Village
On your second lap, there is a snowplough at the base of the track. Knock over the cones in front of the snowdrift to the left of the plough. Now the plough will clear the snowdrift, giving way to the doors that let you onto the next lap.

Cheat Codes
Enter the following cheats on the main menu screen (1-Player, Options):

All the other cars jump ⬆ + ▧, ⬆ + ●, ⬆ + ▧, ⬆ + ●, ⬆ + ▧, ⬆ + ●, ⬆ + ▧
Car jumps ▧, ●, ▧
Choose your own car parameters ⬅ + ●, ➡ + ▧ + **Select**
Drive the black prototype Porsche ➡ + ▧, ⬅ + ● + **Select**
Extra long tracks **Select** + ⬆, **Select** + ⬇, **Start**, **Select**
High pitched voices ⬆, ▲, ⬆, ▲
Hyper car **Select** + ▧, **Select** + ●, **Select** + ▧ + ●
Invisible car ▧ + ●, L2 + R2, ▧ + ●, L1 + R1, ▧ + ●
Mirror mode ⬅ + ●, ⬇ + ▲, ➡ + ▧
Takes you straight to the 'interactive' versions of the tracks, where the road alters as you race ⬇ + **Start**, ⬆ + **Start**, **Select**, **Start**
Takes you to the end credits ▧, ●, ⬅ + **Select**, ➡ + **Select**
Unlimited re-entries L1 + L2, R1 + R2 + ▧
Your opponents swerve all over the track ⬆, ⬅, ➡ + **Select**

POWER MOVE PRO WRESTLING

Play As Gorgon (the announcer)
Go to the title screen and press the following: **L1, L1, L2, R2, R2, R1, ▲, ⬇, ✖, ⬆, Select**. Highlight Agent Orange at the wrestler select screen, then press **Select**.

Play As Sallie (the referee)
Press the following at the title screen: ⬆, ⬇, ⬅, ⬅, ▲, ✖, ▧, ⬅, **L1, R1, L2, R2, Select**. Then highlight El Temblor at the wrestler select screen and press **Select**.

Play as Sparrow
Go to the title screen and press the following sequence: ⬅, ➡, ▲, ⬆, ▧, ⬅, ✖, ⬇, ✖, ⬇, ▧, ⬅, ▲, ⬆, ⬅, ➡, **Select**. Highlight Commandant at the wrestler select screen, and then press **Select**.

PREMIER MANAGER '98

Cheap Quality Players
At the start of the game switch the ageing option on, and invest in your youth team policy so that it is 25%. Then in the game buy quality old players at the end of their careers and when they retire they will keep their stats and appear as a young player with cheap wages!

Raising Cash
Buy players on the transfer list under the Free Bosman ruling. If you do it at the end of a season you will not have to pay them heavy wages for very long. Put them in your side, put them on the transfer market, and you sell them for some good quick bucks.

PREMIER MANAGER '99

Five star players
Enter your name as **MATT IS GOD**. You will now have really athletic players.

PROJECT OVERKILL

Cloak
If you would like to have a cloak, pause the game and select Review Mission. Hold t and press ■, ●, ●, ■, then release ▲. Next hold ✖, then press ▲, ▲ and release ✖.

End Level
Pause the game and select Review Mission, then press ✖, ⬆, ⬇, ⬆, hold ■, press ●, release ■, hold ✖ and press ▲ to get to the end of the level.

Life Refill
To refill your life bar, press pause during the game and then select Review Mission. Hold ■ and press ●, ✖, ▲, then release ■. Next hold ●, press ■, ✖, ▲ and then release ▲.

Maximum Ammo
For maximum ammunition, pause the game and select Review Mission. Next hold ●, press ■ and release ●. Hold ▲ and press ✖, then release ▲. Hold ● and press ✖, then release ●. Hold ✖ and press ■.

Speed Up
To be speedier, pause during a game and select Review Mission. Hold ⬆ and press ▲, ▲, ▲, then release ⬆. Hold ⬇ and press ✖, ■, ●, then release ⬇.

Test Mode
To have a test mode, pause the game and select Review Mission. Next press ⬅, ➡, ➡, ⬅ and then hold ✖ while you press ▲. Release ✖, hold ▲ and press ✖.

PSYBADEK

Passwords
GOANYWHERE   Level Select
DEKPOWERUP   Faster Dek

RAGE RACER

Advanced Colour Palettes
If you would like more choice in colours that you can use for your team logo, carry out the following functions:
Go to the main options and select Customise.
Select Design and choose a logo or design one of your own.
Select Paint and press any direction to move the cursor off the painting area.
Move onto the colour palette by pressing a button.
Press **L1**, **L2**, **R1**, **R2**, and **Select**.
There should now be some extra boxes labelled RIGHT, G and B. The letters represent the amount of hue for the palette that is highlighted by the cursor. Use ⬆ and ⬇ to change which hue you alter. By pressing **R1** and ⬆ or ⬇, you can change the number in the hue box.
Put the cursor onto the painting area, then press **L1**, **L2**, **R1**, **R2** and **Select**. You can now use the cross-hair in the smaller picture area to target for more accuracy.
To rotate the design, press **L1** and **R1** along with any direction while keeping the cursor inside the painting area.

Infinite Money
To have infinite money, first complete the Normal GP (all the classes), and wait for the end of the credits. Go to the Save/Load screen and save the game into a new block. Next go to play the Normal GP at class five, and you should find that there is only one car that you can choose - GNADE. Select it and press Race Start. During the countdown to 'Go', press **Start** and select Retire, to quit the race without losing a chance. Enter the Normal GP again and choose class one. Now you should have infinite money.
You can carry out the same steps at Extra GP to get infinite money there as well.

Mirror Mode
In Mirror Mode the tracks are reversed so that everything including the writing is back to front. To enter Mirror Mode go to the main options and select Race Start. Next hold **L1**, **R1**, **Select** and **Start** until the race begins.

Mirror Toggle
To remove your rear view mirror, pause the game while in internal mode. Hold ▲ and press **L1**. To have the mirror back again, use **R1**.

RAGING SKIES

All Enhancements
Start a game with the following password in order to already have the special capsules (Double Air Dash, Hyper Charger, Super Armour, I Tracer):

6414, 4155, 6872, 3356.

Extra Time
For extra time, hold the following as the game loads: **L1** + **L2** + **R1** + **R2** + ✖ + ⬅ + ▲ + ■ + ⬅.

Final Stage
Highlight the 'X' logo on the stage select screen. Then quickly press ⬇ + ■ + ✖. The code is confirmed by the cursor moving to the bottom of the screen.

Zero's Light Sabre
You can play with Zero's light sabre by entering the following as a password to start a game: 7357, 7533, 6462, 7835.

RAIDEN PROJECT

Extra Options
You can make adjustments to the resolution and move the screen around by accessing a special screen. Just hold **L1**, **L2**, **R1** and **R2** together during the game.

Full Credits
There are two ways of doing this. Either press **Select** when you have died (at the countdown) and this will give you full credits, or you can press ▲, ●, ■ and ✖ at the same time at the option screen where you set the number of credits. This way gives you FREEPLAY.

Mission Select
Select Difficulty at the Settings Menu, then hold **R1**, **R2**, **L1**, **L2** and press **Start**.

Power-Up Pixie
To release a pixie that gives you power-ups, you need to look out for trees that are a slightly different colour. They tend to be on the right side of the screen. Get close to these trees and unload into them to release the pixie which you must capture. The pixie will release power-ups when you die.

RAINBOW SIX

Level Select
On the main menu, hold **L1** and press ●, ✖, ●, ■, ■, ▲, ▲. Begin a game and you will be able to select any mission.

RALLY CROSS

The following passwords can be entered as either the Lap/Course Record name or the New Season name:

PASSWORD	ACTION
banzai	You can drive straight through other cars as if they weren't there at all.
fat_tires	Gives your car fatter tyres, although their grip does not seem to be affected.
feather	Makes the cars lighter so they bounce around.
float	When the cars bounce up, they float through the air for longer.
im_a_pro	This gives you four more cars, and the Gardens and Stadium tracks.
no_wheels	The cars float around the track with no wheels.
noviscous	Water and mud etc don't slow you down.
radbrad	This returns gravity back to normal when you have been using the 'float' cheat.
spinner	More sensitive steering that allows you to turn more quickly.
stone	Makes the cars grip the road so they hardly jump at all.
vet_me	This gives you four extra cars and access to the Alpine track.
weeoo	Allows you to select the three pick-up trucks.
wheels	Just the four wheels of the car float around the track, with no body.

RALLY CROSS 2

Start a new season and enter your name as one of these names to access the extra bonus tracks and cheats.

SISAO	Oasis Track
ELGNUJ	Jungle Track
FOSTER	Little Woods Track
NIVEK	Frozen Trail Track
MIT	Dusty Road Track
KCIN	Rocky Creek Track
CIRE	Dry Humps Track
BSIRHC	Hillside Track
MOOBMOOB	All Cars
PREALL	All Tracks And Most Of The Cars
PREVENT	Veteran Level Cars And Tracks
PREPRO	Pro Level Cars And Tracks
INCORPEREAL	Turn Off Collision Detection
AIRFILLED	Low Gravity
LEADSHOT	Original Rally Cross Physics
MOONEY	Normal Rally Cross 2 Physics

RAPID RACER

Enter these cheats on the Name Selection screen in one-player mode:

Extra Boats	_BOA
Duck mode	_QAK
Hurricane	HURR
Mirror Track	M__? (? - select track number)
Day Track	D__? (? - select track number)
Night Track	N__? (? - select track number)
Random Track	FRAC

RAPID RELOAD

Passwords

At the title screen, using controller one, hold **L1**, **L2**, **R1** and **R2**. Press **Select**. Now you should see 'Secret Code' which has two letters beside it which you can change by pressing ↟ and ↡ for the Left hand letter, and ▲ and ✖ for the right. Use the following codes:

Stage 2: MA
Stage 3: UT
Stage 4: RH
Stage 5: MK
Stage 6: HT

Debug Mode

Set the MA code, then press **Select** and change the code to SV. Now press **Start** and enter the following using controller two:
Boost weapon power to a ten-second duration: ↟
Change selected weapon type from Axel to Ruka: ■
Gunlock type change: ←
Increase number of bombs: ●
Increase weapon power-up time in 30-second increments: ✖
Invincibility on/off (although falling will cause damage): ▲
Skips area (disengages invincibility): →
Voice mode on/off: ↡

Special Codes

999 weapon power-up	SS
Begin with 9 bombs	YI
Big Character	QB
Small character	CM
Small windows	MV
Weak Axel and Ruka	TY

RASCAL

Level and Room Select

Enter the password HOUSE and during the game press R1 to select a new level or R2 to select a room.

RAYMAN

Picture In Picture

Pause the game and hold **R2** while you press ●, ●, ←, ●, ●.

Removed 'Paused' Text

To remove the '*game paused, press **Start** to continue*' graphic, Pause the game and hold **R1** and **R2**.

Passwords

Start = 38W8Z92W9M
Pink Plant Woods = **L8W8Z9LW9M**
Anguish Lagoon = **LOW8ZH2W9M**
Swamps of Forgetfulness = **L04JPHLW9M**
Mosquitoes Nest = **LO44Z9LNHM**
Bongo Hills = **BOD4?HL29X**
Allegro Presto = **BOD4?1L29X**
Gong Heights = **BO4DG13L9K**
Mr Sax's Hullaloo = **BOD4?R33HP**
Twilight Gulch = **BH4N?1!3NP**
Hard Rocks = **T9DN?R33NF**
Mr Stone's Peaks = **49DN?1!!WF**
Eraser Plains = **DW44?1!CN7**
Pencil Pentathlon = **4NBN?1!5NF**
Space Mamma's Crater = **DCT4G13CDF**
Crystal Palace = **DCTW81!CD7**
Eat at Joe's = **NWTDDR!346**
Mr Skop's Stalactites = **NW?WD15!4Q**

RAYSTORM

Free Play Mode

When 'Press Start 'appears on your screen, press and hold **L1** + **L2** + **R1** + **R2** and **Start**. Continue to hold these buttons and press ↟, ↟, ↟, ↟, ↟, ↟, ↟, ↡, ↟, ↟, ↟, ↟, **Start**. You should hear 'Limiter Released'. Go to the options menu and turn off the credit limit to enable free play.

Level Select

Complete the 'Combat Mode'.

RAY TRACERS

Drive as Tsumujikaze

Beat the T man in Time Attack mode to play the game as him.

Drive White Vestal

Finish the game with each car, using no continues.

Drive Black Vestal

Finish the game with the White Vestal.

R/C STUNT COPTER

Fly as a Pilot
Complete the training with an average of silver.

Fly as a Captain
Complete the training with an average of gold.

Fly as an Ace
Complete all the training levels with a gold.

REBEL ASSAULT II

Passwords
The following codes may be entered at the password screen:

Easy level	✗ ● ✗ ● ✗ ▲
Medium level	✗ ▲ ▲ ■ ✗ ▲
Hard level	▲ ■ ■ ■ ✗ ▲
Invulnerability	▲ ● ● ▲ ■ ✗
Level Skip	▲ ▲ ● ● ▲ ■ ■
Movie mode	▲ ■ ● ▲ ● ●
Open all levels	✗ ▲ ■ ● ✗ ▲

RESIDENT EVIL

Guide For Jill
The Mansion

1) When you first take control, you will be searching for Chris in the Dining Room (2). Before doing anything make sure you figure out how to run and the method of attack.

2) Arming yourself with the beretta, head towards Barry and take part in some enthralling conversation. Remove the emblem from the mantlepiece behind Barry, and go to corridor 3.

3) Exploring this corridor will put you head to head with a white zombie, hunched over a pool of blood. Remove any thoughts of attacking from your head. Apart from a massive chance of dying in the first five minutes of the game, it uses up precious ammo. Instead, leg it back to Barry who will relish in the glory of removing head from torso.

4) Upon returning to the Main Hall (1), you find that Wesker has disappeared. (Ooh! How mysterious). After yet more Oscar-Nominated script, return to the corridor where the zombie was. Search the decapitated mess that is Kenneth a few times to gain two clips of ammo.

5) Now go to room 5. Push the (obviously out of place) cupboard out of the way to reveal the music for 'Moonlight Sonata'. Now go to the piano and *use* the music. Head into Room 12. Remove the gold emblem and replace it with the one from the Dining Room. Put this gold emblem in the slot in the Dining Room and, hey presto! The mansion key is yours.

6) Next to the stairs in the Main Hall are a typewriter and some ribbon. If you are feeling unsure, save here.

7) Go to Room 14. Push the steps to the appropriate place and remove the map from the statue. Push the drawers out of the way and walk round the corner. Avoid the floored zombie and take the ribbon from the shelves at the end.

8) Use the lock-pick to enter Room 15. Turn 180 degrees and walk backwards. When the devil dog lands, shoot it once. Don't shoot it again until it starts to run. On turning the corner a second devil dog will jump you. Deal with it in the same way as before. Moving the drawers in this section of the corridor will reveal another clip. Now you have plenty of ammo.

9) As you enter Room 16, you will notice a green herb by you feet. If you are injured use it. Otherwise leave it, but remember its position.

10) Travel to Room 20 via Room 19 and you will be presented with a beast of a weapon; the shotgun. Return to Room 19 to be confronted with certain death! Or maybe not. Barry's quick talking fails to impress and you suddenly feel very alone.

11) Stick with the pistol for the time being. Go to Room 21 and take out the zombies as described at the start. Enter Room 22.

12) Whatever you do don't shoot at the crows. If you want to know why... well, okay then, try it! The sensible ones among you are still alive. The pictures on the wall are of a person at different stages of life. Flick the switches underneath them in the correct order; newborn to old man. Now hit the switch right at the end of the corridor. Do this incorrectly and you'll know about it! Success will leave you with the star crest.

13) Being careful not to annoy any of the crows, go to Room 25. Take out the massive rotweiler, and place the crest in the slot at the end of the corridor. There! Only three more to go, and you'll have unlocked the back door.

14) Take out another zombie in Room 23, and a welcome break is your reward in the form of a save point in Room 23b. This is a recommended place to save.

15) The chest in the corner can be used to store things, and by some form of magic, items in one chest will appear in chests throughout the game. (Funny that, quite handy though!) There's a bag of chemical stuff on the floor. Put this in the chest along with the ribbon. If you are low on ammo, take an extra clip from the chest. Now the shotgun can entertain you!

16) Climb the stairs in Room 23 to get to Room 51. Wait for the zombie to get close, then aim up and take it's head clean off. Turn around quickly and deal with the one behind you.

17) Go into Room 56 via Room 55 and read the green book on the table. This information is vital to surviving further on in the game.

18) Room 55 houses two zombies, which should be taken out using the pistol. Following the corridor will take you to the first floor of the Main Hall, where Barry gives you some acid rounds. Why is he so confident about himself?

19) Go to Room 44 via Room 43. Get the bazooka and run.

20) Go to Room 32. Kill the two zombies, then push the statue.

21) Go to Room 33. Kill the zombies with the shotgun.

22) Go down the stairs to Room 7. Shoot three zombies with the shotgun, and then go to Room 8. You are probably low on ammo, so get the clips. Save if necessary.

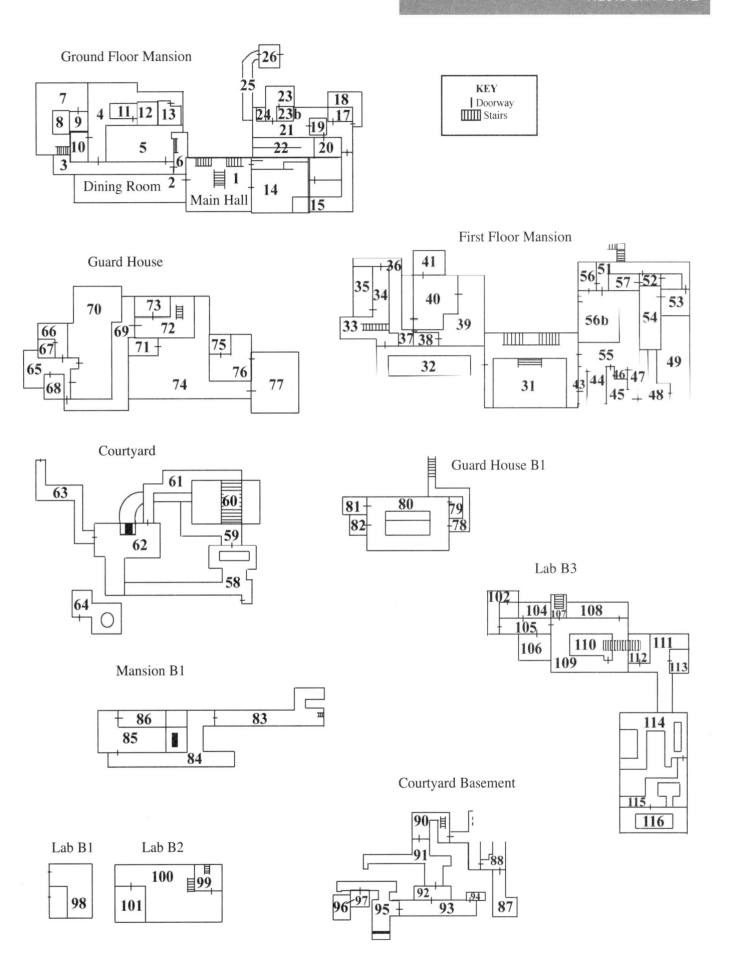

Ground Floor Mansion

Guard House

Courtyard

Mansion B1

Lab B1   Lab B2

First Floor Mansion

Guard House B1

Lab B3

Courtyard Basement

KEY
Doorway
Stairs

23) Kill the two zombies in Room 4. Next go to Room 13 and put the chemical in the pump. Get the key and then combine the herbs.

24) Go to the Dining Room and get the blue jewel. Now go to Room 11 and put the jewel in the tiger's eye. Get the wind crest.

25) Go to Room 8. Store the bazooka, herbs, ribbon and knife.

26) Go to Room 10. When reading, kill the zombie using the bazooka. Then get the shotgun and the beretta ammo.

27) Go to Room 50 via Room 52. Hit the switch on the insect display. Push the now empty tank out of the way so that the bookcase can be pushed into the corner, revealing the ammo. Some ribbon can be found in the hanging coat.

28) Store these items in Room 23b.

29) Go to Room 57 via Room 52. Get the clip from the corner and take the lighter from on top of the cupboard.

30) Go to Room 53 and light the fire to unveil the map of the second floor.

31) Go to Room 56. Push the statues over the grills in the floor at the end of the room. Now push the switch in the centre. Collect the sun crest from the case at the end.

32) Store the lighter and the crest. Go to Room 45. Find Richard and get him the serum from Room 8. While you are in Room 8 get rid of your clips and beretta, and any excess shotgun rounds. Instead, load up with the bazooka, acid rounds, explosive rounds, and lighter. Then take the serum to Richard in Room 45.

33) After laughing at Richard's fate go to Room 48 and take out the zombie. Light the candle in Room 47 and push the cupboard away to get to Room 46. Take the acid rounds from the cupboard.

34) Go to Room 49 and discard the mansion key. When you see the snake just keep shooting at it. About five normal bazooka rounds and four or five acid rounds should scare it away. Collect the crest from the hole where the snake runs to, then get out of there. Oh no! You're poisoned! You must be dead, right? Hey, isn't that Barry? How convenient!

35) Leave everything in the chest except the beretta, some clips and the mansion key. Take the opportunity to go to Room 13, and mix the remaining herbs. Now go to Room 27.

36) Arm yourself and collect the clip on the dressing table. You should have at least 70 shots available to you now. Take out the zombie and open the drawers he is guarding. Collect the shotgun shells. Go to Room 29. Collect the two green herbs and try to avoid the floored zombie. If he chews just kick his head off. Go to Room 23b.

37) Collect the three crests and put them in the slots in Room 25. Enter Room 26.

38) Push the steps against the high shelves and collect the crank.

39) Go to Room 23b. Make sure you have the shotgun and ammo and the beretta and ammo, the crank and the mansion key. SAVE!! Put the ribbon in the chest.

Courtyard

1) Go to Room 58. Stay where you are and wait for the dogs then shoot them - three shots will do. Use the radio and get the map from the wall on the far side.

2) Go to Room 59, use the crank and walk across the bridge (60). As soon as you climb up to area 61, run to the lift and get to Room 62 as the snakes are poisonous. Take out both dogs in Room 62.

3) Go to Room 63. Run past the dogs to the far end, turn and shoot both dogs.

Guard House

1) Get the shotgun out! Go to Room 68. Get rid of the crank, fill up your shotgun, and get rid of any excess shells. You'll need three free shots. Put the spray and explosives in the chest.

2) Go to Room 66. Decapitate the two zombies. Get the shells from the desk. Take the red book and go to Room 67. Unplug the bath and get the key. Store the book and get out the bazooka.

3) Go to Room 70. Kill the spiders by shooting with the bazooka. This will flip them over. One shot from the shotgun will burst their bodies. Kill the babies by stepping on them. Get the ammo from the corner.

4) From here on you must use common sense on what to take and what to store, as what you have depends entirely on how well you play.

5) Push the statue onto the hole in Room 65. Go to Room 74 via Room 69 and get the key from under the wasps nest. Quickly get out. Go to Room 72, beware of the zombies! Get the map and the Plant 42 notes. Sort out the zombie in Room 73. Go back to Room 72 and move the cupboards to reveal a stairway.

6) Go down to Room 78 and push the crates to make a walkway. Go to Room 82 via Room 80. Drain the water and hit the flashing light to get to Room 81. Get the key and ammo from this room.

7) Go to Room 76 and sort out the zombies in Room 75. Take the V-Jolt report from the cupboard.

8) Go to Room 71. Get in by hitting the corresponding buttons that are NOT lit up. Once the entire board lights up, you're in. Create the V-Jolt using your knowledge and the scribbles on the wall. Once you have V-Jolt, use it on the roots in Room 79. Now get the mixed herbs, bazooka rounds and shotgun rounds and put the red book in the empty space in the cupboard in Room 76. Now face Plant 42 in Room 77.

9) Stay around the edge of the room, otherwise it will grab you. Avoid the acid droplets, and when you get the chance, fire off the bazooka using exploding rounds as a preference. After a while, Barry should come and help.

10) Get the key from the fireplace and head back to the mansion. Try to store and combine all the herbs you come across. You'll come across Wesker on the way. SAVE!! (Before you get to the mansion).

Back In The Mansion

1) Hunters are everywhere, be very careful, a couple of shells or a well-aimed bazooka round will take them. Don't get too close, and avoid them if at all possible. Beware! They are very

fast!

2) Go to Room 24. Turn the light on, get the magnum rounds and the Doom Book. Go to Room 23. There is a hunter here.

3) Read the note on the stairs, enter 23b and store the magnum rounds and Doom Book. Go to Room 16. There is a hunter here. Run through Room 15, don't stop to kill the spiders. Kill the two hunters in Room 32. Go to Room 33 and take out the hunter there. Then go to Room 35.

4) Switch the light on by the door. Push the stairs in front of the head and get the red jewel.

5) Go down the stairs to Room 7 and take out the hunter.

6) Go to Room 8, save and store.

7) Go to Room 4, be careful of the two hunters in the same position as the zombies were before. Put the red jewel in the tiger's eye in Room 11 to get the Colt Python. Now get your entire magnum rounds.

8) Go to Room 23b, taking out the hunters on the way. Store everything except a mixed herb, shotgun and ammo, bazooka and ammo. Go to Room 53 and decapitate both zombies. Go to Room 54 and prepare to battle the snake for the second time. Use the same method as before.

9) Jump down the hole and hit the switch. Don't go down the stairs, but wait for Barry to come back and see you. Then go down the stairs into Room 83. Take out the zombies and go into Room 85.

10) Take out the zombie, and go to Room 86. Go up the stairs and out of the door to Room 6. Go to Room 8 and take weapons and ammo only. Leave plenty of free slots.

11) Now go back to Room 6 and get in the lift, up to Room 39. Take out the zombie, go to Room 38 and grab the ammo and the battery.

12) Go to Room 40. Get the rounds and the notes, and take out the zombies.

13) Go to Room 42. Hit the red switch and push the statue into the light. Go into the office and get the MO disk.

14) Push the bookcase in Room 40 to get to Room 41. Look out of the window. WOW! The helipad. Or maybe not!

15) Go to Room 8 and get the Doom Book, square crank, battery, guns and ammo. Go to Room 25 and take out the hunter.

16) Go to Room 62 and put the battery in the faulty lift. Go up and check everything out.

17) Go to Room 62 and down the steps behind the waterfall.

Courtyard Basement 1

This area is full of hunters. Whenever you enter a room, have the Colt at the ready and listen for their footsteps.

1) Explore Rooms 90,89,88,and 87. In Room 87, you'll meet Enrico. Rooms 78 and 77 now hold four hunters! Pick up the second crank in Room 78.

2) Go to Room 76 and encounter Barry who has been injured.

3) Use the new crank to get to Room 91. Once the boulder has been triggered run back into the doorway to avoid it.

4) Room 92 contains a giant spider. Make sure you are all right and have at least a round each of shotgun and bazooka, or some magnums and beretta rounds.

Run around the spider and shoot when you get the chance. Don't get trapped in the corner! When the snake dies, its body will release baby spiders. Go back into Room 91, then come back into Room 92. Use the knife on the barrel to cut the cobwebs covering the door.

5) Go straight to 94, the save room. The blue herb will help if you are poisoned. Go to Room 95 and use the crank to get to Room 96.

6) Move the statue so that it is against the moving wall section. Use the crank twice to push the statue out. Now you can move the statue onto the switch and get Doom Book 2.

7) Go back to Room 94. Turn both the Doom Books on their sides (look at them). Press the action button to open them and take the medals. Store the crank and take the weapons and ammo. Save!

8) Go to Room 64 via the lift in Room 95. Put the two medals in the appropriate places on the side of the round fountain to reveal a staircase. That'll be the underground labs then! Oooh, scary! Go down the stairs and into the lift to Room 98.

Umbrella Labs - The Final Horror

1) Go to Room 98. Go straight down the ladder to Room 99. Take the weapons and the MO disk with you. Store the rest in the chest.

2) Go to Room 100. Take out the zombies, grab the MO disk and go down the stairs to Room 107.

3) Don't kill anything; go straight to Room 106 via Room 105. Press the switch and read the letter. Look at the painting and use it to decipher the password in the letter.

4) Room 109 holds loads of zombies, shoot them if you must! Go to Room 108 and start up the computer.

Name: John
Password 1: ADA
Password 2: Mole
(Open B2 and B3 doors before switching off)
Take the slides.

5) Go to Room 101 and watch the slides. Get the security system file. Open the panel on the wall and hit the switch. Get the key.

6) Go to Room 111. Be careful of the increasing numbers of zombies.

7) Go to Room 113, a save room. Take the shotgun/bazooka and Colt and MO disk. Save!

8) Go to Room 112 and put the boxes on the grates. Put the steps on the switch. Go through the air-duct into Room 110. Use the disk to get the password.

9) Go to Room 93 and put the password in. Go to the opposite side of the level and activate the power panel on your way to Room 114.

10) Go to Room 114. Beware of ceiling hunters. The best method is to shoot them down with the beretta or shotgun, then hammer them when they are down. There are only two of them in Room 114, and one in 115. In one corner of 114 is a terminal from which you can get password three.

11) Go to Room 116, the main generator, and activate the

terminal. Get out!

12) Go to Room 104. Four zombies await you. Get the fax from the wall and use the MO disk to get password one. Go to the terminal in Room 105 and enter the passwords.

13) Go to Room 103 via 102 and see Chris.

14) Go to Room 113 and save. Grab the Colt and shotgun.

15) Get in the lift and meet Wesker. Your confrontation with the Tyrant is easy enough. Using the Colt, run away to the other side of the room and take a shot or two. Keep doing this; it doesn't take long.

16) Use the terminal to unlock the door.

17) Go to Room 103 and free Chris.

18) Go to Room 113 and save. Take weapons and ammo - leave a couple of slots free.

19) Go back up to Room 98. There are zombies everywhere! Try to avoid them if you can. Go through the emergency door in Room 98. Run along the passageway and put the battery in the socket. Go up in the lift.

20) Take and use the flare on the heliport. At some point the Tyrant will return. Attacking is hopeless; just keep running away until Brad drops the rocket launcher. You know what to do!

Note: If you did this in three hours or less, you can start again with the rocket launcher and unlimited ammo!

RESIDENT EVIL: DIRECTORS CUT

Double Items
To get a duplicate of every item, firstly go to the Skill Level screen, highlight "Advanced" and hold ➡. It should turn green. Once you commence playing you will get double of every item collected.

Resident Evil 2 Demo skill level
To change the skill level, highlight "New Game" and hold ➡. Both Normal and Rookie skill modes should now be available.

RESIDENT EVIL 2

Alternative Scenarios
Both characters have an alternative scenario, which are linked to the other character's basic game. Once you've completed the game with one character, you can save the other character's alternative scenario to your memory card. This scenario runs parallel with your previous game and differs depending on the choices you made in the previous game. There are two alternative scenarios, one for each character. Claire's alternative scenario is obtained by completing Leon's basic game and Leon's alternative scenario is obtained by completing Claire's basic game.

Game Rankings
Once you've completed either scenario, you will be awarded with a grade between A to F. The higher the grade the more secrets you can unlock. Your grade is determined depending on the amount of time it takes you to complete the game, how many times you saved during the game and if you use any of the super secret weapons.

Alternative Costumes
Each character has a alternative costume locked in a locker near the dark room. To obtain the locker key you need to reach the police station without picking up any items on the normal difficulty setting. Once you reach the police station, venture down the steps just outside the main police station entrance and you will be confronted by a zombie version of Brad Vicars. Once you've killed Brad search his body for the locker key. Once you've reach the police station it is possible to enter and collect items and return to kill Brad later in the game. The easiest way to kill him is to collect the shotgun if you are Leon or the grenade launcher if you are Claire before you fight him. From the locker, Leon can collect two new costumes. Claire can only collect one costume but has access to a new six shooter pistol.

Super Weapons With Unlimited Ammo
If you complete the game in under a certain amount of time with a high ranking, you'll gain access to three weapons with infinite ammo. These can be found in chests once you start a new game.

Rocket Launcher
Complete either character's first scenario in under two hours and thirty minutes with an A or B grade.

Machine Gun
Complete either character's second scenario in under three hours with either an A or B grade.

Mini Gun/Gatling Gun
Complete either character's second scenario in under two hours with an A grade.

Super Shotgun And Spark Shot
When playing as Leon you can upgrade your basic shotgun and as Claire you can collect the spark shot. After riding the underground train you enter a series of narrow corridors. If you head left you'll come to a zombie lying on the floor, he's dead and won't attack you. Stand above him and pick up, Leon will get the shotgun extension which can blow not only a zombies head off but also their arms and most of their body. Claire will collect the spark shot, a rifle which fires electricity.

Dr Birkin's Laboratory Locker Key
The key to the locker in Dr Birkin's laboratory can be found near the flare gun after riding the underground train, just before reaching the vacant factory. Light the flare gun with the cigarette lighter to fire the flare gun, just right of the flare gun is the laboratory locker key. Leon will find the magnum extension while Claire will find additional grenade rounds.

Capsule Room

You can only open this room situated on the top floor of the Umbrella Labs during a character's alternative scenario, but you have to use your other character's handprint during their basic scenario. When playing on a character's basic scenario, make your way to the capsule room and scan your handprint into the console. You'll be told that to open the door you need two hand prints. At this point in the game you cannot open the capsule room door, so go on to complete the game. Once you've completed the game, restart but on the others character's alternative scenario. Once you reach near the end of the game, return to the capsule room. You'll find that there is already one handprint scanned into the computer. Scan in your handprint to open the door. Inside you'll find a machine gun or grenade rounds depending on which character you're playing.

The Giant Crocodile

There are two methods of killing the Giant Crocodile. The easiest way is to use the gas canister on the left wall of the tunnel. As the crocodile chases you down the long tunnel, hit the switch holding the canister to release it. When the crocodile reaches the canister, it will pick it up in it's mouth. Fire at the canister to blow it up along with the crocodile's head. The hardest way is to open fire on it with every thing you've got. If you try to use this method remember to only retreat a small distance from the crocodile before you turn and face it. If you run to far from it, the crocodile will charge after you giving you less time to kill it. There are three outcomes to using this method, the crocodile either kills you or you kill it, or the crocodile will escape by crashing through the sewer wall. If this happens be prepared to tangle with the crocodile again during the other character's alternative scenario.

Defeating Tyrant 103

Near the end of Leon and Claire's alternative scenario you'll be confronted by the Tyrant 103 as you try to activate the emergency train. The Tyrant 103 can only be defeated using the rocket launcher. If you damage the Tyrant a certain amount or avoid it's attacks for long enough Ada Wong will appear and throw you a rocket launcher. Use this to destroy the Tyrant.

Final Boss

To reach the final boss you need to complete either character's second scenario. Once you've defeated the final boss you're get to see the real ending.

Hunk

Complete the game with Leon or Claire basic scenario in under two hours and thirty minutes to get an A grade and the alternative costume locker key. Then complete the other character's alternative scenario in under two hours and thirty minutes with another A grade. You'll then be able to save a special Hunk file to your memory card. Load this file from the main title screen to play the 4th Survivor scenario with a character called Hunk, an Umbrella special forces agent.

Tofu

To unlock Tofu you need to complete the game three times. First play either character's basic scenario, then the other character's alternative scenario. Then play the game for a second time, complete a character's basic scenario and then the other character's alternative scenario. Again play the game for a third time and complete a character's basic scenario and the other character's alternative scenario. Each scenario must be completed in under three hours, with less than twelve saves per scenario and the super weapons with unlimited ammo cannot be used (the normal limited ammo super weapons found in the game such as the machine gun and rocket launcher can be used). You must also start the game from a newly created Leon or Claire save file and the Hunk save file must exist on your memory card before you start playing the game for a third time.

Hidden Rebecca Chambers Camera Film

There is a hidden camera film of Resident Evil one star Rebecca Chambers. Search the main desk in the S.T.A.R.S room of the police station fifty times to get the film. Take this to the dark room and develop it to see a picture of Rebecca in her sports gear.

Smash The Camera

At certain points in the game you can turn to the camera and smash it. With Leon go to the basement near the morgue. Take the corridor to the left (the right leads to the underground car park) to the man hole cover (two dogs usually jump down from the street above). With the shotgun, turn to the camera and fire to smash the camera.

Walkthrough

The nightmare continues. You can choose to play as Leon or Claire. Both characters are covered in the following solutions.

Scenario 1: Leon

The Streets of Racoon City

As soon as you gain control of Leon, follow the road, avoiding all of the zombies until you get to the gun shop. Talk to the owner and collect the two lots of ammo from behind the counter. When the zombies attack, get into position behind the counter. You should be able to take them all out before they get to you. When the music stops, you know that you are safe. Collect the Shotgun from the owner but don't equip it.

Escape by the back door and go down the alleyway until you get to the van. Collect the ammo. Run back to where the zombies just appeared. If you run into them, wiggling the directional pad should see them off whilst avoiding injuries and saving ammo. Run through the playground. Follow the stairway. At the bottom, near the bins, there is some ammo. Avoid or shake off the next set of zombies.

Ignore the zombies huddled around the corpse and head straight for the bus. Take out the crawling zombies with three shots and shake off the other. Grab the ammo and head for the other end of the bus. Once off the bus, zig-zag carefully through the group of zombies. Quick short bursts of speed will confuse them. Head for the gate. Go down the stairs and collect a herb from the plant pot. You will probably need it straight away. Head straight for the R.P.D front entrance.

Secret!!

Don't pick up any items on your way to the R.P.D and you will find a special Brad Vickers zombie. It will take all of your ammo to kill him, but your reward will be a Special Key which you can use in room 8.

Racoon Police Department

Go straight to 10 and talk to the injured officer. Get the Keycard and use it with the computers in the main hall. Get the ammo and the ribbon. Go to 2. Put the knife and ammo in the storage chest. File the Police Memorandum and go to 3. Get the ammo from the headless body and continue to 4. Your first confrontation with the licker should be brief. For now, run around it and head for 5. Pick up the Operation Report. Go into the secondary room behind the briefing room and get the ammo from the far end. Use the lighter on the fireplace to get the Red Jewel. Go to 7. Take out the four zombies with the handgun. On your way to 8 pick up the green herbs. Room 8 is a safe room and guarantees to be free of enemies. Pick up the ammo and the Operation Report. You can save here by using the ink ribbon with the typewriter. If you managed to get the Special Key you can also open the locker. Store the herbs. Now go upstairs to 25. Push the two statues onto the clean floor tiles so that they both face each other. Pick up the Red Jewel. Kill the three zombies in 24. Go to 23. This is the S.T.A.R.S office. Collect the Shotgun from the locker if you don't already have it. Also collect the First Aid Spray, Unicorn Medal and some ammo from behind the desk. After talking to Claire, make your way back to the main hall. Whilst back-tracking through 4, keep away from the windows. When you reach 3, remember to take out the licker with two shotgun blasts. Pick up the herb. Store everything in 2, except weapons, ammo and the medal.

The Spade Key

Go to the statue in the main hall. Put the medal in the slot and take the Spade Key. Now go to 3. Get the patrol report and the ammo. Push the steps against the cupboard to get the Crank. Go to 22. There is a group of zombies here. Take them out two or three at a time by letting them get close before firing straight up. Collect the ammo from the open locker and go to 21. Go up the stairs to the third floor. Go to 34 via 33 and use the crank to lower the steps. Now go back to 32 where you can fall through the floorboards to a hidden area. Press the power switch and move the shelves in accordance with the picture in the hidden area. Collect the Bishop Plug and red herb. Proceed to 20.

Forget about the zombies on the west side, but kill the ones on the east side. Lower the Emergency Ladder but don't go down it. Instead, go to 26. Leave the small key for now, but

pick up the Secretary's Diary. Store the red herb and the Bishop Plug. Go to 29. This room will soon be full of crows, so just run straight to 31. Go down the stairs to 31a. Avoid the zombies and go to 31b. Pick up the ammo and the Valve Handle, then make your way back up to 31. Behind the fence is a valve. Use the handle to put out the fire. Collect the ammo from the helicopter and go to 29. Most of the crows will have gone, so you will have time to get the ammo from the corpse. Go to 30 and collect the green herbs. Go back up to 27 and kill the two zombies. Store the herbs and the Valve Handle and get the two Red Jewels. Put the small key in the chest.

The Diamond Key

Go to 28. Here you can pick up an ink ribbon, some Shotgun Shells and the Diamond Key. Put the Red Jewels into the statues to receive the King Plug. Store the King Plug in 26. Go to room 18 via 30. Collect the ammo from the floored zombie. Take out the others using the Handgun. Open the safe using the code that you found earlier (2236) and take the shells and the map. Pick up the two green herbs from behind the desk and head for 11. Use the Shotgun for this group of zombies. Grab the green herb by the vending machines. Go to 14 and kill the four zombies with the Handgun. Collect the red herb. If you don't have room, combine the herbs. Go back to 2 and store everything apart from the Diamond Key. Use the small key to get the ammo from the drawer. Go to 12 via 14. Take the small key. Go to 13. Collect the Card, First Aid Spray and the Rook Plug. Taking the Rook Plug triggers a licker attack. Just run straight past it and back to 2. Store the Rook Plug, Card and Spray and get your weapons back out. Go to 22 via the stairs in 7. Use the small key to get the Handgun Parts. Combine these with your Handgun for an upgraded weapon. Head for 6 and use the Shotgun. Use caution, as there are two zombies around the corner. Take the shells and the film. You can develop the film in 8 but it is not necessary.

The Heart Key

Go to 10. When the officer zombifies, kill him with your Shotgun. Collect the Heart Key. Get the ammo from the locker, the Memo to Leon, and the green herb. Head to 2. Store everything except the Card, Heart Key, weapons, ammo and a green herb.

Go to 17. Collect and combine the green herbs. Use the Card to close the shutters and collect the shells from the shelves. Go down the stairs.

R.P.D Basement

Kill the three dogs in 35 using the upgraded Handgun. Go to 36, get the map and herb and use the power switches as follows:

Switch 1	UP
Switch 2	UP
Switch 3	DOWN
Switch 4	UP
Switch 5	DOWN

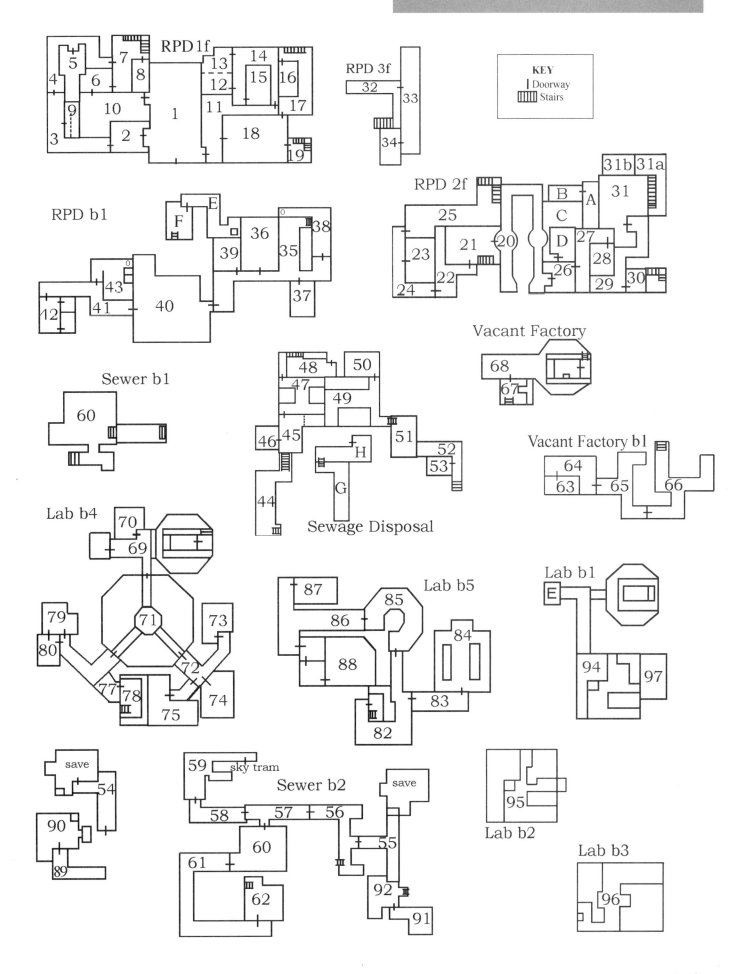

KEY
| Doorway
||||| Stairs

RPD 1f
RPD 3f
RPD 2f
RPD b1
Vacant Factory
Sewer b1
Sewage Disposal
Vacant Factory b1
Lab b4
Lab b5
Lab b1
Sewer b2
Lab b2
Lab b3
sky tram
save
save

Take out both the dogs in 38 and go down the manhole. Go to 53 and get rid of all the herbs. Now go back to 40 and talk to Ada Wong. Go to 43. As soon as you take the herb, the dogs will attack. Kill them and get the Map from the kennel. Go to 42.

The Club Key

Talk to Ben and get the Manhole Opener. Go to 43 and go down the Manhole. A couple of well aimed Handgun shots should finish off each spider. Go to 46, get rid of the herbs, equip the Chess-Plugs and save. Go to 47 and put the plugs in the relevant places. Go back out to 45. As Ada, take out the two dogs and go to 50. Drop into the big hole and push the crates to form a bridge. Go back up and push the switch. Cross over the bridge and get the Club Key. Get the shells from 51. Return to 45.

As Leon, Take the shells and the Club Key and go back up to 40. Get the green herb from the far side, then go to 35. There are now two lickers in this corridor, so get the shotgun out. Go to 39 and get the Keycard from the cupboard. It isn't worth wasting ammo on the zombies in here, just shake them off and run. Use the Keycard to get into 37. Collect the ammo and the shells. Equip the Side Pack, leave the Machine Gun for Claire. Go to 16. Get the Ink Ribbon, the Watcher's Diary and the Magnum. Go to 15. Pick up the Film and read the Clue on the wall. Using the Lighter, light the fire. Now push the switches under the statues in this order:

1	MIDDLE
2	RIGHT
3	LEFT

Take the Cogwheel and go to 34. On the second floor balcony there is a licker, so be careful. Once in 34, go up the steps and use the Cogwheel. Collect the Knight Plug and go down the chute.

G-Virus Mutant 1

Go to see Ben in 42 and witness his death. Go to 46. Make sure that you have the Knight Plug and the Magnum. Equip the Magnum and save your progress. Go to 47. Watch the Mutant grow, then aim and fire. Seven shots should do it. As soon as it falls to the ground, run back to 46 and heal yourself. Get rid of the Magnum, as you won't need it until the end of the game. Save.

Racoon City Sewers

Use the final Chess-plug and meet up with Ada. Get the blue herbs and continue until you get to the save-room. Get the Sewer Manager's Fax. Collect the ammo from the drawers and the First Aid Spray from the locker. Push the main locker away to reveal a hidden stairway to a warehouse. Light the lamps to get the Magnum rounds and the shells. Store any herbs and equip the Valve Handle. Go down the lift.

As Ada, collect the map and go to 56. There are two spiders here. Take them out yourself to save Leon's ammo. Go up the ladder to the shaft. Run straight through, avoiding the cockroaches. After talking to Annette Birkin, go down the ladder to 62.

As Leon, you won't be able to go up the ladder in 56 as the fan is on. Remember to pick up the Wolf Medal and the Shells from the dead S.W.A.T team members. Go to 57 and kill two spiders with the Handgun. Place the Wolf Medal in the slot and go to 60. Use the blue herbs if you need them. Use the Valve Handle to bridge the gap. Once on the other side, use it again to raise the bridge. Get the shells and the green herb and go to 61. Go down the corridor and read the Gas Cylinder Warning Sign. On finding Ada, lure the Giant Crocodile to the Gas Cylinder. Pull it off, and once the creature eats it blast its head off with the Handgun. Cross the waste dump to Ada. Go up the ladder, across the bridge and up the ramp. Get the Eagle Medal and the Sewer Manager's diary. Use the Valve Handle to stop the fan and go to 57. Use the Eagle Medal to uncover the door to 58. Go to 59, switch on the power and get in the Sky-Train.

G-Virus Mutant 2

Just before this boss strikes, dust will fall from where his claw will appear. Simply move away from this area and let Ada shoot him.

Vacant Factory

When you get out, set off the Flare and get the W-Box key. Go to 65. Take out the zombies by using Ada. Shoot them once and Ada will finish them off. Get the Shotgun Parts and combine them for an awesome weapon. Get the green herbs from 66 and go up the ladder to 67. Store the Magnum rounds, herbs and the W-Box key. Get the items from the room. Take two First Aid Sprays with you and save. Go to 68. Get the ammo from the far end. Get in the train and use the keys from the control room to start up the lift outside.

G-Virus Mutant 3

Once Ada gets attacked, go outside armed with your new Shotgun. Always avoid the side that its claw is on. Get some distance between you and the monster and blast it once or twice. Then run past it and start again. Keep an eye on your energy. When it gets weaker, just stand there and blast it.

Umbrella Labs

Get the ammo and the herb from the save room and save your progress. Equip the W.Box key. Go to 73. Get the spray and the Fuse Case. Use the Fuse Case with the Mechanical Arm to get the Main Fuse. Use the Main Fuse in 71 to regain power to the area. Go to 79 and get the User Registration. Use the lighter to set fire to the petrol and then get the Lab Security Manual. Turn on the Gas Sprinkler. Get the Flame Thrower, arm yourself with the Shotgun and go through the air duct to 80 where two lickers await you. Kill them and get the ammo from the locker. Go to 77 and use the Flame Thrower on the mutant plants. Go to 78. Take out another plant and collect the herbs. Go down the ladder. In area 82, there are three lickers. Take them out with the Shotgun and get the herbs. Go to 85 and get the map from the computer. Go to 88, take out the zombies and get the

Red Keycard and the Magnum parts. Go to 87 and kill the giant moth with about six Shotgun blasts. Remove the larvae from the computer using the Handgun. Log-in with "Guest" and register your fingerprint.

Upon entering corridor 82, another licker will attack. Make your way back up to 78. Take out the two plants with the Flame Thrower. Go to 74. Take out the four zombies. Get the spray, the M.O disk and the Magnum rounds. Talk to Annette. Use your fingerprint identification to open the first lock to the room you haven't entered yet. Do not proceed with the second phase. Go to 71 and meet up with Ada. Then go to 82 and use the M.O disk with the computer. Be careful of the naked zombies. Go to 85 and save. Get the Shotgun and shells, Magnum and rounds and the herbs and spray. Save. Go to 84.

G-Virus Mutant 4-Final Boss

Quite easy really, as long as you keep an eye on your health regularly. Using the Shotgun, run to the end of the room and blast him. After eight shots, he will turn into his second form. Let it get next to you, and continuously blast it with the Magnum, remembering to heal yourself. Once the lift opens, get the hell out of there

Scenario 2: Claire

The Streets of Racoon City

Avoid all of the zombies and go through the gate.

Racoon Police Department

Get the Cabin-Key from the office at the far end and use it to get into 31b. Collect the ammo and go up to 31. After seeing how the helicopter got there, go to 29. Get the herb and the ammo from the corpse. Get another green herb from 30. Go to 26, forget the licker in 27. Get the ammo and go to the second floor balcony.

The Spade Key

Go past the library door and take out the zombies. Get the Unicorn Medal from the wall and use it in the main hall. Get the Spade Key and the Grenade launcher. Take out the licker in 27 using the Grenades. Go to 18 via 30 and 19 collecting the herbs on the way.

Get the ammo from the corpse and take out the zombies with the Handgun. Get the Valve Handle, green herbs and Acid Rounds from the safe. Go to 11 and use the Handgun. Unlock the door to the main hall. Go to 12. Pop the licker with the Handgun to get it off the ceiling, then blast it with a grenade. Get the ammo and the red herb outside.

Go back to 26 and store all but one of your herbs. Go to 31 and use the Valve Handle. Get the Acid Rounds from the helicopter and go back. Blast the Tyrant 103 with four acid grenades and collect its ammo. Go to 28 and get the Blue Keycard. Ignore the licker for now and use the Keycard in the main hall.

Go to 2. Kill the three zombies, get the spray and store it and the Valve Handle. Go to 9, collecting the ammo on the way.

Use the steps to get the Lighter. Get the herb from 3 and go to 4. Take out the zombies and go to 5. Get the ammo and use the lighter with the Red Jewel. Go to 8, collecting the herbs on the way. Get the ammo and store the herbs and the Red Jewel. Go to 25 and get the second Red Jewel.

The Diamond Key

Meet Leon in the S.T.A.R.S office. Get the Bow Gun and the Diamond Key. Leave the room and save Sherry. Take out the group of zombies in 22 with a grenade. Get the ammo from the drawer and go to the library. Solve the puzzle to get the Serpent Stone. Go to 8 and store the Red Jewel, the Serpent Stone and the herbs. Go to 6. Collect the Plastic Explosive, Bows and film. Kill the zombies in 10 and get the ammo, herb and Detonator. Combine the Detonator with the Explosive. Go to 13. Get the Eagle Stone. Taking the spray triggers off the licker, so get the spray last and run straight out.

The Heat Key

Now, go up to 27 via the emergency ladder. Use the Bomb to blow away the wall next to the helicopter. Get the two Red Jewels and the two stones. Go to 28, take out the licker and use the jewels. Take the stone and go to A. Go to B and talk to Chief irons. Go to D and switch on the light to find Sherry. Get the ammo and go back to the Chief's office. Push the switch under the painting behind the desk and use the Eagle and Serpent stones. Get the Heart key and go to 26. Store the Blue Stone. Go to 17. Collect the herbs and kill the zombies with the Bow Gun. Get the Acid Rounds. Go down to 35. Take out the zombies with the Bow Gun and switch on the power in 36. Go to 38 and kill the dogs. Go down the manhole to 52. Go into the save room. Come out and talk to Sherry.

The Club key

Sherry's mission is pretty much the same as Ada's. Sherry can avoid the zombies as she is so small. Get the Club Key and the Grenades. The next section requires a lot of running back and forth so that you can get all of the items. As Claire, take the items, go to 53 and save. Go to 39 and take out the lickers. Get the Red Keycard and go to 37. Take the ammo, Grenades and the Sub-Machinegun. Go to 40 and take out the dogs. Go to 41 and kill the dogs there. 43 holds two more dogs, a herb, a Map and the vital Crank. 42 holds the Film, herbs and some Bows. Go to 16, killing the zombies on the way. Take the Acid Rounds. Go to 15. Use the Lighter to get the Cogwheel. Tyrant 103 will burst through the wall so be ready with the Acid Rounds. Get the Cogwheel and make your way to 34 via the Emergency Ladder. On passing the hole in the wall, Tyrant 103 will charge again. Take him out and get the Bows.

On the way to 34, stop in at 2 and get the Blue Stone and Crank. Use the Crank and the Cogwheel and combine the two halves of the Stone to make the Jaguar Stone. On entering the library, Tyrant 103 strikes again. Floor him and get his grenades. Go to B and use the Jaguar Stone. Get the Mail to the Chief. Make sure that you have the Grenade Launcher and some herbs and go down the lift. Talk to the Chief, get the Acid

Rounds and go down the ladder.

The Sewers
Go down the ladder to G

G-Virus Mutant 1
Stand your ground and blast him with Acid Rounds. Go up the second ladder to H. Unfortunately, to get into the sewers you need Sherry, so go all the way back and get her. Go to 90. Get the spray, the Fax and the ammo, then go down the lift and talk to Leon. Go back up to 90 and the ladder to 92. Kill the zombie and get the Bows and Grenades. 91 is a dead-end. Go back down to 55 and get the map. Annette will be in 60. Get the two medals from 56 and 60 and use them.

Vacant Factory
Go to the Sky Train with Sherry. Pick up the W-Box key. Take out the zombies and pick up the Spark Shot and the herbs. Go to 67 and get the Grenades and the spray. Go down the lift in 68 and get the C.Panel Key. Look at the monitor before you leave. Get the Acid Rounds, go back to 67 and save. Use the C.Panel Key and get out the Grenade Launcher.

G-Virus Mutant 2
On your way down he attacks again. About ten Acid-Grenades should do it. Just try to avoid his four-arm combo as this does massive damage.

Umbrella Labs
Go to 95. Get the report and the Grenades. Store them. Go to 96 and flick the elevator switch. Now go back up to 94 and go in the elevator. Sherry will have disappeared. Go to 70 and get the ammo, herb and grenades. Go to 79, take out the zombies and get the Red Keycard and the Bolts. Go through the shaft to 80 and kill the two lickers. Get the Grenades. Take out the plants in 74 and get the spray and Main Fuse. Use it in 71. The next part is similar to Leon's mission. Make your way down to 88 and get the herbs, Grenades and the P.Rom Key. Kill the moth and enter your name as before, remembering to register your fingerprint to get into the locked room upstairs. Store the P.Room Key and go back up to 75, killing the licker on the way. 75 holds three lickers. Sort them out with the grenades or the Sub-Machinegun. This room holds Machinegun ammo. Go up the elevator. Get the P.Room Key from the chest in B1. Push the crate on to the lift and make a stairway with it in B2, so that you can get to 97. Go to 97 and watch the cut-scene. Go back to 71 and get the Master Key. Use it in the elevator.

Escape!
Go to the far end of the train, get the Key and save. Get out the Sub-Machinegun, Flame Grenades, spray and herbs. Leave one slot free. Use the Platform Key to get through the gate. Go over the bridge and get the two Plugs. Go through the door and put the Plugs in the sockets. Prepare yourself!

Boss 1-Ultimate Tyrant
This is the Tyrant 103 when he's angry. Before the cut-scene finishes hold the fire button down so that you can let off a grenade as soon as you're in control. Standing your ground is pointless. Try as hard as you can to get away. Run in big zig-zags so as to put him off charging. His charge move hurts a lot! It is possible to put the corner of the fencing between you and the Tyrant. When you are in this ideal situation, simply blast it with grenades. Six or seven shots should do it. At this point, Ada will drop the Rocket Launcher. Equipping it isn't easy as the Tyrant knocks you about a lot. Once you've equipped it let him come near and blast him to pieces. Whatever you do, Don't Miss. Once he is no more, go to the chest on the other side of the platform behind the stairs. Get any weapons and health you can and go back through the gate. Mow the zombies down with the Submachine Gun and open the tunnel gate. Hit the lever in the train and get out of there.

Boss 2-Ultimate G-Virus Mutant
Hmmm..... forgot about him didn't you. Firstly, fire off the last Rocket you have. Then use your remaining Grenades and then, if necessary, the Sub-Machinegun. It should die before it gets to you. Ahhh! The End!

RESIDENT EVIL 2: DUAL SHOCK EDITION

Unlock Extreme Battle Mode
Complete both scenario A and B with both characters and then save to a memory card. Original Resident Evil 2 files work.

Play As Ada Wong
Complete level 1 on Extreme Battle Mode.

Play As Chris Redfield
Complete level 2 on Extreme Battle Mode.

Unlimited Ammunition
Start a game and press **Select** to enter the ingame option screen. Select the Key Config option, then hold **R1** and press ■ **x10**. The word 'Auto' will turn red.

RESIDENT EVIL NEMESIS

Jill Valentine makes an explosive entrance as her apartment block is engulfed in fire and finding herself surrounded by the living dead. Run down the street and evade the lone zombie blocking your path, try not to use your gun, ammunition is in short supply at the beginning of the game. Climb over the bin. A short cut scene will take place where Jill finds herself surrounded by a group of zombies but manages to escape down an alleyway.

Uptown
When the screen fades in, you will find Jill in an abandoned

warehouse with a man named Dario. Scared to death of being eaten alive, Dario will lock himself in a storage container. Search the ground floor for a first aid spray and some handgun bullets from the locker. Head up the stairs onto the gantry. The door to the left is the only way out but is locked. Head right along the gantry and up the stairs. Enter the office at the end of the gantry. Inside, search the key hooks by the door for the warehouse key. Search the office for two pots of gunpowder and an ink ribbon. Deposit any unwanted items in the storage crate. Combine the gunpowder with your bullet maker to form handgun bullets. Leave the office and use the warehouse key to unlock the warehouse door. Outside, run down the alley and out through the door at the end. Head up the street and enter the door on the right. Make your way down the alley. Suddenly the door to the left will burst open and you will get a glimpse of S.T.A.R.S helicopter pilot Brad Vickers being pursued by a pack of zombies. Kill all the roaming zombies and then head through the open door and down the steps. Blast the lone zombie and collect the lighter oil and shotgun. Return up the steps and head down the alley in the direction Brad ran. Go through the door at the end of the alley. You will find yourself on a main street. Dodge the two zombies roaming around and run down the street. Climb the crates on the corner and take the map of uptown from the wall. Climb the fire escape and pick up the two green herbs. Return down on to the street and continue down the street. Avoid the two zombies feasting on the corpse and head through the door at the end. Run down the alley and then down the steps on the left. Here you will find Brad fighting three zombies. He will flee as soon as you appear. Avoid the remaining zombies and follow Brad down the alley and through the door at the end.

The Bar
In the bar you will find Brad wrestling with a lone zombie. Take the clock tower postcard from the counter and the handgun bullets that are found near the cash register. After killing the lone zombie, Brad will ramble about a creature that is hunting down the remaining S.T.A.R.S members. After he has left, take the lighter from the table near the door. Combine the lighter oil with the lighter. Head out via the door you entered through. Run down the alley and up the steps. Head right and at the intersection turn right and head out through the door at the end. At the end of this alley are police barriers holding back a horde of around seven or eight zombies. To the right of the barrier is a gate bound closed by rope. Use the lighter to burn the rope. Suddenly the barrier will fall and the zombies will flood towards you. Luring them towards the explosive barrel and then blowing it up will take down the majority of them. You can find two red herbs at the end of the alley. Go through the gate. Run down the path and enter the single door on the right. As you go a dog will jump from the flames. In the save room take the gunpowder from the shelf by the door, deposit any items and save. Head back outside and run through the gate at the end. You will find yourself on yet another deserted Main Street. Head up the street past the burst fire hydrant and through the gates of the police station.

The Police Station – First Floor
Just as Jill prepares to enter the police station Brad will stumble in. Before he has a chance to warn you, a large,

tyrant style creature will drop from above and kill Brad in a very, very nasty way. This is the Nemesis, one of Umbrella's tyrants similar to Mr X from Resident Evil 2. While Mr X's mission was to retrieve William Birkin's G Virus sample, the Nemesis's mission is to eliminate any S.T.A.R.S members remaining in Racoon City. This includes Jill. You can encounter the Nemesis one of two ways. Here you will be given a choice of what to do next. Here you can either fight the Nemesis or dive into the police station. Your actions change how the game progresses. While diving into the police station seems like the safest option, it will mean you will have to spend more time in the police station as you search for Jill's S.T.A.R.S card to gain access to the station's computer. If you choose to fight the Nemesis, after Jill evades the Nemesis's blow, run over to Brad's body and search for his card case. Avoid the Nemesis's next attack and head into the police station. Examining Brad's card case will reveal his S.T.A.R.S card allowing you access to the station's computer. Actually fighting the Nemesis can reap rewards but you are likely to use up valuable ammunition and health. With Brad's S.T.A.R.S card head over to the far side of the lobby. Take the handgun bullets and the station map then insert Brad's S.T.A.R.S card into the computer. Here you will be informed that the key to the S.T.A.R.S room has been locked in the evidence room. The computer will give you a random four figure password (write this down). Head through the single door into the station office. Fight your way through the zombies into the sergeant's office in the corner of the room. Examine Officer Branagh's body and read his report. Go through the door opposite. You will find yourself in the station's evidence room. Open the lit locker near the door. Inside you will find a blue gem. Work your way around the lockers until you come across another lit locker. To open the locker you will need to input the four-figure code you got from the computer. Inside you will find an emblem key, this will open the S.T.A.R.S room on the top floor. Go through the other door. Fight your way down the corridor ignoring the door on the right and the stairs and enter the room at the end. Once inside, examine the locker for some gunpowder, take the ink ribbon and read David's memo. When you have finished, head back into the corridor and head upstairs.

The Police Station – Second Floor
Fight your way down the corridor, past the statue and through the door at the end. Unlock the door and enter the S.T.A.R.S room. Open the locker to discover a magnum. Examine the desk on the far right (Rebecca's desk) and look at the first aid bag to reveal a first aid spray. Examine the next desk along (Jill's own desk) and you will find a lock pick. Search the desk on the far left (Barry's desk) for some handgun bullets. As you prepare to leave, Jill will receive a garbled radio message from one of the surviving Umbrella mercenaries, named Carlos. Backtrack your way downstairs. At the bottom of the stairs, the Nemesis will suddenly burst through the window. Armed with a rocket launcher, the Nemesis will track you from room to room until you eventually lose him (save rooms are safe havens but the Nemesis will wait patiently outside). Run down the corridor and dart into the evidence room. From here run through the office

out into the lobby. Head out of the police station and out onto the street. Run down the main street and use the lock pick to unlock the door on the right. Run down the alley avoiding the Deimos creatures crawling across the walls and examine the dead mercenary's body. He holds handgun bullets and his diary. With this in hand run down the alley and through the door at the end. To the left is a fire hose but you cannot remove the bolts yet. Head right and through the door at the end; note there are some blue and green herbs to the left of the door. Fight your way through the dogs and around the crashed bus to where you will find a dead mercenary. Search him for more gunpowder. Head into the parking lot. Kill the two dogs creeping around the room. Take the power cables from the car engine and head into the office on the opposite side of the garage. Inside, take the handgun bullets and the ink ribbons. Go out the door and run past the dogs patrolling this area. Run down the street and through the door at the end. Take the downtown map from the wall. Jill will notice the body of another mercenary, when she draws closer to the corpse, two large Deimos creatures drop from above. These genetic creatures can poison you so it is best to try and avoid them. Head left and out the door on the end.

Downtown

Depending on if you go to the restaurant first or the newspaper office will effect the following; where you first meet Carlos, where the Nemesis's attacks and the location of the green gem. If you go straight to the restaurant, the green gem can be found in the newspaper office, if you go there first, you will find it in the basement of the restaurant. Walk down the street and you will get a glimpse of a mercenary capping a lone zombie. Follow him down the street and into the restaurant at the end. Inside, search the tables for the city guide. Head through the kitchen to the back door. Here you will find a locker, use the lock pick to open it. Inside you will find a fire hook. Return into the kitchen and use the fire hook on the hatch. At this point you will get your first face to face conversation with Carlos Oliviera, one of the remaining Umbrella mercenaries. Before you can finish your conversation you will be interrupted by the Nemesis. You will be presented with two choices, either hide in the basement or hide in the kitchen. Hiding in the basement only gives you limited safety as the room begins to fill with water forcing you back upstairs to the waiting Nemesis. Hide in the kitchen and Jill will throw a lamp at the gas cylinders in the kitchen. The ensuring explosion will temporarily stun the Nemesis. Examine his body to discover the Eagle parts. Before you and Carlos can leave the restaurant, the Nemesis will regain conciseness and charge after you. Carlos will offer you a hand but if he dies it is game over. Run out of the restaurant. Outside Carlos will ask you to join him before running off. Run back down the street and enter the door at the very end. You are now in the shopping arcade area of the city. The door found at the top of the stairs leads back into the restaurant. Take the path leading off to the right and enter the door on the right. You will find yourself in a save room. In here you will find a rusted crank and some

shotgun shells. Leave and continue down the path and out the door at the end. As soon as you walk through the door you will be set upon by the Nemesis. Dodge his attacks and run up the street. Turn right and through the double doors.

The Newspaper Office

Inside collect the first aid spray and then push the stepladder towards the drink machine on the left. Climb the stepladder and turn on the power. Take the photo from above the pay phone. Press the green switch to the right of the fire shutter. Walk up the stairs avoiding the patches of fire. Enter the door on the top floor. Head into the office and kill the lone zombie. Search the office for a green gem, a reporter's memo and another photo. When you try to leave you will again be cornered by the Nemesis. Evade his attack, backtrack down the stairs and head outside. As you reach the corner the street, the Nemesis will drop from above. Continue to run down the street and dive through the door on the right. Enter the save room, make sure you have both the blue and green gems in your inventory before you leave. Head back to the street and the Nemesis. Run straight to the Racoon city hall gate and place both gems into the clock style gate control. Dive through the gate before the Nemesis can attack. Run down the path and at the intersection take the left path entering the door at the end. Fight your way past the zombies and through the door at the end. Follow the path until you reach another door. Here you will be confronted by a group of zombies. Blow up the explosive barrel before they draw too close. Search the body to the right of the door for some shotgun shells. Climb over the barricade and head around the corner. Kill the three zombies and enter the cable car.

The Cable Car

Inside the cable car, read the mechanics memo. You will get a brief and abrupt conversation with the mercenary leader, Nikolai Ginovaef and his wounded comrade Mikhail Victor. Enter the next carriage. Inside you will be reunited with Carlos. The team will agree to use the cable car to reach the extraction point, but the cable car needs to be repaired first. Carlos will give Jill a utility belt enabling her to carry two extra items in her inventory. Collect the wrench from the seat and exit the cable car. Climb over the barrier and go through the door. Follow the path and through the door at the end. As you pass the car, a zombie will jump out. Kill the zombie and search the car for gunpowder. Continue down the path and through the door at the end. At the intersection turn left. As you pass the house, the door will slam open and four zombies will flood towards you. Kill the zombies and head through the open door. You will find a statue of Racoon City's mayor. Press the green switch and take the bronze book. Head back to the path and through the door on the right. Run straight across the street and through the door on the right. Follow the path to the end and enter the door leading onto the street. Run down the street up to the monument. Place the bronze book in the slot and then take the bronze compass on the left. Run back to the statue of the mayor and place the bronze compass in his hands. This will reveal a battery. Head back to the save room and place the battery in the storage crate and take the rusted crank and the wrench. Leave the save room and head back to the statue. At the intersection, head down the right path and through the door at the end. You will find yourself outside a gas station.

The Gas Station

At the shutter use the rusted crank. The rusted crank will break, then use the wrench to lift the shutter. Head inside. Collect the gunpowder from the table. Head around the counter and examine the electronic locker. To open the locker you will need to randomly press the buttons until you light only the panel selected. Inside the locker you will find the machine oil. As you prepare to leave the gas station, the gasoline flooding the floor will catch alight. Run outside. The gas station will explode. Make your way to the save room in the shopping arcade. Deposit the machine oil and take the battery. Leave the save room and head down and onto the street. Go through the door on the left. Quickly examine the dead mercenary's body before you get attacked. Avoid the attacking creatures and run up the steps. Place the battery in the elevator control panel. Ride the elevator down. Fight your way through the horde of zombies and enter the power station via the far right gate.

The Power Station

Go inside the power station. Press the flashing red button. To open the two doors opposite you need to create the correct flow of electricity. To open the left door you will need to create between 15V to 25V of electricity. The correct combination to open the door is Red, Blue, Blue and Blue. Inside the room you will find a fuse. To open the right door you will need to create between 115V to 125V of electricity. The correct combination to open the door is Blue, Blue, Red, and Red. Inside the room, search the locker for a grenade launcher. After opening one of the doors a group of zombies will attack the power station. You will be presented with two options, increase the electrical output or try the emergency exit. Pick the first option and you will create an electric fence, electrocuting all the zombies. Backtrack to the elevator and ride it up. Take the door leading to the parking lot. Fight your way to the door at the end of the street. In the parking lot save room, deposit the fuse. Before you leave make sure you have the wrench. Head out via the door opposite and run through the parking lot. Outside the parking lot, run down the street and through the door at the end. Run to the end of the alley and use the wrench to remove the fire hose. Go through the door on the right. Run down the alley avoiding the creatures and out the door at the end. Go through the door on the left. Use the fire hose on the fire hydrant. Jill will then put out the fire blocking the path. Head down the path and through the door. Run down the alley and out the door at the end. Pick up the crank directly in front as you enter. Head around the corner and enter the building.

Business Area

Inside you will find Nikolai standing over the body of a mercenary that he just executed. Read the managers report. Use the television remote control and take a note of the advert shown on the television. Access the computer to the left of the television remote and input the name of the advert you saw on the television. This will unlock the door to the storeroom. Head through the door and down the corridor to the storeroom. Search the shelf for gunpowder and the oil additive. As you leave, the building will flood with zombies. Shoot the steam valves to burn the zombies as they trickle towards you. Fight your way through the office and outside. Run past the Deimos and through the door. Run down the alley and through the door at the end. When you run past the fire hydrant you will be attacked by the Nemesis. You now have all the items needed to repair the cable car but there are a number of extra items you can collect before continuing. Head to the area behind the bar. Use the crank to open the shutter. Inside you will find grenade rounds. Now head to the warehouse where you started. Examine the storage container, which you will find is open. Take the gunpowder and read Dario's memo. Now make your way to the parking lot, avoiding the Nemesis as you go. You will face the Nemesis as soon as you pass the fire hydrant and are in the alley where you collected the fire hose. As you head through the parking lot, the floor will shake and collapse. Again you will be given a choice, either climb up or jump off. If you climb up, you will narrowly miss the two crates that are sliding towards you. If you jump off you will find yourself in the sewers and will have to fight your way passed large tapeworms that swim in the water to reach the ladder. After this event enter the parking lot save room. Inside, mix the machine oil with the oil additive to create the mixed oil. Before you leave make sure you have the mixed oil, the fuse and the power cable in your inventory. When you are ready, make your way to the cable car. When you reach the intersection near the statue of the mayor, the Nemesis will again attack. Either avoid or fight him (if you decide to fight him, remember to search his body after he falls), then continue down the left path towards the cable car. Run down the alley and through the gate at the end. As you run down the path there will be a sudden tremor, as you continue there will be another but this time the floor under Jill will collapse and she will fall into the sewers below.

The Gravedigger

Here you will face the Gravedigger, a large monstrous worm. To defeat this creature, run near one of the holes to lure it out. Quickly turn and run towards the wall, then turn around and open fire. You should be able to get two or three shots in before it backs off. Repeat until it flees. Press the two switches on either side of the sewer to lower the ladder, then climb up. Once topside, climb over the barrier and enter the cable car. Repair the cable car using the mixed oil, fuse and power cable. Enter the front carriage. Return into the rear carriage when you hear Mikhail. You will discover the Nemesis has found you again. Mikhail will take on the Nemesis, so head back into the front carriage. Mikhail falls to the Nemesis, but not before he releases a grenade blowing the Nemesis from the cable car. With no brakes the cable car will speed out of control and you will be presented with two options, either jump out or use the emergency brakes. Your decision will decide where you start at the clock tower.

The Clock Tower – Jump Out of Cable Car Route

If you decided to jump out of the cable car you will find yourself in the rubble of a town house bedroom. Collect the gunpowder and the clock tower key, you will find this behind the picture. Head through the door. In here you will find a storage crate. Head through the door. Here you will be reunited with Carlos. When he leaves, take the grenade rounds from the table. Search the room for an open drawer containing an art picture and an ink ribbon. Head through the door into the main lobby. Collect the first aid spray and the map of the clock tower. Search the body for the mine thrower and the instructions on how to use it. Head through the door opposite. Take the grenade rounds and head through the next door where you will find yourself in a room with a piano. Head through the door on the opposite side of the room into the chapel. Take the key from the cabinet and use the storage crate if you need to. Return into the piano room. When you enter a horde of zombies will come crashing through the windows. Fight your way to the lobby and climb the stairs.

The Clock Tower – The Emergency Brakes Route

If you decided to use the emergency brakes, you will find yourself in the garden of a town house. Head through the door in the corner of the garden and you will be in a room with a piano. Head through the door into the chapel. Search the chapel for a key and some gunpowder. Return into the piano room and fight your way through the zombies that come smashing through the windows and through the door opposite. Here you will be reunited with Carlos. Once he has left, take the grenade rounds and go through the double doors. You will be in the lobby of the house. Search the corpse for the mine thrower and operation instructions. You will also find a first aid spray and the map of the clock tower in the lobby. Head through the door on the opposite side of the lobby. In the library, search for an ink ribbon and an art picture and then head out the door at the end of the corridor. Go through into the next room. Inside collect the clock tower key. Backtrack to the lobby and climb the stairs.

The Evacuation

Once at the top of the stairs, run along the balcony avoiding the spiders and through the door at the end. On the outside balcony, use the clock tower key to lower the ladder. Search the shelf next to the typewriter for a silver gear. Go to the music box behind you. To solve the music box puzzle you will need to move the six notes either up or down to find the correct note. After hearing the sixth note, play the entire tune. If you are correct you will be presented with the Chronos chain. Combine this with the other key in your possession to create the Chronos key. Return down the ladder and you will come face to face again with the Nemesis. Out of the two choices you are given, select use the cord. Jill will electrocute the Nemesis, while he is stunned you can search his body for the eagle parts.

Head through the door. Run along the balcony and down the stairs. Go through the door on the left. Inside, use the Chronos key to unlock the green door and enter inside. Blast your way down the spider invested corridor, searching the body of the dead mercenary for grenade rounds. Head through the door at the end. Examine the clocks then take the three balls from the statues on the right. You need to get all the clocks to read 12:00. By placing the balls in different positions you can affect the time. Once you have completed the puzzle you will be given the gold gear. Backtrack your way upstairs and up into the clock tower. Once there, combine the gold gear with the silver gear and place them in the large gears next to the storage container. This will start the bells ringing. Open the storage container and arm yourself with your best weapons and a number of health sprays/herbs. Head back down the ladder. Just as the rescue helicopter comes into view, the Nemesis makes an unwelcome appearance and blows up the helicopter. Trapped in the courtyard you are forced to fight the Nemesis, but not before he infects you with a virus via one of his tentacles. If you pulled the emergency brake when you were on the cable car, Carlos will appear and destroy the Nemesis's rocket launcher before being knocked out. If you jumped out of the cable car, you will have to face the Nemesis armed with his rocket launcher. The best strategy is to try and keep your distance, use the hedge as cover and fire your grenades from a distance. When the Nemesis drops, run up to him and keep firing until he stumbles into the fire. Carlos will appear and carry Jill to the chapel. Infected with the virus it is up to Carlos to find a cure. From the chapel, head to the room with the three clocks. In the next room you will find a bell blocking the door. Push the bell out of the way and head through the door. You will find yourself back on the streets. Head up the street fighting the zombies as you go. At the end of the street you will find a hospital, head inside.

The City Hospital

Inside you will encounter a couple of Hunters. Head through the door into a room containing a typewriter and storage container. Search the shelf for a first aid spray and then head into the next room. You will find yourself in an office. Search the locker for some handgun bullets and the desk for a tape recorder. The elevator is voice activated so you will need to use the tape recorder. Once in the elevator, select the fourth floor. Once there, head into the room at the end of the corridor. Inside you will find Nicholai about to kill another mercenary. Before he can the mercenary releases a grenade, blowing himself up and Nicholai out of the window. Search the rear of the room for a sick room key. Return into the corridor and enter the first room in the side corridor. Examine the note in the dead doctor's hand (remember the numbers). Head outside and into the next room. Inside, push the shelf onto one of the pressure pads in the corner of the room. If you activate the correct pad, a picture will fall revealing a safe. The numbers from the note the dead doctor had opens the safe. Inside you will find the vaccine base. Head back to the elevator and ride it down to the basement. Head down the corridor and through the door at the end. Inside you will face two more Hunters. Head into the next room. Take the medium base from the shelf and the instruction manual from the desk. In the corner you will find a console. Press the power switch to its right to activate it. Use the medium base with the machine. You will need to move the different levers to get the two gauges on the left into a centre position. Once you have done this you will have created the vaccine medium. Combine this with the vaccine base to create the vaccine. Before you get a chance to leave, the creatures in the cylinders awake and break free. Run out of the room. Fight your way through the Hunters to the elevator. Ride the elevator up to the first floor. As soon as the elevator doors open, a flood of zombies will start to pore into the elevator. Fight your way through the office and into the save room. Continue into the lobby. In the main lobby, Carlos will notice a time bomb, with seven seconds left before detonation, so run out of the hospital. Outside, the hospital will be levelled by Nicholai's bomb. Head back through the clock tower to the chapel. In the lobby the Nemesis will drop in, who has mutated since your last encounter. Continue into the piano room (the Nemesis will come running through the large windows) and into the chapel. Once there give Jill the vaccine. With the virus cured you will take control of Jill. You will need to back track Carlos's route back outside. The only problem is that the Nemesis is waiting for you and will chase you through the clock tower until you get outside. The street towards the hospital is now rubble. Use your lock picking skills to open the door next to the steps. Inside you will find another typewriter and storage container. Search the room for extra ammunition and the park key. Head outside and up the steps. Unlock the gate using the park key.

The City Park

Inside you will find yourself in the City Park. Here you will face either leeches or several Hunters. Head down the path on the right side and down the steps. Fight your way across the docks and then through the path winding through the trees. Search the body you find near the explosive barrel for another park key. At the end of the path you will find a locked gate. Search the body nearby for additional magnum bullets. Now you will need to backtrack to the park entrance. Go through the gate on the opposite side of where you appear. Here you will find a water fountain. Examine the chart on the wall. Drop into the water and walk around the fountain. Here you will find another chart showing you how to drain the water. Head back out of the water and position the gears into the pattern shown to drain the water. With the water drained, climb down the hatch that has opened. In the sewers, run forward avoiding the leeches and up the ladder at the end.

The Graveyard

Once up the ladder you will find yourself in a graveyard. Fight your way through the graveyard and unlock the gate at the end. In the woodsman's hut search the cupboard for an iron pipe and the gunpowder from the table. The other door leads to another save room. Take your lighter and return to the main room. Use the lighter in the fireplace then use the iron pipe to break through the bricks revealing a hidden room. Inside the room you will find a third park key and some grenade rounds. When you try to leave, you will encounter Nicholai. The ground will shake and he will leave. Before following him, return into the save room and stock up on ammunition and additional health. When you are ready, head outside. Here you will face the gravedigger for the second and final time. At this point there is one way to escape. When the ground opens up, back off and open fire. The gravedigger should retreat. Continue this until it is defeated. If you take too long, the lampposts will begin to collapse. Move near to the water and when the gravedigger attacks, shoot the lamppost. This will electrocute the beast. Use the ladder that falls down to escape. Run down the sewer tunnel avoiding the spiders. Climb up the ladder. Back at the fountain you will again need to backtrack through the park, along the dock and along the path winding through the trees to the locked gate. Unlock the gate using the park key you found in the woodsman's hut. Climb the steps and cross the bridge. As you do so you will ambushed by the Nemesis. The two choices presented to you are either to push him off or to jump off.

The Dead Factory – Jump Off the Bridge Route

Landing safely in the water, Jill will pull herself up out of the water, in front of he is a spillway leading into a deserted factory. Once inside enter the right doorway. Inside take the water sample from the machine and then go through the other door. At the bottom of the stairs, use the water sample on the machine opposite. To solve this puzzle you need to line up all three bars so they all match the sample at the top. To do this you will need to move each of the three bars left or right until they are in the correct position. If the sample has a tall bar then underneath you will need to have a bar on each of the three bars, if the sample has a clear space then there must be a space on all three of the bars underneath. Once you have solved this puzzle, the water level will be passed. Head back up the stairs and through the door opposite. Continue down the tunnel and you will be surrounded by a pack of zombies. Luckily Carlos will appear and save you. Once he has gone, head through the door at the end. Fight your way through the next room, collecting the shotgun ammo from the right side of the room. Ride the elevator up. Fight through the zombies and take the system disk from the console. Unlock the door in the corner and continue on. As you near the corner a shot will ring out causing Jill to dive to the ground. Before you can act Nicholai escapes. Head through the door behind you. You will find yourself in another save room. Search the room for gunpowder and a facility key. When you are done, go through the door with the red light. You will now be in a room with numerous jets of steam. Push the first switch and then head around the corner. Press the next switch and then the far switch. Head back, round the corner and press the switch. Head around to the other side and press the far switch. Press the right switch and then head back around to the other side. Press the switch and then the far switch. You can now activate the console. Press the far, left switch and then the next switch to leave. Backtrack through the save room and then through the passage back into the room where you found the system disk. Open the door to the right of the elevator. In the passage, use the system disk in the wall console.

The Dead Factory – Push the Nemesis off the Bridge Route
Darting forward Jill pushes the Nemesis off the bridge. Run straight through the doors of the factory. Continue down the passage and enter the door on the left. Inside you will find another save room. Carlos will enter and tell you that the government has decided to launch a nuclear missile against Racoon City. Search the room for the facility key. Go through the door with the red light. You will now be in a room with numerous jets of steam. Push the first switch and then head around the corner. Press the next switch and then the far switch. Head back, round the corner and press the switch. Head around to the other side and press the far switch. Press the right switch and then head back around to the other side. Press the switch and then the far switch. You can now activate the console. Press the far, left switch and then the next switch to leave. Head back through the save room and out into the passage. Fight or avoid the Deimos and head through the door opposite. Fight through the zombies and take the system disk found on the console. Ride the elevator down. Collect the shotgun rounds from the right side of the room, head down the steps and through the door. Run down the leech filled passage and through the door on the opposite side. Inside take the water sample from the machine and then go through the other door. At the bottom of the stairs, use the water sample on the machine opposite. To solve this puzzle you need to line up all three bars so they all match the sample at the top. To do this you will need to move each of the three bars left or right until they are in the correct position. If the sample has a tall bar then underneath you will need to have a bar on each of the three bars, if the sample has a clear space then there must be a space on all three of the bars underneath. Once you have solved this puzzle, the water level will be passed. Backtrack to the elevator and ride up. Now you can enter the door to the right of the elevator. Inside, you will be fired upon by Nicholai, but Jill will dive safely out of the way. When you regain control use the system disk in the wall console to unlock the door.

The Last Escape
Head through the door. Once inside the door will automatically lock and a countdown will begin. Worst still, you are locked in here with the Nemesis. During the Nemesis's first attack, he hits a valve spraying a type of acid. To defeat the Nemesis you need to get him near the valves and then shoot them open spraying the Nemesis. With a combination of sprayed acid and gun rounds the Nemesis will fall. A key card will fall out of a researcher's pocket. Take this and unlock the door. Head back to the save room. Inside, save your position and replenish your ammunition and

health. When you are ready head through the door with the red light. Ride the elevator down and collect the grenade rounds. Head back up the elevator and through the save room into the passage. Go to the shutter near the entrance. The key card in your possession will open the shutter. Fight your way past the zombies and into the control room. Search the room for useful items including a portable radar. If you saw Nicholai die then Carlos will contact you, but if not Nicholai will appear a final time. You will be given a choice in how to reply to him. Negotiating with him will save you ammunition and health but will allow Nicholai to escape. Returning fire will repay you nothing but the satisfaction in knowing he is dead. Head down the ladder and head through the door at the end of the room filled with what appears to be dead zombies. Run through the scrap yard and through the door. You will find yourself in a scrap yard with what appears to be a super weapon of some kind. To activate the console you will need to restore power. Head back to the door you entered by and push the first power unit into position. Suddenly a super mutated Nemesis will drop down. Ignore its attacks and push in the second and third power units. With the power restored the super weapon will begin charging. The weapon will create a path through the rubble. You need to keep the creature within this path so it is in the super weapon's line of fire the next time it fires. Keep running behind the creature to keep it in the weapons path. After three or four hits from the cannon, the creature will be dead. Head to the door.

The End ??
Before you leave, you notice that the creature is not completely dead. You will be presented with a choice, either exterminate the monster or evacuate. Your decision will not alter the ending, but if you want to finish the job completely you can decide to finish off the beast, but remember the nuclear missile closing in on the city. Ride the elevator to safety. Your earlier decisions will affect if you escape with Carlos or if you and Carlos will be saved by an unknown helicopter pilot. Could that be Barry Burton from the original Resident Evil. I wonder if Wesker is still alive, I wonder...

RETURN FIRE

One-Player Level Codes
By entering the following codes at the password screen you can get to the section that you desire:

Level 2	Umbrella, Bird, Butterfly, Flower
Level 3	Smiley, Cup, Rabbit, Umbrella
Level 4	Rabbit, Umbrella, Bird, Bird
Level 5	Flower, Umbrella, Rabbit, Cup
Level 6	Bird, Cup, Butterfly, Bear
Level 7	Bear, Bear, Shamrock, Bird
Level 8	Rabbit, Cup, Umbrella, Heart
Level 9	Shamrock, Butterfly, Bird, Heart
Level 10	Heart, Butterfly, Cup, Heart

Level 11	Umbrella, Umbrella, Bird, Flower
Level 12	Flower, Cup, Shamrock, Butterfly
Level 13	Heart, Umbrella, Shamrock, Heart
Level 14	Rabbit, Smiley, Flower, Shamrock
Level 15	Rabbit, Smiley, Bear, Bird
Level 16	Flower, Umbrella, Bird, Rabbit
Level 17	Flower, Bear, Heart, Umbrella

Two-Player Level Codes

Level 2	Butterfly, Umbrella, Bear, Heart
Level 3	Bear, Rabbit, Flower, Shamrock
Level 4	Umbrella, Heart, Shamrock, Flower
Level 5	Umbrella, Bear, Rabbit, Heart
Level 6	Cup, Bird, Butterfly, Flower
Level 7	Heart, Flower, Shamrock, Rabbit
Level 8	Rabbit, Cup, Umbrella, Heart
Level 9	Bear, Rabbit, Shamrock, Flower
Level 10	Butterfly, Smiley, Umbrella, Shamrock
Level 11	Bear, Flower, Smiley, Flower
Level 12	Cup, Bear, Flower, Umbrella
Level 13	Heart, Bird, Flower, Shamrock
Level 14	Smiley, Bird, Shamrock, Cup
Level 15	Cup, Bird, Shamrock, Bear
Level 16	Umbrella, Cup, Bird, Flower
Level 17	Smiley, Bear, Rabbit, Flower
Level 18	Shamrock, Shamrock, Shamrock, Shamrock

RIDGE RACER

Extra Cars

To gain access to eight new cars, wait for the PlayStation logo as the game loads and press ✖ several times until the Galaga game appears. You will find that you will already be firing. As you shoot at the enemy, work your way to the left and blast the alien hordes as you go. Destroy all of them to get the new cars.

Mirror Tracks

You can play the tracks mirrored - this is different to when you play them in reverse after winning on a track. Start the race and when you get to the junction where you would normally turn left, turn around and head for the start before you reach the checkpoint. Keep going towards the steel barrier, which disappears to let you onto the mirrored track.

The Black Car

To drive the black Diablo, you must win every race (including the time trial and the 4 backward tracks). The Diablo will be in the race with you on the final Time Trial. Although you will be unable to overtake him, on the second lap he will park, and it is now that you must get ahead and stick to the racing line without crashing. If you do this he will not pass you. If you win after 3 laps, you get to drive the Diablo.

RIDGE RACER REVOLUTION

Buggy Mode

There are 2 ways of turning the cars into buggies. One is to complete the Galaga game and score a 100% hit ratio. The other is to carry out the following when you switch on the PlayStation: Press and hold **L1**, **R1**, **Select**, ⬇ and ▲. You will find that your ship in Galaga has a powerful laser beam. Start the game as you normally would, and the buggies should be there for you.

Extra Cars

To gain up to 12 extra cars, shoot all 40 enemy craft on Galaga 88 loading game.

Mirror Mode

To drive the track backwards (corners and writing back to front), start a game and after driving a short distance along the track, turn the car around. Drive through the barrier at exactly 100km/h to enter the mirror mode track.

Secret Options

To set the racing time from Normal, Morning, Evening and Night, you must not use the fire button in the game Galaga '88. Once all the ships have passed by (which you have not shot at), there will be a small burst of fireworks. Go to the 'Other' screen to set the racing time.

Special Cars

Try 3 new cars: the Devil #13 in Novice, Kid Car #13 in Advanced, and the White Angel #0 in Expert mode. In order for you to be able to drive these cars, you must win Novice, Advanced and Expert in Time Trial after completing them in normal mode.

Spinning Mode

To spin your car at 3 spinning points on the track, choose a Time Trial race. Press and hold the accelerator and brake when Start is highlighted. Begin the race, and when you get to the first corner, the message 'Spinning Point' will appear. Now spin the car by letting go the accelerator button and quickly pressing it again. It is possible to achieve 360, 540 and 720-degree spins, upon which you will be marked.

Spotlight Control

To have control of the direction and intensity of the spotlight, go to the main screen and hold **L1** and **R1**.

Toggle Mirror On/Off

To remove the rear-view mirror, pause the game, hold ▲ and press **L1**. Use **R1** to put the mirror back again.

Zoom Car In/Out

Zoom in and out on your car by pausing the game in the external view mode. Hold ▲, press **L1** to zoom in, and **R1** to zoom out.

RIDGE RACER TYPE 4

Four player mode
Connect two PlayStations via a link cable. A "Link Battle" mode that allows a simultaneous four player game will appear.

Bonus vehicles
Unlock all 320 cars in the game. The Pac-Man character, which can run at 252 km/h, and the Sony Eat'em Up car may now become selectable in time attack mode.

RISE 2: RESURRECTION

Access Bosses
To have 5 playable boss characters, go to the character select screen and press the following:

Anil 8	↑, →, →, →, ↑, ←, ↑.
Assault	→, ↑, ↑, →, →, ↑, ↑.
Mayhem	←, →, ↓, ←, ↑, ←, ↓, ←, ↓.
Supervisor	↓, →, ↓, ↑, →, ↓, ←, ↓, ↑, →, ↑.
Vitrol	→, →, →, ↑, ↑, ↓, ←, ←, ↓, ↓.

RIVAL SCHOOLS

Extra Hinata Costume
Complete Arcade mode using a combination of Hinata, Batsu and Kyosuke.

Extra Tiffany Costume
Complete Arcade mode using a combination of Tiffany, Roy and Boman.

Extra Natsu Costume
Complete Arcade mode using a combination of Natsu, Shoma and Roberto.

Extra Kyoko Costume
Complete Arcade mode using a combination of Kyoko and Hideo.

Gain All Extra Costumes
Complete Arcade mode then hold **L2** while selecting either Tiffany, Hinata, Natsu or Kyoko.

Alternative Evolution Costumes
On the character selection screen, highlight your chosen character and press either ■, ▲, ●, ■, **R1**, **R2**, **L1** or **L2** to select your character in one of eight different coloured costumes.

Kyoko's Office
Complete the Evolution disc with Kyoko.

Target Mode
Complete the Evolution disc with any character.

Service Mode
Complete the Evolution disc with Natsu.

Home Run Mode
Complete the Evolution disc with Shoma.

Shoot Out Mode
Complete the Evolution disc with Roberto.

RIVEN

Temple Island
Examine the mechanism. Go back to the cage and up the stairs. Turn left to the Gate room. Push the button four times then exit. Go down the stairs then bear left to get to a locked gate. Crawl under the gate. Go up the ladder and over the plank to the Gate room. Go into the cave and pull the lever on the left of the Gate room doorway. Push the chamber rotation button twice. Go in and walk to the doorway. Pull the lever by the door. Push the chamber rotation button twice. Go back to the other door and push the button here twice. The other doorway is now open. Go to the golden dome. Walk across and look at the plaque on the floor: It shows you the pipe layout. Following the winding stairs outside and look at the leaking pipe. Hit the lever. Go back to the main walkway and go through the cave. Look at the pipe and hit the lever. Go to the gate room and go across to the far door. Go over the bridge to the temple.

Walk down the corridor and go into the room on your left. Raise the cage around the throne. Look at the thing on the right hand wall. Hit the switch and walk down the previous corridor. Go through the door to Gehn's temple. Look around and go out near the pillars. Go to the steps and press the blue button. Get in the tram. Hit the left-hand knob to turn the tram, then hit the lever.

Jungle Island
Walk forward and look at the wooden ball on your right. Hit it. Go into the cave and up the stairs. At the top is a tram call button. Go down the stairway. When you see the animals on the rocks, stop. Only move when they stop moving. Walk down onto the beach, be careful not to scare the animals. Go down the beach then go left. Look at the wooden ball on the whale like rock structure. Walk back to the original path from the cave and down it until you get to some more stairs. Go through the tunnel, over the walkway and down the ladder. Fill the basin with water and look at the eye. Go back to the stone stairway. Keep going up past the cave and cross the suspension bridge. Go right at the first fork and left at the next. Hit the bug on the gatepost. Hmmmm, familiar sound! Go through the forest, down the stairs and through the tree trunk. Follow the steps near the giant dagger and look at the wooden eye.

Keep going down the main pathway and bear right until you get to the whale statue. Hit the switch on the right hand lamppost. Go into the mouth and up the stairs. At the top of the stairs is a tram call button. Push the elevator lever to go up.

Walk along the tree top walkway and go left at the fork. Look at the Fire Marble Dome. Now take the alternative path to the spinning mechanism. Look at the eyepiece and push the button on the eyepiece. Do this quickly or it won't work. Go back to the Fire Marble Dome. Go up the stairs to the tower. Go in and sit on the throne. Hit the left handle to rise. Hit the right handle to close the cage. Go back to the whale rock structure and exit through its mouth. Go to the cave and take the right fork up the red stairs to the gate. Turn right and go to the blue cave. Follow the walkway to the village. Climb the ladder to the mud building. Knock on the door, go left, and climb up another ladder. Find the submarine. Hit the left lever to lower it into the water.

Go back to the water basin. Go through the tunnel and down the ladder to the submarine. Hit the centre lever and then the right lever. Hit the right lever again. Get out and climb up the ladder. Move all the levers up. Get back in the submarine and go back. Take the left route. Get out and go into the house. Look at the hangman and pull the ring. Use this game to figure out all the D'ni numerals.

Numerals on the wooden eyes
Bug-2.
Frog-3.
Sunner-4 (seal creature).
Whark-5 (whale creature).
Turn the submarine around and go left. Get out and go to the central gallows. Pull the triangular handles and grab the bar. Go to the cage. Bear right and continue to the button. Hit the button to open the cage. Open the grate on the floor and pull the ring in the water. Go down the tunnel and hit the switch to the left to turn the light on. Turn on the other lights and find the switch to open another door. Go through. For this puzzle you need to click the five pillars in the correct order. However, at the moment you don't know what number one is. Go back to the cage. Go right and climb down the ladder. Keep going through the blue tunnel and out of the woods. Go left then right. Get in the car and hit the left handle.

Book Assembly Island

Get off the wood chipper and go down the pier. Move the valve handle to the middle. Get off the pier and go left to the boiler. Go up to the controls on the walkway. Move the handle up to turn off the furnace. Turn the wheel to alter the water level. Pull the valve lever towards you. Turn around and hit the switch at the top right. This will turn off the red boiler door light. Go into the boiler. Climb down the drain and follow the pipe to the rocks. Turn left and when you get to the balcony, jump over the rail, and go down the hatch. Return to the valve

box at the pier and move the handle to the right. Go back to the balcony and through the doors. Closing the double doors from inside will reveal secret tunnels. Choose the right-hand one.

Go down the path and hit the lever to the right to shut down the fan. Remember the location of this fan for later. Follow the path to the raised bridge. Lower it to get to the Golden Dome. Walk around and turn the wheel. Keep walking and take the first left. Seem familiar? Hit the right hand switch and go back to the walkway. Find the gap in the walkway (a couple of right turns) and press the button to bridge it. Keep going and hit the switch to open the door. Go back to the Golden Dome, turn left, and go down the stairs. Keep going and hit the button to go down. Follow the tunnel and go up the stairs.

Hit the scope and remember the symbol. Go back to the double doors on Book Assembly Island and go forward through the passage to Fire Marble Dome. Follow the walkway and look up at the ceiling to see a strange shape. Go back to the door and close it to find the secret passage. Find the scope and turn it off by hitting the button as before. Note the symbol and go back to the fan duct. Go down it and through the grate. Read everything in Gehn's lab. Look at the wooden eye to learn D'ni number one. Read the papers. Read Gehn's journal and note the five numeral code. Translate this to normal numbers and keep it handy. Unlock the door and hit the tram call button. Go through the door and down to the tram. Turn it around and go forwards.

Survey Island

Go down the steps and follow the path to the building. Go up in the lift. Look out over the balcony. Go to the far side until you see the brown/red building. Go down to it and up to the control panel. Use it to get the grid references of all the Fire Marble Domes. Go back out and at the intersection go right to the Fire Marble Dome. Note the symbol and go to the scope. Once you know it's broken, go back to the tram. Turn it around and exit to get onto the other side of the rails. Go through the door and hit the lever. Get into the car and push the button. Walk down the passage and follow the man. Remember this tram station. Go back to the passageway and go left and up the stairs. Sit on the chair and hit the red button. Hit the lever and look at the code-wheel. Use the wheel to find the colour for each symbol.

Dome	Colour
Prison	Blue
Temple	Green
—	Yellow
Survey	Orange
Jungle	Red
Book Assembly	(Won't work)

Hit the right lever, then the left lever. Rotate the viewer to see a fish. This is the creature for D'ni No1. Go to the tram station where the man escaped. Turn it around and go forward.

Jungle Island

Go up in the lift and get out of the whark. Follow the path going right at the Fire Marble Dome. Go right again and then up the ladder in the blue cavern. Find the secret door in the cage and go through.

Hit the stone pillars from 1 to 5

1 = Fish
2 = Bug
3 = Frog
4 = Sunner
5 = Whark

Look at the book to get the moiety age. Walk up to the idol and you'll be knocked out - literally! Go through the door and stand at the central table. Read the journal that you brought. Note the locking pin, the 5 number code and Catherine's release code. Look at the linking book to return to the pillar room. Go back through the blue cavern. Go up the steps, out of the forest, and across the suspension bridge. Go down and into the cave. Press the tram call button and go down. Turn the tram around and get going.

Temple Island

Go up into the temple and turn left. Go through the door between the pillars and continue across a bridge. Take the far doorway in the gate room and go up the ramp to the Golden Dome. Look at the grid puzzle. You have to put the appropriately coloured marbles at the correct grid reference. The following grid references are to be taken from the top left:

	Horizontal Row	Vertical Row
Blue	1	16
Green	1	22
Orange	22	6
Red	17	9
Purple	4	2

Hit the switch on the wall to lower the press. Hit the white button. Go back to the gate room. Go out of the far door and hit the rotation button three times. Go back in and out of the far door. Go along the walkway and go left at the junction. Follow the stairs out of the dome to a tunnel entrance. Go down in the lift. Solve the sliding puzzle using the 5 number code from Gehn's journal. Push the button and look at the linking book. Look at the window and go to Gehn's Age. Push the button in the cage and talk to Gehn. When he opens the prison book, look at the window. Now you're in his office. Go to the globe and move the lever to the right. Hit the lever to lower the cage. Climb down the ladder and read the personal journal. Touch the small metal ball to get the code for Catherine's cage. Go back up the ladder and get inside to go to prison island.

Prison Island

Press the button on the floor to rise up. Go to the lift. Inside is a puzzle. Use the code from Gehn's bedroom and hit the lever. Now save Catherine. Go back to the dome and use the scope, hitting the top button to switch if off. Go up to the dome and set the sliding puzzle as before. Open the linking book to get Gehn's age. Open the temple island book (5 squares) to get there. Press the button on the floor and go to the button to lower the lift. Go up and then to the Golden Dome. Follow the walkway to the drawbridge. Cross it and take the far door at the gate room. Turn right and go down to the star fissure. Look at the hatch and use the telescope code from Catherine's journal. Open the hatch. Use the viewer. Get the locking pin from just left of the hatch. Hit the lever on the right and push the button five times. There it is.

ROAD RASH

Dismount Bike

To see your rider get off his bike, stop him when he is racing and press **↑**, **L1** and **R1** together.

ROAD RASH 3D

Lazy Rider

Press **✖** twice to pull a wheelie then keep tapping **✖** until you ride over a car. If you brake at the right time you will be able to get a lift.

ROAD RASH: JAILBREAK

Four Nitros

Go to the options menu and highlight Multiplayer selection. Hold **L1 + R1 + R2 + ← + ✖**. Go to the cheat code entry screen and enter **FDMFG**. Start the game in Jailbreak mode and you will start with four nitros.

ROADSTERS

Level Select

On the main menu screen, press **R2, L1, L1, L1, R2, R1, L2, R2, R2, R1, L2, L2, L1.**

ROBO PIT

Choose Stage

To select a stage, go to the menu screen and hold **R1, L1, R2** and **L2** while you press **Select**. You will now see 'Stage 00' above the robot. Use **←** and **→** to change the stage number.

ROBOTRON X

Power-Ups
To ease the frantic action, enter the desired cheat during play:

Pulse Wave	↑, ●, ↓, →, ■
Shield	↓, ←, ■, ●
Speed Up	←, ←, →, →, ▲
Flame-Thrower	↓, →, ↓, →, ●
2-Way Gun	↑, ▲, ↑, ▲
3-Way Gun	→, →, ■, ✖
4-Way Gun	↓, ↓, ↑, ●

ROGUE TRIP

Cheat Mode
Press **L1 + R1 + R2 + Select** while playing. Then hold **L1 + R1** and press

↑, ↓, ←, →	Invulnerable.
↑, ↓, ↑, R2	Infinite Weapons.
R2 + ✖ + ↓	Mega Guns.
L2 + ▲ + ←	Hornet Nest.
R2 + ↑, ↓, ↑	God Mode.
←, →, ←, →	Upgrades All Weapons.

Play As Big Daddy
Enter ▲, ■, R2, ✖, ▲, R2 as a password, select Challenge Mode and choose the Nuke York level.

Battle Boss 1
Enter ●, R2, R1, ■, L1, R2 as a password.

Battle Boss 2
Enter ●, ●, L2, L1, ▲, ▲ as a password.

Battle Big Daddy
Enter ■, ▲, ●, ●, R2, R2 as a password.

Infinite Jumps
Enter ●, ■, R2, ✖, ▲, R2 as a password.

ROLLCAGE

Unlock Everything
Enter MAXCHEAT as a password.

Eighties Air Horn
Enter AIRHORNS as a password.

Designers High Scores
Enter BESTLAPS as a password.

All Tracks (Easy)
Enter EEFNIEBA as a password.

All Tracks (Hard)
Enter EEFPHMBC as a password.

All Tracks (Expert)
Enter HEMPCMDD as a password.

All Tracks (Expert), Bonus Car, Mega Time Trial, Mirror Mode, All Deathmatch Modes
Enter HHMPNEED as a password.

ROLLCAGE 2

Cheat Mode
Enter **I.WANT.IT.ALL.AND.I.WANT.IT.NOW!** complete with full stops to unlock everything the game has to hide.

ROSCO MCQUEEN

Passwords

Level	Password
Laundry 2	FLUFFY
Laundry 3	SWEATY
Auto 1	HOTROD
Auto 2	GREASE
Auto 3	BIGEND
Harolds 1	SMELLY
Harolds 2	WIDE TV
Harolds 3	PILLOW
Leisure 1	TRICEP
Leisure 2	MOTION
Leisure 3	HIPHOP
Residential 1	KENNEL
Residential 2	BARREL
Runaround	SPLASH

RUGRATS: THE SEARCH FOR REPTAR

Easier Putt in Mini Golf
While putting in the mini golf game, hold down the walk button to slow down the aiming line making it easier to aim.

Jumping Down the Stairs
While you are in the house, stand at the top of the stairs and face the staircase. Now when you jump you will leap jump the whole staircase.

Play On Playground Equipment
Go to the game Grandpas teeth "medium". Go up to the playground equipment and press ●. You will see a small movie of the Rugrats playing on the equipment.

Play With Spike
You can play fetch with Spike outdoors by picking up the small ball, the bone, and the stick.

Secret Reptar Bars
When playing hole 8 on Ice Cream Mountain, search around the pyramid for the entrance. Head inside and you will discover a large stash of Reptar Bars and Mr Friend's mummy.

Shortcut in Incident Isle 7
On Incident Isle 7, near the plants you will find three balloons tied together. Run into the three balloons and press ● and you will be transported to the middle part of the board.

SAMPRAS EXTREME TENNIS

All The Courts And Players
Enter **ELIBDEANPAOCAAABJGEMIAAACKKKI** as a Tournament password.

SAMURAI SHOWDOWN

Play as Zankuro
To access this character, firstly select Vs Mode and go to the character selection screen. Next, hold down **Start** and highlight the following characters in this order: Haohmuru, Ganjuro, Basara, Kyoshiro, Ukyo, Rimruru, Haohmaro, Shizmaru, Nakoruru, Hanzo, Amakusa, Gaira, Galford and Shizmaru. Finally, hold **Start** and press ✖ + ●. Zankuro will now appear.

SAN FRANCISCO RUSH

More Cars
On the car selection screen press ● to select either a Viper, a 60's hippy van, a VW Beetle or a McLaren.
Hidden UFO
Hold **R1 + R2 + L1 + L2** at the car select screen and choose a car. Keep all four buttons held down and on the transmission select screen press ✖. Then hold ▲ until the race begins.
Hidden Truck
Select any vehicle and hold **L1** until the race begins.
Hidden Buggy
Select any vehicle and hold **R1** until the race begins.
Hidden Car
Select any vehicle and hold **R1 + R2** until the race begins.
Extra Cars
Select any vehicle, then on the transmission selection screen press ⬇ to cycle between a low rider, a bus, a rocket engine car, a taxi and a police car. The number of vehicles you can select depends on the amount of keys you've collected.
Change Car Colours
On the car select screen press ■.
Reversed Tracks
Complete the Circuit mode.

Stunt Mode
Complete the Tournament mode and then select the Golden Gate Bridge.

SCARS

Car and Cup Passwords
RUNNER - Cheetah Car
MYSTER - Panther Car
DESERT - Scorpion Car
RATTLE - Cobra Car
ALLVID - All Cars

XPERTS - Master Mode
GLASSX - Crystal Cup
ROCKYY - Diamond Cup
ZOPEAK - Zenith Cup

SHADOW MASTER

Game Cheats
On the first level, kill the two shadowfists from the first room that opens, then enter the room and enter the following codes

Invincibililty
Press **L1 + L2 + R1 + R2 + ✖** at the same time, the screen should flash blue.

All Weapons
Press **L1 + L2 + R1 + R2 + ●** at the same time, the screen should flash red.

Level Select
Press **L1 + L2 + R1 + R2 + ▲** at the same time, the screen should flash green. Quit the game and on the title screen there should be a level select.

SHELLSHOCK

Invulnerability
To be invulnerable, quit the game when you are in the Pen. When the main title screen appears press the following:
⬆, ⬆, ⬆, ⬇, ⬇, ⬇, ➡, ➡, ▲.

Test Menu
You can bring up a special menu that gives you a choice of options including playing with maximum fire power, starting on any level, viewing all FMV's, and seeing the credits. To see this menu, go to the title screen which displays the copyright message, and press ⬆, ⬇, ⬅, ➡, ⬇, ⬇, ➡, ➡, ▲.

SILENT HILL

Extra Options
While on the Option screen, press **L1 + L2 + R1 + R2**. An Extra Options screen will appear.

The Nightmare
Follow Cheryl through the fog and down the alley. Once you reach the end of the alley you will be attacked by a number of knife wielding children. You cannot escape and are soon killed.

The Café
When you awake you will find yourself in a café. Here you meet Cybil Bennet, a district cop who has come to Silent Hill to discover why there has been no contact from the town. After speaking with Cybil, collect the health drinks, flashlight, the map of Silent Hill and the kitchen knife. Equip the gun then head to the door. As you leave the radio will begin to buzz. When you move closer to investigate a strange winged creature will smash through the window. Use your gun to kill the creature.

Old Silent Hill
Once outside, use the map to return to the alley where you were attacked by the knife wielding children. At the end of the alley, read the "To School" note and collect the steel pipe. Leave the alley and head down Matheson Street towards the school. You will discover the road is blocked. Collect the "Levin Street Doghouse" notes then head up Levin Street. The dog house is on the left side of the street. Search the dog house and you will find the house key. Use the house key to enter the house. At the back of the house you will find a locked door which requires three keys. Examine the map on the left which marks the locations of the three keys. Before leaving collect the two boxes of ammunition, the health drink and save on the note pad.

Leave the house and head up to Finney Street. Enter the Convenience Store on the corner of Finney Street and Bachman Street. Collect the 1st aid kit and the three health drinks. You will also find the secret channeling stone here in 'Next Fear'. Leave the store and head to the end of Finney Street to find an abandoned Police Car. Search the car for the key of 'Lion' and a box of ammunition. Return down Finney Street and head down the alley between Ellroy Street and Bachman Street. Enter the basket ball court behind the café and collect the key of 'Woodman' and the health drink. Head down the alley and turn left onto Ellroy Street. The final key is found in a mailbox. You will have to cross the plank to reach it. When you have got all the three keys, return to the house on Levin Street. Once inside, unlock the back door and head into the backyard. Once outside, the foggy day will turn into the blackness of night. Turning on the flashlight will provide you with some light but will also allow the creatures of the night to pin point your position. Collect the two health drinks from the table and head onto Midwich Street. Head up Midwich Street to the collapsed freeway and collect the box of ammunition and the health drink. Then head down Midwich Street towards the school. Ignore the school entrance for the moment and enter the school bus. Collect the two health drinks then leave the school bus and enter the school.

Midwich Elementary
Collect the map of the school from the lobby and head into the corridor. Turn left and enter the reception. Read the list of teachers and the three poems written in blood. Then collect the box of ammunition from the back room. Return to the corridor and head right to the infirmary. Collect the 1st aid kit and the health drink from the medicine cabinet then save at the note pad. Return to the corridor and head through the double doors into the courtyard. Kill the two knife wielding children, stomping on their heads to finish them off. Examine the clock tower. Head through opposite double doors. Kill or avoid the children and enter the doors opposite. Collect the box of ammunition, the shadow babies are harmless for the moment. Leave and head up the stairs to the second floor. Enter the door opposite and enter the lab equipment room. Collect the chemical.

Return to the corridor and enter the laboratory. Walk up to the desk with the stone hand. Use the chemical on the hand to release the gold medallion. Take the gold medallion and return downstairs. Head into the courtyard and place the gold medallion in to the clock tower. The clock will now read 12:00. Return upstairs and make you way to the music room. Inside you will find an open piano. To release the silver medallion above the chalk board you will need to play the dead notes in the order told in the poem. White coloured birds represent white keys while black coloured birds represent black notes. First press the second white key from the left, then the second white key from the right, then the black key on the far right, the third white key from the right, then finally the black key on the far left. Take the silver medallion, return downstairs and enter the courtyard. Place the silver medillion into the clock tower. The clock will now read 5:00. Head down to the boiler room and press the switch. The door in the clock tower will now be open. Head inside and descend the ladder. Enter through the door labelled "Keep Out" and you will appear.......

Alternative Midwich Elementary
You will find yourself in a darker mirror world. Head through the top double doors. Enter the doors opposite and collect the 1st aid kit and the box of ammunition. Return to the corridor and enter the room on the right. Inside, collect the rubber ball. Return to the corridor and head left down the corridor and through the door on the left. Inside collect the picture card. Head through the opposite door. Make your way to the infirmary. Collect the 1st aid kit, the health drink and save at the note pad. Leave the infirmary and enter the lobby. Collect the ampoule then return to the corridor. Enter the reception and use the picture card to open the strangely decorated door. Enter the girls rest room then leave and you will find yourself

transported to an inaccessible part of the second floor. Enter the second floor boys rest room, collect the two boxes of ammunition and the shotgun shells. Return into the girls rest room, leave and you will find yourself on the first floor again. Enter the first floor boys rest room and collect the shotgun from inside the stall. Enter the teachers room and collect the box of ammunition. As you leave, a phone on the table will ring even though its disconnected.

Leave the room and take the stairs to the roof. Search the hole in the drain and you will find a key but it is just out of reach. Place the rubber ball in the hole in the corner then turn the water valve. The water will flush the key down the drain. Head down the stairs and into the courtyard. Collect the classroom key from the bottom of the drain pipe. Head back up to the second floor. Collect the box of ammunition from the top left classroom and the shotgun shells from the room below. Enter the locker room and open the shaking locker. There nothing inside but a corpse will fall out of a locker behind you and drop the stack room key. Enter the stack room and collect the health drink. Enter the library, collect the box of ammunition and read the 'Beast Book'. Make your way through the classrooms to reach the stairs on the right side of the building. Enter the storage room and collect the ampoule and the two boxes of shotgun shells. Head into the boiler room and you will find yourself in a room with a turnstile. Examine the right hand valve and then turn it twice to the right. Then examine the left valve and then turn it twice to the left. You should now be able to head down the narrow corridor. Ride the elevator down to the boss.

Boss One: The Lizard

For the first part of the fight, constantly fire at the giant beast's head while backing away. After you have inflicted enough damage, it will open its mouth and try to ensnarl you in its huge jaws. When it opens its mouth, fire several shots from your shotgun while backing away.

To Central Silent Hill

After defeating the beast, you will find yourself in the original school boiler room. Collect the key and head to the reception. You will discover the key you hold opens the house of one of the schools teachers. With the house marked on your map, leave the school. Make your way to the house. Inside, collect the two boxes of ammunition and save at the note pad. As you leave the house, collect the health drink on the steps. Head down Bradbury Street and up onto Bloach Street. Enter the church. Here you will meet Dahlia Gillespie. When she leaves, collect the Flauros and the key from the altar. Leave the church and head to the gas station. Collect the box of ammunition. If you are playing a second time (Next Fear), you will find the secret item, the gas tank here. Then head to the bridge. You will find a 1st aid kit on the steps on the left and a box of ammunition on the steps on the right. Climb the stairs and enter the drawbridge station. Collect the map of the Shopping District and the health drink. Insert the key into the console and press the button to lower the bridge. Return outside. If you are playing a second time (Next Fear), enter the room below the drawbridge station and you will find the Rock Drill. There is also a chainsaw to collect from the window of the Hardware Store. Head across the bridge.

Central Silent Hill

Enter the Police Station on the corner of Sagan Street and Crichton Street. In the lobby collect the two boxes of ammunition and the shotgun shells. Enter the office, collect the box of ammunition, the shotgun shells and save at the note pad. Before leaving read the black board. Before entering the hospital, collect the alley off Koontz for a box of ammunition and a health drink. Then collect the health drink from the café on Koontz Street. Enter Alchemilla Hospital

Alchemilla Hospital

Collect the map of the hospital from the reception then head into the consultation room. Here you will meet Dr Kaufmann. Once he has left, enter the door on the left. Head through the next door and you will find yourself back in the reception, but behind the desk. Collect the 1st aid kit. Make your way back to the consultation room and head through the opposite door. Head through the next door into the corridor. Go through the unlocked door on the right and collect the map of the basement. Go into the next room and collect the basement key from the table. Return to the corridor and enter the next unlocked door. You will find yourself in a kitchen. Collect the plastic bottle (this item is essential to getting the best ending). Return to the corridor and head into the next room. Search behind the desk to find a strange liquid on the floor. Use the plastic bottle to collect some of the strange liquid. Use the basement key to unlock the next door in the corridor, then head down the stairs to the basement. Enter the generator room and switch on the generator. This will restore power to the elevators. Enter the elevator and head to the second floor. You will find the double doors locked, return to the elevator and ride up to the third floor. On the third floor you will find the double doors locked, but when you return to the elevator a fourth floor mysteriously appears. Ride up to the fourth floor.

Alternative Alchemilla Hospital

As you step off the elevator onto the fourth floor you will discover you have crossed over to an alternative hospital filled with nightmarish creatures. Head through the double doors and dash down the corridor to the next set of doors. Head down the next corridor to the staircase and descend to the third floor. Head through the doors and enter the men's rest room on your right. Collect the plate of 'Turtle'. Return to the corridor and head into room 302, take the shotgun shells and save at the note pad (remember the VCR). Return to the corridor and enter the room opposite. Make you way through the room and exit through the door. Head into the room opposite, collect the blood pack from the shelf, the box of ammunition and the 1st aid kit. Head down the corridor and enter room 306 on the right of the double doors. Collect the plate of 'Cat'. Return back to the stairs and descend to the second floor. Head through the doors on the right and enter the room 201. Collect the lighter. Return to the corridor and head to room 204. Throw the blood bag at the tentacles and collect the plate of 'Hatter'. Return to the stairs and descend to the first floor. Head through the double doors.

Head down the corridor and enter the director's office. Collect the final plate, the plate of 'Queen'. Examine the drinks machine for three health drinks. Make your way back to the stairs and ascend to the second floor. Enter the room opposite room 201. In the Alice in Wonderland room, examine the door then place the plates in this clockwise order, Blue, Green, Yellow, then Red. Head through the door. Enter the doors opposite and enter the doors on the right. Collect the basement storage key. Return to the corridor and enter the next set of doors. Collect the medicinal alcohol. Collect the 1st aid kit from room 206 then take the elevator down to the basement. Enter the generator room and collect the hammer. The hammer is such a powerful weapon that you should use it for the rest of the hospital. Enter the morgue and collect the two health drinks and the ampoule. Enter the store room and pick up the box of ammunition and the shotgun shells. Push the cabinet in the corner of the room and head through the wooden door. Use the medicinal alcohol on the ivy then set it alight with the lighter. Head down through the hatch.

Head down the corridor and through the door at the end. In the next corridor enter the metallic door on the left. Enter the door on the right and collect the video tape. Return to the corridor and enter the last door on the left. Examine the picture and take the consultation room key. At this point you can return to room 302 and play the video tape in the VCR or head straight for the consultation room on the first floor. In the consultation room you will meet a frightened nurse named Lisa Garland. You will soon lose consciousness, when you awake, you will find yourself back in the original hospital. After speaking with Dahlia Gillespie, collect the antique shop key and make your way to the reception. Save at the note pad then leave the hospital.

Shopping District

The Antique shop you are looking for is found at the end of Simmons Street. Use the key to enter the shop. Once in the shop, push the cabinet aside to reveal a secret passage. Cybil will appear, after a brief conversation head through the passage. Collect the axe from the wall, after examining the altar head back through the passage. After a dream sequence with Lisa, you find yourself back in the alternative Silent Hill. Leave the Antique shop and head through the gap in the fencing and head into the shopping mall. As you move towards the escalator the video screen to your right will come to life. When you reach the top of the escalator head into the Jewelry Store and collect the 1st aid kit, the two rifle shell boxes and save at the note pad. As you approach the corpse, the floor

gives way and you fall to the floor below.

Boss Two: Larva

As soon as you recover from the fall, grab the hunting rifle from the broken case. The Larva has two attacks, it emerges from beneath you and then spits a red liquid at you. Equip the shotgun and back up into a corner. This should prevent the Larva from attacking from below. When it appears fire a number of shots at its head before it returns into the ground. When you have inflicted enough damage it will flee.

Head through the broken glass. You will appear behind the shopping mall. Head down to Sagan Street past the Police Station, where you can save your game. Then head down Crichton Street and enter the hospital.

Alternative Alchemilla Hospital

Head inside and go to the examination room. Lisa will tell you about the water works which leads to the lake. Leave the hospital and head across the street. Climb the steps up onto the roof of the Post Office.

Boss Three: Giant Moth

While you were in the hospital, the Larva has transformed into a giant moth and wants a second chance at killing you. Climb the steps to the water tank and use it as cover. It only takes five or six shots from the shotgun or the hunting rifle to kill the giant moth. With the giant moth dead, night will turn to day. Head back down to the street and head up Crichton Street. Return back across the bridge to Old Silent Hill.

Water Works

Once at the water works, use the axe to break the lock on the gate. Climb down the hatch. Head down the narrow passage and turn left. Take the next left and collect the health drinks and ammunition. Head across the plank and grab the rifle shells. Follow the sewer until you reach a door. Head inside and you will find yourself in the maintenance office. Collect the map of the sewers, the sewer key and save at the note pad. Backtrack and head past the passage leading South. Use the sewer key to unlock the gate. Head down the passage until you reach a ladder. Climb the ladder and collect the 1st aid kit. The gate leading to the ladder is locked, the sewer key is found in the water on the other side of the passage. Examine the bloody pool at the waters edge. Once you have the key a number of creatures will attack. Quickly run to the locked gate and climb the ladder.

Resort Area

Enter the old hut and collect the map of the Resort Area, the 1st aid kit, rifle shells and the box of ammunition. Head to Annie's Bar. Here you will run into Kaufmann. Once he has gone search around the pool table for the receipt and the motel room key. Head to the Indian Runner Store on the corner of Weaver Street and Craig Street. Use the code 0473 on the lock. Open the draw next to the counter and collect the safe key, the health drink and the rifle shells. Examine the wall near the safe and you will find the code for the motel manager's room, 0886. Open the safe with the safe key to discover a shipment of drugs. Leave the Store and head down Weaver Street. Use the code to unlock the back door to the motel. Read the note and the newspaper once you are inside. Collect the magnet from the desk. Head through the door to the right. Once in the garage, collect the health drink and the shotgun shells. Before leaving examine the motorcycle. Go to motel room number 3 and use the key you found in Kaufmann's wallet. Once inside the motel room, push the dresser and use the magnet to retrieve the motorcycle key. Collect the health drink from the bathroom.

Return to the garage. Use the motorcycle key to open the bike's gas tank. Inside you will find a bottle filled with red liquid. At this point, Kaufmann will appear and snatch the bottle from you. Leave the motel and head down Sanford Street. Suddenly the world will transform into the alternative, nightmarish world of Silent Hill. Head down the dock and enter the houseboat. Once inside the houseboat you will meet up with Cybil and Dahlia again. Dahlia will tell you to go to the lighthouse why Cybil checks out the amusement park. Before leaving, collect the box of ammunition, rifle shells, the health drink and save at the note pad. Leave the houseboat via the double doors and make your way to the lighthouse. Once in the lighthouse, climb the stairs to the roof. Once at the top, you will see Alessa who disappears just as you arrive. Return back down the stairs and make your way back to the houseboat. Head back to Sanford Street and enter the gate leading to the second sewer.

Sewers

Collect the map of the sewers leading to the amusement park. Head straight down the passage and turn right. Go right down the next passage then take the left passage. Climb the ladder at the end of the final passage up to the amusement park.

Amusement Park

First, find the ice cream stand and save at the note pad. Head to the merry-go-round. Upon entering the ride, you will confront Cybil but she is being controlled by a strange parasite attached to her back. Cybil will suddenly attack you. You need her to run out of bullets, so stay in range and dodge her shots. If you get hit, instantly use a 1st aid kit or health drink and get up before she attacks again. Once she has run out of bullets, she will try to strangle you. Wait until Cybil grabs you around the neck, then use the red fluid in the bottle you found in the hospital. This will force the parasite to release Cybil. Alessa will appear and casts a force field around herself. The flauros will then begin to glow and attacks Alessa. Dahlia will then appear and whisk Alessa away.

Nowhere

You will awaken in a room with Lisa. After a disturbing conversation she will leave the room. Head out through the door on the right of the desk. Follow the corridor to the elevator. Once you leave the elevator head down the corridor and check all the unlocked rooms to familiarize yourself with the layout. You will eventually encounter the ghostly image of Cheryl and will pass through a door with the word 'Phaleg' carved into it. Enter the door to the right and you will find yourself in the antique shop. Save at the note pad and examine the clock. Before leaving collect the shotgun shells and the 1st aid kit. Once back in the corridor, head through the last door on the right. Descend the stairs and enter the door at the end. You will find yourself in a classroom. Examine the desk then head into the next room and collect the pliers and the screwdriver. Return back to the first corridor and enter the room with the faucet. Use the pliers on the faucet to retrieve the key of 'Ophiel'. Return to the corridor and unlock the door with the word 'Ophiel' carved in it. You will find yourself in another corridor. All but one door is unlocked, inside you will find a zodiac puzzle. Examine the pictures on the wall, each number represents a month. You have to reassign new numbers for each month. For example, Leo is the eighth month of the year, but if it is numbered 10, then Sagittarius the twelve month will be 2 and not 12. Once you have solved the puzzle collect the stone of time.

Return to the corridor and head to the double doors with the keypad. To unlock the door you need to find the Grim Reaper's list and reorder the names according to age, youngest to oldest. Then input the first initial of each name, spelling ALERT. Head through the next room to the morgue. Collect the amulet of solomon and then leave. As you leave you run into Lisa, after another disturbing conversation her entire body will begin to bleed. After her screams have stopped, return into the room and read her diary. Return to the corridor and enter the second door on the right. You will find yourself back in the original corridor. Return to the antique shop room and use the stone of time on the clock. The glass face will shatter, enabling you to grab the key of 'Hagith. Head into the corridor and unlock the double doors with the word 'Hagith' carved into it. Ride the elevator to the second floor. Enter the third door on the left and collect the crest of mercury and the ring of contact. Return to the corridor and head through the double doors. Go into the room on the right and collect the camera and the box of ammunition. Head back through the door and go to the end of the corridor, entering the last door on the left.

Examine the steel plate, then remove it using the screwdriver. You find a key but cannot collect it until you cut the power. Head back to the elevator and ride up to the third floor. Examine the altar, then use the camera on the two paintings to reveal three symbols. Input the symbols into the each door to unlock them. Enter the left door and collect the birdcage key. Enter the right door, collect the health drink and read the book. Return to the elevator and ride down to the first floor. Enter the room with the birdcage. Unlock the cage and collect the key of 'Phaleg'. Unlock the door with 'Phaleg' carved into it. Once in the passage, enter the first door on your right. Use the ring of contact to fasten the chains, then grab the dagger of melchior. Enter the next room on the right and collect the health drink and the box of ammunition. The key of bethor is found in the bag of jellybeans. Head into the next room and play the video tape in the VCR. Return to the passage and enter the second room on the left. Collect the ankh from the wall. Return to the passage and unlock the room using the key of Bethor. Inside you will find a generator. Turn off the generator, then return to the room with the electrified key and collect the key of Aratron. Open the door with 'Aratron' carved into it. After the flashback, examine the picture and collect the disk of Ouroboros. Enter the final door and save at the note pad. Examine the door at the rear of the room. Place the dagger of Melchior, the Ankh, the Amulet of Solomon, the crest of Mercury and the disk of Ouroboros into the door. Then head through the door.

Dahlia's House
Once you have stepped through the door you will find yourself in Dahlia Gillespie's house. Both doors are locked, so descend the stairs.

Final Boss: Winged Demon
After an informative conversation, Kaufmann will shoot Dahlia and cause the demon she has summoned to split from Alessa. The demon itself is not very hard to beat. There is no real way in avoiding its lightning attacks. Just continue to fire clean shots at the demon, first with the shotgun and hunting rifle then finally with the handgun. Heal yourself after each attack and continue to attack until it falls.

Endings
There are a number of different game endings.

Bad Ending: You will get this ending if you head straight for the houseboat after leaving the waterworks. By not visiting the resort area such as Annie's bar, the Indian Runner store or the motel, you do not get to learn Kaufmann's part in the story. At the end of the game you will face the possessed Alessa/Cheryl and not the demon. You get the bad ending even if you do or do not save Cybil at the amusement park.
Good Ending: You visit the resort area but do not save Cybil at the amusement park.

Good Ending+: You visit the resort area and save Cybil at the amusement park.

Secret Items
Once you complete the game you are given a rank depending on which ending you got, how many times you saved, how many items you collect etc. You are ranked in stars and you can only unlock certain secret weapons and items by achieving a certain number of stars.

After completing the game once you will be awarded the chainsaw, the pneumatic drill and petrol can.
Six stars of more rewards you with the katana.
Ten stars rewards you with the hyper blaster.
For collecting over 180 items you are rewarded with the channeling stone.

Next Fear
Once you have completed the game you can play again from a save file named, 'Next Fear'. The game is harder but you will have access to the secret weapons.

SIM CITY 2000
Free Credit
Have bonds at 0% interest by going to the Budget screen, holding ▲ and pressing **L1, L2, L1, L2, R2, R1, R2, R1**.

Loads Of Money
Increase your money by $1 million, by carrying out the following instructions: Access City Info/Budget while you are in a game. Hold **R1** and press ✕, ●, ▲, ■ at the Budget screen. Release **R1**, and hold **L1** while you press ✕, ●, ▲, ■. Release **L1**. Now hold **R2** while you press ✕, ●, ▲, ■, then release **R2**. Finally hold **L2** while pressing ✕, ■, ▲, ●, and release **L2**.

Helicopter View
When you are in the 3D Drive-Thru mode press **R2, L2, R2, L2, R2, L2**.

SKELETON WARRIORS
Invincibility
Pause the game during play and press ↓, ●, ■, ■, ↑, ✕.

SKULL MONKEYS
Passwords
These passwords should ease the clay-related mayhem!

Level	Code
Monkey Shrines	R2, R2, ●, ■
Hard Boiler	R2, ■, R2, R1, ■, ✕, R1, ✕, ✕, R1, ▲
Sno	●, ▲, ■, ▲, ●, R1, R1, L1, ✕, R1, ■
Elevated.. of Terror	L1, L1, ■, L1, ■, R1, ■, L1, ■
Castle De.. Muertos	●, L1, ✕, ▲, ■, ✕, ✕, ✕, L1, R1
YNT Death Garden	■, R1, ●, L1, ●, R1, ●, L1, ✕, ✕, ■, R2
YNT Mines	✕, ■, ✕, ▲, ✕, ✕, ■, L1, ■, ■
YNT Weeds	▲, R2, ▲, ▲, ■, ✕, ●, L1, ■, ▲, ■, ■
Evil Engine No. 9	✕, ▲, ✕, ✕, R1, ■, ●, ✕, L1, ✕

SMALL SOLDIERS
Medal Of Honor Demo
On the password screen enter ▲, ▲, ✕, ●, ●, ●, ■, ✕.

Level Passwords
Gorgon	✕, ✕, ▲, ■, ■, ✕, ●, ✕.
Dimensional Temple	■, ✕, ▲, ■, ■, ■, ●, ✕.
Floating Fortress	●, ✕, ▲, ■, ■, ●, ●, ✕.
Sprit Bog	▲, ✕, ▲, ■, ■, ▲, ●, ✕.
Canyon Village	✕, ■, ▲, ■, ■, ▲, ●, ✕.
Creepy Caverns	■, ■, ▲, ■, ■, ■, ▲, ✕.
Space Ship	●, ■, ▲, ■, ■, ●, ▲, ✕.

Hall Of Patroits	△, ■, △, ■, ■, △, △, ✕.
Graveyard Of War	✕, ●, △, ■, ■, ✕, ✕, ■.
Nuclear Mine	■, ●, △, ■, ■, ■, ✕, ■.
Launch Centre	●, ●, △, ■, ■, ●, ✕, ■.
Ulhaden Fier	△, ●, △, ■, ■, △, ✕, ■.
Garrison	✕, △, △, ■, ■, ✕, ■, ■.
Inner Sanctum	■, △, △, ■, ■, ■, ■, ■.

SOUL BLADE

Altering Ending

To change the ending sequence, wait for the screen to go from being letter-boxed to full-screen at the beginning of the Game Over sequence, and immediately press all of the buttons and rotate the joypad. The only end sequence that will not be affected by this method is during Mitsurugi's ending where you fight Tanegashima in a first-person perspective. In this case, use ← and → to avoid the arrows, and keep pushing forward. Use a slash button to finally kill him.

Alternative Outfits

Use the following codes to find every costume for each of the characters:
Costume 1 - ■
Costume 2 - ✕ and ■
Costume 3 - ●
Costume 4 - △
Costume 5 - ✕ and △

Play As Sophitia!

To play as Sophitia!! who wears even less, you need to complete the Blade Master Mode with every character, and get every one of the weapons.

Play As Soul Blade

There are two ways of accomplishing this. Either play for 20 hours, or take the quicker option of completing the game with every character. After doing this, you will find that there is a picture of the fighters on the title screen, signifying that the cheat has worked.

Voice Change

Alter the voice at the main title screen when the gruff voice says 'Soul Edge', by carrying out the following examples while the voice is speaking:

Hold **L1** and **L2** and press ↓ for a husky, slow voice.
Hold **L1** and **L2** and press ← or ↑ for a fast girls voice.
Try other directions on the pad for variations.

Play As Han Myong

To have the choice of Han Myong on the character selection screen in Arcade and Versus mode, go to the 'game over' sequences of Seung and Hwang, and when the screen changes from letter-boxed to full-screen, repeatedly press the buttons and rotate the D-pad. When you have carried this out with both characters, Han Myong should be selectable.

Play As Sophitia!

Obtain Sophitia's eighth weapon after using her to complete the Blade Master Mode. Then go to the character select screen in Arcade or Versus mode and Sophitia! should be at the end of the list. When you play as Sophitia! you will find that she is basically no different to the original Sophitia apart from the fact that she wears white, and no body armour.

Play As Siegfried!

This version of Siegfried wears armour of a different colour, and he also has the Soul Blade sword. To put Siegfried! onto the character select screen in Arcade and Versus mode, use Siegfried to complete the Blade Master mode and get his eighth weapon.

SOUL REAVER

Controlling Raziel is very similar to controlling Lara Croft. Raziel can run, walk and jump but also has the ability to sneak up on his enemies. All the lower vampire ranks need to be impaled or they will regenerate. By mastering sneaking, you can creep up on distracted vampires and kill them in relative safety.

Head down the passageway directly in front of you. Walk onto the gate to open the passage way across the room, then head down the passageway.

Feed until your strength is maximised. Continue straight ahead to the passage way with steps leading upwards. Jump across the chasm and continue along the tunnels. Move to the wall opposite from where you entered the chamber, and jump up twice to continue through the corridors. Enter the portal for instructions, go into the Portal Plane. Head down the corridor to the right of the one you entered the room.

Jump the water and stand next to the door, then enter the room. Now first jump the water, move to the box, and stand next to the box. Drag box to the light on the opposite wall. Climb onto the box, so if you jump you can see the corridor that you need to go through. Jump up to corridor and continue along the corridor to a door and go through it.

Raziels Clan Area

Head down the corridor opposite the gates. Continue along the corridor to the right and go across the rope bridge. Jump to the passageway on the left, and go through wooden door. Attack the vampires and the gate will open, go through and up the stairs.

Go through the door to the left, turn right, and follow the passageway. Go through the gate, continue on, and go up the circular stairs. Enter the room, go to the switch and operate. The draw bridge now lowers, which you can cross and follow the passageway. Jump up the slope, jump down, go through the gate on the right, and jump up to enter the next clan.

Melchahim clan area
Jump the wall and head to the box. Drag the box back towards the entrance to the room, then drag it to the left corner. Jump on the box allowing you to jump up to the next corridor. Head up either ramp, go through the gate where the sunlight shines and continue down the spiral staircase. Go straight across the room, jump the pillars to cross, and go through two gates. Move on down the slope, head to the gate on the right and change to spectral realm whilst facing away. Platforms will emerge. Jump up to Portal Plane and change back to Material Realm. Walk along the raised platform, jump to the ledge on the left side, and move the block. Follow the instructions to slot the block into the gap and the gate will open.

Enter room and go across to opposite wall. Pull the block out and shift it into the gap next to the gate, which will then open. Shift back to Spectral Realm and climb back to the top as before. Go through the top gate and jump up to the beam, then to either the left or right of the platform. As the platform descends jump and float to the upper level. Move the blocks stacked on top of each other toward one of the corner blocks next to the gate. Jump on the corner block and push the top of the stack of blocks off. Flip the blocks over until the pattern matches the pattern on the wall. Insert both blocks into the gaps and the gate will open. Go up the slope and through the wooden door. Push the block off the ledge and jump down.

Pull the blocks out and drag them to the right hand side of the furthest right pillar. Jump up and go down the corridor. Go to the right and follow the ledge round. Go through the door and up the slope then pull the switch on wall. Go either left or right and continue until you reach a door. Go through and pull the switch on the near wall, then head to the far wall and turn the crank. Return to the elevator and pull the lever to lower the floor. Jump down to the lower level, go through the open entrance and head down the passageway. Drag the blocks in the large room until they set fire to beam, which will then collapse. Do this for each of the four blocks and the floor will the drop down. Drag each block along the tracks into the corner slots, you will hear a click once they are in the correct position. The floor will then drop again. Head down the passageway to meet Melchan. To defeat Melchan, jump up through the gap by the gate, pull the lever and wait for Melchan to pass

underneath. Release the switch to impale him. Repeat this at the other gate. Next head up towards the crank and wait for Melchan to cross the centre of the room. He will then get mangled when the crank is released.

Change to the Spectral Realm. Go towards the unopened gate and pass through. Head all the way back to where you entered the level. Change to spiritual mode and pass through the gate on the right. Fight the monsters and the door will open, here you shall meet Kain.

Kain fight.
Attack Kain quickly when he appears, eventually he will smash the blade.

Leave the pillars the way you entered and go through the gate. Return to the Portal. Activate it and go back to the training area. Take the path, as before, up the steps and you will come across a gate. Head through and continue along the passageway. Go over the bridge to the moat. Use Reaver to open the gate then switch to Spectral Realm. Pass through second gate, go right and change back to Material Realm. Turn back and go left through the double wooden gate. Next to the gate jump up to the ledge until you can see a passageway to your right. Jump across but do not go down this passageway. Instead jump to the roof on your left where a large jump will take you up to another ledge. From this ledge jump on to the roof. Look around and you will see a gap in the wall, jump across and head down the passageway.

Push open the large double gate and enter the cathedral. Change to spectral realm enabling you to climb up the far-left pipe. Press **L1** to crawl up the pipe. Once up shift back into the Material Realm, jump up on the next ledge and move around the room. Go past the wooden door and activate a switch. Jump onto the wooden platform then continue along the ledge to another wooden door. Go through and head downwards to a wooden gate. Change to Spectral Realm and pass through gate. Change back to Material Realm and manoeuvre the blocks into the holes matching the markings on the wall. Once this is done a platform will appear. Go back to the passageway you passed before the switch, go down and pull the switch. Go back, step on the second wooden platform, jump into the centre of the room, open your wings and float upwards. Go up the slope into a large room. Go through the wooden door on the right, head up the slope past the bell and go through the wooden door on the left. Continue until you reach a wooden gate. Change into Spectral Realm and pass through. Jump up to the ledge on the right and change back to Material Realm. Move the blocks to create a conduit. Head back past the bell, go through the wooden door and continue to a large gate. Change to spectral realm and pass through. Change back to Material Realm and push the blocks onto the floor. As with the previous puzzle, move them into the correct position. Return to the bell and ring it. Go back through the wooden door and turn down the passageway on the right. Ring another bell. When the window smashes, head back and turn the crank on the wall. A door will open. Change to spectral mode and freeze time. Head through where the window used to be then head across the room and down a sloping corridor. On the right is the entrance which opened. Find the portal and change back to material realm. Go back to the large wooden door, turn the knob and go though the passageway to the left of the door. Follow the pipe until you come to a large gate. Change to Spectral Realm, pass through, then change back to Material Realm. Head down either passageway and remove the lids. Return down the other passage to a similar room and remove the other lids. Head back through the gate and turn the four handles on the floor, which operate the fans. Jump into the air and float upwards and onto the yellow pipe. Push the raised pipe forming a link, repeat this on the other side. Go through the passageway at the top.

Turn the two handles on the floor to the right, this will open a passageway at the top of the room, You will need to return to this room later to defeat the level boss. Jump onto the platforms enabling you to enter the passageway at the top of the room. Pass through he gate at the end. Drop down into the room and change back to Material Realm. Turn the knob and return via the pipes to the top passageway. Go down towards the gate and pass through. Run up the pipes and continue down the next passageway. Jump down and you will come across some stacked blocks. Pull the bottom one out causing them to fall down. Drag the box to the yellow pipe with the wheel, jump up and turn the wheel. Next jump up and go through the next doorway. Move along the passageway into a room and jump onto the pipes. You will now need to push a raised pipe to create a link. Crawl up the pipe to the turn the wheel. Go back to the room with the three pipes, which should now be blowing air. Jump into the air stream and float up to the next ledge. Go down the passageway where you will find a warp gate to your right. Return back to the training level for instructions from the elder. Go back to the portal and return to fight Zephon.

Zephon fight
Move in close, wait for the leg to stick in the ground. Attack it to release an egg. Carry the egg to the flame, light it and throw it at Zephon. Do this 3 times to defeat him. Return to the pillars where your first battle with Kain took place. Scale up the column to the right with your new ability and walk around the ledge to the doorway. Continue down the passageway, go through either door then drop down into the courtyard. Head through the gap ignoring the large gate and head down the passageway.

To the left there is a passageway high up which leads to a warp gate. Continue through the gate in Spectral Realm. Go through the door, jump down and pull out the block in front of you.

Change to Spectral Realm and the floor will give way. Head towards the gate and pass through. Jump to the portal and change to Material Realm.

Morlock Mini Boss will appear. Jump across and attack him until he is weak enough to throw into the water. You will then get the Force Projectile. Shoot at the square in the wall, pushing the Morlock back. Enter the room and turn left. Drop down and head into the water. Follow the path straight ahead. This will lead you out of the water. Jump to the far side and crawl up the wall. Turn around and jump to the nearest pillar. Jump to the next pillar where you will see a block. Shoot a Projectile from the Reaver to knock the block off the top, then jump across to the staircase. Go through the door and head down the passageway to the right. Go through the fence and change to Material Realm. Use the Force Projectile to move the block back against the wall. Change to the Spectral Realm and pass through the gate. Jump onto the block, up to the higher passageway and glide down to the boat below. Jump to the top of the boat and change to Spectral Realm. Jump up to the ledge on the right and follow it until you reach two doors. Go through the one to the left and continue. Stand close to the door at the end of the passage and use the Soul Reaver to open.

Glide to the pillar on the right and follow them around until you reach a gap. Go through and open the wooden door. Follow the corridor and go across a circular floor. Head straight across and pass through two wooden gates. Jump from pillar to pillar across the water in the next room. Once you are safely across the water follow the passageway. Go through the wooden gate and continue until you enter the water. Carry on until you reach a chequered floor. Go to the right and you will see a ledge. Jump up, then up to the next ledge. You can then climb the wall to another ledge. About turn and jump across the beams to the passageway on the left. Use the Soul Reaver to shatter the glass. Jump across the ledges that stick out on the right of the circular building. Go to the right hand side and jump over to the bell tower. Ring the bell. You will see a staircase. Go down the steps then climb up to Rehab's room. Enter the circular room and change to the Spectral Realm. Jump up to the staircase and change back to the Material Realm. Rahab will appear in the water. Use the Reaver to smash all the windows. Once Rahab has been defeated you will have the ability to swim.

Return to the underwater room with the beams. Go to the circular building and open the door using the Reaver. Go down the staircase and turn left when you reach the bottom, following the wall. You will see three windows. Swim to the third one and you will see a staircase going down go through. Carry on swimming until you reach a large room, then continue on to another room where you will see some alcoves. Look for the one that leads out and follow it. Once you have reached the room where you met the first Vampire continue swimming up the stairs and turn left, this will take you out of the water. Return to the cliffs where the vortex is, this will let you enter the next area.

Dumanhim Clan Area

Go past the vortex and enter the water. Look for the ledge above and jump up. Follow the passageway until you find yourself out in the snow. Go through the archway and go towards the wall. Climb up the pillar to the top and jump across the canyon. Float to the wall on the opposite side and drop down into the courtyard. Go through the doors to the next courtyard, change to Spectral Realm and move through the gate. Next you will need to go to the Portal on the far side of the room. You will see a block in the middle of the fenced area, jump onto the block and to the ledge above. Change back to material realm. Float down to the passageway below, go left and continue until you see a block at the end. Pull this out so that it is next to the wall with the ledge above it. Jump up to the ledge, and then glide across the courtyard to the entrance on the other side. Continue down the passageway until you reach a room with two areas of water. Head towards the crank and turn it, this will empty the room of water. Go to the blocks and stack them on top of each other and climb up to the ledge. Go down the passageway to a large room with furnaces. Find the wheel on the wall and turn it, this will turn on the gas. Next, go to the opposite wall and turn the other wheel switch, this will turn on the fire.

Go to the passageway behind the fire and continue until you reach a stone block. Push this off the ledge and jump down. Put one block onto the other and drag them to the other side of the room. Jump onto the blocks and up to the ledge then continue down the next passageway. Change to Spectral Realm, which will change the form of the room. Jump up and follow the ledges until you come to the Portal Plane, then shift back to the Material Realm. Jump and float over to the switch and activate it. This will open the door at the bottom of the room. Jump down and go through the passageway. Go right when the passageway splits in two. Pull the block from the wall and drag it to the right next to the pillar with the fence around it. Jump over the fence using the block and flip the pillar over. This will break the gate leading to Dumah.

To defeat Dumah get him to follow you to the furnace and burn him, this will give you the ability to Constrict.

Once you have done this head back to Ash Village and climb up the front gate to the other side. Go to the left and continue until you reach a sundial. Run around the dial using the Constrict ability, which will open the doors. Go through the doors and continue down the passageway leading to a Warp Gate on the right. Carry on until you reach the large door. Change to Spectral Realm and the room will shift to reveal an opening to a room on the left. Go through to another sundial. Change back to Material Realm and use Constrict on the sundial, which will open the doors to the side. Go through the one on the right and change back to Spectral Realm. Pass through the gate and continue to the left of the next passageway until you see two blocks. Change back to Material Realm, pull out the block on the left and push it into the area to the right. Next pull out the other block and position it where the first block was.

Go back to the Sundial and go down the opposite passageway. Go back to Spectral Realm and pass through the gate. You will see the first block you removed from the wall and dropped down. Move it to the wall with the letter Z above it. Return to the place where the blocks first came from. Remove the second block from the position you left it, pull it out and place it in the hole with the letter O above it. A door with OZ will now open in the lower area. Return again to the room with the sundial. Constrict the sundial, then go through the door with OZ above. Go right then left and continue down the passageway until you reach a gate. Change to Spectral Realm and pass through. Continue until you reach the edge of the cliff jump and then head to the right. You will see a Portal Plane on the right. Go to it and shift back to the Material Realm. Go back to the cliff and head to the room with two stone blocks. Move the blocks in front of where they should go, then use the Soul Reaver to shoot the blocks back into their place.

Enter the next room, you will see a number 9 with four columns around it. Use Constrict around the pointers that will turn them to face the 9. This will then open the door with a 9 symbol. Drop down through the trap door. Go to the cauldron in the centre of the room and use Constrict. A door will then appear. Go down the passageway until you reach a room with a clock and two switches. Go to the switches and operate them. This will operate the hands on the clock. Move them until the time says 6 o'clock. Drop down to the room below where you will see four lenses and a reflector in the centre. Use Constrict so that the lenses match the area behind each. Turn the blue and red lens to blue then turn the red and green lens to green. When you see two lenses next to each other, turn the red and blue one to make purple. Constrict the central light to each lens to open the door. Go through and continue until you reach another set of doors. Go through into the next room with a clock on the floor with three knobs. Look at the symbols on the wall and you will see they match the ones on the floor. Constrict each knob to turn the hands on the clock until they match the markings on the floor. Once you have done this an exit will open.

Go down this passage and you will reach a room with a stone block and some large gears. Go to the block and lift it. The gears will then start turning. Go to the pillar and jump up. Change to Spectral Real and the room will shift causing the pillar to move to the edge of the room. Go to the Portal Plane and change back to the Material Realm. Continue along the ledge until you reach a pendulum. Jump onto it and when it swings to the door jump off. Go down the next passageway until you reach the fence on the right. Use the Soul Reaver to force the stone block back on the other side of the fence where it will drop down. Next go down the passageway until you reach another fence. Once again use the Soul Reaver to push another block past the fence until it drops down. Carry on until you reach another room with four blocks. Arrange these to form the correct pattern, which matches the one on the floor. A door will then open. Go through and continue until you reach a hole. Jump down and head to a large area that has three other rooms. You will see in each room incomplete symbols and a knob next to each one. Constrict each knob, then turn it until it completes the symbol. Do this in each room. Once you have done this jump onto the platform that appeared when the symbols were completed. Swing over to the switches and activate them all. This will open a door in the main passage and Kain will appear.
Use the Soul Reaver Projectile at Kain when he is on the lower level. Hit him and he will appear on the next level. Do this until he reaches the top level then follow Kain into the star portal and move to the area with Mobius. Watch the ending.

SOUTH PARK

Master cheat:
Enter ZBOBBYBIRD to unlock all codes (all multi-player characters, invincibility, unlimited ammunition, all weapons, and level select).

Chef in multi-player mode:	**YLOVEMACHINE**
Wendy in multi-player mode:	**BCHECKATACO**
Terrence in multi-player mode:	**SRAFT**
Phillip in multi-player mode:	**PPHAERT**
Ned in multi-player mode:	**JHAWKING**
Mr. Macky in multi-player mode:	**ACHEATINGSBAD**
Officer Barbrady in multi-player mode:	**DELVISLIVES**
Big Gay Al in multi-player mode:	**GOUTRANGE**
Starvin Marvin in multi-player mode:	**MSLAPUPMEAL**
Mr. Garrison in multi-player mode:	VDOROTHYSFRIEND
Pip in multi-player mode:	EFISHNCHIPS
Jimbo in multi-player mode:	QSTARINGFROG
Ike in multi-player mode:	HKICKME
Ms. Cartman in multi-player mode:	KALLWOMAN
Mephisto in multi-player mode:	NGOODSCIENCE
Alien Visitor in multi-player mode:	TMAJESTIC

SOUTH PARK RALLY

Cheat Mode
Complete championship mode without using a token to unlock all tracks, cars, skins and cheat options.

SOVIET STRIKE

Level Codes
Use the following codes at the password screen:
Level 1: WORSTCASE
Level 2: GRANDTHEFT
Level 3: GROZNEY
Level 4: CHERNOBYL
Level 5: CIVILWAR

You can start Campaign 4 with five lives by entering the password NOSFERATU.

The following passwords can be entered after inputting a level code. You can use them all at once if you wish:

CODE	ACTION
VULTURE	Double mileage (slow fuel depletion).
QUAKER	Enemies don't fire at you.
GHANDI	Helicopter is viewed as friendly.
FUGAZI	Infinite ammo, fuel, and lives.
THEBIGBOYS	Infinite ammo, fuel, and double damage.
MIDNIGHOIL	Infinite ammo, fuel, and invincibility.
ELVISLIVES	Infinite choppers.
DAVEDITHER	More powerful weapons.
ANGRYLOCAL	Soldiers and hostages crowd the chopper.
STRANGELUV	Unlimited ammo.
IAMWOMAN	Unlimited armour.
MOUNTANDEW	Unlimited fuel.
EARTHFIRST	Unlimited fuel.

SPACE HULK

Cheat Menu
Walk the path of the Emperor. For a full cheat menu hold down L1 and press ✖, ■, ➜, ✖, ▲, ✖, ↓, ✖, ■, ➜, ✖.

SPACE JAM

Extra Options
To receive more options go to the options screen and highlight

"Game Options" (do not click on it). Next hold **L1, R1, L2, R2, ↑** and hold **✖**.

SPAWN

Level Skip
Pause the game, hold **L1 + L2 + R1 + R2** and press **▲, ✖, ▇, ●, ●, ●.**

Shield
Pause the game, hold **L1 + R1** and press **▲, ▲, ✖, ✖, ▇, ●.**

Power Ups
Pause the game, hold **L2 + R2** and press **▲, ●, ▇, ✖, ▲, ✖.**

Every Item
Pause the game, hold **L2 + R2** and press **✖, ▇, ●, ▲, ▇, ●.**

Invisibility
Pause the game, hold **L1 + R1** and press **▇, ▇, ●, ●, ▲, ✖.**

Reset Energy
Pause the game, hold **L1 + R1** and press **✖, ●, ▲, ▇, ✖, ●.**

Reset Magic
Pause the game, hold **L1 + R1** and press **▲, ●, ✖, ▇, ▲, ●.**

Energy Restore
Press **L1 + L2** during play to restore your energy, you must first activate the power up cheat.

Todd McFarlane Interview
If you want to listen to an interview with Spawn's creator, listen to track 16 on an CD player or through the audio menu on your Playstation.

SPEED FREAKS

Race as Cosworth
Beat the EASY tournament coming first in every race. Then beat Cosworth on millenium park.

Race as Tetsuo
Beat the MEDIUM tournament coming first in every race. Then beat him on the city course withmasses of turbo pads.

Race as Beamer
Beat the HARD tournament coming first in every race.

SPEEDSTER

Go to the Speedster screen with the message 'PRESS A KEY' to enter the following codes:

CODE	ACTION
L1, R1, L1, ▇, R1, ↑	Heavy Metal Cars.
✖, ↑, ▲, ↓, R1, L1	Hidden track.
↑, ←, →, ✖, ●, ▇	Performance cars.
←, ▲, R1, ●, L1, ↓	Reverse tracks.
→, ▇, ←, ●, ↑, ✖	Super Championship.

SPICE WORLD

Giant Spice
At the menu screen where your character walks across the globe hold the **Start** button and press **●, ▇, ●, ▇.** Your code will appear on the screen to confirm it and your character will be blown up to giant size.

Handbag Code
At the "globe" menu, hold the **Start** button and press **▇, ▲, ●, ▲.** With that code on the screen, enter the television studio with your "act" prepared. Instead of standing in a line, the Girls will be crowded around a pile of handbags on the floor.

Hidden Messages
At the screen where your character walks across the globe, hold the **Start** button and press **●, ▲, ▲, ●.** You will see the code on the screen to confirm. Now hold **Start+Select** and press **●, ●, ●, ●.** Also try **▲, ▲, ▲, ▲** and **▇, ▇, ▇, ▇.**

Naked Spice
First, enter the first part of the "Hidden Messages" code as described. Then, press **L1 + L2 + R1 + R2 + Select + Start** simultaneously to reset the game.

Alternative Title Screen
At the global screen hold **Start** and press **●, ▲, ▲, ●.** Release **Start** and press **L1, L1, R1, R2** and **Select.**

SPIDER

Recharge Weapons and Energy
Pause the game and enter the following:
▲, ✖, ✖, ✖, ●, ✖, ▇, ▲, ✖, ▲, ●

Shrink
Pause the game and enter the following:
▲, ▇, ●, ▲

Passwords	CODE
Laboratory	
Lab Floor	1FMLC939GPR8F3BF7KT1
Sinks	CHMLC939GPR8F3LWGTS3
Lab Top	86MLC939GPR8F3VFQ5S4
Seventies Room	FW1MC939GPR8F3BF7KT1
Factory	
Boxes	FW1MC939GPR8F36DTTS3

Conveyors	BSRMC939GPR8F3VTKKT1
Machine Room	WDRQC939GPR8F3LM8S95
Tubes	8WV5L939GPR8F36DTTS3
Mechanical Arm Boss	8WV5L939GPR8F3G10JB4

City

Up The Street	9WV5L939GPR8F3LRT6S4
Side Of Building	6SXXS939GPR8F3LRT6S4
Park	W9PNT839GPR8F3B9LVS3
Under The Street	N7KB3Y19GPR8F3V95HR5
Along The Street	N7KB3Y19GPR8F3GGK4T3

Museum

Display Cases	P7KB3Y19GPR8F3BPFGC3
Volcano	G7KB3Y11GPR8F3BPFGC3
Dinosaur Bones	H7KB3Y1QFPR8F3QXSDS4
Model City	J7KB3Y1GWPR8F31766D1
Temple	K7KB3Y1B15S8F3QXSDS4
Museum Boss	K7KB3Y1B15S8F3BTQBB4

Sewer

Wells	V7KB3Y1B15S8F3QS7QC1
Along The Sewer	W7KB3Y1VBVP8F3LC1M95
Food Carton	X7KB3Y1VLN7BF31CH1C3
Up The Well	Y7KB3Y1VV16QF3QS7QC1
Ryan's World	Q7KB3Y1LDRTQD3VKCDT1

Evil Lab

Circuit Boards	Q7KB3Y1LDRTQD3LCQSR3
Lab Top	R7KB3Y118H56T1WTY4R4
Hard Drives	S7KB3Y118H56T1TCQSR3
Brian's Folly	T7KB3Y118H56T1FNY4R4
On The Ceiling	T7KB3Y118H56T1TC4LD1
Kip's Bonus	68KB3Y118H56T151P6C4
Brain Boss	68KB3Y118H56T1TMVM35

SPIDERMAN

All Cheats
Go to the password screen and enter **EEL_NATS** to unlock all the comics, costumes, levels etc.

More Cheats
Enter these via the cheats menu:

Big Head Mode	**DULUX**
Level Select	**XCLSIOR**
Unlimited Webbing	**STRUDL**
Unlock Joel Jewett	**RULUR**

SPOT GOES TO HOLLYWOOD

Access To All Levels
To have access to all levels, go to the title screen and press the following to bring up the new Cool option: ▲, ↑, →, ↓, ←, ▲, ←, ↓, →, ↑, ▲. When you select this option it will give you access to the levels.

Infinite Lives
You can gain infinite lives by entering the Access To All Levels code above, and then starting a continued game. Next press pause along with ✖ and ■.

SPYRO THE DRAGON

Level Select
During the game, press **Select**, enter the inventory screen and press ■, ■, ●, ■, ←, →, ←, →, ●, ↑, →, ↓.

99 Lives
During the game, enter the inventory and quickly press ■ **x6**, ●, ↑, ●, ←, ●, →, ●. Return to the game and your lives will start to increase to a maximum of 99.

Open All Worlds
Go to the inventory and quickly press ■, ■, ●, ■, ←, →, ←, →, ●, ↑, →, ↓. Then go to the balloonist to access the world menu.

STARBLADE ALPHA

Rapid Fire
At the Title screen press ↑, ↑, ↓, ↓, ●, ▲, ■.

Infinite Continues
Fame! I wanna live forever! On the Title screen press ↑, →, ↓, ←, ✖, ✖, ✖.

STARFIGHTER 3000

Crystal Awards
Use the following crystal combinations to build up your ships fire power:

Beam Laser x 250	Magenta, Green, Magenta, Green
Bonus Wingpod	Green, Yellow, Green
Bonus Wingpod x 2	Cyan, Red, Cyan, Red
Bonus ATG x 10	Blue, Blue
Bonus ATA x 10	Magenta, Magenta
Control Damaged	Magenta, Green, Blue
Control Upgrade	Red, Yellow
ECM x 50	Cyan, Green, Cyan, Blue
Engine Damaged	Magenta, Red, Blue
Engine Upgrade	Blue, Yellow
Fast Adder Crystals	Star, Star, Star, Star
Laser Upgrade	Red, Red
Mega-Bomb x 15	Magenta, Red, Magenta, Red
Mega Ship (limited time)	Star, Star, Star, Red
Mines x 10	Magenta, Orange, Magenta, Orange
Multi-Missile x 10	Magenta, Blue, Magenta, Blue
Multi-Missile x 5	Cyan, Yellow

Shield Damaged   Magenta, Yellow, Blue
Shields Upgrade   Yellow, Yellow

Enter Cheat Mode

To gain access to various cheats, go to the 'Enter Name' screen and enter the following: **COFFEE N PICKLE**. You will see the words 'Cheat Now' at the bottom, the next time that you go to this screen.

Hidden Bonuses

Make the invisible secret bonuses visible, by entering **SHOW ME** at the 'Enter Name' screen.

Mission Select

To select any mission, enter the cheat mode as described, then enter **ROGER THE CAT** at the 'Enter Name' screen.

Pyramid Select

To have a new option on the main options screen that allows you to switch between the different 'pyramids' of mission, go to the 'Enter Name' screen and enter **WAG**.

Super Ship

To load your ship with all sorts of powerful weapons, enter **DANIEL DEFOE** at the 'Enter Name' screen.

STAR GLADIATOR

Big Head Mode

To give your character a big head, after selecting him hold ➡, **Start**, ●, ■. Do not release them until the game has begun.

Fight As Bilstein

In one-player mode, go to the character select screen, go to Hayato and then hold **Select**. Next go to Gore and press the following sequence: ✖, ●, ✖, ●, ■, ■, ■, ▲, ▲, ▲, ✖, ●. Now Bilstein should appear on the right of Gore, and the cheat can from now on be accessed in two-player mode also.

Fight As Blood

To add Blood to the selectable characters, you must first carry out the Bilstein and Kappah cheats. Next go to the character select screen and Bilstein. Hold **Select** while you enter the following sequence: ✖, ■, ✖, ■, ✖, ■. Now go to Kappah (you must not highlight any other character on the way) and press ●, ▲, ●, ▲, ●, ▲, then press **L1** and **R1**.

Fight As Kappah

This must be performed in one-player mode, and the first thing that you need to do is carry out the Bilstein cheat. Then go to the character select screen, go to Bilstein and hold **Select**. Next go to Hayato and press the following: ●, ■, ▲, ■, ✖, ■, ▲, ■, ●, ■, ✖, ▲. Now Kappah should appear on the Left of Hayato. From now on you can also access the

character in two-player mode.

Fighting In The Dark

To fight your opponent in the dark, select a character and then hold ⬇, **L2**, and **R2** until the fight starts.

Invisible Walls

To turn the invisible walls on or off, win a game on any skill level and then go to the options screen. You will see that there is now a new option.

Shrunken Head Mode

For a shrunken head, select your character and then hold ⬅, **Start**, ●, ■. Again you must hold them until the game starts.

Super Bilstein

To fight against Super Bilstein who is bigger than the original Bilstein, set all options to default, and complete the game in six minutes or less. You will find that when you fight Super Bilstein, the stage will be different also.

STAR WARS EPISODE ONE: PHANTOM MENACE

Trade Federation Droid Control Ship

After speaking with Qui Gon Jinn, TC14 a federation protocol droid will enter the room. At this point the room will begin to fill with gas. Head straight out through the blast door and you will be confronted by five Federation Battle Droids. Ignite your lightsaber and deflect their laser blasts back at them. Enter the room on the right and press the switch located near the Gonk droid to reveal a blaster. Return to the hallway and head into the room opposite. Press the switch to reveal a thermal detonator and enter the small circular room for full health. Return to the hall and continue forward. Enter the small circular room on the right and press the switch to open the blast doors. Press the switch on the left to reveal another full health power up. Head right down the hall destroying the battle droids as you go. At the blast door, enter the control room on the right and press the switch. The wall opposite will lower revealing another battle droid and a switch. Pressing the switch will open the blast door. Before you can reach the Viceroy, the blast door leading to the control room will shut tight and you will encounter a number of Destroyer Droids. At this point you are no match for this heavy armed and shielded droids and have no choice but to run. Head right down the hall and head through the opening on the left. As you run along the gantry you will slide down to the airshaft below. Follow the airshaft past the destroyed Republic Cruiser and you will find yourself in an area with three maintenance droids. Attack from the rear to avoid being electrocuted. Press the switch in the top right to open the door on the right. Destroy the droid which appears from behind the door, then press the switch found inside. Quickly make your way to the door in the top left before it closes.

The left path leads to a full health power up, but is guarded by three Battle Droids. You can return to this room once you reach the hangar. Head right and drop back into the main hallway. There are two Battle Droids ahead and three appear from the right blast door. If you wait, the centre blast door will open but reveals nothing more than several Battle Droids. To open the left blast door you will need to cut the power. Head through the right blast door and ride the elevator down. Destroy the four Battle Droids you encounter before activating the switch and lowering the wall behind. Ignore the Neimoidian and enter the small circular room. Inside destroy the power generator. Return via the elevator to the intersection and head through the door opposite. You will find yourself in a hangar. Destroy the Battle Droid on the right and collect the small health power up found above. The droid fighter will take off and flee if you move in and attack. Ride the elevator up and destroy the lone droid. The blast door returns you back to the end of the airshafts where there is a full health power up guarded by three Battle Droids. Head through the opening opposite the elevator and continue forward.

You will briefly be reunited with Qui Gon. Follow the gantry forward and you will find an elevator but with no switch to activate it. Head right and press the switch located on the left. Continue to the right and press a second switch. Once the gantry has moved, you will have access to a third switch. Press the switch and wait for the gantry to move back to the first switch. Once you have pressed the first switch again you can return to the elevator and activate the switch to ride down. Destroy the Battle Droid and head down the right gantry. Continue forward and a platform will rise from below containing three Battle Droids. Continue along the gantry. Once you reach the two platforms, destroy the two Battle Droids on the right before riding the left platform down onto the drop ship.

Naboo Swamp

Jump into the water and swim forward avoiding the rocket blasts until you reach the shore. Destroy the five Battle Droids you confront and collect the blaster rifle. Jump into the water and swim to the left. Pull yourself from the water and head left up the slope. Here you will meet Jar Jar Binks, an exiled Gungan. When the Battle Droids attack, head right and slide down into the swamp. Swim to the left and destroy the Battle Droid. There are two routes from here. Crossing the log is a quicker route but you will encounter eight Battles Droids and have to avoid falling trees. Jumping through the bushes towards Jar Jar is a safer but slower route. Push the log up to the cliff and use it to reach Jar Jar. Follow Jar Jar across the logs avoiding the blaster fire from the Battle Droids. Climb up the ledge and drop to the swamp floor on the left. Continue to follow Jar Jar destroying the six Battle Droids as you go. Drop down and collect the small health power up on the right. Continue to follow Jar Jar avoiding the two legged chicken creatures. When you drop into the water, head right around the large tree to reveal a full health power up. Return to the water and head left. Destroy the Battle Droids and jump up the ledges

to the top. Head forward avoiding the falling trees then left. Collect the small health power up from the rock. Head right. Jump from ledge to ledge across the swamp. Follow the path to the right and jump from the log to the opposite ledge. Speak to Jar Jar.

Ask Jar Jar
'Who are you?'
'Have you seen anyone like me?'
'Can you show me where he is'
Jump up to the vine above and shimmy across the gap avoiding the Battle Droid riding the Staps. Drop down to Jar Jar and follow him through the chasm. To reach the other side, push the log into the ditch and use it to climb the other side. Jump to the vine and shimmy to the right until you reach the ledge. As you and Jar Jar enter the clearing, activate the laser cannon and destroy all the Battle Droids. Avoid hitting the crates or you will activate Destroyer Droids. Once it is safe to continue, follow Jar Jar down the path to be reunited with Qui Gon Jinn.

Otoh Gunga

Head through the tunnel until you reach Qui Gon Jinn. After speaking with Boss Nass, talk to Qui Gon.
Ask Qui Gon
'What about Boss Nass and the Gungans'.
Answer
'I'll find him Master'.
Head back to the previous chamber. The left tunnel leads to 3 Gungan energy balls. Speak to the Gungan standing next to the fish tank.
Ask the Gungan
'What has become of Jar Jar'
'Can you show me where to find him?'

When you have finished, head right and ride the bubble lift down. Head down the tunnel on the right. To get past the Gungan guards use your force push to knock them off their feet. In the next chamber, head down the left tunnel. Use force push to pass the Gungan Guard. Before you can reach Jar Jar, his bubble lift descends. Talk to the Gungan near the lift.
Ask the Gungan
'What has become of Jar Jar'
'Is there another way to reach the detention area?'
'Can you help me'

The Gungan will give you a pass. Head through the next tunnel. In the large chamber, wait until both pillars rise, then use them to reach the opposite ledge. Use force push to clear a path through the two guards. Enter the bubble lift at the end of the tunnel. Leave the bubble lift and follow the tunnel to the water filled chamber. You will need to jump from pillar to pillar to reach the opposite side. You will need to be quick because the pillars will lower into the water once you have stepped on them. Follow the tunnel into the long chamber and avoid the Gungan Guards as you make your way through the room. Collect the Gungan energy balls from the left and right bubbles, then head into the bubble lift at the end of the tunnel. Head down the left tunnel. In the large chamber, press the switch then quickly run up the balcony and down the tunnel before the door closes. Talk to the Gungan Guard.

Ask the Gungan
'I need to find the detention area'
Answer
'I have the security key'
'<I must be very important if I have a passcard>'

The Gungan Guard will then open the door. Head down the left tunnel. The switch which opens the door on the right is found beneath the glass panel on the floor. Stand just outside the doorway to lower one of the pillars, then push the block so you can reach the switch. Press the switch to lower another pillar. Continue until you have lowered all four pillars and pressed all four switches. The floor panel will slide away allowing you to activate the floor switch. Return back to the chamber and head into the tunnel opposite. Drop to the floor and move the block so you can reach the switch. Activate the switch, climb up onto the pillar and jump to the ledge. Talk to the Gungan at the control panel.

Ask the Gungan
'What are you doing with those controls?'
'Can you raise the bubble lifts for me?'
The Gungan will open the bubble lift which leads to the detention area. Head through the right tunnel and enter the bubble lift. Use force push to move the Gungan Guard. Take the left tunnel down to the detention block . Talk to the Gungan at the control panel.
Ask him,
'I'm here for Jar Jar Binks!'
Answer
'<It is dangerous to have Jar Jar here, I will take him away>'
The Gungan will allow you to take Jar Jar with you. Descend the stairs and talk to Jar Jar.
Tell Jar Jar
'Boss Nass will provide us with a bongo which we will use to reach Theed and warn the Naboo. You must help us navigate'
Finish with
'Let's get going!'
Follow Jar Jar to the bubble lift. Leave the bubble lift and you will rejoin Qui Gon Jinn at the Bongo.

Theed

When you begin, the bridge leading directly to the palace will be destroyed by a Federation AAT and you will be seperated from Qui Gin and Jar Jar. Run and jump to the centre pillar. From here jump from pillar until you reach the stone ledge on the left. If you fall, swim against the current to the shore in the top right corner. Then climb the steps to the higher pool. Jump into the water and swim to the stone ledge in the top

left corner of the pool. Avoid the large fishes as you go. Follow the path up the steps, then jump from pillar to pillar across the waterfall. Use force push to move the lever and extend the bridge. You will need to destroy two Battle Droids as you ascend the steps. There are three Battle Droids in the clearing on the left. Once you have secured the area, use force push to move the lever to the left of the force field. As you jump across the gap, be wary of the Battle Droid who ascends the steps opposite. Collect the small health power up on the left. Descend the stairs and follow the path round to the left. You will come across a small band of Naboo Royal Guards under attack from a group of Battle Droids. Destroy the attacking group of Battle Droids then head back and up the stairs on the right. Speak to the Naboo Soldier.
Ask the Naboo Soldier
'I must find the Queen, She's in grave danger!'
'I need to reach the palace. Can you tell me the fastest route?'
Answer with
'The bridge is gone!'
Reply with
'The force has shown me the way. I must brave the garden!'
The guard will give you a light repeater. Return down the stairs and follow the path to the left. You will find yourself on the outskirts of the city gardens. Descend the steps and head to the left, destroying any Battle Droids you encounter. Follow the path through the grassy area collecting the small health power up as you go. Cross the path and head into the second grassy area. To the left you will find a wounded Royal Guard and a light repeater. First clear the area of any roaming Battle Droids then talk to the Guard.
Tell the Guard
'I am a Jedi searching for the Queen'
Ask him
'Tell me how to get into the city'
'Do you know the pass code?'
The Guard will tell you the pass code to get past the garden gate leading into the city.
Finally ask
'Can I help'

Head left through the grassy area. Wait until the AAT patrols to the far left, then run and jump over the balcony opposite. Destroy the two Battle Droids, then collect the small health power up. Make your way around the AAT and head down the path to the left. You will encounter two Battle Droids at the intersection. Continue left and through the grassy area. The lower right path leads to a small health power up. Cross over to the next grassy area. Avoid hitting the crates while you fight the Battle Droids or you will activate Destroyer Droids. Make your way through the grassy area to the path beyond. Collect the small health power up near the rubble. Follow the path around to the right. Take down the three Battle Droids guarding the crates again avoiding destroying the crates. There is a Battle Droid to the left and two in the top right corner. Head down the path to the left and you will find a Naboo Soldier trying to get through a locked gate. Talk to the Naboo Soldier.

Answer his question with
'Try J-154'

The Naboo Soldier will input the correct pass code and unlock the gate. Follow the Naboo Soldier down the street. He will lead you to a group of Naboo Guards surrounding a damaged Droid fighter. When you move closer to the group the fighter will explode killing the Naboo and injuring you. Collect the full health power up from the rubble then return to the street. Head left down the street and up the steps to your left, destroying the Battle Droid as you go. Press the switch you find at the top, this will raise the water level below enabling you to swim to the opposite side. Jump into the water and swim to the left. Ignore the path on the right and climb the steps. Pressing the switch lowers the water enabling you to activate the switch at the base of the waterfall. Once you press this switch, a bridge behind you will extend. Head up the steps and take the right path. Continue right ignoring the extended bridge for now. Head into the courtyard and destroy the lone Battle Droid. Press the switch on the right and open the blast door on the balcony above.

Head back down the path and cross the bridge. Use force push to move the switch, extending the bridge. Head up the steps and climb through the open window on the right. Collect the thermal detonator and head out onto the balcony. Jump up and grab the wire above and shimmy to the opposite balcony. Collect proton missile launcher and the small health power up. Either jump down into the courtyard below returning back across the bridge or use the wire to shimmy back across to the opposite balcony. Avoid the mines as you head up the steps to the left. Head right avoiding the incoming fire from the AAT. Climb through the window on the right. Destroying the Battle Droid found in the next room and collect the full health power up. Return outside and use the window ledges to the right of the large steps to reach the room at the top. Pull the lever and the first palace gate will open. Return outside and climb up on the pillar on the left of the large steps. Use force push to move the lever on the balcony opposite. The second and final palace gate will open. Head up the large steps and enter the palace.

The Royal Palace
From an attack by the Droid army both Obi Wan and Queen Amidala are separated from Qui Gon and the royal entourage. Quickly follow the Queen Amidala. Head down the steps and destroy the Battle Droid. Continue around to the right and destroy the droid which descends the stairs. Go down the steps into the garden. Push the block in the top right corner to reveal the hidden stairs. Head up the stairs and follow the balcony to the right. Stop at the closed door. A Battle Droid will appear from the left. Deflect its shots back at it. Run and jump across the gap to the opposite balcony. Drop to the balcony below and collect the proton missile launcher. Jump back up and head through the open phwindow. Press the switch and open the door. Collect the blaster and the small health

power up. Exit through the door and head down the steps. Destroy the droid which appears from the room at the base of the steps, the two Battle Droids on the left and the group which appears from the right. Queen Amidala will stay at the steps. Return up the steps and enter the room on the left. Talk to the distressed woman.

Ask the woman
'What tragedy has befallen you?'
Answer with
'Don't worry. I promise that you will have your son back soon!'
Return outside and head down the left street. Enter through the door on the right. Inside you will find a small boy.
Tell the boy
'Don't be afraid. Are you lost?'
Ask
'How can I help?'
Answer with
'Your mother is waiting for you. Go to her. You are safe now'.

Jump up to balcony and collect the full health power up from behind the screen. Return outside. Jump up to the ledge on the right and enter the room. Destroy the Battle Droid you will find inside and collect the light repeater. Quickly head back to Queen Amidala and defend her from a group of Battle Droids which appear from the right path. Once the area is clear, head down the right path. When you reach the courtyard, clear the area of Battle Droids while avoiding fire from the AAT. Return back to the path leading back to Queen Amidala and jump over the small wall. Follow the path around and up the stairs and you will find yourself in a room containing a water flask, a Naboo Fusion Coil and a shield. At this point Queen Amidala will come under attack. Race back the way you came back to her. Once she is safe, head back to the courtyard with the AAT. Head down the left side of the courtyard, safe from the AAT. Head up the steps in the top left corner of the courtyard. Follow the path around to the left destroying any Battle Droids you encounter. Talk to the wounded Naboo soldier you come across.

Tell the soldier.
'I am in an urgent mission, but Jedi are sworn to protect the innocent. How can I help you'.
Answer his plea with.
'Here take some water'.
Ask him
'Is there a way past the tank?'

Leave the guard and head across the balcony. Destroy the Battle Droid who appears from the door in front of you. Inside you will find a small health power up. Race across the balcony and through the open window. Destroy the Battle Droid found inside. Head through the left door and down the hall. Destroy the Battle Droid then collect the blaster from the room on the right. Head down the hall to the left and exit through the door in the top right of the room. Turn to your left and climb through the window. Inside, collect the light repeater and collect the full health power up by pressing the switch. Return back through the window you came in from. Head down the steps and you will find yourself behind the AAT. Leave the Battle Droid repairing the AAT and press the switch. The blast door in the courtyard will now be open. Head up the steps to the left and follow the path round. Head down the stairs and release the prisoner. After a short conversation he will give you a thermal detonator. Head back up the stairs and return back around to the top of the steps. Jump over the balcony down into the courtyard. Head up to the intersection and deflect the laser bolts back at the Battle Droid in the window. Return through the open blast door to the right back to Queen Amidala.

Ask Queen Amidala

'Follow me!'

Head to the left side of the courtyard and speak to Queen Amidala again.

Tell her

'The gate is open. We must go now!'

Run across the courtyard through the open blast doors. Queen Amidala will wait at the bottom of the steps just beyond the blast door. Further down the street are a group of Battle Droids and a heavy repeater. If you attack them, you will trigger extra Destroyer Droids. Speak to Queen Amidala.

Answer her with

'Let's go!'

Run up the steps and race past Queen Amidala. If you are fast enough she will stop on the balcony and not follow you into the blue lit room. It is crucial that she does not follow you further as you have to face a number of Destroyer Droids. Press the switch to reveal a full health power up and collect the proton missile launcher. Wait at the top of the steps until the Destroyer Droid rolls out of view. Equip the proton missile launcher and head down the steps. Wait until the Destroyer Droid rolls into view and fire a proton missile directly at it. It can take up to three missiles to take out a Destroyer Droid. Head down to the lower path and wait for a second Destroyer Droid to appear. Again wait for it to roll directly into your line of sight before firing proton missile against it. Go around to the right and then left down the street. Head across the street and up the stairs on the right. Head through the door on the left. Talk to the old women you find inside.

Tell the old woman.
'Don't be afraid. I've come to help!'
Ask her
'Do you know where I can find the controls for the gate?'
Finish with
'Thank you'.

Collect the full health power up, then exit through the window. Run and jump over to the opposite roof. Head through the glass doors. Inside head left down the hall. Destroy Battle Droid then press the switch in the top right corner to open the gate. Head

down the stairs and press the switch to the left of the door. Head outside. Return back to Queen Amidala. Escort Queen Amidala down the street and through the gate. Head left down the street. Destroy the mines using your thermal detonators. You will encounter a lone Battle Droid. A second droid will appear from the door on the right. When you reach the river, jump over the raised section of the bridge and cross over to the barge. Go through the door and up the stairs to the balcony. Use your force power to activate the lever on the opposite side of the street. The raised section of the bridge will lower allowing Queen Amidala to cross. Return to Queen Amidala and escort her across the bridge to the courtyard. Once there you will find yourself surrounded. Head back down the slope and take out the four Battle Droids which move in from behind you. Return to Queen Amidala and jump to the balcony above. Head to the end of the balcony and you will find yourself behind the heavy repeater. Drop to the street and destroy the Battle Droids roaming around the heavy repeater and the two droids that appear from the left. Attacking the Battle Droid operating the heavy repeater alerts a Destroyer Droid. Quickly destroy the droid and take control of the heavy repeater, ready to fire as a Destroyer Droid rolls around the corner. Return to Queen Amidala's side and protect her from any roaming Battle Droids. From the courtyard head left down the street. Head into the room on the right and talk to the Naboo citizen inside.

Reply with
'Your insight serves you well. I must see her safely to the hangar'.
Ask
'We would greatly appreciate any help you could provide!'
He will unlock the storage room next door. Head into the storage room and collect the full health power up and the Remote Droid. The Remote Droid will wait outside for you to collect it. Leave Queen Amidala and continue down the street. To the right will be a group of Naboo Soldiers. Talk to the nearest soldier.
Tell the Naboo Soldier
'I'm a Jedi in the service of the Republic. I am trying to deliver the Queen safely to the hangar.'
End with
'Thank you'.
The Naboo Soldiers will cause a diversion. Destroy the group of Battle Droids between Queen Amidala and the hangar. Avoid roaming over to the right or you will stumble into two Destroyer Droids. Return to Queen Amidala.
Reply to her question with
'Let's go!'
Lead Queen Amidala to the hangar. Head through the hangar door and destroyer the three Battle Droids which attack as you enter. The hangar will now be safe for Queen Amidala to enter. Return back to Queen Amidala.
Explain to her
'Lets try to reach your ship'.
Head to the far end of the hangar and you will be met by Qui

Gon, Captain Panaka and the Queen's Handmaidens.

Mos Espa

You will need to find a T-14 hyperdrive generator so that the Queen's royal star ship can be repaired and she can be taken to Coruscant. After speaking with Obi Wan, lead Jar Jar and Padme along the path and through the canyon. As you pass through the canyon you will be attacked by a group of Tusken Raiders. Several of the Tusken Raiders are armed with projectile weapons that cannot be deflected using your lightsaber. Once through the canyon you will find yourself on the outskirts of Mos Espa. Deactivate your lightsaber before entering the spaceport or you will find the local inhabitants will become hostile and attack you. Padme will ask you to find the T-14 hyperdrive generator while she and jar jar collect supplies. Your main objective is to find Anakin Skywalker who will take you to Watto a local junk dealer, but there are various sub quests you can complete to receive certain objects.

The Scrap Merchant
If you are after some extra health and information head down the main street and turn down the second street on the right. Opposite the first corner you will find a scrap merchant. Speak to him.
Ask the merchant
'I'm looking for a T-14 hyperdrive generator'.
He will tell you that the only person who may have a hyperdrive generator is a junk dealer named Watto.
'Tell me how I can find Watto'.
The merchant will tell you to find Watto's servant, a young boy named Anakin.
'Where is Anakin?'
Offer the merchant
'Here are ten credits'.
Use your Jedi mind powers
'<You'll tell me where I can find him>'
'Go ahead, I'm listening'.
The merchant will tell you Anakin lives in the slave quarters, located at the end of the street.
Ask the merchant
'Do you have anything else for sale?'
He will tell you about his Podracer
'Can you show me the Podracer?'
Follow the merchant into his backyard. There is a full health power up in the corner of the yard.

Rescuing Tomo
Head to the end of the main street. You will find a Hammer Head dressed in red sat at the base of a set of stairs. Talk to the Hammer Head.
Ask him
'What can I do to help you?'
The Hammer Head will explain that his son has been imprisoned by one Captain Neg.
'I will speak with this Captain Neg'.
Head up the stairs and walk up to the door. A model DX5 droid

will appear.
'I would like to speak with Captain Neg'.
Continue with
'I'm here for the child called Tomo'.
With no luck finish with
'Never mind'.
Unable to enter through the main entrance you will have to find another way into the building. Head down the main street and turn down the alley on the right. Go up the stairs on the right and into the room at the top. Make your way through the room and out onto the ledge. Head around the ledge until you reach the wire. Jump up and grab the wire. Shimmy along to the opposite ledge. Inside the room, listen to what the blue Twi'lek tells you, then head up the stairs. If you collect the blaster you will activate a drone gun. Head out onto ledge and around to the wire. As soon as you try to shimmy across the wire a thug will appear from a side entrance to Captain Neg's home and begin firing at you. Drop to the ground and dispose of him. Remember to quickly deactivate your lightsaber before continuing.

Return back up to the wire and shimmy across to the balcony. Collect the full health power up only if you really need it. Rush the Rodian at the top of the stairs, then drop into the courtyard. Tomo is in the small cage but do not release him yet. Moving in proximity to the large cage will release the fur and spike covered wild beast. When the beast is released jump up onto its cage and strike at the wild beast. Standing above the cage door will lure the beast back into the cage. When the beast is back in the cage, drop to the ground and swing at the wild beast through the cage wall. When the beast leaves the cage, jump back onto the cage and lure the beast back into the cage. Continue until the beast falls. If you become low on health during the fight with the wild beast you can find a small health power up in the corner of the courtyard. Open Tomo's cage.

Ask Tomo
'Where is Captain Neg?'
He will tell you that Captain Neg is out in the Dune Sea hunting Banthas.
'Is there a way to escape?'
'Lets go. Hurry!'
Head down the side alley. Use your lightsaber on the generator to release the door. Return back to Tomo's Father. Tomo's Father will thank you for saving his son.
'Thank you'.
In gratitude Tomo's Father will present you with a Repulse Booster.

Ishi Tibb Storekeeper
Head through the market and you will find Padme.
Ask Padme
'Where is Jar Jar?'
'I'll help you find Jar Jar'.
Padme will suggest you find the slave boy Anakin.

'Did you learn anything?'
'Go on. I'm listening'.
Padme will explain that Anakin knows a local junk dealer known as Watto.
Head forward into the slave quarters.
A slave boy will ask you why you are in the slave quarters. Explain with.
'I'm searching for a boy named Anakin. Do you know him?'
Further down the street you will meet a Yak Face.
Ask Yak Face
'What can I do to help you?'
'Why did they throw you out?'
'I will talk with them for you'.
Head up the stairs on the left and enter through the open door. Talk to the first thug you encounter.
'What are you doing here?'
'I will not allow this crime to continue'.
When the thug threatens you continue with.
'If you resort to violence. You will find that I am a formidable opponent'.

At this point, both thugs will attack you. Strike them both down and head out onto the balcony. Jump down into the courtyard. Here you will find two Rodians attacking an Ishi Tibb storekeeper. Strike down both Rodians then speak to the Ishi Tibb. He will ask you to step into his store. Follow him inside.
Ask the Ishi Tibb storekeeper.
'I'm looking for a T-14 hyperdrive generator'.
The storekeeper will explain he has nothing like that in his store.
'Never mind'.
Leave the store through the main entrance and you will find yourself opposite Captain Neg's house. Head back to the slave quarters. At the end of the slave quarters you will find a women standing in a doorway. Talk to the slave women.
Introduce yourself
'I'am Qui Gon Jinn, a jedi in the service of the Republic. I'am searching for a boy named Anakin'.
The slave women will reveal she is Shmi Skywalker, Anakin's mother.
'Can you take me to Anakin?'
'Go on'.
'Yes. Anakin will be free before I leave this planet'.
Follow Shmi, she will take you to Anakin. You will find Anakin working on his Podracer.
'You must be Anakin. I've heard much about you'.
'Hmm....The Force is strong with you'.
'I must repair my ship. Anakin can you help me?'
Anakin will tell you that Watto, a local junk dealer may have the part you need.
'Can you introduce me to him?'

Anakin will agree to take you to Watto. Follow Anakin through the gap in the junk yard wall and head right. Anakin will crawl through a small gap in the wall. Jump onto low wall on the left. Jump forward to the opposite pillar. Run and jump to

the centre pillar. Turn to the right, then run and jump to the junk wall. Walk across the girder. The girder will break and you will drop to the floor below. Examine the wall in the right corner and a group of scavenger Jawa's will blow down the wall. Head through the gap, then go left down the ally between the wall and junk. Push the movable block to the left, then use it to climb over the wall. Drop down and then follow Anakin to Watto's shop.

Watto's Shop
There are two different routes through the next part of the game:
Hydro Spanner Route
Watto is the blue, winged Toytarian. Talk to Watto.
Ask Watto.
'I'm looking for a T-14 hyperdrive generator'.
Offer
'I will give you 500 credits for a T-14!'
Use your Jedi mind powers.
'<You will take credits for the T-14>'
Because Watto is a Toytarian, your Jedi mind powers will not work on him.
'Could you possibly sell it for less?'
Insulted, Watto will fly off. Talk to him again.
'I will give you a portable fusion coil from Naboo in exchange for the T-14'.
Watto will agree to exchange portable fusion coil for a hydro spanner.
'We have reached an agreement here!'
Collect the hydro spanner. Head outside and talk to Anakin.
'What do you need to fix your Podracer?'
'I have a hydro spanner. Would that be of any use?'
Anakin has no use for a hydro spanner, but he suggests that you may be able to trade it for what he needs.
'I'll see what I can do'.
In the centre of the courtyard are two blue Twi'lek twins owned by the Podracing champion, Sebulba. Go up to the twins and talk to them. They will explain that if you are looking for money, Jabba the Hutt a local crime lord will lend you money.
'Why would Jabba lend me money?'
'What makes you think I'm a Jedi'.
'How do I contact Jabba?'
The Twi'lek tells you she will meet you when you reach the Podracing arena.
Talk to Padme outside Watto's shop.
'Did he say anything before he disappeared?'
'I'll find him'.

Head back towards the slave quarters. Before you actually enter the slave quarters, head through the door on the left. You will find Jar Jar here.
Tell Jar Jar
'Find Watto's shop and wait there 'till I return!'
Head back towards Watto's shop. Head into the building opposite the blue Twi'lek twins. In here you should find the

Gran, Barbo. If the room is empty, wait until Barbo returns.
Ask Barbo
'Do you have any Podracer parts that you wish to trade?'
Barbo is after a repulse booster and a fuel converter.
'I have a repulse booster'.
Before you can make a trade you will need to find a fuel converter.
'Never mind'.
Head to the Ishi Tibb storekeeper.
Ask the Ishi Tibb storekeeper.
'I need a mass coupler'.
'I am searching for a servo control system'.
Finally ask
'Do you have anything I could use?'
The storekeeper will give you an engine binder.
'Thank you'.

Head to the market. On the left is a Podracer. Head into the room behind the Podracer and you will meet a Podracer known as Mawhonic.
Ask Mawhonic
'Do you have any Podracer parts that you wish to trade?'
Mawhonic wants a hydrospanner and an engine binder in exchange for a mass coupler.
'We have reached an agreement here'.
Collect the mass coupler.
Head to the bar. Talk to drunk Podracer called Teemto Pagalies.
'Would you be interested in trading any podracing parts?'
'You must be drunk, friend. I'm not that tall'.
'I'm trying to help Anakin repair his Podracer'.
'Do you have any Podracer parts that you wish to trade?'
The drunk Podracer agrees to trade you the part you need.
'We have reached an agreement here'.
Collect the servo control system. Return back to Anakin.
'You are a talented boy Anakin. I'm certain you will succeed'.

Fuel Converter Route
Watto is the blue, winged Toytarian. Talk to Watto.
Ask Watto.
'I'm looking for a T-14 hyperdrive generator'.
Offer
'I will give you a portable fusion coil from Naboo in exchange for the T-14'.
Watto agrees to exchange the portable fusion coil for a fuel converter.
'Perhaps two fuel converters?'
Watto kind of reluctantly agrees.
'We have reached an agreement here!'
Collect the both fuel converters. Head outside and talk to Anakin.
'What do you need to fix your Podracer?'
'I have a two fuel converters. Would that be of any use?'
Anakin has no use for two fuel converters, but he suggests that you may be able to trade it for what he needs.
'I'll see what I can do'.

In the centre of the courtyard are two blue Twi'lek twins owned by the Podracing champion, Sebulba. Go up to the twins and talk to them. They will explain that if you are looking for money, Jabba the Hutt a local crime lord will lend you money.
'Why would Jabba lend me money?'
'What makes you think I'm a Jedi'.
'How do I contact Jabba?'
The Twi'lek tells you she will meet you when you reach the Podracing arena.
Talk to Padme outside Watto's shop.
'Did he say anything before he disappeared?'
'I'll find him'.
Head back towards the slave quarters. Before you actually enter the slave quarters, head through the door on the left. You will find Jar Jar here.
Tell Jar Jar
'Find Watto's shop and wait there 'till I return!'
Head back towards Watto's shop. Head into the building opposite the blue Twi'lek twins. In here you should find the Gran, Barbo. If the room is empty, wait until Barbo returns.
Ask Barbo
'Do you have any Podracer parts that you wish to trade?'
Barbo is after a repulse booster and a fuel converter.
'We have reached an agreement here'.
Talk to Barbo again.
'Do you have any Podracer parts that you wish to trade?'

He will tell you he does not but opens the back door and tells you to ask his friend in the backyard. Head outside and you will be attacked by two Ishi Tibbs and a Nitko. Strike down all three while avoiding the drone gun which appears. Collect the fuel converter in the left corner of the yard then climb up the block and jump over the wall. Head to the market and talk to the scrap merchant.
'I'm looking for a mass coupler'.
'Will you take anything in trade?'
'We have reached an agreement here'.
Collect the mass coupler. Return back to Anakin.
'You are a talented boy Anakin. I'm certain you will succeed'.

The Mos Espa Arena
Make you way straight to the blue female Twi'lek.
Ask her.
'Lets us find this Jabba now'.
'I must deal with Jabba before the race!'
Use your Jedi mind powers.
'<You will take me to Jabba now>'
Follow the blue female Twi'lek up the stairs and through the previously locked door. The blue female Twi'lek will tell you to follow the path down to meet Jabba. Head down the path until you reach a room with a switch. Press the switch and you will drop into a pit. You will find yourself before Jabba the Hutt.
'Jabba is even more grotesque than I imagined'.
'I'm listening'.
Jabba's protocol droid will tell you that you are to provide entertainment for Jabba and his guests.

'What sort of entertainment?'

Jabba's protocol will explain that you are to fight Jabba's champion.

'I am ready. Lets proceed'.

Collect the Duggets. A gate will open and Jabba's champion will enter the pit. Jump back and forward while slashing with your lightsaber. Continue this strategy while avoiding its strikes and the spikes it occasionally throws. With Jabba's champion defeated, Jabba will throw down a small health power up. Head down the open passage and you will find yourself in a bar. At the bar you will find the drunk Podracer, Teemto Pagalies.

Ask Teemto Pagalies.

'I am looking for Watto. Do you know where I can find him?'

'<I'm certain that you know where to find him>'.

Teemto will agree to take you to one of Watto's employees.

'Please take me to him'.

Follow Teemto. Talk to Watto's employee.

'Do you know where I can find Watto?'

'Is it not true that you work for Watto?'

Head to the bar.

Ask the bar keeper.

'Give me a juri juice'.

Take the juri juice back to Watto's employee.

'Here, take this juri juice, my friend'.

'Now can you help me find Watto?'

Head back to the bar and get another juri juice. Return back to Watto's employee and give the juri juice to his friend.

'Here, take this juri juice, my friend'.

Now ask Watto's employee.

'Now can you help me find Watto?'

Watto's employee will agree to go and ask Watto if he will meet you. Follow him through all the previously locked doors. Head out onto the balcony and you will find Watto.

Tell Watto

'I still need a T-14 hyperdrive generator'.

'Agreed. But if Anakin Skywalker wins the race, you will grant the boy his freedom and give me the T-14. If he loses, you can keep one of the fastest Podracers ever built. In either case, you can have my money'.

'He will be piloting my Podracer. It is the fastest in the galaxy'.

Watto will agree to your wager.

'Agreed Anakin deserves this opportunity to earn his freedom'.

Return back the way you came to the bar. If you need some extra health, head left down the stairs. Head outside, then turn right and go up the stairs. Use the boxes to reach the window ledge. Turn left, then run and jump to the ledge opposite. Head inside. Talk to the sleeping creature.

Answer the creature's question with.

'Not yet'.

'Why is this race so important'.

'I'm certain he will surprise everyone. In fact, I sense that he will win this race'.

The creature will ask you if you are a friend of Anakin's.

'Yes I'am'.

The creature will supply you with a full health power up. Return to the bar. Head around the bar and down into the stadium. Drop to the track and make your way to Anakin's Podracer. When you reach Anakin's Podracer, a small reptile creature will steal an important part from Anakin. Race after the thief. He will lead you around the stadium, past all the other Podracers and eventually back to Anakin's Podracer, up the steps and into the dome building behind Anakin's Podracer. Head inside and you will find the reptile creature but no missing part. Push the block in the wall to reveal a hidden workshop. In the main room you will find a giant thug. The only way to retrieve the stolen part is to defeat the giant thug. The only way you can harm the giant thug is to deflect his laser bolts back at him with his lightsaber. During the fight, drone guns will appear from the floor and begin firing at you. If you need extra health return back to the entrance where you will find two small health power ups. If you leave the building altogether the large thug's health will refill. Once you have defeated the giant thug, collect the stolen part and return to Anakin.

Encounter In The Desert

Leave Mos Espa and follow the path. Just beyond the town's outskirts you will be attacked by four Sith probe droids. Deflect their laser bolts back at them or use force push to stun them. To the right you will find a landspeeder with a full health power up in its cockpit. When you reach the canyon, a rock slide will bar your way and the Sith Lord, Darth Maul will ambush you. Jump up onto the lower boulder, then push the boulder to the left revealing a gap. Once through the gap make your way to the end of the canyon. Here you will find Darth Maul attacking the T-14 hyperdrive generator. Use force push to lure Darth Maul away from the hyperdrive generator, he will then turn his attention to you. You do not have to defeat Darth Maul, just hold him off long enough for the Queen's star ship to take off. Once the Queen's star ship takes off you will automatically jump inside, leaving Darth Maul behind.

Coruscant

Collect the R-65 heavy blaster, then follow the senate guard to the air taxi. Just before you are about to board, a hover cannon appears and blows up the air taxi. Equip the heavy blaster and destroy the hover cannon. Escort Queen Amidala to the opposite side of the landing platform. Collect the light repeater to the right of the floating platform. Board the floating platform and talk to the protocol droid.

Answer his question with.

'Yes, please'.

The floating platform will stop at a large blast door. Head through the blast door and talk to the protocol droid behind the counter.

'Can you tell us how to find the Senate?'

'Where do we take the tour?'

'Thank you'.

Head down the hall to the left. You will find yourself in a

control room. Ignore the blast door to the left and head through the door on the opposite side of the room. There is a full health power up on the right near the astromech. Follow the passage to the end. Talk to the protocol droid behind the counter.

'Does the tour stop at the Senate chambers?'
'How much are tickets?'
'When does the next tour leave?'
'I'll return with some Republic credits'.

Return back to the control room and head out the centre door. Head out onto the landing platform and go up to the man on the far left.
Tell the man
'I'm trying to sell these electrobinoculars'.
'No I am the legal owner of these electrobinoculars I assure you'.
The man will agree to buy the electrobinoculars for 100 Republic credits.
'Yes Thank you. I hope you enjoy these'.
A hover cannon will appear so either destroy it using your heavy blaster or avoid it. Run over to the opposite side of the landing platform and you will find a horned man.
Reply to the man's plea
'Yes, how can we help?'
'How much are you asking?'
The man will offer to sell you two tickets for 100 Republic credits.
'Yes, that sounds like a good plan'.

Head back to the ticket office while avoiding the thugs. Once you have reached the ticket office, the protocol droid will open the blast door. Head through the blast door. Before you can reach the tour bus, a hover cannon will descend and destroy it. Blast the hover cannon then go right. You will need to raise the gantry to allow Queen Amidala to cross over to the bridge. Drop down to the cargo hold. Move the crate found in the bottom right over to the ledge in the top right. Use the crate to reach the ledge. Head left to the control room. You will find a full health power up on the far side of the control room. Pull the red lever to raise the gantry. Head back the way you came to Queen Amidala's side. Before you can reach her, Queen Amidala will be kidnapped. As they escape, they blow up the bridge just beyond the gantry. Head back to the control room and lower the gantry.

Return to the cargo hold and move the crate found just below the control room onto the lowered gantry. Return back to the control room and raise the gantry. Return to the cargo hold and move the crate you used to reach the control room over to the gantry. Use this crate to climb up onto the gantry. Move the crate on the gantry over to the destroyed bridge. Pull the lever to the right of the destroyed bridge then climb onto the crate. A platform will appear, jump up onto it. The platform will take you across the destroyed bridge. When you reach the other side, drop off to the left and run towards the closed blast door. To

the right of the door you will find a thin ledge. Jump onto the ledge and enter through the second window. Follow the passage around to the right. Push the switch at the end, then head out of the window and onto the ledge. Jump to the next ledge and head through the window. At the end of the passage you will find yourself in a storeroom. Push the movable crate to the side to reveal a hidden passage leading to a small health power up. Return to the storeroom and head out to the plaza.

Talk to the red clothed market dealer.
'I'm looking for a girl and two armed men'.
The market dealer will tell you he saw them taking one of the turbo elevators.
'I must be going now'.
Head up the steps and enter the far left turbo elevator. As soon as you leave the turbo elevator you will be ambushed by six thugs. Once you have cleared the area search all the doors. One holds two small health power ups, a light repeater and 5 flash grenades. When you have finished, stand on the cargo elevator. When the elevator has stopped, head right down the passage, then go left into a small room. Talk to the man in the corner.
'I won't hurt you'.
'Yes I am. Where did they take her?'
The man will tell you they took Queen Amidala into the restricted area.
'Why is that area restricted?'
'How do you prevent outlaws from leaving the restricted area?'
The man will tell you that there are security doors which can be only opened using a password.
'What is the password?'
The password is – Coruscant has lovely sunsets.
'I have no time to talk to you right now'.
Exit the room. Head through the security doors to the left.

Restricted Area
Head down the left passage and press the switch. The wall in front of you will lower. Stand on the lowered wall and you will be raised to the upper level. Press the switch to lower the wall, head into the room straight in front of you. Turn and face the passage. Quickly, press the switch to the right switch, then the switch to the left then run down the passage to the right. Pull the lever and head into the room straight in front of you. Climb onto the crate to the right and then push the white crate onto the floor. The crate will break revealing a white key card. Pull the lever and head down the right passage. Use the white key card to open the white cell door. Inside the cell you will find Queen Amidala guarded by a Rodian. Blast the Rodian and collect the red key card he drops. Escort Queen Amidala from the cell. Pull the lever, then head into the room straight in front. Use the red key card to activate the elevator. Follow the passage to the end. In the room with the bridge, first pull the right lever. A lever to your left will appear. Pull this and the bridge will rotate allowing you to cross to the opposite side. Pull the lever to the left then pull the lever to the right. Return back to the first right lever. Pulling this will open the blast door. Head back and pull the upper right lever. Head through

the open blast door. At the end of the passage, pull the lever. Step onto the elevator and press the elevator switch. Step off the elevator and walk up to the security door.

The security door will ask for a password.
Answer with
'Coruscant has lovely sunsets'.
Once you step through the security door you will face the Coruscant Mercenary responsible for kidnapping Queen Amidala. Use the heavy blaster and fire directly at the mercenary's left side. If you fire at his right side, he will deflect your shots with his force pike. Another strategy is to lure the mercenary near one of the power generators then blow it up, catching him in the ensuing explosion. Once you have dealt with the mercenary, head through the blast door opposite. Ride the elevator up. Step onto the floating platform and you will be escorted to the Senate chambers where you will find Senator Palpatine waiting for you.

Assault on Theed
Collect the light repeater left from your starting point, then head into the hangar. Inside the heroes are confronted by Darth Maul, a Dark Lord of the Sith. During this part of the game, you will swap between Queen Amidala and Obi Wan Kenobi.

Capture the Viceroy 1
You will take control of Queen Amidala, who needs to reach the Royal Palace and capture the Federation Viceroy, Nute Gunray. The streets are crawling with Federation Battle Droids so stay close to Captain Panaka. As long as you provide Captain Panaka with covering fire, he will destroy any Destroyer Droids you may encounter. Head down the main street and enter the room on the left. Once inside, talk to the Naboo citizen.
'Thank you, but time is short. We are trying to reach the palace'.
Answer his statement about the Gungans with.
'If I can reach the palace, I might be able to save them'.

The Naboo citizen will unlock the storage room to the left. Head inside and collect the blaster and remote droid. Continue down the street until you reach the square. A Battle Droid will appear from a door to your left. Destroy the droid and enter the room. Collect the thermal detonator you will find inside. A group of Battle Droids will appear from the right. As you fight the Droids, a Destroyer Droid will roll in behind you. Use the fountain to hide from the Destroyer Droid and left Panaka deal with it. There is a full health power up on the opposite side of the square. Head down the right street. Jump to the balcony and collect the small health power up. Head down the stairs and collect the proton missile launcher. Return to the balcony and drop to the street. Cross the bridge and take control of the heavy repeater. Clear the narrow street of all the Battle Droids and any Destroyer Droids. Head down the street. When you near the street corner you will face a fourth Destroyer Droid. Either let Panaka deal with the Destroyer or run back to the heavy repeater and use it to blast it. Head into the room on the left and you will find another proton missile launcher and a full health power up. Head down

the street towards the city gate.

Battle Against Darth Maul 1
You will find yourself in control of Obi Wan Kenobi teamed with Qui Gon Jinn against Darth Maul. You can only cause damage against Darth Maul with your lightsaber. Try to let Qui Gon do most of the work. If Maul turns his attention to you, step backwards while swinging with your lightsaber. You will block some of his strikes while attacking him at the same time. Jump to avoid the crates Maul throws at you. You can find a small health and a full health power up littered around the hangar floor. After you have diminished half of Maul health, he will retreat. Follow Maul.

Capture the Viceroy 2
Avoid the Destroyer Droid which rolls up the steps to the left and let Panaka deal with it. Head down the street and talk to Panaka when he stops.
Tell Panaka
'Follow me!'
Head right, blasting the Battle Droid in the far corner as you go. Go up the steps on your left. Press the switch to reveal a full health power up. Continue forward along the balcony and down the steps. Head up the right street. Talk to the wounded Naboo Soldier.
Ask the wounded Naboo Soldier.
'The security gate is locked. Can you open it?'
'Who can open the door to the machinery room?'
Turn around and head to the astromech droid.
Ask the astromech
'The security gate is locked. Can you open it?'
The astromech will unlock the machinery room door. Go inside and destroy the power generator. Collect the full health power up. Return outside and run through the open gate. Head through the archway on the right. Go up the steps to the right and follow the balcony around to the left. Talk to the Naboo citizen.
Answer his statement with.
'So am I. Who are you?'
'I need to return to the palace'.
'What are you doing?'
'It is happening now. Show me the weapons'.

The Naboo citizen will give you a proton missile launcher and 10n flash grenades. Return back down the stairs and through the archway into the large courtyard. Run up to Captain Panaka. To continue you need to destroy the field generator. There are two ways to do it. Either make your way to the balcony to the right of the field generator. Drop off the balcony so that you are behind the field generator. Then fire proton missiles and thermal detonators at the power generator found behind the field generator. Or tell Captain Panaka that he is the only one who can destroy the field generator. He will then destroy the field generator using a thermal detonator. Once the field generator has been dispersed make your way down to the end of the street. When you turn the corner you will be confronted

187

by a number of reprogrammed astromechs. Destroy the astromechs as they roll towards you. Head left up the steps. Enter the room on the left. The woman inside will open a room in the back leading to a light repeater. Return outside and continue up the steps. Collect the full health power up and head out through the door opposite. Follow the balcony around down into the garden. Head up the steps to Captain Panaka.

Battle Against Darth Maul 2
Continue the assault against Darth Maul, you will find a small health power up along the corridor. Eventually Darth Maul will retreat along the gantry. When you follow him across the gantry it will break and you will fall to the ground below. Head through the blast door.

Final Battle 1
Head right down the hall. On your left you will encounter two Battle Droids. Once you have blasted both of them you will be faced by three doors. Head through the right door. Inside there are two Battle Droids. Pull the block to the doorway. Behind the block you will find a small health power up. Return to the hall and head into the left room. Inside you will find two more Battle Droids. Return to the hall and pull the block from the room opposite into the left room. Push the block under the switch. Climb onto the block and activate the switch. A secret passage will open. Enter the secret passage. You will find yourself in a room filled with captive Naboo Soldiers. Talk to the Naboo Commander.
Ask him
'I need all the pass keys you are hiding'.
The Naboo Commander will give you the white pass key.
'Thank you. Please help these men escape. I must continue on towards the throne room'.
Head back through the secret passage. Return to the hall and enter the white pass key into the computer to the left of the main door. Press the switch and head through the door.

Battle Against Darth Maul 3
Make your way through the blast door. Destroy the patrolling Battle Droid. Follow the gantry around to you reach the far side. Ride the platform up to the higher level. Jump to the platform opposite and head through the blast door. Destroy the two Battle Droids beyond the first blast door. Press the switch and continue forward. You will find yourself on a thin gantry. Press the switch to the left to activate the lights. Destroy the Battle Droid patrolling the gantry and the one which appears from the room opposite. Make your way to the end of the gantry and press the switch. This will shut off the energy barriers. Use force push to activate the switch on the opposite gantry which extends the bridge. From the extended bridge, jump to the opposite gantry. Turn right and go through the blast door. When the blast door opens you will be confronted by five Battle Droids. Once you have cleared the area, press the grey wall to reveal a full health power up. Press switch to open the next blast door.

Final Battle 2
Destroy the fist two Battle Droids you encounter. Stay close to the left wall, and move slowly forward. Press the switch then slowly move back. The door in the corner will now be open. Make your way through the door and up the stairs. Enter the control room and blast the two Battle Droids you find inside. Open the panel to the right to reveal a proton missile launcher. Climb out of the window and make your way across the window ledge. Enter through the window. Press the panel between the stairs to reveal a full health power up and a thermal detonator. Head through the door to return to the hall. From a distance, fire a proton missile at the heavy repeater. Once the heavy repeater is destroyed, you can move forward. Let Captain Panaka deal with any wandering Battle Droids. Repeat against the next heavy repeater then move forward. Two Destroyer Droids will then roll out from the room on the right. Leave the Destroyer Droids to Captain Panaka.

Enter the room on the left and collect the small health power up, blaster and the light repeater. There is a third Destroyer Droid lurking around which is likely to appear when you leave this room. There is a final heavy repeater at the end of the hall. Once this has been disintegrated you can enter through the door on the left. Destroy the four patrolling Battle Droids then head to the end of the corridor. Enter the far left door and collect the blue pass card. When you return into the corridor you will come under attack by more Battle Droids. Enter the first left door and enter the blue pass card into the computer. At any time if you need more health, you will find a full health power up in the first room on the right. Make your way to the end of the corridor and go through the centre door. Destroy the two Battle Droids on your left and right then drop off the balcony. Drag the block over to the opposite side and place it under the gap in the balcony.

Return to the balcony and enter the room to the left of the entrance. Inside you will find another block. Pull the block out onto the balcony and push it through the gap in the balcony onto the first block. Drop off the balcony and push the two blocks to the left, next to the pillar. Return up onto the balconyand jump onto the two blocks. From the blocks, jump onto the pillar and collect the red pass card. Return to the balcony and input the red pass key into the computer. Drop off the balcony and enter the red room on the left. Inside you will find a light repeater and two small health power ups. Return outside and climb the stairs at the end. Head through the doors.

Battle Against Darth Maul 4
Make your way forward and ride the platform to the level below. From here jump to the gantry opposite. Continue forward and jump to the next gantry. Ride the platform up. Make your way through the blast door. Press the switch to

raise elevator. Stand on the edge of elevator and jump to the ledge to the right. Press switch. Drop to the ground and press the switch to lower the elevator. Press the switch a second time then ride the elevator up. The bars on the left will have slid across allowing you to drag the block. Push the block over the elevator to the ground below. Drop down and push the block through the gap to the left. Push the block to the left, then climb on the block and enter the control room. Press the switches in this order. The first switch is next to the door.

Press the 1st switch twice
Press the 2nd switch once
Press the 3rd switch once
Press the 4th switch once
Press the 5th switch once

There will now be a clear path through the energy bars. Once past the energy bars, press the switch and ride the elevator up. Head left and through the blast door.

Final Battle 3
Blast the two Battle Droids and the one in control of the heavy repeater but do not destroy the heavy repeater. Take control of the heavy repeater and blast all the Battle Droids and Destroyer Droids at the base of the stairs. Once the area is clear, make your way up the stairs. There are a number of Battle Droids lurking around the top of the stairs and two Destroyer Droids will roll into battle, one from the left and one from the right. There is a full health power up hidden within the statue near the left door. Head through the door and out of the window. Make your way around the window ledge and through the next window. Destroy the two Battle Droids and collect the full health power up found in the corner of the room. Head through the door on the right and you will find yourself in the throne room. Destroy all the Battle Droids then confront the Viceroy sitting on the throne. Reply with
'That's impossible!'
When he asks you to surrender and sign his treaty. The main door will open and six Battle Droids will stalk in. Destroy all the droids then confront the Viceroy.

Battle Against Darth Maul 5
Jump to the rising platform on the right and ride it down to the lower level. Follow the gantry to the end and ride the platform up to the higher level. Follow the gantry towards the central gantry. Jump to the central gantry and head left and through the blast door. Wait for the energy barriers to open before continuing. As you near the end you will see Darth Maul strike down Qui Gon. Charge at Darth Maul. Stay close to Darth Maul or he will fire dark lightning at you. If you are in need of more health you will find two full health power ups in secret compartments at the top of each slope. Continue the assault against Darth Maul until he falls. Return to Qui Gon's side to receive his final request.

STAR WARS: JEDI POWER BATTLES

Hidden Characters
Darth Maul
Complete the game with Qui Gon Jinn on either difficulty setting. Highlight Qui Gon and press **Select**, Qui Gon's portrait will be replaced with Darth Maul's.

Queen Amidala
Complete the game with Obi Wan Kenobi on the Jedi level setting. Highlight Obi Wan and press **Select**, Obi Wan's portrait will be replaced with Queen Amidala's.

Captain Panaka
Complete the game with Plo Koon on the Jedi level setting. Highlight Plo Koon and press **Select**, Plo Koon's portrait will be replaced with Captain Panaka's.

Hidden Levels
Droidekas
To unlock the eleven level complete the game with Plo Koon.

Kaadu Race
To unlock the twelve level complete the game with Adi Gallia

Gungan Roundup
To unlock the thirteenth level you will need to collect the three hidden Gungan artefacts.

Ultimate Saber and Survival Mode
To unlock the ultimate saber that kills with one hit and the final level, complete the game with Mace Windu.

STAR WARS: MASTERS OF TERAS KASI

Character moves based on your character facing right, reverse directional controls when facing left.

Basic Moves
Dash Forward = ➡, ➡
Run = ➡, **Hold** ➡
Dash Backwards = ⬅, ⬅
Throw = ◼ + ● / ▲ + ✖
Jumping Attack On Prone Opponent = ⬇ + ✖ / ⬆ + ✖
Left Punch = ◼
Right Punch = ▲
Left High Kick = ✖
Right High Kick = ●
Forward Low Kick = ➡ + ●
Forward Roll = ➡, ↘, ⬇
Forward Flip = **Running** + ◼ /▲
Ground Slide = **Running** + ✖ / ●
Low Jumping Punch = ◼ (**In The Air**)

High Jumping Punch = ▲ **(In The Air)**
Low Jumping Kick = ✖ **(In The Air)**
High Jumping Kick = ● **(In The Air)**

Force Bar

Each character has a force bar that is situated at the bottom of the screen. As you fight and score hits against your opponent this fills up. Your force bar can be used to perform super moves or the more powerful force power moves.

Super Force Power Moves

To maximise your super force power move, your force move must be full. Some power moves will work with only partially filled force bars, but have a less powerful effect then a fully charged power move. Most super force power moves lose their effectiveness from long range, others can be stopped at the beginning of the move.

Weapons

Every character except Arden Lyn and Thok can fight with or without their weapon drawn. To draw your weapon tap **R2**.

Defence

To block simply **Hold Away** from your opponent. To perform a crouching block **Hold ↓ + Away**. To avoid oncoming attacks each character can side step into and out of the screen. To side step press **L1** to step into the foreground, or **L2** to step into the background.

Throws

Each character has several throws, two with weapons drawn, and two without. Most of these are the same regardless of your weapon status.

Hidden Characters

There are five hidden playable characters in Masters of Teras Kasi, here is how to get them.

Princess Leia dressed in slave gear

With all settings on default, set the difficulty to Jedi. Then complete the game using Princess Leia.

StormTrooper / Scout Trooper

With all settings on default, set the difficulty to Jedi. Then complete the game with Han Solo.

Darth Vader

With all settings on default, set the difficulty to Jedi. Then complete the game with Luke Skywalker.

Jodo Kast

You must defeat seven opponents in survival mode in less then three minutes, thirty seconds.

Mara Jade

Hold down **L1**, **L2** and **R2** and enter team mode on Jedi difficulty. The computer will automatically choose your team (Rebel characters) and you must defeat the computer team (the Empire) to unlock Mara Jade.

Cheats

Change Clothes
> **Hold L1 On The Character Select Screen**

Big Head Mode
> **Hold Select During Loading**

Super Deformed Mode
> **Hold Select + ↓ + ✖ During Loading**

Tiny Mode
> **Hold Select + ↓ + ✖ + R2 During Loading**

Full Screen / Removal Life Bar, Force Bar etc.
> **Hold Select + ↓, L1 + R2 During Loading**

Power And Life Regeneration
> **Hold ↘ + ✖ During Loading**

STEEL HARBINGER

Full Health

To enable full health (up to five times per game) pause during play and press **L2, L2, R2, R2, ↑, L1, ↑, R1**. A beep will confirm your success.

All Weapons

To gain all of the weapons (up to three times per game) pause during play and press ✖, ▲, **R2**, ▲, ✖, **L2, R2**, ↓, **L2**, ■, ➔. A beep will confirm your success.

STREET FIGHTER ALPHA

Extra Playable Characters

To play as the extra characters, follow the instructions below:

Akuma

To select Akuma, whilst in the Character Selection screen go to the Random selection box and hold **L2**. Now enter the following code: ←, ←, ←, ↓, ↓, ↓, ■, ▲. Akuma should then appear as your character selection. To play in his other strip, simply substitute ■, ▲ at the end of the code with ●, ✖.

Dan

To play as Dan, go to the Random selection box on the Character Selection screen and hold **L2**. Now enter the following code: ▲, ■, ✖, ●, ▲. Dan should then appear as your character selection. To play in his other strip, put the code in backwards.

M Bison

To play as the old master, go to the Random selection box on the Character Selection screen and hold **L2**. Now enter the following code: ←, ←, ↓, ↓, ←, ↓, ↓, ■, ▲. M Bison should then appear as your character selection. To play in his other strip, simply substitute ■, ▲ at the end of the code with ●, ✖.

STREET FIGHTER ALPHA 2

Hidden Characters
For a little variety, follow the codes below:

Old-Skool Chun-Li
Hold down **Select** for five seconds before pressing any other button to select her.

Turbo Akuma
To get a real advantage over the opposition, firstly highlight Akuma on the Character Selection screen and hold **Select** for a few moments. Next, enter the following code: ↓, ➡, ➡, ↓, ⬅, ↓, ⬅, ↓, ➡, ➡, ➡. Your cursor should start and finish on Akuma. Now hold **Select** again and press any button to get Turbo Akuma.

White Dhalsim and Vega
To get white versions of these characters, firstly select Training mode, choose Dhalsim or Vega, then commence playing. Perform the Teleport move, and at the instant the character disappears press **Start**, go to the Menu, and highlight "Normal" mode. Start again, and your character will appear white.

STREET FIGHTER ALPHA 3

Extra World Tour Stages
In World Tour mode, build your character to level 30+ and you gain access to three extra stages.

Play As Guile
Complete the first extra stage in World Tour mode, where you fight Guile.

Play As Evil Ryu
Complete the second extra stage in World Tour mode, where you fight Evil Ryu.

Play As Shin Gouki/Super Akuma
Complete the third extra stage in World Tour mode, where you fight Shin Gouki/Super Akuma.

Unlock Dramatic Battle And Final Battle Modes
Complete Arcade mode on difficulty level 8.

Unlock Team Battle And Survival Modes
Complete World Tour mode with a level 10+ character.

Classic Characters
Accumulate 3 hours of game play or complete Arcade mode on

difficulty level 6 or higher. On the character election screen, press **Select** to switch to a classic character.

Saikyou Mode
Accumulate 4 hours of game play.

Mazi Mode
Accumulate 5 hours of game play or complete Arcade mode on difficulty level 7 or higher.

Hidden Character Game Intro
Accumulate 48 hours of game play.

STREET FIGHTER COLLECTION

Super Street Fighter 2
Play As Akuma/Gouki
On versus mode, highlight Ryu and press **L1 + L2 + R1 + R2.**

Street Fighter Alpha 2 Dash
Play As Cammy
In arcade mode, select M.Bison and complete the game. You need a score which places you on the top of the score board. The default high score is 50,000. Enter you're initials as **CAM.** Select verses mode, highlight M.Bison and press **Start** three times. Cammy can only be played in versus mode or practice mode.

Play As Evil Ryu
Highlight Ryu and press **Start** three times.

Play As Super Akuma/Shin Gouki
Highlight Akuma and continue to press **Start** until Akuma's gi changes colour to purple.

Play Classic Street Fighter 2 World Warriors
Highlight the Alpha version of classic characters, Ryu, Ken, Chun Li, Sagat, M.Bison, Dhalsim, Zangief and press **Start** twice. These characters appear like Alpha characters but don't possess super moves, alpha counters, air blocking, landing from throws just the two or three special moves which they possessed when they appeared in the original Street Fighter 2.

STREET FIGHTER COLLECTION 2

Secret Boxes
Complete Arcade mode on Street Fighter 2 World Warrior to unlock 18 pieces of artwork.

Complete Arcade mode on Street Fighter 2 Championship Edition to unlock 22 pieces of new artwork.

Complete Arcade mode on Street Fighter 2 Turbo Hyper Fighting to unlock a sound test.

Complete all three games and you get the sound remix option and the Deluxe Versus mode.

STREET FIGHTER EX PLUS ALPHA

Bonus Barrel Game
Highlight 'Practice' option on mode selection and press start then press ↑, ↑, ➡, ↑, ➡, ↑. A message will appear to confirm correct code entry. Select the 'Bonus' option under practice mode to play the bonus barrel game from Street Fighter 2

Computer controlled team in Battle Round
Select team battle mode. Hold **L2** + **Select** at the Vs Loading screen until the match begins. The computer will now control your fighter for this round. However this can only be used once per team battle mode.

STREET FIGHTER EX2

Hidden Characters
Play as Garuda
On the menu screen highlight Arcade and press **Select** three times, move ➡ and press **Select**, twice then move down and press **Select** three times.

Play as Shadow
On the menu screen highlight Versus and press **Select** three times, move ⬇ and press **Select** four times, move ↑ and press **Select** three times.

Play as Kairi
On the menu screen highlight Options and press **Select** once, move ➡ and press **Select** three times, move ⬇ and press **Select** twice.

Play as Hayate
On the menu screen highlight Bonus Game and press **Select** twice, move ↑ and press **Select** four times, move ↑ and press **Select** once, move ⬅ and press **Select** five times.

Excel Break and Satellite Bonus Games
On the menu screen, highlight Bonus Game and press **Select** five times, move ⬅ and press **Select** three times, move ↑ and press **Select** once, move ➡ and press **Select** twice.

Maniac Mode and Demonstration
On the menu screen highlight Practice and press **Select** once, move ⬇ and press **Select** once, move ⬅ and press **Select** once, move ↑ and press **Select** once, move ↑ and press **Select** once, move ➡ and press **Select** once, move ↑ and press **Select** once, move ⬅ and press **Select** once, move ↑ and press **Select** once, finally move ➡ and press **Select** once.

M Bison Bonus Game
On the main menu highlight Bonus Game and press **Select** thirteen times, move ↑ and press **Select** four times, move ⬇ and press **Select** thirteen times.

STREET FIGHTER: THE MOVIE

Choose Akuma
To become Akuma you must highlight Guile and press the following: ↑, **R1**, ⬇, **L2**, ➡, **L1**, ⬅, **R2**.

Secret Configuration
Pause the game while you are fighting and press **Select**. A menu should appear which allows you to configure your buttons.

STREET RACER

Level Codes
Select the desired level with the following codes:

Silver	TRAFIK
Gold	NEJATI
Platinum	DOUGAL
Super	TURGAY

When you enter the password DOUGAL you will get the Rabbit car with three new personalised tracks.
When you enter the password TURGAY you will obtain the Secret Options screen.

STREET SKATER

Opening The Gates
Completing all three stages with a skater will open two of the gates for the previous courses.

Extra Skaters
Complete all three stages a second time with one of the standard characters to unlock the bonus skaters. TJ unlocks Sarah, Jerry unlocks Mick, Ginger unlocks Bonobo the monkey and Frankie releases Saho.

Extra Boards
Completing all three stages with a bonus skater will earn you five new board designs.

Mirroir Courses
Compete the game a second time with Sarah, Mick and Bonobo will open mirrored versions of all three tracks.

Day Or Night Mode
Complete the game a second time with Saho and you will earn the option to race in the day or at night.

STREET SKATER 2

Cheat Codes
Enter these on the main menu:

Unlock all Characters	←, ←, ●, ●, L2, ■, →, R2
Unlock all Tracks	←, →, ←, →, ●, ●, R1, ■
Max Out Stats and Trick Level	L1, ■, ←, ←, R2, ←, R1, ←
Unlock all Movies	R2, R2, L1, L2, L1, R1, R1, R1
Unlock all Boards	●, ●, ■, ●, ■, ■, ●, R1

Alternative Costumes
Hold either **L1, L2, R1, R2** when selecting your character.

STRIKER '96

Special Teams
If you would like to enter a bonus Special Cup tournament starring teams of characters from Star Trek, and Warner and Rage teams, all you have to do is win the World Cup.

SUPER PUZZLE FIGHTER II

You can select hidden characters in all modes except Street Puzzle Mode:

Play As Akuma
Place the cursor on Morrigan, hold **Select** and press the following for player one to play as Akuma: ↓, ↓, ↓, ←, ←, ←, ●.

For player two to play as Akuma, you must place the cursor on Felicia, hold **Select** and press the following: ↓, ↓, ↓, →, →, →, ●.

Play As Amanda
For player one to play as Amanda put the cursor on Morrigan and hold **Select** while you go to Donovan and press ●. For player two to play as Amanda put the cursor on Felicia and hold **Select** while you go to Donovan and press ●. You can use this method in V's, Arcade, and Master Arcade mode.

Play As Anita
For player one to play as Anita place the cursor on Morrigan and hold **Select**, then move the cursor two squares to the right and press ●. For player two to play as Anita, place the cursor on Felicia, then hold **Select** and move the cursor one square to the Left and press ●.

Play Against Dan
To play against Dan you must carry out the following before you reach stage 6, and without using a continue:
- win one round within 1 minute
- perform at least 1 Super Combo

- perform a maximum chain of 4 or more
- have a maximum Power Gem of at least 20 units

Play As Dan
To play as Dan in V's, Arcade, or Master Arcade mode, go to the character select screen and press **L1**, **R1** and ●.

Play Against Devilot
To play against Devilot, you must carry out the following before you reach stage seven, and without using a continue:
- defeat an opponent within 1 minute in one round
- perform at least 1 Super Combo
- perform a maximum chain of 4 or more
- have a maximum Power Gem of at least 20 units

Play As Devilot
For player one to play as Devilot, he must place the cursor on Morrigan, then hold **Select** and press ←, ←, ←, ↓, ↓, ↓. Press ● when the timer reaches exactly 10 seconds.
For player two to play as Devilot he must highlight Felicia, hold **Select** and then press →, →, →, ↓, ↓, ↓, and press ● when the timer reaches 10 seconds.

Play As Devilot
Go to the character select screen and press **R1** and ● in any of V's, Arcade, or Master Arcade mode.

Play As Hsien-Ko's Sister
Player one must highlight Morrigan and hold **Select**, then move the cursor one square to the right and press ●. Player two needs to put the cursor on Felicia, then hold **Select** and move the cursor two squares to the Left and press ●.

Play As Lei-Lei
The following can be used in V's, Arcade, and Master Arcade mode:
For player one to play as Lei-lei, put the cursor on Morrigan and hold **Select**, then go to Hsien-Ko and press ●. For player two to play as Lei-Lei, put the cursor on Felicia and hold **Select**. Then go to Hsien-Ko and press ●.

Lei-Lei's Talisman
You can access Lei-Lei's talisman by going to Morrigan and holding **Start** whilst you go to Lei-Lei and press any button.

Stage Select
Select a character, then hold **L2**, **R2** and **Select**. Choose you handicap, then whilst still holding **L2**, **R2** and **Select**, press one of the following codes:

Donovan: ●		Chun-Li: ↓	
Hsien-Ko: ✖		Ryu: ←	
Sakura: ▲		Ken: →	
Felicia: ■		Morrigan: ↑	
Devilot: R1		Dan: No button	
Akuma: L1			

SWAGMAN

Invincibility
Pause the game and press ●, ■, ✖, ■, ●, ■, ●, ■, ▲, ■, ●, ▲, ●, ■, ▲, ■.

SYNDICATE WARS

Eurocorp Missions
Part One
Tip: Other than following the guide, always make sure you have completed the objective and satisfied all orders.

Level 1- London
Go west while killing the unguided that are indicated on the radar. Then go north-west. When all the targets are killed go back to the Headquarters.

Level 2 – Detroit
Go west, turning the corner and going northwards. Steal a car so you can get around faster and also run over targets. Beware of cops near your base when evacuating.

Level 3 - Hong Kong
Steal a vehicle and drive into the fusion plant. Exit the vehicle and kill the attacking security. Equip the Persuadertron and go after the targets. Wait in the car for the technicians to follow then off to the Evacuation point.

Level 4 - Mantochkin Star
Walk south to the river, then west and north up the incline. Kill the unguided citizens on the fly-over. Go to the guarded compound in the Northwest. This is where the scientists are. Blast your way into the Northeast corner base. Steal a hovercar and fly to the scientists. Get them and go back to base.
Skin 1: Cross the river to the south side. Go over the bridge to the east, and to the right-hand church base. Four Zealots guard the skin.

Level 5 - Singapore
Take one of your men to the building south of the Headquarters and get the guards rifles. Regroup and head south where you can take out the bullion guards. Drive the bullion vehicle to the evacuation point.

Level 6 - Phoenix
First take out the police who are shooting at you. Get together an army, and after removing the Zealots, enter the temple. Persuade about half a dozen civilians. In the temple, get a suitcase that contains cult technology. Kill the owner - a Zealot - grab the suitcase and go back to HQ.

Level 7 - Rome
Take your armed Cyborgs up the ramp to the garrison, entering the south side. Work your way through, kill the rebel agents, and leave. Kill the Spiderbots outside by using long-range rifles.

Level 8 - Phoenix
The city has degenerated. Arm your troops and head for the base in the north west corner: use either a car or explosives to get in. Find the rogue agent inside and kill him. Return to HQ.

Level 9 - New York
Use clone shields and go to the south east corner. Persuade the NAA employee to join you and head for the NAA HQ in the north west corner. Protect the NAA employee at all costs! Go over the fly-over to the NAA HQ. Persuade Jennifer Taks to join you and return to HQ.

Level 10 - Cape Town
The enemy immediately attacks so use a Cerberus IFF, and your red mist drug and shields. Head south to the church's base. Enter the base by blasting you way through the side of the building. Persuade the scientist to join you, but be quick about it.

Level 11 - Adelaide
Make your way to the church temples in the east, taking out the enemy on your way. A good way of getting rid of the Zealots is to get in a car and use long range rifles to pick them off. When your car gets too badly damaged, get out. Persuade the scientist to join you. He is in the south eastern temple.

Level 12 - Nuuk
There isn't much point in using a hovercar. Just draw the enemy into the open areas. Use some Ceberus IFFs inside the fence and a trigger wire. Lure the enemy in and take them out with the flamer as they come through.

Level 13 - Tokyo
Get yourself some miniguns and go south to the Zealot's base. Go to the police station opposite the base and kill the Zealots by luring them into the laser fire. Go into the base, get the scientist and go to the evacuation point.

Level 14 - Bangkok
Kill the church members. The main objective is to protect Professor Drennan. Do this by sticking close and watching the scanner.

Level 15 - Hawaii
Set up some trigger wires to take out the Zealots. Leave one man with the personnel, take three men to take on the tank. Destroy it but attacking and running away. When the tank comes back, attack again. Now go to the evacuation point. Use the fourth man to guide the personnel to the evacuation point.

Level 16 - Johannesburg
Get to Agent Wu via the Matter Transporters. Upon persuading him, you will receive the location of Lucy. Persuade her to return to HQ.

Level 17 - Cairo
Get to Lucy as quickly as you can. Don't try to destroy the patrol tanks. Zealots can be removed by dropping explosives and trigger wires. Kill Lucy and get to the evacuation point.

Level 18 - Bahrain
Go to the AI building in the Southeast corner via the small Access Bridge. Set up and ambush for the unguided. Use trigger wires and ion mines along the road. Take out the rest with pulse lasers.

Level 19 - Colombo
Set up a trap and lure the Zealoys in with one of your men. This should remove most of their men. Take out the hovercars and then enter the tower. Kill everyone!

Level 20 - The moon
Use the graviton gun to remove the Spiderbots. Quickly go to the back of the main building taking the longer route to avoid the guards. Use your scanner to locate the Nine. Destroy them.

Part Two - Church of the New Epoch
Level 1 – Detroit
Kill the police and guards at the start, then go west and steal the police car. Drive to the Eurocorp base and kill the guards. Go in the Target Bunker to plant the virus.

Level 2 – Tripoli
Go north from the temple then to the east of the city killing as you go. Kill the unguided in the south-east then back to the temple.

Level 3 – Santiago
Drive south-west and kill the gang of agents then get Disrupters from the bodies. Build up a small army then go to the police compound north of where you started. Persuade the officers through the fence. Run to the IML in the north-west, going to the centre island and leaving your persuadees behind. Persuade the guards and target agent and get out with the flying car.

Level 4 - Johannesburg
Before the convoy arrives, get to the Eurocorp vault from the Southwest corner. Kill the guards and get the money off the agent when he arrives. Two groups will attack you before you get to HQ.

Level 5 - Hong Kong
Go to the temple at the northern part of the town. Make the Zealots join you, one by one. Now kill the rest of the unguided. Return to HQ.

Level 6 - Rome
Get out of your HQ before it is bombed. Go west to the Unguided base. Kill the agents and steal their weapons. Gain control of the base and then take out the remaining Unguided. Return to HQ.

Level 7 - Buenos Aires
When you have dealt with the Eurocorp APC, go to the barracks in the north. Keep away from the roads to avoid APC's. Get your energy up and go into the base. Take out twelve agents, then get the agents at the outposts in the west and any remaining APC's.

Level 8 - Santiago
Head for the church in the north, watching the radar for any Unguided. Blast your way through the side of the church, kill the desecrators and return to HQ.

Level 9 - Cairo
Put on a clone shield and go to the Eurocorp building in the Southeast. Kill Kotosek and when the guards come in, self-destruct! (■ + ● + ▲ + ✖) This should kill loads of guards. This building holds a skin.

Level 10 - Bahrain
The only way to do this is to get an army by persuading the citizens and then the police. Attack the main bridge barricade from the south by crossing the smaller bridge. Once you've taken out the barricade, drive the tank from the Northeast over the bridge and kill the agents in the Southeast.

Level 11 - New York
Follow the contact to where he starts a riot (Southeast). Let the contact distract the APC's. Steal a hovercar and park in the car park. Go to the Eurocorp base (south) and enter with the stolen car. Get out of the car, kill the six remaining agents and grab the secret grenade.

Level 12 - Cape Town
Get your most powerful weapons out. Go to Lucy who is in the Northwest. Don't make contact with her until you have dealt with the Unguided. Then go to the IML link (Southwest).

Level 13 - Bangkok
The captive is on an isolated island in the east. Get to this via the 'link' in the south. Before going to the link, lower the Eurocorp count by throwing grenades at them from across the river. Now go round, knock them out with gas and then kill them. Persuade the agent, then it is back to HQ.

Level 14 - Cape Town
This area is occupied by an army of the Unguided. Avoid the main body, go to the eastern street, then north. Attack Lucy's position from the north taking out the hovercars and Spiderbots. Kill Lucy.

Level 15 - Johannesburg
Ignore the car outside your HQ. Go south and use knockout gas at the Unguided outpost. Blow up the temple to kill the leader of the uprising. Back to HQ.

Level 16 - Adelaide

Go to the Southwest to get a car. Use this to gain entrance to the Eurocorp base where you can get the tank. Now destroy the other tanks on the map. Go to the centre, kill the agents, and lead the VIP out.

Level 17 - Colombo

Leave one man at the start. Go to the Southwest to get the tank. Take the tank back and kill the Zealots and the Scorpions. Get into the Orbital Elevator.

Level 18 - The moon

Same as for level 20 - The Moon in Syndicate Wars - Eurocorp missions guide.

SYPHON FILTER

Level Select

During the game, press **Start** to go to the option screen. Go to 'Options' and highlight 'Select Mission', then press and hold ← + **L1** + **R1** + **Select** + ■ + ✖.

Super Weapons

During the game, press **Start** to go to the option screen. Highlight ' Weapons' and hold ➡ + **L2** + **R2** + ■ + ✖ + ●.

Movie Theatre

On level one, go to the theatre opposite the alley where you use the service elevator. Stand in the doorway and press **Start**. Highlight 'Map' and hold ➡ + **L2** + **R1** + ✖. Walk through the curtains to view all the games cut scenes.

Hard Difficulty Setting

Highlight 'New Game' on the title screen, then press ← + **L1** + **R2** + **Select** + ■ + ● + ✖.

SYPHON FILTER 2

Level Skip

Pause the game during any level, highlight the Map option and hold ➡ + **L2** + **R2** + ● + ■ + ✖. Go to options and select the Cheats option and pick End Level.

View Movies

Pause the game during any level, highlight the Briefing option and hold ➡ + **L1** + **R2** + ● + ✖. Go to options and select the Cheats option and pick Movies.

Level Select

Enter both the level skip and the view movies cheats. On the pause screen, select Options, then Cheats and Disc 1 Movies. In the cinema, press **Start** and select Options, then cheats and then End Level. The game will quit, start a new game and pause mid play. Return to the cheats menu and select Select Level option. From here you can choose any level.

Super Agent

Pause the game during any level, highlight the Weaponry option and hold **L2** + **Select** + ● + ■ + ✖. Go to options and select Cheats. Turn on the Super Agent option and you can kill enemies with a single shot.

Hard Mode

On the title screen, highlight New Game and hold ⬆ + **L1** + **R2** + **Select** + ● + ■ + ✖. The game will now begin on hard mode.

Secret Items

Mission 1: Secret Items:	H11 Sniper Rifle found in the waterfall cavern. Unlocks Colorado Rockies arena.
Mission 2: Secret Item:	Complete in under 3:00. Unlocks silly extra characters.
Mission 3: Secret Item:	Binoculars. Unlocks Caves Arena.
Mission 8: Secret Item:	Kill Archer with one shot. Unlocks Jungle arena.
Mission 9: Secret Item:	Girlie Magazine, found in locker. Unlocks Syphon Filter 1 characters.
Mission 11: Secret Item:	Kill Bodyguards quickly at the start of the level. Unlocks Disco Basement arena.
Mission 12:Secret Item:	PK-102 found in crashed car after grabbing bar above. Unlock's Rhoemer's Bunker arena.
Mission 13: Secret Item:	BIZ-2 found in white car at the start of the level. Unlocks Surreal arena.
Mission 15: Secret Item:	Complete the level without using the crossbow. Unlocks the Ajir Prison arena.
Mission 18: Secret Item:	M-79 found above the autopsy room. Unlocks the Agency computer lab arena.
Mission 19: Secret Item:	Dirty Laundry found in the washing machine. Unlocks the DC City Car Park.
Mission 20: Secret Item:	M-79 found at the top of the stairs. Unlocks all the Syphon Filter 2 characters.

T'AI FU

Level Select

Complete the first level, then while on the map screen press **R1** + **R2** to bring up a list of the games levels.

TARZAN

Extra Life
If you are low on lives in the later stages of the game there is an easy way to build them up again. If you replay earlier levels again and again you can clock up as many lives as you like. Do not save the game on these earlier levels however, restart where you were getting stuck before saving.

TEKKEN

Galaga Cheats
The following cheats can be carried out during Galaga to have an effect upon Tekken:
You can play with 2 ships by pressing and holding the following on controller 2 when you see the screen stating 'Licensed by Sony': ↑, **L1**, ▲, ✖. The other method of getting 2 ships is to complete stage 1 in less than 18.5 seconds. (Playing with 2 ships means that you will not be able to play as the devil)

Play as Heihachi
To play as Heihachi in Tekken, you need to clear the whole of Galaga with one coin only. To select Heihachi, use **Start** instead of the usual punch or kick.

Play as Kazuya
To play as Devil Kazuya or any of the middle bosses in Tekken, you must get a perfect hit rating in all of the stages of Galaga.

Alternate Colours
Change your characters clothes by placing the cursor over your character on the selection screen in Arcade mode, then press either a punch or a kick button, each of which gives a different set of clothes.

Easy Heihachi
To play as Heihachi you must not lose a single round in the game. If you set the fights to just one round each (of 20 seconds each) you will have a much better chance of accomplishing this.

Play the Bosses
Play as one of the bosses by defeating one, and then pressing ← or → on the character selection screen. If you have a memory card you can save the data when you make the defeat, so that you can play as the boss again.

TEKKEN 2

Big Head Mode
To fight with a big head, acquire all the hidden fighters in the game, then start again. When you choose your character, hold **Select** and don't release it until the first round starts.

Bigger Head Mode
Carry out the Big Head Mode cheat, then if you are in Arcade Mode you can increase the size of your arms and head again by going to the continue screen and holding **Select**. If you are in Vs Mode, hold **Select** for a second time at the character select screen.

Devil And Angel
Add the Devil and Angel by fighting with Kazuya and completing the game.

Fight Roger Or Alex
To fight against Roger or Alex you must obtain the Devil and Angel, then start a new game. You can fight with any character in this game. At the third fight you must defeat your opponent with a particle of energy left in the final round. When you hear 'Great', you know that the cheat has activated.

First-Person Perspective
To play with a first-person perspective, you must acquire all the hidden characters in the game, then at the character select screen, hold **L1** and **L2** while you choose a character.

Obtaining Kazuya Mishima
To obtain Kazuya Mishima you must complete the game using the original 10 characters to acquire the sub-bosses. Then complete a game using a sub-boss.

Pick A Pose
Choose your victory pose after you have won by pressing and holding ■ or ✖ throughout the replay, or by holding ● or ▲ throughout the replay. Each gives a different pose.

Purple Kazuya
To fight with Kazuya wearing a purple costume, acquire all the hidden characters in the game, then start a new game and highlight Kazuya. Hold **Start** while you select him.

Roger And Alex
You can obtain Roger and Alex by first making sure that all the characters are selectable (including Kazuya, Devil and Angel). Then carry out a 10-hit combo with any character in practice mode, with the tool bar at the bottom of the screen turned off.

Sky Mode
Play in Sky Mode where you can send your opponent into the sky with uppercut moves, by collecting all the hidden characters in the game. Then when you choose a character, press ↑ and **Select**, holding these buttons until the fight begins. You will find that this also activates the big Head Mode.

Thought Bubbles
Play in practice mode, then leave your character alone until a thought bubble appears over his or her head.

TEKKEN 3

Secret Characters

Like Tekken one and two, each time you complete the game with a different character you gain access to new previously unplayable characters. Tekken 3 is slightly different because each of the secret characters are released in a set pattern.

1st hidden character = Kuma/Panda
2nd hidden character = Julia Chang
3rd hidden character = Gun Jack
4th hidden character = Mokujin
5th hidden character = Anna Williams
6th hidden character = Bryan Fury
7th hidden character = Heihachi
8th hidden character = Ogre
9th hidden character = True Ogre

Gon

To play Gon, you must enter Tekken Ball Mode and play against Gon. If you win Gon will become a selectable character.

Doctor Boskonovitch

To play the Russian scientist, you must enter Tekken Force Mode and complete all four stages three times. On the fourth time after defeating Heihachi you're fight against the doctor himself. If you beat him, Doctor Boskonovitch will become a selectable character.

Secret Costumes

Each character has two costumes. The standard costume is accessed by selecting your character with a punch button. The alternative costume is accessed by selecting your character with a kick button. Six of the characters have three costumes. This special costume is accessed by selecting your character with the **RP** button after these requirements are met:

Forest Law's "Way of the Dragon" costume is instantly selectable.
To unlock Gun Jack's "Jack" costume you need to play as Gun Jack at least ten times in any game mode.
To unlock Eddy's alter ego, Tiger, you need to complete Arcade Mode with at least sixteen different characters.
To unlock Anna's "1920's" costume, you need to play Anna at least twenty five times in any game mode.
To unlock Jin's "School Outfit", you need to play Jin at least fifty times in any game mode.
To unlock Ling's "School Girl Outfit", you need to play Ling at least fifty times in any game mode.

Tekken Ball Mode

After you beat the game with all the ten standard characters, Tekken Ball Mode will become available.

Theatre Mode

After you beat the game with all the ten standard characters, Theatre Mode becomes available. Here you can watch any of the movies for the characters you've completed the game with.

To access the Sound and Disc options in Theatre Mode, complete the game with every character except Doctor Boskonovitch and True Ogre.

The Sound option allows you to listen to all the music from Tekken 3.
The Disc option allows you to replace your Tekken 3 disc with either Tekken 1 or 2 and allowing you to access all the movies and music.

To access Gun Jack's "Good" ending you must complete the game as Gun Jack twice.

TEMPEST X3

Level Skip

To be able to skip a level at any time, press and hold the following during any game to set up the cheat: **L1**, **R1** and ↖ on the D-pad, ▲, ●, **Start** and **Select**. Release the buttons as soon as you hear a loud grinding sound. Next, quickly press and hold **L2**, **R1**, ✖, ▲, and ↓ on the D-pad. A spoken word will signify that the cheat is now ready to be used at any time. Whenever you want to skip a level, press the following four buttons simultaneously: **L1**, **L2**, **R1**, and **R2**. This will let you go to the next level as soon as there are no enemies on the web.

Psychadelic Mode

For loads of colours, press and hold the following during any game: **L1**, **R1**, ↖ on your D-pad, ▲, ●, **Start** and **Select**. Let go of the buttons as soon as you hear the grinding sound, then press and hold **L2**, **R1**, ✖, ▲, and ↑ on the D-pad.

Tempest 2000

To play Tempest 2000, you need to first get the #1 High Score, then enter your name as either 'YIFF!' or 'H V S'.

TEN PIN ALLEY

Taunts

Taunt the opposition during their approach by pressing the following during Team Play mode: **L1**, **L2**, **R1**, and **R2**. Now you can use the following:

'Choke!'	▲
'Loser!'	■
'Miss!'	●
'You Suck!'	✖

TENCHU

Increase Item Capacity
On the item selection screen hold **R2** and press ■, ■, ▲, ▲, ➡, ➡, ⬆, ⬇.

Gain Secret Items
On the item selection screen hold **R1** and press ■, ■, ▲, ▲, ➡, ➡, ⬆, ⬅.

Increase The Number Of Items
On the item selection screen hold **L2** and press ■, ■, ▲, ▲, ➡, ➡, ⬆, ➡.

Restore Your Health
Pause the game and press ■, ■, ▲, ▲, ➡, ➡, ⬆, ⬅.

Mission Select
On the mission selection screen hold **R1** and press ■, ■, ▲, ▲, ➡, ➡, ⬆, ➡.

Enemy Pattern
On the mission selection screen hold **L2** and press ■, ■, ▲, ▲, ➡, ➡, ⬆, ⬅.

Debug Mode
Pause the game, hold **L1 + R2** and press ⬆, ▲, ⬇, ✖, ⬅, ■, ➡, ●, release **L1 + R2** and slowly press **L1, R1, L2, R2**. Return to the game and press **L2 + R2** to bring up the debug menu.

TENCHU 2

AYAME
First you must completed the four training exercises, then proceed to Shiunsai's House, which is at the top of the cliff. Shiunsai will then give you one last test before he considers you a true ninja, he will pull a cord and you will plummet into a heavily guarded cave beneath the house.

Go past the torches and jump up the ledge, then immediately press against the wall on the left. Now slide along the wall until you are able to see the enemy. When the enemy faces away from you quickly run towards him and kill him. Put your weapon away and climb the step. Now stand in front of the wooden wall and jump. You should grab onto the ledge so pull yourself up. Run forward. Around to your left is a big pit with an enemy in it. Crouch down and look over the edge, wait until he walks to the right hand side then drop down and kill him. Use your grappling hook to get up the other side. Walk straight forwards but keep to your right. Push up against the wall and you will see a guard stood at the back wall. Once again wait until he is not facing you then run out to make your attack.

In this corridor are 6 distinctly marked tiles. Make sure you don't stand on these for too long because they will fall under your weight. Make your way up the slope, stop just before the edge then crouch and look over the edge. This guard walks about a lot so wait until he walks from the middle of the room to the right. You will have to be quick so start running before he stops. If you fall the gap will release poisonous gas so do a big jump. Now push up against the right hand wall. The enemy will only just come into view, so as soon as he walks away run as fast as you can to get there in time. In front of you is an arrow pointing up, go past this as you will go back later.

Walk up the slope on the right and keep to the right as there is a spear that comes out of the wall. At the end on the left above you is a gap. Use your grappling hook as the spear is right below it. Walk forward and to your right the wall goes in at an angle. Look down this and you will see the enemy. Wait for the right moment to strike. Now you can either go back the way you came or you can drop down in front of it and make your way back around. Now go where the arrow points using your grappling hook. Go through the tunnel (don't worry there are no guards). You will now find an arrow pointing down, there is water below so you're safe to jump. Turn to your right and swim forwards until you reach shallow water and a big pool. Dive down to your right and you will see a tunnel leading to another room. Make your way to the far end of the room and to your left, then rise to the surface and peep around the corner from which you came. There is a guard standing in the middle of the platform. Wait until he turns away then get out the water and kill him. Around the corner where you were hiding is a ledge. Jump up here but be slow and quiet as there is an enemy immediately around the corner. There is also another ledge to hide below. Once again wait for the right moment. Now head right and there will be a big drop into a room with a guard who will walk towards you in between the 2 pillars. Wait until he turns and walks away then quickly drop down and kill him. In this room is a big steel door. Walk towards it and it will open.

THE MOUNTAIN BANDITS
Equip lots of blades and health packs, but don't use them as you will need to save them for the end boss.

Run towards the boulder. Turn slightly to your right and you will see a small house with a sleeping guard in it, kill him. Turn around and walk around to your left, head up the slope and ahead of you is a series of ledges. Go to the top where there is a hut, be careful not to walk into the traps as they make a lot of noise. Go around the right hand side of the hut and up against the wall. In the background is a bandit who will disappear behind the rock; this is when you should strike. You will now be stood in front of a hut. Go around the right hand side beyond the fence and walk along side it. Just to your right is a little hut run behind this and wait until the bandit's back is turned before making the kill. Down the slope to your right is a well, where there is another bandit.

Stand at the top of the slope and wait for the bandit to start walking away from you. Carry on walking forwards and when you reach the cliff turn right and use your grappling hook to get to the top of the watch tower. This bandit is asleep. Jump off and walk in the direction you were walking in before, until you see a bridge. DON'T cross it. Instead walk around to your left until you reach a fence. Walk along it a little way and you will see the bandit walking around the other side of the bridge, wait until he is stood on the far side of the bridge then run.

Jump through the gap in the building. Exit, turn right and walk into the building to pick up the potion. If you turn you will see a big watch tower. Use your grappling hook to get up. This bandit is not asleep so you will have to hang there until he starts walking away from you. Look over the sides for the building with the torch in front of it (not the one you just came from). In this building is a sleeping bandit, go and kill him. Now turn and head for the fence. You will see in the distance on the other side a bandit patrolling. Jump the fence and stay out of sight, waiting to kill. Head up the steps but before you reach midway check the bandit is not in sight, if not walk forward and hide behind the wall until he walks down. When he is walking away you know what to do. Go to the bottom of the steps and head to the other side, passing the building with the last sleeping bandit in. When you reach the first tree look about and check the bandit isn't near. If he is not make your way forward to the next tree. You should now see a bandit. Only strike when he is on your right because there is another bandit on your left on top of the ledges who will see you. Wait until the bandit is walking left, get up to the first ledge and hang off the second. You will have to wait until he is walking left and passes you before you can make your strike. Make your way to the very top to meet the boss.

BOSS: Goron
As soon as you start, try to get onto the balcony as this is where you can use your blades. This should take of a good bit off his life but probably not all. If not do a jumping attack and then keep hitting so as not to give him a chance to fight back.

ACT 1 The red Lotus
LADY KEI IN DANGER
On this level only kill the soldiers with green armour on and stay out of the way of the women as they panic and it alerts the soldiers.

Turn left and approach the first door. Lean up against the wall and peer in. You will find a woman. Go past this door to the end of the wall, always looking out for patrolling soldiers. Go round the corner and down to the next door and again lean against the wall. You will find a soldier in this room. Wait for him to turn and kill. Take the top left door in this room and go straight around to the right to the next door. Stop and lean

against the wall to look in and find a soldier. Walk through this room and into the next, then turn right and go through that room too. Lean against the wall and wait for the patrolling soldier to pass the door before killing him. Walk straightforward and you will pass a friendly soldier, now keep right and walk up that wall. A soldier is patrolling along the top of the corridor. Once you have killed him take the door in the top right corner, go to the right hand side and go through that door.

There is a door on the opposite wall with a soldier in. You can kill him if you want but your not going that way so it's up to you. Head towards the door on your left and lean on the wall to check the room. You might not be able to see a soldier at first but there is one so be patient and he will present himself. When he does wait for him to show you his back then show him your weapon. Take the door on the left and go through the next 2 rooms. You will then see 2 doors in front of you, don't go through either. Instead turn left and peer round the corner to make sure there is no soldier there. If there is not go up to the top and smash the wooden door open. Then make your way up the stairs slowly, as there is a soldier at the top. The best time to strike is when he walks from the middle of the room to the left. You will have to move fast and to the top right corner as he will soon turn around. Even if he does you can still run along the wall to kill him. Now enter the room of fire (don't worry its safe) and turn left toward the door.

BOSS: Jenbu
This is easy. Just block his attack and then attack him. You only have to get his life down to about 145 then he will give in.

TO SAVE A PRINCESS
You must not let yourself be seen at all on this level.

When you start turn right and head towards the watchtower. Sneak along the wall, check no one is about then do ninja rolls all the way along the wooden barriers until you get to the end of the white pen. You will see a soldier patrolling. Wait until he starts walking away and then strike. Make sure you get it right or the alarm will be raised. Now turn left, go to the edge and drop down near the wooden logs towards the right. You will see a soldier. When he turns jump over the logs into the gap in front, wait for him to walk towards you and then turn so you can kill him. Go to your right up the slope; be aware of a soldier walking about. You should see a hut in front of you. This is where the princess is being held. Hide behind the tree nearest the hut and wait for the soldier to turn and walk away. Now go to the hut but watch out for the traps.

ACT 2 The shifting sands
KUBON ISLAND
All you need to do on this level is make your way clockwise around the island.

You start on a beach so just turn around, get in the water

and swim clockwise around the island. Make sure you pick a quiet spot to come up for air or you will be seen. Keep going until you come to another beach, get out and hide by the edge of the water until you feel confident on taking the kill. Carry on heading clockwise being cautious going around every corner. Make your way to the fence and jump it..

THE ISLAND FORT
Jump up over the ledge in front of you and wait for the guard in front to start walking away. On your right you will see a wooden pathway, follow this using your stealth skills to avoid the guards on the way up. You will come to a tunnel. When you come out the other side go left to kill the bad guy. Now walk back up and go left down to a bridge. Do a big jump over the bridge. Do not walk over it because it creeks and eventually breaks. There is also a sleeping guard on top of the watchtower who will wake up if it creeks too much. When you are across use your grappling hook to get up there and kill him. Carry on following the path and you will find it ends shortly. Go left and a wooden walkway takes you up a couple of ledges, or you can go right and take that walkway instead. Either way you come across a hut. Get on top of it and then use your grappling hook to get you on top of the cliff. Go around the side of the large building, drop down one ledge and jump on top of the building in front of you. Use your grappling hook to get up to the top of the cliff. Here is a little ledge. Go onto that one first as there is a guard in front of the entrance to the prison. Enter the prison and go straight forward to the large cell in front of you.

BOSS: Wang Dahi
Simple really. Block his attacks then either do a simple normal attack back or do lunge attacks that take off more life.

THE QUARANTINE VILLAGE
Immediately after you start turn 180° and head down to the stone walls watching out for the ninja women with 2 daggers. Once you have killed her follow the fence all the way round and watch out for the big hole in the ground, When you get to some stone you must crouch and wait for the villager to turn and walk away. If he sees you he will make a noise and a nearby ninja will be made aware of your presence. Now walk up to the bottom of the stairs.

BOSS'S: Snake, Frog and Slug
Try and keep them in close vicinity of one another as Slug is a bit heavy handed with his weapon and will damage his friends, which helps an awful lot. Do full on attacks through them all and when on the other side do a flip jump (Down, Up and the Jump button) and immediately block. Repeat this and you should to fine.

CHERRY TREE HILL
Go left and head for the trees. Crouch behind the second one and look to your right. In time you will see a blue ninja woman. Wait until she turns and follow her down the gauge. Stop at the end in front of the stream where you will see a bird lady on the

other side. Run out to your right, do a big jump over the stream and run after her when she starts walking to the left. Turn around and head toward the blossom tree. When you get to it turn right and you will see a sleeping ninja to kill. Jump the stream and head toward the boulder. On the ledge in front of you is a ninja (use the look button to find him). When you do wait for the right moment to strike. Make your way around the left-hand side of the hill and stop by the sloping ledge. If you look over it you will see a bird woman. Also watch out as there is a wolf nearby. The woman will walk across to the other side of the ledge. This is when you should attack. Head forward to the next ledge but keep along the right hand wall as there is a ninja down to your left. You should also see another bird women just ahead. Now all you have to do is go up and to the right.

IN PURSUIT OF TATSUMARU
Make sure you equip, as many blades as you can and about three health potions, but don't use them until you get to the boss.

Head right and follow the rocky ledges watching out for mines. Stop at the edge of the bamboo trees and ahead you will see a birdman. His back should be turned, if not just wait. Jump up the ledge in front of you and keep right. If you keep to the far right you will come across a sleeping birdman. Stay as far right as possible as there is a mine guarding him. There is also a mine for you to pick up. Follow the bamboo around to your right watching for any ninjas. You should come across a sleeping ninja with big claws. Jump the stream and try to land behind the first tree then duck behind it. There is a ninja patrolling around this area so wait until the right moment to move in for the kill. Just keep following the trees around to your right, always on the lookout for patrolling ninja. You will come across a claw ninja walking in-between the trees who should be no problem to kill. Follow the path around to the left and you will see a lone bamboo tree ahead. Stop around the corner just before and wait for the birdman to walk up and back again. Run forward to the big opening.

BOSS : Byakko The White Tiger
Start off by throwing all your ninja blades at the tiger then wait for him to attack before striking with your combo attack. When you attack again you will find that he will pass you a little bit. Make sure you turn and face him or you won't be able to block.

THE KANSEN CAVERNS
Turn right, drop down into the water and swim to the left-hand ledge. If you fall down the waterfall swim to the far right corner. There is a green women on the ledge above so wait until she has gone then look out to the water. You will see a ledge slightly higher. Do a big jump onto it and turn right into a brown cave. Inside the cave is a man, watch him and when he isn't looking run and jump into the hole in the wall. Turn left up the slope. There is a mine in the middle of this room so walk around to your right, then jump up the ledge. You will now see

a ledge in front of you but you will have to do a big jump to get to it. Now jump over. This where you would have got out if you had not fallen.

There is a birdman stood by the first pillar. Once you have killed him turn and wait behind the pillar. You will see a woman patrolling. Make sure you kill her on the right hand side of the room, as there is an archer further up to the left. Kill the archer by sneaking up behind him. To the right of the big wooden gate is a ledge. Use your grappling hook to get up there. On the ledge above is a ninja patrolling with big claws. Go to the back right and you will see a trap laid across a doorway. Jump this and make your way down the slope. About halfway down there will be a little alcove on your right. Jump past this as it shoots arrows. Follow the corridor to the bottom and turn right. You will need to go straight across this room, but watch out for the room on your right as you go past. At the end is a sleeping ninja. Take care as there is another ninja the other side of the wooden fence and if he sees you first the sleeping Ninja will wake up. Now turn around and go round to your right. Halfway down the slope is a trap and the following room is full of mines so tread carefully. Turn left into the next room and take the exit on your left. Down the bottom of this corridor is a birdman. Do a big jump off the ledge to just clear the trap then run up and kill him. There is another trap to your right, walk around it and through this room. At the end is a slope, walk halfway up and wait for the green woman to start walking away. Kill her. Do a couple a ninja rolls backwards so the ninja in the next room doesn't see you then go and kill him. Start walking down the slope on your left but not all the way as a ninja will present himself. When he walks around the corner chase after him and kill him. Walk around the right hand side of the wooden fencing.

ACT 3 Solitude
THE FIRE DEMON
Go down the right hand side passage and drop down the stairs, then walk along the left hand side of the room and jump down the hole. Walk forward and jump up the step on the right hand side then press against the wall and wait for the ninja to turn around. Walk round to the left into the next room and right down the slope. Wait just past the bottom for a ninja to turn and walk to the left. Now lean against the left-hand pillar, wait for the clawed ninja to move away, then kill him. On the right hand side of the room is a passage leading up. Go up to the top and smash open the door. Check there are no ninjas about then run up the stairs stopping just before the top. Look forward and you will see a ninja walking towards you. Wait and kill. Enter the next room slowly, as there are two sets of stairs and a ninja in between. Wait until he faces away and run up the right stairs stopping before the top. Look to your left to see a ninja walking about. Kill him. Head left down this corridor watching out for any ninja lurking around the pillars. Now drop down to the left and head left. Follow this path all the way round to the front were you will meet Jenbu.

BOSS: Jenbu
All you have to do is block his swings then strike back. If you have any blades throw them when he isn't too close then immediately attack.

BOSS: Tatsumaru
Block his combos and as soon as he finishes attack like mad and don't stop. You will have to be quick as he will start again very quickly. Always make sure you stay in front of him. Now sit back and enjoy the superb graphics.

RIKIMARU
First you must have completed the four training exercises, then proceed to Shiunsai's house which is at the top of the cliff. Shiunsai will then give you one last test before he considers you a true ninja. He will pull a cord and you will plummet into a heavily guarded cave beneath the house.

Go past the torches, jump up the ledge and then immediately press against the wall on the left. Now slide along the wall until you are able to see the enemy. When the enemy faces away from you quickly run towards him and kill him. Put your weapon away and climb the step. Now stand in front of the wooden wall and jump. You should grab onto the ledge so pull yourself up. Run forward and around to your left is a big pit with an enemy in it. Crouch down and look over the edge. Wait until he walks to the right hand side then drop down and kill him. Use your grappling hook to get up the other side then walk straight forwards keeping to your right. Push up against the wall and you will see a guard stood at the back wall again. Wait until he is not facing you then run out to make your attack. In this corridor are 6 distinctly marked tiles on the floor. Make sure you don't stand on these for too long because they will fall under your weight. Make your way up the slope, stop just before the edge, crouch and look over the edge. This guard walks about a lot so wait until he walks from the middle of the room to the right. You will have to be quick here so start running before he stops. Do a big jump over the gap because if you fall in it will release poisonous gas. Now push up against the right hand wall. The enemy will only just come into view.

As soon as he walks away run as fast as you can and you should get there in time. In front of you is an arrow pointing up. Go past this as you will go back later. Walk up the slope on the right and keep to the right as there is a spear that comes out of the wall. At the end on the left above you is a gap. Use your grappling hook as the spear is right below it. Walk forward. To your right the wall goes in at an angle. Look down here and you will see the enemy. Wait for the right moment to strike. Now you can either go back the way you came or you can drop down in front and make your way back around. Now go where the arrow points using your grappling hook and make your way up. Go through the guard-free tunnel. You will now find an arrow pointing down. There is water below so you're safe to jump. Turn to your right and swim forwards until you reach shallow water. Here there is a big pool. Dive down and to your right and under the water you will see a tunnel leading to another room. Make your way to the far end of the room and to your left. Rise to the surface and peep around the corner from which you came. There is a guard standing in the middle of the platform. Wait until he turns away then get out the water and kill him. Around the corner where you were hiding is a ledge. Jump up here taking extreme care as there is an enemy immediately around the corner. There is another ledge here to hide below. Once again wait for the right moment. Now head right and there will be a big drop into a room with a guard walking around, he will walk towards you in between the 2 pillars. Wait until he turns and walks away then quickly drop down and kill him. In this room is a big steel door. Walk towards it and it will open.

THE GANG OF THIEVES

Run towards the boulder and turn 45° to the right. You should be able to see a hut and an enemy inside. Crouch near the rock. Wait a few seconds for him to lose his guard and fall asleep. Once asleep, approach the enemy, unsheathe your blade and kill him. Step back outside and pivot approximately 45°. Head for the mound of dirt next to a house. Hide behind the mound and wait for the enemy on the rooftop to turn his back on you. Use your grappling hook to get up and kill him. Jump off the roof and head for the stack of logs next to the watchtower. Grapple up to the top of the watchtower, wait for the right moment, and then attack the unsuspecting archer. Jump off of the side opposite to the logs. Run towards the house with the fence and then to the overturned tree. Drop down into the ravine along the right hand side of the tree and run to the end. Crouch when you reach the end peer over the tree. You should see an enemy walking about. Wait for him to walk close then run out and attack before he moves again. Now turn 90° to the left and head for the well, watch out for the woman. If she sees you she'll shout, alerting the enemy. When you get to the well crouch behind it. There is an enemy on the other side slightly up ahead, wait for the enemy to turn his back and kill him. Just ahead you will find a house and a tower. Walk between the two and press against the house. Peer around the right corner. You should see an enemy by a tree and in front of the bridge. He will only turn occasionally.

Wait for the right moment when his back is turned. Go over the bridge and continue running straight. Stop next to the large tree. Use your grappling hook to get up the tower in front of you. Hang onto the sides as there is a guard at the top. This enemy won't see you so wait until his back is turned. Look over the left-hand side where you can see an enemy patrolling. Drop down carefully and wait for him to walk in your direction. When he turns to walk away run after him and kill him. Turn around, head past the tower, jump over the fence and immediately crouch. The enemy ahead is guarding the entrance to the shrine. Wait until he walks to the left and kill him. Be careful walking up the stairs. Stop halfway and look up the rest of the

stairs. He will turn around at some point. When he does kill him. Now head up to the shrine.

BOSS: Garan

Don't wait for him to attack you just keep giving all the attacks you can. If you do miss or make a mistake block his attack and then start again.

ACT 1 The Red Lotus
TREASON AT GOHDA CASTLE

Walk through the doorway to your right. This room is on fire but just avoid the fire and you'll be fine. Head to the other side of the room then climb the stairs. Make your way through the three rooms until you reach a dead end. Slice the black and white wall panel. On the other side will be a soldier. Wait for his back to turn. Take a right, ignore the stairs and carry on around the corner. Turn left into the next room where there will be a soldier either in the doorway to the room in front or just past it. Walk through the next couple of rooms and you will see a staircase on your left. Stand by the doorway at a safe distance. You will see a soldier walking in and out of the room. When he turns to exit, run and attack. Now go up the stairs. In the room to the right there is a soldier. Enter slowly If he is not in the room he will be patrolling the next room. Take a left and crouch in the right corner between a torch and the wall. Look into the hallway and wait for a soldier to walk into view from the right. He will stop, turn around then continue to the left. As he starts to walk left, run out and attack. Go right down to the end and enter the room on your left, stopping just after you enter. There is a soldier standing in the room in front. He will only turn on the spot. Go to the left, smash the black and white door and go up the stairs. Head out into the corridor and up and across the raised walkway where there will be a soldier at the end. There will be a door on your right with stairs to the right of it. Climb both sets of stairs. While crouching, move forward until you spot the enemy. Keep heading up to the end of the level.

BOSS: Gohda Motohide

He has a sword and a gun so stay close. At least then you can block his sword. Reduce his life to approximately 50 to win.

LORD TODA'S WAR CAMP

A soldier stands directly in front of you, but he can't see you. Turn right and run in between the 2 piles of logs. Wait for the enemy to turn his back and strike. Jump on top of the hut and jump onto the ledge. Keep looking to the left to avoid an archer. Keep running forward constantly watching for any enemies. When you come across a big white fence turn left and head for the middle.

BOSS: The Red Sparrow

He will throw knives at you if your are at a certain distance so stay close and slash like mad. Reduce his life below 100 to win.

ACT2 The Shifting Sands

DEMON MOUNTAIN

When you start the level run forward to the ledges and use your grappling hook to the first ledge. Now grapple up to the next ledge and hang on. There is an enemy here. Wait for him to turn his back on you. Climb up and turn left to see a mossy ledge. Use your grappling hook to reach it. Now turn right around and grapple to the ledge just up from you. Turn around again and you should see a series of ledges. Climb up the first of these, then hang onto the second ledge where there is an enemy right above you. Walk past the bridge and stop at the ravine. On the other side should be a patrolling enemy. Do a big jump and you should manage to grab on to the other side. Wait for the enemy to walk past you then pull yourself up and kill him. Now traverse your way across the multiple pillars to the highest one on the far side. If you fall there are two enemies at the bottom; one guard and a big Grey bear that is hard to see. This little bit could keep you entertained for hours if you don't get it right, so take your time. When on the top one turn left and do a big jump to the next ledge. Hide behind the hut and wait for the enemy to walk past you. Go to the grassy ledge on the right and grapple to it. Pull yourself up when the enemy passes to your right. There are a couple of ledges in front of you Jump up these and cross the bridge.

BOSS: Kamadoma

This boss has a combo that you must avoid. Just keep hacking into him or he will use grenades and smoke bombs on you. Once again stay close.

THE SECRET HARBOR

Draw your blade and crouch behind the wall to your left. Wait for the guard to turn and walk away. Now follow the path around to the left. When you pass a slope on your right wait at the end. There is an enemy around the corner. Now walk up through the passage to the other side and walk across the little slope with the boulder at the top. Keep running forward and out onto the beach. Now follow the water line to the left until you come to a walkway with a guard at the bottom. When he is not looking kill him. Stand at the bottom of the wooden plank and wait for the guard that is halfway along to turn then run up and kill him. Go onto the ship, turn left and jump into the hole to complete the level.

BOSS: Wang Xiaohai

This boss is deadly. He has no weapons other than his hands which is to his advantage as they are much harder to block. Don't give him any chances to attack. Use your ninja blades as soon as you start, After throwing a couple unleash a combo to take maximum damage off. When he stands up do it again.

THE TEMPLE OF DREAMS

This is very easy. When you start walk to the left of the bridge and jump in the water. Swim around the left-hand side of the building, go under the boat and stick to the side of the building. Make sure you come up for air. When you get to the end of the building turn right and swim between two blocks, then over a little ridge. You will see a boat in front of you. Get on it and draw your weapon. Go to the back of the boat and you will see a little pier in front of you. You will need to do a big jump to get to it. If you don't make it don't just get straight up onto it use the boat again. You'll need your weapon drawn straight away against this boss as you will have no time to get it out.

BOSS: Yukihaturo

This boss is quite hard, she has a strong combo plus she will throw 4 blades at a time. So stay close and don't stop laying into her. Give her an inch and you're dead.

THE NINJA VILLAGE UNDER ATTACK

When you start immediately step back. There is a ninja on the roof in front of you and he can see you. Turn around and grapple to the top of your master's house. Go to the back, stand near the edge and look below. There is a ninja. After you have killed him walk towards the hot water pool, there is a ninja in green. Don't kill him as he's on your side. Stop near the edge and wait for a ninja to come into view, when he does wait for him to start walking away then kill him. You should be near a big tree. Wait by the side of it and look to the left of the burning log. In between 2 trees will be a ninja lady. Time this well because you have quite a distance to run. Now turn right up the slope and crouch behind the tree stump, up behind the fence is another ninja. He will walk across the entrance then turn to look your way for a second then turn and walk away. Run at this point. Once you've killed him go back out, go to your right and go up the left hand side of the building Wait in between that and the second building. Look around the corner and you will see a ninja. If he is walking towards you run to the other end of the wall, wait until he turns to walk back down then chase after him. Run to the end of the building and look around the corner to make sure there is no ninja (there shouldn't be). Now keep on walking down the path and stop just before you get to the turning on the right. Just ahead will be a ninja. Just wait for the right time. Carry on down the path and there will be a watchtower in front of you. Grapple up but hang off the edge until the ninja turns his back on you. Now drop down the same side and you will be next to a bridge Stop at the top of the bridge and you will see a ninja by the slope in front of you. Kill her when she walks away. Go in front of the building and wait. There will be a ninja walking in front of the larger building the other side. When he walks in the other direction go and get him. Now walk back down to the bridge by the watchtower and go left around it. You should be in front of another bridge. Cross it, turn to your right, crouch and wait. A ninja will approach and stop by the entrance to the bamboo forest. He will stand here for a while then walk away. Now he is out of the way stand by the entrance yourself. If you wait you will see a ninja inside. Walk back out and across the bridge then turn left. Go and wait behind the tree for a ninja to walk up to you. When he walks away he must die. Follow the stream along until it goes to the right. When it does stop and look up to see a ninja walking up the slope. When he gets halfway run up after him. At the top you will find another ninja. She walks around a lot so she could be anywhere. Take your time and you should do all right. Once you have killed her head back to your master's house. The best way is to jump over the fence to the ninja on your side, walk between the buildings and straight forward. When you get to the second noise trap turn right and grapple up to the ledge with the other friendly ninja, then up again. Look to the building on your right. On the roof will be your last enemy to kill.

Done!

BOSS: Tatsumaru

He only punches and kicks you so it is simple to block. Take your time in retaliating as he may start before you get to hit him. Get his life down to about 35 to beat him.

THE PURSUIT OF TATSUMARU

Draw your sword and turn right. Walk up to the bamboo and look up the slope where you will see a ninja. If you wait she will fall asleep. Run up and take a swipe. Now turn left and head up the path. There is a mine on your left in a gap so don't walk into it. Just around the next bamboo there will be a ninja below and one ahead slightly and up. Try to time this perfectly. Run past the Ninja below and up to the ledge, then hang from it and wait until the one above is not looking, then pull yourself up and kill him. Keep to the right all the way round, watching out for the little dirt mound. Keep following the trees a little more then, before the end, stop and crouch. Up ahead you will see a ninja. When he starts walking away run forward and turn to your right totally ignoring him. Walk a little way forward to see the ninja ahead. If you can't see his head popping up over the top of the slope then he is asleep. Kill him then jump across the stream. Hide behind some bamboo and wait for a woman to become visible. She will look away but don't run as she will turn to come in your direction very quickly so wait until she turns around again. Keep following the trees around to the right, always on the look out for ninjas. Walk past the trap and stop at the corner. There will be a ninja around the corner so just wait. Walk past the lone bamboo tree and wait just at the edge of the corner on the left-hand side. A black ninja is on the prowl so wait for him to turn then kill. Walk to the end of the path..

BOSS: BYAKKO

This bloke is a little soft, but still has a sword. He has a 4-5 hit combo so wait, then just lay into him. If you give him a chance he will use a smoke bomb so jump back quick. He doesn't have much life so it won't take long.

THE KANSEN CAVERNS

Turn right, drop down into the water and swim to the left-hand ledge, if you fall down the waterfall swim to the far right corner. There is a green women on the ledge above so wait until she

has gone then look out to the water and you will see a ledge slightly higher. Do a big jump onto it and turn right into a brown cave. Inside the cave is a man, watch him and when he isn't looking run and jump into the hole in the wall. Turn left up the slope. There is a mine in the middle of this room so walk around to your right, then jump up the ledge. You will now see a ledge in front of you but you will have to do a big jump to get to it. There is a ninja stood by the first pillar. Once you have killed him turn and wait behind the large pillar to your left where you will see a woman patrolling. To the right of the big wooden gate is a ledge. Use your grappling hook to get up there. On the ledge above is a ninja patrolling with big claws. Go to the back right and you will see a trap laid across a doorway. Jump this and make your way down the slope. About half way there will be a little alcove on your right, jump past this as it shoots arrows. Follow the corridor to the bottom and wait at the edge. Look around the corner to see a ninja. She may be asleep. If not wait until she is then kill her. At the end is a sleeping ninja but be careful as there is another ninja to the left just before. Kill him first then kill the sleeping one. Now turn around and go round to your right. Halfway down the slope is a trap and the following room is full of mines so tread carefully. Turn left in the next room but watch for a patrolling ninja. Take the door to the right of the one you came in but move slowly as there is a ninja right by it. Down the bottom of this corridor is a couple of traps. Jump down and walk around the first one then slide up against the wall and peer around the corner. There are 2 ninjas in this room. The nearest one will fall asleep if he isn't already. When he is wait for the second one to turn and walk away. Run around the trap, kill him, then turn around and kill the sleeping one. At the end of the room is a slope. Walk halfway up, wait for the ninja to start walking away, then kill her. Do a couple a ninja rolls backwards so the ninja in the next room doesn't see you then go and kill him. Start walking down the slope on your right but not all the way as a ninja will present himself out of the middle of the fencing. Chase after him and kill him. Walk around the right hand side of the wooden fencing.

ACT3 Solitude

THE SEA BATTLE Part 1

Turn left and follow the pier to the end then jump in the water to your left. When in the water turn to your right slightly and you will begin to see some boats. Swim under them. When you need air come up slowly and quietly or you will be seen. Keep following the boats until you come across a huge one with a plank leading down to concrete steps. Climb up out of the water, draw your sword, stand at the bottom of the plank and look onto the boat. You will see a green ninja. You don't have to kill him if you don't want to. Instead you can just run to the far left of the boat.

BOSS: The Red Sparrow

This boss has a killer combo so avoid it at all costs. Like all bosses just keep attacking giving him no chance to attack back. When you first start back off and drop down the ledge as there is more space to fight in the middle of the ship. If you need to you can run to either end of the ship and use your grappling hook to get to one of the masts, but you must be super quick. Here you can use your health potions and wait for him to lose you and turn away. When he does drop behind him and immediately unleash a combo attack.

Part 2

Turn left and grapple on to the roof. Turn right and walk to the end, look down you will see a ninja. When he walks away jump down and cross the bridge. Stand at the end of the bridge and grapple up to the roof of the building in front of you. Walk to the other side, check below to make sure no ninjas are looking, then jump down and cross the bridge. When on the other side walk around the right hand side of the mast and walk to the edge. Drop down and go around the right hand corner. Jump over the raised pathway in front of you and press up against the right hand wall. Wait for the ninja to turn his back then run straight across to the other side. Just keep running to the end of the level.

BOSS: Kagami

Stage 1

She will have a little dagger. Just keep up an unrelenting attack. Get her life down to 125.

Stage 2

She will now get out a very large sword and run down the steps at you. Before she has chance to attack, you must attack her and keep going. She will also use blades and grenades so keep on guard.

TATSUMARU

ACT1 The Red Lotus

A SHADOW

Go straight forward and up the slope to the soldier in front of you. Now turn to your right and grapple to the roof. Go around the right side of the building until you get to a high wall, follow this wall all the way around to your left, watching for soldiers along the way. You will come to a double roof, grapple to the top one and you will be able to get over the wall. When at the top turn right and walk forward to a very large building. Grapple all the way to the top to meet the boss.

BOSS: Seiryu

This boss only has a 2 hit combo but is quite powerful. Hit and punch him continuously and he wont stand a chance. It's best to start another combo as he is getting up.

THE HEAD OF LORD TODA

Walk down and into the pen in front of you. Walking back out of the same exit, turn right into the fencing and turn left. Jump on top of the hut. A ninja is in front of you so wait and jump onto the ledge. Keep running forward and stop at the top of the little slope. A soldier will walk to the other side of the tree

stump on your left. When he does go and kill him. Carry on in the direction you were going and stop when you get to a tree stump in front of a ledge. Look to your right and you will see a ninja. He will walk halfway along then turn and walk back again. Strike now. Go to the top of the mound, stop and look down to your left. You will see a soldier walking around by some boxes. Wait until he's walking away then go down and kill him. Turn right and you will be in front of the large white pen. Go to the front.

BOSS: TODA

Toda will call 2 guards to help him, an archer and a spearman. Try to get Toda in between you and the archer so when the archer shoots an arrow at you it hits him. When Toda is near you keep attacking him. If the spearman is close enough you will hit him too. When your health gets to about 40 try to get into a space to renew it as you will probably be hit a couple of times in the process. Keep going and you will soon get rid of the spearman, which will make Toda a darn sight easier to finish off.

ACT2 The Shifting Sands

LABOR SHORTAGE

You cannot be seen on this mission otherwise you will be killed.

Turn left at the start, go to the next street and follow the passage way on the left of the street, but stop before it turns. Look down it and you will see a guard. He will disappear behind the building. This is the best time to strike. Carry on ahead and another guard should usually be asleep (go slow to make sure). If he is asleep go up and hit him. Keep on going but stay to the left-hand side, a guard will be walking up a little alleyway so stop by the wall, he won't come as far as you so don't worry. When he turns to walk away make your move. Now turn around, go to your right and then stop at the beginning of the alleyway. If you wait long enough a guard will walk by. Run and kill him. Turn left, grapple onto the roof and head straightforward. When you come to the end look down to see a guard walking up and down. Wait until he is walking to the right then drop down and kill him. Once you have killed him turn right down the alleyway and around to your left. Ahead in the corner should be a sleeping guard. Go and kill him. Step back and grapple onto the roof. Turn right and you will see a watch tower with a guard on top. Sometimes he is asleep. If he is grapple to the edge. If not wait until his back is turned then grapple to the edge, hang off and wait until he turns his back again. When you are ready pull yourself up and kill. In front of you on the ground is a patrolling guard, When he walks from below you to the middle of the 2 torches jump down and run up to kill him. Now go left until you get to a bridge, stop by the white post, crouch, look to the top and wait. Eventually a guard will walk up and over to this side then turn to walk back. When he does go and kill him.

GUARDING THE SECRET HARBOR

On this mission you must kill all the enemies again but this time it doesn't matter if you are seen.

Run down the passage and around to your left. There will be a guard on the ledge to your left. Go right down the next passage and crouch half way down. On the ledges in front of you there will be a guard. When he walks around to the left jump up and kill him. Turn around and wait. A guard will come from the same direction you did. Now run down towards the opening but wait by the first ledge. Another patrolling guard will come into view. If you feel he's getting too close just roll backwards. Wait for him to turn and then kill him. Run diagonally to your right until you get to a tree with grass at its base. Crouch and wait and a guard will come near. If its too near roll backwards again. When he walks away go and get him, but be careful as on the other side of the tree is a mine. Keep walking down until you **see** a torch on a ledge. When you do you should also be able to see a guard. When he walks towards the torch jump up and kill him. Now turn to go through the alcove and turn right over the edge. You should be able to see a sleeping guard. Jump over to him a put him to sleep indefinitely. Go back out and walk into the middle of the beach.

Kill the guard by a square box watching out for the little mounds on the floor (they're mines). Now head back up to the cliffs and you will see another guard walking around by the large square rock. Turn right and go forward. On top of three ledges will be another guard. Go down past the hut and to your left. There will be some more ledges around the corner with a guard on top. Jump back down and follow the wall along. When you reach the end stop just ahead and you should see a guard walking around. Wait for the right moment then strike. Follow the torches forward. There will be a guard stood at the bottom of the plank. Turn slightly to your right and jump into the sea. Once in the water swim for a little bit. Turn slightly more to the right and you should come across a little island. Be very quiet as there is a guard on it. Make sure you time this well as there isn't a lot of fighting space. Once he is dead, head back to the ship. Stand by the middle section of the plank and look onto the ship. Here will be a patrolling guard. When he walks to the left go with him. You should have now killed all the guards. If you have missed a couple check around the beach area.

BOSS: Elderly Guard

You can't help but feel sorry for this poor old chap, as he seems so frail. He has a powerful four hit combo and a spin attack. But as he is such a feeble old man you should be able to kill him quite easy. Just keep laying the punches on.

NO MERCY

On this mission you have to kill all the guards.
When the level starts immediately roll to the right and run up the wall. A guard will have walked out from the end of the building. Run behind him and kill him. Wait behind this corner and a guard will walk from between the two buildings on your left. As he walks back down go and attack him. Turn left and walk all the way to the end. Watch out on your first right as there is villager down there. When you get to the end you will see a well. Turn right, keep going and you will see two rocks. Go past these to the next building and wait by the end. A guard will walk just past you. Kill him before he turns around. Go right along the building with the pool on your left and stop at the end to see a guard in front of a big tree. When he looks at the pool run to kill him. Now if you turn to look up the embankment by the washing there is a guard patrolling around it, stay back until he has passed you and gone back up, now run up and kill him. Turn left and follow the path down the hill you will see another guard walking around, stay out of sight and when you think the time is right do your thing.

Walk around the left-hand side of the building with the fence. Walk up the left-hand wall and look down to see a guard. He will walk all the way up to you. Kill him before he has time to turn. Wait a little way inside the alley looking in the direction you came. A guard will walk towards you but will then turn and go back down the building. Run and kill him. Now turn back around, go back to the last guard, walk down the alley and go left. Stop near the end of the wall. In front should be a well with a guard nearby. Wait for the right time then strike. Turn right and go slowly up a little hill. There is a guard walking on the top. He will walk away slightly. When he does run up and out across the pool. You now need to go back to the house with the fence. If you go to the right of it there is a steaming pool. Go around to the right but be careful as there is a villager around there. Sneak past him and follow the pool around. When you come to an angled corner stop and look ahead of you. There will be an archer standing on the wall. You will need to sneak up on him, hide below the wall and, when he isn't looking, finish him. Now follow the fence and stop just past a big hole. A guard will be walking nearby soon. Bide your time and strike when you are ready. Watch the left as you go past the three stones then wait. You will find a guard nearby. Go to the building opposite the steps and look down the right hand side of the building. A guard will walk to the nearest bit of grass, stop, and turn around. Quickly go and kill him. That was your last man.

ASSAULT ON THE AZUMA NINJA VILLAGE

When you start turn right slightly and walk towards the hill. Go around the right side of the hill and ahead will be a little green ninja. Now go around the left of the building in front, passing two upturned baskets. Use your grappling hook to get on top of the roof. Now turn left look above the cliff and a ninja will be walking up and down. Wait for him to be as far to the left as possible then do a big jump on to the cliff. Head right and up to the building to complete the level.

BOSS: Master Shiunsai

He is the master ninja and a very hard one at that. He knows how to use his sword so always be on guard. When he breaks attack. He will step back out of the way so learn when to stop and block. Keep repeating this and he will soon lose all his life.

THE FINAL DAWN
Again you must eliminate all guards on this huge boat.

Run forward and drop down the step. There will be a guard down the next one. Now drop down that step and just ahead will be another guard. Turn right and do ninja rolls forward until you see another guard. Watch your left side as there is another one who may see you. When you have killed these two go to the left or the right hand side of this area up a ramp and turn left or right accordingly up another ramp, but not all the way. Look to the top and you will see a guard. Wait for his back to turn then kill him. Now on the left hand side is another guard up towards the top. When you have killed these go to the right hand side and keep going along the bottom rampway where you will pass a torch on your right. When you reach a big pillar go slowly as there are two guards down below. Watch their movement and when you can kill one without the other seeing do it. Once you have killed both of them run down the right hand side of the ramp you came from past some spare cannons. Stop just inside the corner, wait for the guard to stroll in and then quickly kill him before he turns around. Now walk out, wait behind the big pillar and look around it. When the guard is facing away run and kill him. Now grapple onto the room around the right hand corner, go straight over and drop down.

Go to the wall and jump. You should grab on to the edge, if not grapple up. When hanging look about for a guard. You should see one up by the cannon. There will also be another one walking about the big pillar. Time this right because the other one will see you killing his chum. When you have killed those two there will be another one up on the raised platform walking up and down. Run up to the edge and crouch behind it and, when he isn't looking, jump up and kill him. Go back down, turn right to go across a bridge, go to the wall opposite the ramp and look around the corner. A guard will walk up and then turn around. Go and kill him. Now run all the way down to the other ramp and wait on that corner. Look around it and you will see yet another guard. Just wait for the right moment as this one only turns on the spot. Drop down and go right across the bridge. Stop half way and crouch. You will see a guard just up ahead. He also only turns on the spot so just wait until he turns away. Go and wait by the edge of the wall and look down the passageway where a guard will be walking up and down. He will stop a little way before you. Quickly kill him because he will soon turn your way again. Now jump up the wall on your right and there will be another guard. He will walk away towards the pillar. Pull yourself up and kill him. Drop back down and carry on around the corner to the end. There will be a ramp on your right leading to a room. Wait here and there will be a guard around to your left. When he turns to go in the other direction go and kill him. Now go down to the bottom of the ramp and wait at the left-hand side of the entrance.

Inside you will see a guard. Strike when he reaches the far wall. That was your last kill.

BOSS: Jubai
This boss has a deadly four hit combo. If you block it then attack you will gradually take down his health. You can use your ninja blades, although he will sometimes block them.

TEST DRIVE 4

Hidden Cars
To get ALL of the hidden cars, firstly select a normal game with checkpoints and traffic. When you get into the top 10, simply enter your name as "SAUSAGE".
Mirrored Tracks
Follow the same steps as above but this time enter your name as "KNACKED"
Nitro
Follow the steps as above then enter your name as "WHOOOSH"
Micro Cars
Follow the steps as above then enter your name as "MJCIM.RC"

TEST DRIVE 4X4

School Bus
Select Single Race or World Tour mode, choose any vehicle then on the transmission selection screen press **L1, ↑, L2, ↓, ↓, L2, L2, R2**. Start the race and you will be driving a school bus.

Ice Cream Van
Select Single Race or World Tour mode, choose any vehicle then on the transmission selection screen press **R2, L2, L2, ↓, ↓, L2, L2, R1**. Start the race and you will be driving an Ice Cream Van.

TEST DRIVE 5

Unlock All Game Modes
Enter your name as **VRSIX** on the high score screen.

Access All Cars and Tracks
Enter **RONE, NTHREE** and **MTHREE** as names on the high score table.

Bonus Cars
Enter **NOLIFE** as a name on the high score table.

TEST DRIVE OFFROAD

Try out these effects by entering the codes as the player's name:

CODE	EFFECT
sprinter	4X4 Buggy

alltrack	All Tracks Available
friendly	Dirt Track
fifty	Hot Rod
beefy	Monster Truck
lowrider	Stock Car

TETRIS PLUS

Stage Select

To access the stage select option, firstly select Puzzle Mode, then select Password. As soon as the Password screen appears, press ⬇, ⬇, ➡, ⬆, ⬆, ➡, ⬆, ⬆, ⬆, ➡. Do this a second time then press ✖ and a Stage Select option will be available when the game starts.

THEME HOSPITAL

Passwords

Level 2	✖, ●, ■, ▲, ▲, ●, ■, ✖
Level 3	●, ●, ▲, ■, ✖, ▲, ●, ▲
Level 4	■, ▲, ●, ■, ✖, ✖, ▲, ●
Level 5	●, ▲, ■, ●, ✖, ▲, ●, ■
Level 6	■, ▲, ■, ●, ✖, ■, ✖, ●
Level 7	■, ▲, ▲, ●, ✖, ■, ▲, ●
Level 8	✖, ▲, ■, ●, ▲, ●, ■, ✖
Level 9	▲, ■, ✖, ▲, ●, ✖, ▲, ■
Level 10	●, ■, ✖, ▲, ■, ✖, ●, ■
Level 11	▲, ●, ■, ●, ▲, ■, ●, ✖
Level 12	●, ■, ✖, ✖, ■, ●, ■, ▲

THEME PARK

Instant Millions

Gain $10 million by entering BOVINE as your nickname. Then hold the following for 10 seconds during play: ●, ■ and ✖

THEME PARK WORLD

Special Awards

Follow these tips to win special gold tickets:

Aesthetics	Build at least eight rides and spend over $3,000 on features.
Security	Install cameras that can see at least 80% of the park.
Green	Build at least five shops each with a litter bin within one square of each shop.
Upgrade	Upgrade at least ten rides.
Path Economy	After building ten rides you must use less than one hundred squares of path.

Gold Tickets Cheat

On the map screen or inside the park, press ⬆, ⬇, ⬅, ➡, ●, ➡, ⬅, ⬇, ⬆, ●, repeat this four more times and you will be rewarded with 255 gold tickets.

Buy Everything For Free Cheat

Press ⬅, ⬇, ✖, ●, repeat this eight times and you will be able to buy everything for free.

Everything Researched Cheat

Press ⬆, ⬇, ⬆, ⬇, ⬅, ⬆, ⬇, ⬆, ⬇, ➡, repeat this eight times and every item will be researched to max.

THRASHER SKATE AND DESTROY

Bumblebee Suit

Go to the character select screen and pick Roach (without the hat). Enter your name as **BEESUITGUY.** You will now be skating in a bumblebee suit.

THREE LIONS

England 1966
On the team selection screen press **L1, L1, L1,** ➡. Move to Europe and press ⬅ to change to Secret. Below it will appear the England 1966 team for you to select.

Brazil 1970
On the team selection screen press **R1, R1, R1,** ➡.

Die Mannschaft
On the team selection screen press **R2, R2, R2,** ➡.

All Time
On the team selection screen press **L2, L2, L2,** ➡.

Z-Axis
On the team selection screen press **R1,** ⬇, ⬇, ➡.

Europe Stars
On the team selection screen press **L2,** ⬇, ⬇, ➡.

S America Stars
On the team selection screen press **R2,** ⬇, ⬇, ➡.

N America Stars
On the team selection screen press **L1,** ⬇, ⬇, ➡.

African Stars
On the team selection screen press **R2,** ⬆, ⬆, ➡.

Australasia Stars
On the team selection screen press **R1,** ⬆, ⬆, ➡.

Azzuri
On the team selection screen press **L2,** ⬆, ⬆, ➡.

Oranje
On the team selection screen press **L1,** ⬆, ⬆, ➡.

Team BMG
On the team selection screen press **L2,** ⬅, ⬅, ➡.

Ocean Colour Scene Team
Highlight 'England 1966' and press **R2,** ➡.

TIGERSHARK

Invincibility
To become invincible, simply enter **"KURSK"** as a password.

Passwords

Level	Password
2	AKULA
3	PASHA
4	MIRAS
5	NAKAT
6	REZKY
7	TUCHA
8	ZARYA
9	VOSTA

TIGER WOODS '99

2X Higher Terrain
Enter **PUMPZ** as your name from the Edit Name option on the player select screen.

4X Higher Terrain
Enter **MAXIMUMZ** as your name from the Edit Name option on the player select screen.

Destroy Your Golf Cart
Select Practice Facility mode and choose Driving. If you hit the golf cart three times you will cause it to explode.

TIME COMMANDO

Restore Health
Restore your life bar at any point in the game by pressing pause and highlighting Sound FX. Then press ✖, ▲, ▲, ●, ✖, ▲, ▲, ●, ■, ■, ✖.

Secret Level
You can fight new enemies in a secret boxing ring by entering COMMANDO at the password screen.

Passwords
Go to the level of your choice by entering one of the following codes at the password screen:

TUHOUEFY	Roman Empire
ADSAZGLY	Japanese
ZJFKYGLZ	European Middle Ages
EBELPWNF	Conquistadors
EVXXGPWNN	Western
ENQOEQHJ	Modern Wars
NDWMHGEC	Future
XXEMJBDFS	Beyond Time

TIME CRISIS

Easy Arcade Mode
Select 'Arcade Mission' from the main selection screen. On the next screen shoot outside the screen. If the cheat has worked you will see the word 'easy' appear over the story mode option. Select it and start playing. You will now have five lives and more time to complete the game.

Alternative Reload
An easy way to play this game arcade-style is to plug a second joypad into port 2 and press a button with your foot to duck and reload.

TINY TANK

Level Select
On the New Game menu, hold **L1 + L2 + R1 + R2 + ← + ● + Select.**

Cheat Password
On the Options menu, hold **L1 + L2 + R1 + R2 + ← + ● + ▲ + ■** and press ✖ to display the cheat code screen.

TOCA TOURING CAR

Hidden Track
To gain access to the hidden fire track, simply input your name as JHAMMO.

Moon Mode
For reduced gravity, enter your name as CMLOGRAV.

Cartoon Mode
For that cow and chicken feel, enter your name as CMTOON.

Hummer Mode
To get a grenade launcher, enter your name as TANK.

Kart mode
Go kart mayhem! Enter your name as CMCHUN.

T.V Mode
To get a chase-cam view, enter your name as CMFOLLOW.

Irish Rain
Enter your name as CMRAINUP for upside down precipitation.

Glue Factory
Stick to the road better. Enter your name as FLEXMOBILE.

Disco Mode
Enter your name as CMDISCO for a real boogie night.

Helicopter View
Enter your name as CMCOPTER

Upside Down Mode
Enter your name as CMUPSIDE

Speed-Up
Enter your name as XBOOSTME

No Collisions
Enter your name as CMNOHITS

Mad Drivers
For maniac drivers enter your name as CMMAYHEM.
Big Hand Mode
Enter your name as CMHANDY.
Raining Cats and Dogs
Enter your name as CMCATDOG.
All Cars
Enter your name as CMGARAGE, or GONGOGO for all of the cars.
Star Filled Sky
Enter your name as CMSTARS
Overhead View
Enter your name as CMMICRO

TOCA TOURING CAR 2

Enter your the passcode as your name during a single race:

MINICARS	Micro Machine style camera view
PADDED	Bouncy barriers
LUNAR	Low gravity
LONGLONG	Propeller head championship
PUNCHY	No kick out of championship
BANGBANG	Battle made
TECHLOCK	Lock frame rate during qualification
BCASTLE	Bouncy crashes
DUBBED	Over the top crashes
ELASTIC	Stretch the track vertically
TRIPPY	Blur the horizons
JUSTFEET	Wheels only
FASTBOY	Go faster
DINKYBIT	Oulton Park Island circuit

TOCA WORLD TOURING CARS

Game Codes
Select options, then bonuses to enter these codes:

Mirror Mode	WEFLIPPED
Double Height	TWINPEAKS
Motion Blur	ETHANOL
Extra Power	GRUNTSOME
Low Gravity	EUROPA
Chrome Cars	T2
Nitro Boost	GLYCERINE
Slot Cars	RAILROAD
Exploding Kerbs	KERBKRAWL
70s Springs	VANISHING
Invincible Car	MADCAB
Tough Bonus Cars	REARFEAR

TOKYO HIGHWAY BATTLE

The following codes can be used after you have won your first race in Scenario mode. Use a second controller to enter the codes during the next race:

To display the best time:	➡ + **Select**
To display the fastest lap time:	⬆ + **Select**
To display the prog number:	⬇ + **Select**
To have a white speedometer:	**L1** + **Select**

Change Your Car Colour
Use controller one to enter **R2** at the car select screen, after winning the first race in Scenario mode

Extra Cars And Colours
When you defeat the Drift King there will be three extra cars available to you (Supra, NSX, and GT-R). If you defeat him in one of these cars, go to the car selection screen and use **R2** to change the colour.

Free Upgrade Points in Scenario Mode
You can get 9,999,999 upgrade points by going to the title screen and holding the following simultaneously on controller two: **L1, L2, R1, ⬇, Start**. Now press **Start** on controller one while still holding the buttons on controller two. When the Speed Shop screen appears, you can release them.

Maximum Money
Immediately after the opening demo when the checkered flag title appears, press and hold the following buttons on controller two: **L1 + L2 + R1 + Start + ⬇**. Keep holding them until the title flashes and letters finish flying in.

Maximum Points
As the game is starting up and you see the 'Jaleco' logo displayed, press and hold the following on controller two: **L1 + L2 + R1 + ⬇ + Start**. When the FMV intro begins, press **Start** on controller one while still holding the buttons on controller two. When you see the title screen, select Scenario mode and go to the Speed Shop. When you enter you should see that you now have 9,999,999 points to spend on car modifications.

Race The Drift King
Select Vs. CPU to race the Drift King. You can also choose different enemies at the Course Select screen.

TOMB RAIDER

Level Skip
If you are using the default control system (Type 1), enter the following at the inventory screen: **L2, R2, ▲, L1, L1, ●, R2, L2**. If you are using Type 2, press **L2, R2, ●, ▲, ▲, L1, R2, L2**. For Type 3, press **L2, R2, R1, ▲, ▲, L1, R2, L2**.

Maximum Weapons
To gain all of the weapons and unlimited ammo, use the level skip cheat to complete the game quickly, then start a new game.

Maximum Weapons Cheat

Go to the inventory screen and press **L1**, **▲**, **L2**, **R2**, **R2**, **L2**, **●**, **L1**. Now return to your game. When you next go to the inventory screen, the weapons will be there.

For Type 2 press: **▲**, **●**, **L2**, **R2**, **R2**, **L2**, **L1**, **▲**.

For Type 3 press: **▲**, **R1**, **L2**, **R2**, **R2**, **L2**, **L1**, **▲**.

Rough Guide

Level 1: The Caves

The best way to avoid the blow darts is to jump over them. Take out wolves by shooting them, jumping away while you do so will preserve your health. In the room with the closed door there is a secret room in the centre of the left-hand wall. To open the door you must quickly pull the switch on the right-hand wall and jump to the platform with the door. To do this side flip to the lower block then turn and walk to the edge, perform a forward standing jump grasping the ledge, then pull yourself up and run through the open door.

Level 2: City Of Vilcabama

The best way to defeat the bear is to run into the building in which he is hiding (next to the pool of water) and quickly climb up onto the ledge inside. From there safely shoot down at him. Dive into the pool of water, turn right and swim to a water-filled room with pillars. In two of the corners lie switches. One opens a trap door above you, the other opens a secret room near the entrance of the pool (turn left instead of right).

In the skull room (with collapsing floors) push the lightly coloured block forward to discover a hidden room. At the end of this room there is a golden idol and a skull key. To exit this room climb onto the block you pushed to enter the room to reach the roof. Avoid the bats and exit through a hole in the wall, which returns you to the main complex. Use the skull key to enter the temple, take the left corridor, and make your way to the top. Pull the switch and quickly make your way down to the newly opened door, (if you are not quick enough the door will close and you will have to pull the switch again). Again climb to the top and pull another switch that will open the central passage, then quickly make your way to the door before it closes.

Level 3: The Lost Valley

To exit the level you need three cogs. When you place them in the cog machine they will divert the river, opening the entrance behind the waterfall. The shotgun can be found near the cog machine by the source of the river, (head up river in the opposite direction then the waterfall). You will need it to defeat the T-Rex. Make your way to the waterfall and climb through the caves opposite. Climb vertically to discover the lost valley, there will be a number of skeletons on the way. Beware of the raptors as you enter the valley. To kill the T-Rex lure him from the shadows then run and hide in one of the caves situated around the right side of the valley. From here shoot the T-Rex, but first make sure the cave you are in is free of raptors.

The three cogs are hidden:

A) In the temple at the end of the valley. Dive to the bottom of the waterfall inside, and swim to the right.

B) On the opposite side of the broken rope-bridge, above the valley. Head to the left side of the temple and climb the cliff, following the path to the rope-bridge. Walk to the edge, jump back and perform a running jump then grab the opposite side. At the end is a cog.

C) In the corner of the valley under a small waterfall. Swim underneath to discover a hidden cave (beware of the raptor). Climb the left wall to the top to find the final cog.

Place the three cogs in the machine at the river source and pull the lever. The water will be diverted revealing the exit. Return to the waterfall and climb into the passage that was hidden behind the waterfall.

Secrets:

a) Climb to the right of the temple entrance and jump off the roof.

b) By the cog mechanism. You should drop off the bridge and shimmy to the rivers source.

c) 3rd cog. Climb to the Left of the waterfall, and shimmy across to the top of the waterfall.

d) The secret is where you found the 3rd cog.

e) Use the 3 cogs and swim to the end of the water. Go to the tomb by walking behind the first waterfall.

Level 4: Tomb of Qualopec

Pull the lever on the right wall next to the statue to open the right gate. Kill the raptors and follow the passage. At the junction take the right passage. Push the blocks to discover a hidden passage. The floor before the lever collapses so quickly run across, pull the lever, (this will open one of the gates in the main room), then do a standing jump from the edge to return across. At the junction take the central passage, walk to the switch and fall through the collapsing floor. Push the blocks and climb to the top to pull the second lever. Take the final passage at the junction. Here you must pull levers to move the blocks in the centre of the room in order to gain access to hidden rooms. First move the block in the top left corner, then the block in the bottom right corner, then finally move the top right corner block so it is close to the room in the top right corner. Jump from the bottom right block to the top right block, then jump at an angle from this block to the opposite room and pull the switch to open the final gate.

Make your way to the main room, take the left passage, run past the blow darts to the throne room and take the scion. As the room collapses run through the central passage into the main room and towards the level entrance, (beware of the rolling block behind you and the blocks falling from the roof).

Secrets:

a) Side flip over the darts. Climb up the statue, then run over the collapsing platform.

b) After getting the first secret, jump back to the doorway. The next bit has to be done with small steps. Walk to the edge and face the item under the platform. Make sure you are one step away from the edge and do a standing jump. With any luck you will land just after the spikes.

Level 5: St Francis Folly

Kill the lions. Push the block in the trench over the omega symbol. This opens the door of the temple for you to head inside. Pull the lever opposite the door, head up to your right, and pull the lever. The door above the main room will now be open. Climb up on to the pillars and on to the ledge. Make your way to the newly opened door. Follow the passage past the crocodile to a room filled with platforms and a long drop. There are four levers, each opens one of the four god rooms. In each of them is a key that unlocks the door at the bottom of the level. In the top room swim to the bottom of the water filled tunnel and pull the lever to open up the gate and grab the key. In the room with the swords, make your way though the room into the tomb. When you pick up the key the swords will come alive. As you move through the room to the exit the swords will begin to fall, so quickly run and dodge to escape. In the room with the boulder run towards it and jump up and over as it rolls at you. Climb the left wall to gain the third key. In the last room run past the lightning into the room with the giant hammer. Wait under the hammer until you hear a click then quickly dive out the way. Move the blocks to gain access to the high pillar, perform a running jump to the opposite ledge, and retrieve the last key. To escape perform a running jump. Make your way to the bottom of the level, killing the lions on the way down, and use the four keys to exit the level.

Secrets:
a) Position Lara near the sloped block. Backflip off the slope onto the second slope. Jump and grab towards the ledge.
b) After the second locked door, you can slide down a slope. Just before the bottom, jump and Lara will land on the slope platform. Jump and grab to the door.
c) Don't drain the water, go in and find the room in the ceiling bit.
d) Behind the Gods' Hall door in the corner

Level 6: Coliseum

To pass the crocodile pit, jump and grab the ledge on the left-hand wall, then safely shimmy over the pit. In the main coliseum make your way into the room in the top left corner, and pull the switch to open the room in the right hand corner. Climb out of the pit and kill the lions. If the lions come to close climb back into the pit and shoot them as they look over the edge. Step on the stone in the right hand corner to open the left gate, run into here, and pull the lever to open the right hand gate. Quickly run through and into the right hand corner. Pull the lever and return to the main room. Go through the open door. Go past the spike pit and climb up to the right corner of the coliseum. From here jump from block to block and then to the balcony. Pull the block out to discover a lever that opens one of the three rooms in the corner of the coliseum. Visit each of these, pulling the levers to open the door to the next, eventually you will discover a key. Return to the balcony

above the coliseum and open the gate on the right wall. Fall into the water and swim to the next level.

Secrets:
a) Jump to the right of the crocodile pit entrance. Shimmy across the crack over the pit.
b) Get to the Lions Den puzzle area by climbing to the crack above the pit. Walking over the plate opens the gates. Hit the switch on the left gate and go into the next room.
c) Before you jump to the Gorilla room, climb up the rocks. The key is behind the block near the Gorilla Room door switch.

Level 7: Palace Midas

To exit the level you must collect three lead bars and turn them to gold. Make your way to the room with pillars and four closed doors. Head to the top-left corner and climb onto the pillar. Jump from pillar to pillar until you reach the balcony. There are five switches, each one represents on or off. Above each door is a symbol representing on or off. Match the switches to those above the doors to open them.
Room 1: Shoot the rats then run and jump across the platforms. If you get set on fire jump into the water and try again. Grab the lead bar and drop in the water.
Room 2: Make your way past the spikes to the room at the far end. Move the block to reveal a switch. Carefully jump from block to block to the room at the far right-hand corner. Inside is a lead bar.
Room 3: Head into the corridor at the opposite end and go down to find a block. Pull the block to cause the roof to collapse. Head up to the top and jump from block to block to the exit high above. Jump from here to the pool of water. Drop down to the high archways to find yourself above the first level of arches. Jump to the long stretch of archways. Near the end you have to jump to the rock face opposite, move left, then jump back to the exit. Follow the passage around the level, across the high ledges that pass the level start, until you reach the temple roof. Here you will find the final lead bar.
Room 4: This is the level exit. You need to place the three gold bars here. To turn them into gold you have to go to the garden. To unlock the gate go to the temple with the lever inside. In the garden climb onto the far right ledge, then the low roof. Here is a passage that leads to a broken statue of Midas. Place each lead bar into the giant hand to turn them to gold. Do not stand on his hand or Lara will turn to gold. Return to room 4 and place the three gold bars onto the platforms to open the level exit.

Secrets:
a) Below you once you complete Room 3.
b) Swim under the ledge of the T-shaped water. Go to the V-shape, and jump forward twice. Go to the gap between the door and the T-shaped pool. Do a running jump and grab to the opposite side via the arches.

Level 8: The Cistern

To reach the exit you must fill and drain the level with water.

You will now be able to gain all the keys and pull all the levers. To drain the level of most of its water head to the central passage on the right-hand wall. Here there is a lever which when pulled drains or fills the level. The exit is on the right hand corner opposite the entrance.

Key 1: This can be found on the corner platform in the main room.

Key 2: Go to the room just next to the cistern. You can go through the grill and climb to another room.

Grey Keys: Go through the entrance in the pool.

Secrets:

a) In the tunnels, underwater in the main room.

b) Adjust the water level in order to get to the secret room with the gold key.

c) After the Gold Key area a block can be pushed and climbed up on to reach a ledge.

Level 9: Tomb Of Tihocan

Quickly swim to the end of the passage and down to find a lever. Pull this and return back up. Pull the lever to open the door and then kill the crocodile. Climb to the top of the room avoiding the arrows. Move the block over each symbol to open each door in turn. There are two keys to be collected, use these to exit the room. When you land in the water quickly swim away from the crocodile, climb to dry land, and shoot the crocodile safely from there. Make your way to the underground temple. As you move towards the gates one of the statues will come alive. Kill it or avoid it by running into the temple. Once inside defeat Natlia's man and retrieve the second scion. Enter the tomb to exit the level.

Level 10: City Of Khamoon

This is the first level which you are introduced to mummies and large undead panthers. Once you have released the boulder in the open cavern stand next to the point it stops. Look towards the cat statue to find a secret passage. When you find yourself next to a gong, instead of dropping to the ground, make your way around the top of the cavern to the temple roof. Along the way pick up ammo and medi packs. Once you have reached the panther room, go to the central column, and jump to the top left corner to find additional ammo.

Level 11: Obelisk Of Khamoon

You need four Egyptian artefacts that are situated in the middle of the complex. There are four bridges which need to be lowered so you can gain access to the artefacts. These are then placed in the Obelisk in the large open cavern. Once you are opposite the top of the central column (with the artefacts) perform a running jump to reach the top of the column to discover extra medi packs.

Secrets:

You can get to Level 10 again by going down near the switch which releases the sand.

Level 12: Sanctuary of The Scion

You begin at the bottom of a line of steps. Kill the creatures and climb to the top. You will find yourself on the top of a Sphinx. Climb down to the left-hand side. Head around the bottom of the Sphinx until you reach its right side. Climb onto the pillar and jump until you reach the cliff. Climb around the edge until you reach a lever, and pull it. Climb down killing the winged creature and head to the front of the Sphinx. Climb the cliff until you reach a hidden room. Inside you will find an artefact.

Place the artefact in the top of the Sphinx to open the door between its legs. Enter here and drop to the cavern below. Swim down to the feet of the left-hand statue and pull the lever, which will have you sucked into the statue. Here climb the pillars and pull the lever to drain some of the water. Climb down and around the statue to find a lever that opens a passage in the right statue. Swim up this and make your way to the top. You will find yourself back at the start. Make your way down into the crypt to exit the level.

Level 13: Natla's Mines

You begin the level with no weapons. Climb out of the water and into the room with the digger. In the left-hand corner is a pile of rocks, climb these to find the first lever. You need to find four batteries to get a weapon (this will make facing Natlia's henchmen slightly easier).

Fuse 1: Next to the crane.

Fuse 2: Hit the switch by the conveyor belt and wait at the end.

Fuse 3: Just inside the cavern with one of Natlia's hench men and the lava pit.

Fuse 4: In the secret room near the cabin. Walk up to the gate to open it.

You must quickly jump past all the boulders before they squash you or bar your exit. The best way to defeat Natlia's henchmen is to keep moving while using the auto aim. They can also be avoided but will stay in pursuit of you. The shotgun is in the tunnel next to the lava pit and pillars. Jump up into the secret room before the boulder crushes you. Make your way above the boulder then drop into the passage behind it, and grab your weapon. There is an exit above the way you came in. To avoid the oncoming boulders after defeating the skateboard henchmen side-jump left and right. Near the end of the level you will meet the last henchman. To open the Pyramid jump from flat surface to flat surface to the opening on the top-left corner.

Level 14: Atlantis

Be careful as you jump from ledge to ledge in the centre of the pyramid as there is no chance of survival. All the obstacles you encounter are similar to those already overcome during the game. Take great care, as most of these are unforgiving and usually lead to certain death. You will come across a creature that does not attack but mimics your movements. Climb the cliff with the lever, and pull it to open a shaft. Quickly move to the same place on the opposite side of the room to send your mirror image to its death.

Level 15: The Great Pyramid

Jump to the central platform, and when the boss appears, begin shooting. When it comes close drop off the edge and grab the ledge. It will then move away. Climb back up and continue firing and repeat until you have won. Alternatively run around the boss while continuing to fire, but beware of the edge. Make your way back to the Great Pyramid, and take the scion. The next sequence is the hardest in the game. You have a continued amount of hazards and the screen constantly shakes as Atlantis collapses, making jumping more difficult. To escape, leave the Great Pyramid and drop into the right hand side of the moat (now filled with rocks). There is a small hole to drop down. Once you have made it past all the traps, (these are all similar to what you have encountered during the game), you will find yourself in a large room with tall pillars. Here Natlia herself will attack you. Once you beat her the first time she will grow wings and attack you from above for a second and final attack. Keep moving and avoid her fireballs. Once you kill her use the tunnels to gain access to the pillars, and climb these until you reach a long corridor. Run to the end and slide down to escape. Tada!

TOMB RAIDER 2

The Great Wall-Level 1

Stride through the water and follow the blocks up to the top of the canyon. Forget the tigers. On the way up, look around for a platform that leads to *Secret One*.

Climb up into the room and fall into the water below. Pull the switch and exit through the door. Kill the three crows. Dive down into the pool and find the key from one of the underwater caves. Kill the tiger and climb back up to the great wall. Use the key to open the door and kill the spiders. Grab the key from the top of the room.

In the next room, kill the spiders and move the block to reveal a hole in the wall. Slide down and cross the water by shimmying across using the ledge at the top of the side walls. Keep running and bear right. In the boulder room, run away and jump over the spikes. Jump up to the gap. Keep running and grab the *Secret Two*. Go down the slope and fall through the tiles. Run past the wheels and shoot the spiders.

Before using the rope slide, look over the edge to see a platform on the right. Lower yourself and shimmy across the rock face. What follows is more jumping and climbing. Kill the T-Rex's and grab *Secret Three*. Climb back up and go down the rope slide. Kill the tigers and go through the red door.

Venice-Level 2

Kill the dogs and the man. Grab his item. Press the switch in the hut and go up the ladders. Smash the window and go through it. Go across to the balcony where the other gangster is and kill him. Take the key. Jump down into the water. Go under the doors to where the boat is. Hit the switch and use the key.

Go back up the ladders, this time going through the window and turning left. Take out the dogs and hit the switch. Smash the window in the previous room and do the appropriate acrobatics across the red canopies to the secret door.

Hit the switch, then go and get the boat. Drive the boat into the sewers. On the right is a corridor leading to *Secret One*. Follow the water in the boat, until you get to the waterfall. Dive down at the base of the waterfall to get *Secret Two*. Get back in the boat and go to the big gate.

Swim to the wooden dock, then climb out and crash through the window. Kill the rat and the man. Swim under the large doors and hit the switch. A lot of lever pulling follows, with you being able to drive the boat through this area at the end of it. Get out near the gondolas. Get to the bridge via the block and the canopy and kill the man and his dog. Go right and get the key from the man. Open the nearby door and drop through the hole. Hit the switch, go back to the bridge and kill the gangster. Drive the boat past the lock, then left, then right. Climb the wooden slope, and grab *Secret Three* from the room. Go through the window and drop down. Kill the bloke and the rats and hit the switch. Go all the way back to the boat and find the door that you just opened. Get the iron key and use it to open the lock.

Kill the man and hit the switch. Take the boat through the open grates and through the maze of alleys to a room on the right. Hit the switch. To clear the minefield, drive the second boat towards the mines and jump out at the last minute. Get in the first boat and power up the wooden slope. Make sure that you get to the exit before the chimes stop.

Bartoli's Hideout-Level 3

Kill the rats and the bloke and hit the switch at the far end. This opens up the big doors. Go through and kill the men. Smash the windows on the left and grab the items. Go past the swordsmen statues and hit the switch. Go back to the main room and then do a backwards rebound-jump off of the slope to jump forwards and reach the ledge.

By moving the right hand block, you can jump to the ledge where the block was previously. Jump to the opposite side. Do a bit of ladder climbing and ledge shimmying and fall to the edge outside. Jump toward the left end of the red canopy and grab it. If you try to climb up you will slide back. Before you fall, jump back to the balcony. Make your way across to the wooden ledge and the red canopy, dropping off at the end. Go into the opening.

Go up the stairs and kill the gangster. Pull the switch and grab *Secret One*. Go through the window to the balcony and take out the guard. At the other end of the balcony is another window, which you can enter. Push the block twice and kill the rat.

Jumping to the slope from the block triggers off some traps, so jump to the right, into the water. Hit the switch to turn off the flame sand jump over them. Kill the bloke and the two dogs. Get on the chandelier and jump to the ledge. Hit the switch and get to the next chandelier. Eventually, you'll get to the topmost rafter.

Jump over to the wooden platform, then to the back. Kill the guard and go back to the brick wall. Jump forwards to get the switch. Hit the switch and drop down to the wooden floor. Make your way down to the bottom chandelier. Jump to the opening and grab the key. Go back up to the highest chandelier and hit the switch. Jump to the ledge as before and go out of the window. Drop into the water and pull the lever. Swim through the hole and get to *Secret Two*. Hit the switch. At this point you'll need some air, so find somewhere you can surface. Go back to where you dropped in.

Unlock the door at the top of the stairs and take out the man. Climb the bookcase and from here, jump onto the block. Hit the switch and kill the man. Go into the other room, and climb up the other bookcase. On the opposite side of this room is another bookcase. Jump across to this and climb up to the window. Slide-jump down to the canopy and on to the platform, then jump to the roof area. Get the detonator key from the hut, via the wall and the water. Climb up and find the windows. Go through and hit the switch. Go through the windows and jump up to the sloped roof for *Secret Three*. Go through the wooden door and set off the detonator. Jump into the water and go to the brick-block. Jump up to the right hand block. Go down the hole and slide down.

The Opera House-Level 4
Avoid the crate and jump into the water. Go up the ladder and hit the switch. Carry on up the ladder, then jump to the ledge opposite. Make your way up to where you began and get the key from the man. Go up the stairs and carry on going up. Get to the window by shimmying across the sloped-rooftop. The only way to get through this room is to walk, not run. Climb the ladders and use your key. Kill the gangsters and make your way right to the swinging crate.

Once across, hit the switch. This triggers another room to open along with two enemies. Hit the gate-switch and drop into the next room. Run away from the boulder and press the switch. At the top of the ladder you shimmy to the ledge from where you can drop down. Avoid the boulders by not stopping in one place for to long. Jump up and take out the enemies. Find the switch, hit it, and head back. Go to the new doorway minding the glass. Find the raised-bridge area, jump across, and hit the switch. Stand on the platform in the middle of the room.

Jump to the lowered section, then to the wooden beam. Avoid the swinging sandbags and hit the switch. Jump off the slope and swim left, then dive down to find the *Secret One*. Get out of the water and grab the relay-box. Hit the switch. Climb up to where the enemy was. Go along the corridor, drop down and hit the switch. Slide down the slope and jump off to get the key. Climb up, jump to the slope, and go to the duct. Jump over the fans and find *Secret Two* at the end of the dark corridor. Jump over the last fan and pull the block away to reveal the switch. Pull the block to the next room and go through the window. Push the block so that you can climb up to the other windows. Use the key. Now you are just to the left of where you started. Use the relay-box and hit the switch. Whilst on the lift, jump up to the opening for *Secret Three*. Hit the switch and go back to the bottom.

Send the lift up and go into the water. Follow the steps to get the circuit board. Hit the switch and go in. keep jumping up until you reach the main room. Drop down, then climb up the ladder, hitting the switch on the way. Use the circuit board and hit the right-hand switch. Go out and hit the first switch again. Go back to the stage in the main room.

In the crate room you will have to avoid sandbags and kill enemies. Pull away the block and hit the switch. Climb up to the hanging-light. Hit the switch in the sandbag room, and continue through here and the swinging crate room. Climb up the crates, hit the switch, and drop down. Kill the man and go through the door to be welcomed by an agent and his dogs. Get his grenade launcher and kill the other agent. Hit the switch and climb up.

Offshore Rig-Level 5
Pull the block to reveal the corridor. Hit the switch and run out. Taking time to kill the guards is perilous, so ignore them for now. Once at the top go through the window to the hanger area. Hit the switch and find the switch in the plane by swimming underneath it. Get to the plane wing via the previous window. Get the items from the plane and swing back.

Get the Yellow Pass from the guards. From the smashed window another ledge can be seen. Jump to it and down the corridor to a switch in the water. *Secret One* is behind the blades. Use the Yellow Pass to open the door. Hit the switch and go along the corridor. Go right at the T-junction. Follow the rooms through, picking up the harpoons and the harpoon gun on the way. Hit the switch by the top bunk and get out. Climb up near the hatch. At the end of the corridor is a slope. Grab on to the edge and go down the ladders.

Use the block to get over the wall. Climb up the ladders and get the Red Pass from the man. At the top of the ladder is *Secret Two*. Follow the stairs, through the water to the corridor. Go through the Yellow Pass door and go left at the T-junction. Kill the enemies, avoid the barrels and use the Red Pass. Take out the guards and push the block into the gap. Climb up and jump to the hallway. Get to the bottom. Hit the switch and drop into the water. Get out on the opposite side and hit the switch behind the pipes.

Go to the Green Pass room and go down the hatch. Swim to the ladder. At the bottom is *Secret Three*. Jump across the multiple gaps and go through the window to get the Green Pass. You would have seen a hole in the wall on your way. Jump up to the corridors and drop down. Use the Green Pass and hit the switch. Go through to the pool of water. Go through the tunnel, hit the switch, and go through the gate. Go up the stairs.

The Diving Bit-Level 6
Go up and through the corridor. Hit the switch. Now grab the underwater switch. Go into the now opened room. There is a dog here. Get in the water and go through the doorway. Climb out, kill the enemies and get over to the other side of the room. Go through to where the agents were and slide down the slope backwards. Get *Secret One* on your way down. Jump off the end of the slope to avoid the toxic waste. Go up the ladder. To shorten your fall grab on to the ledge halfway down. Drop down, kill the bloke and grab the Blue Pass from the grey area.

Find the corridor through the right hand door and go to another walkway. Get to the Blue Pass door. Be careful, there are four dogs and a guy with a flame thrower. Open the doors and go into the room. Dive in and swim to the gap. Get the frogman to chase you and kill him from the surface. Hit the switch underwater and go through the grate, hitting the other switch to open the helipad area. Go back to the helipad room. Keep going and hit the switches to shut the flames off. Get the machine-gun and the chip.

In the frogman area move the block and use the chip. Go through the door and kill the enemies. Jump in the water and take out the frogmen. Swim through the gap and get out. Climb up and hit the switch. Swim through and kill the agent. Go through the computer-panel door and hit the switch. Go back underwater to get *Secret Two*.

Go to the Control Room and hit the switch. Jump to the other side via the crane. Hit the switch behind the blocks. Go back to the helipad and then to the new area. Take out the enemies. Grab the chip and go to the door in the side room. Use the chip in the slot behind the buzz-saw in the Control Room. Get the Red Pass and use it. Follow the corridor round and go through the water. Climb out, kill the enemies and find *Secret Three* through a small door. Talk to the prisoner.

40 Fathoms-Level 7
Follow the debris to the ship-wreck. Go to the top left to get some air. Swim through various gaps in the walls and hit the switch. Go through and surface for air. Go to the gap under the crates. Climb out and hit the switch. This drains the water. Go

to the dry area and get to the ledge by jumping between the blocks. Get *Secret One* and fall through to the room below.
Get to the raised doorway in this room by jumping off the slope and then run-jumping. Jump over the pipes and hit the switch. Go left and swim to *Secret Two*. Go back and this time take a right turn. Jump up and hit the switch. Go down and follow the corridor to a switch. Hit it and run along to find another switch. Hit it and go back to the *Secret Two* area. Go through the new door and hit the switch. Leg-it back to the flame-corridor and hit the switch by the door. Swim through the gaps and hit the switch which opens another gap. Go through and find another switch. *Secret Three* is around here.

Swim back to land and drop into a new room. Drop down into another room and pull the block back. Climb up and hit the switch. Go to the left-hand gap in the wall and jump up to the room above. Get to the hole in the ceiling and hit the switch. Now do the same for the right-hand gap in the wall.
Go to the hole in the corner and follow it to the water. Take out the frogman and swim through the gap to the new room. Kill the enemies, hit the switch, and go through the door.

Maria Doria-Level 8
Kill the frogman and swim through the tunnel. Slide down the slope, then drop down to the room with the enemies. Go to the new room and jump to the gap in the ceiling. Follow the corridor and get *Secret One*. In the previous room were some blocks. Move them to find a corridor. Go down the right corridor and drop down. Keep going, walk through the glass and drop down, grabbing the ledge below. Get the key and jump back up to the glass area. In the block room is another room. Go through and use the key. Hit the new switch, kill the agent, and hit the second switch.

Hit the first switch again and head for the broken glass room. Use the raised tile to get to the ledge above. Follow the platform round and run-jump to the corner platform. Get the circuit breaker. Starting from the raised tile repeat what you just did, but along the way jump up to an area above you. Climb up to the door, open the airtight door and open the second airtight door at the other end. Drop into the room via a ledge.

Move the block to hit the switch. Move another block to get to the hole. Go through the corridor. Move another block to get to the switch. Get the key and climb up to the corridor. Use the key on the door in the airtight area. Drop down to avoid being hurt. Move the block to get to a metal platform. Move the other blocks to reveal a corridor. Run over the collapsing floor and avoid the barrels. Go up the slope. A corridor holds *Secret Two*.

Go down the slope and head right. Take out the guard. Hit the switch in the water and get back up. Hit the switch in the new room and go down the slope. Use the metal floor to get to the ledge above. Hit the switch and then make your way back to the room with the boat. Go to the higher gap in the wall and kill the agents. Hit the switch on the left, drop through the gap, and hit a second switch. Get the circuit breaker. Go back to the boat room via the hatch. Go through the airtight door, drop down and hit the switch. Get the circuit breaker. Go back up and head right. Drop into another room.

Go to the big room at the start of the level. Swim through the gaps in the pool and hit the switch. Climb out and kill the agents. Use the circuit breakers to put out the fire. Move the block to get to the hole in the ceiling. Hit the switch and jump to a metal beam. Keep doing this to get to a new room. Swim through the water, kill the fish, and then kill the agent. Go through the air-tight door and hit the switch. Move the block to reveal another switch. Pull it. Go down the corridor with the lantern, then go right and get the Cabin Key from the water. *Secret Three* can be found in a cave around here.

Go back and use the key. Hit the switch and drop into the pit that is now open. Move the block to hit the switch. Go through the hatch in the cabin. Drop into the room and into the water. Mind the enemies and head for the barrel on the seabed. Go through the gap and keep going.

Living Quarters – Level 9
Swim through the cave and hit the switch. Go in the hatch. Go left and head for the large machine filled room. Jump up to the main section. Drop off the other side and follow the corridor. Go to the top of the slope and jump to the ledge. Shimmy past the fire and drop down. Hit the switch, jump up and follow the corridor to another switch. Drop down to the large machine filled room. Jump onto the towers, you can reach *Secret One* from here.

Jump to the opening, push the block, then go down the unveiled corridor. Push the block and drop down. Hit the switch again and climb back up. Go back to the towers and jump right to the switch platform. Pull it and head back toward the fire room, which is now flooded. Hit the new switch. Go out of the new door and head for the cave. Hit the switch. Go back out and find the new hatch. Climb up and hit the switch. Go through the new door and hit the right then the left switch. Jump to the ledges and shimmy past the glass. Climb up, hit the switch and drop down, leaving the same way as you came. Jump off the sloped pillars to get to the ledge. Jump to the opposite ledge. Move the block to get past and shimmy off the ledge to get to a ledge. Keep going, slide down the slope and head right, over the vent to the opening.

Go down the corridor and turn right. Jump over the gap. Make the tiles collapse, but don't fall with them. Fall down the gap behind you. Get *Secret Two* and climb up. Go down the corridor and jump off the slope into the water. Kill the eels and find *Secret Three* outside the wreck by going down a tunnel.
Head back towards the eel pool. Go towards the sloping pillar room and stand between the tall pillars. Jump forward onto the step by the sloping block. Jump to the crack and climb up. Go

through the doorway and drop down. Go up the stairs and take out the agent. On the balcony is a block. Push it forwards and go down the stairs. Go to the lower area and move the block to get the Theatre Key. Go back up the stairs and move the block. Go down the new corridor and use the key. Kill the enemies and jump to the balcony. Hit the switch; this moves the curtains. On the stage move the block to get to the gap above. Drop down the other side, go left and hit the switch. Go back to the pool of water and climb out on the other side.

The Deck – Level 10
Head right and take out the enemies. Get the items and climb to one of the ledges near where you started. Jump into the water and climb to the pillar. Follow the pillars to the Stern Key. Swim through the opening to the Rusty Ship. Climb into the opening and find the wooden blocks on the right. Move the blocks accordingly to find a doorway. Use the key. Go through and swim right to the switch. Hit it and go back to where the flame-thrower man was. Go down the hatch.

Climb the ladder, hit the switch. Go up the ladder. Go back to the Stern Lock. Drop into the drained area and pull back the block. Climb up through the cavern. Take out the frogmen and climb out to the craters. Kill the agent, dive back in and get *Secret One* from the weeds. Swim through the hole and climb up.

Go up the slope and heal yourself fully. Drop backwards to the lifeboat, grabbing the ledge on the way down. Get the Cabin Key. Swim back through the hole. Go back toward the slope and this time go left down a corridor. Climb up to an opening. Go to the deck. Get *Secret Two* by the panel on the wall. Go down the narrow alleyway. Explore to find two steam-vents. Get to the roof by climbing and shimmying. Go through the hatch and the corridor. Move the block to get to the room above. Hit the switch and go through the door at the end of the previous corridor. Go through another door and use the Cabin Key.

Jump to the only stable tile in the room and hit the switch. Jump back to the entrance and go back to the corridor with the block. Go up and through the cave, then up some ledges. You'll come to a room with a hole. Fall through and get the Storage Key. Drop down through the decks and get *Secret Three* from the swimming pool. Return to the start of the level to the room with multiple block pushing in it. Use the Storage Key in the left corner of the room and get the Seriph.

Tibetan Foothills – Level 11
Climb up to the right hand gap and slide down. Jump over the boulders and climb up to the hole. Run through the ice-wall and jump right to a hole in the wall. Follow the path and drop backwards. Slide down and grab the edge. Shimmy right and jump to the left of the rock below.

Climb up to the Skidoo. *Secret One* can be found on a right hand ledge. Follow the dark cavern and power over the ramp. Carry on over various ramps and get off at the blocks. Move the blocks and drive the Skidoo into the cavern. Get off when you come to a multiple path room. Go right and hit the switch. Drive the Skidoo over the drop. Get *Secret Two* from a ledge on the right. Drive the Skidoo through the gate onto a bridge. Accelerate over the jump and avoid the boulders. At the turning, hit the switch and go back to the ladder in the boulder area. Jump up and fall down backwards, grabbing the ledge of the opening. Get the Drawbridge Key and drop down. Be careful of the falling-ice and hit the switch. Climb up to the opening. Go over the ladder and get the items. Get to the bridge and take out the leopards.

Get back to the Skidoo and go right. Use the Drawbridge Key. Drive past the boulders and over the ramp. Go to the ledge on the right to get back to the Keyhole area. Get the Hut Key. Drive back to the Skidoo Hut Area (you'll have to do the last part on foot). Use the key, hit the switch and take out the agents. Kill the Skidoo guy and go down the ladder to *Secret Three*. Jump to the ledge above the drop. Shimmy right to a new bit. Move the block and go into the room. Drop backwards in stages to get to the water. Run down the tunnel.

Barkhang Monastery – Level 12

DO NOT kill the Monks, only kill the agents. Go up the ladder, jump to the ledge and jump over the gaps. Slide down the rocks to the ledge below. Shimmy across and climb up. Go through the windows and through the corridor then left to another room. Get the items and go down the other corridor. Follow the monk and help him out. Go down the corridor to a ladder. Once on the next floor, go right, then left. Grab the Main Hall Key. Go back down the ladder and use the key.

Kill the enemies and go right, down a corridor. Carry on to the right. Once over the first blade, go into the room and get the Strongroom Key. Use it in the area where you shot the windows. Get the Rooftops Key. Go towards the main hall and turn right. Run past the blades and use the key. At the top of the stairs go right, between the statues. Turn right and hit the switch. Run over the flames.

Bear left and help out the monks. Hit the switch and drop down the hatch. Go through the windows to collect the gemstones. There's another switch on the left. Pull it and go up the ladder. Head for the flame area. Take the alternative route and find the two Dog Statues. Use the gemstone. Go behind the Star Statue, move the block and get the Prayer Wheel.

Go to the main hall and go up the ladder to get to the statue. Get to the head via the hand. Get to the ledge via the shoulder. Use the second gemstone. Drop down. Jump up the slope to the alcove to find *Secret One*. At the statue's base is a hole, drop down and hit the switch. Go through and find *Secret Two* in the stream. Push the block into the stream. Get out of the room, turn left and drop down. Jump up the ledge and move the block for another Prayer Wheel. Go up the ladder and turn

left. Help out the monk. Go to the room with two swinging blades. Avoid them and get the Trapdoor Key. Get to the corridor via the alcoves and get *Secret Three*.

Go back to where you got the Trapdoor Key. Follow the corridor and drop down. Just before the steps go left, jump over the grate, go right, then left. Drop into the courtyard and go up the ladder near the archway. Keep climbing up to get the third Prayer Wheel. Go to the main hall and hit the switch. Use the Trapdoor Key on the grate. Drop down and climb to the opening. Climb the ladder and follow the ledge right. Cross the bridge to the building. Climb the rocks to get tot the ledge. Climb to the roof and get the fourth Prayer Wheel. Hit the switch. Go down the hill and pull the switch. Go back through the main hall to where you picked up the Main Hall Key. Go to the new opening and follow the corridor up a hill. Dodge the boulders and go down the slope. Push the block and follow the slope to the water.

Avoid the centre and swim to the gap. Climb out and into another pool. Follow the corridor to a ladder. Move the two blocks and get the last Prayer Wheel from the dark room. Jump over the flames and go down the newly found corridor. Climb the ladder to the Main Hall. Go to the gap near the statue and use the Prayer Wheels. Put the Seraph in the Gold Door and go through the new door.

Catacombs of the Talion-Level 13

Avoid the stalactites and go into the room. Grab the ledge on your left. Climb up and drop down to get *Secret One*. Go back out and drop down. Mind the Yeti. Go down the stairs and hit the switch. Go back and find the ladder. Climb up. Jump off the end of the slope and get onto the ledge. Avoid the stalactites. Go down and towards the boulders. Dodge them by jumping into the water to your right. Climb out and jump off the slope up to a ledge. Hit the switch and get the mask from the cage.

Drop down and find the pool. Go down the hatch and along the corridor. Open the door using the mask. Dodge the boulders and kill the leopards. Go back to the slope just before this room. Climb up to the ledge. Drop down and go right. There are loads of leopards here. Climb onto the rocks. Get the mask from the water and go back to the leopard area. Go back out towards the building and use the mask to open the door. Go up the ladder and shimmy across to get to the door. Hit the switch, go in the new room, and take out the Yeti's with the grenades. Go back to the switch area and find the corridor. Move the block to jam the gate and go back to hit the switch.

Go down the steps and through the door near the slope and boulders that was previously locked. Go along the bridge avoiding the boulders. Jump to the next bridge and grab on. Get *Secret Two* from this room by doing a well timed double-jump on the fly. Swim left and get to the tall block. Jump to the ladder, then to a ledge. Hit the switch and go down through the big doors. Hit the switch in the middle and go right, to the ledge. Jump down. Return to the door at the top of the stairs. Jump over the pit and make the boulders come down. The boulders open a doorway. In this room are timed pressure-tiles. Go to the left door and jump over the spikes to the next door. To get *Secret Three* walk through the spikes to get to the wall that you can climb. Grab the ladder and gradually make your way down.

The Ice Palace-Level 14
Hit the bell to open the door. Use the springboard to get up to the ledges. Get to the top and hit the switch. Jump down into the cage and move the block. Find *Secret One* on a tall block. Get there via the invisible bridge. Go to the next room and hit the switch.

Find the next springboard and use it to hit the bell. Jump up to the slope. Go through the archway and using the springboard go up and shoot the bell. Go back down and through the now open gates. Use the springboard to get to the right hand ledge. Jump between sloped platforms in order to shoot the bell. Go back down and spring up to the ladder. Jump to the next room and take out the yeti. Go through the gap and drop down to the tigers. Go down the corridor to *Secret Two* and a mask. Go back to where you dropped in. At the top of the right-hand slope is *Secret Three*. The left-hand slope has a drop at the end. Keep going and drop down twice. Now climb up onto a ledge and use the mask in the hole. Go through the door and over a bridge to a switch. Pull it and drop down to the tigers. Get the gong-stick from the water and swim to the yetis. Kill them and go up the stairs. Go to the slope and grab on. Shimmy and climb up. Jump to the wall, go through the gap and drop down. Use the gong and jump over the slope to the gap. The Talion is here. Go back to the cave and kill the boss.

The Temple of Xian-Level 15
Follow the corridor, slide and avoid the blades. Shimmy across to *Secret One*. Go down the waterfalls and to the temple. Kill the tigers and spring up. Hit the switch and drop down. Swim to the corner and go up the ladder. Go along and down another ladder to a ledge. Under this is *Secret Two*. Go left to another ledge and to a ladder. Climb up to a corridor. Drop down into a room, go across the spikes, climb up and jump back. Jump to the wall and climb up. Go to the last tile and fall through. Slide down, avoiding the spikes and grab the ledge. Climb up and hit the switch. Go back to the water. Go into the Temple, walk down the middle, then go right. Go up the stairs and slide down until you can grab on. Climb up and jump to the block. Jump to the switch and drop down. Hit the switch and run out. Go up the slope, avoiding the boulders, and on up the ladder. Watch the blades! Go through the doorway on the left to a ledge above the statues. Kill the eagles. Jump to the switch. Hit it and quickly get to the opposite doorway. Go past the maces and hit the switch on the right, then the left. Go through and run. Jump to the ledge and up into a room. Hit the switch and go through the other door. Go down and jump to the centre of the room. Double-jump off the sloped block

to the next block. Jump off to the ledge. Jump back to the Dragon Seal ledge. Jump to the wooden block. Get to the springboard and spring to the slope. Jump back to the ledge, Go right, then double back to avoid the boulder. In this room is *Secret Three*. Get to the other side of the room, then jump to the higher blocks. Get to the doorway above and move the block. Go through, hit the switch and drop down.

Keep running, slide down and take out the tigers. Drop down and put the Dragon Seal into the slot. Go through and past the spinning blades. In one of the alcoves is a slope. Go down, hit the switch near the waterfall, then hit the other two. Go through and make your way up to a high ledge. Drop into the water and kill the fish. Hit the switch under the water. Go down the tunnel, ignoring the first switch. Keep going through the next tunnel and hit the switch. Swim through the grate and hit another switch. Go back to the switch that you ignored and hit it. Go through the new gate and hit the switch. Now go and hit the main-pool switch. Swim up and climb out of the hatch.

Go through the door and hit the switch. Run to the hatch. Grab the Gold Key from the water and swim out to the temple. Use the key and swim through to the pillar room. Hit the switch and double back. Go up through the hole to the cave. Kill the spiders and jump from block to block. Climb up various ledges and make your way to the next room. Climb up, get the Silver Key, and swim back to the temple. Use the key to get through the locked door.

Jump from block to block avoiding the boulders. Go left through a corridor. Watch for tigers just past the rope-bridge. Double-jump over to the sloped block and jump into a room with a spinning blade. Carefully climb up into another room and across another bridge. Hit the switch and go back to the spinning blade room. Go down to the springboard. Use it and the others to get to the next room. Go across the blocks and climb up the ladder. Climb another ladder and move along the corridor. Hit the switch and go back along the corridor. Jump to a ledge, then jump to the pillar. Get the Chamber Key. Slide down the tail to a wooden block. Jump to the gap and go back to the keyhole in the room after the springboards. Jump to the new ledge and climb the ladder. Climb the next ladder and into a new statue room. Make your way into the statue. Go up the ladder and avoid the blade by jumping off the slope to a ladder. Go up, avoid the blade and flip around to grab another ladder. Climb, shimmy and drop down.

The Floating Islands-Level 16
Find the cage and jump into the gap. Hit the switch and drop down from the entrance. Kill the guard and climb up to the start level. Return to the cage and go down the slope, jumping at the end. Get out a big gun and destroy the guards. Climb up and grab the Mystic Plaque. *Secret One* is here as well. Go right and drop down to a ledge. Climb to the cave and hit the switch. Jump to the gateway and on to the green island. Go

left to the centre island. Jump to the block and onto the island with the steps. Get back on to the cage and down to the stone ledge. Get to the triangular block and drop down to the next Mystical Plaque. Go up the steps to the start and climb up onto the cage. Follow the ledge and jump to the next island. Use the plaques and kill the guards. Go across the bridge (from where you can see *Secret Two*). Avoid the boulders. Climb up the wall and slide onto the roof. Jump over the roof and jump across the slopes to the next island.

Slide down the rope to the bridge. Go into the room and kill the statues. Hit the switch, go through the corridor and up the ladder. Go to the opening and back to the rope-slide. Ride it all the way down. Pull the block twice and climb up to the switch. Hit it and drop through the gap in the room on to a block. Hit the switch and climb back to where the rope-slide ended. Go into the room on the left, avoid the stars and blades and swim through a tunnel. Hit the switch and go back to the blades. Climb up, hit the switch, and go back up the steps. Go back to the block and use it to get to the area above the corridor. Go into the room and climb up to the switch. Hit it and go back to the door that you came through. Head right, through the gate, and drop down to the cage-room. Hit the switch and take out the enemies. Carefully kill the statues one by one and hit the switches. Go through the gate and up the stairs, hit the switch, and kill the guards. Head for the new door on the right. Climb the ladder and flip round to the ladder behind you. Flip back once more to another ladder. Jump between the slopes and the corridor. Move the box to get the rocks. Jump over the lava, and get *Secret Three* from the tunnel. Ride the rope-slide to the end.

The Dragon's Lair-Level 17
Kill the statues and hit the switch in one of the alcoves. Hit the switch by the door and kill the statues. Go into the room and take out the enemies. Get the plaque and use it. Jump into the water and grab all the goodies. Get out the Uzi.

The best way to defeat the dragon is just to run around it constantly shooting. When it eventually drops grab the dagger from its body. Run down the corridor.

Lara's Mansion-Level 18
Go to your bedroom and use the key. Grab the items. Go through the mansion killing all the enemies. Kill the enemies in the mansion grounds and well.. that is it!!

TOMB RAIDER 3

Enter these codes while playing the game, (do not pause):

All Weapons
L2, R2 x2, L2 x4, R2, L2, R2 x2, L2, R2 x2, L2 x2, R2, L2 x2, R2.

Level Skip
L2, R2, L2 x2, R2, L2, R2, L2, R2, L2 x4, R2, L2, R2 x4, L2.

All Secrets And Keys
L2 x5, R2, L2 x3, R2, L2, R2, L2 x2, R2, L2 x2, R2, L2 x2.

Full Energy
R2 x2, L2, R2, L2 x6, R2, L2 x3, R2, L2 x5.

Race Track Key
Enter this code while on the mansion training level.
R2, L2 x3, R2, L2 x6, R2, L2 x5, R2, L2 x2.

India
The Jungle
Lara begins her third quest on the outskirts of an ancient Inca temple in the jungles of India. Follow the left path and slide to the green ledge. Drop to the next ledge in front then hang drop off the ledge to the right. After you slide past the log be prepared to jump over a bed of spikes. When you stop collect the shotgun shells and the medi pack. When you collect the medi pack a boulder will roll towards you. Stand where you collected the medi pack and you will be safe. Slide down the rest of the hill and jump the final set of spikes. Head left and collect the first save crystal. Climb the ruins to your left and collect the items scattered around. Return to where you collected the save crystal, the level exit is at the far end of the quick sand. Drop into the shallow quick sand and enter through the doorway in the ruins. Follow the monkey on the left. Collect the small medi pack and pull the lever. Return to the clearing and climb the tree opposite. Enter the doorway. Pull the lever, then quickly roll and climb up onto the window ledge avoiding the wall of spikes. Head left and climb through the gap. Slide across the river and climb the block.

Run and jump into the passage opposite and then drop down. Shoot the tiger then head left. Enter the passage on the left and pull the lever. This will trigger the boulder at the top. Avoid the boulder by walking up the steps. Collect the flares and the small medi pack in the top left. and return past the boulder. Head up and left through the open doorway. Pull the lever then head through the other door. Shoot the lone tiger, another tiger will appear when you reach the end of the passage. Search this area for shells then head right. You will find yourself in another clearing. Avoid the hole in the ground and head for the top left corner. Crawl under the tree log then head right. Collect the save crystal and shoot the tiger who appears from the other end of the log. Cross the log. Avoid the hole at the end of the log. There is a secret inside the log. Jump across the hole and grab the end of the log, then pull yourself in. Collect the items inside then return back. You will need to drop down the hole. You will slide into a bed of spikes but you should only receive minimum damage. Carefully jump out and head through the dark tunnel to your right. Walk through the spikes and climb out at the end. You will need to backtrack under and over the fallen log.

Head through the left passage and walk through the bed of spikes. Jump to the next ledge and collect the small medi pack.

To collect the save crystal, grab the ledge in front and shimmy across to the opposite ledge. Then jump towards the save crystal. Because the ledges in front are sloped you will slide down. Grab the end and shimmy to the flat ledge on the right (above the bed of spikes). Return to the ledge opposite. Jump up and grab the ledge to the left and shimmy until you can pull yourself up. Turn to the right and climb the ledge. Head forward and left into the dark passage. Turn left and head up to the lever. Jump and grab to the left and pull yourself up into a secret area. Collect the items and return back down to the lever. Pull the lever then return outside. The boulder above you will drop and roll towards you. The gate below you will now be open. Drop down to the ground floor and shoot the tiger. Head through the gate and through the trees to the left. Avoid the rolling boulders which appear through the bushes to the left. Head through the bushes and drop through the hole on the left avoiding the spikes below. Collect the save crystal then return back up. Continue forward until you reach the river.

Dive into the water. Swim through the underwater passage in the top right. Once in the temple, climb out of the water and pull both levers. Return into the water and swim into the next chamber. Collect the flares from the centre platform. Enter the doorway opposite and pull the lever. Head right and follow the passage until you reach the water pool. Swim along the left water and climb out when you reach the waterfall with the passage behind it. At the end of the passage, turn around and climb the ladder to the top. Follow the path right, climb to the higher ledge, turn and jump to the opposite ledge. Head left and pull the lever. Dive into the water and climb the stairs on the left. To reach the save crystal, climb the pillar at the end of the stairs and perform a running jump to the opposite ledge. Drop into the water and swim down through the passage on the left. Pull yourself out of the water and shoot the lone tiger. Collect the items from the corners of the room, then climb the ladder. Quickly grab the Indra key before the monkey does. Head right and drop to the lower ledge. Shoot the tiger then drop down. Jump the mud and use the Indra key in the lock. Enter through the doorway to exit the level.

Temple Ruins
Beware, the long grass are filled with poisonous snakes. If you are bitten you will slowly lose health until you use a medi pack. Head forward towards the river avoiding being bitten by the snakes. Drop into the water and swim quickly to the right. Once in the underground passage crawl forward and collect the small medi pack. Head forward, kill the snake as you turn left. Continue forward and climb out the through the left hole. The monkeys on this level are hostile so you should shoot them quickly as they can become a problem when performing tricky jumps. Collect the items on the steps on your right then go to the edge of the water. Wait until the piranhas are at the other end of the river, then dive into the water and quickly swim to the other edge. Pull the lever in the far right then head to the centre of the shallow ledge. When the piranhas swim away from you drop into the water and swim through the passage. Pull yourself out at the other end. Head right and climb the far pillar. Turn right and climb to the higher ledge.

Head left and across the flat mud. Jump to the ledge and follow the path around the right. Collect the save crystal.

Walk to the edge and jump diagonally to the tree. Walk to the edge, then perform a running jump to the ledge opposite. Jump diagonally to the tree. Enter the cave to the left. Continue round until you reach the waterfall. Jump backwards down the slope and grab the ledge. Shimmy along to the right, collect the shells then drop to the ground. Turn to the right and climb up. Jump diagonally to the green ledge, then crawl into the cave. Shoot the snake and slide down the slope. Run through the passageway and shoot the snake on the right. Slide down the slope, close to the right wall, avoiding the rolling boulder. Drop into the green lit room. Collect the shotgun from the statue then pull the block back from the corner of the room. Crawl through into the next chamber. The statue opposite will come to life. You can only cause damage when its arms are open. Wait until it comes close to you and opens its arms, then jump backwards and fire. Continue until it is destroyed. Collect the save crystal from the top of the chamber. Pull the two levers to open the left door.

Enter through the left door and turn right. Climb the block and drop into the next chamber. Shoot the monkeys and continue into the next room. Wait until the fire subsides and drop into the water. Swim to the opposite end and when the fire dies down climb up and pull the lever. Return into the water and swim through the open gate. Stay close to the ground to avoid the poisonous darts. As you enter the next room, ceiling blocks will drop from above. Swim to the left and climb out of the water. Climb the ladder then jump backwards to the opposite ledge. Diagonally run and jump to the ledge near the entrance. Jump to the ledge to the left, turn around and jump and grab the ledge opposite. Pull yourself to the top. Run and jump diagonally to the right ledge, steering yourself around the corner. Run and jump to the ledge with the sleeping snake, then shoot it when it awakens. Jump to the following ledge and then into the temple entrance. As soon as you land a boulder will roll towards you. Jump back and grab the ledge, the boulder will pass safely over you.

Crawl under the darts and the left blade. Collect the medi kit then perform a running jump over towards the save crystal. Push the block just right of the save crystal. Push the block to the right four times. Push the first and third block to the left in. Then push the middle block left or right revealing a lever. Head left and run down the tunnel, two boulders will roll after you. As you near the pit, jump and grab the ledge. Drop down the right side of the following pit into the water below. Swim into the fire room and head into the next room. The pool will be flooded. Drop into the water and pull the level, enter through the open gate and collect the first Ganesha key. Leave the room and return to the statue chamber.

Head towards the opposite door. Stand on the stone panel three blocks from the door to open the floor grating in front. Drop down and pull the lever to the left, this will open the door above. Push the block in front of you to enter a secret room. Return to the chamber above and enter the now open door. Run to the end and drop into the mud. Turn to the left and walk towards the opposite end, Lara will sink into the mud. If you continue forward without stopping you will reach the end without drowning. Climb out of the mud. Turn around and jump to the ledge opposite. Pull the lever at the end and then run through the open door. Run straight forward through the traps is the best method to avoiding the most dangerous traps. Head to the right and pull the lower block from the column. Push the block forward, you can now climb up to the gate. Under the gate is a lever, which when pulled will open the gate. Once you have done this, climb the block and head through the gate. Once in the water, pull the lever to open the gate then swim through the tunnel to the next chamber.

You will need to pull both the lever to the right and to the left to open the gate above the underwater tunnel. Drop into the water and pull the three levers to activate the statues above. Climb out the water. The fire from the statues will reveal invisible platforms, climb these to reach the platform on the opposite side. Pull the lever then quickly drop off to the left and run through the open gate. Head to the right and pull the lever on the left. This will open the gate to your left and activate a wall of spikes to your right. Run to your left and collect the second Ganesha key, roll around then run towards the exit. Drop into the mud and cross to the opposite side, stay close to the right side to avoid the falling blocks. Head to the top of the mud slide and into the passage on the right. At the end there is a passage head right and on the second step turn and run back around the corner, avoiding the activated boulder. Return up the stairs and take the right passage. Pull the lever at the end and head forward. Collect the save crystal then head to the right side of the chamber. Climb down the wall and then drop into the statue chamber.

Insert both the Ganesha keys into the locks to open the giant gate. Jump the pit and quickly climb the wall. Collect the save crystal then pull the block in the bottom right of the room. Climb the block then run, jump and grab the ledge opposite. Pull both levers then drop down to the ground. Avoid the two boulders which appear when you step in front of the open gate. Wait until the fire dies down then run past the statue. Destroy the two statues which come to life and collect the two Scimitar they drop. Place the two Scimitars on the statue on the ledge to open the gate opposite. Enter through the open gate and take either passage into the final chamber. Destroy the living statue as you enter. Walk towards the gate to the left to open it. Run in and pull the lever opposite the entrance. Turn to your right and pull the final lever to open the trap door. Drop down the trap door and collect the Ganesha key. Return to the main chamber and collect the key from beneath the floating central figure. Head forward and collect the save crystal from around the corner. Drop through the hole on the left. Once in the water, swim to the far left or right avoiding the bed of spikes. Pull the lever then swim up the side of the wall and head to the over side. Pull the second lever to stop the current and collect the key from the entrance. Climb out of the water and insert all three keys into the locks. Exit through the gate at the top of the steps.

The River Ganges

Run towards the quad bike, collect the items from the narrow ledge. Mount the quad bike and ride to the mound at the end of the plateau. Rev the bike and jump the river to the cave opposite. Continue around the cave avoiding the drops until you reach a closed gate. Dismount and return back across the previous ramp. Run and jump to the passage to the left of the final ramp. Head through the passage, shooting the snake around the first corner. Jump the hole in the vine tunnel and shoot the snake on the right. Drop down the ledge and push the switch to open the gate. Collect the save crystal. Remount the quad bike and head through the gate. There are two ways through this level. Up stream is quicker but with less items to collect while down stream takes longer to complete but has more items to collect.

Take the left passage and head up the slope. Stop the bike on the right side. Rev the bike and jump the pit. As you near the top turn right into the next chamber. Pass around the hole and head up. Centre the bike with the rock bridge then drive down. Drive at full speed to jump to the opposite ledge. Drive to the left until you reach the bottom of the ramp. Make your way slowly up along the ledges until you reach the cliff edge. You will need to rev the bike up to gain enough speed to reach the opposite ledge. Collect the save crystal then position the bike facing the opposite direction in the far left corner. Rev the bike and jump to the ledge. Ride the bike down the hill and collect the save crystal once you reach the bottom. Dismount once you reach the river. Dive down into the pool at the base of the waterfall and swim towards the shore. Head behind the waterfall and climb up in to the hidden passageway.

Caves Of Kaliya

Go right and stop at the slope. Jump back and perform a running jump down the slope. You will land on the slope near the bottom of the slope, jump again. Once you land run forward and turn left, narrowly avoiding the rolling boulder behind you. In the left passageway, run halfway up then turn and roll running back into the left alcove. This will trigger the next boulder but give you enough time to escape. Race up the slope and climb into the temple ruins. Take the first right and then turn right. Push the block until you reach the end. Head right then left. Follow the passage and drop down the hole at the end. Follow the passage until you reach the green stone area. Go left and continue until you reach the save crystal. Drop down the hole then run to the end. If you time it right, you will avoid being bitten by the snakes. Once you reach the end quickly crawl through the gap on the right. Collect the save crystal then slide down the slope towards the boss.

To defeat the boss, position yourself at the edge of the platform in line with the one next to it. So while facing the boss character and firing, you can side jump between both platforms. Wait until the boss releases a fireball before jumping to the adjacent platform and you will avoid his attack when he fires again return to the first platform. Continue until he is destroyed. Once defeated, collect all the items scattered across the platforms including the grenade launcher from the far platform. To end the level collect the artefact.

South Pacific Islands
Coastal Village

As you swim towards the island, swim to the right and collect the smugglers key. Surface and head towards the hut in the top left corner. Inside, insert the smugglers key in the lock to open the trap door. Drop down and collect the save crystal. Slowly walk down the passage and crawl under the spring trap.

Continue forward until you reach the water. Cross the ledges until you reach the top. Monkey swing across the water to the opposite side. Head up the right path. At the top run and jump to the far ledge. Monkey swing to the rock bridge and head to the other end. Jump to the sloped block and jump to the opposite ledge. Jump over the spikes and grab the ladder. Climb to the top then shimmy over to the left. Collect the save crystal. Drop off to the ledge below, then shimmy to the left. Jump to the next ledge and follow the passage across the rope bridge. Head left at the shrine and crawl under the spinning blades. In the temple head round to the right and press the switch. Jump across the stream and collect the save crystal. Drop down the slope and slide into the village.

Clear the village of hostile natives then head left towards the tree house. Kill the native to the left on the edge of the swamp. Turn the pulley wheel to drop the bridge across the spikes. Return to the village and up into the new village area. Head up the slope and enter the far left hut. Turn the pulley wheel and return down the slope. Climb the ladder up into the tree house and onto the window ledge. Jump diagonally to the ledge opposite and enter the flame passage. Kill the native and head to the right. Jump across to the first roof then cross to the second. Monkey swing across the spikes to the far roof and enter the tree house. Turn the pulley, then return outside. Climb back up the ladder and enter the flame passage. Jump left to the grating covering the flames and cross the fire covered floor. Press the switch in front and kill the native who appears. Head down the right passage and dash past the spinning blades. Turn the pulley to open the gate. Slide back down into the village. Drop into the water and swim through the now open passage. Surface once you have reached the end and climb the ladder. Cross the rope bridge and follow the passage until you reach the tree house. Run and jump to the ledge opposite and enter the tree house.

Crash Site
Once you have finished speaking with the wounded commando, leave the tree house and drop to the ground. Cross the swamp using the swamp map as a guide to which lily pads are stable. In the top left corner of the swamp is a secret area containing extra items. Once you have reached the far side of the swamp, head through the forest and to your first encounter with a raptor. Past through the fog and climb the blocks at the end. Drop through the hole and head to the right side of the crashed plane. Climb the slope and kill the raptor attacking the soldiers. Be careful not to hit the solders or they will attack you. Head back the way you came but enter the cave on your left. At the end of the passage you will enter a room with a dead raptor and solder. Collect the solders MP5 rifle and kill the scavengers. Pull the levers to open the gate.

Return back outside and continue forward and enter the next cave. You will reach a clearing with one solder. As you enter the clearing, two raptors will attack. Climb the tree on the right for a secret area. Slide down the slope and kill the scavengers. Head into the large cave and climb the mound. Collect the key from the dead solder. Once you have collect the key the T-Rex will appear. If you stand still the T-Rex will not notice you. Head to the base of the slope, the gate on the left will be open. You can safely shoot the T-Rex from here. Once dead pull the lever and head to the other gate and pull the lever there.

Return to the first gate and head up the steps.

Return to the plane and head to the right and the large open clearing and the river. Enter the tunnel on the right and follow the passage. Kill the raptor. If you attempt to cross the rope bridge you will drop into the water and be attacked by the piranhas. Climb the rock face then jump to the tree. Kill the raptor in the tree. Grab the rock ledge on the left. Cross over to the tree and kill the raptor. Shoot the hanging raptor and it will drop in to the water. Dive into the water below, you will be safe from the piranhas as they will be eating the dead raptor. Pull the underwater lever, then pull yourself ashore. Kill the raptor which appears and enter the open gate. There are three levers to pull, which will drop the ceiling above. When you pull a lever a raptor will be released. Pull one of the levers and climb on the block, safe from the raptors attacks. After pulling all three levers, climb through the open ceiling and collect the second key. Avoid the raptor and return to the crashed plane. Go to the side of the plane near the door and jump and grab the ledge. Shimmy along to the left until you can pull yourself up. Drop through the hatch and kill the raptor. Enter the cockpit and insert both keys. Enter the hull and enter the small room at the end. Push the button and run towards the cannon. Use the cannon to kill the rampaging raptors. Once their attacks have stopped, fire at the temple walls in the left corner. Leave the gun and jump across the river. Collect the save crystal from the right room then head down the steps towards the temple.

Madubu Gorge
There is a narrow gap in the left building which leads to some hidden items. Shoot the reptiles which appear, avoid their poisonous breath by jumping backwards while shooting. Drop down to the blocks just left of the pillars. Then jump to the block in the river. Run and jump to the opposite side, grabbing the ledge as you side towards the river. Shimmy and climb right and press the switch at the end. Return back across the river and up to where you started. Enter the secret room and drop down the open trap door. Climb into the canoe and paddle down the river. Paddle into the green rope to stop the spinning blades. Continue down the rapids and paddle right against the current. Avoid the red ropes, as you reach the waterfall collect the save crystal. Battle up the right waterfall until you reach the pool with the giant plug. Head down the right passage and collect the save crystal hidden under the waterfall.

Return to the giant plug and paddle up the green lit rapids. At the top is a small pool and a crocodile. Quickly dive into the water and pull yourself ashore. Shoot the crocodile from the safety of the shore. Head left and drop down the step over looking the giant plug room. Jump up and grab the roof. Monkey swing across the chamber past the flames. Drop to the ledge below and cross the water. Collect the rocket launcher and head up through the passage. Climb the wall at the end and again grab the roof. Monkey swing up and then right. Jump across to the blocks next to the spinning blades and run and jump to the climbable wall. Head left across the wall. Enter the doorway and climb down to the bottom. Run to the first step and crouch, a boulder will roll towards and over you. Repeat again when you reach the following step. Run forward then jump to the left avoiding the boulder behind you. Jump the flames then avoid the final boulder.

Follow the passage and climb up. Run and jump to the ledge on the right. Climb the wall to the left to reach the next ledge. Jump to the block in the middle of the water then cross to the next ledge. Jump to the rope slide and ride it down the rapids. Drop down near the chain and climb the wall. Find the switch and raise the plug. Return down the corridor and drop down to passage. Slide down the slope to return to your canoe. Paddle down the rapids to the plug chamber and ride down the hole. Dive into the water and shoot the crocodiles from the shore. Swim under the yellow ledge and pull the lever. Swim quickly back to shore avoiding the crocodiles. Exit through the gates.

Temple Of Puna
Head down the passage and at the cross roads, turn right and shoot the natives. Head right and climb the stairs. Once you reach the top turn right to the edge of the rolling blade room. There are four switches in the room which need to be pressed to open the gate. You can stand in the corners of the room in relative safety if you stay close enough to the wall. Once you have open the door, climb the block and slide down into pit. Pull out the block to stop the lowering spiked ceiling. Hang and drop into the shaft and slide into the boulder chamber. Head towards the base of the boulder and press the switch. Immediately roll around and dash towards the opposite gate. As you enter the next chamber you will encounter another rolling boulder. Quickly turn and dash to the exit. Shoot any remaining natives and head up the stairs. Slide down into the chamber below.

This is the boss chamber. Walk up towards the throne and the boss will swivel round. It fires electric bolts which will instantly kill you. Run left and right from the sides of the room. As you run towards the centre of the room turn slightly so Lara aims at the boss as she passes by. Once you reach the other end of the room, roll and run back. The boss is only vulnerable when it fires its electricity. Eventually the boss will turn towards the side of the room and creates a reptile creature. Stop at the side of the room and face the creature. The boss will not attack until the creature is destroyed. Continue to fire until the reptile creature stops in front of you, at this point it is ready to fire is poisonous breath. Jump back one space and continue to attack, you will be just out of range of its attack. If you are hit, you will only lose small amounts of energy very slowly so do not use a medi pack until you are below 20% energy. Once the creature is destroyed the boss will continue its attack. Continue this strategy until it is destroyed. Once the boss has been vanquished, climb the steps and collect the artefact.

London
Thames Wharf
The actual route through this level can take about an hour to complete but there is a secret route which takes mere minutes. Turn around and run up the long gantry. Turn around and run towards and over the roof. Collect the save crystal on the right. Climb the block and up onto the roof. Jump to the roof to your right and grab the ledge as you slide down. Shimmy to the left and drop to the ground. Turn right and jump over to the opposite block. You should be facing the yellow crane structure. Stand at the edge and jump forward slightly facing right so that you do not hit the crane. If positioned correctly you will land on the platform below. Run and jump to the roof top opposite. Pull yourself up and slowly walk through the barb wire. Jump to the

flat roof to the right then across to the ledge on the left. Run along to the left and shoot the two guards which confront you. Head right and drop through the gap in the fence.

Aldwych
As you slide down, jump from the second slope and grab the ledge. Collect the shells then drop into the water below. Pull yourself from the water and ascend the stairs. Shoot the wooden boards and collect the save crystal. Climb the two ladders to reach the loft. Pull the block out by the pillar. Drop through the hole onto the ticket machine. Jump from ticket machine to ticket machine and climb the block to the top. Drop through the following holes into the ticket office. Collect the maintenance key and press the switch to open the office door. Head down the right escalator. Jump diagonally across the large hole. Shoot the thug and the dog which appear. Head through the pillars and towards the door on the right. Use the maintenance key to open the door and inside switch the platform lights on. Head to the other side of the platform and pick up the old penny near the vending machine. Return across the large hole and up the escalator to the ticket machines. Insert the old penny into the second ticket machine from the right. Collect the ticket. Head down the left escalator and shoot the thug at the bottom. Head through the pillars then right up the stairs. Shoot the dog as you ascend. Jump and shimmy to the tunnel above. Crawl to the end and use the ticket to open the barrier.

Shoot the rats and the lone thug. Head to the right and descend the escalator. Drop into the blue passage, shooting the thug who appears behind you. Jump across the hole and shoot the dog. Follow the stairs to the platform. Shoot the thug at the end. Drop onto the track, at the end is a hole with a large medi pack at the bottom. Return upstairs and jump the hole. Head through the open door on the left. Drop into the large hole. Quickly run left along the track and into the alcove on the right before you are hit by the oncoming train. Shoot the two thugs, then climb onto the crate in the far right corner. Run and jump to the crates on the left then repeat to reach the next crate on the left. Jump backwards onto the middle of the slope, then jump and grab the netting. Climb to the top then jump backwards to the ledge behind. Shoot the thug behind you and climb up to the next ledge. Jump forward and grab the ceiling netting and monkey swing around to the right. Drop down and then slide down the slope. Here you will face a large drill machine. Turn around and slide backwards down the slope, grab the ledge at the end. Drop to the crumbling floor and then quickly jump left to the slope. Jump again and grab the ledge. Drop to the crumbling floor and grab the ledge as you fall. Drop to the slope below then jump backwards to safety.

Climb up to the pool area, then climb the netted wall. Pull yourself up and run past the flames. Climb on the block to extinguish the flames. Climb up onto the ledge then head left until you can jump and reach the netted wall. Jump backwards to reach the ledge and press the switch. This will drop the hatch back in the red room near the train tracks. Walk to the edge and jump and grab the ledge above the netted wall. Hang and drop to the next ledge. Head up left to the steps and then ascend them. Climb up to the left and through the doorway on the right. Shoot the rats then hang and drop through the grating. Head to the right escalator and drop through the large hole. Run down the track to the red room. Climb up as before and head to the drill. Drop onto the top of the machine and collect the Solomon key. Climb up and head through the passage. Return down the large hole and head to the red room. Climb up again but this time head through the open hatch. Shoot the thug and the dog who appear.

Stand on the crumbling tile and drop down. Pull the block back and then climb back up. Drop through the hatch opposite. Follow the passage. Crawl through the tunnel then climb out to the right. Follow the passage until you reach the two switches. Press the right switch then quickly run left up the passage. In the room with the doors enter the right door before it closes. Press the switch inside. Head through the rear passage and return to the switches. Press the right again but enter the middle door. Climb up through the hatch and press the switch on the right wall. Follow the passage and drop back down to the switches. Press the left switch and quickly enter the left door. Climb the ledge to the left, jump to the ceiling grating and monkey swing to the ledge. Drop and grab the ledge. Collect the items and the Solomon's key. Exit through the tunnel in the water. Climb out once you reach the end of the tunnel.

Kill the thug who opens the door and head to the ticket machine area. Head down the left escalator and clear the track of rats. Drop onto the track and head to the right. Dash for the open middle door. Shoot the thug and press the switch. Head back and into the right door, collect the save crystal. Then head right and into the left door. Swim to opposite side and press the switch. Go right and press the triple hands/croc/writing switch. Return to the passage and head right, press the hands switch. Enter the door on the right of the passage and press the croc switch. Then return to the first triple switch and press it again. Head down the passage until you reach the large Masonic room. Use the two Solomon's keys to unbolt the hands at the opposite end of the room. Cross the crumbling tiles and collect the Masonic mallet. collect the save crystal and the uzis from the centre of the room. Exit through the far left door. Drop into the pool and swim along the passage. Surface and climb to tunnel. Pass the open barrier and head down the escalator. Use the mallet to open the door. Inside press the switch then head outside and drop into blue passage. Drop into the hole and crawl through the gap at the bottom. Climb up through the open hatch into the train. Press the switch then drop through the open hatch. Crawl through the tunnel and head down the passage. Slide down either of the two slope to exit the level.

Lud's Gate
From this point onwards do not attack the sewer thugs. Follow the passage down to the pool area. Head through the left doorway and slide down the slope. Once you land, quickly turn to the right and climb the wall to avoid the lowering spikes. Press the switch then climb the block. Climb the wall to the top. There are various items you can collect as you climb up. Crawl through to the middle of the tunnel and climb up through the hole. Drop through the following hole and shoot the guard below. Pull and push the block to the left and press the switch. Shoot the guard in the passage and head right. Once in the Egyptian chamber, climb the steps and enter the

room at the rear. Push the block inside to the doorway, then climb onto the block and through the niche. Head to the top step, jump to the left and grab the monkey bars. Monkey swing across and collect the save crystal. Drop down and return back to the monkey bars. Head to the right and pull up to the ledge and press the switch. Drop down, then jump and climb to the block now blocking the entrance. Climb to the ledge then head right to the niche. Head down the other side and climb up to the ledge. Slide down the slope and drop into the passage.

Head into the room at the end and pull the block. Return to the Egyptian chamber and climb onto the sliding pillar. Jump to the ledge with the switch, press the switch then drop down to the pillar. Climb the ladder with the closed hatch, head left to the ledge. Turn around and jump left to the block then across to the opposite ledge. Drop down and then climb to the right. Slide down the slope backwards so you can grab the end. Pull up then jump backwards and twist in mid air, grabbing the opposite ledge. Climb up and slide down the next slope. Once you land, quickly jump forward and grab the ledge before the floor falls away. Collect the Embalming fluid then crawl through the tunnel in front. Shoot the guard around the corner then crawl through the tunnel on the right. Shoot the guard then press the switch to open the door.

Once you have collect the items behind the door, return into the room and drop through the hole in the right corner. Monkey swing to the opposite side and collect the save crystal then swing back. Halfway across stop and drop onto the Sphinx's head. Slide down the side of the Sphinx and head around to the left. Shoot the guard then head up the stairs. Kill the guard on the stairs and head to the top. Climb up to the ledge and pull the block out. Drop to the ground then jump and climb up the side of the moved block. Climb right to the ledge, then turn around and climb up the passage. Drop down the hole, then down into the brick tunnel. Turn around and push the block, then pull the other block twice. Climb up the block to the grating, then right to the ledge. Climb to passage, then drop through the hole and down the brick tunnel to appear back at the start. Head up the passage back to the throne room and use the Embalming fluid by the blue lit ledge to open the secret door.

Head through the secret door and drop into the water. Swim over to the Propulsion unit and head into the next chamber. Kill or avoid the crocodile and head to the far left corner and up a wide passage. Surface, then climb out onto the ledge. Drop into the next pool and swim to the following pool. Pull the underwater lever then swim back through the tunnel and up the open hatch. Climb up the ledge and press the switch. Return to the water and swim through the open hatch. Swim to the left and climb out. Jump onto the ledge, then to the crate and shoot the guard. Collect the boiler room key from the dead guard then head around to the right. Drop into the water and swim through the tunnel. Avoid the crocodile and enemy divers and head for air in the top left chamber. Collect the propulsion unit from the top right chamber on the right wall and hunt down the crocodile and enemy divers. Return for air when you get low. Head down the low green lit tunnel and pull the lever. Enter the green lit tunnel above the entrance and pull the lever.

Enter the top red tunnel and pull the lever inside. Enter the top blue tunnel and head through the hatch and up the long shaft until you reach the surface. Pull yourself out of the water and press the switch to extinguish the flames. Head across the platforms and into the passage, timing your dashes past the crushes. Climb up and head to the edge of the ledge. Turn to the right and run and jump to the monkey bars. Climb forward then to the left, drop and grab the niche as you fall. Crawl into the niche and descend the other side. Use the boiler room key in the lock. Collect the save crystal and press the switch. Return to the pool and swim back to the large underwater chamber and swim into the top purple tunnel. Continue through the open hatch and up the shaft until you reach the surface. Climb out of the water, then jump to the passage. Head left and into the hole, then slide down the slope. Ascend the steps then run and jump the shaft and grab the ledge. Drop to the blue niche and crawl through the tunnel. Perform a running jump to the purple niche opposite, crawl left then climb downwards. Turn around and head up. Slide down the slope. Then just crawl to the end of the level.

The City
Exit the office through the passage in the top right corner of the room. Outside you will face this levels boss, the evil Sophia. Head up the slope and climb the block. Turn and grab the monkey bars opposite and monkey swing to the platform opposite. Climb up and follow the bridge around to the right. Press the switch and return across the bridge. Climb up through the open hatch. Continue to climb up, then head for the higher bridge. Jump diagonally to the netted wall and climb up. Crawl through the niche, then turn around and climb up. Run and jump over the gap and grab the opposite ledge. Pull yourself up and run forward to find the fuse box. Shoot the fuse box to electrify the grating under Sophia, killing her. Return across the gap then turn to the left and jump to the opposite roof. Make your way up and to the left avoiding the electrified floor. Deactivate the electricity by pressing the switch on the far left of the grating. Once the floor is safe to cross, collect the artefact.

Nevada
Nevada Desert
Head forward and round the right side of the centre boulders. Enter the passage at the end and follow it to the right. Jump up the small slope. Push the left block in and collect the shells. Climb up the steps and head around the corner. Walk to the edge of the slope then run and jump to the ledge opposite. Repeat to reach the end, then head to the right. Cross to the edge of the ledge on the right of the large steel block. Jump to the ledge opposite. Follow the ledge to the left, shooting the snake in the bush. Jump to the opposite ledge and continue round. Drop to the lower ledge just left to the quick sand. Turn to the left and then run and jump to the rocks opposite, grabbing the ledge. Climb up the slope and drop through the hole in the top of the large steel block. Swim through the tunnel to the end. Pull yourself out and head through the arch. You can drop into the water below and collect the items at the bottom of the water, then climb back up to the arch. Head to the right and jump from ledge to ledge. Shoot the vulture which appears, then continue round. Climb the blocks then turn to the left. Run and jump to the climbable wall opposite. Climb to the top then jump to the ledge on the left. Shoot the

vultures and the snake in the bush. Climb up and watch the stealth planes fly over. Drop and grab the left ledge. Climb to the ledge underneath, then monkey swing to the right and then left across the wall to the waterfall. Climb to the top then jump backwards to the ledge behind. Run and jump to the ledge behind the waterfall.

Jump from ledge to ledge until you reach the shore. If you fall into the water you will be dragged down the waterfall. Head to the yellow machine and shoot the mechanic. Climb the ladders on the right to the top of the machine. Head to the right across the wall shooting any vultures. Drop into the water, pull the lever and collect the flares form the open hatch. Climb out of the water and head across to the left. Drop into the water and pull the lever in the corner. Dive between the yellow slopes and enter the open hatch. Pull the lever above you as you enter then pull the second lever as you swim around the right corner. Head to the end of the tunnel and pull yourself out. Press the switch at the end then slide down the waterfall into the water below. Return down the yellow machine and head left. Enter the corner passage and shoot the mechanic. Enter the elevator and collect the detonator switch. Return back across the shore to the waterfall. Cross the ledges to the cave with the detonator.

Use the switch with the detonator then quickly move to avoid the rolling boulder. Follow the cable down into the cave then climb up and around the ledges to the niche. Crawl through until you reach the fenced compound. Head left past the fence and climb into the tunnel. Follow the passage then jump across the hole to the ledge. Climb to the right until you find a pool. Drop into the water and pull the lever behind one of the pillars. Swim through the tunnel and pull the level. Return back to the surface and climb out. Drop down into the hole, climb up and then crawl back outside. Head round to the left and into the rocky passage. Enter the door on the right and press the switch. This will flood the tunnel, return back to the tunnel and swim into the next room. Climb onto the ledge and jump over the compound fence to land open the crate. Head into the hangar and mount the quad bike, ride the quad up onto the roof via the ramp and collect the generator access. Ride down the ramp and enter the room with the pool table. Go through the office and use the generator access on the switch box. Head inside and deactivate the electric fence. Return to the quad and ride to the main gates. Dis mount and open the gates. Ride out of the compound and head left. Ride over the fence at full speed using the large ramp to exit the level.

Security Compound
On this level you have no weapons so you need to release other prisoners to fight the guards for you. Climb on to the window ledge and cross the infra red beams. Turn around and run past the guard who enters. Head left and press the switch to open the other cells. Cross the gantry and press the switch. Enter the left cell. Push the block near the basin until you can crawl to the left. Push the block then return back to the first block forward. Turn around and jump up and grab the ledge above. Jump the barb wire, continue forward walking through the next set of barb wire. Press the switch then climb up to the left. Climb down the ladder then drop to the ledge. Drop through the hatch and head to the left. Press the switch to release the prisoners. Collect the keycard A and use it to open

the set of gates. Head through and then to the left. Press the switch to open the rest room door, enter and press the switch inside. Move the right block under the hatch then climb up. Press the switch then drop down the hatch. Swim over to the hatch and climb up into the dark passage. Jump across the hole and up to the lit steps. Jump the two sets of barb wire and then drop down at the end. Press the switch to deactivate the burners. Press the other switch to open the door and climb up through the hole. Jump the two sets of barb wire then climb up to the passage. Head round and drop down the hole into the kitchen. Press the switch and head through the door.

Open the right door then the left one. Run through the right door. Head through the far left door, go right then to the left. Once the prisoners have killed the guards return through the canteen to the green guard room. Press the switch to raise the grating back in the kitchen. Return to the kitchen and climb past the fans and collect the save crystal. Go to the rear and slide down the left side. Jump from the following slope across the barb wire. Climb up into the tunnel and crawl through to the next ladder and climb up. Head to the left ledge, when the hatch open turn around and jump through it. Follow the passage to the steps. Climb up the grating to the green lit area, head up the slope and run past the guard. Head left near the crate then go to the right. Drop down the steps and press the left switch. Collect keycard B from the dead guard. Return to the crate and unlock the door. Enter inside and head up the steps. Press the switch then return outside. Head right from the crate and climb the ladder at the end. Climb down and press the switch to release the prisoners. Press the second switch and collect the yellow pass from the dead guard. Use the yellow pass to open the locked yellow pass door. Enter and once the guards are dead, head round to the left. Crawl right through the tunnel. Hang drop down and when the guard is turned press the switch. Jump the laser beam and head through the door.

Hang drop into the room at the end, head left around the steps. Hang drop to the ledge below then jump to the passage. Follow the passage and drop into the control room. Press the switch in the corner. Press the switch to open the door, head out then to the right. Back in to the main room. Head to the opposite side and climb the ladder. Follow the passage and pass the guard. Collect the yellow pass from the right tunnel. Climb down into the main room and enter the red lit tunnel. Press the switch and head to the control room using the yellow pass. Climb up the ladder and drop into the pool. Swim through the long passage and pull the lever to open the door. Swim through and up to the surface. Climb out and jump into the red lit area. Swim through the new water channel. Head through the passage and climb the crates to the switch. Open the door and head inside to collect your belongings. Return towards the door and shoot the drone gun. Climb over the crates and up the slope. Head up the right slope and collect the blue pass from the guard. Climb the left ladder then through the right passage and use the blue pass. Press the right switch then head back down the ladder. Descend both slopes and climb the crate on the right and up to the ladder. Monkey swing past the hooks then climb up. Collect the yellow pass from the guard. Hang drop into the main room and use the yellow pass to open the gates. Head through past the

trucks into the crate area. Head into the blue section and the back of the truck.

Area 51
Climb out of the truck and shoot the MP before he can lock the armoury. Press the switch by the vent and crawl through until you reach the large passage. Crawl under the laser beams then head right. Press the switch at the end of the passage, then drop into the courtyard. Kill the MP quickly or he will release the guard dogs on you. Drop down to the grate and press the switch. Crawl through the gap. Head down the red lit cell block and release the prisoners. Head back to the green lit area and across the glass floor. Head down to the control room where you will be ambushed. Press the switch and head up towards the missile silos. Shoot the guard patrolling the gantry in the right silo. Collect the code clearance disk. Head inside the left silo and use the code clearance disk in the terminal to move the missile. Climb the ladder until you reach the rafters. Shoot the guard and collect the hangar access key. Take the passage on the silo floor down to the monorail tracks. Drop down to the side of the track and head to the ladder at the end. Climb the ladder and press the switch. Return down the ladder and crawl under the tracks. Climb the ladder and onto the train. Head towards the front and climb up into the passage above. Monkey swing across the grates. Climb down then jump to the ledge.

Shoot the patrolling MP's and avoid the lasers. Head to the end of the passage and climb the crates. Press both switches on the upper gantry then quickly head through the double doors before they close. Press switches 2, 4 and 5 to open the hangar doors. Return to the hangar and inspect the weather balloon. Press the switch on the opposite side of the hangar. Climb the ladder, then backflip onto the rafters. Cross the rafters until you can drop to the gantry. Drop down and collect the launch code pass. Return to the passage behind the large missile and drop down into the launch control room. Use the launch code pass to open the launch controls. Launch the missile then quickly run to the back of the room. Climb the ladder and return to the courtyard. Shoot the MP and collect the code clearance disk. Return back to the hangar. Enter the control room and use the code clearance disk. Return to the hangar and climb inside the weather balloon. Climb to the top and collect the artefact.

Antarctica
Cross the ice block until you reach the rear of the ship. Turn to the right and climb the ice blocks to the top. Use the handholds and drop onto the deck of the ship. Drop down into the ship's hold and enter the engine room. Press the switch to open the gate to the lower deck. Follow the passage until you reach the door at the end. Enter inside and drop down to the passage at the rear. Press the switch at the end to release the lifeboat. Pull yourself back up into the hallway and make your way to the front of the deck. Backflip over the front of the ship and land in the lifeboat. Ride the lifeboat down the river until you reach the landing. Leave the lifeboat. Use the handholds on the gantry to cross to the opposite side. Follow

the passage to site 1. Enter through the door and follow the passage to the main site. Head left towards the warehouse. Run through the automatic doors and head to the top of the warehouse. Collect the crowbar then leave the warehouse and go to the water tower. Cross to the opposite side of the site and cross the bridge to the kennels. Follow the passage until you reach the ruined headquarters. At the fire, head to the right and enter the generator building. Drop through the hole, then turn the wheels marked number 2 and number 4. Press the switch upstairs to turn the generator on. Return to the kennel and enter the office at the back. Collect the gate control key then return through the main site to the landing. Use the crowbar on the outside the door. Use the key inside in the lock and press the switch to open the river gates. Return to the boat and follow the river to the tunnel. Follow the passage into the RX-Tech mines shooting any guards you encounter. Head around the building to exit the level.

RX-Tech Mines

Climb out of the mine shaft and into the vent above. Follow the passage completely around, then turn and go in the opposite direction. Crawl through the next vent and then follow the tunnel to the mine cart junction. Head to the ground level and take the gantry up to the suspended building. Inside, turn the power on. Climb into the mine cart on the middle track. Ride down the track, braking around the corners and hitting the lever near the end. Leave the cart and crawl under the drills. Follow the passage until you reach the top of the slope. Slide down the slope backwards and grab the edge, then hang drop to the ground. Kill the mutant creature and climb to the exit near the bottom. Enter the pool area and kill both the guard with the flame thrower and the mutant creature. Climb up to the gantry and cross the water. Collect the crowbar. Climb up through the green lit opening. Trip the switch at the end to open up a passage to the main junction. Jump from bank to bank. Climb up past the ice crushers to the mine cart. Climb into the mine cart and head to the main junction. Use the crowbar on the door and collect the battery.

Climb into the lower mine cart and ride to the lower landing. Head into the passage and through the side door. Continue to follow the passage, then slide down to the grate. Follow the passage on the opposite side and stop once you reach the ladder. Climb up and enter the second door. Continue down the passage until you reach the control room. Kill the mutant creature who appears then return back through the way you came. Drop into the pool and collect the winch starter. Pull yourself out and head to the landing. Ride the mine cart back to the main junction. Ride the upper mine cart to the landing. Use both the battery and the winch starter on the winch. Drop into the water and swim quickly down under the observation tank and through the hole on its bottom. Because the water is freezing you will need to use a large medi pack to restore your health before you freeze. Once you have regained your strength, swim down to the green lit lights and through the passage until you appear near dry ground. Dive from the ledge into the water and swim straight across and up through the long tunnel to the top. Pull yourself out of the water. Cross the bridge and enter the building to end the level.

The Lost City Of Tinnos

To escape the first area, climb the ladder on the left. Press the switch to open the doors below. Collect the Uli key from inside and use the key in the lock in the right hand side of the room. Enter through the grating and climb the ladder. Climb out of the window and drop onto the ledge below. Press the switch. Climb up and slide down the ramp. Press the switch you find at the end of the room. Leave the room and run to the room on the left. Climb the wall and turn dials 1, 2 and 5. Climb down and walk to the bridge. Avoid the wasps and run towards the end of the bridge. At the end, jump to the rocks on the left and climb to the left. Jump over to the arch and then to the second bridge. Head left at the end of the bridge. There are three demons waiting in this area. When you reach the centre they are released. Enter the alcove and press the switch, raising the platform. Climb the carved block until you can jump to the high walkway. Crawl through the small passage into the platform room. You need to pull the levers in the correct order to raise and lower the platforms. Pull the top lever on the wall opposite, then the top lever on the wall to your right, then the lower centre lever on the same wall, then lastly the top lever on the first wall. All the platforms should now be in place, make your way across them to the left wall and then to the platform under the bridge. Pull the lever. At the top of the stairs you will face the test of the four elements.

Wind Puzzle - Take the right passage, left, right, left, right, left and right. Continue the end. Side jump from the left ramp to the right ramp and back again to avoid the rolling spiked logs. Collect the first Oceanic mask.
Earth Puzzle - Head right through the quick sand and climb up onto the rocks. Follow the path and collect the Oceanic mask.
Fire Puzzle - Jump to the left safe block, then run and jump to the block by the wall. Turn to the right then run and jump to grab the block by the wall. Stand and jump to the block to the right of the medi pack block then quickly turn to the left and run and jump to the ledge. In the dragon room, hang on the invisible block and pull yourself up. Then perform a running jump to the next block. Pull the lever then return across the invisible block and across to the solid ledge. Avoid the swinging fire and collect the Oceanic mask.
Water Puzzle - Swim down past the two scythes, facing the wall with the four passages enter the left cave for extra air. Pull the lever and quickly swim through the right hand opening. Go through the open side and pull the lever. Head through the opposite side through the gap and collect the Oceanic mask. Pull the lever and return back through the gap, and swim through the crack at the end. Return to the cave with the four passages and swim through the bottom passage.
Head to the puddle room and collect the second Uli key. Use the key and the four masks at the base of the shaft of light to deactivated the force field. Hang drop down the hole and slide into the meteorite cave.

Meteorite Cavern

Once in the meteorite cave you will discover Willard has transformed into a giant spider. Chase him around the centre of the chamber, stopping occasionally to fire at him with the Desert Eagle. Once you have stunned Willard, run to the nearest passage and collect an artefact. Willard will then reawaken. Return to the centre chamber and continue this strategy until you have collected all four artefacts. Willard will be destroyed and the centre core will collapse. Jump and grab either of the ladders and climb up. Enter the passage and then down the left tunnel. Monkey swing to the left ledge, then run and jump to the ledge on the right. Climb up to the right snowy ledge. Run and jump to the rock ledge and climb up. Head into the passage and slide down. Kill the guards you encounter and press the switch. Run back between the buildings and head to the heli-pad. Wait until the helicopter lands, then head through the open gate.

TOMB RAIDER: THE LAST REVELATION

For these cheats to work you must be facing directly North.

Level Skip

With Lara facing North, press Select to bring up her inventory. Highlight 'Load' and then press **L1 + L2 + R1 + R2 + ↑ + ▲**.

Unlimited Items

With Lara facing North, press Select to bring up her inventory. Highlight the small medi pack and then press **L1 + L2 + R1 + R2 + ↑ + ▲**.

All Weapons

You must first activate the Unlimited Items cheat. With Lara facing North, press **Select** to bring up her inventory. Highlight the large medi pack and then press **L1 + L2 + R1 + R2 + ↓ + ▲**.

TOMORROW NEVER DIES

Mission Select

On the mission select screen press **Select, Select, ●, ●, L1, L1, ●, L1, L1**.

Instantly Complete Mission

Pause the game and press **Select, Select, ●, ●, Select, ●**.

All The Levels Weapons

Pause the game and press **Select, Select, ●, ●, L1, L1, R1, R1**.

Invincibility

Pause the game and press **Select, Select, ●, ●, ▲, ▲, ▲, ▲**.

Fifty Medi Packs

Pause the game and press **Select, Select, ●, ●, ▲, Select**.

No Floor Textures

Pause the game and press **Select, Select, ●, ●, Select, Select, ●, ●**

Debug Information

Pause the game and press **Select, Select, ●, ●, L2, R2**. Pause the game again and press **Select, Select, ●, ●, R2, L2** to turn it off.

TOMMY MAKKINEN RALLY

Cheat Mode

Enter the following codes as your name:

STRANGE	Drive a bus
MIRROR	Mirrored tracks
PEUGEOT	Drive a Peugeot
FFSA	Rally Jeunes
THRILLS	Non-stop dual shock rumblings
_MONEY	Absolutely wedges of cash

TONY HAWK'S SKATEBOARDING

To enter these cheats, pause the game and hold down L1.

Special Meter Always Full
✖, ▲, ●, ↓, ↑, ➡.

Level Select
▲, ➡, ↑, ■, ▲, ⬅, ↑, ■, ▲.

Unlock All Levels, Tapes, Officer Dick, FMV and Get Full Stats
●, ➡, ↑, ↓, ●, ➡, ↑, ■, ▲.

Raise Stats to 10
■, ▲, ↑, ↓

Raise Stats to 13
✖, ■, ■, ▲, ↑, ↓

Random Start Locations
■, ●, ✖, ↑, ↓

Big Head Mode
■, ●, ↑, ⬅, ⬅ (Now exit and start a new game)

TONY HAWK'S PRO SKATER 2

Master Cheat

Start a game, pause, then hold **L1** and press **✖, ✖, ✖, ■, ▲, ↑, ↓, ⬅, ↑, ■, ▲, ✖, ▲, ●, ✖, ▲, ●**. This gives you all levels, cheats, skaters and videos.

Secrets

To unlock each secret option you must complete the game with a different character with 100% on all levels.

Beat the game **Code**

1st time	Officer Dick
2nd time	Skip to Restart
3rd time	Kid Mode
4th time	Perfect Balance
5th time	Infinite Special
6th time	Full Stats
7th time	Increase or Decrease Your Weight
8th time	Wireframe Mode
9th time	Slow Motion Ollys
10th time	Big Head Mode
11th time	Sim Mode
12th time	Smooth Mode
13th time	Less Gravity
14th time	Reverse Skate Park

Complete the game with Private Carrera to unlock Disco Mode.

Complete the game with Tony Hawk to unlock 80's style Tony Hawk.

Complete the game with every character to unlock Spiderman and the two hidden stages; Helicopter Drop (Hawaii) and Skate Heaven.

Move List

Flip Tricks

Move Name	Cost	Best Assigned To
Pop Shove-It	$500	↑ + ■
Shove-It	$500	↓ + ■
Kickflip	$500	← + ■
Heelflip	$500	→ + ■
Impossible	$500	↓ + ■
Body Varial	$750	→, → + ■
Varial Kickflip	$750	↙ + ■
Varial Heelflip	$750	↗ + ■
360 Shove-It	$750	↓, ↓ + ■
Hardflip	$750	↘ + ■
Ollie North	$1500	↑, ↑ + ■
Flip	$1500	↓ + ■
Inward Heelflip	$1500	↙ + ■
Front Foot Impossible	$1500	↘ + ■
Kickflip to Indy	$2000	→, → + ■
Heelflip Varial Lien	$2000	←, ← + ■

Grab Tricks List

Mute	$500	← + ●
Melon	$500	← + ●
Stalefish	$500	↘ + ●
Benihana	$500	↙ + ●
Roastbeef	$500	↙ + ●
Nosegrab	$500	↑ + ●
Indy Nosebone	$500	↗ + ●
Tailgrab	$500	↓ + ●

Indy	$500	→ + ●
Japan Air	$500	↖ + ●
Method	$750	→ + ●
Rocket Air	$750	↑, ↑ + ●
Crossbone	$750	↖ + ●
Airwalk	$1000	↓, ↓ + ●
Judo	$1000	↓, → + ●
Indy Stiffy	$1000	↓ + ●
Madonna	$1000	↑ + ●
Varial	$1500	↙ + ●
Sal Flip	$1750	↑, ↑ + ●

Lip Tricks List

Rock N Roll	$1000	↓ + ▲
Axle Stall	$1000	← + ▲
Rock N Roll	$1500	↓ + ▲
Nosestall	$1500	↑ + ▲
Disaster	$2000	→ + ▲
Handplant	$2000	↓ + ▲
Eggplant	$2500	→ + ▲
Nosepick	$2500	↑ + ▲
Mute Invert	$3500	↑ + ▲
One Foot Invert	$4000	← + ▲
Gymnast Plant	$5000	↑ + ▲

Special Grinds

Move Name	Cost	Skater	Default Controls
One Foot Smith	$7500	Bob Burnquist	→, ↓ + ▲
Darkslide	$7500	Created Skater	Assign Yourself
Overturn	$8500	Tony Hawk	↓, ← + ▲
Hurricane	$8500	Chad Muska	↓, → + ▲
Nosegrab Tailslide	$8500	Andrew Reynolds	↑, ↓ + ▲
Madonna Tailslide	$8500	Elissa Steamer	↑, ← + ▲
Rocket Tailslide	$9000	Bob Burnquist	↑, ↓ + ▲
Nosegrind to Pivot	$9000	Kareem Campbell	↓, ↑ + ▲
One Foot Bluntside	$9500	Rune Glifberg	←, ↑ + ▲
The Fandangle	$9500	Eric Koston	←, ↓ + ▲
Rowley Darkslide	$9500	Geoff Rowley	←, → + ▲
Hang Ten	$10000	Steve Caballero	→, ↑ + ▲
The Big Hitter	$10000	Bucky Lasek	←, ↓ + ▲
Beni F-Flip Crooks	$10500	Jamie Thomas	↓, ↑ + ▲
Heelflip Darkslide	$11500	Rodney Mullen	→, ← + ▲
Lazy-A-Grind	$20000	Officer Dick	←, ↓ + ▲
Spidey Grind	$20000	Spiderman	←, → + ▲
Layback Grind	$20000	Available after you unlock Spiderman	
Ho Train	$20000	Private Carrera	→, ↓ + ▲

Special Air Tricks

Triple Kickflip	$7500	Steve Caballero	↑, ← + ■
Hardflip Late Flip	$7500	Andrew Reynold	↑, ↓ + ■
Double Hardflip	$7500	Geoff Rowley	→, ↓ + ■
540 Flip	$7500	Created Skater	Assign Yourself

Trick	Price	Character	Control
Fingerflip Airwalk	$8000	Bucky Lasek	← , → + ●
Christ Air	$8500	Rune Glifberg	← , → + ●
Laser Flip	$9000	Jamie Thomas	↓ , → + ■
Kickflip Mc Twist	$9000	Created Skater	Assign Yourself
FS-540	$9500	Steve Caballero	→ , ← + ●
Triple Heelflip	$9500	Andrew Reynolds	↑ , ← + ■
Half Flip Casper	$9500	Geoff Rowley	→ , ← + ■
Hospital Flip	$9500	Elissa Steamer	← , → + ■
Sacktap	$10000	Tony Hawk	↑ , ↓ + ●
Racket Air	$10000	Bob Burnquist	↓ , ← + ●
Foot Tail	$10000	Rune Glifberg	← , → + ●
1 Foot Japan	$10000	Bucky Lasek	↑ , → + ●
Nollieflip Underflip	$10000	Rodney Mullen	↓ , ← + ▲
Ghetto Bird	$11000	Kareem Campbell	↓ , ↑ + ■
Indy Frontflip	$11000	Eric Koston	↓ , ↑ + ●
Pizza Guy	$11500	Eric Koston	↓ , ← + ●
Mute Backflip	$11500	Chad Muska	↑ , ↓ + ●
Indy Backflip	$11500	Elissa Steamer	↑ , ↓ + ●
The 900	$15000	Tony Hawk	→ , ↓ + ●
Assume the Position	$15000	Officer Dick	↑ , ↓ + ●
Salute	$20000	Officer Dick	← , ↓ + ●
Does What A Spider	$25000	Spiderman	← , → + ■
Spidey Flip	$25000	Spiderman	↑ , ↓ + ●
Pogo Air	$25000	Available after you Assign Yourself unlock Spiderman	
Double Splits	$25000	Private Carrera	← , ↓ + ●

Special Manual Tricks

Trick	Price	Character	Control
Casper	$9500	Kareem Campbell	← , ↓ + ●
One Foot Nose	$10500	Jamie Thomas	← , ↑ + ●
Muska Nose Manual	$11500	Chad Muska	→ , ↑ + ●
Casper to 360 Flip	$12000	Rodney Mullen	↓ , → + ●

Special Handplant Tricks

Trick	Price	Character	Control
Ho Ho Handplant	$25000	Private Carrera	← , → + ▲

Grinds List

Name	Control
FS Bluntside	↓ , ↓ + ▲
FS Nosebluntside	↑ , ↑ + ▲
FS Nosegrind	↑ + ▲
FS 5-0	↓ + ▲
FS Boardslide	▲ (at 90 degrees to the rail)
FS 50-50	▲
FS Lipside	▲ (at 190 degrees to the rail)
FS Tailslide	←/→ + ▲
FS Noseslide	←/→ + ▲
BS Feeble Diagonally	↙/↘ + ▲
BS Smith Diagonally	↙/↘ + ▲
FS Crooked Diagonally	↖/↗ + ▲
FS Overcrook Diagonally	↖/↗ + ▲

Character's Special Moves

Tony Hawk

Flip Tricks
Ollie North- ↑ , ↑ + ■
360 Flip- ↓ , ↓ + ■
Pop Shove It- ↑ + ■
Heelflip- → + ■
FS Shove It- ↓ + ■
Heelflip Varial Lien- ↗ , ■
Varial Heelflip- ↘ , ■
Varial Kickflip- ↙ , ■
Kickflip to Indy- ↖ , ■

Grab Tricks
Nosegrab- ↑ + ●
Indy Nosebone- ← + ●
Melon- → + ●
Tailgrab- ↓ + ●
Mute- - ↗ , ●
Judo- - ↘ , ●
Stalefish- - ↙ , ●
Rocket Air- - ↖ , ●

Lip Tricks
Gymnast Plant- ↑ + ▲
Eggplant- → + ▲
180 Rock N Roll- ↓ + ▲
Mute Invert- ← + ▲

Special Moves
The 900- →, ↓ + ●
Sacktap- ↑, ↓ + ●
FS-Overturn- ↓, ← + ▲

Bob Burnquist

Flip tricks
Body Varial- ↑ , ↑ + ■
360 Flip- ↓ , ↓ + ■
Heelflip- → + ■
Kickflip- ← + ■
FS Shove It- ↓ + ■
Inward Heelflip- ↗ , ■
Varial Heelflip- ↘ , ■
Varial Kickflip- ↙ , ■
Hardflip- ↖ , ■

Grab Tricks
Rocket Air- ↑ + ●
Indy- → + ●
Tailgrab- ↓ + ●

Method- ← + ●
Japan Air- ↗, ●
Indy Stiffy- ↘, ●
Benihana- ↙, ●
Varial- ↖, ●

Lip Tricks
Handplant- ↑ + ▲
Eggplant- → + ▲
Rock N Roll- ↓ + ▲
Disaster- ← + ▲

Special Moves
Rocket Tailslide- ↑, ↓ + ▲
One Foot Smith- →, ↓ + ▲
Racket Air- ←, ↓ + ●

Steve Caballero
Flip trick
Front Foot Impossible- ↑, ↑ + ■
Hardflip- ↓, ↓ + ■
Ollie North- ↑ + ■
Heelflip- → + ■
Kickflip- ← + ■
360 Flip- ↓ + ■
Body Varial- ↗, ■
Varial Heelflip- ↘, ■
FS Shove It- ↙, ■
Kickflip to Indy- ↖, ■

Grab Tricks
Sal Flip- ↑, ↑ + ●
Airwalk- ↓, ↓ + ●
Stalefish- ↑ + ●
Indy- → + ●
Method- ← + ●
Tailgrab- ↓ + ●
Japan Air- ↗, ●
Madonna- ↘, ●
Indy Nosebone- ↙, ●
Madonna- ↖, ●

Lip Tricks
Axle Stall- ↑ + ▲
Rock N Roll- → + ▲
Disaster- ↓ + ▲
Nosestall- ← + ▲

Special Moves
Hang Ten- →, ↑ + ▲

Triple Kickflip- ↑, ← + ■
FS 540- →, ← + ●

Kareem Campbell
Flip Tricks
360 Shove It- ↑, ↑ + ■
360 Flip- ↓, ↓ + ■
Pop Shove It- ↑ + ■
Heelflip- → + ■
Kickflip- ← + ■
FS Shove It- ↓ + ■
Inward Heelflip- ↗, ■
Varial Heelflip- ↘, ■
Varial Kickflip- ↙, ■
Hardflip- ↖, ■

Grab Tricks
Nosegrab- ↑ + ●
Indy - → + ●
Melon- ← + ●
Tailgrab- ↓ + ●
Mute- ↗, ●
Roastbeef- ↘, ●
Benihana- ↙, ●
Crossbone- ↖, ●

Lip Tricks
Nosestall- ↑ + ▲
Axle Stall- → + ▲
Rock N Roll- ↓ + ▲
Disaster- ← + ▲

Special Moves
Nosegrind to Pivot- ↓, ↑ + ▲
Ghetto Bird- ↓, ↑ + ■
Casper- ←, ↓ + ●

Rune Glifberg
Flip Tricks
Ollie North- ↑, ↑ + ■
360 Flip- ↓, ↓ + ■
Pop Shove It- ↑ + ■
Heelflip- → + ■
Kickflip- ← + ■
FS Shove It- ↓ + ■
Inward Heelflip- ↗, ■
Varial Heelflip- ↘, ■
Varial Kickflip- ↙, ■
Hardflip- ↖, ■

Grab Tricks
Nosegrab- ↑ + ●
Melon- ← + ●
Indy Nosebone- → + ●
Tailgrab- ↓ + ●
Mute - ↗, ●
Indy Stiffy- ↘, ●
Judo- ↙, ●
Crossbone- ↖, ●

Lip Tricks
Handplant- ↑ + ▲
Eggplant- → + ▲
Rock N Roll- ↓ + ▲
Disaster- ← + ▲

Special Moves
One Foot Bluntside- ←, ↑ + ▲
Kickflip 1 Foot Tail- ←, ↓ + ■
Christ Air- ←, → + ●

Eric Koston
Flip Tricks
360 Shove It- ↑, ↑ + ■
360 Flip- ↓, ↓ + ■
Pop Shove It- ↑ + ■
Heelflip- → + ■
Kickflip- ← + ■
FS Shove It- ↓ + ■
Inward Heelflip- ↗, ■
Varial Heelflip- ↘, ■
Varial Kickflip- ↙, ■
Hardflip- ↖, ■

Grab Tricks
Nosegrab- ↑ + ●
Tailgrab- ↓ + ●
Indy- → + ●
Method- ← + ●
Mute- ↗, ●
Stalefish- ↘, ●
Benihana- ↙, ●
Crossbone- ↖, ●

Lip Tricks
Nosestall- ↑ + ▲
Disaster- → + ▲
180 Rock N Roll- ↓ + ▲
Rock N Roll- ← + ▲

Special Moves
Indy Frontflip- ↓, ↑ + ●
Pizza Guy- ↓, ← + ●
The Fandangle- →, ↓ + ▲

Bucky Lasek
Flip Tricks
Front Foot Impossible- ↑, ↑ + ■
360 Flip- ↓, ↓ + ■
Ollie North- ↑ + ■
Heelflip- → + ■
Kickflip- ← + ■
FS Shove It- ↓ + ■
Heelflip Variel Lien- ↗, ■
Varial Heelflip- ↘, ■
Varial Kickflip- ↙, ■
Kickflip to Indy- ↖, ■

Grab Tricks
Nosegrab- ↑ + ●
Indy Nosebone- → + ●
Indy Stiffy- ↓ + ●
Melon- ← + ●
Japan Air- ↗, ●
Judo- ↘, ●
Stalefish- ↙, ●
Crossbone- ↖, ●
Lip Tricks
Handplant- ↑ + ▲
Eggplant- → + ▲
180 Rock N Roll- ↓ + ▲
Mute Invert- ← + ▲

Special Moves
One Foot Japan- ↑, → + ●
Fingerflip Airwalk- ←, → + ●
The Big Hitter- ←, ↓ + ▲

Rodney Mullen
Flip Tricks
360 Shove It- ↑, ↑ + ■
360 Flip- ↓, ↓ + ■
Pop Shove It- ↑ + ■
Heelflip- → + ■
Kickflip- ← + ■
Impossible- ↓ + ■
Inward Heelflip- ↗, ■
Varial Heelflip- ↘, ■
Varial Kickflip- ↙, ■
Hardflip- ↖, ■

Grab Tricks
Airwalk- ↑ + ●
Mute- ↗, ●
Indy- ➡ + ●
Stalefish- ↘, ●
Tailgrab- ↓ + ●
Benihana- ↙, ●
Melon- ⬅ + ●
Body Varial- ↖, ●

Lip Tricks
Nosestall- ↑ + ▲
Axle Stall- ➡ + ▲
Rock N Roll- ↓ + ▲
Disaster- ⬅ + ▲

Special Moves
Heelflip Darkslide- ➡, ⬅ + ▲
Nollieflip Underflip- ↓, ⬅ + ■
Casper to 360 Flip- ↓, ➡ + ●

Chad Muska
Flip Tricks
Sal Flip- ↑, ↑ + ■
360 Flip— ↓, ↓ + ■
Pop Shove It- ↑ + ■
Heelflip- ➡ + ■
Kickflip- ⬅ + ■
FS Shove It- ↓ + ■
Inward Heelflip- ↗, ■
Varial Heelflip- ↘, ■
Varial Kickflip- ↙, ■
Hardflip- ↖, ■

Grab Tricks
Nosegrab- ↑ + ●
Mute- ↗, ●
Indy- ➡ + ●
Roastbeef- ↘, ●
Tailgrab- ↓ + ●
Benihana- ↙, ●
Melon- ⬅ + ●
Crossbone- ↖, ●

Lip Tricks
Nosestall- ↑ + ▲
Disaster- ➡ + ▲
180 Rock N Roll- ↓ + ▲
Rock N Roll- ⬅ + ▲

Special Moves
Mute Backflip- ↑, ↓ + ●
FS-Hurricane- ➡, ↓ + ▲
Muska Nose Manual- ➡, ↑ + ●

Andrew Reynolds
Flip Tricks
360 Shove It- ↑, ↑ + ■
360 Flip- ↓, ↓ + ■
Pop Shove It- ↑ + ■
Heelflip- ➡ + ■
Kickflip- ⬅ + ■
FS Shove It- ↓ + ■
Inward Heelflip- ↗, ■
Varial Heelflip- ↘, ■
Varial Kickflip- ↙, ■
Hardflip- ↖, ■

Grab Tricks
Nosegrab- ↑ + ●
Indy- ➡ + ●
Melon- ⬅ + ●
Tailgrab- ↓ + ●
Mute- ↗, ●
Roastbeef- ↘, ●
Benihana- ↙, ●
Crossbone- ↖, ●

Lip Tricks
Nosestall- ↑ + ▲
Axle Stall- ➡ + ▲
Rock N Roll- ↓ + ▲
Disaster- ⬅ + ▲

Special Moves
Nosegrab Tailslide- ↑, ↓ + ▲
Triple Heelflip- ↑, ➡ + ■
Hardflip Late Flip- ↑, ↓ + ■

Geoff Rowley
Flip Tricks
360 Shove It- ↑, ↑ + ■
360 Flip- ↓, ↓ + ■
Pop Shove It- ↑ + ■
Heelflip- ➡ + ■
Kickflip- ⬅ + ■
FS Shove It- ↓ + ■
Inward Heelflip- ↗, ■
Varial Heelflip- ↘, ■
Varial Kickflip- ↙, ■

Hardflip- ↖, ■

Grab Tricks
Nosegrab- ↑ + ●
Melon- ← + ●
Indy- → + ●
Tailgrab- ↓ + ●
Mute- ↗, ●
Japan Air- ↘, ●
Benihana- ↙, ●
Crossbone- ↖, ●

Lip Tricks
Nosestall- ↑ + ▲
Disaster- → + ▲
180 Rock N Roll- ↓ + ▲
Rock N Roll- ← + ▲

Special Moves
Rowley Darkslide- ←, → + ▲
Double Hardflip- →, ↓ + ■
Half Flip Casper- →, ← + ■

Elissa Steamer
Flip Tricks
360 Shove It- ↑, ↑ + ■
360 Flip- ↓, ↓ + ■
Pop Shove It- ↑ + ■
Heelflip- → + ■
Kickflip- ← + ■
FS Shove It- ↓ + ■
Impossible- ↗, ■
Varial Heelflip- ↘, ■
Varial Kickflip- ↙, ■
Hardflip- ↖, ■

Grab Tricks
Nosegrab- ↑ + ●
Melon- ← + ●
Indy- → + ●
Tailgrab- ↓ + ●
Mute- ↗, ●
Body Varial- ↘, ●
Benihana- ↙, ●
Crossbone- ↖, ●

Lip Tricks
Nosestall- ↑ + ▲
Axle Stall- → + ▲
Rock N Roll- ↓ + ▲

Disaster- ← + ▲

Special Moves
Madonna Tailslide- ↑, ← + ▲
Hospital Flip- ←, → + ■
Indy Backflip- ↑, ↓ + ●

Jamie Thomas
Flip Tricks
Sal Flip- ↑, ↑ + ■
360 Flip- ↓, ↓ + ■
Pop Shove It- ↑ + ■
Heelflip- → + ■
Kickflip- ← + ■
FS Shove It- ↓ + ■
Inward Heelflip- ↗, ■
Varial Heelflip- ↘, ■
Varial Kickflip- ↙, ■
Hardflip- ↖, ■

Grab Tricks
Airwalk - ↑ + ●
Melon- ← + ●
Indy Nosebone- → + ●
Ollie North- ↓ + ●
Japan Air- ↗, ●
Stalefish- ↘, ●
Benihana- ↙, ●
Crossbone- ↖, ●

Lip Tricks
Nosepick- ↑ + ▲
Disaster- → + ▲
180 Rock N Roll- ↓ + ▲
Rock N Roll- ← + ▲

Special Moves
Beni Fingerflip Crooks- ↓, ↑ + ▲
Laser Flip- ↓, → + ■
One Foot Nose Manual- ←, ↑ + ●

Officer Dick
Flip Tricks
Front Foot Impossible- ↑, ↑ + ■
360 Flip- ↓, ↓ + ■
Ollie North- ↑ + ■
Heelflip- → + ■
Kickflip- ← + ■
FS Shove It- ↓ + ■
Heelflip Varial Lien- ↗, ■
Varial Heelflip- ↘, ■

Varial Kickflip- ✔, ■
Kickflip To Indy- ↖, ■

Grab Tricks
Nosegrab- ↑ + ●
Melon- ← + ●
Indy Nosebone- → + ●
Tailgrab- ↓ + ●
Mute- ↗, ●
Judo- ↘, ●
Stalefish- ✔, ●
Crossbone- ↖, ●

Lip Tricks
Nosestall- ↑ + ▲
Disaster- → + ▲
180 Rock N Roll- ↓ + ▲
Rock N Roll- ← + ▲

Special Moves
Lazy A. Grind- ←, ↓ + ▲
Assume The Position- ↑, ↓ + ●
Salute!!!- ←, ↓ + ●

Spiderman
Flip Tricks
360 Shove It- ↑, ↑ + ■
360 Flip- ↓, ↓ + ■
Pop Shove It- ↑ + ■
Heelflip- → + ■
Kickflip- ← + ■
FS Shove It- ↓ + ■
Inward Heelflip- ↗, ■
Varial Heelflip- ↘, ■
Varial Kickflip- ✔, ■
Hardflip- ↖, ■

Grab Tricks
Nosegrab- ↑ + ●
Melon- ← + ●
Indy- → + ●
Tailgrab- ↓ + ●
Mute- ↗, ●
Roastbeef- ↘, ●
Benihana- ✔, ●
Crossbone- ↖, ●

Lip Tricks
Nosestall- ↑ + ▲
Disaster- → + ▲

180 Rock N Roll- ↓ + ▲
Rock N Roll- ← + ▲

Special Moves
Spidey Grind- ←, → + ▲
Spidey Varial- ←, → + ■
Spidey Flip- ↑, ↓ + ●

Private Carrerra
Flip Tricks
Pop Shove It- ↑ + ■
Heelflip- → + ■
Kickflip- ← + ■
FS Shove It- ↓ + ■
Inward Heelflip- ↗, ■
Varial Heelflip- ↘, ■
Varial Kickflip- ✔, ■
Hardflip- ↖, ■

Grab Tricks
Nosegrab- ↑ + ●
Indy- → + ●
Melon- ← + ●
Tailgrab- ↓ + ●
Mute- ↗, ●
Roastbeef- ↘, ●
Benihana- ✔, ●
Crossbone- ↖, ●

Lip Tricks
Nosestall- ↑ + ▲
Disaster- → + ▲
180 Rock N Roll- ↓ + ▲
Rock N Roll- ← + ▲

Special Moves
Double Splits- ←, ↓ + ●
Ho Ho Handplant- ←, → + ▲
Fifty-5 Ho Train- →, ↓ + ▲

TOP GUN: FIRE AT WILL

The codes for all the levels are:

Level	Miramar	Cuba	Korea	Libya
1		68353	45610	96430
2	82120	58210	85543	10163
3	23053	98143	75400	82230
4	97920	44010	98033	
5	72653	84933	61200	
6	83720	59810	84823	

7	99743	11800
8		99633
9		17500
10		85433

TOTAL DRIVING

Scotland Warp
Whilst on the Scotland 3 track, hit the cliff on the right just before you get to the woods so that you land on the right of the woods. Drive straight forwards into the sign and you will hit a glowing ball. If hit correctly, you will go to an extra level.

Switzerland Warp
Start Switzerland level 1 and follow the course through the village and underneath the cable car. Go through the tunnel and cross the bridge. Drive off the road and around the back of the buildings and drive into the red spinning shape to go to the bonus level.

Hong Kong Warp
Drive around Hong Kong level 5 and under the small bridge on the dirt track. Drive into the orange ball to enter the bonus level.

Access all Switzerland Levels
Tap out the rhythm to the song "Doe, a deer..." from the Sound Of Music with **R1** on the Main Selection screen. An engine should roar after a few seconds and all of the Swiss tracks will have been completed.

Access all Moscow Levels
Follow the above instructions but simply replace "Doe, a deer..." with "Jingle bells..."

Access all Scotland Levels
As above, but this time use the song "Hark, where the night is falling..." (a classic tune!) from Scotland the Brave.

Access all Multi-player Tracks
As above, but use the song "Zip a dee doo dah..." Now, six new tracks can be raced in split screen mode, and the two player tracks can be played in four player link-up mode.

Access all Tracks
On the main options screen tap the **R1** button to the rhythm of "Ding Dong the Witch is Dead, the Witch is Dead, the Witch is Dead." The cursor will help you get it right. After about four or five seconds you will hear an engine roar and all tracks will be open.

TOTAL NBA '96

All-Star Games
This cheat gives you the opportunity to play either the '94/'95 (Pheonix) or '95/'96 (San Antonio) All-Star Game, with the All-Star Weekend court, and team names from the Eastern/Western conferences. To see the All-Star menu option (which also contains cheats) go to the Exhibition Game screen. For the '94/'95 game press **R1**, **L1**, **R1**, **L1**, **R2**, **L2**, **R2**, **L2**. For the '95/'96 game press **R1**, **R1**, **R2**, **R2**, **L1**, **L2**, **L1**, **L2**.

Crazy Ball
To see the ball flick into the air, do some loops and return to you while scoring you a point, you need to use either Shawn Bradley or George Mureasan. Goal tend, rebound the ball, and shoot a three-pointer.

Remove Stats
You can remove the stats by pressing **L1**, **L2**, **R1**, **R2** at half-time, or during a break.

TOTAL NBA '97

Super Difficulty
Press **L2** + **R1** on the Options screen for a new super difficulty level.

Maximum Skill
Hold **Select** + ◄ + ■ + ● on the Create Player screen to give your players maximum skill.

TOTAL NBA '98

Super Player
Go to the Roster and Create Player. Enter **Nothing Can** as a first name, **Save** as a surname and **You** as a college. Press ▓ for stats and his attributes should be 99.

Small Players
Go to the Roster and Create Player. Enter **Micro** as a first name and **Man** as a Surname. Play in Exhibition mode and players in both teams will be small.

TREASURES OF THE DEEP

For lots of cheats press ✚, ✖, ◄, ■, ↑, ↑, ▲, ▲, ➧, ➧, ●, ● then the following codes:

Banana Harpoons:	✖, ↑, ▲, ✚
Disable Currents:	R1, L1, L2, R2, ✖.
More Shark Attack Time:	L2, L2, L2, R1, R1, R1, R2, L1.
Full Map:	■, ✖, ●, ✖, ■.
Full Screen Display:	▲, ✖, ↑, ✚.
Turbo Mode:	R1, R2, R1, R2, R1, R2.
Level Select:	✚, ➧, ↑, ◄, ▲, ✖
All Levels Complete:	■, ✖, ✖, ✖, ■, ▲, ▲, ▲, ■, ✖, ✖, ✖

All Weapons:	R1, R1, R1, R1, L1, L1, L1, L1,
	R2, R2, R2, R2, L2, L2, L2, L2
Level Skip:	▲, ▲, ▲, ↓, ↓, ↓
Extra Gold:	R1, R2, L1, L2, R1, R2, L1, L2
Extra Continues:	R2, R2, R2, L2, L2, L2
Add Tablet:	L1, L2, L1, L2, ■, ●
Swim Through Obstacles:	■, ■, ●, ●
Unlimited Payload:	▲, ↑, ✖, ↓

Bonus Levels

The Bonus Atlantis can be accessed via the Level Select cheat To enter the Bonus Shark Attack level you must start the Wreck of Concepion level then enter the Level Select and Extra Gold cheat before entering the Level Skip cheat. The bonus level will be automatically selected at the level select screen although it will disappear after one play.

TUNNEL B1

Maximum Weapons And Energy

To gain all of the weapons and a full life bar, press the following simultaneously: **L1, R1, L2, R2, ■, ●, ✖, ▲**.

TWISTED METAL

Level Codes

Freeway	✖ ■ ■ ● ▲
River Park	✖ ▲ ■ ● ■
Cyburbia	✖ ■ ▲ ▲ ▲
Warehouse	● ▲ ■ ● ●
Rooftop	■ ▲ ✖ ● ✖

Fight Minion
Enter ▲, ✖, ●, ■, ▲ at the password screen.
Final Level Cheat
When you get to the final level, you can get all your original weapons and full energy by beating the cars on the rooftop and then driving off the roof.

Helicopter View
To view the race from the air, press the following sequence in either the Arena or the Rooftop stage: ●, ●, ▲, ✖, space (press ➡), then press **Start** and ↑.

Infinite Weapons
Gain infinite weapons by pressing ▲, space (press ➡), ■, ●, ●.

Invincibility
To be invincible press ■, ▲, ✖, space (press ➡),●.
Multi-Cars
To have 5 cars all chasing you at the same time, press ■, ▲, ●, ■, ■.

Play As Minion
If you would like to play as Minion, select the tank, and on the password screen enter ■, ▲, ▲, space (press ➡), ■.

Unlimited Turbo
Enter ▲, ✖, ▲, ▲, ● at the password screen.

TWISTED METAL 2
Advanced Attacks

CODE	EFFECT
➡, ↓, ⬅, ↑	Cloaking Device
⬅, ➡, ↑	Freeze Blast
↑, ↑, ⬅	Jump
➡, ⬅, ↓	Mine Attack
➡, ⬅, ↑	Napalm
⬅, ➡, ↓	Rear Attack
↑, ↑, ➡	Shield lasting three seconds.

Backwards Freeze
When without ammo, press the following during play: ⬅, ➡, ↓, ⬅, ➡, ↑.

Extra Character Codes
Go to the car selection screen for a one-player tournament game to enter the following codes for the extra characters:
To add Minion to the character screen:**L1, ↑, ↓, ⬅**
To add Sweet Tooth to the character screen: **↑, L1, ▲, ➡**
Once you have done this you can select the extra cars in any other mode. (The codes need to be re-entered each time you load the game.)

Extra Level Codes
The following codes can be entered at the track selection screen for a two-player challenge match. A loud noise will indicate that you have entered it correctly and you will advance to the character selection screen. These codes need to be re-entered each time you load the game.

CODE	LEVEL
↓, ⬅, R1, ↓	Rooftops Level (From the first game)
↑, ↓, ➡, R1	Jet Rider Level (Based on Jet Rider)
↓, ↑, L1, R1	Cyburbia Level (From the first game)

Extra Powerful Weapon
If you destroy a train in the subway at Hong Kong, your next weapon will have twice the normal power.

Health Recharge
Recharge your health by running over ten citizens!

Homing Napalm
Carry out the following steps to receive about a dozen extra napalms which will home in on enemies:
1) Firstly you must be holding three napalms.

2) Fire one of them and keep the button held down.

3) Enter this code while you are still holding the fire button: ↑, ↓, ↓, ←, ←, ←, →, →. (If it doesn't work straight away, keep the fire button held down and re-enter the code.)

Minions' Special

You can do this with any character as long as you have full advanced-attack power. Hold **R2** and press ↑, ↓, ↑, ↑.

Weapons For Health

You can exchange your weapons for increased health by pressing the following during play: ↓, ↑, →, ←, ↑, ↑, ↓, ↓. You will see the words 'Sell Your Soul' at the top of the screen. The more weapons you give up, the greater health you will receive.

UEFA CHAMPIONS LEAGUE

Eliminated Team Selection

Complete all the UEFA Champions League Scenarios. Now go back and play an exhibition game. The team selection screen now has Eliminated Teams.

UNHOLY WAR

All Players

Select Mayhem mode and highlight Set Teams. Then press ● + ■, Select, Select, Select, Select, Start, Start, Start, ■, ■, ●, ● + ■.

All Levels

Select Mayhem mode and highlight Accept Teams. Then press ● + ■, Select, Select, Select, Select, Start, Start, Start, ■, ■, ●, ● + ■.

Unlock Wars

Select Strategy mode and highlight Set War. Then press ● + ■, Select, Select, Select, Select, Start, Start, Start, ■, ■, ●, ● + ■.

UM JAMMER LAMMY

Bonus Stages

Beat any 2 stages in the normal game to unlock 2-player Lammies.

Beat 2-player Lammies to unlock 2-player vs. Lammies.
Beat the 1-player game to play as Parappa.
Beat 1-player Parappa to unlock 2-player Lammy Parappa.
Beat 2-player Lammy Parappa to unlock 2-player vs. Lammy Parappa.

URBAN CHAOS

Level Select

On the main menu screen, highlight New Game and press **L1 + R1 + Select + Start**.

Energy Refill and All Weapons

During the game, hold ▲ + ● + ■ + ✖ and press →, your energy will refill and you will have access to all the weapons.

V-RALLY

When the Infogrames logo appears quickly press ↑, ↓, ▲, ●, ↑, ↓, ▲ + ● (together). The words 'Lock Off' should appear. All the tracks in arcade mode will now be available. To access further cheats input one of the following codes before the screen changes.

All Cheats

Press and hold ← + L1 + L2 + R1 + R2.

Debug mode

Press ← then →. Press **Start** to access a memory option.

Jeep Mode.

Press and hold ← + R1. A jeep will now replace the Peugeot 106.

Narrower Tracks

Press and hold ← + L2 to make the arcade tracks narrower.

Restart Race

Press and hold ← + R2 to allow arcade races to be restarted.

Unlimited time

Press and hold ← + L1 to get unlimited time in arcade races.

Rollercoaster track

Access the jeep cheat then select Sweden 1 track in time trial mode.

V-RALLY 2

Hidden Tracks Passwords

Enter your driver's name as one of theses codes to unlock these hidden tracks:

Hidden Track 1 – **CDLC**
Hidden Track 2 – **CDLCA**
Hidden Track 3 – **CDLCB**
Hidden Track 4 – **CDLCC**
Hidden Track 5 - **CDLCD**

VICTORY BOXING 2

General Strategies
Hooks
You can hook the opposing boxer by tapping ↑ or ↓ when you throw a punch. This allows you to get around their guard. The drawback of the hook is that it is slow, however if your opponent is very defensive they work a treat.

Understand The Opponent
When playing the computer controlled boxers you can learn their style of fighting and the patterns of punches they adopt. By recognising these you can anticipate your blocking moves and when best to lunge into a flurry of punches.

Quick Jabs
Use quick jabs to break up an opponent's concentration then follow through with a flurry of harder punches. Use a range of punches so that your opponent does not learn a pattern and therefore block you.

VIEWPOINT

Passwords
Go to the level of your choice by entering the following passwords:

Level 1-1	CGG	Level 1-2	CLL
Level 1-3	CRR	Level 2-1	FGD
Level 2-2	FLJ	Level 2-3	FRN
Level 3-1	HGD	Level 3-2	HLG
Level 3-3	HRL	Level 4-1	KGG
Level 4-2	KLD	Level 4-3	KRJ
Level 5-1	MGJ	Level 5-2	MLD
Level 6-1	PGL	Level 6-2	PLG
Level 6-3	PRD		

Go To The Movies
Pause the game and press ■, ●, ▲, ←, →, ↓, R1, L2, R2, R1 to go straight to the end-of-level movies.

Invincibility
Pause the game and press the following for invincibility: ■, ■, ●, ●, ▲, ✕, ■, ↑, ↑, ↓, ↓, L1, R1, Select.

VIGILANTE 8

Enter these on the password screen:
Big Wheels = **MONSTER_WHEELS**
Homing Missiles Power Ups = **DEADLY_MISSILE**
Low Gravity = **REDUCE_GRAVITY**
No Enemies = **GO_SIGHTSEEING**
Invincibilities = **I_WILL_NOT_DIE**
View FMV = **SEE_ALL_MOVIES**

Select The Same Vehicle In 2 Player Mode = **SAME_CHARACTER**
Expert Mode = **HARDEST_OF_ALL**

VIGILANTE 8: 2ND OFFENCE

Go to the options screen and select Game Status. Highlight any character and press L1 + R1, this will bring up a password screen. Then input any of the cheats below.

Remove Reload Time	**RAPID_FIRE**
Mega Hard Difficulty	**UNDER_FIRE**
Slow Game Down	**GO_SLOW_MO**
Increase Vehicle Weight	**GO_RAMMING**
Play Original Game Arenas	**OLD_LEVELS**
Increase Floating Height	**HI_CEILING**
Only Car in Arcade Mode	**HOME_ALONE**
Floating Cars	**NO_GRAVITY**
Monster Truck Wheels	**GO_MONSTER**
Show All FMV's	**LONG_MOVIE**
Identical Multiplayer Cars	**MIXED_CARS**
Powerful Missiles	**BLAST_FIRE**
High Speed Driving	**MORE_SPEED**
No Propulsion Add Ons	**DRIVE_ONLY**
High Suspension	**JACK_IT_UP**
Fast Action	**QUICK_PLAY**
Disable Codes	**NO_CODE**
Invincibility	**ELBICNIVNI**
All Characters	**LLA_KCOLNU**
All Characters Maximum Statistics	**LLA_DORTOH**

VS

Hidden Bosses
Defeat all members and bosses in each gang. Save to a memory card. The bosses should now become playable characters

WALT DISNEY WORLD QUEST: MAGICAL RACING TOUR

Play as Jiminy Cricket
Collect all the firework machine parts in Adventure Mode.

Play as Shredbetter
Win all nine golden cups in Adventure Mode.

Play as X.U.D.71
Collect all eight fairies.

Race around Splash Mountain
You will need to win all nine first place flags.

WARCRAFT 2

Cheats

To enable these cheats, simply enter them on the Password screen. "Cheat Enabled" should appear at the bottom left of the screen if you are successful.

All Spells and Full Mana	VRYLTTL
Build Faster	MKTS
Build More	DCKMT
Invincible Forces	TSGDDYTD
Lose Level	YPTFLWRM
Gold, Timber and Oil	GLTTRNG
See All Map	NSCRN
Win Level	NTTSCLNS
5,000 Oil	VLDZ
Speedy Wood Chopping	HTCHTXNS.
Disable Total Victory	NVRWNNR.

Tides Of Darkness
Orc Horde Missions

1. Zul'Dare	ZLDR
2. Raid At Hillsbrad	RDTHLL
3. Southshore	RCSTHS
4. Assault On Hillsbrand	SSLTNH
5. Tol Bartad	RCTLBR
6. The Badlands	BDLNDS
7. The Fall Of Stormgarde	FLLFST
8. The Runestone At Caer Darrow	RNSTNT
9. The Razing Of TYR's Hand	RZNGFT
10. The Destruction Of Stratholme	DSTRCT
11. The Dead Rise As Quel Thalas Falls	DDRSSQ
12. The Tomb Of Sargeras	TMBFSR
13. The Siege Of Dalaran	SGFDLR
14. The Fall Of Lordaeron	FLLFLR

Tides Of Darkness
Human Missions

1. Hillsbrad	HLLBRD
2. Ambush At Tarren Hill	MBSHTM
3. Southshore	HSTHSH
4. Attack On Zul'Dare	TTCKNZ
5. Tol Barad	HTLBRD
6. Dun Algaz	DNLGZ
7. Grim Batol	GRMBTL
8. TYR's Hand	TYRHND
9. The Battle At Darrowmere	BTTLTD
10. The Prisoners	PRSNRS
11. Betrayal And Destruction Of Alterac	BTRYLN
12. The Battle At Crest Fall	BTTLTC
13. Assault On Blackrock Spire	SSLTNB
14. The Great Portal	GRTPRT

Dark Portal Levels
Human Missions

1. Allerias Journey	LLRSJR
2. The Battle for Nethergarde	BTTLFR
3. One More Into The Breach	NCMRNT
4. Beyond The Dark Portal	BYNDTH
5. The Shadows Seas	SHDWWS
6. The Fall Of Auchindon	FLLFCH
7. Deathwing	DTHWNG
8. Coast Of Bones	CSTFBN
9. Heart Of Evil	HRTFVL
10. The Battle OfHellfire	BTTLFH
11. Dance Of The Laughing Skull	DNCFTH
12. The Bitter Taste Of Victory	BTTRTS

Dark Portal Levels
Orc Missions

1. Layer Of The Shadowmoon	SLYRFT
2. The Skull Of Gul'dan	SKLLFG
3. Thunderlord and Bonechewer	THNDRL
4. The Rift Awakened	RFTWKN
5. Dragons Of Blackrock Spire	DRGNSF
6. New Stormwind	NWSTRM
7. The Seas Of Azeroth	SSFZRT
8. Assault on Kul Tiras	SSLTNK
9. The Tomb of Sargeras	DTPMBF
10. Alterac	LTRC
11. The Eye Of Dalaran	YFDLRN
12. The Dark Portal	DPDRKP

WARGAMES

WOPR Level Select

Select a two player WOPR Co-operation game. Highlight level 2 and enter the following password:

●, ×, ●
●, ×, ●
×, ×, ●

Return to the main menu and then select the one player WOPR option.

Secret NORAD Mission

Enter the password: ■, ×, ▲
▲, ×, ●
■, ●, ×

Norad

Mission Number	Location Code
2 Czech Republic	●, ×, ● / ●, ×, × / ●, ×, ●
3 Russian Urais	×, ×, ● / ×, ×, × / ×, ●, ●
4 Cairo	●, ■, × / ●, ●, ▲ / ●, ×, ■
5 Cambodia	▲, ×, ● / ●, ×, × / ■, ▲, ●
6 Swiss Alps	▲, ●, ● / ■, ●, × / ×, ●, ×
7 Libya	■, ×, × / ×, ●, ■ / ●, ×, ■
8 Channel Islands	●, ●, × / ■, ■, ▲ / ■, ■, ●

9 Grenadines ■, ■, ● / ▲, ●, ▲ / ✖, ▲, ▲
10 Louisiana Bayou ✖, ▲, ● / ■, ●, ● / ●, ✖, ■
11 China ●, ■, ▲ / ✖, ■, ▲ / ▲, ▲, ■
12 Saudi Arabia ▲, ■, ● / ✖, ▲, ● / ●, ✖, ■
13 Arctic Circle ■, ■, ▲ / ■, ▲, ■ / ▲, ✖, ▲
14 New York ✖, ✖, ● / ▲, ✖, ▲ / ■, ✖, ■
15 Omaha Desert ●, ■, ● / ✖, ■, ✖ / ▲, ●, ✖

WOPR

Mission Number	Location Code
2 Florida Keys	●, ✖, ● / ●, ✖, ● / ✖, ✖, ●
3 Irian Jaya	■, ▲, ● / ▲, ✖, ● / ■, ✖, ▲
4 New England	✖, ▲, ● / ✖, ✖, ● / ●, ●, ▲
5 Russia	●, ●, ■ / ■, ●, ✖ / ▲, ✖, ✖
6 Brussels	✖, ●, ✖ / ▲, ▲, ■ / ●, ✖, ▲
7 South Africa	▲, ▲, ✖ / ✖, ■, ■ ✖ / ✖, ●
8 Hong Kong	■, ✖, ● / ▲, ✖, ✖ ■ / ●, ▲
9 Mexico	■, ●, ▲ / ▲, ✖, ● / ✖, ✖, ●
10 Bering Straight	✖, ●, ■ / ▲, ●, ✖ / ■, ▲, ✖
11 Kremlin	■, ●, ✖ / ▲, ■, ▲ / ●, ■, ●, ●
12 Polynesia	✖, ●, ▲ / ✖, ●, ■ / ✖, ●, ■
13 Congo	✖, ●, ■ / ■, ✖, ✖ / ●, ✖, ●
14 Washington DC.	●, ▲, ● / ●, ▲, ■ / ✖, ▲, ■
15 Tokyo	▲, ■, ▲ / ●, ✖, ■ / ●, ●, ■

WARHAMMER: DARK OMEN

View Videos

To view the in game sequences screen enter the following on the main menu

Black Grail	←, L1, ●, L2, ▲, R2
Hand Of Nagash	R2, ←, R2, ↑, ↓, ←
Carnstein and Jewel	R1, ▲, R2, R2, ■, R1
Libermortis	●, ▲, ■, →, R1, R2
End Credits	←, →, ■, →, R1, R2
Victory	L2, →, ■, →, R1, R2

Fighting Cheats

Press **Select** on the deployment screen, enter the following codes then Resume

More Money	R1, L1, R1, L2, R1, R2
Touch of Death	R1, L1, R2, R2, R1, R1
Battle Skip	R1, R1, L2, L2, R1, R2
Fast Reload	R2, R1, R2, R1, L2, R1
Choose Enemy	L2, L2, R2, L2, R1, R1

Level Skip

On the options screen in the main menu enter **R2, R1, L2, R2, R1, R2** then Resume

WARHAMMER: SHADOW OF THE HORNED RAT

Cheats

Enter the cheats on the Caravan screen.

Infinite Magic Points

Place the pointer on the Book of Magic, hold **Select** and press ←, ↑, →, ↓, **L1, R1**.

Free Troops

Place the pointer on the Troop Roster, hold **Start** and press ●, ▲, ✖, ■, ←, →.

All Units

Place the pointer on the Spare Book on the left, hold **Select** and press **R1, L1, L2, R2**.

WAR OF THE WORLDS

Level Codes:

Level 2	✖, ✖, ✖, ●, ▲, ✖, ●, ■
Level 3	■, ✖, ✖, ▲, ●, ●, ●, ▲
Level 4	●, ●, ■, ■, ▲, ✖, ▲, ●
Level 5	▲, ▲, ▲, ■, ●, ▲, ✖, ✖
Level 6	■, ●, ▲, ▲, ●, ■, ✖, ■
Level 7	●, ▲, ●, ■, ■, ■, ▲, ▲
Level 8	●, ▲, ●, ✖, ■, ▲, ✖, ▲
Level 9	■, ✖, ●, ●, ●, ▲, ✖, ●
Level 10	▲, ✖, ✖, ●, ●, ▲, ●, ✖
Level 11	✖, ▲, ●, ●, ■, ■, ✖, ■
Level 12	●, ●, ■, ▲, ▲, ✖, ●, ▲
Level 13	●, ▲, ▲, ●, ✖, ✖, ■, ■
Level 14	●, ●, ▲, ✖, ■, ■, ✖, ●

WARZONE 2100

When you turn on your PlayStation hold **Start** on pad 2 until the main menu appears. Then press **L1, R1, R2, L1, Select, Start**. Cheat Mode is now enabled and campaigns 2 and 3 will be unlocked. With cheat mode enabled enter the following:

Additional Structures	During a game press **R1** on pad 2.
Additional Units	During a game press **R2** on pad 2.
All the Items	During a game press ✖ on pad 2.
God Mode	During a game press ▲ on pad 2.
Infinite Power	During a game press ● on pad 2.
Level Skip	During a game press **Select** on pad 2.
Super Unit Strength	During a game press ↑ on pad 2.

WCW MAYHEM

Passwords

Enter each of the following cheats as a Pay-Per-View password.

Unlock Hidden Wrestlers	**PLYHDNGYS**
Special Area Select	**CBCKRMS**
Doppelganger	**DPLGNGRS**
Bionic Created Wrestlers	**MKSPRCWS**
Quest Cheat Enable	**CHT4DBST**
Classic Nitro Setting	**PLYNTRCLSC**
Masked Ray Mysterio Jr	**MSKDTLRY**
Transformed Wrestlers	**NGGDYNLN**
Stamina Meter	**PRNTSTMN**
Momentum Meter	**PRNTMMNTM**
Thusday Thunder	Enter **PLYHDNGYS** then press ✖, then on the line below enter **MSKDLTLRY** and press ✖.

WCW NITRO

Unlock All 48 Wrestlers

On the character select screen press **R1, R1, R1, R1, L1, L1, L1, L1, R2, R2, R2, R2, L2, L2, L2, L2, Select**.

Extra Rings

On the option screen press **L1, L2, R1, R2, L1, L2, R1, R2, Select**.

YMCA Dance

Select the Disco ring, then press **L2** during a fight to make both wrestlers do the YMCA dance.

Swelling Heads

On the option screen press **L1, L1, L1, L1, L1, L1, L1, L2, Select**. Each time the wrestlers are hit their heads will swell.

Big Head Mode

On the option screen press **R1, R1, R1, R1, R1, R1, R1, R2, Select**.

Big Heads, Hands and Feet Mode

On the option screen press **R2, R2, R2, R2, R2, R2, R2, R1, Select**.

WCW VS THE WORLD

Hidden Wrestlers

Enter league challenge and defeat each league. Defeat the boss in each and you will be able to play as him in most modes. Defeat all the leagues and a new one will appear. Defeat these and you will get two more hidden wrestlers.

WILD 9

Cheat Codes

Pause the game then enter a code:

Full Energy	▲, L1, ←, ▲, ●, ✖
Extend Red Beam	→, ↑, ←, ●, ↑, ●, ●
Ten Bombs	✖, ●, R1, →, ▲, ✖, ▲

WILLIAMS ARCADE GREATEST HITS

Debug Mode

To get to the Operators Options screen, hold **L1, L2, R1** and **R2** simultaneously and then push **Select**. Repeat this again. You can use this on all of the Greatest Hits games.

Mortal Kombat 3 Sounds

To hear over 5 minutes of MKIII sounds, turn on your PlayStation with no CD in it, then access the audio CD player from the menu. Insert the game CD to see 2 tracks. Choose track 2 and press a button to play it.

WING COMMANDER IV

Kill A Ship With One Shot

Once you have activated the Scene Select cheat, you have the ability to kill any ship with one shot. Just press **L1 + L2 + ■**.

Scene Select

Enter the following at the game copyright screen: ↑, ↓, ↓, ↑, **R2**. Now use **R1** or **R2** to select any scene.

WING OVER

Plane Select

On the game mode screen press ↑, ↑, ↓, ↓, ←, →, ←, →, ✖, ▲.

WIPEOUT

Access Rapier Class

To access Rapier Class without first having to complete Venom Class, go to the startup screen and highlight One Player. Next hold down **L2, R2, ←, Start** and **Select** while you press ✖. Now you can access Venom Class through the Class screen.

Hidden Track

You can access the hidden Firestar track by completing the tracks in Rapier Class, but there is also another way. Go to the startup screen and highlight One Player. Then hold **L1, R1, →, Start, ■** and ● while you press ✖.

WIPEOUT 2097

To access the Ship and Track cheats go to the opening options menu and hold down **L1**, **R1** and **Select**. Then enter the code:

Piranha Ship
Press ✖, ✖, ✖, ✖, ●, ▲, ■. On the team selection screen you will find the super-ship.

Phantom Class
Press ▲, ▲, ▲, ●, ● and ●. The Phantom class is now selectable from the track selection screen.

Vector Cheat
Press ■, ●, ▲, ●, ■. You can now race in the Vector class.

The Following cheats must be entered during play:

Infinite Energy
Pause the game and hold down **L1**, **R1**, **Select**. With those buttons held, enter the code ▲, ✖, ■, ●, ▲, ✖, ■, ●.

Infinite Time
As before, Pause the game and hold down **L1**, **R1**, **Select**. Still holding them press ▲, ■, ●, ✖, ▲, ■, ●, ✖.

Infinite Weapons
Pause the game and hold down **L1**, **R1**, **Select**. Still holding them press ✖, ✖, ■, ■, ●, ●, ▲. Unpause the game and you are also able to cycle through your armament using the "Drop Weapon" button.

Machine Gun
Pause the game and hold down **L1**, **R1**, **Select**. Still holding them press ■, ●, ✖, ■, ●, ✖, ▲.

Farm Animals
Hold down **L1**, **R2**, **Select**, **Start** when you switch on your PlayStation. When the Start screen appears let go of **Start** and press it again. The Craft will now be animals.

WIP3OUT

Enter the following names for the following cheats:

Phantom class	AVINIT
Extra vehicles	JAZZNAZ
All tracks	WIZZPIG

Link-Up Options
You need two PlayStations, two TVs/monitors, two copies of Wip3out, and a link cable. Use the cable to link the machines and load the game on both. On each machine in turn, select Options, Game Setup, Default Names, and Default Name Player One. Enter your name as LINK. The screen flashes to confirm the cheat is working. Return to the main Options screen, where you'll now find the new option Establish Link. Select the Establish Link option on both machines. Choose the number of players (two per machine for four-player action), then chose Single Race or Eliminator Mode. In four-player mode only your four vehicles will be in the race. In two-player mode all the other opponents will be there.

WORLD CUP '98

World Cup Classics
To play classic football matches you need to win the world cup. You can then replay the first World Cup Final. If you win, you'll gain access to another classic final. Repeat the process to gain all the matches.

WORLD LEAGUE SOCCER '98

Proper Players Names
Go to Options and select Player Editor. Choose English League, then any team. Now edit any players name and change it to **'TEAMTWO'**. Click on it to make it a new 'Default 2' option appear. Choose this to bring up the real names for that team, to change the names in all the other English teams, choose on 'Back To Teams' then on 'Default 2'. This only works for the English Teams.

WORMS

Extra Weapons
To gain some great new weapons, go to the Weapons Options screen and place the cursor so that it is not touching any words then press ✖ and ■ together 7 times.

WRECKIN CREW

Unlock Everything
Enter this password to unlock all the secrets, ●, ●, ■, ▲, ▲, ■, ■, ■, ✖, ●, ●, ●, ▲, ■, ■, ✖.

WWF ATTITUDE

Random wrestler
Press **R1** at the character select screen.

Career Mode bonuses
Select a wrestler and win the WWF title in career mode to unlock all the hidden wrestlers and other bonuses, such as Ego Mode, Squeaky Mode, Big Heads, Bleep Mode, and Additional costumes. A new feature will be awarded for each victory.

European title
Sable, Marc Mero Trainer, New Custom Options, Squeaky Mode
Intercontinental title
Jaqueline and Chyna, Extra Attribute Points, Big Head Mode
WWF Heavyweight title
Beep Mode, Ego Mode, Head
King of the Ring PPV
Kurrgan and Taka Michinoku

Summer Slam PPV
Sgt. Slaughter and Shawn Michaels
Royal Rumble PPV
Jerry Lawler and Paul Bearer

Bonus details:
Squeaky Mode
Wrestler voices are squeaky and fast.
Extra Attributes
Gives three extra attributes points for your created character.
Big Heads
Gives the wrestlers big heads.
Ego Mode
When the crowd is chanting the wrestler's name their heads swell.
New Custom Options
More clothes and options available in the creation mode.
Beep Mode
Unlock "Bleeped Out" option on the Language menu under Utilities. Enable that option to bleep out all foul language.
Alternate costumes
Hold **R2** and press ✖ while selecting on the wrestler selection screen.

WWF IN YOUR HOUSE

Combos On
You can keep the combos on by Pausing the game and pressing **R1, L2, R2, L2** and ➡

Computer Players Off
Turn computer players off by Pausing the game and pressing ⬅, ⬅, ⬆, down, and **R2**.

More Pain
You can cause more damage by Pausing the game and pressing ⬆, ⬆, **L1, L2** and ⬇

Superpins On
To have superpins on, Pause the game and press ⬇, ⬇, ⬇, ⬇ and **L1**.

WWF SMACKDOWN

Season Extras
As you play through the season game you will unlock these extras features after each season:

1 season – Ivory
2 seasons – Prince Albert
3 seasons – Jacqueline
4 seasons – Viscera
5 seasons – 80 creation points
6 seasons – Mideon

7 seasons – Pat Patterson
8 seasons – Gerald Brisco
10 seasons – 90 creation points
20 seasons – 100 creation points

Extra Characters
Follow the following events to unlock the characteristics of these superstars.

Stephanie Mcmahon
1. Lose the first five matches.
2. Say thanks to Debra
3. Lose the next two matches
4. Tell the Hardy's to shut up.
5. Lose the next three matches
6. Tell the Godfather to shut up.
7. Lose the Royal Rumble.
8. When Triple H tells you to attack Vince Mchon, tell him no.
9. Lose the next match.
10. Say thanks to Vince and Stephanie.

Stevie Richards and New Steve Austin
1. Win the first six matches.
2. Lose the next match against Mankind.
3. Win the next two matches.
4. Tell Kane to shut up.
5. Lose the Royal Rumble.
6. Refuse to attack Ken Shamrock and fight Chyna and X Pac.
7. Win the next match.
8. Refuse to fight The Big Show.
9. Win the next three matches.

New Rock and The Blue Meanie
1. Lose your first four matches.
2. Win the next one.
3. Tell Debra to shut up.
4. Win the next four matches.
5. Win the Royal Rumble.
6. Save Al Snow and tell him not to worry about it.
7. Beat him.
8. Say thanks to Triple H, Mr Ass and Road Dog.
9. Win the final tag match.

Change Weapons in Hardcore Match
To change your weapon during a hardcore match, pick up a weapon, climb out of the ring and stand next to the ring. Press **R1** and the weapon your holding will magically change into another item.

WWF WARZONE

View FMV Sequences
On the main title screen press: ⬆ + ▲ ➡ + ●, ⬇ + ✖, ⬅ + ■, ⬅ + ■, ⬅ + ■, ⬅ + ■, R1 + L1, R2 + L2, R2 + L2. Then

use ↑ or ↓ to select a FMV sequence you want to watch.

View Unlocked Cheats
When you are in the elevator press **L1 + R1** to view a list of the cheats you have unlocked.

Play As Cactus And Dude
Win the WWF title in challenge mode with Mankind on either medium or hard difficulty setting.

Play As Trainer
Enter training mode and select 'Custom' followed by 'Trainer' on the character select screen.

Play As Sue
Win the WWF title in 'Challenge' mode with either Bret Hart or Owen Hart on either medium or hard difficulty setting.

Extra Clothing
Win the WWF title in 'Challenge' mode with Kane on either medium or hard difficulty setting.

Goldust Variations
Win the WWF title in 'Challenge' mode with Goldust on either medium or hard difficulty setting. Highlight Goldust and then hold **L2, R1** or **R2**.

Cold Variation
Win the WWF title with Stone Cold on either medium or hard difficulty setting. Highlight Stone Cold and then hold **L2, R1** or **R2**.

Rattlesnake Variation
Win the WWF title in 'Challenge' mode with a user created wrestler on either medium or hard difficulty setting.

Female Bodies
Win the WWF title with HHH or Shawn Michaels on either medium or hard difficulty setting.

No Metres
Win the WWF title in 'Challenge' mode with the Undertaker on either medium or hard difficulty setting.

Big Head Mode
Win the WWF title in 'Challenge' mode with British Bulldog on either medium or hard difficulty setting.

No Blocking Mode
Win the WWF title in 'Challenge' mode with Ken Shamrock or Farooq on either medium or hard difficulty setting.

No Manners Mode
Win the WWF title in 'Challenge' mode with either Mosh or Thrasher on either medium or hard difficulty setting.

Ego Mode
Win the WWF title in 'Challenge' mode with Ahmed Johnson on either the medium or hard difficulty setting.

Random Select
Hold ↑ and press **Block** on the character select screen.

Alternative costumes
Hold **L2** and select a wrestler on the character select screen.

Fight In the Wrestlemania Ring
Win both titles in 'Challenge' mode and defend the WWF titlefrom all the wrestlers. The title match will be fought in the Wrestlemania ring.

Taunts
Taunt 1 = ▲ + ✖
Taunt 2 = ● + ■

WWF WRESTLEMANIA
Auto Refill Combo Meter
You can automatically refill your combo meter, by going to the character select screen and holding **L1** and **L2** while you press ■, ✖, ●, ▲.

Character Select Codes
Go to the character select screen and enter the code for the cheat that you wish to activate:
Combos on: **L1** and **R2**, ■, ✖, ●, ▲.
Hyper mode: **L1** and **R2**, ↑, ↓, ↑, ↓, ▲, ▲, ➡, ⬅.

Invincibility: ✖, ▲, **R2**, ↑.
More powerful hits: ✖, ▲, **L2**, ↓.
Stop timer: ✖, ▲, **R2**, ⬅.
Two times less powerful hits: ✖, ▲, **L2**, ➡.

Pause Codes
To activate the following cheats, pause the game and enter the relevant code:
Half power hits- ✖, ▲, **L2**, ➡.
No human damage- ✖, ▲, **R2**, ↑.
Powerful hits- ✖, ▲, **L2**, ↓.
Reset cheats- ■, ●, ▲, ✖.
Stop timer- ✖, ▲, **R2**, ⬅.

X2
Password Cheats
Go to Options and select Password. Now enter the code for the cheat that you would like to activate:

267776 - Begin with eight credits
220969 - Begin with nine ships

180771 - Invulnerable ship
216409 - Criticus
300167 - End sequence
713948 - Level 2
900277 - Level 3
213490 - Level 4
866141 - Level 5
321904 - Level 6
196861 - Level 7
040186 - Level 8
841003 - Level 9

X-COM-TERROR FROM THE DEEP

Money Cheat
Enter the Base Name AEIOU when you start to get loads of cash, and cheap items.

Hard-Nut Army
Enter the Base Name JUSTLIKEME and all the soldiers you build will have a high-rank and full armour.

XENA: WARRIOR PRINCESS

Highlight New Game on the title screen and enter one of the following:

Full Shield and Attack ▲, ■, ▲, ■, ■, ↑, ↑, ↑

Invincibility ↑, ↑, ↑, ●, ■, ↑, ➔, ⬅

XENOGEARS

Basic Fighting
Your attacks are based on AP (Attack Points), and you have a certain amount of APs per turn. You have three levels of attack, each uses a certain amount of AP. A light attack uses 1 AP, a strong attack uses 2 APs and a heavy attack uses 3 APs. You can use a combination of light, strong and heavy attacks epending the amount of APs you have to use per turn.

Combo Attacks
When fighting you can create combos using a combination of light, strong and heavy attacks. For example if you have 3 AP you can attack with three consecutive light attacks, a light attack followed by a strong attack or vice versa. Every character has a number of more powerful combo attacks, which once learnt cause more damage. Your character will pause during the attack and charge up before performing a volley of attacks.

28 AP Super Combo Attacks
Through out the game you will face bosses who can only be defeated using a 28 AP combo attack. Any APs you do not use during your turn are stored. The maximum APs you can store is 28. Once you have stored 28 APs, select the Combo icon and manually select as many Combo Attacks you can from the selection you have learnt. Your character will then perform a Super Combo, combining a multitude of attacks into a single series of attacks.

Deathblows
Unlike many of the attacks in the game, you will not learn them as you progress through the game unless you take the time to learn them yourself. To learn a Deathblow, you will need to press the corresponding key command over and over until you accumulate 100 points on your status bar.

Gear Battles
Fighting in a Gear is slightly different from fighting on foot.
Attacking - In a Gear you cannot store unused AP and so cannot perform 28 AP Super Combos. You must rely on level 1 and 2 combos to cause the most damage.
Fuel - An addition to the health bar is a fuel bar. If you run out of fuel your Gear will stop and become defenceless.
Charging - You can increase your fuel during battle by Charging. Charging takes up all your turn preventing you from attacking but will increase your fuel by 50 units.
Booster - This will speed up the time between each of your turns but uses up your fuel quicker. Use this when you need to defeat an enemy quickly.
Special Options – A special move which uses up your Gear's fuel.

X-FILES

Day 1. FBI Field office
1. Respond to Mark Cook.
2. Enter your office.
3. Sit at your desk.
4. Answer the phone.
5. Use the tape dispenser.
6. Pick up and examine your case files.
7. Look down at the drawers.
8. Open the drawers.
9. Take the FBI Badge, gun and handcuffs.
10. Look up.
11. Go to the meeting room.

Meeting Room
1. Open the cabinet marked 'Authorized Agents only.
2. Take the camera, flashlight, evidence kit, binoculars, goggles and lockpick.
3. Close the cabinet.
4. Leave the meeting room.
5. Enter Shank's office.

Shank's Office
1. Ask all questions to Skinner.
2. Examine the travel requisition form.

3. Ask all questions to Shanks.
4. Go to the hallway.

Hallway
1. Respond to Cook then enter his office.

Cook's Office
1. Ask agent Cook what he's working. Do not ask him to put out an APB.
2. Hand your case files to Cook.
3. Exit the office and return to yours.

Willmore's Office
1. Look at the bulletin board.
2. Sit down at your desk.
3. Switch on your computer.
4. Enter the name CRAIG WILMORE and the password SHILOH.
5. Select APB, Send, then Quit.
6. Exit to the hallway.

Hallway
1. Meet Skinner.
2. Select your PDA from your inventory then select Everett and Comity Inn.

Comity Inn front Desk
1. Ring the bell twice and show your FBI badge to the clerk. Ask all questions.

Mulder's Room
1. Look at the ashtray.
2. Examine Mulder's report in the briefcase.
3. Pick up the Jose Chung book.
4. Turn on the Television.
5. Examine the bottle.
6. Enter Scully's room.

Scully's Room
1. Examine the bible.
2. Take the laptop.
3. Talk to Skinner.
4. Select the phone icon.
5. Ask all questions.
6. Exit into the parking lot.
7. Go to the front desk.

Front Desk
1. Speak to the receptionist.
2. Select the phone icon.
3. Look at the numbers on the record.
4. Call the Washington number.
5. Call the Seattle number.
6. Go to the field office in Seattle.

Field Office
1. Go into your office after talking to Skinner.

Willmore's Office
1. Access the computer and select ING.
2. Enter the Seattle number under the search section.
3. Once you get the address, quit.
4. Go to the dockside warehouse.

Warehouse
1. Find and collect a sample of the bloodstain using the evidence kit.
2. Find the bullet in the post to the right of Skinner; collect it with the evidence kit.
3. Find the cigarette butt on the floor and collect it.
4. Use the flashlight and head up the steps.
5. Select the toolbox and take the crowbar.
6. Go back to the office to where Skinner will tell you the phone is dead.
7. Use the crowbar on the crates near the front door.
8. Collect a sample of the black powder.
9. Go back to the office and talk to Skinner.
10. Ask all questions and suggest all ideas.
11. Go to the boat dock via the back door.

Boat Dock
1. Find James Wong washing his boat.
2. Show James your badge and ask all questions.
3. Use the fish stocks idea.
4. Meet Skinner in his car at the front of the warehouse.
5. Go forward then quickly photograph the Sedan.
6. Go to the crime lab.

Crime Lab
1. Ask John all questions and show him all the evidence.
2. Go to the Field office.

Field Office
1. Go to the meeting room and ask all questions and use all evidence on Skinner.
2. Go into your office.

Willmore's office
1. Cook will turn up when you sit at your desk.
2. Talk to cook and agree to him calling the computer crime division.
3. Run a check on James Wong on your computer by selecting ING, then search. Then type WONG under category and Criminal under database then Search.
4. Run a search on the Sedan by selecting photo followed by download. Clicking on the thumbnail will enlarge the licence plate. Type the number under search category and Government/ Military under Database.
5. Go to the Warehouse.

Warehouse

1. Hide until the men close the warehouse door.
2. Use your lockpick on the back door.
3. Use your binoculars to view the men in the warehouse from a safe distance.
4. Take another look at the bloodstain.
5. Select the spot to the left of the blood.
6. Go to your apartment.

Willmore's Apartment

1. Go through the door and switch on the television.
2. Look at the mess on the settee.
3. Go to the bedroom and look at the ties on the dresser.
4. Look through the journal then go to bed.

Day Two:
Willmore's Apartment

1. Look in the mirror in the bathroom then head for the field office.

Field Office

1. Revive Cook then look in the evidence cabinet.
2. Pick up the phone in your office.

Willmore's Office

1. Ask Cook all questions then head for the Warehouse.

Dockside Warehouse

1. Show your badge to Mendoza.
2. Ask the medical examiner all the questions.
3. Ask Mary Astadourian all questions.
4. Board the boat then use both questions on Mary.
5. Examine everything on the boat. Make sure you get the Slicker idea.
6. Open the cabinet door and select the drugs.
7. Go back onto the deck.
8. Use the slicker and drugs ideas on Mary.
9. Ask the harbour master all questions and use all ideas.
10. Go to the Tarakan in Seattle.

The Tarakan

1. Enter via the gangplank then go through the open hatch into the hold.
2. Look closely at the crates.
3. Open the box to the left of the crates and take the sphere.
4. Exit the hold and go through the open passageway.
5. Enter the Crew cabin area.
6. Pick up the journal in the first cabin and the payroll log in the second.
7. Step onto the upper deck walkway.
8. Look at the white figures on the hull.
9. Go up the stairs and into the wheelhouse.
10. Click on the prints next to Mary.
11. Use your mobile phone to call John Amis.
12. Ask Amis to lift the fresh prints.

13. Use the payroll log idea on Mary.
14. Share your evidence.
15. Use the lead sphere idea.
16. Use the white shadows idea.
17. Go back to the wheelhouse an approach Mary again.
18. Go to the Coroners office in Seattle.

Coroners Office

1. Select the organ trays in the autopsy room.
2. Select the slug.
3. Ask all questions to the coroner.
4. Look at Wong.
5. Use the drugs idea on the coroner.
6. Use the Tarakan idea on the coroner.
7. Ask who the FBI agents were.
8. Ask Mary any question.
9. Go to the Crime Lab.

Crime Lab.

1. Ask Amis all questions, use the fingerprints and give him all the evidence.
2. Go to your apartment.

Willmore's Apartment

1. Check your telephone messages and E-mail.
2. Read the Amis e-mail and download the file attachment.
3. Use the ING interface to search the FBI database.
4. Quit the computer and answer the door.
5. Ask all questions to Cook and use the fingerprints idea.
6. Go to the dockside warehouse.

Dockside Warehouse

1. Quickly get into the truck via the drivers door, get the scrap of paper from the glove compartment and exit via the passenger door.
2. Go back to your apartment and sleep.

Day 3
Wilmore's Apartment

1. Ask Mary all questions.
2. Watch the tape then answer Mary any way you like.
3. When you receive the fax from Amis give him a call on your mobile.
4. Use all ideas on Mary.
5. Get the paper from the fax machine.
6. Share all the information with Mary.
7. Take a shower then go to the coroner's office.

Coroner's office

1. Use all questions on the coroner.
2. Go to Gordon's Hauling.

Gorden's Hauling

1. Enter the office and pick up the logbook.
2. When you get attacked grab the shovel from the floor and use it to open the grate next to the refrigerator.
3. Try to kiss Mary in the yard.

4. Use all ideas on her.
5. Go to your apartment.

Wilmore's Apartment
1. Run a search on Tarakan, Russia, UFO, Wong, Smuggling, Plutonium and Georgia.
2. Quit the computer read the journal and sleep.
3. When you wake go to the FBI field office.

FBI Field Office
1. Ask all questions on Cook in the meeting room.
2. Go to the Crime Lab.

Smol's Warehouse
1. Arm your handgun.
2. Kill two guys on the first floor and three on the second.
3. Go up the spiral staircase on the top floor.
4. Talk to Smol and Mary.
5. Find the gun and logbook on the first floor. Look at the crates.
6. Talk to Mary and Smol about the gun and log.
7. Go to the Crime Lab.

Crime Lab
1. Run a test on the gun.
2. Go back to Smol's warehouse.

Smol's Warehouse
1. Talk to Smol about the gun.
2. Once Amis has finished talking go to your apartment.

Wilmore's Apartment
1. Listen to your answerphone and check your e-mail.
2. Download the fingerprints and check them on the government search database.
3. Talk to Mary.
4. Check your field notes then sleep.
5. When you wake, go to the Sand Point Hangar 4.

Day 5
Hangar 4
1. Pay attention to X.
2. Talk to Mary then head for Goldbar Hospital.

Hospital
1. Show the Doctor your badge.
2. Talk about Scully and Skinner then ask all questions.
3. Go into the room where you will see Scully.
4. Tell Scully Skinner has sent you and your name is Wigmore.
5. Tell her about the black guy.
6. Click the stiletto.
7. Discuss the case with Scully, ask all questions.
8. Show her the photograph of Smol.
9. Ask all questions and use all ideas.
10. Go to RR 1121.

RR1121
1. Climb the telephone pole and use the binoculars to look at the roof of the train.
2. Talk to Mary then explore the train car.
3. Play the game with the tramp (he has a videotape).
4. Buy the tape.
5. Go to the field office.

Field Office
1. Put the video in the machine.
2. Select capture then search under Government/Military.
3. Exit the computer then talk with the gunmen, ask all questions.
4. Open the e-mail and download the co-ordinates.
5. Go to Alaska.

Rauch's House
1. Go into the house and straight upstairs.
2. Try talking to Rauch.
3. Pull the rope to drop the ladder, go up to the attic.
4. Talk to Mulder.
5. Shoot or run away from the NSA hitmen.
6. If you shoot them, go to your car.
7. If you run away you must head for the woods and hide under the log. You will be automatically returned to your car.

Secret Base
1. Meet Scully and search for Mulder, shoot everyone you find (except Mulder and Scully).
2. Find Mulder in the Locker room.
3. Tell Scully to RUN.
4. Shoot the soldier in the storeroom and head back to the locker room.
5. Enter the supply room.
6. Talk to Scully.
7. Go around the outside of the control room and enter the medical exam lab.
8. Pick up the cattle prod.
9. Select the prod to hit agent Cook with.
10. Go further around the control room to the isolation chamber control.
11. Listen to Scully.
12. Pull the green knob.
13. Push the red button to open the door.
14. Open the other chamber door.
15. Once both doors are pen go into the central control room.
16. Push the blast door control button.
17. Go back around to the left of the isolation chamber.
18. Go through the open security door.
19. When Scully asks, go right.
20. Shoot the guard and quickly take his key.
21. Go through the isolation chamber and push the red button to shut Mulder in.
22. As soon as you can, give the stiletto to Scully.

23. Sit back and watch the ending unfold.

X~MEN CHILDREN OF THE ATOM

Quick Continue
When you want to continue with the same character on the continue screen, hold **L1 + L2 + R1 + R2**, then press **Start**.

Play As Akuma/Gouki (Player One)
On the character select screen highlight Spiral for three seconds, then move to Silver Samurai, Psylocke, Colossus, Iceman, Colossus, Cyclops, Wolverine, Omega Red, Silver Samurai. Stay highlighting Silver Samurai for three seconds. Then hold all three punch buttons and Akuma should drop from above.

Play As Akuma/Gouki (Player Two)
On the character select screen highlight Storm for three seconds, then move to Cyclops, Colossus, Iceman, Sentinel, Omega Red, Wolverine, Psylocke, Silver Samurai, Spiral. Stay highlighting Spiral for three seconds then press all three Kick buttons.

Play As Magneto And Juggernaut
On the title screen, highlight options and hold **L1 + R1 + ✕** until the option menu appears. Go to Configuration and select System, there should be a new option, Boss Select. Turn it on and go to versus mode. Choose any character and hold either **L2** for Juggernaut or **R2** for Magneto until it says now loading.

Free Play
Once you've activated the boss code, scroll through the number of credits available until you find free play, giving you infinite continues.

X~MEN MUTANT ACADEMY

Cerebro Codes
On the main menu press **Select, ↑, L2, R1, L1, R2**

X~MEN VS STREET FIGHTER

Hidden Characters
There is only one hidden character in X-Men Vs Street Fighter which is the demon Akuma / Gouki. To access him highlight any of the top row characters and press **↑**.

Team Supers
Both of your team members can join together and combine their super moves for a mega size super combo. To do this you must have at least a level 2 super meter, then press **↓, ↙, → + Fierce Punch + Roundhouse Kick**.

Air Raves
Air Raves are combo's which are performed in the air. Knock your opponent into the air, then push **↑**. Your character will leap into the air following your opponent. Now perform a chain combo (e.g. **Jab Punch**, **Strong Punch**, **Roundhouse Kick**) to carry out an air rave.

Energy Regeneration
Your character will slowly regain lost energy during a match. After you have sustained major damage you can back away from your opponent for long enough to regain most of your lost energy. If you cause damage to your opponent do not allow them to retreat, as they also will regain energy.

Z

Enter the following cheats on the password screen:

Enable port 2
✕, ▲, ■, ●, ▲, ●, ✕, ■
During the game you can now press ▲ on pad 2 to destroy the enemy base or ■ to destroy your own.

Full Metal Jacket
■, ●, ✕, ▲, ▲, ✕, ●, ■

Invincibility
■, ▲, ●, ✕, ✕, ●, ▲, ■

Level Codes

Level	Code
Level 2:	■, ▲, ✕, ●, ▲, ■, ●, ✕.
Level 3:	■, ✕, ●, ▲, ▲, ■, ✕, ●.
Level 4:	■, ▲, ✕, ●, ●, ▲, ✕, ●.
Level 5:	✕, ●, ■, ✕, ▲, ■, ✕, ●.
Level 6:	■, ●, ▲, ✕, ●, ✕, ■, ●.
Level 7:	✕, ●, ■, ✕, ▲, ▲, ✕, ●.
Level 8:	✕, ✕, ●, ▲, ✕, ●, ■, ✕.
Level 9:	●, ✕, ●, ■, ✕, ●, ■, ●
Level 10:	●, ▲, ●, ●, ■, ▲, ✕, ●.
Level 11:	✕, ■, ●, ✕, ✕, ■, ■, ●.
Level 12:	✕, ✕, ●, ✕, ●, ✕, ■, ●.
Level 13:	●, ▲, ✕, ●, ▲, ■, ✕, ●.
Level 14:	■, ▲, ✕, ●, ▲, ✕, ●, ■.
Level 15:	■, ▲, ✕, ●, ■, ▲, ✕, ●.
Level 16:	●, ✕, ●, ■, ■, ✕, ■, ✕.
Level 17:	●, ■, ▲, ✕, ▲, ✕, ●, ■.
Level 18:	■, ●, ■, ✕, ✕, ●, ●, ▲.
Level 19:	✕, ●, ✕, ●, ▲, ▲, ✕, ●.
Level 20:	▲, ▲, ✕, ●, ▲, ▲, ✕, ●.

ZERO DIVIDE

Area Select
To choose your area of battle in VS PLAY mode, you must play

in 2P VS mode with Zulu and Xtal, winning a round with each of them in less than 5 seconds (05"00). When you have accomplished this you will be able to choose your battle area.

Colour Select
You can choose from 16 colour schemes after beating the game. Just hold **Select** and press any one of the eight attack buttons. You will find that players one and two each have their own set of eight colour pallettes.

Fight As Neco
Fight through the entire game with both Zulu and Xtal, then you will have the chance to fight as Neco.

Fight As Zulu
To play as Zulu you need to defeat him with every character as you play the entire game.

Fight As Xtal
You can fight as Xtal by playing the entire game without continuing. You may fight as any character to do this, and at the Normal or Hard setting.

Hidden Comics
You can view the comic strip featuring Neco by beating the game in Easy mode without continuing or losing a round. Then go to the title screen and highlight the Option icon. Hold the following on controller two: **L1**, **L2**, **R1**, **R2**, **Start** and **Select**.

Hidden Game
Turn off the machine. Now hold **Start** and **Select** on the second controller and start the game. Don't release the buttons until after the Zoom logo has appeared. Now you can play the secret 'Tiny Phalanx' game. You can fight Neco if you beat the game and get a high score. To be invincible, go to the option screen and press ↖, **L2**, **R2** and ▲ together. You know the cheat has worked when the background turns red.

Manual Memory Save
You can save the current fight to a memory card by pressing **Select** after a round which brings up the option to save. This way, there is no need to keep the Replay Save option in all the time.

Special Congratulations Scene
When your total playing time exceeds 200 hours, you will see a congratulations screen that displays the characters.

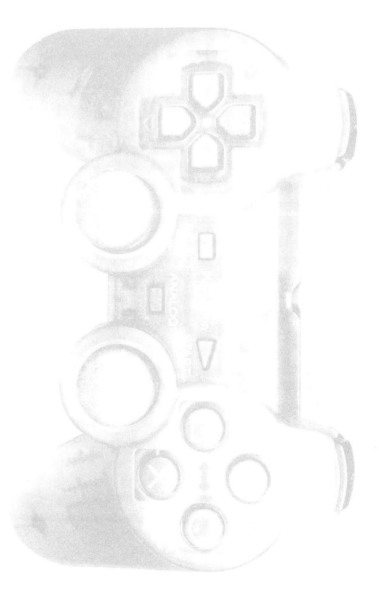

www.**chart**deals.co.uk

©**chart**deals 2000

Find the cheapest games
on the Internet in an instant